THE PROPERTY RIGHTS OF COHABITEES

The Property Rights of Cohabitees

An Analysis of Equity's Response in Five Common Law Jurisdictions

JOHN MEE

BCL, LLM (National University of Ireland);
LLM (Osgoode Hall);
Ph.D (University of Dublin);
Barrister at Law (King's Inns, Dublin)
Lecturer in Law (University College Cork)

•HART•
PUBLISHING

OXFORD – PORTLAND OREGON
1999

Hart Publishing
Oxford and Portland, Oregon

Published in North America (US and Canada) by
Hart Publishing
c/o International Specialized Book Services
5804 NE Hassalo Street
Portland, Oregon
97213-3644
USA

Distributed in the Netherlands, Belgium and Luxembourg by
Intersentia, Churchillaan 108
B2900 Schoten
Antwerpen
Belgium

Distributed in Australia and New Zealand by
Federation Press
John St
Leichhardt
NSW 2000

Hart Publishing Ltd is a specialist legal publisher based in Oxford, England.
To order further copies of this book or to request a list of other
publications please write to:

Hart Publishing Ltd, 19 Whitehouse Road, Oxford, OX1 4PA
Telephone: +44 (0)1865 434459 or Fax: +44 (0)1865 794882
e-mail: hartpub@janep.demon.co.uk

British Library Cataloguing in Publication Data
Data Available
ISBN 1 901362–76–0 (cloth)

Typeset by Hope Services (Abingdon) Ltd.
Printed in Great Britain on acid-free paper
by Biddles Ltd, Guildford and King's Lynn.

"The courts should not become alchemists transmuting the ashes of dead passion into gold". *Seidler* v *Schallhofer* [1982] 2 NSWLR 80, 103 per Hope JA.

"Nor should . . . [those] who have provided 'women's work' over their adult lifetime . . . be told condescendingly, by a mostly male judiciary, that their services must be regarded as 'freely given labour' only or, catalogued as attributable solely to a rather one-way and quaintly described 'love and affection', when property interests come to be distributed". *Bryson* v *Bryant* (1992) 29 NSWLR 188, 204 per Kirby P.

"The mistakes are all out there, waiting to be made". Attributed to Dr Savielly Tartakower (Chess master and teacher).

To Mary

Preface

This book is a considerably modified version of a Ph D thesis which I completed at Trinity College Dublin in 1997. I am grateful to Professor William Binchy, who supervised the thesis, and to Dr Andrew Lyall and Dr Hilary Delany, who acted as examiners. I would also like to thank Professor Robert Pearce (now of the University of Buckingham) who supervised an LLM thesis on a related topic in 1987.

In addition, I would like to acknowledge the assistance I received from the following: Professor David Hayton and the staff of King's College London; Eoin O'Dell of Trinity College Dublin; Professor Peter Watts, Professor Charles Rickett and Paul Rishworth of the University of Auckland; Charles Harpum of the Law Commission; Rick Snell and Gino Dal Pont of the University of Tasmania; Olivia Smith, Siobhan Mullally, Aine Ryall, Darius Whelan, Valerie King and Patrick Crowley of University College Cork; Andrew Webster of the Australian Bureau of Statistics; Brendan and Claire Mee; and the many people who were helpful to me in my time as visiting scholar at the University of Auckland (1994), Osgoode Hall Law School, Toronto (1995) and the Institute of Advanced Legal Studies, London (1997). I am also grateful for the financial assistance which I received from the President's Research Fund, University College Cork.

Closer to home, I should not omit to mention my son Cormac, who arrived just in time to lend his critical voice to the conclusion of this project. Finally, and above all, I would like to thank my wife and colleague, Mary Donnelly, who read countless drafts and ensured numerous improvements of style and substance.

I remain solely responsible for any errors which remain. I have discussed the law on the basis of materials available to me on November 1st 1998.

John Mee
University College Cork
February 3rd 1999

Contents

Detailed Table of Contents

Table of Cases

Table of Statutes

Introduction

This book concerns itself with the doctrines of equity as they apply to the determination of the property rights of cohabitees upon the termination of their relationship. It is proposed to examine the law prevailing in five common law jurisdictions, i.e. England, Ireland, Canada, Australia and New Zealand. These jurisdictions have been chosen for a number of reasons. First, and most obviously, there is the fact that they share a common heritage in terms of the influence of English law, language and culture. Secondly, there is, to some extent, a common debate being carried on in these jurisdictions, with (to take the example of the most "cosmopolitan" jurisdiction) the New Zealand courts regularly citing cases from England, Canada and Australia.[1] Finally, it appears that the doctrinal developments in the five jurisdictions examined in this book come close to playing out the full range of intellectual options in the area. Therefore, while there would clearly be benefits in an examination of the position in civil law jurisdictions[2] or in an attempt to negotiate the "seething chaos" of American law,[3] these worthwhile endeavours must be the subject of another work.

[1] By way of contrast with the New Zealand experience, the courts of Ireland (the other small jurisdiction considered in this book) have been very slow to take any notice of foreign developments. In turn, the Commonwealth jurisdictions have shown no interest in the Irish approach to this area. Nonetheless, the Irish cases reflect an independent approach, quite distinct from that of any of the other four jurisdictions considered, and are therefore worthy of discussion in the present comparative survey.

[2] Of course, the benefits of such a study would be rather more indirect, since such jurisdictions do not have any direct equivalent of the law of equity. The position upon the termination of a cohabitation in such jurisdictions appears to depend to a large extent on the interpretation of relevant provisions (governing e.g. unjust enrichment) of the Civil Code of the jurisdiction in question. See generally Muller-Freienfels "Cohabitation and Marriage Law—A Comparative Survey" (1987) 1 *International Journal of Law and the Family* 269; Neilson "Family Rights and the 'Registered Partnership' in Denmark" (1990) 4 *International Journal of Law and the Family* 297; Szlezak "Cohabitation Without Marriage in Poland" (1991) 5 *International Journal of Law and the Family* 1; Bradley *Family Law and Political Culture: Scandinavian Laws in Comparative Perspective* (London: Sweet and Maxwell, 1996) pp 95–105; 151–160; 213–222. For a brief discussion of the French position, see Chauveau and Hutchinson "A Short History of Cohabitation and Marriage" (1995) 145 NLJ 304; 391, 392. See also Estrada Alonso *Las uniones extra-matrimoniales en el derecho civil espanol* (1991), cited by Piconto-Novales "Family Law and Family Policy in Spain", ch. 6 in Kurczewski and Maclean (eds) *Family Law and Family Policy in the New Europe* (Aldershot: Dartmouth, 1996). For the Scottish position, see Norrie "The Proprietary Rights of Cohabitants" [1996] *Juridical Law Review* 209; Jackson "Scottish Cohabitation" [1997] *Fam Law* 754.

[3] See Meagher "Constructive Trusts: High Court Developments and Prospects" (1988) 4 *Australian Bar Review* 67, 71, who suggests that it could be said of many American jurisdictions "(as

II. UNMARRIED COHABITATION

Arguably, Adam and Eve were the first couple to live together without the benefit of a formal marriage. Even in the more regulated world of today, an increasing number of couples do the same. It is not possible to come up with a simple definition which will cover all types of human cohabitation, whether "heterosexual or homosexual, dual or multiple in nature".[4] The possibilities range from, at one end of the spectrum, a union "which has all the characteristics of a marital relationship save the blessing of the law"[5] to, at the other end, "a relationship which is no more than that of two persons . . . who, finding each other sexually attractive, decide, for the convenience of their primary interest in each other, to occupy the same dwelling, neither intending the relationship to have the quality of permanence".[6]

Not only is definition almost impossible, exceptional difficulty also surrounds the lesser task of finding a convenient label to describe those involved in non-marital cohabitations.[7] In the past, terms used to describe female cohabitees have included "paramour"[8] "mistress",[9] "consort"[10] and "concubine",[11] while older cases referred to cohabitation as a "meretricious" relationship (thus implying that "it pertained to and encompassed prostitution").[12] Such labels have fallen from favour and, when they occur in modern cases, may sometimes give an indication that the judge concerned will be slow to recognise any prop-

---

it was once said of the Irish Court of Chancery) that no case is certain and yet none is hopeless". For discussion of the leading American case of *Marvin* v *Marvin* (1976) 18 Cal (3d) 660, see Kay and Amyx "Marvin v Marvin: Preserving the Options" (1977) 65 *California Law Review* 937; Anon "Comment: Property Rights upon Termination of Unmarried Cohabitation" (1977) 90 Harv Law Rev 1708. See also Krause *Family Law*, 2nd edn (St Paul: West Publishing Co, 1983) pp 120–140; Bruch "Cohabitation in the Common Law Countries a Decade after Marvin: Settled In or Moving Ahead?" (1989) 22 *University of California, Davis Law Review* 717; Rotherham "The Contribution Interest in Quasi-Matrimonial Disputes" (1991) 4 *Canterbury Law Review* 407, 418–419; Wadlington *Cases and Other Materials on Domestic Relations* (Westbury, New York: Foundation Press, 1990) pp 82–121.

   [4] *Allen* v *Snyder* [1977] 2 NSWLR 685, 689 per Glass JA.
   [5] *Hollywood* v *Cork Harbour Commissioners* [1992] 1 IR 457, 465 per O'Hanlon J.
   [6] *Crick* v *Ludwig* (1994) 117 DLR (4th) 228, 235 per Southin JA. Cf. Chapter 1 *infra*, text to and following n 98. The range also includes an intimate relationship between two people which lacks a sexual element: *Hamilton* v *Jurgens* [1996] NZFLR 350.
   [7] See Girard "Living Together" (1983) 28 *McGill LJ* 977, 979 n 1; Freeman and Lyon *Cohabitation without Marriage* (Aldershot: Gower Publishing, 1983) pp 5–6; Sparkes "The Language of Cohabitation" [1989] *Fam Law* 328; Parry *The Law Relating to Cohabitation* (London: Sweet and Maxwell, 1993) pp 1–4.
   [8] See e.g. *Forgeard* v *Shanahan* (1994) 18 Fam LR 281, 295 per Meagher JA (whose use of language was criticised by Kirby P *ibid*, 282).
   [9] Cf. *Crick* v *Ludwig* (1994) 117 DLR (4th) 228, 228 ("mistress and lover" used to describe a relationship lacking a strong emotional commitment). Cf. Parry, n 7 *supra*, pp 2–3.
   [10] See e.g. *Hollywood* v *Cork Harbour Commissioners* [1992] 1 IR 457, 464.
   [11] See e.g. *Hill* v *Estate of Westbrook* (1950) 95 Cal App (2d) 599, 603.
   [12] See the discussion in *Marvin* v *Marvin* (1976) 18 Cal (3d) 660, 683 per Tobriner J. Note also the references to "living in sin" and "masquerading . . . as husband and wife" in *Gammans* v *Ekins* [1950] 2 KB 328, 331 per Asquith LJ.

erty claim arising outside the matrimonial context. In this book, the relatively neutral terms "cohabitation" and "cohabitees"[13] will generally be employed.[14] However, in dealing with a particular jurisdiction, some concessions will be made to the locally prevalent terminology. Thus, in relation to Australia and New Zealand, the term "de facto relationship"[15] will be employed since this usage is almost universal in the judgments emanating from those jurisdictions.

III. PROPERTY DISPUTES UPON THE TERMINATION OF A RELATIONSHIP

Given that, in Western societies, there is generally no legal prohibition on unmarried cohabitation,[16] the major legal problems are presented when such relationships break down. Unfortunately, "in the case of separating unmarried couples, [their] distress and bitterness is often found, paradoxically, to have been increased rather than diminished by their decision not to undertake a commitment to each other in marriage".[17] Thus, property disputes between cohabitees constitute "a new field of discord liable to explode into litigation".[18]

Despite the absence of a formal legal marriage, it is still quite possible that the parties to a cohabitation will fall into the assumption that their relationship will last indefinitely and that there is no need to safeguard their separate property entitlements. This tendency "to rely upon the relationship itself rather than the proprietary rights to secure to them . . . their enjoyment of the property"[19] may leave cohabitees in an extremely vulnerable position upon the termination of their relationship. The difficulties are compounded by the fact that, in most jurisdictions, there is no established legal structure within which to resolve property disputes between cohabitees.[20] As one English judge put it:

[13] The difficulty with prefacing these terms with the word "unmarried" is it is quite possible that either or both cohabitees may be legally married to someone other than their present partner (see Freeman and Lyon, n 7 *supra*, p 5). For consideration of the problems surrounding terms such as "quasi-matrimonial" or "quasi-spousal", see Chapter 1 *infra*, n 100 and accompanying text. The terms "common law husband" and "common law wife" are technically inaccurate, since they refer to a form of marriage recognised by the law before Lord Hardwicke's Act 1753. See Parry, n 7 *supra*, pp 1–2.

[14] Notwithstanding certain undesirable commercial connotations, the convenient term "partner" will generally be used to describe the relationship of one cohabitee to another. The same terminology will be used to describe cohabitations which take place in the context of a same sex relationship. Cf. Norrie, n 2 *supra*, 210, referring to those in a heterosexual relationship as "ungay cohabitants".

[15] Cf. Chapter 1 *infra*, n 100.

[16] Contrast the position in countries governed by Islamic law. See e.g. Pakistan's Offence of Zina (Enforcement of Hudood) Ordinance (VII of 1979) (prohibiting *inter alia* fornication), discussed in Medhi *The Islamisation of the Law in Pakistan* (London: Curzon Press, 1994) pp 116–117. Note also the remarkable persistence of archaic laws in the USA. According to Rotherham, n 3 *supra*, 418, in 1991 unmarried cohabitation was still technically illegal in 16 States.

[17] *Hammond* v *Mitchell* [1991] 1 WLR 1127, 1139 per Waite J.

[18] *Allen* v *Snyder* [1977] 2 NSWLR 685, 688 per Glass JA.

[19] *Ibid*, 705 per Mahoney JA.

[20] Note, however, that a number of Australian jurisdictions have introduced legislation allowing for the re-adjustment of property entitlements upon the termination of a cohabitation. See further Chapter 1 *infra*, n 96.

"[A] husband has a legal obligation to support his wife even if they are living apart. A man has no legal obligation to support his mistress even if they are living together . . . The courts possess neither a statutory nor an inherent jurisdiction to disturb existing rights of property on the termination of an extra-marital relationship, however long established the relationship and however deserving the claimant".[21]

Thus, an unmarried claimant must somehow show that the formal legal ownership does not truly reflect the "existing rights of property" as between the parties. This will generally involve resort to the principles of equity.

As will be seen in the chapters which follow, a claimant in the situation under discussion may argue that she[22] has made "contributions" to the property of the defendant. The range of possible contributions includes paying a portion of the purchase price of property, contributing to the repayment of a mortgage, financing or personally undertaking the making of improvements to a property, working without pay in the defendant's business or working in the home and in the rearing of children. A claimant may also argue that she has been led to undergo various forms of sacrifice for the benefit of the relationship. She may argue, for example, that she has given up a lucrative career (or a secure home) in order to live with the defendant and bring up the children of their relationship.

Although the nature of the contributions and sacrifices of the claimant are obviously very important, it is clear that there is another factor of major significance. This is the question of the intention of the parties. It may make a crucial difference whether, on her side, the claimant expected anything in return for her contribution or sacrifice and, on the other side, whether the defendant shared that expectation or at least led the claimant to believe that he did. All of the equitable doctrines which will be considered in this study are built around these two main themes of contribution/sacrifice and intention. It will be seen also that the two main themes are interrelated and that, under some doctrines, the making of certain contributions permits the inference (rebuttable by contrary evidence) that the parties had the intention required to justify the granting of a remedy.

As a last point at this preliminary stage, it is necessary to draw attention to the gendered nature of property disputes between (heterosexual) cohabitees. In the majority of cases, the male partner is in an economically stronger position and is left with the legal ownership of the greater part of the assets of the family. Despite recent social changes, it is still more commonly the female partner who subordinates the advancement of her career to the demands of the relationship and who undertakes a greater proportion of the domestic labour and child-rearing.[23] This point should be borne in mind when considering the manner in which domestic labour is accommodated by the doctrines of equity. It will

---

[21] *Windeler* v *Whitehall* (1990) 2 FLR 505, 506 per Millett J. Cf. *Ennis* v *Butterly* [1996] 1 IR 426.

[22] For an explanation of the choice of the feminine pronoun, see text following n 27 *infra*.

[23] See generally Neave "Living Together—The Legal Effects of the Sexual Division of Labour in Four Common Law Countries" (1991) 17 *Monash University Law Review* 14.

be seen in due course that the English[24] and the Irish[25] courts (but not those of the major Commonwealth jurisdictions)[26] have operated on the basis of doctrines which generally refuse any remedy to a claimant who relies on work in the home. Many commentators have seen this as unjust and as reflecting an inherent male bias in the law.[27] While this book takes a predominantly doctrinal approach to the area under discussion, it will be necessary throughout to maintain an awareness of the gender issues which lie beneath the surface of the formal legal rules.

Consistent with the foregoing, the practice will be adopted in the book of assuming, when referring in the abstract to a claimant, that the claimant is female. This usage has the advantage of emphasising the social reality of the problem as it arises in heterosexual relationships. It is also completely appropriate in the context of female same sex cohabitations but is, of course, completely inappropriate in the context of disputes between gay men. Despite this last important problem, it remains true that the majority of claimants are female and, given the convenience of the usage and its contribution to clarity of explanation, it appears to be defensible once it is understood that there is no attempt to suggest that all claimants are, in fact, female.[28]

---

[24] See Chapter 5 *infra*, text following n 68.

[25] See Chapter 3 *infra*, text to and following n 136.

[26] See Chapter 7 *infra*, text following n 60 (Canada); Chapter 8 *infra*, text following n 53 (Australia); Chapter 9 *infra*, text to n 65 (New Zealand).

[27] See e.g. Neave, n 23 *supra*; Flynn and Lawson "Gender, Sexuality and the Doctrine of Detrimental Reliance" (1995) 3 *Feminist Legal Studies* 105 (exploring also the special problems of same sex relationships). Cf. Halliwell "Equity as Injustice: The Cohabitant's Case" (1991) 20 *Anglo–American Law Review* 500; Bottomley "Self and Subjectivities: Languages of Claim in Property Law" (1993) 20 *Journal of Law and Society* 56; Wong "Constructive Trusts over the Family Home: Lessons to be Learned from Other Commonwealth Jurisdictions?" (1998) 18 *Legal Studies* 369.

[28] Cf. *Pettitt v Pettitt* [1970] AC 777, perhaps the most famous of all family property cases, which involved an (unsuccessful) male claimant. See also Chapter 1 *infra*, text to and following n 136 (discussing the special problems facing male (homosexual) claimants); Chapter 9 *infra*, n 178.

1

The Social and Legal Background to the Problem

Before moving on in later chapters to consider the doctrinal developments which have taken place in the various jurisdictions, there are a number of important preparatory tasks to be accomplished in this chapter. First, in Part I, in order to set the legal problem in its proper social context, it will be necessary to venture some general observations on the phenomenon of unmarried cohabitation, heterosexual and homosexual, in Western industrialised societies. Part II will consider generally the problems surrounding the law's attempt to adjudicate upon property rights in the context of intimate personal relationships. It will be pointed out that much of the legal learning on this question is derived from cases dealing with married couples. This Part will, therefore, trace briefly the (recent) history of equity's treatment of disputes over matrimonial property, outlining the rejection of solutions based on the law of contract in favour of an approach through the law of trusts. Part II will conclude with an examination of the extent to which principles derived from the matrimonial property cases can be applied in the rather different context of unmarried cohabitation. Next, Part III will deal briefly with the question of the private regulation of property rights by means of cohabitation contracts and of express declarations of the beneficial interests in family homes. Finally, Part IV will explain the manner in which the material will be tackled in the remainder of the book.

I. COHABITATION WITHOUT MARRIAGE

A. Heterosexual Cohabitation

Although it is tempting to see heterosexual cohabitation without marriage as a modern phenomenon, this is clearly at variance with the historical record.[1] Reviewing the literature on the question, O'Donovan[2] points out that cohabitation without formal legal marriage has been a recurrent phenomenon in

---

[1] See Harrison *The Law of Athens: The Family and Property* (Oxford: Clarendon Press, 1968) pp 13–15; Treggiari *Roman Marriage: Iusti Coniuges from the Time of Cicero to the Time of Ulpian* (Oxford: Clarendon Press, 1994) pp 51–54.

[2] "Legal Marriage—Who Needs It?" (1984) 47 MLR 111–113.

Western society and that it "is legal regulation which is the late arrival at this particular feast".[3] The rate of cohabitation has varied over the centuries, partly in reaction to the varying influence of agents of social control such as church-wardens, constables, Justices of the Peace and church courts.[4] However, in general, the "all-important problem of legal property transfer was sufficient to restrict mere concubinage largely to the propertyless poor . . . and the very rich who were indifferent to public opinion".[5] As Freeman and Lyon[6] point out, "[m]arriage has always been of greater significance for the propertied classes than for the others".[7]

In modern times, one can certainly trace a dramatic increase in cohabitation in Western societies over the second half of the twentieth century.[8] It was estimated that in the USA in 1996 there were seven times as many unmarried (heterosexual) couples as there were in 1970.[9] The rate of cohabitation in both Australia and Canada increased by just over one quarter from 1991 to 1996.[10] The increase in New Zealand was even sharper, with the numbers rising by more than 50 per cent from 1991 to 1996 (and by more than 100 per cent from

---

[3] *Ibid*, 112. The picture is somewhat clouded by the fact that private "contract" marriages were only outlawed in England with the passing of Lord Hardwicke's Act 1753. Until then, and for some years afterwards, many in the community saw relatively informal private arrangements as a moral justification for starting sexual relations. See Stone *Uncertain Unions: Marriage in England 1660–1753* (Oxford: Oxford University Press, 1992) pp 16–17.

[4] See Stone, n 3 *supra*, p 17.

[5] *Ibid*, pp 16–17.

[6] *Cohabitation without Marriage* (Aldershot: Gower Publishing, 1983).

[7] *Ibid*, p 46.

[8] This may be simply another example of the cyclical variation in cohabitation in a society founded upon marriage or it may prefigure an eventual "withering away" of the institution of formal marriage. Cf. Glendon "Withering Away of Marriage" (1976) 62 *Virginia Law Review* 663; O'Donovan, n 2 *supra*; Clive "Marriage—An Unnecessary Legal Concept?", ch. 8 in Eekalaar and Katz (eds) *Marriage and Cohabitation in Contemporary Societies: Areas of Legal, Social and Ethical Change* (Toronto: Butterworths, 1980). The increased prevalence of cohabitation has prompted a flurry of academic comment, much of it emanating from the late 1970s and early 1980s. In addition to the sources cited above, see e.g. Pearl "The Legal Implications of a Relationship Outside Marriage" (1978) 32 CLJ 252; Oliver "The Mistress in Law (1978) 31 CLP 81; Deech "The Case Against the Legal Recognition of Cohabitation" (1980) 29 ICLQ 480; Holland *Unmarried Couples* (Toronto, Carswell Publishing, 1982); Girard "Living Together" (1983) 28 *McGill Law Journal* 977; Binchy *A Casebook on Irish Family Law* (Albingdon: Professional Books, 1984) pp 102–173; Barton *Cohabitation Contracts* (Aldershot: Gower Publishing, 1985); Parry *The Law Relating to Cohabitation*, 3rd edn (London: Sweet and Maxwell, 1993).

[9] See Saluter and Lugaila *Marital Status and Living Arrangements: March 1996*, Current Population Reports, Series P20–496 (Washington DC: US Bureau of the Census, 1998) p 5. Note also the suggestion by Freeman and Lyon, n 6 *supra*, p 59 (in the context of earlier American figures) that, given the likely extent of under-reporting of cohabitation, a more accurate estimate might be obtained by doubling the official figure.

[10] Based on Australian Census figures, there was a 27 per cent increase from 584,100 people cohabiting in 1991 to 744,100 in 1996. It appears from other family surveys that this increase is partly attributable to an increased willingness of people to identify themselves as cohabiting. (Information supplied in a personal communication to the author by Mr Andrew Webster of the Family Statistics Unit, Australian Bureau of Statistics). The increase in "common law" families in Canada from 1991 to 1996 was 28 per cent, more than 16 times greater than the increase in married families over the same period. See Statistics Canada *1996 Census: Marital Status, Common-law Unions and Families* (The Daily, October 14 1997) (available at Statistics Canada's worldwide website).

1986 to 1996).[11] Recent figures also show a striking increase in cohabitation in the United Kingdom. In 1993, the cohabitation rate was roughly twice that in 1979.[12] Furthermore, as Haskey[13] points out, the percentage of "spinsters" who live with their future husband before marriage increased from around 5 per cent in the mid-1960s to 70 per cent in the early 1990s. In relation to second marriages, the figure was even higher at 90 per cent.[14]

Rather than undertake further recitation of figures, it may be more helpful to conclude this section with Table 1.1 showing the rates of cohabitation in the countries dealt with in this book[15] (and, for the purposes of comparison, in Norway and the USA).

Concomitant with the increase in the prevalence of cohabitation in Western societies has been an increased social and legal[16] acceptance of the practice. As Kirby P pointed out in the Australian case of *Bryson v Bryant*,[17] "[d]e facto relationships, akin to marriage, are neither uncommon nor (in most circles today) a source of opprobrium".[18]

From the experience of a number of countries, it appears that cohabitation tends to change in pattern once it has achieved a certain level of social

[11] See Statistics New Zealand *1996 Census: Population Structure and Internal Migration* (Wellington: Statistics New Zealand, 1997) p 48 (the numbers of people were 111,537 in 1986, 154,713 in 1991 and 236,394 in 1996; these figures relate to those usually resident in New Zealand and aged over 15).

[12] See Haskey "Trends in Marriage and Cohabitation: the Decline in Marriage and the Changing Pattern of Living in Partnerships" (1995) 80 *Population Trends* 5, 14 (an increase from an 11 per cent cohabitation rate in single, widowed, divorced or separated women aged 18–49 in 1979 to 22 per cent in 1993). The rate of increase has been more gradual in more recent years, with the figure reaching 25 per cent in 1996 (the same as in 1995). See *Living in Britain: Preliminary Results from the 1996 General Household Survey* (London: Stationery Office, 1997) p 5.

[13] See n 12 *supra*.

[14] *Ibid*, 8.

[15] Note that the figures for the United Kingdom include Scotland, even though the law of that jurisdiction is not considered in this book (cf. the Introduction, n 2 *supra*). Similarly, the Canadian figures include Quebec (where the rate of cohabitation is by far the highest in Canada (see the source cited in n 10 *supra*)), even though this book deals with the position in the common law jurisdictions of Canada. Cf. *Vien Estate v Vien Estate* (1988) 49 DLR (4th) 558, 565.

[16] Many jurisdictions now treat unmarried cohabitees on a par with married couples in legislation dealing with matters such as social security, taxation, compensation in the law of tort for the wrongful death of a partner, protection from domestic violence etc. In addition, the decisive trend in family law is towards an emphasis on "the significance of parentage, rather than the relationship between the child's parents, as the most relevant factor in determining a child's legal position". (See Cretney and Masson *Principles of Family Law*, 6th edn (London: Sweet and Maxwell, 1997) p 5). Note also recent English legislation giving unmarried cohabitees the right to apply for provision from the estate of their partner: see s 2 of the Law Reform (Succession) Act 1995. In Canada, the effect of the Charter of Rights and Freedoms has been to allow the courts to insist upon equal treatment even where a different legislative choice has been made. See e.g. *Miron v Trudel* (1995) 124 DLR (4th) 693 (SCC) (holding that the Charter prevents the exclusion of unmarried members of family units from motor vehicle accident benefits). Note also *Taylor v Rossu* (1998) 161 DLR (4th) 266 (Alberta CA): contrary to the Charter to exclude de facto spouses from right to alimony; suggested by Court (*ibid*, 319) that other aspects of matrimonial legislation, including provisions on property division, might also have to be extended to de facto spouses.

[17] (1992) 29 NSWLR 188.

[18] *Ibid*, 194. See also *Barclays Bank plc v O'Brien* [1994] 1 AC 180, 198 per Lord Browne-Wilkinson; *WO'R v EH* [1996] 2 IR 248, 286 per Murphy J.

Table 1.1: Rates of Heterosexual[a] Cohabitation

Country	Estimated percentage of population cohabiting outside marriage	Estimated ratio between unmarried and married couples
Canada (1996)[b]	6.4%	1:6
Australia (1996)[c]	4.2%	1:10
New Zealand (1996)[d]	6.5%	1:6
Ireland (1996)[e]	1.7%	1:21
United Kingdom (1996/1997)[f]	[9.5% in age group 16–59][g]	[1:6 in age group 16–59]
USA (1996)[h]	3.0%	1:14
Norway (1997)[i]	10.2%	1:4

[a] With the exception of New Zealand, Ireland and the United Kingdom (see respectively nn d, e and f *infra*), the figures in this table do not cover those living in same sex relationships. See also text following n 31 *infra*.

[b] See Statistics Canada *1996 Census: Marital Status, Common-law Unions and Families*, n 10 *supra*: 920,635 "common law couples" and 5,779,715 married couples. "Common law couples" are defined as "two persons of opposite sex who are not legally married to each other, but live together as husband and wife in the same dwelling". The population of Canada was 28,846,761 as at the 1996 Census.

[c] Information relating to the 1996 Census supplied in a personal communication to the author by Mr Andrew Webster of the Family Statistics Unit, Australian Bureau of Statistics: 744,100 people cohabiting in a heterosexual de facto relationship and 7,415,500 married people. A "de facto relationship" exists where two people live together as a couple and consider their relationship to be a marriage-like relationship. The population of Australia was 17,892,423 as at the 1996 Census.

[d] See Statistics New Zealand *1996 Census of Population and Dwellings: National Summary* (Wellington: Statistics New Zealand, 1997) p 21; p 52: 236,384 people "living as married" ("i.e. in a consensual union, de facto relationship etc"), 1,345,578 married people and a total (usually resident) population of 3,618,302. The category of "living as married" includes approximately 3,000 same sex couples: see n b toTable 1.2 *infra*.

[e] See (Irish) Central Statistics Office *Census 1996—Principal Demographic Results* (Dublin: Stationery Office, 1997), Table 17: 31,298 cohabiting couples (those "living together as a couple"), 646,421 married couples and a total population of 3,626,087. The category of "living as together as a couple" includes an unspecified number of same sex couples.

[f] See *Living in Britain: Preliminary Results from the 1996 General Household Survey* (London: Stationery Office, 1997) p 4 (in age group 16–59, 56 per cent of men and 58 per cent of women were legally married and living with their partner); p 28 (in the same age group, 10 per cent of men and 9 per cent of women were cohabiting). The figures were said (p 23) to include "a small number of same sex couples". (These statistics are based on a survey conducted from April 1996 to March 1997 of a sample of those living in private households).

[g] The percentage of the total population would, of course, be substantially lower given the extremely low rate of cohabitation outside of the age group 16–59.

[h] See Saluter and Lugaila, n 9 *supra*, Table 1; Table 8: 7,916,000 people in "unmarried couple households", 111,405,000 married people (excluding separated married people) and a total population of 264,485,000. An "unmarried couple household" is composed of two unrelated adults of the opposite sex (one of whom is the householder) who share a housing unit. Note the comments on this definition *ibid*, p 5.

[i] See Statistics Norway *Weekly Bulletin Number 23 1997* and *Weekly Bulletin Number 21 1997* (available in English at Statistics Norway's worldwide website): 225,000 cohabiting couples, 850,000 married couples and a total population of 4,397,000.

acceptability. In the early stages of its development in a society, cohabitation tends to serve as a trial period for an ultimately intended marriage. In this phase, the birth of a child is normally the occasion for formalising the relationship into a legal marriage. However, in Scandinavia[19] and in the Commonwealth countries and, more recently, in the United Kingdom, it has become more common for a non-marital cohabitation to continue despite the advent of children.[20] This changed pattern shows cohabitation operating more as an alternative, rather than a precursor, to formal marriage.

However, it is also possible to have a cohabitation which bears no relationship to conventional notions of marriage. One Canadian judge[21] has usefully pointed to the difficulty with phrases such as "common law relationship", "quasi-spousal" or "quasi-matrimonial relationship". She suggested that such phrases are often euphemisms for a cohabitation which simply serves the convenience of a sexual relationship and which has none of the qualities of commitment and permanence which usually characterise a marriage.[22]

Thus, it seems fair to say that, at all stages of a society's development, cohabitation is entered into for a variety of reasons. It may be useful to review some of the motives which have been suggested as underlying the decision to cohabit outside marriage. Freeman and Lyon[23] identify four major factors in the growth of cohabitation.[24] These are (1) "the ideological response" whereby couples reject "the traditional marriage contract and the assumption of roles which necessarily seem to go with it";[25] (2) "the law-avoidance response" which is relevant where one or more partner is legally unable to marry due e.g. to restrictions on the availability of divorce;[26] (3) "the financial response" whereby those involved (often in second unions) seek to avoid leaving themselves open to financially and emotionally costly legal proceedings in the event of an ultimate breakdown of the relationship;[27] and finally (4) "the postponement response", which Freeman and Lyon subdivide into the self-explanatory subcategories of the "trial marriage response" and the "pre-marital sexual experience response".[28] Of Freeman and

---

[19] Note the recent figures suggesting that one in three babies born in Norway are born to parents who are cohabiting. See Statistics Norway *Weekly Bulletin No 26 1997* (available in English at Statistics Norway's worldwide website).

[20] See Harding *Family, State and Social Policy* (Basingstoke: MacMillan Press, 1996) p 83.

[21] Southin JA in *Crick v Ludwig* (1994) 117 DLR (4th) 228, 235. Cf. *Evans v Marmont* (1997) 42 NSWLR 70, 89–90 per Mason P.

[22] Cf. text to and following n 98 *infra*.

[23] See n 6 *supra*, p 50 *et seq*.

[24] They do not claim that their list of factors is exhaustive. See also the list of eleven reasons for cohabitation set out in Hoggett, Pearl, Cooke and Bates *The Family, Law and Society: Cases and Materials*, 4th edn (London: Butterworths, 1996) p 38, referring to Meade "Consortium Rights of the Unmarried—Time for a Reappraisal" (1981) 12 *Family Law Quarterly* 213.

[25] See n 6 *supra*, p 51.

[26] Note that this issue would have been of considerable importance in Ireland until the introduction of divorce through the Family Law (Divorce) Act 1996.

[27] This category also includes those who decline to marry on the basis of perceived financial advantages accruing to the couple from the avoidance of marriage.

[28] See n 6 *supra*, p 55.

Lyon's categories, the first three (the "ideological response", the "law-avoidance response" and the "financial response") would all tend to map onto a pattern of long-term cohabitation involving child-rearing whereas the "postponement response" would appear to indicate a pattern of shorter term cohabitation without children.

As will be pointed out later in this chapter, the differing motives of the parties in entering into a cohabitation are likely to be of significance in the assessment of their property rights. However, the whole question is a very difficult one, since people's motives may change over time. Consider the case of a couple who move in together at an early stage in their relationship, seeing their cohabitation as a trial period before a possible marriage. If for some reason (probably the reluctance of one partner) they never actually marry, they will not necessarily separate. Many of the cases in this area involve relationships which drift on for many years, even after it has become apparent that the originally envisaged marriage will never take place. Such a relationship begins as a "trial marriage" and ends, in effect, as an alternative to marriage. Moreover, the two parties to such a relationship may have acted with different motives, with perhaps one party attributing the failure to marry to the "ideological response" while the other is selfishly thinking in terms of protecting himself or herself in the event of a breakdown (the "financial response"). Therefore, while courts have sometimes sensibly insisted on the need to take into account the reasons for the decision not to marry,[29] this is made very difficult by the fact that the parties may have shifting and competing motives for their actions.

B. Homosexual Cohabitation[30]

1. *Prevalence of same sex cohabitation*

It is now necessary to consider the question of cohabitation between partners of the same sex. Presumably as a result of the tendency to marginalise same sex relationships, it is difficult to find statistics revealing the extent of homosexual cohabitation.[31] However, in the 1996 Censuses in Australia and New Zealand, information was for the first time collected on same sex cohabitation. The resulting figures were comparatively low and probably do not reflect the full extent of the social phenomenon of same sex cohabitation in either country. Statistics from the USA reveal the rate of homosexual cohabitation in that

---

[29] See e.g. *Bernard* v *Josephs* [1982] Ch 391, 403B–C per Griffiths LJ. Cf. Cretney and Masson, n 16 *supra*, pp 146–148.

[30] For general discussion of the law's construction of homosexuality, see Collier *Masculinity, Law and the Family* (London: Routledge, 1995) pp 90–110.

[31] The statistics available in the United Kingdom and Ireland do not distinguish between couples who cohabit in same sex and heterosexual relationships. See nn e and f to Table 1.1 *supra*. In Canada, on the other hand, the Census statistics are based around a definition of "common law partner" which covers only opposite sex couples. See n b to Table 1.1 *supra*.

country to be many times higher than that indicated for Australia and New Zealand. One suspects that the social stigma which has been attached to same sex relationships may have dissuaded people in Australia and New Zealand from responding accurately to a novel Census question.[32]

Table 1.2: Rates of Same Sex Cohabitation

Country	Same sex couples as percentage of all unmarried couples	Same sex couples as a percentage of all couples
Australia (1996)[a]	2.6%	0.2%
New Zealand (1996)[b]	2.8%	0.4%
USA (1995)[c]	29.8%	2.7%

[a] The Census showed 11,300 male couples and 8,300 female couples. See also n c to Table 1.1 *supra*. Information supplied in a personal communication to the author by Mr Andrew Webster of the Family Statistics Unit, Australian Bureau of Statistics.

[b] The Census showed 6,510 people living in same sex couples. Female same sex couples made up 55.7 per cent of the total. See Statistics New Zealand, n 32 *supra*, p 18. See also n d toTable 1.1 *supra*.

[c] See Saluter and Lugaila, n 9 *supra*, Table 8: 1,760,000 men and 1,610,000 women living with a partner of the same sex. See also n to Table 1.1 *supra*.

2. *Legal treatment of same sex cohabitation*

Same sex cohabitation takes place against an unaccommodating legal background. Lesbians and gay men do not have the option of formalising their relationships in a legally recognised marriage.[33] Therefore, whereas patterns of heterosexual cohabitation are affected by the fact that many couples choose marriage ahead of cohabitation, same sex cohabitation covers the full range of possible relationships, from casual to deeply committed. This means that it will

[32] See also Statistics New Zealand 1996 *Census of Population and Dwellings: Families and Households* (Wellington: Statistics New Zealand, 1998) p 18, suggesting that it is likely that the figure given underestimates the true number of same sex couples in New Zealand "because of inconsistencies in the way people have responded to the Census question".

[33] See Lord Penzance's influential definition of marriage in *Hyde* v *Hyde* (1866) LR 1 P&D 130, 133 "marriage, as understood in Christendom, may . . . be defined as the voluntary union for life of one man and one woman, to the exclusion of all others". Cf. *Quilter* v *Attorney General* [1998] 1 NZLR 523; Woolley "Excluded by Definition: Same Sex Couples and the Right to Marry" (1995) 45 *University of Toronto Law Journal* 471. Some jurisdictions have made moves to address this discrimination. See Neilson "Family Rights and the 'Registered Partnership' in Denmark" (1990) 4 *International Journal of Law and the Family* 297; Henson "A Comparative Analysis of Same-Sex Partnership Protections: Recommendations for American Reform" (1993) 7 *International Journal of Law and the Family* 282; Bradley *Family Law and Political Culture: Scandinavian Laws in Comparative Perspective* (London: Sweet and Maxwell, 1996) pp 101–105; 151–155; 217–222; Nygh "Homosexual Partnerships in Sweden" (1997) 11 *Australian Journal of Family Law* 11; Eekalaar "Registered Same Sex Partnerships and Marriages—A Statistical Comparison" [1998] *Fam Law* 561; *Fitzpatrick* v *Sterling Housing Association Ltd* [1998] Ch 304, 334D–G per Ward LJ.

not always be possible, for the purpose of legal analysis, to assimilate same sex couples with their heterosexual counterparts. Obviously, for example, it will never be relevant to inquire, as it might be in relation to a heterosexual couple, as to whether the partners' rejection of marriage indicates a lack of commitment to their relationship.

In discussing same sex cohabitation, it is also essential to remember that homosexual relationships have long been regarded with suspicion and hostility by heterosexual society in the jurisdictions considered in this book.[34] It appears that there is now a trend towards "a greater openness in, and the removal of public censoriousness towards, gay and lesbian cohabitation"[35] and it has been optimistically contended that "the tide in favour of equality rolls relentlessly forward".[36] However, whether or not the situation is improving,[37] same sex couples are still subjected to discrimination in many areas of their lives.[38] Attempts to challenge the discriminatory treatment of same sex couples have, as yet, met with limited success in the courts.[39] Given the difficulties generally faced by same sex couples, it will be necessary, at a later point in this chapter, to examine carefully the special features of property disputes in the context of homosexual unions.[40]

II. DETERMINING SEPARATE PROPERTY OWNERSHIP IN THE CONTEXT OF INTIMATE RELATIONSHIPS

Now that the sociological phenomenon of cohabitation without marriage has been briefly discussed, it is possible to move on to consider the difficult problems surrounding the determination of property rights in the context of an intimate cohabitation.

---

[34] Of course, there is (and has been) a variation in treatment across the five countries (and across the various jurisdictions within some of those countries). Tasmania, for example, was particularly slow in eliminating the legal prohibition on certain male homosexual acts. See Purvis and Castellino "A History of Homosexual Law Reform in Tasmania" (1997) 16 *University of Tasmania Law Review* 12. See also *Norris* v *Attorney General* [1984] IR 36 and the Irish Criminal Justice (Sexual Offences) Act 1993.

[35] *Fitzpatrick* v *Sterling Housing Association Ltd* [1998] Ch 304, 308 per Waite LJ.

[36] *Ibid*, 340 per Ward LJ. Cf. *Toonen* v *Australia Communication* [1994] 1–3 IHRR 97 (Art 26 of the International Covenant on Civil and Political Rights held to cover discrimination based on sexual orientation); Resolution of the European Parliament (OJ C 61 28.2.94) on equal rights for lesbians and gay men in the European Community.

[37] Note the comparatively recent introduction of s 28 of the English Local Government Act 1988, which prevented a local authority from promoting "the teaching in any maintained school of the acceptability of homosexuality as a pretended family relationship".

[38] See Henson n 33 *supra*, 283.

[39] See e.g. *Fitzpatrick* v *Sterling Housing Association Ltd* [1998] Ch 304; *A-G of Canada* v *Mossop* (1993) 100 DLR (4th) 658; *Egan* v *Canada* (1995) 124 DLR (4th) 609 (contrast *Miron* v *Trudel* (1995) 124 DLR (4th) 693); *Grant* v *South-West Trains Ltd* [1998] 1 CMLR 993. Cf. *R* v *Ministry of Defence, ex p Smith* [1996] QB 517; *R* v *Secretary of State for Defence, ex p Perkins* [1997] IRLR 297; *Re T, Petitioner* 1997 SLT 724; *Re W (A Minor) (Adoption: Homosexual Adopter)* [1998] Fam 58; *M* v *H* (1996) 142 DLR (4th) 1; *Vriend* v *Alberta* (1998) 156 DLR (4th) 385.

[40] See Part II(B)(3) *infra*.

The strict rules of property law become difficult to apply when the parties to a transaction are not strangers but are intimately associated with one another. In these situations it may prove very difficult "to unravel the tangled skein of human association, and apply to it considerations of legal principle".[41] Much of the law's experience in this area has been in dealing with married couples rather than with those cohabiting outside marriage. Therefore, the story of the development of matrimonial property law is an important part of the background to the problem of the property rights of cohabitees. However, while there are many similarities between married and unmarried couples, there are also a number of significant differences. Therefore, having examined the learning developed in the matrimonial cases, it will then be necessary to consider what modifications are necessary in applying this learning to disputes between unmarried couples.

A. Matrimonial Property Disputes

1. *The inherent difficulty in resolving matrimonial property disputes*

Over the years, the courts in all the jurisdictions under discussion have encountered various difficulties in dealing with disputes over matrimonial property.[42] In the first place, there are evidential problems in ascertaining the precise ownership of matrimonial property. The parties may feel that "to talk of property matters at all indicates a distrust, or at least an attitude inconsistent with that which is appropriate amongst persons newly living together".[43] Lord Hodson in *Pettitt* v *Pettitt*[44] regarded it as "grotesque" to imagine a "normal married couple spending the long winter evenings hammering out agreements about their possessions".[45] Another, and perhaps more fundamental, difficulty is that the parties are unlikely to contemplate the breakdown of the marriage.[46] Their belief in the permanency of the relationship leads them to order their affairs purely on the basis of mutual convenience. In the marriage situation "it would happily often have been a matter of indifference and, in very many cases, almost a matter of irrelevance whether ownership was in one spouse or in the other or whether ownership was joint".[47] Furthermore, it is important to note that it was, until comparatively recent times, the normal practice when a married couple were acquiring a house to convey that house into the sole name of the husband. This would have had the *prima facie* effect of giving him the full ownership of the house.

---

[41] *Allen* v *Snyder* [1977] 2 NSWLR 685, 689 per Glass JA.

[42] For discussion of the historical background, see Holcombe *Wives and Property: Reform of the Married Women's Property Law in 19th Century England* (Oxford: Martin Robertson & Co, 1983).

[43] *Allen* v *Snyder* [1977] 2 NSWLR 685, 705 per Mahoney JA.

[44] [1970] AC 777.

[45] *Ibid*, 810. See also *Heavey* v *Heavey* (1974) 111 ILTR 1, 3 per Kenny J.

[46] As Dohm J put it in *Anderson* v *Luoma* (1986) 50 RFL (2d) 127, 148: "What reasonable person reads the end of a book first?"

[47] [1970] AC 777, 801 per Lord Morris.

The above considerations made it seem harsh to apply to married couples the normal rules of law which would be applicable between strangers. This perceived harshness prompted attempts by the English courts in the 1950s and 1960s to step entirely outside the existing framework of legal doctrine in the particular area of marital breakdown.

2. *Early judicial attempts to develop special rules for matrimonial disputes*[48]

The first attempt was based on a rather wishful interpretation of section 17 of the Married Women's Property Act 1882, which provides that "[i]n any question between husband and wife as to title or possession of property, either party . . . may apply by summons or otherwise in a summary way to any judge . . . and the judge . . . may make such order with respect to the property in dispute . . . as he thinks fit".

The early history of section 17 is "regrettably obscure"[49] but a number of post-war decisions of the English Court of Appeal clearly proceeded on the basis that the section afforded to the court some discretion in the determination of property rights on the breakdown of a marriage. Judicial opinions as to the extent of this discretion varied greatly. The claim for a discretion under section 17 was couched in its most extreme form by Lord Denning MR in *Hine* v *Hine*[50] where he said:

> "It seems to me that the jurisdiction of the court over family assets under s 17 is entirely discretionary. Its discretion transcends all rights, legal or equitable, and enables the court to make such order as it thinks fit. This means, as I understand it, that the court is entitled to make such order as appears to be fair and just in all the circumstances of the case".[51]

Certain *dicta* of Lord Upjohn in *National Provincial Bank Ltd* v *Ainsworth*[52] cast doubt on the validity of the claim for a discretion under section 17. Perhaps partly as a result of this, the Court of Appeal developed an alternative solution, the so-called "family assets doctrine". Again, it is necessary to turn to Lord Denning MR for a statement of this doctrine:

> "[W]here a couple, by their joint efforts, get a house and furniture, intending it to be a continuing provision for them for their joint lives, it is the prima facie inference from their conduct that the house and furniture is a 'family asset' in which each is entitled to an equal share".[53]

---

[48] See generally Brady "Trusts, Law Reform and the Emancipation of Women" (1984) 6 *Dublin University Law Journal* (ns) 1.

[49] See the comments in Murphy and Clark *The Family Home* (London: Sweet and Maxwell, 1983) p 75 n 29.

[50] [1962] 1 WLR 1124.

[51] *Ibid*, 1127–1128.

[52] [1965] AC 1175, 1235–1236.

[53] *Gissing* v *Gissing* [1969] 2 Ch 85, 93 (CA).

The section 17 discretion and the family assets doctrine enabled the courts to move well beyond the established principles of law which would otherwise have applied to these cases. Clearly, these developments reflected a feeling amongst the English judiciary that those traditional principles were inadequate to deal justly with the fact-situations which were confronting them in the courts. Nonetheless, in two decisions of the House of Lords, *Pettitt* v *Pettitt*[54] and *Gissing* v *Gissing*,[55] these new doctrines were given their quietus.

In *Pettitt*, the Lords were unanimous that section 17 was purely procedural in nature and conferred no discretion on the court to interfere with existing property rights.[56] This refusal "to substitute the uncertain and crooked cord of discretion for the golden and straight metwand of the law"[57] was not surprising in view of the wording of section 17 itself. The "family assets" doctrine was also decisively rejected in *Pettitt*. Lord Reid, for example, said:

> "I would therefore refuse to consider whether property belonging to either spouse ought to be regarded as family property for that would be introducing a new conception into English law and not merely developing existing principles".[58]

This rejection of the family assets doctrine was reaffirmed in *Gissing* v *Gissing*.[59]

3. More recent attempts to develop a broader approach: imputed contract and imputed common intention

In *Pettitt*,[60] both Lord Reid and Lord Diplock advanced suggestions as to how the law might be developed within existing principles in order to avoid the injustice attendant upon a strict application of the general rules of property law to disputes involving spouses. Lord Reid, while rejecting the "family assets" doctrine, took the view that "even where there was in fact no agreement, we can ask what the spouses or reasonable people in their shoes would have agreed if they had directed their minds to the question".[61] Thus, Lord Reid was willing to impute an agreement to the parties, thereby creating a fictional contract.

In assessing this suggestion, it is important to bear in mind the limitations of ordinary contract doctrine in such circumstances. As well as the unlikelihood of a married couple concluding an agreement which would be sufficiently precise

---

[54] [1970] AC 777.

[55] [1971] AC 886.

[56] [1970] AC 777, 793D per Lord Reid; 799C-D per Lord Morris; 808D per Lord Hodson; 813C per Lord Upjohn; and 820E per Lord Diplock. Note also the similar view taken by the Supreme Court of Canada (*Thompson* v *Thompson* (1960) 26 DLR (2d) 1), the High Court of Australia (*Wirth* v *Wirth* (1956) 98 CLR 228 and *Hepworth* v *Hepworth* (1963) 110 CLR 309), the New Zealand Court of Appeal (*Barrow* v *Barrow* [1946] NZLR 438 (as explained in e.g. *Masters* v *Masters* [1954] NZLR 82)) and the Irish High Court (*MB* v *EB*, 19 February 1980, unreported).

[57] [1970] AC 777, 808 per Lord Hodson (borrowing the language of Coke).

[58] *Ibid*, 795. See also *ibid*, 801A–C per Lord Morris; 809G–810G per Lord Hodson; 817A–H per Lord Upjohn.

[59] [1971] AC 886, 899–900 per Viscount Dilhorne.

[60] [1970] AC 777.

[61] *Ibid*, 795.

to be enforceable,[62] one must also reckon with the rule in *Balfour v Balfour*[63] that spouses in making arrangements with each other do not normally intend to create legally binding contracts.[64] As Lesser[65] argues, if one accepts the validity of the presumption laid down in *Balfour*,[66] then in imputing a contract to the parties in the fashion suggested by Lord Reid, the court "is fixing on them outstanding legal rights and duties which the House accepted they would probably not have provided for if they *had* thought about the matter".[67]

Lord Diplock's solution appears similar to that of Lord Reid. He felt that the court could impute to the parties "a common intention as to their respective property rights which as fair and reasonable men and women they presumably would have formed had they given their minds to it at the time of the relevant acquisition or improvement of a family asset".[68] However, a close examination of Lord Diplock's speech in *Pettitt*[69] shows that the fictional common intention which Lord Diplock favoured would serve to create a trust rather than a contract.

The importance of the distinction between the approaches of Lord Reid and Lord Diplock is reduced by the fact that the majority of the House of Lords in *Pettitt* found them equally unacceptable. Lord Morris stated firmly that:

"In reaching a decision the court does not and, indeed, cannot find that there was some thought in the mind of a person which was never there at all. The court must find out exactly what was done or what said and must then reach conclusion as to what was the legal result. The court does not devise or invent a legal result".[70]

Lord Hodson[71] and Lord Upjohn[72] made similar observations. This rejection of the device of the legal fiction[73] was reiterated in *Gissing*.[74]

---

[62] See text to n 45 *supra*.

[63] [1919] 2 KB 571.

[64] Note also that s 4 of the Statute of Frauds 1677 and its modern equivalents state that a contract for the sale of land (e.g. a family home) or any interest therein will not be enforceable unless it is evidenced by "a note or memorandum in writing". Section 2 of the English Law of Property (Miscellaneous Provisions) Act 1989 goes further and requires such a contract to be in writing. Cf. *United Bank of Kuwait plc v Sahib* [1997] Ch 107.

[65] "The Acquisition of Inter Vivos Matrimonial Property Rights in English Law: A Doctrinal Melting Pot" (1973) 23 *University of Toronto Law Journal* 148.

[66] But see Freeman "Contracting in the Haven: Balfour v Balfour Revisited", ch. 4 in Halson (ed) *Exploring the Boundaries of Contract* (Aldershot: Dartmouth Publishing, 1996).

[67] See n 65 *supra*, 165–166.

[68] *Pettitt* [1970] AC 777, 824.

[69] See *ibid*, 822C–D. See also *ibid*, 823G.

[70] *Ibid*, 804.

[71] *Ibid*, 810.

[72] *Ibid*, 816.

[73] See the comments of Lord MacDermott LCJ in *McFarlane v McFarlane* [1972] NI 59, 71.

[74] [1971] AC 886, 898 per Lord Morris; 900 per Viscount Dilhorne; 904 per Lord Diplock. Lord Pearson appears to have taken the same view (although note his unfortunate use (*ibid*, 902) of the loaded word "imputed"). Lord Reid "adhered" to the opinions he had stated in *Pettitt*, although he did express his views in somewhat different terms, accepting (*ibid*, 896) that the correct approach was through the law of trusts rather than the law of contract.

Since those cases there have been rare attempts to revive the controversy. Lord Denning on occasion found it convenient to make use of the minority opinions in *Pettitt*. For example, in *Hardwick* v *Johnson*[75] he relied on the views expressed by Lord Diplock in that case, without giving the slightest hint that those views had been rejected by a majority of the House of Lords. More recently, in *Burns* v *Burns*[76] Waller LJ quoted extensively from the minority speeches and it was only with "reluctance" that he allowed himself to be persuaded by the views of his Court of Appeal colleagues that the law did not permit the imputation of a deemed common intention in the circumstances of the case.[77]

Despite these isolated *dicta*, it seems that the "imputed common intention" approach has been rejected in England. Interestingly, the courts of New Zealand have in recent years spoken favourably of this approach and have seen it as one of the (many) foundations for their "reasonable expectations" doctrine.[78] However, the imputed common intention approach has not found favour in the other jurisdictions with which this work is concerned.[79]

4. *The modern equitable approach through the law of trusts*

As the previous discussion has shown, without the possibility of resort to a legal fiction, it is unlikely that the law of contract will be of assistance to a married claimant. The Lords in *Gissing* v *Gissing*[80] therefore focused their attention more closely on the law of trusts. The equitable device of the trust, "the most distinctive achievement of English lawyers",[81] makes it possible for ownership in equity to differ from that at law. The equitable (or beneficial) ownership will *prima facie* follow the legal ownership but they may be separated in a number of ways. For example, the legal owner may make a declaration of trust, thus leading to the creation of an "express" trust. Such a declaration of trust need not

---

[75] [1978] 1 WLR 683, 688.

[76] [1984] Ch 317.

[77] *Ibid*, 326.

[78] See the detailed discussion of this doctrine in Chapter 9 *infra*.

[79] See *Allen* v *Snyder* [1977] 2 NSWLR 685, 694 per Glass JA; 701 per Samuels JA; *Muschinski* v *Dodds* (1985) 160 CLR 583, 595 per Gibbs CJ; *McGill* v *S* [1979] IR 283, 294 per Gannon J. Some sympathy was shown with Lord Reid's approach in the minority judgments in the earlier Canadian cases: see *Murdoch* v *Murdoch* (1974) 41 DLR (3d) 367, 388–389 per Laskin J; *Rathwell* v *Rathwell* [1978] 2 SCR 434, 452–453 per Dickson J. However, although it may continue to exercise a subliminal influence, the imputed common intention doctrine does not feature expressly in modern Canadian statements of principle. For full discussion of the Canadian position, see Chapter 7 *infra*. Interestingly, the courts of many American jurisdictions have, in the wake of the leading case of *Marvin* v *Marvin* (1976) 18 Cal (3d) 660, adopted a solution based on implied contract. However, this approach has not been universal; see e.g. *Monroe* v *Monroe* (1980) 429 NYS (2d) 592 (NY CA). A detailed discussion of the position across the range of American jurisdictions falls outside the scope of the present work.

[80] [1971] AC 886.

[81] Maitland *Lectures on Equity*, 2nd edn by Brunyate, (Cambridge: The University Press, 1936) p 23.

take any particular form but it is necessary to demonstrate that the creation of a trust was intended.

Significantly in the present context, given that the family home is often the most valuable item of family property, each of the jurisdictions under discussion has attached formal requirements to declarations of trust which concern land. The requirement is generally that the trust be evidenced in writing.[82] Where a home is held at law in the sole name of one of the parties to a marriage (or similar relationship), it will rarely be possible for the other party to establish a suitably evidenced declaration of trust in his or her favour.[83] There are, however, other classes of trust, "implied, constructive and resulting trusts", which are excluded from the formal requirements which govern express trusts.[84] In all the jurisdictions under discussion, it has been the law of implied, resulting and constructive trusts which has governed equitable claims to a share in the ownership of a matrimonial home or other matrimonial property.

5. The advent of legislation and the continuing relevance in the matrimonial context of the equitable rules

The House of Lords tempered their strict approach in *Pettitt* with strong hints that legislation was necessary to remedy the potential injustices in the area of matrimonial property.[85] Shortly afterwards, the Matrimonial Proceedings and Property Act 1970 was introduced, giving the courts a wide discretion to adjust property rights upon the granting of a divorce. The modern equivalent of this legislation,[86] and similar legislation in the other jurisdictions under consideration,[87] allows the court to make a wide range of property adjustment orders consequent upon the granting of a divorce. Thus, for example, in an appropriate case the court could order that the ownership of a family home, originally held in the sole name of one spouse, should now be transferred (in whole or in part) to the other spouse. In making property adjustment orders, the court must have regard to a range of factors identified in the relevant statute. For example, the factors specified in section 25 and section 25A of the English Matrimonial Causes Act 1973 give the court a wide discretion in relation to the redistribution

---

[82] See s 7 of the Statute of Frauds, 1677 and its modern equivalents (for example, s 53(1)(b) of the English Law of Property Act 1925).

[83] Note, however, the impact of the principle in *Rochefoucauld* v *Boustead* [1897] 1 Ch 196, discussed in Chapter 5 *infra*, text following n 237. Where the home is in joint names, it is normal practice in England (but not to the same extent in other jurisdictions) for there to be a declaration, at the time of the conveyance, as to how the beneficial interests shall be shared. For discussion of the effect of such a declaration, see Part III(B) *infra*.

[84] See s 8 of the Statute of Frauds 1677 and its modern equivalents (for example, s 53(2) of the English Law of Property Act 1925).

[85] [1970] AC 777, 797A per Lord Reid; 803A per Lord Morris; 811D per Lord Hodson.

[86] See the consolidating Matrimonial Causes Act 1973.

[87] See e.g. Australia's Family Law Act 1976. Note, however, that some jurisdictions have taken a further step and operate on the basis of an equal sharing of matrimonial assets rather than on the basis of a generalised statutory discretion. See e.g. New Zealand's Matrimonial Property Act 1976.

of property. Significantly, the court is entitled to take account of "the contributions made by each of the parties to the welfare of the family, including any contribution made by looking after the home or caring for the family".[88] Thus, in the event of divorce, the statutory jurisdiction will generally displace the more restrictive rules which had previously been relied upon by the courts. This legislation has greatly reduced the significance of the rules of equity in the context of matrimonial disputes and in recent years an increasing number of the reported family property cases have involved couples living together outside marriage.

There are, however, a number of important circumstances in which it will still be necessary to determine the ownership of matrimonial property without the benefit of the statutory rules. These circumstances include cases where (for religious or other reasons) no formal divorce or judicial separation[89] is obtained. Without the trigger of a divorce or judicial separation, the ancillary property adjustment jurisdiction of the court is not available. There are also other, rather different, circumstances where the separate entitlements of the spouses will suddenly become of great significance.[90] The first is where either spouse dies. In order to apply the rules of the law of succession, it will be necessary to determine what property actually forms part of the deceased spouse's estate and what property already belongs to the surviving spouse.[91] Likewise, separate ownership will be vital if a creditor seeks to enforce a security against the property of one of the spouses[92] or if either spouse is adjudicated a bankrupt.[93] In this type of case, where the rights of creditors are at issue, very different considerations will motivate the parties when they argue their separate property entitlements in court. For example, it will obviously be in the interests of the family as a whole if a bankrupt husband can demonstrate that his wife is entitled to a share in the beneficial ownership of their home, thereby removing that share from the grasp of his creditors.[94]

In all the situations described above, one must have resort to the ordinary rules of the law of property and equity in order to determine the separate property entitlements of the spouses.[95] This means that, when one comes to consider developing the common law rules in order to solve disputes between unmarried

---

[88] Matrimonial Causes Act 1973, s 25(2)(f).

[89] Note that the English Family Law Act 1996 abolishes the decree of "judicial separation" in favour of the power to make a "separation order". For discussion, see Cretney and Masson n 16 *supra*, pp 385–389.

[90] Cf. Cretney and Masson *ibid*, 118–120.

[91] See e.g. *Bryson v Bryant* (1992) 29 NSWLR 188.

[92] See e.g. *Lloyds Bank plc v Rosset* [1991] 1 AC 107; *Midland Bank plc v Cooke* [1995] 4 All ER 562.

[93] See e.g. *Re Densham* [1975] 1 WLR 1519.

[94] Cf. *Midland Bank plc v Dobson* [1986] 1 FLR 171.

[95] Although the issue will generally have more symbolic than practical importance, the ownership of property at any point in the currency of a subsisting marriage must also be determined by reference to the ordinary rules of the law of property and equity. Cf. English Law Commission *Third Report on Family Property: The Matrimonial Home (Co-Ownership and Occupation Rights) and Household Goods*, Law Com No 86 (London: HMSO, 1978) pp 3–4.

cohabitees, one must bear in mind the continuing significance of those rules in the marital context. Accordingly, although this book concerns the problem of unmarried cohabitation, it will be necessary at various points throughout the book to consider whether the various doctrines under consideration might have a negative impact upon the position of married couples.

B. Disputes Between Cohabitees

With the important exception of a number of Australian jurisdictions,[96] there are no statutory provisions applicable to the determination of property rights in the context of a relationship which never involved marriage. Therefore, disputes involving unmarried couples (whether upon the termination of the relationship or the death or bankruptcy of either partner) must generally be dealt with under the general law. Thus, one begins with the position reached by equity in its efforts to resolve matrimonial property disputes (i.e. a rejection of the law of contract in favour of the rules of implied, constructive and resulting trusts). However, in applying the rules of equity to unmarried rather than married couples, there is a danger that assumptions deriving from the matrimonial property cases will be unquestioningly carried forward into the new situation. It will be useful, at this stage, to explore briefly the relevant assumptions and to test them against the reality of unmarried cohabitation.

1. *The matrimonial property "mind-set"*

It seems fair to suggest that very few judges and commentators felt comfortable with the application to married couples of the strict rules of law applicable between strangers. There was an almost universal feeling that the rules of equity were too crude and inflexible to deal with matrimonial property and that they led to extreme injustice in many cases. Upon reflection, one can see that a number of aspects of the matrimonial context conspired together to create this injustice.

First, as has been mentioned already, there was the fact that it was, for many years, customary for a family home to be conveyed into the sole name of the male bread-winner. Since the family home was often the primary family asset, this practice gave a crucial advantage to the husband in the event of an eventual breakdown of the marriage. Secondly, and of course related to the previous point, there was the typical pattern of married life which involved the husband

---

[96] See New South Wales' De Facto Relationships Act 1984; Victoria's Property Law (Amendment) Act 1987, adding a new Part IX to the Property Law Act 1958 (regime applicable only to real property); the Northern Territory's De Facto Relationships Act 1991; the Australian Capital Territory's Domestic Relationships Act 1994; and the South Australian De Facto Relationships Act 1996. Of these statutes, only the penultimate is applicable to same sex couples. Cf. New Zealand's De Facto Relationships (Property) Bill 1998; Owusu "Union Other Than Marriage Under the Barbados Family Law Act 1981" (1992) 21 *Anglo-American Law Review* 449.

going out to work and the wife staying at home to raise a family. Society actively worked against allowing married women access to the job market, both in obvious ways, in the shape of direct discrimination, and in more subtle ways, at the level of societal conditioning as to the proper role of women within the home. The tendency for married women to work exclusively in the home left them in a very weak position in the event of a breakdown in the marriage. Lacking training or experience, they often found it difficult to return to the labour force. Moreover, from a legal point of view, their contribution to the family in the home was not easy for the courts to accommodate within the traditional structure of the law of trusts. This difficulty was due in part to the sort of gender bias which had, in the first instance, relegated work in the home to the category of "women's work". However, it was also due to the fact that the relevant parts of the law of trusts had not been developed with the problem of matrimonial property in mind and therefore could not really be expected to respond sensitively to its demands. Thirdly, there was the fact that it was perfectly understandable, given the central role of marriage within the organisation of society at the time, for a wife to expect that, having committed herself to marriage, she would be protected by the law.

These various factors led commentators and judges to regard the strict rules of equity as "[V]ictorian and unjust"[97] in their application to matrimonial property disputes. However, one must now examine whether or not these same factors operate in the context of unmarried cohabitation.

2. *The position in relation to unmarried cohabitation*

When one comes to look at unmarried cohabitation, it is immediately obvious that matters are rather different. In the first case, there was no tradition of automatically putting the family home into the name of the male cohabitee. Therefore, if his name appears on the title one cannot assume, as one might have in relation to the earlier matrimonial cases, that this was merely a matter of form and revealed nothing about the true intentions of the parties. Furthermore, it is important to remember that an unmarried cohabitation, unlike a marriage, will not always have a clearly identifiable starting point. Therefore, the beginning of a cohabitation is less likely than the start of a marriage to be the occasion for the purchase of a house intended to be the family home for life. The home of an unmarried couple may well have been purchased by one partner at an earlier point in time and with an intention entirely unrelated to the relationship which eventuated.

A second point is that the parties to an unmarried cohabitation will have less justification for assuming that their relationship will be permanent. Obviously, it will depend to a large extent on the nature of the particular cohabitation. It may be that the parties are living together in a "trial marriage", in which case it

---

[97] *Per* Mackenzie J in *B v B*, Irish High Court, 22 April 1986 unreported, p 8 of the transcript.

would be clear that both are keeping their options open as to the permanence of the relationship. Another possibility is that one party has expressly refused to commit himself or herself to marriage. Again, this fact may militate against the other party assuming that the relationship will necessarily last indefinitely. It would appear that an assumption of permanence would be most likely (and most justifiable) in only one subcategory of cohabitation, where the relationship has settled into a "quasi-matrimonial" pattern and the claimant has been given the impression that his or her partner is committed to him or her for the indefinite future.

Unfortunately, while the reality is that unmarried cohabitations vary in the expectations of permanence which they engender, there is a tendency for judges to assimilate all such cohabitations with the familiar model of marriage. As Southin JA explained in her dissenting judgment in *Crick v Ludwig*,[98] "most judges, at least in the higher courts, come from a time when reputable members of society did not openly live together without benefit of clergy or marriage commissioner".[99] The judge went on to emphasise the danger of judges assuming that "young people who live together must intend the relationship to have the permanent quality of a formal marriage, albeit without the piece of paper".[100] In fact, Southin JA believed "[t]he social reality . . . is that many of these couples have no such intention . . . [and] are simply having a good time without intending any commitment, emotional or economic, to each other".[101]

A third point, which is again related to the previous point, is that it is by no means "grotesque" to think of an unmarried couple giving conscious thought to their property rights in the event of an ultimate separation. Despite the reservations of some commentators,[102] this is both an entirely rational and a relatively frequent response by those who live outside the cocoon of protection which the law provides for married couples. While some unmarried partners fit the stereotype of dewy-eyed infatuation inconsistent with any self-interested thought,[103] many others are conscious of the need to protect their position as against their partner. This is especially true of those who have previously been involved in an unsuccessful marriage (a category of people who are heavily represented in the

---

[98] (1994) 117 DLR (4th) 228.

[99] *Ibid*, 236.

[100] *Ibid*. As Southin JA emphasised (*ibid*, 235), this danger is increased by the use of terms such as "quasi-spousal" or "quasi-matrimonial" to describe an unmarried cohabitation. Interestingly, the analogy with marriage is often partly hidden in the terminology. For example, in Australia and New Zealand it is common to speak of "de facto" relationships, with no apparent perception that all human relationships are "de facto" in nature. What has happened is that the phrase "de facto marriage" has been shortened to provide an alternative which does not overtly refer back to marriage. A similar transformation seems to have occurred in relation to the (less common) term "common law relationship" (as against "common law marriage").

[101] *Ibid*.

[102] See Hayes and Williams *Family Law: Principles, Policy and Practice* (London: Butterworths, 1995) p 563 n 20 (couples are often "vague and haphazard" about their financial affairs "[y]et surely such a trusting approach is to be encouraged").

[103] See the Australian case of *Woodward v Johnston* (1991) 14 Fam LR 828, 830: "I was like a little puppy dog. I was doing it because I loved him in them days".

cohabitation statistics).[104] The trauma of a divorce and consequent property settlement will frequently be enough to clear the vision of the most romantic soul. The reported cases from the Commonwealth jurisdictions show many examples of vulnerable cohabitees who have sought to persuade their partner to provide them with "security"[105] and, on the other hand, cohabitees who feel they have been wronged in relation to a previous property settlement and are determined to give nothing away to their new partner.[106] Thus, while relatively few couples actually conclude formal cohabitation contracts governing their property rights, it is clear that the conduct of more couples is influenced (at least to some degree) by an awareness of the possibility of an ultimate breakdown in their relationship.

Finally, it is necessary to address the assumption that the female partner will work in the home and will necessarily be damaged economically by the relationship. The interesting aspect of this assumption is that it is no longer true even of married couples. Digressing slightly, it may be pointed out that much of the social thinking on family property disputes has been frozen at a point in the early 1970s. After that time, legislation has taken matrimonial property disputes largely out of equity's remit in many jurisdictions and, as a result, equitable thinking on the matter has tended to stagnate. One is left with the danger of applying to unmarried cohabitation stereotypes based on the different situation of marriage which, moreover, are largely outdated.[107] Returning to the point under discussion, what is sometimes forgotten is that it is now very frequent for both partners to a relationship to work outside the home. As a result, the assumption that women are necessarily dependent on men has increasingly been questioned.[108] Therefore, while not forgetting that more women than men work in the home (and that women who work outside the home earn less on average than men),[109] it must also be remembered that this is not a universal trend and that each case must be treated on its own merits.

This section has identified a number of differences between marriage and unmarried cohabitation. The ultimate conclusion must be that one cannot unthinkingly apply the same assumptions to both situations. While some of the leading cases have involved relationships akin to marriage,[110] by no means all

---

[104] See text to n 14 *supra*.

[105] See e.g. *Atkinson v Burt* (1989) 12 Fam LR 800 (female cohabitee concerned that her partner's estranged wife might evict her if he were to die; he, in turn, feared that his partner might leave him if he put the property into joint names).

[106] See e.g. *Booth v Beresford* (1993) 17 Fam LR 147.

[107] Thus, for example, it is also no longer the case that matrimonial homes are automatically put into the sole name of the husband. Changes in social thinking and the dictates of lenders have combined to ensure that it is normal practice in all jurisdictions to convey property into the joint names of the spouses.

[108] See e.g. Deech "The Case Against the Legal Recognition of Cohabitation" (1980) 29 ICLQ 480, 485–489.

[109] Cf. Wong "Constructive Trusts over the Family Home: Lessons to be Learned from Other Commonwealth Jurisdictions?" (1998) 18 *Legal Studies* 369, 373.

[110] See e.g. *Burns v Burns* [1984] Ch 317 (19-year cohabitation); *Sorochan v Sorochan* (1986) 29 DLR (4th) 1 (42 years).

cases involving unmarried partners fall into this pattern. It is proposed to conclude this Part with a brief discussion of the British Columbia case of *Crick* v *Ludwig*[111] which should provide a counterweight to the "matrimonial property mind-set".

The cohabitation in *Crick* v *Ludwig*[112] lasted for a little over two years. Both parties were "young, attractive, accomplished and experienced".[113] The plaintiff was a flight attendant and the defendant a businessman. Both parties continued to work throughout the relationship. As a result of the relationship, the plaintiff was able to enjoy an exalted lifestyle. The defendant paid "the vast majority of the expenses" for the couple's seventeen holidays to destinations such as Bali, Thailand and Hawaii. When the defendant fell ill with cancer, the plaintiff took two months off work to care for him. When he had recovered, he took her on a long skiing trip to Europe "to do something special for her". The plaintiff helped with the renovation of the defendant's house, primarily by helping to select certain materials and supervising aspects of the decorating. However, she made no financial contribution and the contractor testified that her work "had no effect whatsoever on the cost of the project to the defendant".[114] She also acted as hostess when they had visitors. She lived rent free in the defendant's house and the defendant "paid for the upkeep of the house and most of the living expenses, including groceries".[115] Both parties had married other people by the time the action came to be tried.

The majority of the British Columbia Court of Appeal, reversing the trial judge, held that the plaintiff was entitled to $45,000 from the defendant under the doctrine of unjust enrichment. The majority believed that "provision for her living expenses" had not adequately compensated the claimant for her contributions to entertaining and housekeeping, in helping with the renovations and in caring for her partner while he was ill. However, Southin JA dissented, finding no unjust enrichment. She concluded that:

"[U]pon viewing what I perceive to be the full picture of this short relationship, I see neither enrichment nor a corresponding deprivation. She helped with the renovation of the house, the gardening and the entertaining. She looked after him for two months while he was ill, although I do not understand that he required nursing as such. She did not give up her job and, so far as I can tell, suffered no significant loss of seniority from their time together. He spent lots of money on her. They had some good times and the good times ended".[116]

The decision of the majority in *Crick* provides an example of a case where, judging from the report, injustice was done to a defendant who had made no commitment to, and taken no advantage of, his erstwhile partner. The case is

---

[111] (1994) 117 DLR (4th) 228.
[112] *Ibid.*
[113] *Ibid*, 237 per Southin JA (dissenting).
[114] *Ibid*, 233.
[115] *Ibid.*
[116] *Ibid*, 239.

considered at this point in order to demonstrate the point that glib moral judgments in this area are not secure. *Crick* v *Ludwig* shows that the problems presented by unmarried cohabitation are, if anything, more intractable than those arising out of the marriage situation. The challenge for the courts is to derive from the general principles of equity a doctrine which is sufficiently sophisticated to deal with the full variety of cohabitation, from "good times" liaisons to true "quasi-matrimonial" partnerships.

3. *Special problems relating to homosexual cohabitation*[117]

It has already been noted that lesbians and gay men suffer from systemic discrimination in all the jurisdictions with which this book is concerned. It is therefore likely that a homosexual cohabitee will face special difficulties in attempting to claim a share of his or her partner's property after their relationship has broken down.

Upon reflection, it appears that many of these problems will arise, not as a result of deficiencies in the relevant equitable doctrines, but rather because of the manner in which judges may apply them in the context of homosexual cohabitation. The point is that, as will emerge in the chapters which follow, in cases dealing with heterosexual cohabitation, equity has traditionally refused to make any doctrinal concessions to the reality of the relationships involved. The rules applied are those which would be equally applicable as between strangers. Thus, at least in England and Ireland, there is no specially generous equitable model designed to do justice between heterosexual cohabitees, into which homosexual couples might be admitted or from which they might be unfairly excluded. Thus, in *Tinsley* v *Milligan*,[118] a dispute over the ownership of the family home of a lesbian couple, the House of Lords applied the purchase money resulting trust doctrine[119] without comment. Moreover, Lord Browne-Wilkinson took the view[120] that the claimant's entitlement to a share could equally be explained in terms of authorities such as *Gissing* v *Gissing*[121] and *Lloyds Bank plc* v *Rosset*,[122] cases which set out the "common intention" trust doctrine generally applied in England to disputes between heterosexual cohabitees.[123]

In the other jurisdictions considered in this book, Canada, Australia and New Zealand, there does appear to be a degree of emphasis on the nature of the relationship between the parties. However, as will emerge in later chapters, none of the relevant doctrines depends on a rigid policy of according a particular status

---

[117] See generally, Flynn and Lawson "Gender, Sexuality and the Doctrine of Detrimental Reliance" (1995) 3 *Feminist Legal Studies* 105, discussing *Wayling* v *Jones* (1995) 69 P & CR 170.

[118] [1994] 1 AC 340.

[119] Discussed in detail in Chapter 2 *infra*.

[120] [1994] 1 AC 340, 371.

[121] [1971] AC 886.

[122] [1991] 1 AC 107.

[123] For detailed discussion of the relevant doctrine, see Chapter 5 *infra*.

to certain types of relationship; the doctrines depend on the fact that, in the circumstances of an intimate cohabitation, the parties may neglect to protect their separate property entitlements. Thus, to apply these doctrines to homosexual couples, the courts would not be required to take the step of affirming that homosexual relationships are as valuable and worthwhile as heterosexual relationships. The courts must simply recognise that in the circumstances of a homosexual cohabitation, as much as in a heterosexual cohabitation, the partners may make contributions and sacrifices which (on the basis of the various doctrines in the different jurisdictions) justify a remedy. There has been no suggestion in the courts that the doctrines developed by the Canadian, Australian and New Zealand courts are not, at a formal level at least, equally applicable to disputes between homosexual couples.

This point is supported by the Australian case of *Bell* v *Elliot*,[124] one of the few available written decisions which concerned a same sex couple. The lesbian couple in *Bell* had lived together for the sixteen years prior to the sudden death of one partner. The deceased woman had left no will and so her parents were *prima facie* entitled to all her property under the rules of intestate succession. The couple had owned the family home as tenants in common in the proportion of one quarter to the plaintiff and three-quarters to the deceased. The plaintiff claimed that, notwithstanding this legal position, she was entitled to a one-half share under a resulting or constructive trust.

Macready J took the view that the parties were "in no different situation, given their close emotional and sexual involvement, from a de facto man and wife".[125] The judge held that, given the common intention of the parties, the plaintiff was entitled to succeed in her claim to a one-half share in the family home. This conclusion involved the application of the older "common intention" analysis[126] but Macready J also felt that a very similar result[127] would follow upon the application of the more radical "unconscionability" doctrine which has been central to Australian law in this area since *Baumgartner* v *Baumgartner*.[128]

The *Bell* case, and similar isolated cases from Canada[129] and New Zealand,[130] suggest that there is no doctrinal obstacle to a claim by a same sex

---

[124] NSW Sup Ct, November 26 1996 (LEXIS). See also *Harmer* v *Pearson* (1993) 16 Fam LR 596 (Qd CA) (unsuccessful claim by gay man).

[125] *Ibid*, p 13.

[126] *Ibid*, pp 19–20. See Chapter 5 *infra* for discussion of the relevant doctrine.

[127] *Ibid*, p 20.

[128] (1987) 164 CLR 137.

[129] *Anderson* v *Luoma* (1986) 50 RFL (2d) 127 (female couple); *Forrest* v *Price* (1992) 48 ETR 72 (male couple); *Regnier* v *O'Reilly* (1997) 31 RFL (4th) 122 (male couple). It is worth noting that the claims in all three cases were successful.

[130] See *Julian* v *McWatt* [1998] NZFLR 257 (Dist Ct). See also *Hamilton* v *Jurgens* [1996] NZFLR 350, 358 where Anderson J held it to be irrelevant that parties were of the same gender. Note, however, that the relationship was presented as involving "an intense loving bond" without sexual intimacy. One may observe in passing that it is possible that, for a variety of reasons, homosexual cohabitees might be tempted to suppress the true nature of their relationship in framing their legal claim. Cf. *Thwaites* v *Ryan* [1984] VR 65, 87.

cohabitee. This does not mean, of course, that homosexual cohabitees might not be subjected to discriminatory treatment at a practical level. Unfortunately, since there are so few relevant decisions from any of the jurisdictions with which this work is concerned, it is difficult to identify precisely the nature of such possible discriminatory treatment (which would, of course, depend heavily on the particular facts and on the attitude of the particular judge or judges hearing the case). It is possible, however, to venture a number of tentative observations.

First, it is necessary to address the possibility that an unfocused judicial hostility to homosexual relationships might manifest itself in a tendency to favour defendants over claimants. Judges might subconsciously (or at least without admitting it) conclude that the law should not get involved in a dispute arising out of a "questionable" relationship and should (as in cases where the litigants had both been involved in some illegality)[131] allow property rights to lie where they fall.[132]

A second possibility, again leading to difficulties for plaintiffs, is that judges might fail to take seriously the level of commitment involved in a homosexual union.[133] This could mean that judges would tend to underestimate the extent of the contributions and sacrifices of a homosexual claimant or would refuse to regard them as having been undertaken on the basis of the relationship. Of course, it would be somewhat paradoxical if judges insisted on regarding homosexual cohabitations as inherently more casual than heterosexual cohabitations; as has already been pointed out, the reality is that homosexual couples, however great their commitment, do not have the option of formal legal marriage, while heterosexual cohabitees will very often have made a deliberate choice to eschew the commitment of marriage.[134]

The discussion thus far has not addressed the cluster of issues surrounding the simple fact that the parties to a homosexual cohabitation will be of the same sex. The development of the rules applicable to the resolution of disputes between cohabitees has been greatly influenced by the dynamic of male-female power relationships. Although disputes between lesbians or gay men take place outside that dynamic, it is clear that their resolution will nonetheless be affected by it.

---

[131] Cf. *Muckleston v Brown* (1801) 6 Ves 52.

[132] Cf. *Harmer v Pearson* (1993) 16 Fam LR 596, where the Queensland Court of Appeal rather perfunctorily held that a gay man was bound by a separation agreement whereby he accepted a small share of the beneficial ownership in a jointly-owned home (in circumstances where, but for the agreement, he might have been entitled to a far larger share).

[133] See *Egan v Canada* (1995) 124 DLR (4th) 609, 677 per Cory J, deprecating "the stereotype that homosexuals cannot and do not form lasting, caring mutually supportive relationships with economic interdependence in the same manner as heterosexual couples". See also the discussion in Collier, n 30 *supra*, p 100. Cf. *Fitzpatrick v Sterling Housing Association Ltd* [1998] Ch 304, 318 where Waite LJ wondered "[i]f succession rights are to be extended to couples of the same sex in a sexually-based relationship, would it be right to continue to exclude friends?"

[134] On the other hand, there is a danger that the courts might set unrealistically high standards of fidelity, stability and altruism in homosexual relationships, failing to make the allowances for human nature which they would make in relation to a heterosexual relationship. Cf. *Fitzpatrick v Sterling Housing Association Ltd* [1998] Ch 304, 318C–D per Waite LJ.

It may be relevant that in Canada, Australia and New Zealand, where the doctrines of equity have been strained in an attempt to do justice for predominantly female heterosexual claimants, there has been an awareness of the deep-seated imbalance in the relationship between men and women. The equitable doctrines developed in these countries have been designed, in part, to remedy that imbalance.[135] It is perhaps possible that a court might (below the surface of doctrinal reasoning) have less sympathy for a gay man or a lesbian woman who sought to avail of these doctrines, given that the hardship faced by such claimants must arise, not from systemic discrimination against people of their gender by people of the gender of the defendant, but rather from factors peculiar to their particular relationship with a partner of the same sex.

It is also possible, however, that the fate of claims by same sex partners might be influenced by judicial stereotypes of male and female roles. A gay man claiming against his partner might suffer simply because he is a male claimant. In cases involving heterosexual couples, there have been comparatively few successful claims brought by men.[136] One might argue that the judicial construction of males is as emotionally strong, rational and worldly agents who are fully capable of safeguarding their own interests. This stereotype could operate against a male homosexual claimant who was in the weaker position in his relationship and who did not insist on safeguarding his rights from an early stage. The reverse argument would be to suggest that a gay man might stand less chance of success than a female heterosexual claimant because he cannot take advantage of a judicial stereotype which rewards female claimants because it regards them as irrational, dependent and unable to take full responsibility for the way in which they arrange their affairs. Conversely, this kind of stereotyping might operate in favour of a woman claiming in the context of a lesbian relationship.

Stereotyping might also impact upon the prospects of a homosexual claimant who brings a claim based on work in the home and in child-rearing.[137] Such work has traditionally been associated with women and has been undervalued as "mere women's work". While the relationships of lesbian women fall outside the male-female power relationship which initially led to the undervaluing of work in the home, it seems likely that a lesbian claimant would be in a similar position to a heterosexual woman in relying on such work. Thus, as will be seen in due course, a claimant relying on work in the home would generally fail in jurisdictions such as England or Ireland and would generally succeed in Canada

---

[135] Note, for example, the reference by McLachlin J to the "feminization of poverty" in *Peter* v *Beblow* (1993) 101 DLR (4th) 621, 648.

[136] For examples of unsuccessful claims, see *Thomas* v *Fuller-Brown* [1988] 1 FLR 237; *Gillies* v *Keogh* [1989] 2 NZLR 327.

[137] In 1996, approximately 6 per cent of all same sex couples in the USA shared a household with children under 15 years of age. This figure conceals a significant difference between female couples (11 per cent) and male couples (1.6 per cent). See Saluter and Lugaila, n 9 *supra*, pp 71–73 (Table 8).

and New Zealand.[138] In the case of a gay (or heterosexual) man who worked in the home or in child-rearing, it is not impossible that a court might be influenced by the fact that such a claimant has strayed far beyond the male stereotype. Perhaps a court might feel that for a man to perform this "woman's work" constitutes a particularly serious form of detriment and might be quicker to find in his favour than if he were a woman.[139]

A final, more general, point is that some judges may lack what has been described as an "epistemological familiarity"[140] with the reality of homosexual relationships. In other words, judges who are reasonably secure in the inferences they draw from the conduct of the parties to a heterosexual cohabitation may be less sure of themselves in dealing with the uncharted territory of a same sex relationship. Presumably, the extent of this problem will diminish to some extent as judges are educated by involvement in a number of cases involving homosexual cohabitees.

In conclusion, it appears that, at a doctrinal level, there is nothing to exclude homosexual claimants from successfully relying on the equitable doctrines which will be discussed in the later chapters of this book. At a practical level, however, various problems may be encountered, some of which have been discussed above. Inevitably, more cases involving homosexual cohabitees will reach the courts in future years and the availability of more judgments will make it easier to comment on the suitability of the doctrines of equity to do justice in such cases.

III. PRIVATE CONTRACTUAL REGULATION OF PROPERTY RIGHTS

As a final preliminary before proceeding to consider the equitable doctrines developed in the various jurisdictions, it is necessary to consider in this Part the possibility that the parties might make such doctrines irrelevant by opting for a private regulation of their property rights.

A. Cohabitation Contracts

By the end of this book, it will have become clear that, in at least some of the jurisdictions considered, the rules of equity provide very limited protection for unmarried cohabitees. To a large extent in England and Ireland, the law is that people who live together outside marriage do so at their own peril. In view of

---

[138] The position is less certain in relation to Australia. For the position in the various jurisdictions, see Chapter 5 *infra*, text following n 68 (England); Chapter 3 *infra*, text to and following n 136 (Ireland); Chapter 7 *infra*, text following n 60 (Canada); Chapter 8 *infra*, text following n 53 (Australia); Chapter 9 *infra*, text to n 65 (New Zealand).

[139] Cf. *Wayling v Jones* (1995) 69 P & CR 170, discussed by Flynn and Lawson, n 117 *supra*. See also *Forrest v Price* (1992) 48 ETR 72, 74.

[140] See Flynn and Lawson, n 117 *supra*, 115.

this, a number of commentators have drawn attention to the possibility of drawing up a cohabitation contract which would regulate *inter alia* the property rights of the parties in the event of the termination of the relationship.[141] Such contracts are comparatively rare at present but could, at least in theory,[142] provide a valuable method of protecting the rights of vulnerable cohabitees.

Although older decisions have suggested that such contracts would be unenforceable,[143] due to the "immoral" context in which they arose, it seems reasonable to suggest that such an argument would be rejected by a court in modern times. The issue was famously addressed in *Marvin v Marvin*,[144] where the Supreme Court of California concluded that "[t]he courts should enforce express contracts between non-marital partners except to the extent that the contract is explicitly founded on the consideration of meretricious sexual services".[145] It seems clear that a similar attitude would be taken by a court in Canada,[146] Australia[147] or New Zealand and, in a number of jurisdictions in these countries, the position has been clarified by express legislative recognition of cohabitation contracts.[148] It has generally been assumed that the same view would be taken in England,[149] although reservations have been expressed concerning the enforceability of a cohabitation contract between partners of the same sex.[150] Interestingly, an Irish court has recently refused to enforce an express cohabitation contract on the grounds that to do so would be contrary to

---

[141] See, in particular, Barton, n 8 *supra*.

[142] Of course, there is a natural resistance among those living together to the whole idea of a formal legal contract regulating their rights. However, as has already been pointed out, unmarried couples are probably somewhat more willing than their married counterparts to turn their minds to their separate rights.

[143] See *Walker v Perkins* (1764) 1 Wm Bl 517; *Lowe v Peers* (1768) 4 Burr 2225; *Beaumont v Reeve* (1846) 8 QB 483; *Spiers v Hunt* [1908] 1 KB 720; *Upfill v Wright* [1911] 1 KB 506; *Fender v St John Mildmay* [1938] 1 AC 1, 42 per Lord Wright; *Diwell v Farnes* [1959] 1 WLR 624; *Campbell v Campbell* [1976] Fam 347, 352 per Sir George Baker P. See Pawlowski "Cohabitation Contracts—Are They Legal?" (1996) 146 NLJ 1125; Poulter "Cohabitation Contracts and Public Policy" (1974) 124 NLJ 999 and 1034; Dwyer "Immoral Contracts" (1977) 93 LQR 386.

[144] (1976) 18 Cal (3d) 660.

[145] *Ibid*, 665 per Tobriner J.

[146] See *Chrispen v Topham* (1986) 28 DLR (4th) 754, 758 (Sask QB) per Kindred J; *Wray v Rubin* (1987) 45 DLR (4th) 637, 640 (Ont Div Ct) per Smith J.

[147] See *Andrews v Parker* [1973] Qd R 93; *Seidler v Schallhofeer* [1982] 2 NSWLR 80.

[148] See, for example, ss 45–50 of New South Wales' De Facto Relationships Act 1984 (setting out the role of cohabitation contracts within a legislative scheme which empowers the courts to adjust property rights upon the termination of a cohabitation). See also New Zealand's Property Law Act 1952, s 40A.

[149] See, for example, Pawlowski, n 143 *supra*, 1125; Cretney and Masson, n 16 *supra*, pp 150–151.

[150] See Pawlowski, n 143 *supra*, 1126 (who does not, however, cite convincing authority on the point). Cf. Bullock "Applying *Marvin v Marvin* to Same-Sex Couples: A Proposal for a Sex-Preference Neutral Cohabitation Contract Statute" (1992) 25 *University of California, Davis Law Review* 1029. There would appear to be a stronger public policy argument in cases where either or both of the cohabitees are still married to someone else. However, in this case (as in the case of same sex couples) it may still be argued that, unless the consideration involves the provision of sexual services, the sexual relationship of the contracting parties is entirely irrelevant to the enforcement of their contractual promises.

the pledge in the Irish Constitution to guard the institution of marriage and protect it from attack.[151] This decision, however, appears to involve an unreasonably conservative interpretation of the Irish Constitution and to be inconsistent with the Irish Supreme Court's more realistic attitude to unmarried cohabitation in *WO'R v EH*.[152]

B. Express Declarations of Beneficial Interests in the Family Home

An alternative, albeit more limited, form of private regulation is for the parties to make an express declaration of the beneficial interests in the family home.[153] Such a declaration (which would be contained in the conveyance itself in the case of a transfer of unregistered land and in a separate document in the case of registered land) creates an express trust over the property. It has been clearly established in the English case law that, in the absence of fraud or a mistake which would justify making an order for rectification, an express declaration is conclusive and excludes the possibility of a resulting or constructive trust.[154] The use of an express declaration is standard practice in England and it has been hinted in the case law that a solicitor might be negligent if he or she failed to elicit from a couple their intentions in relation to the beneficial interest in the property.[155] It appears that the declaration gains its binding force from the doctrine of estoppel by deed.[156] There is a somewhat technical flavour to English law in this area, with the courts being willing to bind the parties to a declaration even where they had never read it and probably would not have understood it even if they had.[157]

The device of an express declaration appears to play a lesser role in the discourse of jurisdictions besides England and Ireland.[158] One explanation for this appears to be that, unlike the English "common intention" approach, the various doctrines favoured in Canada, Australia and New Zealand do not lay great emphasis on the intentions of the parties at the time of the original acquisition

---

[151] See the decision of Kelly J in *Ennis v Butterly* [1996] 1 IR 426 (High Court), relying on Art 41 of the Irish Constitution 1937. See further Mee "Contract Law: Public Policy for the New Millennium" (1997) 19 *Dublin University Law Journal* (ns) 149.

[152] [1996] 2 IR 248.

[153] See generally Miller "Conveyances and Beneficial Interests" (1970) 34 Conv (ns) 156.

[154] See *Pettitt v Pettitt* [1970] AC 777, 813E per Lord Upjohn; *Leake v Bruzzi* [1974] 1 WLR 1528; *Goodman v Gallant* [1986] Fam 106. Cf. *Pink v Lawrence* (1978) 36 P & CR 98; *Re Gorman* [1990] 1 WLR 616; *Harwood v Harwood* [1991] 2 FLR 274; *Huntingford v Hobbs* [1993] 1 FCR 45; *Roy v Roy* [1996] 1 FLR 541.

[155] See *Walker v Hall* [1984] FLR 126, 129 per Dillon LJ.

[156] Cf. *City of London Building Society v Flegg* [1988] AC 54 (declaration cannot bind those who were not party to the deed).

[157] See Gray *Elements of Land Law*, 2nd edn (London: Butterworths, 1993) p 382 commenting on the "appalling result" in *Pink v Lawrence* (1978) 36 P & CR 98.

[158] For discussion of the special problems which arise in Irish law, see Chapter 3 *infra*, text following n 71.

of the property. Thus, for example, the Australian approach[159] favours the assumption that the intentions of the parties at that time were conditional on the continuation of the relationship. This means that there would be no great objection in principle to overriding an intention originally expressed by the parties as to the manner in which ownership would be shared.[160] Similarly, under Canadian law,[161] the parties' intention, at the time of acquisition, to own one asset in certain proportions does not logically preclude a finding that the defendant was unjustly enriched by the subsequent conduct of the plaintiff (although it might be capable of impacting upon the question of whether the plaintiff had a "reasonable expectation" of proprietary relief). Finally, under New Zealand's "reasonable expectations" doctrine,[162] there would again seem to be no technical magic in an express declaration. Such a declaration would seem to be only one factor in determining the nature of the reasonable expectations of the parties.

IV. PROGRAMME FOR THE REMAINDER OF THE BOOK

The five jurisdictions discussed in this book have come up with a range of doctrinal developments to deal with the property rights of cohabitees. The remaining task of this book is to consider these doctrines and to assess their strengths and weaknesses from a theoretical and a practical point of view. A necessary first step, undertaken in Chapter 2, will be to examine the orthodox resulting trust doctrine, an equitable doctrine which applies in all the jurisdictions under consideration. Although the resulting trust is relatively limited in its scope, it represents an important aspect of the context to the modern developments considered in later chapters. This is particularly so in relation to the developments in Ireland (considered in Chapter 3), where the resulting trust has been extended in an attempt to do justice in family property disputes. Chapter 4 will examine the scope of the principles of estoppel in this area, facilitating the analysis in Chapter 5 of the English "common intention" doctrine. The discussion will then focus in turn on Lord Denning's abortive "constructive trust of a new model" (Chapter 6), the Canadian unjust enrichment doctrine (Chapter 7), the Australian "unconscionability" approach (Chapter 8) and New Zealand's "reasonable expectations" doctrine (Chapter 9). Finally, the Conclusion (Chapter 10) will attempt to draw together the various themes running through the book.

---

[159] Discussed in detail in Chapter 8 *infra*.

[160] Cf. Hayton "Remedial Constructive Trusts of Homes; An Overseas View" [1988] Conv 259, 262.

[161] See Chapter 7 *infra*.

[162] See Chapter 9 *infra*.

2

The Orthodox Purchase Money Resulting Trust

In the previous chapter, consideration was given to the difficulties surrounding the resolution of disputes over family property and to the early reaction of the courts to these difficulties. It was seen that, in *Pettitt*[1] and *Gissing*,[2] the House of Lords rejected the possibility of developing special rules in the family context and reasserted the primacy of the "bleak and inflexible rules of property law".[3] The rules which the House had in mind were, in particular, those governing resulting and constructive trusts. Much of the remainder of this book will be taken up with an examination of the radical development of the constructive trust which has taken place in England, Canada, Australia and New Zealand in the quarter of a century since *Pettitt* and *Gissing*. The task of this and the next chapter is to consider the long-established doctrine of the purchase money resulting trust.[4]

In modern times, the purchase money resulting trust plays a secondary role in the resolution of disputes over family property. The only exceptional jurisdiction is Ireland, where an expanded version of the resulting trust represents equity's primary response in such cases. However, despite the limited scope of the resulting trust doctrine in most jurisdictions, it is impossible to gain a full understanding of the modern law without an appreciation of the traditional resulting trust. This is particularly true in relation to the English common intention constructive trust, the theoretical roots of which are tangled with those of the resulting trust. Even in relation to the more radical doctrines developed in Canada, Australia and New Zealand, one can still detect the subliminal influence of the resulting trust (for example, in a continuing tendency to speak in terms of a claimant's "contribution", a term which really only makes sense in the resulting trust context).[5]

This chapter attempts to establish the general boundaries of the orthodox resulting trust and to understand its possible role in the family context. The next chapter, which focuses primarily on the Irish case law, will explore the possibil-

---

[1] [1970] AC 777.

[2] [1971] AC 886.

[3] See *Hofman* v *Hofman* [1965] NZLR 795, 789 *per* Woodhouse J.

[4] See generally Scott "Resulting Trusts Arising Upon the Purchase of Land" (1926–27) 40 *Harv Law Rev* 669; Chambers *Resulting Trusts* (Oxford: Clarendon Press, 1997), especially pp 11–39.

[5] See further Chapter 10 *infra*, Part II (A).

ity of extending the resulting trust doctrine to give it greater scope in the context of family property disputes.

I. THE BASIC DOCTRINE

The purchase money resulting trust was explained in the following classic terms by Eyre CB in the leading case of *Dyer* v *Dyer*:[6]

> "The clear result of all the cases, without a single exception, is that the trust of a legal estate . . . results to the man who advances the purchase money".[7]

The doctrine recognises that the person who advances a portion of the purchase price of property has an equitable claim to a share in the ownership. While the point is sometimes obscured by an emphasis on the presumptions of resulting trust and advancement (which will be discussed shortly), it is important to realise that the doctrine proceeds on the basis of the simple assumption that it is just to impose a trust on the legal owner in favour of a person who (1) put up a portion of the purchase price and (2) intended to gain a share in the ownership.[8]

The operation of the doctrine may be illustrated by a series of examples. If A pays for property (real or personal) which is transferred into the legal ownership of B,[9] but with the intention of retaining all the beneficial interest in that property himself, B will hold the property on a resulting trust for A. The identical result would follow if the property had been put into the joint names of A and B. The position is similar if both A and B contribute to the purchase of property with the intention of gaining a share in that property and only A's name appears on the legal title.[10] In that case a resulting trust will arise whereby A holds the property on a resulting trust for himself and B. If their contributions were equal, they will be joint tenants in equity;[11] if not, they will be tenants in common in equity in the proportions of their contributions.[12]

---

[6] (1788) 2 Cox Eq Cas 92.

[7] *Ibid*, 93.

[8] If one were to accept the position advanced by Chambers, n 4 *supra*, pp 19–27, the stipulation under (2) in the text should read "did not have an intention to benefit the legal owner". For discussion, see text to and following n 60 *infra*.

[9] The doctrine of resulting trusts also applies in the case of a voluntary transfer of real or personal property. In relation to transfers of real property, there has been considerable controversy as to whether there is a *presumption* of resulting trust in this situation. See Chambers, n 4 *supra*, pp 14–19; Hovius and Youdan *The Law of Family Property* (Scarborough, Ontario: Carswell Publishing, 1991) pp 49–54; *House* v *Caffyn* [1922] VLR 67, 75–81; *Wirth* v *Wirth* (1956) 98 CLR 228, 236–237 per Dixon CJ. Legislation in some jurisdictions has expressly provided that a resulting trust will not be presumed in the case of a voluntary transfer of real property. See e.g. s 60(3) of the English Law of Property Act 1925.

[10] See Scott and Fratcher *The Law of Trusts*, 4th edn (Boston: Little, Brown and Co, 1989) Vol V pp 226–238 for discussion of the strange "aliquot part rule" sometimes applied in the American courts.

[11] *Lake* v *Gibson* (1729) 1 Eq Cas Abr 290; *O'Connell* v *Harrison* [1927] IR 330. Note that legislation in some jurisdictions has had the effect of modifying this rule so that such purchasers will take the beneficial interest as tenants in common. See s 26 of the Conveyancing Act 1919 (New South

As pointed out already, two requirements must be satisfied in order for a purchase money resulting trust to arise. First, the claimant must have advanced all or part of the purchase price and, secondly, this advance must have been made with the appropriate intention. It will be necessary in due course to consider the problem of deciding when a claimant may be said to have made a contribution towards the "purchase price". First, however, it is proposed to consider the role of intention within the resulting trust.

II.   INTENTION AND THE RESULTING TRUST

A. The Presumptions

In the absence of contrary evidence, equity presumes that the intention of the person advancing the purchase money was that he should have a beneficial interest in the property. This is known as the presumption of resulting[13] trust. The presumption has its historical antecedents in the unstable political climate which prevailed in England around the time of the War of the Roses.[14] In modern times, the presumption of resulting trust is based on what one judge termed "the solid tug of money".[15] The assumption is that "people who pay money nor-

---

Wales) (as interpreted in *Delahunt v Carmody* (1961) 161 CLR 464); s 35 of the Property Law Act 1974 (Queensland). Cf. Chalmers and Dal Pont *Equity and the Law of Trusts in Australia and New Zealand* (North Ridge NSW: LBC Information Services, 1996) p 421.

[12] In the family context, it may not always be simple to determine the precise contributions of each party. There is, therefore, a temptation to say that "equity delights in equality" and to share the beneficial interest equally. The English courts flirted for a time with this straightforward approach (see especially *Rimmer v Rimmer* [1953] 1 QB 63) but the House of Lords frowned on the practice in *Gissing v Gissing* [1971] AC 886. Lord Pearson suggested (*ibid*, 903) that in previous cases there had been "excessive application of the maxim 'equality is equity'". He conceded that, if both parties had made contributions which were very substantial but could not be quantified more precisely, it might be fairest to conclude that they were equal. However, his Lordship went on to insist (*ibid*) that "if it is plain that the contributing spouse has contributed about one quarter, I do not think it is helpful or right for the court to feel obliged to award either one-half or nothing". (See also *ibid*, 897 per Lord Reid).

[13] In this sense, the word "resulting" comes from the Latin "resultare" meaning to leap back. Thus, the trust "leaps back" to the person who provided the purchase money. See Gray *Elements of Land Law*, 2nd edn (London: Butterworths, 1993) p 384. But compare Birks *An Introduction to the Law of Restitution*, revised edn (Oxford: Clarendon Press, 1989) p 60 (from Latin word "resalire").

[14] During the fifteenth and sixteenth centuries it became an almost universal practice for land to be held on trust for (or "to the use of", as it was then described) persons other than the legal owner. If property was transferred to a stranger and no use was declared, it was assumed that the grantor intended to declare a use over that property at some time in the future. In the meantime, given that the legal owner had probably been intended to be a mere trustee, equity presumed a resulting use of the beneficial interest in favour of the grantor. At a later stage in the development of the law of trusts, the presumption of resulting trust was developed by analogy with the original presumption of resulting use. See *Dullow v Dullow* (1985) 3 NSWLR 531, 535 per Hope JA.

[15] Per Woodhouse J in *Hofman v Hofman* [1965] NZLR 795, 800, quoted by Gray, n 13 *supra*, p 385.

mally expect to get something for it".[16] It is certainly arguable that it would be rational now to abolish the presumption of resulting trust and to put the burden on the claimant, in all cases, to prove that she made her contribution with the requisite intention.[17] Nonetheless, the general view appears to be that the presumption is "too well-entrenched [a landmark] to be simply discarded by judicial decision".[18]

There are, however, some circumstances where the presumption of resulting trust will not apply. From a very early stage, it was accepted that the existence of a close relationship between the parties was sufficient to rebut the presumption of resulting trust. Therefore, equity developed the rule that a presumption of "advancement" (i.e. of gift) arose when a father (or other person *in loco parentis*) paid for property which was transferred into his child's name.[19] In the nineteenth century, the presumption of advancement was extended to cover the situation of a husband paying for property which was conveyed to his wife.[20] No such presumption arises, however, in the reverse situation, where it is the wife who has paid for property for her husband.[21] The sexist nature of the presumption of advancement in the matrimonial context has provoked widespread criticism and has led to suggestions that the significance of the presumption has much diminished in modern times.[22] A number of jurisdictions have abolished the presumption by statute.[23]

---

[16] Gray, n 13 *supra*, p 385. See also Hovius and Youdan, n 9 *supra*, p 77, quoting Spence J's view in *Goodfriend* v *Goodfriend* (1972) 22 DLR (3d) 699, 703 that equity "assumes bargains, and not gifts".

[17] See Scott, n 4 *supra*, 670, 711. Cf. *Calverley* v *Green* (1984) 155 CLR 242, 264–265 per Murphy J.

[18] *Calverley* v *Green* (1984) 155 CLR 242, 266 per Deane J.

[19] Traditionally, the presumption was held not to apply as between mother and child. However, times are changing. See Chambers, n 4 *supra*, pp 28–30.

[20] See *In re Eykyn's Trusts* (1877) 6 Ch D 115, 118 per Malins V-C. It seems that the presumption also applies where a man pays for property transferred to his fiancee: *Moate* v *Moate* [1948] 2 All ER 486; *Wirth* v *Wirth* (1956) 98 CLR 228, 237–238 per Dixon CJ; *Jenkins* v *Wynen* (1992) 1 Qd R 40, 46–47. See, however, *Eeles* v *Wilkins*, 3 February 1998 (LEXIS, CA) p 22 per Nourse LJ. The presumption does not apply after the spouses have separated. See e.g. *Wilson* v *Wilson* [1963] 1 WLR 601, 611 per Russell LJ; *Cossey* v *Bach* [1992] 3 NZLR 612, 630 per Fisher J. But see *RF* v *MF* (1985) [1995] 2 ILRM 572.

[21] *Mercier* v *Mercier* [1903] 2 Ch 98; *Containercare (Ireland) Ltd* v *Wycherley* [1982] IR 143, 152 per Carroll J. See also Chalmers and Dal Pont, n 11 *supra*, p 427 n 76.

[22] See *Silver* v *Silver* [1958] 1 WLR 259, 261 per Lord Evershed MR; *Pettitt* v *Pettitt* [1970] AC 777, 793 per Lord Reid; 811 per Lord Hodson; 824 per Lord Diplock; 813 per Lord Upjohn (defending the presumption); *Falconer* v *Falconer* [1970] 1 WLR 1333, 1335–1336 per Lord Denning MR; *Harwood* v *Harwood* [1991] 2 FLR 274, 294 per Slade LJ; *McGrath* v *Wallis* [1995] 2 FLR 114, 115 per Nourse LJ. Note the similar approach in the Canadian courts: *Rathwell* v *Rathwell* [1978] 2 SCR 436, 452; *Mehta Estate* v *Mehta Estate* [1993] 6 WWR 457 (Man CA); *Aleksich* v *Konradson* (1995) 5 BCLR (3d) 240 (BC CA). For the position in Ireland, where the presumption continues to play a significant role, see Delany *Equity and the Law of Trusts in Ireland* (Dublin: Round Hall Sweet and Maxwell, 1996) pp 142–153. See also Chalmers and Dal Pont, n 11 *supra*, p 427; Lesser "The Acquisition of Inter Vivos Matrimonial Property Rights in English Law: A Doctrinal Melting Pot" (1973) 23 *University of Toronto Law Journal* 148, 173–175; Gray, n 13 *supra*, pp 409–411.

[23] See e.g. s 4(2) of New Zealand's Matrimonial Property Act 1976. Note also s 14 of Ontario's Family Law Act (RSO 1990, c F-3) (abolishing the presumption of advancement but including a proviso that the fact that the spouses hold the property as legal joint tenants is *prima facie* proof that

The presumption has not been extended to cases involving unmarried cohabitation.[24] One of the main problems with such an extension was outlined by Mason and Brennan JJ in *Calverley v Green*:[25]

> "The term 'de facto husband and wife' embraces a wide variety of heterosexual relationships; it is a term obfuscatory of any legal principle except in distinguishing the relationship from that of husband and wife. It would be wrong to apply . . . the presumption of advancement . . . to a relationship devoid of the legal characteristic which warrants a special rule affecting the beneficial ownership of property by the parties to a marriage".[26]

The point is that it is undesirable to allow the operation of a presumption to depend on "an imprecise question of degree"[27] (i.e. whether the particular relationship between the parties is sufficiently close to make it probable that a gift was intended). In view of this, and given its doubtful status in the marital context, it appears unlikely that the presumption will be extended to non-marital relationships in the future.[28]

B. Rebutting the Presumptions

1. *The nature of the presumptions*

The presumptions of resulting trust and of advancement are mere "evidential" presumptions, which are decisive only in the absence of convincing evidence of intention. As one American judge put it, "presumptions may be looked on as the bats of the law, flitting in the twilight but disappearing in the sunshine of actual facts".[29] It appears, therefore, that once relevant evi-

---

they intended to own the property as beneficial joint tenants). Cf. the modified operation of the presumptions envisaged by Lord Upjohn in *Pettitt v Pettitt* [1970] AC 777, 815E–G.

[24] See *Rider v Kidder* (1805) 10 Ves Jun 360; *Soar v Foster* (1858) 4 K & J 152; *Clark v Mandoj*, 19 March 1998 (LEXIS, CA) p 12 per Hobhouse LJ; *Collins v Sanders* (1956) 3 DLR (2d) 607, 615; *David v Szoke* (1974) 39 DLR (3d) 707, 716; *Wilson v Munro* (1983) 42 BCLR 317; *Wirth v Wirth* (1956) 98 CLR 228, 231–232 per Dixon CJ; *Hepworth v Hepworth* (1963) 110 CLR 309, 317 per Windeyer J; *Allen v Snyder* [1977] 2 NSWLR 685, 690 per Glass JA; *Napier v Public Trustee (Western Australia)* (1980) 132 ALR 153, 158 per Aickin J; *Calverley v Green* (1984) 155 CLR 242, 268–269 per Deane J; *Cossey v Bach* [1992] 3 NZLR 612, 630 per Fisher J. Contrast the minority view of Gibbs CJ in *Calverley v Green*, *supra*, 250–251.

[25] (1984) 155 CLR 242.

[26] *Ibid*, 260. See also *Nelson v Nelson* (1995) 132 ALR 133, 170–171 per Toohey J; 184–185 per McHugh J.

[27] See Hovius and Youdan, n 9 *supra*, p 64 n 99.

[28] See further Hovius and Youdan, n 9 *supra*, pp 63–64 n 99; Chalmers and Dal Pont, n 11 *supra*, pp 428–429; Morris "Equity's Reaction to Modern Domestic Relationships", ch. 12 in Oakley (ed) *Trends in Contemporary Trust Law* (Oxford: Clarendon Press, 1996) pp 281–288; Gray, n 13 *supra*, 409 n 16; Maxton "De Facto Spouses and the Presumption of Advancement" (1986) 12 NZULR 79; Scott and Fratcher, n 10 *supra*, pp 184–188. Although the argument is somewhat stronger in the case of homosexual cohabitees (who do not have the option of marriage), it also appears unlikely that the presumption will be extended to cover their situation. See Morris, *supra*, p 285.

[29] *Mackowik v Kansas City* (1906) 94 SW 256, 264, quoted by Gray, n 13 *supra*, p 402.

dence is available,[30] the presumption of resulting trust does not continue to weigh in the balance and does not influence the result in the direction of a finding of a resulting trust.[31] However, it is sometimes suggested that the decisive importance of the presumption would return in a case where the available evidence is evenly balanced or neutral as to the possible intention of the contributor.[32] Presumably, the courts should make a serious endeavour to resolve the matter on the basis of the evidence before returning to the presumption to decide the issue.[33]

2. *Whose intention is relevant?*

In order to determine whether the applicable presumption has been rebutted, it is obviously necessary to be clear as to whose intention is at issue.[34] As a matter of basic principle, it is submitted that the only intention relevant to the creation of a resulting trust is the intention of the party whose contributions to the purchase price are alleged to have created the resulting trust. Unfortunately, this proposition has lately been called into question and it has been suggested the intentions of both parties are relevant in this context.[35] It has even been assumed, on occasion, that the presumptions can only be rebutted by reference to the common intention of the parties.[36] These departures from orthodoxy are, it is submitted, largely due to confusion with the "common intention" constructive trust analysis put forward by Lord Diplock in *Gissing* v *Gissing*.[37]

---

[30] It was held in *Shepherd* v *Cartwright* [1955] AC 431, 445 that, while acts or statements before or around the transaction are admissible in favour of either party, subsequent acts or statements are admissible against the party making them but not in his or her favour. See also *Clemens* v *Clemens and Crown Trust* [1956] SCR 286; *Charles Marshall Pty Ltd* v *Grimsley* (1956) 95 CLR 353, 365; *RF* v *MF* (1985) [1995] 2 ILRM 572, 576–577. Furthermore, evidence of intention is not admissible if it discloses a fraudulent or improper motive: see *Muckleston* v *Brown* (1801) 6 Ves 52; *Tinsley* v *Milligan* [1994] 1 AC 340; *Tribe* v *Tribe* [1996] Ch 107; *Martin* v *Martin* (1959) 110 CLR 297; *Nelson* v *Nelson* (1995) 132 ALR 133; *Scheuerman* v *Scheuerman* (1915) 52 SCR 625; *Goodfriend* v *Goodfriend* (1972) 22 DLR (3d) 699; *Parkes* v *Parkes* [1980] ILRM 137.

[31] See *Fowkes* v *Pascoe* (1875) 10 Ch App 343.

[32] See *Gissing* v *Gissing* [1971] AC 886, 907C per Lord Diplock.

[33] See also text to and following n 58 *infra*.

[34] See generally Chambers, n 4 *supra*, pp 33–38.

[35] See *Calverley* v *Green* (1984) 155 CLR 242, 251 per Gibbs CJ; 261–262 per Mason and Brennan JJ; *Muschinski* v *Dodds* (1985) 160 CLR 583, 590 per Gibbs CJ. Following these Australian authorities, Gray, n 13 *supra*, p 403 asserts that: "Where one person has contributed all of the purchase money, it is his or her intention which is relevant; where two persons contributed, the intentions of both are material". Note the similar view of Meagher and Gummow *Jacobs' Law of Trusts in Australia*, 6th edn (Sydney: Butterworths, 1997) pp 299–300.

[36] See, in particular, *Springette* v *Defoe* [1992] 2 FLR 388, discussed in detail in the text following this footnote. Cf. *Calverley* v *Green* (1984) 155 CLR 242, 261–262 per Mason and Brennan JJ. Note also the early identification of the problem in Hardingham and Neave *Australian Family Property Law* (Sydney: The Law Book Company, 1984) pp 81–82.

[37] [1971] AC 886. Cf. *Tinsley* v *Milligan* [1994] 1 AC 340, 371 per Lord Browne-Wilkinson; *Westdeutsche Landesbank Girozenrale* v *Islington LBC* [1996] AC 669, 708C per Lord Browne-Wilkinson (in both cases failing properly to distinguish between the purchase money resulting trust and the common intention constructive trust). See the criticism by Chambers, n 4 *supra*, p 37.

A useful starting point for discussion is provided by *Springette* v *Defoe*.[38] In the respectful view of the present author, the English Court of Appeal made a fundamental error of principle in *Springette* which led to a demonstrably incorrect result on the facts. The disputed property in *Springette* had been conveyed into the joint names of the parties, with no express declaration of the beneficial interests. The plaintiff had contributed three-quarters of the purchase price and her partner had contributed one-quarter. The plaintiff sought to establish that she was entitled to three-quarters of the beneficial interest.

Since the property was in joint names, the defendant had no need to establish a resulting trust in his favour. He could simply rely on his legal ownership. It was for the plaintiff to establish that, notwithstanding the joint legal ownership, there should be a resulting trust in her favour entitling her to a share greater than one-half.[39] This required her to show that she had advanced more than half of the purchase price with the intention of gaining a proportionate share for herself.[40] However, she made the fatal concession in her evidence that she had had no such intention and had, in fact, regarded herself and her partner as equal beneficial owners.

It is submitted that this evidence of her intention should, as a matter of course, have sufficed to rebut the presumption of resulting trust which had been triggered by her larger contribution. Unfortunately, the Court of Appeal took the view that it was for the defendant to show that there was a common intention that he should be entitled to an equal share in the beneficial ownership. Although both parties had independently intended equal ownership, there was no evidence that they had ever communicated this belief to each other. The Court of Appeal concluded that the uncommunicated beliefs of the parties were insufficient to constitute a "common intention".[41] The Court therefore held that the presumption of resulting trust had not been rebutted and that the female partner was entitled to three-quarters of the beneficial ownership.

One thus sees the very strange outcome in *Springette* that a resulting trust arose in favour of a party who, the evidence clearly showed, had had an intention inconsistent with this result. The Court's confusion with the common intention analysis led it to the view that the presumption of resulting trust could only be rebutted by evidence of a (communicated) common intention between

---

[38] [1992] 2 FLR 388. Cf. Chapter 5 *infra*, text to and following n 50.

[39] There was also no possibility of her establishing a common intention constructive trust (see Chapter 5 *infra*) in her favour since, as will be discussed shortly, no intention had been communicated between the parties (and, in any case, the intention which was privately held by each party was that the property should be owned equally).

[40] Or, according to Chambers (see text to and following n 60 *infra*), without intending to benefit her partner. Acceptance of Chambers' view does not affect the argument in the text.

[41] As will be discussed in Chapter 5 *infra*, text to and following n 50, this was a perfectly orthodox view of the nature of the "common intention" required to form the basis of a constructive trust. The mistake of the Court of Appeal was to think that a common intention was required to rebut the presumption of resulting trust.

the parties. This, however, is clearly contrary to principle.[42] One's conclusion must be that, in *Springette*, distracted by the Byzantine complexity of the common intention analysis (addressed in detail in a later chapter),[43] the Court of Appeal wrongly decided a simple resulting trust case.

The above discussion of *Springette* sought to establish that a common intention is not *always* necessary in order to rebut the presumptions. However, it remains to consider the more difficult question of whether a common intention will *ever* be necessary. Consider the following scenario: M sees a good opportunity to invest in property but is short of funds. He obtains the necessary money (say, half of the purchase price) from W, the woman with whom he is cohabiting, and purchases the property in his own name. M regards this money as a gift (or, in a more plausible variant of the problem, as a loan). W, on the other hand, had no intention of making a gift (or a loan) of the money and, although she is aware that the property has been purchased in M's name, believes that she now owns half of the property. How should this problem be resolved?

One solution[44] would be to apply the test advanced by Lord Diplock in *Gissing*[45] (in the different context of the common intention constructive trust) and to treat the intention of a party as "the intention which was reasonably understood by the other party to be manifested by that party's words or conduct". If one applied that test to the scenario above, the focus would remain on the intention of W, the person who contributed the funds; however, one would also be interested in the mental state of M to the extent that W would not be able to rely to her own advantage on an intention which she had not, on an objective test, made apparent to M by her words or conduct.[46] Thus, the resolution of the problem outlined above would depend on whether M, judging from W's actions, should have known that she was not making a gift (or a loan) but was contributing as a purchaser in her own right.

Although the above solution seems plausible at first sight, upon closer inspection it appears to be too severe on the contributor. Imagine that W, although honestly intending to obtain a share for herself, failed to make this clear to M, who reasonably understood that she was making a gift (or a loan) to him. Is M then to be allowed to keep W's money (or to repay it as a loan without allowing her to share in any increase in the property's value), even though the court believes that W did not intend this result? What if M, who could not have raised

---

[42] Cf. Chambers, n 4 *supra*, p 35 n 192 and accompanying text (discussing cases where the recipient was unaware of the transfer of the property in question and therefore of the grantor's intention). See also *Martin v Martin* (1959) 110 CLR 297, 304 per Dixon CJ, McTiernan, Fullagar and Windeyer JJ; *Calverley v Green* (1984) 155 CLR 242, 251 per Gibbs CJ; 270 per Deane J.

[43] See Chapter 5 *infra*.

[44] See Chambers, n 4 *supra*, pp 36–37.

[45] [1971] AC 886, 906.

[46] However, as has already been argued in the context of *Springette v Defoe* [1992] 2 FLR 388, if W had had a subjective intention to benefit M, she could not subsequently rely on the fact that she had not made this intention manifest in her dealings with him.

the money without W's help, would have acted in precisely the same way if W had communicated to him her true wishes?

It is submitted that the proper approach is to adhere to the basic proposition that it is the intention of the contributor which is determinative for the purposes of the resulting trust. Therefore, a resulting trust should come into existence if the court believes the contributor to have had the appropriate intention, irrespective of whether this was communicated to the legal owner.[47] However, an estoppel might arise if the contributor led the legal owner to believe that she was advancing the money with some other intention, and if the legal owner acted to his detriment on the basis of this belief (for example, by not obtaining the funds elsewhere). The use of estoppel in this context has the attraction of allowing the court to penalise the contributor only to the extent that the legal owner was led to act to his detriment.[48] Of course, if the contributor had acted in a fraudulent manner, deliberately setting out to deceive the legal owner, the court might apply the maxim that "he who comes to equity must come with clean hands" and deny the claimant any remedy by way of resulting trust.

It has been contended thus far that a "common" intention is not always necessary to rebut the presumptions and, in fact, is arguably *never* relevant in the narrow context of the resulting trust doctrine. This is not, of course, to deny the practical importance of the separate "common intention" constructive trust analysis.[49] The relationship between the two doctrines is well illustrated by the case of *Drake* v *Whipp*.[50] The couple in that case had decided to purchase a barn for conversion into a dwelling-house. The male partner contributed approximately 60 per cent of the purchase price and his partner contributed the remaining 40 per cent. However, after the purchase of the property, a great deal of money and labour had to be put into the conversion of the property. Both parties contributed to the conversion, although the male partner put in the bulk of the work and capital. The female partner discharged various household expenses out of her earnings and took care of the household for both of them. On these facts, the doctrine of resulting trusts would have suggested a presumption that the shares of the couple were in the proportions of their contributions to the initial acquisition of the property (ignoring the costs of renovation).[51] However, the Court of Appeal concluded that there had been a common intention between the parties that the property would be shared on a basis which would take into account, not only their contributions to the purchase, but also the male partner's larger contribution to the renovation of the property *and* the parties' other contributions to the relationship. The applica-

---

[47] And, clearly, it will be difficult for the claimant to convince the court that, notwithstanding her failure to communicate it to M, she actually had such an intention.

[48] For full discussion of the principles of estoppel, see Chapter 4 *infra*.

[49] See generally Chapter 5 *infra*.

[50] [1996] 1 FLR 826.

[51] See text following n 92 *infra* for discussion of the principle that contributions towards the improvement of property cannot be regarded as contributions to the purchase price for resulting trust purposes.

tion of the doctrine of resulting trusts was precluded by the fact that the parties had acted on the basis of this common intention. The Court of Appeal ultimately held that the claimant was entitled to a one-third share under a common intention constructive trust. This was a lesser share than she would have obtained if she had been successful in establishing a resulting trust. However, in many other cases, the displacement of a resulting trust by a common intention constructive trust will operate to the advantage of the claimant rather than the legal owner.[52]

On the basis of *Drake* and other cases, it is possible to suggest how the courts might deal with the overlapping doctrines of resulting trust and common intention constructive trust. The simplest solution (which may not be the only one) appears to be for the court to begin by examining the facts to see if the requirements of the common intention analysis are satisfied. If not, then the court must return to apply the traditional purchase money resulting trust. In doing so, the starting point is the presumption (either of resulting trust or of advancement) which arises on the facts. However, and this was the mistake in *Springette*,[53] it must not be supposed that the absence of a common intention (which would have been necessary to trigger a remedy under a distinct equitable doctrine) necessarily precludes the rebuttal of the applicable presumption. Once it has been established that the common intention analysis is inapplicable on the facts, then the doctrine of resulting trusts should be applied on the basis of the principles which were established centuries before the waters were muddied by *Gissing* v *Gissing*.[54]

3. The problem of "neutral" intention

Where the presumptions are relegated to the background by the presence of relevant evidence, the court is faced with the very difficult task of examining the actual intention of one of the parties and coming to one of only two possible conclusions i.e. that it is consistent with the creation of a resulting trust or that it is not so consistent. The troublesome reality is that a cohabitee contributing to a purchase is unlikely to be conversant with the intricacies of the resulting trust doctrine. His or her motives in making the contribution are likely to be complex and not directly concerned with the question of whether or not he or she should get a beneficial interest.

The point may be illustrated by reference to the Irish case of *M* v *M*.[55] A husband had contributed to the purchase of a bed-and-breakfast establishment which was conveyed into the name of his wife. Finlay P was satisfied that "it was not a gift or advancement to his wife but rather it was intended as . . . the acquisition of property as a source of income and revenue for the whole

---

[52] See e.g. *Midland Bank plc* v *Cooke* [1995] 4 All ER 562.
[53] [1992] 2 FLR 388.
[54] [1971] AC 886.
[55] (1978) 114 ILTR 46.

family".[56] Finlay P felt that the existence of this intention allowed the contribution to give rise to a resulting trust. However, one may ask whether this intention was really consistent with the creation of a trust. The fact that the husband did not intend a "gift" in the usual sense does not conclude the matter. Even if he did intend the property to be "a source of income and revenue for the whole family", could this purpose not have been achieved just as effectively if the wife held the beneficial interest and no resulting trust arose? It is, of course, arguable that the court in *M* v *M*[57] reached the appropriate conclusion on the facts. The case has been highlighted simply to demonstrate the intrinsic difficulty in trying to force the complex motivations of a real person into legal pigeon-holes.

The problem which has just been discussed arises in its most extreme form in a case where the claimant admits in evidence that she never directed her mind to the status of her contribution to the purchase price. Consider, for example, *Midland Bank plc* v *Cooke*,[58] where the claimant was held to have made a direct contribution to the purchase price of her family home. A presumption of resulting trust therefore arose in her favour. However, in her evidence she conceded, in effect, that she had never given a thought to the question of the ownership of the family home. Although the case raised many other issues,[59] the important question in the present context is whether the claimant could establish a resulting trust in these circumstances. This question raises fundamental issues concerning the intention required to trigger a resulting trust. Is it sufficient if the claimant lacked a positive intention to benefit the legal owner or, on the other hand, is it necessary that she positively intended to gain a share for herself?

Chambers, in a recent monograph, argues strongly for the former proposition.[60] This approach is consistent with the assumption by the Court of Appeal in *Cooke* that a resulting trust would arise on the facts of that case.[61] However, there is also strong support in the case law for the view that, as a prerequisite to the creation of a resulting trust, the claimant must have made her contribution "in the character of purchaser"[62] and must have intended (or be presumed to have intended) to gain a share for herself.[63] Without purporting to deal fully with the point, one might venture the view that the tendency in the family context has been to dodge the theoretical issue by, as it were, letting the presumptions do the work. What seems to happen in practice is that evidence that the plaintiff had no positive intention with respect to her contribution is treated as being neutral on the question of intention and, therefore, as insufficient to rebut

---

[56] (1978) 114 ILTR 49.

[57] (1978) 114 ILTR 46.

[58] [1995] 4 All ER 562.

[59] See the discussion of the case in Chapter 5 *infra*, text to and following n 88, text to and following n 95 and text to and following n 130.

[60] See n *supra*, pp 19–37.

[61] In fact, the Court of Appeal held that the claimant was not restricted to a resulting trust remedy and should, under the common intention analysis, be entitled to a one-half share in the home. For criticism, see Chapter 5 *infra*, text to and following n 95.

[62] See the authorities cited by Chambers, n 4 *supra*, p 27 n 120.

[63] See the authorities cited by Chambers, *ibid*, p 19 n 63.

whichever presumption is applicable on the facts of the case. By this expedient, the troublesome category of intention ("no positive intention either to benefit the legal owner or to gain a share for oneself") is effectively rendered invisible. If the presumption of resulting trust applies, a resulting trust will be declared in the claimant's favour because evidence of her "neutral" intention will not suffice to rebut that presumption. If, however, the presumption of advancement applies, no resulting trust will be created because, once more, the claimant's "neutral" intention will not be regarded as sufficient to displace the presumption that she intended to make a gift to the legal owner.[64] The approach outlined in this paragraph is, like Chambers' analysis, consistent with the result in *Cooke* and similar cases.[65]

C. Joint Ownership at Law

Finally, it is necessary to consider the special features of cases where the disputed property is held in joint names at law. While much of the existing case law focuses on property which is held in the sole name of the male partner, this arrangement is now becoming less common. Changed perceptions of the roles of men and women, combined with the pragmatic preference of lending institutions for joint mortgages, have led to a new paradigm of joint ownership at law of family homes. Therefore, future disputes will increasingly depart from the fact patterns of the older cases.[66]

In principle, the doctrine of resulting trusts entirely ignores the fact that legal ownership is in the joint names of the parties.[67] Irrespective of who holds the legal ownership, the beneficial ownership will (in the absence of rebutting

---

[64] Consider a case involving a married couple where the husband pays the purchase price of the home and puts it into the joint names of himself and his wife. There is no express declaration of the beneficial interests of the spouses. The husband admits that he had never given a thought to the ownership of the property. On the approach discussed in this paragraph of text, no resulting trust would arise in favour of the husband in this situation. On Chambers' view, it would seem that such a trust would arise, a result which could lead to difficulties in practice (particularly because, in at least some jurisdictions other than England, there does not appear to be a tradition of including an express declaration of the beneficial interests in a conveyance of a matrimonial home).

[65] The author's own preference would be to regard a claimant as intending a gift (within the terms of the resulting trust doctrine) where she makes a contribution to the purchase price of property in someone else's name but has no positive intention to gain a share for herself. However, this strict view does not appear to find support in the case law. It is not necessary in the present context to comment on the different situation where the funds of the claimant are, without her knowledge or permission, put towards the purchase of property. See *Ryall v Ryall* (1739) 1 Atk 59; Chambers, n 4 *supra*, pp 21–23 and contrast Scott and Fratcher, n 10 *supra*, p 145 (suggesting a constructive trust solution).

[66] Cf. the discussion in Chapter 3 *infra*, text following n 77 of the treatment of joint mortgages within the Irish "extended resulting trust" analysis.

[67] Some judges have had difficulty in accepting this aspect of the doctrine. See the suggestion by Lord Upjohn in *Pettitt* [1970] AC 777, 815 that "if a wife puts property into [the spouses'] joint names I would myself think that a joint beneficial tenancy was intended, for I can see no other reason for it". See also *Cossey v Bach* [1992] 3 NZLR 612, 629 per Fisher J and the approach of Carroll J in *Containercare (Ireland) Ltd v Wycherley* [1982] IR 143.

evidence) be owned in the proportions of the contributions to the purchase price. Therefore, in the absence of evidence as to intention (and where the presumption of advancement does not apply) there is no particular advantage in this context in having one's name on the legal ownership.

This has led to some harsh decisions in the English courts. The case of *Walker* v *Hall*[68] provides a convenient example. Mr Hall and Mrs Walker lived together in a house which they had purchased in their joint names. Three-quarters of the purchase price had been contributed by Mr Hall and one-quarter by Mrs Walker. Since the parties were not married to each other, no presumption of advancement arose in the case. The Court of Appeal refused to hold that the house belonged to the parties in equal shares. In the absence of specific evidence as to their intention, their shares would be determined by their respective contributions to the purchase price. Therefore, perhaps to her surprise, Mrs Walker was entitled to only one-quarter of the beneficial interest.

Although the mere fact of joint ownership at law is not sufficient in itself to displace the presumption of resulting trust, where a couple put property in joint names comparatively slight evidence[69] should suffice to rebut the presumption. Ordinary people cannot be expected to understand the difference between legal and beneficial ownership and it must very often happen that a couple will have asked for their home to be put into joint names with the intention of ensuring an equal sharing of the beneficial ownership. As Parker suggests, "[s]uch an intention should always be looked for and if it can be inferred on the facts the presumption of resulting trust in proportion to the respective contributions should surely be overridden".[70]

It is clearly undesirable that the doctrine of resulting trusts should frustrate the desire of a couple to ensure joint ownership. However, within the law of trusts there is a relatively straightforward method whereby a couple may specify precisely their intention as to the beneficial interests. This involves making an express declaration of the beneficial interests at the time of the initial conveyance of the property. This device was discussed in the previous chapter.[71]

III. CONTRIBUTIONS UNDER THE RESULTING TRUST DOCTRINE

One cannot establish a purchase money resulting trust unless one has, in fact, made a contribution to the purchase price of property. The position is compar-

---

[68] [1984] FLR 126. See also *Crisp* v *Mullings* (1975) 239 *e.g.* 119; *Lawrence* v *McFarlane, The Times*, 19 May 1976; *Young* v *Young* [1984] FLR 375; *Springette* v *Defoe* [1992] 2 FLR 388.

[69] It should be sufficient if the evidence shows that a legal joint tenancy was created with the intention of benefitting one partner on the death of the other, since such a benefit would not accrue unless the beneficial ownership followed the legal title. See *JC* v *JHC*, 4 August 1982, unreported (Irish High Court); (Binchy *A Casebook on Irish Family Law* (Albingdon: Professional Books, 1984) p 282). Contrast, however, *Harmer* v *Pearson* (1993) 16 Fam LR 596, 598 per Fitzgerald P and de Jersey J.

[70] "Cohabitants, Their Homes and the Winds of Change" [1984] Fam Law 40, 42.

[71] See Chapter 1 *supra*, text following n 152.

atively simple in cases where a property is purchased without the aid of a mortgage. The respective contributions to the purchase price need only be ascertained and the shares arising under a resulting trust will be known. Despite the appearance of simplicity, however, there are a number of issues to resolve. The first question concerns the status of legal fees, stamp duty and other expenses attendant upon a purchase. Secondly, it is necessary to consider whether it is permissible to take into account the "qualifying status" of one of the parties which, pursuant to housing legislation in some jurisdictions, affords that party a discount upon the purchase of their home from their landlord. Finally, it is necessary to consider whether expenditure on improving the disputed property can be treated as constituting a contribution to the purchase price. All of these issues can, of course, also arise in a situation where some of the purchase price has been raised on mortgage.

It is now proposed to look in turn at the three issues identified in the previous paragraph, before moving on, in the next Part, to consider the special problems which arise where some of the purchase money has been borrowed on mortgage.

A. Contributions Towards the Costs of the Purchase

In the case law, the legal fees, stamp duty and other expenses attendant upon a purchase seem generally to have been treated as a part of the purchase price.[72] However, in the Australian case of *Little* v *Little*,[73] Bryson J refused to take into account any expenses whatsoever besides the actual purchase price. He believed that it was necessary "for the law to fix limits as to the directness or the remoteness of the relation, in time and otherwise, between an expenditure and the acquisition of land which it will recognise for the purposes of the law of resulting trusts".[74] He concluded that, for example, "[w]hat one gets for paying stamp duty is a stamp, not a piece of land".[75] This approach was contrary to previous Australian authority[76] and has been received without great enthusiasm in subsequent Australian cases.[77]

---

[72] To take just a few examples from the English case law, see *Gissing* v *Gissing* [1971] AC 886, 907E, 908B per Lord Diplock; *Re Densham* [1975] 1 WLR 1519, 1530H-1531B per Goff J; *Walker* v *Hall* [1984] FLR 126, 129F; *Huntingford* v *Hobbs* [1993] 1 FCR 45, 47F; 56B–C per Sir Christopher Slade; 60B per Dillon LJ. See also *C* v *C* [1976] IR 254; *Malcolm* v *King* (1990) 7 FRNZ 262, 264.

[73] (1988) 15 NSWLR 43. Cf. Starke (1989) 63 *Australian Law Journal* 707.

[74] *Ibid*, 46.

[75] *Ibid*.

[76] See *Currie* v *Hamilton* [1984] 1 NSWLR 687, 691A per McLelland J.

[77] Bryson J followed his own decision in *Little* (1988) 15 NSWLR 43 in *Macchi* v *Scott*, 15 February 1991 (LEXIS, NSW Supreme Court) p 5. See, however, *Walmsley* v *Stanton*, 27 February 1997 (LEXIS, NSW Supreme Court) p 4 per Young J (treating additional costs as part of purchase price without reference to *Little*); *Ramirez* v *Sandor's Trustee*, 23 April 1997 (LEXIS, NSW Supreme Court) pp 13–14 per Young J (showing a reluctance to accept that all one acquires by paying stamp duty is "the pretty stamp on the document").

From a logical point of view, there is some strength in Bryson J's position. Money expended on legal fees or stamp duty is not, in fact, paid to the seller as part of the purchase price. Nonetheless, from a practical point of view, it seems arbitrary to distinguish between a contribution to the purchase price and a contribution, at the same time, towards another necessary cost of achieving the purchase. This latter argument has, it seems, been accepted in most jurisdictions. It is worth mentioning, however, that the cases show little inclination to extend this sort of reasoning further and, for example, to apply it to expenditure on furniture and fittings[78] or on major improvements undertaken shortly after the purchase.[79] Such expenses, even if they are viewed by the parties as necessary to the overall project of acquiring a habitable home, are generally regarded as being sufficiently distinct from the purchase to justify excluding them from consideration for resulting trust purposes. As Bryson J argued in *Little*, a line must be drawn somewhere but it appears that, at least outside Australia, it has been drawn at the aggregate costs of the purchase rather than simply at the actual purchase price.

B. Eligibility for a Discount from the Purchase Price

Another possibility is that a person could make a contribution on the basis of what Gray[80] describes as "qualifying status or eligibility". Under the English Housing Act 1985, and similar legislation in other jurisdictions, certain categories of public sector tenants are entitled to purchase their dwellings at a discount, the value of the discount varying according to the duration of their previous occupation. It was held in *Springette v Defoe*[81] that the discount generated by a person's occupancy should be treated as the equivalent of a commensurate direct cash contribution by that person.

However, in principle, it would seem questionable to treat a discount as constituting a contribution to the purchase price. To do so would appear to open the door to unmeritorious claims by those arguing that they obtained the property at a favourable price because they knew the seller[82] or because of their skill in negotiating a price or their eye for a bargain. There is clearly force in the view of Staughton LJ in the later case of *Evans v Hayward*[83] that it is "difficult to say

---

[78] Cf. *McC v McC* [1986] ILRM 1.

[79] See the discussion of the position of improvements in the text following n 92 *infra*. Cf. the remarks of Lord Reid in *Pettitt* [1970] AC 777, 794C–D.

[80] See n 13 *supra*, p 392. See generally *ibid*, pp 392–393.

[81] [1992] 2 FLR 388, 395G per Steyn LJ.

[82] See *J A Pye (Oxford) Estates Ltd v Ambrose*, 21 March 1994 (LEXIS, ChD), where a woman's grandfather had sold a home at an undervalue to the woman's husband. Citing *Marsh v von Sternberg* [1986] 1 FLR 526 and *Springette* [1992] 2 FLR 388, Arden J regarded the "gift element" in the transfer as constituting a contribution by both the husband and the wife. Therefore, a resulting trust arose in favour of the wife despite the fact that she had made no other contribution to the purchase.

[83] (1992) [1995] 2 FLR 511.

that a discount is, strictly speaking, purchase money provided by either party".[84] It is, instead, "money which is not provided by anybody".[85]

Staughton LJ preferred the approach of Bush J in *Marsh v Von Sternberg*,[86] which involved treating the existence of the discount as evidence supporting the inference that the parties had intended that it should be taken into account in determining their entitlement to the beneficial ownership of the property.[87] This approach has the practical advantage of flexibility and would, as Staughton LJ suggested in *Evans*,[88] allow the court to apportion the benefit of the discount in a case where both parties had been secure tenants and would both have been entitled to some discount on the purchase price. However, it is difficult to see how this approach can be rationalised in terms of resulting trust theory. It is fairly unlikely that the parties would reach an agreement concerning the proportions in which they were to be taken as contributing to the purchase price for the purposes of the resulting trust doctrine[89] and, even if they did, this would effectively amount to an agreement as to the proportions in which they should hold the ownership. This kind of agreement could not be given effect through the resulting trust doctrine[90] and could only be recognised, if at all, through the "common intention" constructive trust analysis.[91] Thus, if one were willing to accept that analysis, the best approach might be to treat the existence of a discount as possible evidence of an understanding between the parties as to how the ownership of the property would be shared (rather than as to how they had provided the purchase price of the property).

C. Improvements

A final issue[92] relates to the status of expenditure on carrying out improvements to the disputed property. It is well-established that a claim to a resulting trust

---

[84] *Ibid*, 516.

[85] *Ibid*.

[86] [1986] 1 FLR 526.

[87] The other judge in *Evans*, Dillon LJ, found it unnecessary on the facts before him to choose between the two approaches.

[88] (1992) [1995] 2 FLR 511, 517.

[89] Cf. the severe criticism in cases such as *Re Densham* [1975] 1 WLR 1519 of the "money consensus" analysis put forward by Bagnall J in *Cowcher v Cowcher* [1972] 1 WLR 425. This criticism proceeded on the false premise that Bagnall J's analysis was based on the type of agreement described in the text. See text following n 119 *infra*.

[90] See *Cowcher v Cowcher* [1972] 1 WLR 425, 431B–E.

[91] See Chapter 5 *infra*. If, as is suggested in that chapter, one were to discard the common intention analysis, resort could possibly be had to the principles of estoppel (discussed generally in Chapter 4 *infra*).

[92] The payment of an ordinary rent will not give rise to a resulting trust (*Savage v Dunningham* [1973] 3 All ER 429, 433) although, of course, a resulting trust can be created by a contribution to the purchase price of a leasehold property. For the situation where a portion of the purchase price is represented by a rack-rent, see *Malayan Credit Ltd v Jack Chia-MPH Ltd* [1986] 1 AC 549 (PC). Cf. the Irish case of *K v K* (1978) 114 ILTR 50.

cannot be founded on the making or financing of improvements. In *Pettitt*,[93] Lord Upjohn made it clear that "in the absence of agreement, and there being no question of any estoppel, one spouse who does work or expends money upon the property of the other has no claim whatsoever on the property of the other".[94] As a matter of principle, the making of improvements (including the erection of a house on a site of comparatively little value)[95] cannot be considered to be a contribution to the purchase price of property so as to attract the resulting trust doctrine.

IV. PURCHASE WITH BORROWED MONEY

The discussion in the previous Part focused on the situation where the entire purchase price has been provided from the parties' own resources. However, not many couples can afford to pay for a house in cash and usually most of the purchase price is raised on loan. The mortgage device allows a couple to buy a home almost entirely on credit. It is necessary for the purchasers to provide from their own resources a certain proportion of the cost as a down-payment. The mortgagee supplies the rest of the money and the mortgage is secured on the property. Over a long period (often twenty years), the mortgage is discharged by means of instalment payments made by the borrower/s to the lender. This elongation of the time-frame of the purchase[96] makes it difficult to apply the classic purchase money resulting trust doctrine.[97]

What is the effect of the fact that the purchase money (or a large proportion of it) has been borrowed? The answer is that, as Gray explains, "there is a primary presumption that the loan moneys should be regarded as the exact equivalent of money contributed from the free available cash resources of the borrower".[98] A simple example may be considered where X buys a house for £1,000. He produces £500 himself and borrows £500 from Y. In this case, X alone owns the house although he owes Y £500. No resulting trust arises in Y's favour because the transaction between himself and X was a loan and therefore Y's intention in providing the money was inconsistent with the creation of such a trust. If X gives Y a mortgage over the house to secure the loan, the position is the same except that, if X defaults on repaying the loan, Y may compel a sale of the property and recover the debt from the proceeds.

A straightforward illustration of these principles is to be found in *Re Rogers' Question*.[99] In this case, a married couple bought a house in the husband's name

---

[93] [1970] AC 777.
[94] *Ibid*, 818.
[95] See *NAD v TD* [1985] ILRM 153.
[96] See Waters "Matrimonial Property—Resulting and Constructive Trusts—Restitution" (1975) 53 *Canadian Bar Review* 366, 375 ("stretching the moment of acquisition over what can be a considerable period of time").
[97] See generally Gray, n 13 *supra*, p 393 *et seq*.
[98] *Ibid*, p 394. See *Aveling v Knipe* (1815) 19 Ves Jun 441.
[99] [1948] 3 All ER 328.

for £1,000. The wife provided the £100 deposit and the remaining £900 was raised by the husband on a loan secured by a mortgage of the house. The wife made it clear from the outset that she had no intention of contributing towards the repayment of the mortgage and in fact never made any such contribution. Thus, the wife had provided one-tenth of the purchase price and the husband nine-tenths (although he had borrowed it from a third party). The English Court of Appeal, applying the doctrine of resulting trust, held that the beneficial interest was owned in those proportions.[100]

Difficulties arise in cases where one party, with the help of a loan, pays part of the purchase price and the other party subsequently pays off some of that loan. Can a resulting trust arise in this type of situation?[101] The basic difficulty is that, in its traditional form, the doctrine of resulting trusts assesses the beneficial interests finally at the point in time when the transaction occurred. Subsequent events (such as an ongoing contribution to the repayment of a mortgage loan) are not readily accommodated within the analysis. On the other hand, it may seem unjust to ignore the practicalities of the situation. As Lord Diplock pointed out in *Gissing*:[102]

"The economic reality which lies behind the conveyance of the fee simple to a purchaser in return for a purchase price which is advanced to the purchaser upon a mortgage repayable by instalments over a number of years, is that the purchase price

---

[100] It might have been argued in that case that the wife should have been given some extra credit for the fact that her payment of the deposit enabled her husband to raise the balance of the price on mortgage. In *Pettitt* [1970] AC 777, 815–816, Lord Upjohn stated *obiter* that he saw "very good reasons" for awarding equal shares to the spouses when one puts up the deposit and the other assumes liability for the mortgage. His Lordship referred to *Ulrich* v *Ulrich and Felton* [1968] 1 WLR 180, a decision of the Court of Appeal made on that basis. This approach has not been adopted in subsequent cases (but see *Re Whitely and Whitely* (1974) 48 DLR (3d) 161 (Ont CA)). In any event, it would not seem to be consonant with resulting trust principles to give extra credit for a contribution to the deposit merely because it facilitates the other party in providing security for the mortgage loan.

[101] Against a background of rising house prices, it will generally be more advantageous for a claimant to seek a proportionate share under a trust than to seek repayment of her contributions. However, where no trust can be established (or where a house has fallen in value), it might suit a claimant to try to recover the amount that she contributed under the principles of subrogation (or, where the parties are co-owners, the rules of equitable accounting between co-owners). See *Rimmer* v *Rimmer* [1953] 1 QB 63, 75 per Romer LJ; *Silver* v *Silver* [1958] 1 WLR 259, 264 per Lord Evershed MR; *Cowcher* v *Cowcher* [1972] 1 WLR 425, 432G–433C per Bagnall J; *Re Nicholson (deceased)* [1974] 2 All ER 386, 391 per Pennycuick V-C; *Escritt* v *Escritt* (1982) 3 FLR 280, 281 per Arnold P; *Walker* v *Hall* [1984] FLR 126, 131B–D per Dillon J *(semble)*; *Calverley* v *Green* (1984) 155 CLR 242; *Currie* v *Hamilton* [1984] 1 NSWLR 687, 692C. Cf. *Boscawen* v *Bajwa* [1996] 1 WLR 328. See also Mitchell *The Law of Subrogation* (Oxford: Clarendon Press, 1994) p 123; Cooke "Equitable Accounting Between Co-owners" [1995] Conv 391; *Forgeard* v *Shanahan* (1994) 18 Fam LR 281 (NSW CA); *Young* v *Peachey* (1996) 72 P & CR D46. Of course, in the context of an intimate cohabitation, contributions towards the repayment of a mortgage will often have been made with the intention of conferring a gift on the partner legally liable on the mortgage. If this can be established, it should preclude any claim to be reimbursed. See *Cowcher* v *Cowcher*, *supra*, 433C per Bagnall J. Contributions made after the breakdown of the relationship will, however, normally be in a different category and a claimant is more likely to be successful in obtaining repayment of such contributions.

[102] [1971] AC 886.

is represented by the instalments by which the mortgage is repaid in addition to the initial payment in cash".[103]

The question is, therefore, whether the doctrine can be modified so that account can be taken of contributions to mortgage repayments which take place after the time of the formal purchase.

The case law reveals two possible solutions to the problem under discussion. The first, and more modest, doctrinal modification was canvassed by Bagnall J in *Cowcher v Cowcher*.[104] As will be discussed shortly, his (frequently misunderstood) "money consensus" analysis involves taking account of any agreement between the parties, at the time of the purchase, as to the manner in which they would repay the mortgage. This approach remains within the confines of the orthodox resulting trust since it is still possible to determine the beneficial interests of the parties at the time of the purchase of the disputed property. The "money consensus" analysis will shortly be considered in Part V.

The second, and more drastic, theoretical option is simply to treat mortgage repayments as constituting a "contribution" to the purchase price. On this basis, a resulting trust could arise in favour of a claimant who, irrespective of any prior agreement that she would do so, contributed to the repayment of the mortgage. This "extended resulting trust" represents a considerable modification of the orthodox resulting trust in that it moves away from an exclusive concentration on the time of the purchase. As will be explained, this approach has been adopted in Ireland but, on balance, has been rejected in the other jurisdictions considered in this work. The "extended resulting trust" is sufficiently distinct to warrant separate treatment. It will be considered in detail in the next chapter.

Before moving on to the extended resulting trust, however, it is necessary to conclude this chapter's consideration of the orthodox resulting trust by examining Bagnall J's "money consensus" analysis.

V. THE MONEY CONSENSUS THEORY

A. Money Consensus

In *Cowcher v Cowcher*,[105] Bagnall J made an attempt to include contributions to the mortgage instalments in the reckoning, while still preserving the basic principle that the beneficial interests had to be determined as at the date of the purchase. His careful analysis has been largely misunderstood in later decisions[106] and this misunderstanding no doubt explains the ease with which some commentators have felt themselves able to dismiss it.

---

[103] *Ibid*, 906.
[104] [1972] 1 WLR 425.
[105] *Ibid*. For brief discussion of the facts of *Cowcher*, see n 136 *infra*.
[106] See discussion in the text following n 119 *infra*.

Bagnall J felt that if A borrowed part of the purchase price on mortgage, he should, *prima facie*, be treated as the source of the money borrowed. However, this presumption could be overturned if it were possible, on the evidence, to infer the existence of what he termed a "money consensus". By this he meant an agreement between the parties as to the manner in which they would contribute to the repayment of the mortgage.

Bagnall J explained his approach by reference to an example where a house has been bought for £24,000 and conveyed into the name of A. In a case where A has provided £8,000 from his own funds and B has raised the remaining £16,000 by means of a mortgage, then "prima facie B will . . . have a two-thirds interest because he or his obligation to repay a loan has been the source of £16,000 of the purchase money".[107] Bagnall J then continued as follows:

> "But suppose that at the time A says that as between himself and B he, A, will be responsible for half of the mortgage repayments, a different result ensues. Although as between A and B and the vendor, A has provided £8,000 and B £16,000, as between A and B themselves A has provided £8,000 and made himself liable for the repayment of half the £16,000 mortgage namely a further £8,000, a total of £16,000; the resulting trust will therefore be as to two-thirds for A and one-third for B—the reverse of the former situation".[108]

Thus, what Bagnall J was willing to take into account was an agreement[109] between the parties, at the time of the purchase, to reallocate the responsibility for paying off a loan representing a portion of the purchase price.[110]

---

[107] [1972] 1 WLR 425, 431.

[108] *Ibid.*

[109] Bagnall J took the view in *Cowcher* [1972] 1 WLR 425, 436D that a money consensus need not be "enforceable as an executory contract". See also *Re Nicholson (deceased)* [1974] 2 All ER 386, 390 per Pennycuick V-C ("unenforceable undertaking"). However, what of a situation where the disputed property falls in value and the legal owner is left with "negative equity"? It seems unjust that the other party to the money consensus could, in such circumstances, simply walk away from her unenforceable undertaking to contribute (which, had the house increased in value, she could have relied upon as the basis for a resulting trust). Contrast Scott and Fratcher, n 10 *supra*, p 276, apparently requiring "an oral contract" between the parties (a requirement which would rarely be satisfied in the family situation).

[110] Interesting problems arose in *Re Nicholson (deceased)* [1974] 2 All ER 386, where the claimant had agreed that, as soon as she received an inheritance she was expecting, she would pay off whatever amount was owing on the mortgage. Although Pennycuick V-C (*ibid*, 391) regarded this undertaking to contribute as "totally incapable of precise quantification", he felt that it could not be ignored. Also taking into account the claimant's contribution to the deposit, he held that the beneficial interest was owned equally. While Pennycuick V-C purported to follow *Cowcher*, there are some difficulties in reconciling his approach with the money consensus analysis. One could possibly argue that an undertaking to make a contribution which is very substantial but unquantifiable could be treated as equivalent to an undertaking to contribute half of the mortgage debt. Cf. *Cowcher* [1972] 1 WLR 425, 437D per Bagnall J. Note also *Bloch v Bloch* (1981) 37 ALR 55 (where the agreement at the time of the purchase was, it is submitted, too uncertain to constitute a money consensus).

B. Support for the Money Consensus Approach

Interestingly, Bagnall J's approach was by no means novel. More than seventy years ago, a similar position was taken by Scott in a seminal American article on the purchase money resulting trust.[111] Although the money consensus approach does not appear to have been made explicit in the English case law before *Cowcher*, its subliminal influence may be discerned as early as *Re Rogers' Question*.[112]

Since *Cowcher*, Bagnall J's approach has been accepted in a substantial number of English cases. In *Huntingford v Hobbs*,[113] for example, both parties were legally liable under the mortgage but "there was a clear agreement or understanding as between the two of them"[114] that the male partner would be responsible for all payments under the mortgage. Applying *Cowcher v Cowcher*,[115] a majority of the Court of Appeal[116] held that the male partner should be credited with having contributed all the money raised on mortgage. Clear support for Bagnall J's analysis is also found in a number of other English[117] authorities, both at High Court and Court of Appeal level.[118]

The next section attempts to explain why, in spite of this strong foundation in authority, Bagnall J's theory has tended to be dismissed by commentators.[119]

---

[111] Scott, n 4 *supra*, 705–707 (discussing, in particular, *Fox v Shanley* (1920) 94 Conn 350). See also *Ingram v Ingram* [1941] VLR 95, 102 per O'Bryan J; *Pearson v Pearson* [1961] VR 693, 700–701 per Scott J. Cf. *Kronheim v Johnson* (1877) 7 Ch D 60.

[112] [1948] 3 All ER 328. See the discussion in Chapter 5 *infra*, text to and following n 211. Cf. *Diwell v Farnes* [1959] 1 WLR 624, 640 per Willmer LJ.

[113] [1993] 1 FCR 45.

[114] *Ibid*, 55 per Sir Christopher Slade.

[115] [1972] 1 WLR 425.

[116] Steyn LJ dissenting.

[117] There appears to have been little consideration of the money consensus analysis outside England. See, however, the clear explanation and application of that analysis by McLelland J in the Australian case of *Currie v Hamilton* [1984] 1 NSWLR 687, 691. See also *Stockbridge v Lupton*, 14 March 1989 (McLelland J) (LEXIS, NSW Sup Ct); *Ramirez v Sandor's Trustee*, 23 April 1997 (Bryson J) (LEXIS, NSW Sup Ct). Cf. *Richardson v Richardson* [1955] St R Qd 277; *Olsen v Olsen* [1977] 1 NSWLR 189. Contrast the hostility towards *Cowcher* manifested in *Allen v Snyder* [1977] 2 NSWLR 685 (see text to n 123 *infra*). Cf. *Calverley v Green* (1984) 155 CLR 242, 267–268 per Deane J (appearing to accept the money consensus analysis, although concluding that it was not applicable on the facts). See also *Malone v McQuaid*, May 28 1998, unreported (LEXIS, Irish High Court).

[118] *Re Nicholson (deceased)* [1974] 2 All ER 386; *Power v Brighton*, 14 November 1984 (LEXIS, CA); *Marsh v von Sternberg* [1986] 1 FLR 526, 534 per Bush J. See also *Crisp v Mullings* (1974) 233 e.g. 511, 511 per Megarry J; *Bernard v Josephs* [1982] Ch 391, 403G–H per Griffiths LJ; *Re Gorman* [1990] 1 WLR 616, 624B–G per Vinelott J; *Harwood v Harwood* [1991] 2 FLR 274, 292D–G per Slade LJ. Cf. *Ivin v Blake* [1995] 1 FLR 70, 83–84.

[119] See n 124 *infra*.

C. Misunderstanding of the Money Consensus Approach

It appears that the neglect of Bagnall J's analysis can be traced to a misunderstanding in *Re Densham*.[120] In that case, Goff J took the view that a money consensus exists "where the parties agree that they shall be treated as having subscribed in particular shares other than those in which they had in fact subscribed".[121] On this basis, Goff J concluded that the concept was hopelessly artificial and argued that "[i]n the vast majority of cases, parties do not direct their minds to treating payments as notionally other than they are".[122]

This opinion was echoed by Glass JA in the important Australian case of *Allen* v *Snyder*[123] and has, unfortunately, been accepted by many commentators over the years.[124] The only remark[125] in Bagnall J's judgment which would support this understanding of "money consensus" is where Bagnall J considered the possibility that one party who had, for example, paid a deposit of £8,000 might agree to treat the other as having provided half of that money—"in effect a gift of £4,000".[126] The rest of Bagnall J's speech makes it clear that he was only considering such a possibility (which has no relevance to the status of money borrowed on mortgage) for the sake of completeness and that it was by no means central to his analysis. For example, when considering the possibility of inferring a money consensus from the conduct of the parties, the question he puts in the mouth of the "officious bystander" is "Ought you not to record that *you are intending to pay* for this house in equal (or some other) shares?"[127] This passage, together with Bagnall J's earlier detailed explanation of his position,[128] shows that "money consensus" means an agreement to contribute in certain shares, rather than an agreement to pretend that the contributions made are of a different amount than they actually are.

---

[120] [1975] 1 WLR 1519.

[121] *Ibid*, 1525.

[122] *Ibid*.

[123] [1977] 2 NSWLR 685, 691–692.

[124] See, for example, Levin "The Matrimonial Home—Another Round" (1972) 35 MLR 547, 548, 550–551; Zuckerman "Ownership of the Matrimonial Home—Commonsense and Reformist Nonsense" (1978) 94 LQR 26, 45 ("difficult to think of another instance where so much ingenuity was so lavishly diverted in such a futile quest"); Glover and Todd "The Myth of Common Intention" (1996) 16 *Legal Studies* 325, 329; Chambers, n 4 *supra*, p 37. An alternative misunderstanding is to regard "money consensus" as "an agreement . . . to treat indirect contributions as direct for the purposes of the presumption [of resulting trust]" (see Hardingham and Neave, n 26 *supra*, p 88; see also Hovius and Youdan, n 9 *supra*, pp 104–105). Contrast the accurate treatment of "money consensus" by Gray, n 13 *supra*, pp 395–397.

[125] It is also arguable that on two occasions Bagnall J gave a somewhat misleading summary of his position on "money consensus" (see [1972] 1 WLR 425, 432B, 436A–B). However, it is submitted that, if read in context, these summaries do not in any way contradict the interpretation of *Cowcher* put forward in the text.

[126] *Ibid*, 432A.

[127] *Ibid*, 437 (emphasis supplied).

[128] See the passage quoted as text to n 108 *supra*.

D. The Relationship Between "Money Consensus" and "Interest Consensus"

It has been argued thus far that Bagnall J's money consensus analysis constitutes a reasonable development of the traditional purchase money resulting trust. However, a more controversial aspect of Bagnall J's approach in *Cowcher* was his attempt to argue that his approach exhausted the range of theoretical possibilities in the area.

Bagnall J distinguished in his judgment between a "money consensus", which could give rise to a resulting trust in the manner which has been discussed in previous sections, and what he called an "interest consensus", which was incapable of giving rise to a resulting trust. An interest consensus was, according to Bagnall J, "a consensus as to what the beneficial interests of the spouses are to be . . . irrespective of the source or sources of the purchase money".[129] Bagnall J felt that "an interest consensus" could only take effect as an express trust and, therefore, would be ineffective unless evidenced in writing as required by section 53(1)(b) of the Law of Property Act 1925. Unfortunately for Bagnall J, his rejection of the possibility of a trust based on an "interest consensus" ran directly counter to Lord Diplock's "common intention" analysis in *Gissing* v *Gissing*.[130] Bagnall J was therefore compelled to make the implausible argument that the references to "common intention" in *Gissing* (and in subsequent decisions of the Court of Appeal) actually connoted a money consensus rather than an "interest consensus".[131]

Although history has gone against Bagnall J's rejection of a trust based on an "interest consensus", it does not necessarily follow that his money consensus analysis must similarly be discarded. There is no reason why one cannot recognise the money consensus theory as a gloss on the traditional purchase money resulting trust while at the same time accepting the applicability of Lord Diplock's common intention analysis. The modern English case law appears to illustrate such a co-existence of "money consensus" and "interest consensus".[132]

E. Inferring the Existence of a Money Consensus

The most obvious way in which a money consensus could be proven is by reference to an express agreement between the parties, as occurred for example in *Huntingford* v *Hobbs*.[133] What is less clear is whether it is possible to infer the

---

[129] [1972] 1 WLR 425, 436.

[130] [1971] AC 886.

[131] [1972] 1 WLR 425, 436.

[132] Admittedly, the relevant case law is not entirely satisfactory and, not surprisingly given the tendency to misunderstand Bagnall J's analysis, the distinction between the money consensus resulting trust and the common intention constructive trust is not always clearly drawn. See e.g. the judgment of Sir Christopher Slade in *Huntingford* v *Hobbs* [1993] 1 FCR 45.

[133] [1993] 1 FCR 45.

existence of such a consensus from the conduct of the parties. Bagnall J himself believed that a money consensus could be inferred from conduct "antecedent, contemporaneous or subsequent".[134] However, Bagnall J felt that, except for "a simple case where a couple have consistently applied a system of all purchases out of a common fund",[135] the evidence would rarely permit the inference of such a consensus.[136]

This seems a sensible conclusion. Admittedly, one might be tempted here to draw an analogy with the more familiar "common intention" analysis, under which the English courts have been willing to draw very generous inferences of fact from the making of financial contributions.[137] However, there seems to be no reason to import this sort of artificiality into the money consensus context. Therefore, it would not seem justifiable to conclude that there must have been a money consensus between the parties simply because, as things turned out, one party ended up making more repayments to the mortgagee than he was legally obliged to make.[138]

F. Conclusion on the Money Consensus Analysis

From a theoretical point of view, the money consensus analysis has the advantage of confining itself to a consideration of events at the time of the initial purchase. Therefore, while making some concession to the reality of family financial arrangements, it minimises the damage to the theoretical integrity of the resulting trust.[139] It might well be protested that, in practice, any cases covered by the money consensus analysis could more easily be dealt with on the basis of Lord Diplock's "common intention" constructive trust analysis (which

---

[134] [1972] 1 WLR 425, 432.

[135] *Ibid*, 437. The point, presumably, is that in this situation it is reasonable to infer that the parties are agreeing that the mortgage will be repaid in the proportions in which they own the common fund out of which they make all payments.

[136] In *Cowcher* itself, the claimant wife had, over the years, made a number of contributions towards mortgage repayments and general household expenses. However, she had only been able to do so because of "unexpected legacies and gifts". Bagnall J felt (*ibid*, 441) that the wife's subsequent conduct was incapable of supporting any inference as to the parties' state of mind at the time of the purchase. He therefore held that no money consensus had been established on the facts.

[137] See Chapter 5 *infra*, text following n 63.

[138] Cf. *Power v Brighton*, 14 November 1984 (LEXIS, CA); *Harwood v Harwood* [1991] 2 FLR 274, 292E–F per Slade J. *A fortiori* the existence of a money consensus will not be inferred simply because the claimant made payments towards general family expenses. However, it seems possible that a money consensus could be established where the parties agree that the claimant will take responsibility for a specific portion of the mortgage repayments and will discharge that responsibility indirectly by paying other expenses. Cf. Hardingham and Neave, n 36 *supra*, p 91 (criticising this position in the mistaken belief that it represented the thrust of Bagnall J's analysis). See also *Crisp v Mullings* (1975) 239 *e.g.* 119 (where, pursuant to "a man-and-wife discussion", the parties had agreed that the wife was to pay for food and other household expenses and the husband was to pay the mortgage instalments, rates and ground rent). Cf. *Calverley v Green* (1984) 155 CLR 242, 258 per Mason and Brennan JJ; 265 per Murphy J; 267, 271 per Deane J.

[139] Note, however, the problem mentioned in n 109 *supra*.

will be discussed in detail in Chapter 5). Under the "common intention" analysis, an agreement by the claimant to take responsibility for a portion of the money borrowed on mortgage could be seen as evidence that there was a common intention between the parties as to how the ownership of the property would be shared. If the claimant then acted to her detriment on the basis of that common intention, for example by making the promised contribution towards the mortgage, then a constructive trust would arise to give effect to the common intention. Since the common intention analysis fully covers the ground, it might seem unnecessary to complicate the resulting trust by accepting the money consensus refinement.

In response to this, one can only point out that (as is argued in detail in Chapter 5) the common intention analysis is indefensible in theoretical terms and should find no place in a rational legal system. This argument is unlikely to be accepted in the short term in England and it may well be true that, so long as the common intention trust is recognised in that jurisdiction, there is no real need for the money consensus analysis. It is, nonetheless, interesting that English judges have, in quite a few modern cases, found it convenient to decide cases on the basis of Bagnall J's analysis (albeit sometimes seeming to treat that analysis as one aspect of the common intention analysis). In Canada, Australia and New Zealand, where there is a real prospect of discarding the common intention trust in the near future, there seems to be no reason why the money consensus analysis should not occupy a modest place in the theoretical scheme of things. However, one must remember that *Cowcher* received a very frosty reception in the Australian case of *Allen* v *Snyder*[140] and does not appear to have been considered in Canada[141] or New Zealand. It remains to be seen whether the money consensus analysis will ever establish itself in these jurisdictions.[142]

VI. CONCLUSION ON THE RESULTING TRUST

Because of the limited nature of the contributions which it can accommodate, the resulting trust has a relatively limited role to play in the resolution of family property disputes in England, Australia, Canada and New Zealand. The versions of the constructive trust developed in those jurisdictions have the capacity to take account of various forms of contributions besides simply the payment, at the time of the acquisition of the property, of a share of the purchase price.

---

[140] [1977] 2 NSWLR 685. But see n 117 *supra*.

[141] See Hovius and Youdan, n 9 *supra*, p 105 n 78.

[142] As will be discussed in detail in the next chapter, the Irish courts have favoured an approach which simply treats mortgage repayments as constituting contributions to the purchase price. This expansive approach seems to preclude recognition of the more conservative money consensus analysis. See, however, *Malone* v *McQuaid*, 28 May 1998, unreported (LEXIS, Irish High Court) where, although O'Sullivan J regarded the money consensus analysis as inapplicable on the facts, he gave no indication that it did not form part of Irish law.

This makes it unnecessary for those jurisdictions to stretch the resulting trust doctrine to take account of events after the initial purchase.

It is only in Ireland, where no real development has taken place in relation to the constructive trust, that the resulting trust has retained its position in the centre of the stage. As will be discussed in detail in the chapter which now follows, the Irish courts have simply extended the resulting trust to cover direct and indirect contributions to a mortgage. It will be seen that this straight-forward approach has enabled the Irish courts to do justice in a number of cases, although the inflexibility of the resulting trust analysis leads to difficulty when one is dealing with a claim based on work in the home or contributions towards improvements.

3

The Extended Resulting Trust

Under the money consensus approach, which was examined at the end of the previous chapter, it is possible to give credit for an undertaking, at the time of the purchase, to contribute towards the discharge of a mortgage representing a portion of the purchase price. This chapter discusses a more direct approach to the problem which involves simply treating contributions towards the mortgage as "contributions" for the purposes of the resulting trust doctrine, irrespective of the existence of any undertaking, at the time of the purchase, to make those contributions. For convenience, this approach will be termed "the extended resulting trust".

Part I of this chapter will examine the status of the extended resulting trust in England, Canada, New Zealand and Australia. It will be seen that, despite support in some cases, the extended resulting trust has not established itself in these jurisdictions. However, the Irish courts have been willing to extend the resulting trust and have, indeed, centred their treatment of family property disputes around this modification of orthodox legal theory. Part II of this chapter will consider the Irish experience, which illustrates both the strengths and the weaknesses of the extended resulting trust.

I. THE EXTENDED RESULTING TRUST IN ENGLAND, CANADA, AUSTRALIA AND NEW ZEALAND

A. The Point of Legal Principle

As a matter of strict legal theory, the point of principle is a relatively simple one. The payment of mortgage instalments does *not* amount to a contribution to the purchase price for the purposes of the purchase money resulting trust.[1] The most authoritative statement of this orthodox position came in *Calverley* v *Green*.[2] In *Calverley*, the High Court of Australia held that it was "understandable but erroneous to regard the payment of mortgage instalments as payment of the purchase price of a home".[3] Mason and Brennan JJ went on to explain

---

[1] See generally Matthews "Resulting Trusts and Subsequent Contributions" (1994) 8 *Trust Law International* 43.

[2] (1984) 155 CLR 242.

[3] *Ibid*, 257 per Mason and Brennan JJ. See also *Ingram* v *Ingram* [1941] VLR 95, 102; *Jasco* v *Vuong* (1988) 12 Fam LR 615; *Ammala* v *Sarimaa* (1993) 17 Fam LR 529. Contrast *Bloch* v *Bloch* (1981) 37 ALR 55 (High Ct), which was unconvincingly distinguished in *Calverley* (*ibid*, 263 per

that "[t]he purchase price is paid in order to acquire the property; the mortgage instalments are paid to the lender from whom the money to pay some or all of the purchase price is borrowed".[4]

B. The Position of the Extended Resulting Trust as a Matter of Authority

The straightforward approach taken in *Calverley* is clearly logical from a theoretical point of view. However, given the economic realities of the situation,[5] there is an obvious temptation to bend the strict rules in order to provide a remedy for a claimant who has contributed (whether directly or indirectly) to the repayment of a mortgage. Unfortunately, there has been a surprising lack of direct consideration in the case law of the simple question: is it permissible to treat mortgage repayments as constituting a "contribution" to the purchase price?

The earliest relevant English authority appears to be the rather unsatisfactory case of *Gravesend Corporation* v *Kent County Council*,[6] a judgment of Lord Wright, sitting as an additional judge of the King's Bench Division. In *Gravesend*, Lord Wright concluded, without detailed analysis, that a local authority had acquired a beneficial interest in a property by virtue of financial contributions it had made towards the discharge of loans which had funded the erection of a school on that property.[7] This conclusion was doubly unorthodox from the perspective of resulting trust theory, in that the loan in question did not even represent the actual purchase price of the property but rather the cost of subsequent improvements. It is also worth noting Lord Wright's surprising conclusion that, on the facts, the local authority which had earned a resulting trust by virtue of its contributions would, nonetheless, be entitled to enforce repayment of those contributions in certain circumstances.[8] The reasoning in *Gravesend* was recently criticised by Scott V-C in *Foskett* v *McKeown*[9] and its authority must now be open to question.

One might have expected that the status of mortgage contributions would have been resolved in the line of matrimonial property cases which began shortly after the Second World War. Unfortunately, however, in the 1950s and 1960s the principled development of the law of resulting trusts was greatly impeded by the attempt on the part of the English Court of Appeal to develop

Mason and Brennan JJ). The parties in *Bloch* had expressly agreed that their beneficial interests were to be determined on the basis of their total contributions to the purchase and to the discharge of the relevant mortgage. Therefore, the decision in the case may be rationalised on the basis of the common intention analysis (discussed in Chapter 5 *infra*).

[4] *Ibid.*
[5] See Lord Diplock's comments in *Gissing* v *Gissing* [1971] AC 886, 906G.
[6] [1935] 1 KB 339.
[7] The only authority cited by Lord Wright was *The Venture* [1908] P 218, an orthodox application of resulting trust principles which was not, in fact, directly relevant to the point in question.
[8] [1935] 1 KB 339, 353.
[9] [1998] Ch 265, 280–281.

special rules to deal with disputes involving married couples.[10] This project, which was ultimately condemned by the House of Lords in *Pettitt*[11] and *Gissing*,[12] for many years distracted attention from basic doctrinal questions. The most interesting case for present purposes is *Diwell* v *Farnes*.[13] This case involved an unmarried couple and, therefore, the Court of Appeal was constrained to consider the general doctrines of equity. All three judges took the view that, on the facts of the case, the claimant's contributions to mortgage repayments should be treated as equivalent to contributions to the purchase price.[14]

Thus, there was some (by no means overwhelming) support for the extended resulting trust in the case law prior to *Pettitt*.[15] This decision of the House of Lords, however, involved a reaffirmation of orthodoxy on a number of points. As well as condemning the various discretionary doctrines which has been developed by the Court of Appeal, the House of Lords also appears to have ruled out the extended resulting trust. If it had formed part of the law, one would surely expect the doctrine to have been mentioned. On the contrary, however, there are a number of clear statements to the effect that it is necessary to concentrate exclusively on the time of the initial acquisition of the property. Lord Upjohn, for example, made the following comment:

> "[T]he court can only ascertain the title to property by considering the circumstances at the time of acquisition . . . This decides the question of title for all time and in all circumstances".[16]

These comments, although directed primarily against the suggestion that the parties' beneficial interests could have been affected by the fact that their marriage had ultimately failed, also appear to rule out any possibility of taking account of subsequent contributions made over the twenty or twenty-five year life of a mortgage.[17]

In the subsequent case of *Gissing* v *Gissing*,[18] similar comments were made by Viscount Dilhorne.[19] Lord Morris merely stated that he adhered generally to the

---

[10] See Chapter 1 *supra*, text following n 48.

[11] [1970] AC 777.

[12] [1971] AC 886.

[13] [1959] 1 WLR 624.

[14] *Ibid*, 629 per Hodson LJ; 632–633 per Omerod LJ (taking the view that "each case falls to be decided on its own facts"); 638–639 per Willmer LJ. Somewhat equivocal support for the extended resulting trust may also be found in *Moate* v *Moate* [1948] 2 All ER 486; *Silver* v *Silver* [1958] 1 WLR 259 (as interpreted in *Diwell* v *Farnes* [1959] 1 WLR 624, 629 per Hodson LJ and *ibid*, 633 per Omerod LJ). Contrast *Dunbar* v *Dunbar* [1909] 2 Ch 639, 646 per Warrington J; *Rimmer* v *Rimmer* [1953] 1 QB 63, 75 per Romer LJ.

[15] [1970] AC 777.

[16] *Ibid*, 816. See also *ibid*, 813D also per Lord Upjohn; 800F–G per Lord Morris.

[17] In general, in attempting to interpret the *dicta* in *Pettitt* and *Gissing*, one is hampered by an ambiguity which goes to the heart of the point at issue. The phrase "the time of acquisition" could be taken to refer exclusively to the moment of purchase or, if one were sympathetic to the extended resulting trust, it could be understood to cover the lifetime of a mortgage which represents a portion of the purchase price.

[18] [1971] AC 886.

[19] *Ibid*, 900B–D per Viscount Dilhorne.

views he had stated in *Pettitt*. The minority opinion of Lord Reid, on one reading, reveals an assumption that the extended resulting trust formed part of English law[20] and that the other Lords merely favoured a more strict version of that doctrine. In a rather brief treatment of the question, Lord Pearson also appears to have indicated support for the extended resulting trust.[21] The speeches of Lords Pearson and Reid, although not central to the eventual development of the law in England, increased the uncertainty surrounding contributions to mortgage instalments.

Ultimately, however, the most fertile source of confusion has been the speech of Lord Diplock in *Gissing*. Lord Diplock implicitly rejected the extended resulting trust by accepting that it is necessary to concentrate upon the time of the initial acquisition of the property.[22] However, Lord Diplock advanced a new analysis in *Gissing* which treated contributions to mortgage instalments in a misleadingly similar fashion to the extended resulting trust. Under Lord Diplock's "common intention" analysis, which now represents English orthodoxy and which will be discussed in detail in Chapter 5, a constructive trust arises in favour of a claimant who has acted to her detriment on the basis of a common intention between the parties that she is to share in the beneficial ownership. Under this analysis, the fact that a claimant contributed to mortgage instalments can be seen as evidence of a common intention between the parties. The (rather implausible) argument is that, as a matter of probability, the claimant would not have made such contributions if it had not been understood between the parties, at the time of the purchase,[23] that she was to get a share in the ownership. Once the existence of a common intention has been established on this basis, the claimant's conduct in making the contributions can be seen as constituting detrimental reliance on the common intention. A constructive trust will then be imposed to give effect to the common intention. The extent of the claimant's beneficial interest reflects the share which she was commonly intended to obtain. However, in cases where the existence of the common intention has been inferred from the claimant's conduct in making contributions to the mortgage, it is difficult to determine precisely what share in the beneficial ownership she was intended to have. As one solution to this problem, Lord Diplock discussed the possibility that the claimant might have been intended to obtain a share which would be quantified at a later stage on the basis of the extent of her total contribution to the initial deposit and towards the repayment

---

[20] *Ibid*, 896F. This was more clearly the view of Lord Reid in *Pettitt* [1970] AC 777, 794D. However, it is arguable that, in his speech in *Gissing*, Lord Reid accepted that it was necessary to concentrate on the time of the initial purchase: see [1971] AC 886, 896G; 897C.

[21] Lord Pearson commented ([1971] AC 886, 903) that: "Contributions are not limited to those made directly in part payment of the price of the property or to those made at the time when the property is conveyed into the name of one of the spouses". See also *ibid*, 902B.

[22] *Ibid*, 905D; 908B–D.

[23] Note also that in exceptional circumstances a common intention could be formed at a later stage. However, in this situation also, subsequent mortgage contributions would only be relevant if they could be related back to this prior agreement.

of the mortgage.[24] Where (as has tended to happen in the subsequent case law)[25] the court decides this to have been the common intention of the parties, then the final result is identical to that which would have been reached on the basis of the extended resulting trust: the claimant's share is proportionate to her contribution to the purchase price, with contributions towards mortgage repayments being taken as part of that contribution. However, the important point for present purposes is that, although the final result is similar, the theoretical path to that result is quite different (and far more complicated).

As has just been explained, Lord Diplock's rather tortuous analysis makes it possible to take mortgage repayments into account while giving lip-service to the idea that conduct subsequent to a purchase is relevant only for the light which it sheds on the intentions of the parties at the time of the purchase. Since Lord Diplock's common intention analysis is broader than the extended resulting trust, and can generate the same results for claimants in cases involving contributions to mortgage instalments, its acceptance appears to remove the need for English law to recognise the latter analysis. Unfortunately, in his speech in *Gissing*, Lord Diplock did not adequately clarify the distinction between his analysis and the traditional resulting trust. Therefore, there has been a reluctance in some subsequent cases[26] and commentaries[27] to accept that the extended resulting trust does not form part of English law.

However, in recent years a more orthodox view appears to be gaining acceptance amongst English judges[28] and commentators.[29] Perhaps the most con-

---

[24] [1971] AC 886, 909C–E.

[25] However, the courts have sometimes taken a more generous approach. See the discussion of cases such as *Midland Bank plc v Cooke* [1995] 4 All ER 562 in Chapter 5 *infra*, text following n 129.

[26] See *Davis v Vale* [1971] 1 WLR 1022; *Falconer v Falconer* [1970] 1 WLR 1333; *Re Densham* [1975] 1 WLR 1519; *Bernard v Josephs* [1982] Ch 391, 398B–E per Lord Denning MR; 407G–H; 408E–F per Kerr LJ; *Young v Young* [1984] FLR 375. Cf. the critical comments of Meagher and Gummow *Jacobs' Law of Trusts in Australia*, 6th edn (Sydney: Butterworths, 1997) p 294. Note also the Northern Irish position, which appears to be based on a resulting trust analysis: *McFarlane v McFarlane* [1972] NI 59; *Allied Irish Banks Ltd v McWilliam* [1982] NI 156.

[27] See the apparent support for the extended resulting trust in O'Hagan "Quantifying Interests Under Resulting Trusts" (1997) 60 MLR 420; Dixon "A Case Too Far" [1997] Conv 66; Dal Pont and Chalmers *Equity and Trusts in Australia and New Zealand* (North Ridge NSW, LBC Information Services: 1996) p 423 (commenting on English law); Stevens "Equitable Tracing into the Proceeds of a Life Insurance Policy Partially Funded with Misappropriated Trust Money" [1998] Conv 406, 408–409.

[28] The extended resulting trust appears to be inconsistent with the following authorities (many of them supporting Bagnall J's rival "money consensus" analysis): *Cowcher v Cowcher* [1972] 1 WLR 425; *Re Nicholson (deceased)* [1974] 2 All ER 386; *Richards v Dove* [1974] 1 All ER 888, 894C–D per Walton J; *Jeffries v Stevens* [1982] STC 639, 651 per Walton J; *Power v Brighton* 14 November 1984 (LEXIS, CA); *Marsh v von Sternberg* [1986] 1 FLR 526, 533 per Bush J; *Re Gorman* [1990] 1 WLR 616, 624E–F per Vinelott J; *Harwood v Harwood* [1991] 2 FLR 274, 292A–G; 294B–D per Slade LJ; *Huntingford v Hobbs* [1993] 1 FCR 45, 54B–55G per Sir Christopher Slade; 61F–62A per Dillon LJ. Cf. *Escritt v Escritt* (1982) 3 FLR 280, 282; *Boscawen v Bajwa* [1996] 1 WLR 328. See also the *dicta* from *Pettitt* and *Gissing* referred to in the text to and following n 16 *supra*; *Bernard v Josephs* [1982] Ch 391, 404C per Griffiths LJ; *Burns v Burns* [1984] Ch 317, 326E–327D per Fox LJ (all suggesting that the central focus is on the time of the original purchase). One may also refer to the cases where contributions towards the repayment of a mortgage are dealt with under the mainstream common intention analysis, e.g. *Passee v Passee* [1988] 1 FLR 263.

[29] Most academic commentators now appear to reject the extended resulting trust. See

vincing evidence for this[30] is the fact that, in the leading case of *Lloyds Bank plc v Rosset*,[31] the House of Lords stated the law governing disputes between unmarried cohabitees without reference to the extended resulting trust.[32] Although one would have liked a more clear-cut judicial statement of principle on the point, it appears that, on the balance of authority, the extended resulting trust does not form part of English law.

There is less authority on the matter in other jurisdictions but the position appears to be similar in New Zealand[33] and (probably) Canada[34] and, as has already been seen, the High Court of Australia has decisively rejected the extended resulting trust.[35] Given the development of the constructive trust which has taken place in these Commonwealth jurisdictions, it is difficult to see any necessity for their courts to stretch the natural boundaries of the resulting trust.

If direct contributions to the repayment of a mortgage are not considered in these jurisdictions to constitute "contributions" to the purchase price for the purposes of the resulting trust doctrine, then *a fortiori* a claimant will not be able to establish a resulting trust by relying on mere "indirect" contributions to the mortgage (e.g. paying other household bills while the legal owner pays the mortgage instalments). Similarly, contributions in the form of housework and child-rearing will not be sufficient to establish a resulting trust.[36]

Matthews, n 1 *supra*; Ferguson "Constructive Trusts—A Note of Caution" (1993) 109 LQR 114, 125, 127; Glover and Todd "The Myth of Common Intention" (1996) 16 *Legal Studies* 325, 337. Cf. Gray *Elements of Land Law*, 2nd edn (London: Butterworths, 1993) pp 387–388. Note also the development of Hayton's views from "Equitable Rights of Cohabitees" [1990] Conv 370, 383 to *Underhill and Hayton: The Law Relating to Trusts and Trustees*, 15th edn (London: Butterworths, 1995) p 320.

[30] Matthews, n 1 *supra*, 45–46 regards *Winkworth* v *Edward Baron Developments Ltd* [1986] 1 WLR 1512 as a leading authority against the extended resulting trust. However, it does not appear to have been necessary in *Winkworth* for the House to form a view on the question, given that the claimant's contribution could not be linked in any way to the purchase price of the disputed property. See *ibid*, 1515D–G. Moreover, Lord Templeman (speaking for the House) stated the relevant equitable principles in rather general terms, appearing in one passage (*ibid*, 1516C–D) actually to support the extended resulting trust.

[31] [1991] 1 AC 107.

[32] See, in particular, *ibid*, 132G–133A per Lord Bridge. See also *Grant* v *Edwards* [1986] 1 Ch 638. Cf. *Foskett* v *McKeown* [1998] Ch 265, 279–281 per Scott V-C.

[33] See *Cossey* v *Bach* [1992] 3 NZLR 612, 630, where Fisher J took the view that it was necessary for a contribution to the purchase price to be made "upon or before the acquisition of the property". Contrast *Hendry* v *Hendry* [1960] NZLR 48, followed in *Donovan* v *Beeson*, 28 March 1990, unreported (NZ High Court). See Atkin *Living Together Without Marriage: The Law in New Zealand* (Wellington: Butterworths, 1991) p 78. Atkin (*ibid*) feels that contributions towards mortgage repayments "fit less well under the resulting trust model and are better dealt with under another heading".

[34] See Hovius and Youdan *The Law of Family Property* (Scarborough, Ontario: Carswell Publishing, 1991) p 92 (suggesting, without the citation of case law, that Canadian courts have in the past treated mortgage repayments as constituting a portion of the purchase price) and p 106 (advocating a more restrictive approach to the resulting trust given the radical development of the constructive trust in Canada).

[35] See text following n 2 *supra*.

[36] Cf. *Burns* v *Burns* [1984] Ch 317.

It has already been mentioned that, by way of contrast to their counterparts in other jurisdictions, the Irish courts have fully embraced the extended resulting trust. The Irish case law shows both the advantages and the limitations of an approach based on this doctrinal option. It will be convenient to address the Irish experience separately and this task will now be undertaken in Part II.

II. THE EXTENDED RESULTING TRUST IN IRELAND[37]

A. Introduction

It was explained in the previous Part that Ireland, unlike the other jurisdictions considered in this book, has accepted the "extended resulting trust". This simple doctrinal development has formed the basis of the Irish treatment of family property disputes. It will emerge from this Part that the Irish theoretical model, although not overly sophisticated, has made it possible to do justice in many cases. However, the Irish resulting trust approach, being based around contributions to the "purchase price" of property, has proven incapable of providing a remedy for a claimant who has worked in the home and in child-rearing or who has paid for improvements to the home.

It is worth stressing at this preliminary stage that the vast majority of the Irish cases to date have involved married couples. Thus far, despite the increasing prevalence of unmarried cohabitation in Ireland,[38] there have only been two Irish cases dealing directly with the position of unmarried cohabitees.[39] Neither of these cases suggest that disputes involving unmarried couples should be treated differently than those involving married couples.[40] The logic of the Irish theoretical approach would also dictate that the same general rules should apply in both situations. However, the unsympathetic treatment of an alleged cohabitation contract in *Ennis* v *Butterly*[41] serves as a reminder of the conservative tendency of some Irish judges. It remains to be confirmed that the Irish courts will be willing to apply to unmarried cohabitees the equitable doctrines developed in the marital context.

---

[37] See generally Mee "Trusts of the Family Home—Boiling Oil From the Ivory Tower" (1992) 14 *Dublin University Law Journal* (ns) 19; Mee "Trusts of the Family Home: The Irish Experience" [1993] Conv 359; Delany *Equity and the Law of Trusts in Ireland* (Dublin: Round Hall Sweet and Maxwell, 1996) pp 153–165; Shatter *Family Law in the Republic of Ireland*, 4th edn (Dublin: Butterworths, 1997) pp 772–806, 1000–1004; Brady "Trusts, Law Reform and the Emancipation of Women" (1984) 6 *Dublin University Law Journal* 1; Cooney "Wives, Mistresses and Beneficial Ownership" (1979) 14 *Irish Jurist* (ns) 1; O'Connor *Key Problems in Irish Family Law* (Dublin: Round Hall Press, Dublin, 1988) pp 170–226; Binchy *A Casebook on Irish Family Law* (Albingdon: Professional Books, 1984) pp 261–288.

[38] See Chapter 1 *supra*, Table 1.1 and accompanying notes.

[39] See *Power* v *Conroy* [1980] ILRM 31; *McGill* v *S* [1979] IR 283.

[40] See the further discussion of this point in the text following n 111 *infra*.

[41] [1996] 1 IR 426, discussed in Chapter 1 *supra*, text to and following n 151.

The course of Irish law was set in the first modern Irish case in the family property area, *C v C*.[42] In *C*, a married couple bought a house and had it conveyed into the sole name of the husband. The wife paid the 10 per cent deposit and the expenses of the purchase. The remainder of the price was borrowed by the husband on mortgage. Afterwards he made most of the repayments. However, on a number of occasions when he was unable to find the cash, the wife borrowed from her family and gave him the money to pay the amount due. There was no evidence of an advance agreement between the parties that the wife would take any responsibility for the repayment of the mortgage. The issue before the court was whether a resulting trust could arise in this type of situation.

Kenny J held that, on the basis of the wife's contributions to the deposit and the mortgage repayments, she was entitled to one-half of the beneficial interest in the home. Unfortunately, the judgment of Kenny J was extremely vague. He simply stated that:

> "I think that the correct and most useful approach to these difficult cases is to apply the concept of a trust to the legal relationship which arises when a wife makes payments towards the purchase of a house, or the repayment of the mortgage instalments, when the house is in the sole name of the husband. When this is done, he becomes a trustee for her of a share in the house and the size of the share depends upon the amount of the contributions which she has made towards the purchase or the repayment of the mortgage".[43]

Given Kenny J's view that the size of the share will depend on the extent of the contributions, it appears that the remedy granted in *C v C* was in the nature of a resulting trust. It is also clear that Kenny J was willing to take into account contributions towards the repayment of the mortgage. However, beyond this generalised acceptance of the extended resulting trust, there was no explanation of the process whereby contributions to the mortgage would serve to create a trust.

Since *C v C* left the theoretical problem untouched, one must look to later Irish cases for guidance on the relationship between mortgage repayments and the doctrine of resulting trusts. Within the Irish case law, one may detect two different views on the basic problem. It is now proposed to outline the two different ways of explaining the extended resulting trust and to make an attempt to establish which is preferable.

B. Explaining the Extended Resulting Trust: Two Irish Solutions

The first of the two competing theoretical models, which will be described as the "economic reality" approach, treats the repayment of the mortgage as the

---

[42] [1976] IR 254 (High Court). See also *Heavey v Heavey* (1974) 111 ILTR 1.
[43] [1976] IR 254, 258. Kenny J cited *inter alia Pettitt v Pettitt* [1970] AC 777 and *Gissing v Gissing* [1971] AC 886.

economic or practical equivalent of the payment of the initial purchase price. On this basis, mortgage repayments are recognised as capable of generating a proportionate share under a resulting trust. This simple approach has various theoretical and practical drawbacks, as will be discussed in due course,[44] but it is not without its attractions.

The second Irish model (the "purchase of the equity of redemption" model) derives its main support from two judgments of Finlay CJ. This second approach treats the repayment of the mortgage as a process of gradually "buying" the equity of redemption from the mortgagee. It is to this "purchase", rather than to the initial purchase of the house, that the resulting trust doctrine has been applied by Finlay CJ. As will be discussed in due course, the practical difference between the two competing Irish models emerges clearly in the context of the repayment of mortgage loans which do not represent the initial purchase price of the property.[45] It will be submitted that the second model (which unfortunately is in the ascendancy in Irish law) is based on a fundamental misunderstanding and should be discarded to avoid the perpetuation of serious anomalies in Irish law.

1. *The "economic reality" model*

As mentioned above, this approach treats payments towards the mortgage as a "contribution" for the purposes of the doctrine of resulting trusts. Although it has never been made explicit in an Irish case, one assumes that the rationale is that when a couple purchase a house they regard themselves as paying for it over the full period of the mortgage.[46] This "economic reality" logic appears to explain the willingness of the Irish courts to award a share on the basis of direct contributions to the mortgage repayments. Speaking for the Supreme Court in *McC v McC*,[47] Henchy J stated that "contributions towards the purchase price or towards the discharge of mortgage instalments" would generate a share "roughly corresponding with the proportion of the purchase money represented by the wife's total contribution".[48] This comment appears to indicate an assumption that the mortgage instalments in reality represent a portion of the purchase price of the house.

In a sense, the economic reality model is as straightforward as that. Once the mortgage is seen to represent the purchase price, one can deal with a case like *C v C*[49] by simply assessing the claimant's contribution towards the deposit and the mortgage repayments. It is not necessary that the contributions to the mortgage be referable to any prior "consensus" as to how the mortgage will be

---

[44] See Section C *infra*.
[45] See text following n 58 *infra*.
[46] Cf. the comments of Lord Diplock in *Gissing v Gissing* [1971] AC 886, 906F–G.
[47] [1986] ILRM 1.
[48] *Ibid*, 2.
[49] [1976] IR 254.

repaid[50] or to any "common intention" that the ownership will be shared.[51] Instead, mortgage repayments (even if made many years after the original purchase) are treated as contributions to the purchase price and, therefore, as triggering the presumption of resulting trust.

Although this development has largely been taken for granted in Ireland, it will be recalled from the discussion earlier in this chapter that a different position has been taken by the other jurisdictions considered in this book.[52] However, it will also be recalled that each of the other jurisdictions had, at various times, shown some sympathy with the type of approach adopted in Ireland. The discussion in this chapter will reveal that, although the economic reality model leads to various theoretical and practical problems, it does have the advantage of comparative simplicity at a theoretical level and may not compare unfavourably in practice with the more artificial English common intention analysis. However, if in the future the Irish courts were to adopt any of the more radical Commonwealth solutions to the problem of family property, there would be a strong argument for restoring the theoretical purity of the resulting trust by refusing to recognise mortgages repayments as contributions to the purchase price.

2. The "purchase of the equity of redemption" model[53]

It is now proposed to examine the second model discernible in the Irish case law. At the outset, it should be explained that this second approach is in many respects similar to the "economic reality" model which has just been discussed. Both are variations on the extended resulting trust and both lead to the same conclusion on many important matters. The "purchase of the equity of redemption" model has independent significance for two reasons.

First, the misconception upon which it is founded gives the false appearance of inevitability to the decision to treat mortgage contributions as "automatically" capable of generating a share under a resulting trust. This may provide a partial explanation of why the Irish courts, unlike those of the other common law jurisdictions considered in this book, have favoured a simple extension of the doctrine of resulting trusts to cover mortgage repayments. Secondly, the "purchase of the equity" model has important practical consequences. These arise most obviously in the context of mortgages which do not represent the purchase price of the property being mortgaged.

---

[50] As required by Bagnall J in *Cowcher* v *Cowcher* [1972] 1 WLR 425. See Chapter 2 *supra*, Part V.

[51] See Chapter 5 *infra* for discussion of the English common intention analysis.

[52] See Part I *supra*.

[53] See generally Mee "Trusts of the Family Home—Boiling Oil From the Ivory Tower", n 37 *supra*, 26–33; Mee "Trusts of the Family Home: The Irish Experience" n 37 *supra*, 362–364.

(a) The basis of the "purchase of the equity" model

The purchase of the equity model treats the repayment of a mortgage as a process of gradually "buying" the equity of redemption from the mortgagee. This view was given its first expression in *W v W*,[54] a decision of Finlay P (as he then was). Having explained that contributions to mortgage repayments could generate a share in the beneficial interest, Finlay P added this explanation:

> "It is not expressly stated in the decisions to which I have referred,[55] but I assume that the fundamental principle underlying this rule of law is that the redemption of any form of charge or mortgage on property in truth consists of the acquisition by the owner or mortgagor of an estate in the property with which he parted at the time of the creating of the mortgage or charge and that there can be no distinction in principle between a contribution made to the acquisition of that interest and a contribution made to the acquisition of an interest in property by an original purchase".[56]

Speaking for the Supreme Court in the more recent case of *EN v RN*,[57] Finlay CJ quoted this passage and confirmed that he "would adhere to that view".[58] The effect of Finlay CJ's approach is that the purchase money resulting trust doctrine is applied to the "purchase" of the equity of redemption from the lender, rather than to the purchase of the property from the original vendor. A practical consequence of this understanding of the law is that contributions towards the redemption of any mortgage or charge over property, whether or not the money borrowed was used for the purchase of that property, can generate a resulting trust for the contributor. Thus in *EN v RN*,[59] a claimant who helped to repay various mortgage loans, taken over a period of years for different purposes, was held to be entitled to a one-half share in the beneficial interest, despite the fact that the initial purchase price had been entirely paid in cash by the legal owner.

(b) Difficulties with the "purchase of the equity" model

There is no support to be found for the "purchase of the equity" model in the decisions to which Finlay P referred in *W v W*[60] (nor in "the judicial decisions quoted with approval in them").[61] Under the "economic reality model", the reason why repayment of a mortgage is regarded as capable of generating a resulting trust is that *where the purchase price is represented by the mortgage loan* those payments can be seen as equivalent to the provision of the purchase price. Departing from this doctrine, Finlay CJ's argument in *W v W* and *EN v*

---

54 [1981] ILRM 202.
55 *Heavey v Heavey* (1974) 111 ILTR 1; *C v C* [1976] IR 254; *McGill v S* [1979] IR 283.
56 [1981] ILRM 202, 204–205. See the similar comments of Shortland J in *Hendry v Hendry* [1960] NZLR 48, 51–52. See also Matthews, n 1 *supra*, 44–45.
57 [1992] 2 IR 116.
58 *Ibid*, 123.
59 [1992] 2 IR 116.
60 [1981] ILRM 202.
61 Invoked by Finlay P *ibid*, 204.

RN was that when a person contributes to the repayment of a loan, he or she gains a share, not in what was purchased with the help of the loan, but in the *security* for the loan.

Finlay CJ's approach is based on the idea that in creating a mortgage a borrower is "parting with an estate" in the property and that, as the loan is repaid, he is buying back that estate.[62] In another Supreme Court decision, *BL v ML*,[63] Finlay CJ referred in passing to "the acquisition of the equity of redemption by . . . the clearing off of a mortgage".[64] Unfortunately this is not an accurate conceptualisation of the process. Consider an example where X mortgages his house (then worth £2,000) to secure a loan of £1,000. If, the day after the mortgage, the value of his house were to double, the bank could not claim one-half of the enhanced value of the land. X would still merely owe it £1,000. What the lender possesses is not a proportion of the ownership but merely a security interest for a fixed sum of money. Correspondingly, as the mortgagor gradually repays the mortgage, he is not increasing his proportionate interest in the property; he is merely reducing the extent of the debt charged upon the property. Thus, the approach taken by Finlay P in *W v W*[65] is inconsistent with the essential nature of the mortgagor/mortgagee relationship.

In addition, serious anomalies are created by the fact that Finlay CJ's trust is triggered simply by the repayment of a secured loan. It appears entirely arbitrary that, as was expressly held in *EN v RN*,[66] a share will be gained by a claimant who pays off a mortgage which was raised to finance improvements to a defendant's property, while a claimant who pays for the same improvements in cash will be awarded nothing.[67] Consider also a case where a couple mortgage their family home (which is in the sole name of one partner) to fund the education of their children. Under Finlay CJ's theory, the ownership of the house would be altered if the partners were to contribute equally to the repayment of this mortgage, even though the relevant loan was raised to meet a joint family expense. Further problems arise in the case of someone who repays an *unsecured* loan (e.g. bridging finance or an unsecured loan from an employer or relation)[68] which represents a portion of the purchase price of property. Under Finlay CJ's "fundamental principle" there could be no trust in such a case because, in the absence of security for the loan, there is no question of buying back any estate transferred to the lender.

Although the doctrine in *W v W* now enjoys the unanimous support of the Irish Supreme Court, it is respectfully submitted that it is founded on a

---

[62] At the level of basic theory, the answer to this is that, even though a mortgage takes the outward form of a transfer of ownership to the mortgagee, the courts of equity will uphold the reality that it merely creates security for a loan. Cf. ss 85 and 86 of the English Law of Property Act 1925; Gray, n 29 *supra*, pp 937–942.

[63] [1992] 2 IR 77.

[64] *Ibid*, 107.

[65] [1981] ILRM 202.

[66] [1992] 2 IR 116, 122–123.

[67] See text to and following n 147 *infra*.

[68] See e.g. *M v M* (1978) 114 ILTR 46, 48.

misunderstanding and should be eliminated from Irish law at the first opportunity. In the meantime, it appears that contributions to any mortgage, whatever its purpose, will suffice to trigger the doctrine of resulting trusts. It remains to be seen how seriously the Irish courts will take the doctrine in W v W in a more difficult context, e.g. in relation to a claim based on the repayment of an unsecured loan.

C. Problems With the Extended Resulting Trust

This section considers the various difficulties which attach to the decision to extend the resulting trust in the manner favoured by the Irish courts. These difficulties attach to the extended resulting trust, irrespective of whether one explains it on the basis of the "economic reality" model or the "purchase of the equity" model. The source of the problems is that the Irish approach abandons the principle, fundamental to the traditional purchase money resulting trust doctrine, that the beneficial interests are to be assessed once and for all at the time of the purchase. Under the Irish approach, it becomes necessary to consider events which take place many years after the initial conveyance of the house by the previous owner. This stretching of the time-frame of relevant events gives rise to the following four problems:

1. *Conveyancing difficulties*

It was relatively easy for purchasers to protect themselves from the effects of the purchase money resulting trust in its traditional form. It was only necessary to find out whether at the time of the previous conveyance there had been a contribution to the purchase price by anyone besides the present seller. Unfortunately, in the light of the modern Irish case law, this sort of inquiry can no longer be confined to one fixed point in the past. For example, even if the seller had been living alone at the time he or she acquired the property, he or she might later have begun to cohabit with a partner and subsequently have received assistance in repaying the mortgage.

Moreover, once one makes the concession of considering mortgage repayments as "contributions", further concessions are almost inevitable. Thus, as will be discussed later in this chapter,[69] the Irish courts have been unable to resist a further extension to accommodate a claimant who contributes to general family expenses and thus facilitates the legal owner in making mortgage repayments. This further extension makes it even more difficult for a future purchaser to pin down the existence of a resulting trust over the property. It could also be argued that lending institutions in Ireland have become less willing to

---

[69] See text following n 90 *infra*.

advance money to small businesses on the security of the family home as a result of the widening of the doctrine of resulting trusts by the Irish courts.

The above conveyancing difficulties must, of course, be balanced against the social justice achieved by the increased willingness to provide a remedy for (generally) female claimants who might otherwise be deprived of financial security upon the breakdown of a long-term relationship. An assessment of whether the disruption to conveyancing has been justified must depend, to a large extent, on one's priorities. It is, however, worth reiterating that the major developments in the Irish case law were motivated by a desire to improve the lot of married claimants, a constituency whose rights are now largely protected by legislation.[70] It is likely that the Irish developments would have been more modest if they had taken place solely in the context of claims by unmarried cohabitees. It is, therefore, not impossible that the Irish courts might in the future attempt to restrict the ambit of the equitable rules given that they now exist largely for the benefit of unmarried cohabitees.[71]

2. *Property held in joint names*

As was discussed in Chapter 1, it is highly desirable that a method should exist whereby a couple may deliberately determine the proportions of the beneficial ownership in a family home, irrespective of their financial contributions.[72] Otherwise, even if the legal ownership of the property has been conveyed into joint names, a financially dependent partner will always be vulnerable to a claim to a resulting trust. In England, the preferred method of excluding the doctrines of equity is to utilise an express declaration of the beneficial interests. It has been held in England that such a declaration is decisive in the absence of fraud or mistake. The parties are estopped from denying that their intentions in relation to the ownership were at that time other than those declared in the deed. This prevents any claim to an implied trust on the basis of contributions to the purchase price or the mortgage instalments.[73]

The problem for Irish law is that its version of the resulting trust (unlike the complicated English common intention constructive trust)[74] no longer hinges on the intentions of the parties at the time of the original conveyance.[75] Therefore, it could be argued by a claimant that her intention in relation to ownership at the time of the conveyance (as captured in the express declaration) is irrelevant under Irish law. She could suggest that what is crucial is her intention at the time when, many years later, she makes a contribution to the mortgage repayments. Given the difference between Irish and English law, it is by no means clear that

---

[70] See the Family Law Act 1995 and the Family Law (Divorce) Act, 1996.

[71] Cf. text to and following n 41 *supra*.

[72] See Chapter 1 *supra*, Part III.

[73] See Chapter 1 *supra*, text following n 152.

[74] See Chapter 5 *infra*.

[75] For example, in C v C [1976] IR 254, 258, Kenny J pointed out that the wife's interest arose "when she made the payments" towards the mortgage instalments.

an estoppel would prevent an Irish claimant from overriding an express declaration.[76] This would be a most unfortunate consequence and, indeed, may provide part of the explanation of why the English courts have eschewed the simple extended resulting trust approach in favour of the far more artificial and complex common intention analysis which will be considered in detail in Chapter 5.

It is also worth pointing out that, while the approach of the Irish courts to mortgage repayments was developed in order to benefit claimants, it may prove to be counter-productive in the context of property which is held in joint names. Consider a case where the male partner works outside the home, while the woman stays at home and takes care of the children of the relationship. Assume that the title to the family home and the mortgage are taken in joint names but there is no express declaration of the beneficial interests.[77] Suppose also that the male partner makes all the payments on the mortgage. Under the unmodified doctrine of resulting trusts, the parties would be credited equally with half of the amount borrowed under the joint mortgage. The beneficial interests could not be affected by the fact that the male partner paid (or continued, after the relationship ended, to pay) all of the instalments under the mortgage. Since these instalments would not be classified as part of the purchase price, he would (at best) be entitled, on the basis of the principles of equitable accounting,[78] to credit for the excess payments in the event of an eventual sale of the house and division of the proceeds. On the other hand, under the resulting trust as modified by the Irish courts, the mortgage is treated as representing the purchase price. Therefore, a presumption of resulting trust would arise in favour of the male partner in respect of all the mortgage instalments he paid. It would be very difficult for the female partner to rebut this presumption by producing positive evidence that her partner intended, during the currency of the relationship, to make a gift to her of one-half of the instalments.

The above example gives substance to the suspicion that the rules developed by the Irish courts focus on an outdated paradigm: the case of sole ownership by the male partner. It will be necessary for the Irish courts, in considering possible future developments, to take proper account of the modern practice of joint ownership and joint liability under the mortgage.

---

[76] Under the "purchasing the equity" model (see text following n 53 *supra*), it is possible to base a claim on contributions to the repayment of a mortgage which does not represent the purchase price of the property. Since this type of claim does not focus on the original acquisition of the home, it is very difficult to argue that it should be precluded by an express declaration of the beneficial interests at the time of that acquisition.

[77] Unless the author's strictures (see Mee "Joint Ownership of the Family Home" (1992) 86 *Gazette of the Incorporated Law Society of Ireland* 59) have had any effect, it would appear that the use of an express declaration is still rare in Ireland.

[78] See Chapter 2 *supra*, n 101.

3. *Theoretical untidiness: a wavering equity*

If payments towards the mortgage constitute "contributions", then it would appear that the beneficial interests under the resulting trust will vary each time the claimant pays an instalment. In the English case of *Richards* v *Dove*,[79] Walton J argued that the existence of such a "wavering equity" was contrary to section 53(1)(c) of the Law of Property Act 1925 (the modern English equivalent of section 9 of the Statute of Frauds 1677).[80] Section 53(1)(c) requires that any disposition of a beneficial interest under an existing trust must be made in writing. The argument of Walton J seems to have been that, once the claimant had made her first contribution towards the mortgage, she would obtain a beneficial interest under a resulting trust and that thereafter any variation in the beneficial interests would have to take place in writing. However, the answer to Walton J's concern would appear to be that, with each contribution to the mortgage, a new resulting trust is superimposed on the previous one. Therefore, each variation in the beneficial interests would be due to the creation of a resulting trust, which under section 53(2) of the Law of Property Act 1925 (the modern English equivalent of section 8 of the Statute of Frauds 1677) is exempt from the evidentiary requirements created elsewhere in the Statute.

While the concept of a "wavering equity" does not, therefore, appear to conflict with the Statute of Frauds and its modern equivalents, it is certainly not elegant from a theoretical point of view. It is true that in practice the courts do not need to concern themselves with the history of the respective beneficial interests and may content themselves with declaring the present quantum of the interests. However, in cases where a portion of the mortgage remains unpaid at the time of the hearing, it may be necessary to tolerate beneficial interests which will continue to waver even after a court declaration as to their extent at one particular time.[81]

4. *Mathematical problems*

A final problem is that the calculation of the beneficial interest generated by contributions to the mortgage instalments is a very difficult task. It is by no means obvious how to decide what proportion of the purchase price is represented by a given amount of expenditure on mortgage repayments.[82] Matters

---

[79] [1974] 1 All ER 888. See also *Jeffries* v *Stevens* [1982] STC 639, 651 per Walton J.

[80] The relevant Irish provision is s 6 of the Statute of Frauds (Ireland) 1695.

[81] See n 84 *infra* and accompanying text.

[82] Cf. Murphy and Clark *The Family Home* (London: Sweet and Maxwell, 1983) pp 52–58; Sparkes "The Quantification of Beneficial Interests: Problems Arising from Contributions to Deposits, Mortgage Advances and Mortgage Instalments" (1991) 11 OJLS 39. The standard Irish method of calculating shares based on contributions to the repayment of a mortgage is illustrated in *K* v *K* (1978) 114 ILTR 50; *L* v *L*, 21 December 1979, unreported (High Court). For discussion of the problem of calculating the share in cases (such as *W* v *W* [1981] ILRM 202) where the mortgage being repaid does not represent the purchase price, see Mee "Trusts of the Family Home: Boiling Oil from the Ivory Tower", n 37 *supra*, 30.

are complicated by various factors e.g. the interest element in mortgage repayments,[83] the possibility of the relationship's breaking up before the mortgage has been fully repaid,[84] the effects of inflation, the possible fluctuation in interest rates over the term of a mortgage and the variety of possible mortgage arrangements.[85]

On the whole, it appears from the case law that the Irish courts have been far from impressive in their attempts to grapple with the difficult mathematical problems which they have set themselves. The mathematical problems are a direct result of the decision to consider mortgage repayments as automatically amounting to contributions under the resulting trust doctrine. A more sophisticated theoretical approach, such as the English common intention analysis, might allow the Irish judiciary to "paint with a broad brush" in some cases, while being able to fall back on a more precise mathematical calculation of the shares where this seemed appropriate.

D. Other Contributions Under the Extended Resulting Trust

1. *Introduction*

Despite the difficulties created by the approach of the Supreme Court in *EN*,[86] it is clear that mortgage repayments are regarded by the Irish courts as capable

---

[83] The Irish courts have generally taken the approach of giving equal credit for mortgage repayments, irrespective of their composition in terms of interest and capital. See e.g. *C v C* [1976] IR 254; *L v L*, 21 December 1979, unreported (High Court, Finlay P); *HD v JD*, 31 July 1981, unreported (High Court, Finlay P); *GNR v KAR*, 25 March 1981, unreported (High Court, Carroll J). Contrast, however, the method of calculation favoured by Carroll J in *Containercare (Ireland) Ltd v Wycherley* [1982] IR 143, 152 and adopted by Barron J in *O'K v O'K*, 16 November 1982, unreported (High Court). Sparkes argues, correctly it is submitted, that the proper approach is to treat all mortgage repayments equally: see n 82 *supra*, 59.

[84] The favoured method of calculation of the Irish courts in this situation is illustrated by the facts of *K v K* (1978) 114 ILTR 50. The parties had contributed equally to the mortgage repayments which had been made thus far. Finlay P took the view that the parties should each be credited with paying half of the entire mortgage, notwithstanding the large amount outstanding. It is submitted that this approach is misconceived because it deserts the fundamental principle that the beneficial interest results to the person who provides the purchase price. The proper method is to give the claimant credit only for that proportion of the purchase price which has actually been paid by her. The remainder of the purchase price should be treated as having been paid by the partner who was legally liable to repay the remainder of the mortgage. As to the problem of mortgage repayments made after the breakdown of a relationship or a court adjudication as to the respective beneficial interests, see the conflicting authorities of *K v K supra*; *MB v EB*, 19 December 1980, unreported (High Court); *O'K v O'K*, 16 November 1982, unreported (High Court); *AL v JL*, 27 February 1984, unreported (High Court); *T v T*, 15 July 1985, unreported (High Court). The author's position is that all contributions should, in principle, be treated in the same way, whether they are made before or after the hearing/break-up.

[85] In relation to the endowment mortgage (as opposed to the more common instalment mortgage), see Sparkes, n 82 *supra*, 56, discussing the inconclusive treatment of the issue in *Cowcher v Cowcher* [1972] 1 WLR 425 and *Heseltine v Heseltine* [1971] 1 WLR 342. Cf. Murphy and Clark, n 82 *supra*, p 57.

[86] [1992] 2 IR 116.

of generating a resulting trust. Subject to a possible *de minimis* test which would exclude trivial contributions,[87] contributions to the repayment of *any* mortgage are to be regarded as "automatically" amounting to a contribution for the purposes of a resulting trust. What is explored in this Part is whether a resulting trust may also be generated by other, less direct, forms of contribution.

In *C v C*,[88] Kenny J considered the possibility that a claimant could contribute to the acquisition of property in the defendant's name "by paying the expenses of the household so that he has the money which makes it possible for him to pay the mortgage instalments".[89] In such cases the claimant's contribution is often described as "indirect". As well as such contributions, this Part will also consider the status of other contributions such as work in the family home and in the rearing of children, the undertaking of unpaid work in a family business and the making of improvements to the family home.

One general point should be stressed at this stage. In order to give rise to a purchase money resulting trust, a contribution must be capable of being linked to the repayment of the purchase price (or, in Ireland, the repayment of a mortgage). Therefore, another type of contribution to family expenditure, a contribution made *after* all the purchase price has been paid (and at a time when no mortgage is outstanding) seems incapable of generating a beneficial interest by means of a resulting trust.[90]

2. Indirect contributions to a mortgage through the payment of family expenses

(a) The status of indirect contributions

There has been much controversy on the subject of the "indirect contribution" made by a non-owning partner who works outside the home and uses her income to pay family expenses other than the mortgage instalments.[91] The status of such contributions in Ireland remained uncertain for a number of years, with some judges imposing a requirement of an "agreement or arrangement" between the parties before indirect contributions could give rise to a beneficial interest.[92] Matters were not clarified until the judgment of Henchy J on behalf

---

[87] See text to and following n 107 *infra*.

[88] [1976] IR 254.

[89] *Ibid*, 257.

[90] See *McGill v S* [1979] IR 283, 291 per Gannon J; *CD v WD and Barclays Bank plc* High Court, 5 February 1997, unreported (High Court) p 11 of the transcript per McGuinness J (also on LEXIS). For discussion of the status of indirect contributions made *before* a purchase, see text to and following n 155 *infra*.

[91] Note that, in a case where a claimant has contributed directly to the mortgage, it would be logical to take account of any "indirect contribution" by the legal owner in the form of paying other family expenses. However, this point does not appear to have been considered in the case law.

[92] See *MG v RD*, 28 April 1981, unreported (High Court) (Binchy n 37 *supra*, p 272) where Keane J based this requirement on the English common intention analysis. (Cf. *McFarlane v McFarlane* [1972] NI 59, another case cited by Keane J, where the Northern Ireland Court of Appeal relied also on certain remarks of Lord Pearson in *Gissing v Gissing* [1971] AC 886, 903B–C). The Irish cases

of the Supreme Court in *McC* v *McC*.[93] In a disappointing judgment, Henchy J failed to advert to the conflict of authority in earlier High Court cases[94] and seemed to regard the law in this area as clear and free of difficulty. He simply stated that:

> "When the wife's contribution has been indirect (such as by contributing, by means of her earnings, to a general family fund) the courts will, in the absence of any express or implied agreement to the contrary, infer a trust in favour of the wife, on the ground that she has to that extent relieved the husband of the financial burden he incurred in purchasing the house".[95]

Despite the lack of analysis, it seems that the Supreme Court came down decisively against the requirement of an "agreement or arrangement". In the later Supreme Court case of *BL* v *ML*,[96] the judges of the Court referred with approval[97] to *McC* v *McC* and clearly regarded it as stating the present law in Ireland.

(b) Calculating the share generated by indirect contributions

The method of calculating the share generated by indirect contributions in Ireland is illustrated by *R* v *R*,[98] a case where both (married) partners worked outside the home and where the husband made the mortgage repayments. McMahon J assumed that the contributions to the mortgage repayments during a given period were made in the same proportions as the spouses' respective contributions to the family purse during that time. When McMahon J came to calculate the contributions to the family budget, he had to take into account the fact that the parties had arranged their tax affairs to their maximum joint advantage which meant that the wife paid more than her share of their joint tax liability. Therefore, McMahon J looked to their gross earnings before tax to decide how much the parties had contributed. During the relevant time, the husband had earned £10,000 before tax and the wife £1,800 before tax. Therefore, they were treated as having contributed to the mortgage repayments, during the years in question, in the proportion of 100 to 18.[99]

---

before *MG* v *RD*, *supra* had, for the most part, made no such requirement (see *C* v *C* [1976] IR 254; *M* v *M* (1978) 114 ILTR 46; *L* v *L*, 21 December 1979, unreported (High Court); *R* v *R* [1979] ILRM 1; *Power* v *Conroy* [1980] ILRM 31; *W* v *W* [1981] ILRM 202), although there was some contrary authority (see *McGill* v *S* [1979] IR 283 and perhaps *MB* v *EB*, 19 December 1980, unreported (High Court). *MG* v *RD* was followed by Murphy J in *SB* v *BD*, 19 March 1982, unreported (High Court) but not by Finlay P in *FG* v *PG* [1982] ILRM 155 and *HD* v *JD*, 31 July 1981, unreported (High Court) or by Barron J in *O'K* v *O'K*, 16 November 1982, unreported (High Court). Cf. *B* v *B*, 22 April 1986, unreported (High Court). For more detailed treatment of the cases discussed in this note, see Brady "Trusts Law, Law Reform and the Emancipation of Women", n 37 *supra*.

93   [1986] ILRM 1.
94   In fact, no authorities were cited in his judgment.
95   [1986] ILRM 1, 2.
96   [1992] 2 IR 77.
97   *Ibid*, 108 per Finlay CJ; 110 per McCarthy J; 113–114 per Egan J.
98   [1979] ILRM 1. Cf. *L* v *L* 21 December 1979, unreported (High Court).
99   In fact, McMahon J simply held that the parties were entitled to the beneficial interests in the property in these proportions, apparently ignoring the fact that the husband had provided the substantial deposit (at least in part) from his own resources.

One interesting gloss on the approach in *R v R*[100] arises from the judgment of Carroll J in *GNR v KAR*.[101] The husband in this case developed "a lifestyle of which his wife did not approve". He bought a twenty-one-foot sailing boat with engine, was a member of a golf club and a yacht club, and went on holidays abroad, while his wife was not keen on any of these pastimes, "preferring walking and home life".[102] The husband's high personal expenditure was taken to have reduced his contribution to family expenses. Therefore, although his earnings represented three-quarters of the total family earnings at the relevant time, he was credited with having contributed only two-thirds of that total.

(c) Is a physical pooling of resources required?

Of possible significance for future cases is the reason advanced by Henchy J for refusing the claim of the wife on the particular facts of *McC*.[103] The wife had paid £600 towards furniture and fittings for the disputed family home. Henchy J commented that:

> "The full purchase price was provided by the husband's employers, who got a mortgage on the house. The employers collected the mortgage payments by means of deductions from his salary. So it could not be said that the [wife's] £600 or any part of it relieved the husband of any share of the financial burden he incurred in purchasing the house".[104]

It is difficult to understand Henchy J's stress on the fact that the mortgage repayments had been deducted directly from the husband's salary. Since the legal owner in cases like this is *ex hypothesi* paying the mortgage instalments, why should it make a difference if he pays them in the above fashion rather than for example by paying his earnings into his bank account and then drawing cheques on that account to pay the instalments? Henchy J referred to a claimant making an indirect contribution "by contributing, by means of her earnings, to a general family fund".[105] The vital question is whether some physical pooling of income, e.g. in a joint bank account or a less formal kitty, is required before a "general family fund" can be said to exist and a resulting trust established.[106]

It is submitted that such a requirement would not make sense. Why should the husband in *McC v McC* have sought some other means of repaying his employers when the money could simply be deducted from his salary? The best

---

[100] [1979] ILRM 1.

[101] 25 March 1981, unreported (High Court). See also *L v L* 21 December 1979, unreported (High Court) p 7 of the transcript.

[102] *Ibid*, p 4 of the transcript.

[103] [1986] ILRM 1.

[104] *Ibid*, 2.

[105] *Ibid*. Note also the comment of Finlay CJ in the Supreme Court in *BL v ML* [1992] 2 IR 77, 107–108 that "a trust could, having regard to the particular features of dealings between the parties in a marriage which was amicable, arise from what are described as indirect contributions by the provision through earnings of money into the family pool". It is submitted that this passing comment does not really shed any light on whether or not a physical pooling is necessary.

[106] Cf. Miller "Family Assets" (1970) 86 LQR 99, 114–119.

approach is to regard the question of a physical pooling of the resources of the couple as merely one of a number of factors which may tend to show the existence of a "general family fund" out of which family expenses are paid. The decision in *McC* itself can be rationalised on the basis that the claimant had not actually contributed to a "general family fund" but had instead made a once-off payment towards furniture and fittings.

(d) A requirement that contributions not be minimal

An interesting comment made by Henchy J in *McC* was that a trust in the proportion which the contribution bears to the purchase price "will be inferred when the wife's contribution is of such a size and kind as will justify the conclusion that the acquisition of the house was achieved by the joint efforts of the spouses".[107] This formulation, with its reference to "joint efforts", is at first glance rather difficult to justify. The notion of "joint efforts", redolent of the discredited doctrine of family assets,[108] has no significance in the doctrine of resulting trusts.

It seems best therefore to read Henchy J's statement as merely requiring that the indirect contribution be large enough to surmount the hurdle of the *de minimis* principle.[109] This appears to have been the approach taken in *CR v DR*,[110] where Lynch J felt that the wife's contributions were "so small relevant [*sic*] to the monies which I am satisfied that the husband was earning . . . that they cannot be regarded as entitling the wife to a share in the property the acquisition of which was directly financed solely by the husband's earnings".[111]

(e) Indirect contributions and unmarried couples

Thus far in this chapter, no attempt has been made to consider the special position of unmarried couples. As a matter of principle, the nature of the relationship between the parties is not crucial to the application of the resulting trust doctrine.[112] Therefore, indirect contributions made in the context of an unmarried cohabitation will be governed by the same general principles as have been developed in the cases dealing with married couples.[113] This is confirmed by the

---

[107] [1986] ILRM 1, 2.

[108] See Chapter 1 *supra*, text following n 52.

[109] Note the comment of Viscount Dilhorne in *Gissing* [1971] AC 886, 900 that a trust would not arise in favour of a wife who paid a single mortgage instalment while her husband was away on holiday. Cf. *RK v MK* 24 October 1978, unreported (High Court) pp 9–10 of the transcript.

[110] 5 April 1984, unreported (High Court).

[111] *Ibid*, p 16 of the transcript.

[112] Except, of course, insofar as the operation of the presumption of advancement is concerned.

[113] Admittedly, the statements of principle in Irish cases involving married couples tend to be phrased in terms relevant to that context. Thus, in *BL v ML* [1992] 2 IR 77, 107–108, Finlay CJ commented that, "having regard to the particular features of dealings between husband and wife in a marriage which was amicable", indirect contributions could be recognised. However, on the same day, Finlay CJ referred in *EN v RN* [1992] 2 IR 116, 122 to the need to confine "the rights to interests in the family home to the broad concept of resulting and constructive trust which would arise between persons other than husband and wife". This suggests that Finlay CJ accepted the logical point that dealings within an "amicable" cohabitation could have the same consequences as those occurring within a marriage.

fact that there was no suggestion to the contrary in either of the two reported Irish cases which involved unmarried couples, *Power* v *Conroy*[114] and *McGill* v *S.*[115]

Power[116] involved a couple who lived together for five years. Towards the end of the cohabitation, a house was purchased for £10,760 in the sole name of the male partner. The claimant paid £1,000 towards the deposit and also a further £1,000 to the builders who were pressing for payment. The defendant borrowed the remainder of the purchase price on mortgage. He had, by the time of the hearing, spent some £1,700 on mortgage repayments. It appeared that, after the purchase, the claimant had continued to contribute to the upkeep of the household.

In a very short judgment, McWilliam J upheld the plaintiff's claim. He made no comment on the fact that the parties were unmarried and simply applied the approach developed in the earlier matrimonial cases. On this basis, he regarded the house "as being held by the defendant on trust for the parties in the shares which they contributed either directly or indirectly towards its purchase".[117] On the limited evidence available, he estimated the claimant's contribution at 55 per cent of the total and, accordingly, he declared her to be entitled to eleven-twentieths of the beneficial interest.

By way of contrast, the claim was unsuccessful in the slightly earlier case of *McGill* v *S.*[118] However, this was not surprising, given the extremely weak factual foundation for the plaintiff's claim. As Gannon J explained, her indirect contributions, such as they were, "all came after the acquisition of the property had been completed (without continuing instalment payments)".[119] Therefore, even under the extended version of the doctrine favoured in Ireland, there was no possibility of establishing a resulting trust.

In the course of his judgment, Gannon J suggested[120] that, because the claimant was unmarried, she "may find it necessary to call in aid" a *dictum* of Lowry J in *McFarlane* v *McFarlane*[121] which showed that the claims of a wife depended "not on her deserts as a wife but on legal principles which are equally applicable between strangers". On the whole, Gannon J's view appears to have been that the general principles derived from the matrimonial cases should also apply to unmarried couples.[122]

---

[114] [1980] ILRM 31.
[115] [1979] IR 283. Cf. Cooney, n 37 *supra*, 7 *et seq.*
[116] [1980] ILRM 31.
[117] *Ibid*, 32.
[118] [1979] IR 283.
[119] *Ibid*, 292.
[120] *Ibid*, 288–289.
[121] [1972] NI 59, 78.
[122] On one reading, there may have been a suggestion in Gannon J's judgment ([1979] IR 283, 289) that unmarried claimants should be treated slightly differently when applying the requirement that an "agreement or arrangement" must accompany indirect contributions. However, this requirement is no longer part of Irish law (see text following n 91 *supra*).

Although the above cases (and the logic of the Irish approach) indicate that the same rules should apply to unmarried couples, it will be necessary for the Irish courts in future cases to be sensitive to the varying attitudes which exist across the spectrum of unmarried relationships. In relation to married couples, it may be fair to assume that, if nothing is expressly said about the matter, it will be understood that the non-owning spouse is to gain a share on the basis of indirect contributions. However, matters may be slightly different with unmarried couples. Considerations of convenience will almost inevitably lead unmarried cohabitees to pool their resources in order to discharge day-to-day family expenses. However, will this always mean that the legal owner of the property, who may well have purchased it long before the cohabitation began, accepts that ownership of the home will thereby be affected?

Consider a case where a single woman purchases a house with the help of a mortgage. Shortly afterwards, she begins a new relationship and her partner moves in. She earns £750 a month and he earns £500. Both contribute £500 each month to pay half of the cost of their food, electricity, telephone bills etc. She spends her additional £250 per month on paying off the mortgage. After two years, the relationship breaks down and he moves out. Should he be entitled to a share in the ownership of the home?

Under the present Irish law, developed to favour married claimants, the male partner in the above example would be entitled to credit for 40 per cent of the mortgage repayments since he contributed 40 per cent of the joint family budget. Given the rather slanted method of calculation favoured by the Irish courts, the fact that this contribution was made over a rather short period of time would probably not prevent him from gaining a substantial share in the beneficial interest.[123] This may seem to be an unfair result, particularly because the claimant contributed no more than his fair share of the living expenses of the couple.

It is tempting to argue that the claimant in this situation should be defeated by the fact that his contributions did not "enable" the defendant to acquire the property.[124] This kind of "causal link" requirement has been mentioned from time to time in the Irish cases.[125] However, a requirement that the claimant's contribution "enabled" the defendant to acquire the property would seem to be unworkable in practice. It would "involve investigation of such questions, really reducing the whole proposition to an absurdity, as whether the [defendant] . . . could have cut down his smoking, or drinking or could have sold his car . . . whether he could have borrowed the money from a money-lender or relative

---

[123] See the discussion in n 84 *supra* (claimant who paid 40 per cent of the mortgage repayments to date would be credited with a similar contribution in respect of the unpaid portion of the mortgage). Clearly, one step forward would be for the Irish courts to develop a defensible approach to the calculation of shares based on contributions to mortgage instalments.

[124] Cf. text to and following n 153 *infra*.

[125] *R v R* [1979] ILRM 1, 2, 3; *FG v PG* [1982] ILRM 155, 158; *Power v Conroy* [1980] ILRM 31, 32. Cf. *C v C* [1976] IR 254, 257. Compare *Burns v Burns* [1984] Ch 317, 329C per Fox LJ (suggesting a similar requirement in the different context of the English common intention analysis).

and other such questions".[126] Furthermore, even if the test could be operated in practice, logically one could only take into account that proportion of the claimant's expenditure which "enabled" the defendant to make the mortgage repayments. Thus, if the defendant "needed" £10 per week and the claimant spent £50 per week, then the excess £40 should be ignored. There is no example of a case where only part of a claimant's expenditure was considered in this fashion. On the whole, it appears that, beyond a possible *de minimis* rule,[127] the Irish courts have not imposed a "causal link" requirement.

If one accepts the argument advanced in the previous paragraph, then it is not easy to see how one could fine-tune the Irish analysis so as to avoid overly generous treatment of the claims of cohabitees. One obvious possibility would be to argue for the English position whereby one requires additional evidence of a common intention between the parties before indirect contributions can form the basis of a successful claim.[128] However, this requirement really only makes sense in the context of the full-blown English common intention constructive trust analysis and cannot readily be fitted into the pure resulting trust approach favoured in Ireland.[129] Moreover, the requirement has been implicitly rejected by the Supreme Court[130] and is unlikely to resurface. Another possibility would be to focus on the requirement of a "family fund", arguing that not all unmarried couples may operate such a fund. However, once more, this argument is not really helpful; the problem is that unmarried cohabitees, whatever their intentions as to ownership, will almost certainly share day-to-day expenses in the interests of economy and convenience.

The best approach seems to be to concentrate attention on the possibility of rebutting the presumption of resulting trust in the context of indirect contributions. It will be recalled that in *McC* Henchy J stated that indirect contributions would earn a beneficial interest "in the absence of any express or implied agreement to the contrary".[131] There has been no written judgment in Ireland in which such an agreement to the contrary has been found. This is explicable on the basis that married couples rarely address their minds to the consequences of their actions while the relationship is still a happy one.

However, the experience of other jurisdictions reveals that, when one is dealing with unmarried couples, there will be some cases where one partner makes

---

[126] *Hazell* v *Hazell* [1972] 1 WLR 301, 306 per Megaw LJ.

[127] Discussed in the text to and following n 107 *supra*.

[128] See Chapter 5 *infra*, text to n 65.

[129] The point is that, for resulting trust purposes, the claimant has either contributed to the purchase price (in which case she may be entitled to a share) or she has not so contributed (and cannot be entitled to a share). A payment which does not constitute a contribution cannot be transformed into a contribution by the mere fact that the parties intend the claimant to gain a share.

[130] See text following n 91 *supra*.

[131] [1986] ILRM 1, 2. In fact, this formulation of the relevant test involves the mistaken assumption (criticised in Chapter 2 *supra*, text following n 35) that a common intention is required to rebut the presumption of resulting trust. It is submitted that, irrespective of any communicated agreement between the parties, no resulting trust can arise if the claimant made her indirect contributions with the intention of making a gift to her partner (or had some other intention inconsistent with the creation of a trust).

it clear that the sharing of family expenses will not affect his ownership of the family home and other property.[132] Although in such cases there may not, strictly speaking, be any "agreement" between the parties, it would appear that no resulting trust could arise in Irish law.[133]

Even in the absence of an express warning by the legal owner, it would seem to be necessary for the Irish courts to take into account all aspects of the relationship between the parties and to be willing, if necessary on the basis of this overview, to find that there has been an implied understanding that the claimant would not gain a share. Of particular significance would seem to be the reason why the property was, in the first place, put into the sole name of one of the partners. Although a great deal of equity's rhetoric is directed towards suggesting that the outward form of legal ownership is not crucial, it is important to remain in touch with reality. Ordinary people, even if they are unfamiliar with the details of the law, do place some weight on the fact of legal ownership. If, after the cohabitation has begun, one partner purchases a home and (to the knowledge of the other) deliberately decides to put it into his sole name,[134] does this not tell us something about the likely intentions of the parties at that point?

In conclusion, it should be pointed out that, while it is easy to urge the court to examine all the features of a relationship, this wholesome activity may not always (or even very often) solve the problem. The fact is that after *McC v McC*[135] the presumption is in favour of a partner who has made indirect contributions. Therefore, the defendant must be able to point to some tangible evidence in order to rebut that presumption. If this seems unfair, then the problem lies at a fundamental level in the Irish theoretical structure and the solution would have to be drastic (e.g. deciding to refuse any remedy on the basis of indirect contributions or entirely abandoning the extended resulting trust).

3. *Unpaid work in the home and in child-rearing*

In the early case of *RK v MK*,[136] it was held by Finlay P that a resulting trust could not be founded upon work in the home and in the rearing of children. This

---

[132] See the discussion of *Gillies v Keogh* [1989] 2 NZLR 327 in Chapter 9 *infra*, text following n 55.

[133] Even if, notwithstanding her partner's warning, the claimant continued to contribute with the secret intention of gaining a share, it seems clear that her claim would fail on the basis that she had not come to equity with clean hands. However, from a wider point of view, one must be concerned with the plight of economically vulnerable women who continue to contribute to a relationship despite their partner's selfish insistence on retaining his separate legal ownership of appreciating assets such as the family home. The problem is to develop a legal framework which would be sensitive to this problem while avoiding injustice in other cases. For an attempt at developing a concept of "oppression" in this context, see Gardner "Rethinking Family Property" (1993) 109 LQR 263, 295–297.

[134] Cf. *Hibberson v George* (1989) 12 Fam LR 725, where the majority of the New South Wales Court of Appeal did not take this point.

[135] [1986] ILRM 1.

[136] 24 October 1978, unreported (High Court).

position was challenged in the High Court in *BL v ML*,[137] where Barr J awarded a claimant a one-half share in the family home on the basis of a rather adventurous application of Article 41.2.2 of the Irish Constitution of 1937.[138] On appeal the Supreme Court unanimously overruled his decision.[139] The Court felt that the adoption of the new doctrine would constitute "a usurpation by the courts of the function of the legislature".[140] The judges of the Supreme Court were also satisfied in *BL v ML*[141] and in *EN v RN*[142] (decided on the same day) that work in the home could not be accommodated within the Irish resulting trust framework.

4. *Unpaid work in the legal owner's business*

Despite their rejection of unpaid work in the home, the Supreme Court were willing to give favourable treatment to unpaid work in the legal owner's business.[143] In *EN v RN*,[144] a family home, which was in the husband's sole name, had been partly converted into apartments for rent. Finlay CJ (speaking for the Supreme Court) awarded a one-half share in the beneficial ownership to the wife, on the basis of her "total management of the bedsitter apartments, the organisation and collection of the rents payable in respect of them and their general maintenance and care".[145] In Finlay CJ's view, "[s]uch activities are different from and not to be identified with the activities of a wife and mother in the home".[146] Thus, unpaid work in the legal owner's business is clearly seen in Irish law as sufficient to trigger a resulting trust.

5. *Improvements*

As was discussed in the previous chapter, the orthodox view is that expenditure on improving the disputed property cannot be considered to be a contribution

---

[137] [1992] 2 IR 77.

[138] This anachronistic provision states that the State shall endeavour "to ensure that mothers shall not be obliged by economic necessity to engage in labour to the neglect of their duties in the home". Barr J reasoned (*ibid*, 99) that, since a woman who worked in the home was precluded from making financial contributions to the acquisition of the home, "her work as home-maker and in caring for the family should be taken into account in calculating her contribution towards that acquisition". Unfortunately, Barr J failed to integrate his new doctrine into the existing trusts law framework and it appears that, quite apart from its dubious Constitutional basis, his doctrine would have led to serious inconsistencies in practice. For further discussion, see Brady "Constructive Trusts, Constitutional Rhetoric and the Non-Owning Spouse", n 37 *supra*; Mee "Trusts of the Family Home: Boiling Oil from the Ivory Tower", n 37 *supra*, 33–35.

[139] [1992] 2 IR 77, 102.

[140] *Ibid*, 107. Cf. *In re the Matrimonial Home Bill 1993* [1994] 1 IR 305.

[141] [1992] IR 77, 111 per McCarthy J.

[142] [1992] 2 IR 116, 122 per Finlay CJ.

[143] The older cases tended to the same view. See *RK v MK*, 24 October 1978, unreported (High Court) p 9 of the transcript; *CR v DR*, 5 April 1984, unreported (High Court) p 15 of the transcript and *BL v ML* [1992] 2 IR 77, 96 per Barr J (High Court).

[144] [1992] 2 IR 116.

[145] *Ibid*, 123.

[146] *Ibid*.

to the purchase price of property so as to attract the resulting trust doctrine.[147] This strict line was followed in the Irish High Court by Finlay P in *W v W*[148] and by Barron J in the later case of *NAD v TD*.[149] The approach in these cases was confirmed by the Supreme Court in *EN v RN*.[150] Citing only *W v W*,[151] Finlay CJ held that a direct contribution towards improvements would not normally generate an equitable share. It appears therefore to be clearly established by the Irish authorities that a claim based on improvements has no chance of succeeding under the resulting trust analysis. Instead, a claimant would be forced to rely on the principles of estoppel, which are reasonably well established in the Irish courts.[152]

F. Is Irish Law Consistent in its Treatment of the Various Forms of Indirect Contribution?

It has been seen in the preceding sections that the Irish courts have been willing to recognise certain forms of contribution as capable of generating a resulting trust (contributions to general household expenses and through unpaid work in the legal owner's business, provided in both cases that a mortgage is being repaid at the time) but have rejected others (work in the home and the making of improvements). This section seeks to establish whether there is any defensible theoretical basis for the manner in which the Irish courts have treated the various forms of contribution.

In considering this question, one begins with the proposition that the Irish courts have been willing to recognise the direct payment of mortgage instalments as constituting a contribution to the purchase price. In order for a more "indirect" form of contribution to trigger a resulting trust, it must be possible to regard that contribution as in some way equivalent to the payment of mortgage instalments. This explains why the Irish courts have refused to recognise a contribution in the form of expenditure on improvements; there is no way of relating this expenditure to the repayment of a mortgage.

How, then, might one relate a contribution to the repayment of a mortgage? It will be helpful to consider this question first in the context of a case where the claimant uses her earnings to pay general household expenses at a time when her partner is paying off a mortgage. It appears that there are two possible ways of

---

[147] See Chapter 2 *supra*, text following n 92.
[148] [1981] ILRM 202.
[149] [1985] ILRM 153.
[150] [1992] 2 IR 116, 122.
[151] [1981] ILRM 202. Finlay CJ did not discuss the far more lax approach which had been taken in a number of earlier cases (see *M v M* (1978) 114 ILTR 46 (a decision of Finlay P himself); *ER v MR*, 26 January 1981, unreported (High Court); *GNR v KAR*, 25 March 1981, unreported (High Court)). Cf. *Friends Provident Life Office v Doherty* [1992] ILRM 372; *McQuillan v Maguire* [1996] 1 ILRM 394, 400.
[152] See generally Chapter 4 *infra*.

explaining why the Irish courts are willing to equate such an "indirect" contribution with a direct contribution to the mortgage. Both of these explanations find some degree of support in the Irish case law.

The first rationalisation, which will be termed the "assistance theory", proceeds on the conceptual basis that the claimant has not actually made a contribution herself but rather has in some way facilitated the legal owner in making *his* contribution. The second theory, "the family pool theory", regards the claimant, by virtue of having paid a share of a joint set of expenses, as having *herself* contributed to the purchase price. It is now proposed to examine these two theories in turn and to see whether either or both is capable of explaining the Irish case law.

1. *The assistance theory*

As has been mentioned earlier, the assistance theory focuses on the fact that the claimant has helped the legal owner to pay the purchase price. It is supported by a number of references in the Irish case law to the claimant's contribution to family expenses "enabling" the legal owner to pay the mortgage.[153] However, as was pointed out in an earlier section,[154] in practice the Irish courts have not gone so far as to require a claimant to show that "but for" her contribution the legal owner would not have been able to acquire the property. The general approach has been that contributions to family expenses, unless they are *de minimis*, will trigger the presumption of resulting trust. Therefore, in order for it to explain the Irish cases, the argument behind the "assistance theory" would have to be that the claimant's contribution (whether or not it was strictly necessary) made it easier for the legal owner to pay the mortgage.

It has just been seen that, as long as it is not expressed in too strict terms, the assistance theory is capable of explaining the treatment of contributions which take the form of paying general family expenses while the legal owner is repaying the mortgage. However, the "assistance theory" does not fare well as a rationalisation of the Irish treatment of other contributions. The basic difficulty is that it explains too much, appearing to require the acceptance of forms of contribution rejected by the Irish courts.

One problem relates to a type of contribution which has not been fully considered thus far in the Irish case law, what might be termed a "pre-purchase indirect contribution".[155] Consider the following example:[156] a couple are living in rented accommodation. Over the years, both contribute equally to the expenses of the family. However, the male partner has a higher salary and manages to

---

[153] See the cases cited in n 125 *supra*.

[154] See text following n 124 *supra*.

[155] See *L v L*, 21 December 1979, unreported (High Court) pp 4–5 of the transcript per Finlay P (rejecting pre-purchase contributions as irrelevant because no savings were being accumulated at the time); *Power v Conroy* [1980] ILRM 31, 32 (events prior to the purchase regarded as irrelevant). See also Cooney n 37 *supra*, 6–7, 13. Cf. *A v B*, 23 May 1997 (LEXIS, English Fam Div).

[156] Cf. the facts of *McFarlane v McFarlane* [1972] NI 59.

save £10,000. Clearly, his partner can have no claim to share in this money under a purchase money resulting trust (there having been no purchase and no repayment of any mortgage). However, the man then purchases a house for £10,000 in cash. Can his partner claim a share in the house? Under the assistance theory, it is difficult to see why not. Her indirect contribution has "enabled" him to pay for the house. However, this result is surely counter-intuitive. The claimant had no interest in the defendant's savings and yet, as soon as he converted those savings into a house, she is suddenly entitled to a share under a resulting trust.

Another, and more serious, problem with the assistance theory is that, logically, it seems fully applicable in respect of the contribution of a claimant who works in the family home and in child-rearing. Her contribution also makes it easier for the claimant to pay for the property. If a woman minds the children, cooks for the family, washes their clothes, maintains the house and performs dozens of other daily tasks, can it sensibly be denied that she lightens the financial burden incurred by her partner in taking on a mortgage?[157] Unless one takes a woman's work in the home for granted, it cannot be denied that it reduces the financial burden involved in a purchase. Yet, as has been seen, the Irish courts have categorically refused to recognise such a contribution.[158]

It appears, therefore, that the "assistance" theory is unable to explain why contributions to household expenses, but not through work in the home, are capable of generating a resulting trust.

2. The family pool theory

Since the "assistance" theory seems insufficient to explain the distinctions drawn in Irish law, it is necessary to consider the alternative "family pool" theory. This theory has never been made fully explicit in the Irish case law but it finds support in a number of *dicta* from the Supreme Court and from the approach in cases such as *R v R*[159] to the calculation of the share generated by indirect contributions.[160]

The argument behind the family pool theory appears to take the following form:[161] in reality, the parties to a matrimonial or quasi-matrimonial relationship regard themselves as having a joint budget. It is only factors of convenience which dictate that the woman pays e.g. for food and clothing and the man meets

---

[157] Note the argument raised by counsel in *EN v RN*, and rejected without explanation by Finlay CJ [1992] 2 IR 116, 122, that the woman who works in the home saves her partner from having to pay a salary to a housekeeper or nanny and therefore makes it easier for him to pay off the mortgage.

[158] See text to and following n 136 *supra*.

[159] [1979] ILRM 1.

[160] See text to and following n 98 *supra*.

[161] Note Finlay P's reference to the concept of a family pool in *BL v ML* [1992] 2 IR 77, 107–108. See also *McC v McC* [1986] ILRM 1, 2 per Henchy J ("family fund"). Cf. the dissenting speech of Lord Reid in *Gissing v Gissing* [1971] AC 886, 896.

other outgoings such as mortgage repayments. It would be unjust to regard the result of the claimant's investment of her money over the years as eaten bread and worn-out clothes, while the result of her partner's investment is an appreciating asset in the shape of the family home. To avoid this injustice, one should (the argument runs) ignore the fact that the parties have never physically pooled their earnings in (say) a joint bank account. They may be regarded, in substance, as having pooled their earnings for their common purposes. This means that each party has contributed to each expense in the proportion that they have contributed to the family pool. Thus, by contributing her earnings to the family pool, the claimant makes what may be regarded as a *direct* contribution to the repayment of the mortgage.

As well as explaining the acceptance of financial contributions towards family expenses, the family pool theory also appears capable of explaining the Irish courts' rejection of work in the home. As explained above, the family pool theory requires a "monied" contribution to a family pool of earnings out of which the mortgage repayments are made.[162] The argument would be that work in the home cannot be conceptualised as a financial payment into a family pool and therefore cannot be treated as, in substance, a *direct* contribution as required under the family pool argument. Therefore, at first glance, one has a rationalisation for the differential treatment of financial contributions into a family pool and non-financial contributions in the form of work in the home.

Unfortunately, the family pool theory is unable to explain why unpaid work in the legal owner's business is seen by the Irish courts as capable of supporting a claim. It will be recalled that in *EN v RN*[163] Finlay CJ asserted that unpaid work in a business was "different from and not to be identified with the activities of a wife and mother in the home".[164] But in what relevant sense are the two sorts of activities "different"?[165] The woman who works without pay in a man's business no more makes a "monied" contribution to a family pool than does the woman who works without pay in the home. In both cases, the woman merely makes it easier for the man to pay off the mortgage *himself*. The genuine economic contribution which both types of activity make to the repayment of the mortgage simply cannot be accommodated within the family pool logic. One suspects that the Supreme Court was engaged in some degree of double-think on the day it decided both *BL v ML* and *EN v RN*. Having used the family pool logic to dismiss work in the home, the Court then subconsciously switched to the "assistance" theory in order to uphold a claim based on unpaid work in a business.

---

[162] See *BL v ML* [1992] 2 IR 77, 108.

[163] [1992] 2 IR 116.

[164] *Ibid*, 123.

[165] Note the unexplained concept of a contribution in "money's worth" mentioned by Finlay CJ *ibid*, 122. The approach of the Supreme Court reflects the traditional dichotomy in social contract theory between the public and the private. Events which take place in the home are often classified as within the private sphere and therefore placed beyond the purview of the law. See e.g. O'Donovan *Sexual Divisions in Law* (London: Weidenfeld and Nicolson, 1985), especially ch. 1.

G. How Could Irish Law Be Made More Consistent?

It has just been suggested that it is impossible to defend a distinction between unpaid work in the legal owner's business and unpaid work in the home. One could base two alternative arguments on this conclusion. The first, and most obvious, line of argument would be to suggest that the Irish courts have made a mistake in relation to unpaid work in the business and that consistency could be restored simply by refusing in future to recognise this kind of contribution. One would then be able to point to a principled distinction between monetary contributions to a family pool from outside earnings and, on the other hand, non-monetary contributions in the home or business which do not feed directly into a family pool. Unfortunately, even this approach runs into problems at a more subtle level.

It is necessary to take into account the effect of the Supreme Court's view in *EN*, criticised earlier in this chapter,[166] concerning the role of the repayment of mortgages under the resulting trust. It will be recalled that Finlay CJ argued that the repayment of a mortgage constitutes the "direct" provision of the price of buying the equity of redemption from the lender. It has already been argued that this was an error and that the repayment of a mortgage is relevant only if it amounts to the economic equivalent of the provision of the purchase price to the original seller. The problem is that the "family pool theory", which allows for a neat distinction between monetary and non-monetary contributions, is based on the assumption that it is of decisive importance if one can categorise a contribution as, in substance, a direct contribution to the repayment of a mortgage. However, if one accepts that the Supreme Court's view in *EN* is mistaken, it is not really important whether or not a claimant has "directly" repaid the *mortgage*. Even to allow the recognition of "direct" contributions to mortgages under the resulting trust doctrine, one must treat the repayment of the mortgage as the economic equivalent of the provision of the *original purchase price of the house*. If one understands that the issue arises at this level, it is hard to see why work in the home does not similarly amount to the economic equivalent of paying part of the purchase price of the house.

This leads one to consider a second possible line of argument which would suggest that work in the home should be recognised as a contribution under the resulting trust analysis. If this appeared to involve undue violence to the traditional resulting trust, it could be retorted that this is merely a logically consistent consequence of the stretching of the doctrine to accommodate contributions to mortgage instalments which take place long after the actual purchase. The Irish courts have gone so far as to recognise the contributions made by claimants who pay household expenses or work without pay in the legal owner's business; it is therefore difficult to see any genuine reason to ignore

---

[166] See text following n 53 *supra*.

work in the family home and in the rearing of children.[167] Although this may be a reasonable argument, it is unlikely, given the view of the Supreme Court in *BL* and in *EN*, that it will be accepted in the near future.

The above arguments concern themselves with the purchase money resulting trust doctrine. For practical purposes, it might be more promising for an Irish claimant who has worked in the home to move outside the context of that narrow doctrine and to invoke the wider principles which have been developed in other jurisdictions. This might allow, over the medium term, for a movement towards rewarding work in the home without departing from the Supreme Court's view on the resulting trust. The relevant principles will be discussed in future chapters.

H. Summary of the Irish Position

The Irish analysis treats mortgage repayments as constituting a contribution to the purchase price of the property. Such contributions therefore trigger the presumption of resulting trust and will generate a beneficial interest in the absence of rebutting evidence. This extension of the resulting trust was by no means inevitable[168] and, in fact, leads to a number of theoretical and practical difficulties.[169]

Nonetheless, the Irish approach does have the advantage of comparative simplicity. Compared with, for example, the far more complicated English position,[170] it is relatively easy for an ordinary person to understand.[171] It is also reasonably straightforward to predict when a claimant will be entitled to a remedy in Ireland. Unfortunately, this ease of prediction is increased by the fact that the Irish approach rejects outright the possibility of affording a remedy based on work in the home or in child-rearing. However, with some lack of consistency, the Irish courts have given recognition to indirect contributions to the repayment of a mortgage through paying other family expenses or working without pay in the legal owner's business.

By way of conclusion, it is worth stressing again a more general limitation on the Irish approach. Since it is based on the purchase money resulting trust, the focus remains firmly on the *acquisition* of property. Therefore, contributions to

---

[167] Cf. the comments of Lowry J in *McFarlane v McFarlane* [1972] NI 59, 78 lines 20–30. If one did accept the argument in the text, it would also seem necessary to recognise "pre-purchase" contributions, despite the problem identified in the text to and following n 155 *supra*. The truth seems to be that, if one is looking for theoretical consistency, the purest approach would be to recognise only direct contributions to the mortgage (or, even better, only direct contributions to the purchase price at the time of the actual purchase). Theoretical untidiness is the price of attempts to bend the resulting trust to do justice to claimants.

[168] See Part I(A) *supra*.

[169] See Section C of this Part *supra*.

[170] Discussed in Chapter 5 *infra*.

[171] Cf. *Phillips v Phillips* [1993] 3 NZLR 159, 168 per Cooke P (emphasising "the desirability of a simply explainable law").

improving property cannot generate a remedy under the principles discussed in this chapter.[172] Moreover, a claimant who contributes to family expenses or undertakes unpaid work in a business will only obtain a remedy if a mortgage is being repaid at the relevant time. It will be seen in later chapters that the other common law jurisdictions have moved beyond the resulting trust and that their doctrines are capable of rewarding contributions which cannot be related to the acquisition of a property.

Having examined, in this and the preceding chapter, the potential scope of the resulting trust, it is next proposed to examine the role of the rather different doctrine of equitable estoppel. The relevant principles will be analysed in the next chapter. Once this has been accomplished, it will be possible to move on to consider, in later chapters, the developments of the constructive trust which have taken place in England, Canada, Australia and New Zealand.

---

[172] See text to and following n 147 *supra*. However, as will be seen in the next chapter, a remedy may sometimes be available under estoppel principles.

4

Estoppel in Equity

As has emerged from the discussion thus far, the purchase money resulting trust, even in its extended Irish manifestation, is really only of assistance to a claimant who has made a financial contribution to the acquisition of a family home. Other avenues of redress must be explored by the claimant who has made other sacrifices, for example raising children of the relationship at the expense of her future employment prospects or carrying out improvements to the home. The most obvious possibility is the equitable doctrine of estoppel.

In fact, estoppel principles, in a somewhat distorted form, already play a central role in the English common intention constructive trust analysis (considered in detail in the next chapter). This overlap has meant that estoppel has had a lower profile in the family cases than would otherwise have been expected. However, recent doctrinal developments in Canada, Australia and New Zealand have raised the possibility of the common intention analysis being discarded in those jurisdictions (and that analysis, of course, never became established in Ireland). Thus, it is important to gain an understanding of the potential of a "pure" estoppel analysis, not just from the point of view of theoretical clarity, but also for the purposes of imagining a doctrinal world without the common intention analysis.

This chapter will begin with a brief discussion of the general principles of estoppel. Once this preliminary work has been accomplished in Part I, it will be possible to move on, in Part II, to a consideration of the application of the relevant principles in the context of unmarried cohabitation. As well as being worthwhile in its own right, this endeavour will also prepare the ground for the examination in Chapter 5 of the English "common intention" analysis.

I. THE PRINCIPLES OF ESTOPPEL[1]

Traditionally, a number of different forms of estoppel have been recognised by the law.[2] The most important form of estoppel in the context of claims to rights

---

[1] See generally Gray *Elements of Land Law*, 2nd edn (London: Butterworths, 1993) pp 312–368; Pawlowski *The Doctrine of Proprietary Estoppel* (London: Sweet and Maxwell, 1996); Parkinson "Estoppel", ch. 7 in Parkinson (ed) *The Principles of Equity* (Sydney: LBC Information Services, 1996); Delany *Equity and the Law of Trusts in Ireland* (Dublin: Round Hall Sweet and Maxwell, 1996) pp 495–515; Mee "Lost in the Big House: Where Stands Irish Law on Equitable Estoppel?" (1998) 33 *Irish Jurist* (ns) 187.

[2] Cf. *McIlkenny* v *Chief Constable of West Midlands Police Force* [1980] 2 WLR 689, 700–701 per Lord Denning MR (estoppel as "a big house with many rooms").

over family property is the doctrine of proprietary estoppel. However, it will also be necessary to consider briefly the doctrine of promissory estoppel.

A. Proprietary Estoppel

1. *The two limbs of proprietary estoppel*

The classic authority on proprietary estoppel is the decision of the House of Lords in *Ramsden v Dyson*.[3] Two limbs of proprietary estoppel emerge from this case. The first originates in the speech of Lord Cranworth, and is generally described as the "mistake limb". The second limb, based on expectation, derives from the speech of Lord Kingsdown (who dissented only on the facts). An understanding of the development of proprietary estoppel will be facilitated by a separate consideration of the two limbs.

(a) The mistake limb

The case of *Ramsden v Dyson*[4] concerned a tenant who had expended money on improving the land he was leasing, allegedly in the belief that he was entitled to demand the grant of a long lease. The general principle of the law, encapsulated in the Latin maxim "*superficies solo cedit*",[5] is that the owner of land owns anything which is built on, or attached to, the land. In other words, the benefit of any improvements to land accrues to the owner of that land. It is to this general principle that the mistake limb of proprietary estoppel forms a limited exception.

In a famous passage in *Ramsden v Dyson*, Lord Cranworth explained the relevant doctrine as follows:

> "If a stranger begins to build on my land supposing it to be his own, and I, perceiving his mistake, abstain from setting him right, and leave him to persevere in his error, a Court of equity will not allow me afterwards to assert my title to the land on which he had expended money on the supposition that the land was his own".[6]

The trigger for this mistake limb of proprietary estoppel is the dishonesty of the landowner in remaining "wilfully passive on such an occasion, in order afterwards to profit by the mistake which [he] might have prevented".[7]

(b) The expectation limb

In *Ramsden*, Lord Kingsdown put forward an alternative formulation of the doctrine of proprietary estoppel. His formulation is regarded as giving rise to the "expectation limb" (or "encouragement limb") of proprietary estoppel.

---

[3]   (1866) LR 1 HL 129.
[4]   *Ibid.*
[5]   The maxim translates as "a building becomes part of the ground". See Gray, n 1 *supra*, p 7.
[6]   (1866) LR 1 HL 129, 140–141.
[7]   *Ibid*, 141. See *Hamilton v Geraghty* (1901) 1 SR Eq NSW 81; *Brand v Chris Building Co Pty Ltd* [1957] VR 625; *McMahon v Kerry County Council* (1976) [1981] ILRM 419. Cf. *Norris v Walls* [1997] NI 45.

Lord Kingsdown stated that:

"If a man, under a verbal agreement with a landlord for a certain interest in land, or, what amounts to the same thing, under an expectation, created or encouraged by the landlord, that he shall have a certain interest, takes possession of such land, with the consent of the landlord, and upon the faith of such promise or expectation, with the knowledge of the landlord, and without objection by him, lays out money upon the land, a Court of equity will compel the landlord to give effect to such promise or expectation".[8]

Lord Kingsdown's statement clearly reflects the fact-situation with which he was dealing. Nonetheless, one can discern in his comments the basic elements of a wider principle. This principle is that an estoppel will arise if (a) a landowner has created or encouraged an expectation in the claimant that she is, or will become, entitled to an interest in certain land; and (b) the claimant has acted to her detriment on the basis of that expectation.[9]

2. *The* probanda

Although both limbs of proprietary estoppel appear to have been recognised by the House of Lords in *Ramsden* v *Dyson*,[10] at an early stage in the years following that landmark decision it became common to regard Lord Cranworth's formulation as an exhaustive statement of the doctrine.[11] This tendency is attributable to the influence of *Willmott* v *Barber*.[12] In that case, Fry J restated the requirements for a claim based on proprietary estoppel. Fry J laid out five propositions (the so-called five *probanda*) which had to be proven as a prerequisite to success in a claim based on proprietary estoppel. The *probanda* are as follows:[13]

(1) The claimant must have made a mistake as to his legal rights.
(2) The claimant must have expended money or done some other act (not necessarily upon the defendant's land) on the basis of his mistaken belief.
(3) The landowner must have been aware of his own rights.
(4) The landowner must have been aware of the claimant's mistaken belief.
(5) The landowner must have encouraged the expenditure or other act of the claimant, either directly or by abstaining from asserting his rights.

The first, third and fourth of the *probanda* emphasise the need for the claimant to be mistaken about his legal rights and for the landowner to be aware

---

[8] *Ibid*, 170.
[9] For examples of the operation of this principle, see *Inwards* v *Baker* [1965] 2 QB 29; *Smyth* v *Halpin* [1997] 2 ILRM 38.
[10] (1866) LR 1 HL 129.
[11] But see *Plimmer* v *Mayor of Wellington* (1884) 9 App Cas 699.
[12] (1880) 15 Ch D 96.
[13] See *ibid*, 105. In the text, Fry J's five requirements have been slightly abbreviated for convenience.

of his own rights and of the claimant's mistake. Therefore, if taken seriously, the *probanda* allow no room for the expectation limb. This is because the expectation limb applies to a claimant who, although not mistaken as to his rights, acts to his detriment on the basis of an expectation created by the defendant. Unfortunately, Fry J (who was dealing with a case where both parties were mistaken as to their legal rights) did not address the possibility that the expectation limb of estoppel could exist alongside the mistake limb which he had formulated.

Although some decisions took a wider view, it seems to have been accepted for a time that the *probanda* were essential prerequisites to a claim based on proprietary estoppel.[14] However, in recent years, the English courts have moved away from a reliance on the *probanda*. The decisive case was *Taylor Fashions* v *Liverpool Victoria Trustees Co Ltd*.[15] In that case, Oliver J undertook a detailed analysis of the case law and concluded that a failure to satisfy all of the *probanda* was not fatal to a claim of proprietary estoppel. In a famous passage, Oliver J explained the position as follows:

> "[T]he application of the *Ramsden* v *Dyson*, LR 1 HL 129 principle . . . requires a very much broader approach which is directed rather at ascertaining whether, in particular individual circumstances, it would be unconscionable for a party to be permitted to deny that which, knowingly or unknowingly, he has allowed or encouraged another to assume to his detriment than to inquiring whether the circumstances can be fitted within the confines of some preconceived formula serving as a universal yardstick for every form of unconscionable behaviour".[16]

According to Oliver J, it was necessary to apply "the broad test of whether in the circumstances the conduct complained of is unconscionable".[17] The central emphasis is therefore on the notion of unconscionability. The issues addressed by the *probanda* are simply factors which, in appropriate cases, should be taken into account in the overall inquiry. Oliver J's views have subsequently been approved by the Court of Appeal[18] and by the Privy Council.[19]

---

[14] See e.g. *Kammins Ballrooms Co Ltd* v *Zenith Investments Ltd* [1971] AC 850, 884–885 per Lord Diplock; *E & L Berg Homes Ltd* v *Berg* (1980) 253 EG 473 (CA). See also *Cullen* v *Cullen* [1962] IR 268. Contrast *Electrolux Ltd* v *Electrix* (1954) 71 RPC 23; *Shaw* v *Applegate* [1977] 1 WLR 970.

[15] [1982] QB 133n.

[16] *Ibid*, 151–152. Oliver J felt (*ibid*, 147) that it might still be necessary to satisfy the *probanda* in cases where the defendant has merely "stood by without protest while his rights have been infringed". However, he commented (*ibid*) that even this point was "open to doubt". See also Finn "Equitable Estoppel" in Finn (ed) *Essays in Equity* (Sydney: Law Book Co, 1985) pp 78–82.

[17] *Ibid*, 154. See generally Finn, n 16 *supra*.

[18] See e.g. *Habib Bank Ltd* v *Habib Bank AG Zurich* [1981] 1 WLR 1265; *Amalgamated Investment & Property Co Ltd* v *Texas Commerce International Bank* [1982] QB 84; *Lloyds Bank plc* v *Carrick* [1996] 4 All ER 630.

[19] *A-G of Hong Kong* v *Humphreys Estate (Queen's Gardens) Ltd* [1987] 1 AC 114; *Lim Teng Huan* v *Ang Swee Chuan* [1992] 1 WLR 113. Contrast the approach of Judge Weeks QC in *Taylor* v *Dickens* [1998] 1 FLR 806, criticised by Thompson "Emasculating Estoppel" [1998] Conv 210. Cf. *Gillett* v *Holt* [1998] 3 All ER 917.

Interestingly, in some subsequent English decisions judges have purported to apply the *probanda* in the family context.[20] The case of *Coombes* v *Smith*[21] is of particular interest because it reveals an intriguing strategy of reinterpreting the *probanda* so that they can accommodate the expectation limb.[22] The strategy is to reclassify the "expectation" created in a claimant by a promise as a "mistaken belief" in a present or future entitlement to an interest in land. Thus, for example, if a landowner promised the claimant that she could remain in a house for her life, this promise would be treated as creating, not an expectation that the promise would not be withdrawn, but rather a mistaken belief in the claimant that she had a legal entitlement to remain in the property. This strategy, at the cost of a great deal of artificiality, allows the court to give lip-service to the *probanda* at the same time as granting a remedy in many cases covered by the expectation principle.

On the whole, however, despite the occasional appearance of the *probanda* in the modern English case law, the weight of judicial and academic opinion in England clearly favours the view that the *probanda* are no longer of decisive importance in that jurisdiction. This means that a claimant in the context of an unmarried cohabitation can have resort to both the mistake limb and the expectation limb of proprietary estoppel without the need to show that she was actually mistaken about her legal rights. The same position appears to prevail in Australia,[23] Canada,[24] New Zealand[25] and (probably) in Ireland.[26]

---

[20] *Coombes* v *Smith* [1986] 1 WLR 808 (Judge Thomas QC); *Matharu* v *Matharu* (1994) 16 P & CR 93 (CA). Cf. *Orgee* v *Orgee*, 5 November 1997 (LEXIS, CA).

[21] [1986] 1 WLR 808 (where the claim was, in fact, unsuccessful).

[22] This strategy was implicit in the speech of Lord Cranworth in *Ramsden* v *Dyson* (1866) LR 1 HL 129, 142. See also *Crabb* v *Arun District Council* [1976] Ch 179, 193–195 per Scarman LJ; *Stilwell* v *Simpson* (1983) 133 NLJ 894; *Griffiths* v *Williams* (1977) 248 EG 947, 950 per Goff LJ; *Matharu* v *Matharu* (1994) 16 P & CR 93; *Tickner* v *Wheeler* (1985) 3 NZFLR 782, 787.

[23] The very broad view of estoppel taken by the Australian courts (discussed in the text to and following n 43 *infra*) is clearly inconsistent with a rigid application of the *probanda*. Cf. *Austotel Property Ltd* v *Franklins Selfserve Property Ltd* (1989) 16 NSWLR 582, 609 *et seq* per Priestly JA.

[24] See *Canadian Superior Oil Ltd* v *Paddon-Hughes Development Co Ltd* (1969) 3 DLR (3d) 10, 15 per Johnson JA (affirmed (1970) 12 DLR (3d) 247 (SCC)) (an estoppel may arise even if owner is unaware of his rights); *Litwin Construction* (1973) *Ltd* v *Pan Ltd* (1988) 52 DLR (4th) 459 (BC CA); *Goutsoulas* v *Liao*, 6 August 1993 (LEXIS, Ont Ct of J) pp 7–8 per Ellen MacDonald J ("a softening of the older approach"). Cf. *Voyager Petroleums Ltd* v *Vanguard Petroleums Ltd* (1983) 149 DLR (3d) 417 (Alberta CA) (*probanda* applied and found to be satisfied on the facts).

[25] See *Andrews* v *Colonial Mutual Life Assurance Ltd* [1982] 2 NZLR 556; *Wham-O MFG Co* v *Lincoln Industries Ltd* [1984] 1 NZLR 641; *Westland Savings Bank* v *Hancock* [1987] 2 NZLR 21; *Stratulatos* v *Stratulatos* [1988] 2 NZLR 424; *Gillies* v *Keogh* [1989] 2 NZLR 327, 331 per Cooke P; 344–346 per Richardson J.

[26] In *Dunne* v *Molloy* [1976–77] ILRM 266 and *Smith* v *Ireland* [1983] ILRM 300 the *probanda* were quoted with approval (although they were not central to the actual decision in either case). There has, as yet, been no direct questioning of the authority of the *probanda* in the Irish courts. See, however, *Smyth* v *Halpin* [1997] 2 ILRM 38 (expectation limb applied without any reference to the *probanda*). It seems likely that, in future cases, the Irish courts will follow the line taken in England.

B. Promissory Estoppel and its Relationship With Proprietary Estoppel

It is now necessary to consider briefly the doctrine of promissory estoppel.[27] This equitable doctrine is an extension of the older common law doctrine of estoppel by representation.[28] Under the older doctrine, a person who made a representation of existing fact may be estopped from subsequently pleading that the facts were otherwise than as he had represented them. As was emphasised by the House of Lords in *Jordan* v *Money*,[29] estoppel by representation applies only to representations of existing fact and cannot extend to statements of intention or promises as to future conduct. However, in the famous *High Trees* case,[30] Denning J (as he then was) developed a new equitable principle which avoided the traditional limitation on the common law doctrine.

Denning J's doctrine, commonly described as promissory estoppel, is summarised in a leading textbook in the following terms:

> "Where by his words or conduct one party to a transaction freely makes to the other an unambiguous promise or assurance which is intended to affect the legal relations between them (whether contractual or otherwise), and, before it is withdrawn, the other party acts upon it, altering his position to his detriment, the person making the promise or assurance will not be permitted to act inconsistently with it".[31]

While there are some similarities between promissory and proprietary estoppel, there are also a number of important differences between the two doctrines.[32] Most significantly, promissory estoppel, unlike proprietary estoppel,[33] provides "a shield and not a sword" and cannot create any new cause of action where none existed before.[34] Thus, promissory estoppel can only operate in a defensive manner, protecting a promisee from an attempt by the promisor to enforce rights inconsistent with the promise.[35] Moreover, also unlike proprietary estoppel, promissory estoppel is suspensory in its effect; the promisor can resile from his promise upon giving notice which allows the promisee a reasonable opportunity of resuming her position.[36] On the other hand, promissory

---

[27] See generally Treitel *The Law of Contract*, 9th edn (London: Sweet and Maxwell, 1995) pp 100–115; 120–124.

[28] See generally Spencer Bower and Turner *Estoppel by Representation*, 3rd edn (London: Butterworths, 1977).

[29] (1845) 5 HL Cas 185.

[30] *Central London Property Trust Ltd* v *High Trees House Ltd* [1947] KB 130.

[31] Baker and Langan *Snell's Principles of Equity*, 29th edn (London: Sweet and Maxwell, 1990) p 571.

[32] See generally Evans "Choosing the Right Estoppel" [1988] Conv 346; Treitel, n 27 *supra*, pp 134–136.

[33] See e.g. *Crabb* v *Arun District Council* [1976] Ch 179, 187E per Lord Denning MR; *Zelmer* v *Victor Projects Ltd* (1997) 147 DLR (4th) 216 (BC CA).

[34] *Coombe* v *Coombe* [1951] 2 KB 215.

[35] It is also possible for a plaintiff to use promissory estoppel to demolish a defence to her claim; in such a case, there is a separate cause of action and the defendant is simply estopped by his promise from asserting a particular defence to the claim against him. See Treitel, n 27 *supra*, pp 108–109.

[36] *Ajayi* v *RT Briscoe (Nigeria) Ltd* [1964] 1 WLR 1326, 1330 per Lord Hodson.

estoppel can apply irrespective of the subject matter of the promise, whereas proprietary estoppel is subject to the important limitation that the representation must concern an interest in specific land.[37]

C. Towards a Unified Doctrine of Estoppel?

In the previous section, the traditional differences between proprietary and promissory estoppel were briefly catalogued. These differences were left untouched by the minor revolution effected in England by *Taylor Fashions*.[38] Even after *Taylor Fashions*, the crucial limitation remained that proprietary estoppel was confined to situations where the claimant was led to expect an interest in *land*.[39] Equally, promissory estoppel was unaffected by *Taylor Fashions*, so that the restrictions on that doctrine (discussed in the previous section) remained in place.

Not all judges (often an indirect method of referring to Lord Denning) have been satisfied with this position. As early as 1982, in *Amalgamated Investment & Property Co Ltd* v *Texas Commerce International Bank*[40] Lord Denning MR expressed the view that all the separate forms of estoppel could now "be seen to merge into one general principle shorn of limitations".[41] This statement was quoted uncritically in a later decision of the Privy Council[42] (although not relied upon directly) and therefore cannot be dismissed out of hand. However, it is fair to say that subsequent English cases have not delivered on the promise of Lord Denning MR's sweeping statement.

Despite its muted reception in England, Lord Denning MR's idea of a unified theory of estoppel has found acceptance in Australia. The landmark case was *Waltons Stores (Interstate)* v *Maher*,[43] a decision of the High Court of Australia which was clarified by the same court in *Commonwealth of Australia* v *Verwayen*.[44] Although the various judges of the High Court of Australia took

---

[37] See Gray, n 1 *supra* p 327, citing *Western Fish Products Ltd* v *Penwith District Council* [1981] 2 All ER 204 and Davis "Proprietary Estoppel: Future Interests and Future Property" [1996] Conv 193, 195–196. See also *Layton* v *Martin* [1986] 2 FLR 227 (vague promises of financial security insufficient); *Lloyds Bank plc* v *Carrick* [1996] 4 All ER 630, 639–641 per Morritt LJ; but see Parkinson, n 1 *supra*, p 220 n 113. It is sometimes suggested that the doctrine can apply in relation to other forms of property. See e.g. Delany, n 1 *supra*, p 499. Davis argues to the contrary (*supra*, 195), suggesting that there is "little authority" for this assertion. Any uncertainty is attributable primarily to the anomalous decision of Judge Nugee QC in *Re Basham* [1986] 1 WLR 1498, criticised by Martin [1987] Conv 211 and Hayton (1987) 46 CLJ 215.

[38] [1982] QB 133n.

[39] See n 37 *supra* and accompanying text.

[40] [1982] QB 84. Note also the earlier case of *Crabb* v *Arun District Council* [1976] Ch 179 where Scarman LJ commented (*ibid*, 193) that he "did not find helpful the distinction between promissory and proprietary estoppel".

[41] *Ibid*, 122.

[42] *A-G of Hong Kong* v *Humphreys Estate (Queen's Gardens) Ltd* [1987] 1 AC 114, 124.

[43] (1988) 164 CLR 387.

[44] (1990) 170 CLR 394. See also *Silvoi Pty Ltd* v *Barbaro* (1988) 13 NSWLR 466; *Austotel Property Ltd* v *Franklins Selfserve Property Ltd* (1989) 16 NSWLR 582; *Foran* v *Wight* (1989) 168 CLR 385;

differing views, strong support emerges from these cases for the view that the different forms of estoppel have been dissolved in Australian law and one form of equitable estoppel has been recognised based on a broad principle of unconscionability. This Australian development goes far beyond *Taylor Fashions*[45] and appear to merge the two forms of equitable estoppel.[46]

Despite the encouragement of the Australian cases, it appears that the various forms of estoppel will remain stubbornly distinct in English law for the foreseeable future.[47] A similar (or, perhaps, more conservative) view is taken in Ireland, although matters have been complicated by a number of carelessly reasoned decisions where the traditional boundaries of the estoppels have been stretched in a desire to do justice *inter partes*.[48] Canadian courts have adopted "a flexible test for estoppel"[49] but do not yet appear to have explicitly adopted the Australian position of a unified doctrine of estoppel.[50] Finally, in New Zealand, the courts have taken on board the modern English developments but, once more, have not explicitly taken the further step of fusing proprietary and promissory estoppel.[51]

Having noted recent theoretical developments, it is worth emphasising that the development of an Australian-style unified doctrine of estoppel, however significant in wider theoretical terms, would not have a huge practical impact in the context of disputes between cohabitees. The most important consequence would be that a remedy would be available to a cohabitee who had relied to her detriment on a promise of general financial security. It would not be necessary, as it is now outside Australia, for the claimant to link her conduct to a representation that she would obtain an interest in specific real property. As is illustrated by *Layton v Martin*,[52] outside Australia, it may be of decisive importance whether a person acts to her detriment in the expectation of gaining rights over

Parkinson "Equitable Estoppel: Developments after Waltons Stores (Interstate) Ltd v Maher" (1990) 3 *Journal of Contract Law* 50.

[45] [1982] QB 133n. Somewhat confusingly, the much more modest revolution launched in *Taylor Fashions* also waved the banner of unconscionability.

[46] It is unclear whether Australia's unified doctrine of equitable estoppel subsumes the common law doctrine of estoppel by representation. See Parkinson, n 1 *supra*, pp 223–229.

[47] Cf. *Taylor v Dickens* [1998] 1 FLR 806, 820G (Judge Weeks QC). Note, however, that in *Sledgemore v Dalby* (1996) 72 P & CR 196, 208–209 Hobhouse LJ quoted with approval a number of "illuminating passages" from the judgments in *Commonwealth of Australia v Verwayen* (1990) 170 CLR 394. See also Pawlowski "Proprietary Estoppel—Satisfying the Equity" (1997) 113 LQR 232. See generally, Lunney "Towards a Unified Estoppel: The Long and Winding Road" [1993] Conv 239.

[48] See *Webb v Ireland* [1988] IR 353; *Re JR (A Ward of Court)* [1993] ILRM 657; Mee, n 1 *supra*.

[49] *Welch v O'Brian Financial Corp* (1991) 86 DLR (4th) 155, 168 per Legg JA (BC CA).

[50] Cf. *Welch v O'Brian Financial Corp* (1991) 86 DLR (4th) 155, which appears to have been the only Canadian case where *Waltons Stores* (1988) 164 CLR 387 was considered. Note also *Litwin Construction (1973) Ltd v Pan Ltd* (1988) 52 DLR (4th) 459 (BC CA); *Revell v Litwin Construction (1973) Ltd* (1991) 86 DLR (4th) 169 (BC CA); *Reclamation Systems Inc v Rae* (1996) 27 OR (3d) 419.

[51] See, in addition to the authorities cited in n 25 *supra*, *Prudential Building and Investment Society of Canterbury v Hankins* [1997] 1 NZLR 114, 121–122 per Hammond J; *Rodney Aero Club Inc v Moore* [1998] 2 NZLR 192, 197–198 per Hammond J.

[52] [1986] 2 FLR 227. See also *Coombes v Smith* [1986] 1 WLR 808, 819B–D.

a particular house (proprietary estoppel applicable) or on the basis of a general promise of financial security (proprietary estoppel unavailable and promissory estoppel unable to provide the necessary cause of action).[53]

II. THE OPERATION OF ESTOPPEL PRINCIPLES IN THE CONTEXT OF UNMARRIED COHABITATION

Having examined the theoretical development of the various forms of estoppel, it is now necessary to look at their practical operation in the context of unmarried cohabitation. It is proposed to begin with an analysis of the two limbs of proprietary estoppel. The discussion will first focus on the expectation limb, which is of the most practical relevance, before moving on to the less commonly invoked mistake limb. Next, a consideration will be undertaken of the independent significance of promissory estoppel. A final section will consider the possibility of affording a remedy to a claimant who has acted to her detriment, not as a result of any representation by her partner, but simply on the basis of an expectation generated by the relationship between the parties.

A. The Expectation Limb of Proprietary Estoppel

The essential elements in the establishment of a claim under the expectation limb of proprietary estoppel are that (i) there must have been a representation or promise; (ii) the claimant must have acted to her detriment; and (iii) this detrimental conduct must have been undertaken in reliance on the representation or promise. Once these three elements are proved to exist it is then necessary to move on to a fourth issue, that of determining the appropriate remedy for the claimant in all the circumstances of the case. It is now proposed to examine these four issues in turn.

1. *The requirement of a representation*

It must be established that there has been a representation or assurance from the legal owner of land that the claimant is, or will become, entitled to some interest in the land.[54] The motive or intention of the legal owner in making the

---

[53] See further text to and following n 125 *infra*.

[54] See n 37 *supra* and accompanying text. Although the requirement of a representation is applied in a flexible manner, it seems clear (under present law) that no claim can arise if no representation has been made by the legal owner. There are, however, one or two Australian authorities indicating a different view. See *Nepean District Tennis Association Inc* v *City Council of Penrith* (1989) NSW Conv R 55–438 and *Beaton* v *McDivitt* (1987) 13 NSWLR 162, 171 per Kirby P, discussed by Gray, n 1 *supra*, p 330. Cf. *Re Sharpe* [1980] 1 WLR 219 (a shared assumption treated as sufficient, albeit in reliance on questionable authorities such as *Errington* v *Errington* [1952] 1 KB 290 and *Tanner* v *Tanner* [1975] 1 WLR 1346). For the status of a "shared assumption" under the "common intention" analysis, see Chapter 5 *infra*, text to and following n 50 (common intention must be communicated between the parties). Cf. Section D of this Part *infra*.

representation is not decisive.[55] What is important is the effect which the representation had on the claimant as a reasonable person.[56] A representation may concern any kind of interest in land, including the fee simple,[57] a share in the equitable ownership,[58] an easement[59] or a lease.[60] Significantly for present purposes, the cases show that it is sufficient if the claimant is led to expect some less formal interest[61] in the land, such as a licence which will not be revoked during the claimant's lifetime.[62]

Given the tendency in an intimate relationship to avoid discussion of separate property rights, it will often be difficult to establish that one cohabitee made a specific representation that his partner would be entitled to continue in occupation of the family home or would be entitled to a beneficial interest therein.[63] Furthermore, any representation made may be of a nature which a judge might not regard as legally relevant; lovers are more likely to promise in vague terms that they will love and take care of each other forever than to specify the precise benefits which their eternal love will confer.[64] Thus, the basic requirement of a representation is likely to prove fatal in the context of many family property disputes.[65]

---

[55] Thus, it does not matter if the person making the representation is telling a deliberate lie. Cf. *Grant v Edwards* [1986] 1 Ch 638; *Eves v Eves* [1975] 1 WLR 1338.

[56] Gray, n 1 *supra*, p 329.

[57] See *Pascoe v Turner* [1979] 1 WLR 431.

[58] Cf. *Grant v Edwards* [1986] 1 Ch 638.

[59] See e.g. *Crabb v Arun District Council* [1976] Ch 179; *Zelmer v Victor Projects Ltd* (1997) 147 DLR (4th) 216 (BC CA).

[60] *Ramsden v Dyson* (1866) LR 1 HL 129.

[61] There seems to be an element of artificiality in the textbook requirement that the claimant be led to believe that she would at present or in the future be *entitled* to an interest (however vague) in the land. It seems much more realistic to admit that the intervention of equity is based upon the abuse of someone's trust. Consider a case where X promises Y that she will be allowed to remain in a certain house. Trusting X, and never considering the possibility that X will resile from the promise, Y acts to her detriment. Must we really pretend that X believed that she owned some kind of legally recognisable interest in the house or that she would get one? In truth, it may be more likely either that (1) she never considered her strict legal position or (2) she realised that Y was, in strict law, entitled to evict her but trusted him not to exercise his right to do so. It is possible that the textbook approach has been influenced by the line of English cases where the *probanda* were twisted so as to cover both limbs of proprietary estoppel. See text following n 20 *supra*.

[62] See *Re JR (A Ward of Court)* [1993] ILRM 657.

[63] Note that in *Gillies v Keogh* [1989] 2 NZLR 327, 346, Richardson P was willing to imply a representation from the attitudes of the parties to the family property during the currency of the relationship and to "draw appropriate inferences from the way they lived their lives together". Cf. *Gibb v MacDonnell* [1992] 3 NZLR 475, 480 per Anderson J. See further Chapter 9 *infra*, text following n 68. Despite the lip-service given by the judges in these cases to the requirement of a representation by the defendant, their approach appears effectively to dispense with this requirement. See further Section D of this Part *infra*.

[64] See *Layton v Martin* [1986] 2 FLR 227, 229–230 where "the lynchpin" of the plaintiff's case was a letter in which her lover promised her "financial security during my life, and financial security on my death". However, the letter also offered less material benefits such as "freedom to do 'your own thing', to write, to share my house and sometimes my bed, to share troubles, joys together". It surely is wrong to parse closely and attribute legal force to the particular words used in such an intimate communication.

[65] Note that, in the somewhat similar context of the "common intention" constructive trust, the English courts have been willing to infer the existence of a common intention simply from the fact

2. *The requirement of detriment*

The second requirement is that the claimant have acted to her detriment. However, as Dixon J explained in the early case of *Grundt v Great Boulder Pty Gold Mines Ltd*,[66] the requisite conduct need not in itself be detrimental or disadvantageous to the claimant; it is only necessary that detriment would arise if the representation were not honoured. Consider a case where a landlord assures his tenant that her lease, which is shortly due to expire, will be renewed. In reliance on this representation, the tenant decides to renovate her apartment at great expense. In one sense, the tenant's conduct in improving her living space is not "detrimental". Nonetheless, if the assumption on the basis of which she acted were falsified, she would have acted to her "detriment", since she would lose all the benefit of the expenditure when the lease expired.

While the seminal case of *Ramsden v Dyson*[67] emphasised the example of a person expending money on improving the land in question, it is now clear that detrimental reliance may take a variety of forms.[68] Gray suggests that detriment may include "the undergoing of any sacrifice which is not of exclusively emotional significance".[69]

A good illustration of the operation of the requirement of detriment in the cohabitation context is provided by *Greasley v Cooke*,[70] where the claimant had, as a young woman, entered a household as a maid. Over the years, her position changed and she became the lover of one of the sons of the family. For many years, she worked in the home and took care of her lover's mentally disabled sister. She was assured on a number of occasions that she would be allowed to remain living in the house for the rest of her life. Her lover died without making provision for her in his will. She was left, at the age of 62, facing eviction at the hands of his successors in title. The Court of Appeal held that she had acted to her detriment by caring for the family and failing to take steps to provide security for herself by leaving the house and obtaining alternative employment. An estoppel arose in her favour and the Court of Appeal held that she was entitled to remain in the house, rent-free, for so long as she wished to do so.

It may be noted that since proprietary estoppel is ultimately based on unconscionability, it is appropriate for the courts, as well as examining the detriment incurred by the claimant, to look also at any countervailing benefits which the

---

that the claimant made financial contributions towards the disputed property. However, this process of inference appears to depend on a dubious analogy with the old purchase money resulting trust. (See generally Chapter 5 *infra*, Part I(A)(2)(a).) In the context of pure proprietary estoppel, which is clearly unrelated to the resulting trust, there is no excuse for "manufacturing" representations in the manner favoured under the common intention doctrine. Cf. *Savva v Costa and Harymode Investments Ltd* (1981) 131 NLJ 1114 (full transcript on LEXIS).

[66] (1937) 59 CLR 641, 674–675.
[67] (1866) LR 1 HL 129.
[68] See generally Pawlowski, n 1 *supra*, pp 60–71; Parkinson, n 1 *supra*, pp 245–250.
[69] See n 1 *supra*, p 336.
[70] [1980] 1 WLR 1306.

claimant has received from the legal owner.[71] For example, the female claimant was unsuccessful in *Cullen* v *Cullen*[72] because she had received far more from her husband's business than she had ever put in. To take another example, a similar result would follow if a claimant who had expended money on improving a property had also received rent-free accommodation in that property for many years.[73]

The case law on detriment in the family context raises very difficult issues in relation to "life-style" choices. People frequently change the course of their lives to accommodate a relationship, perhaps giving up a job and a home in one city in order to move in with their partner in another city. Should this sort of conduct be capable of satisfying the requirement of detriment? Cases such as *Maharaj* v *Chand*[74] suggest that detriment may be established if the claimant gives up a secure home to move in with the defendant. However, it has been argued that detriment cannot be established merely by evidence that the claimant has moved into the defendant's house. Judge Parker QC pointed out in *Coombes* v *Smith*[75] that every claimant who moves in with a defendant must have come from somewhere and that, if the mere fact of a change of address were sufficient, the requirement of detriment would be satisfied in every case. Interestingly, precisely the opposite approach was taken in the Irish case of *Re JR (A Ward of Court)*,[76] where the requirement of detriment was held to be satisfied notwithstanding the absence of evidence as to where the claimant had been living before she moved in with the defendant. Taking a very generous approach, Costello J felt "entitled to assume"[77] that the claimant had given up some house or flat in order to move in with the defendant and had, therefore, acted to her detriment.[78]

The uncertainty in the case law appears to reflect the underlying difficulty in the law's attempt to assess the detrimental quality of "life-style" choices. As any existentialist will testify, we are all imprisoned by the choices available to us.[79] One must have some reservations about concluding that a person acts to her

---

[71] See e.g. *Watts* v *Storey* (1984) 134 NLJ 631; *Beaton* v *McDivitt* (1987) 13 NSWLR 162 (NSW CA).

[72] [1962] IR 268.

[73] See *Sledgemore* v *Dalby* (1996) 72 P & CR 196. Contrast *Re JR (A Ward of Court)* [1993] ILRM 657 (where Costello J seemed to ignore the countervailing benefits received by the claimant). Cf. *Jones* v *Jones* [1977] 1 WLR 438, 442D per Lord Denning MR (claimant treated as acting to his detriment in making financial contribution towards house even though that contribution had already earned him a proportionate share in the beneficial interest).

[74] [1986] AC 898 (PC). Cf. *Stevens* v *Stevens*, 3 March 1989 (LEXIS, CA).

[75] [1986] 1 WLR 808, 816–817.

[76] [1993] ILRM 657. (Note that *Re JR (A Ward of Court)* supra, like *Maharaj* v *Chand* [1986] AC 898, was nominally decided under the heading of promissory estoppel).

[77] [1993] ILRM 657, 663.

[78] Note also two cases decided under the "common intention" analysis: *Thwaites* v *Ryan* [1984] VR 65, 96 (leaving a moribund marriage did not constitute detriment); *Cooke* v *Cooke* [1987] VR 625, 636 per Southwell J (contrary to public policy to classify as "detriment" the decision to allow a normal pregnancy to continue).

[79] See e.g. Sartre *Existentialism and Humanism* (London: Metheun, 1989) p 25 *et seq.*

detriment in making the kind of choice which is an essential feature of life itself. Consider *Green* v *Green*[80] where the claimant was regarded as having acted to her detriment in not ending her relationship with the defendant in Australia and moving back to Thailand. Is such a choice really "detrimental" in the eyes of equity?[81] One is left with the feeling that the reverse choice (e.g. leaving a comfortable life-style in Australia and moving back to an uncertain future in Thailand) might equally be held by a court to be detrimental.

Or consider a case where the claimant gives up her career to take care of the children of the relationship. In one very important sense, this is a clear example of detriment to the claimant. However, how does one take into account issues such as the toll taken on a person by the pursuit of a career? While twenty years in the workplace may leave one with financial security and good future work prospects, one has to pay for this with twenty years of work (which may or may not be fulfilling) and, perhaps, an unsatisfactory relationship with one's children and the likelihood of an early death from a heart-attack. In the end, a great deal in this area appears to depend on the personal preferences of the individuals concerned. If asked whether it is preferable to live in Thailand or in Australia (or to pursue a certain career or to work in the home), one would have to answer that, to a significant extent, it depends on what you want from life. And, of course, what people want from life is often shaped by the attempt to pursue happiness through their relationship with their present partner.

Another, and somewhat different, problem which arises in the family context is that estoppel's emphasis on compensating detriment may lead to the representor becoming, in a sense, a guarantor for the other party. Consider a case where the parties to a relationship are living in different cities. The defendant feels that, if the relationship is to survive, the parties must try living together. Therefore, he urges his partner to come to live with him, promising that he will transfer his home (worth £100,000) into their joint names. Imagine that the plaintiff gives up her job and home and moves in with her partner. The relationship fails at an early stage and the defendant never puts the home into joint names. Imagine that the plaintiff's detriment can be quantified at £30,000. Applying estoppel principles, it would appear that the plaintiff has been led to act to her detriment and that the equity which arises in her favour should be satisfied by a remedy which will erase her detriment. Therefore, one would expect the defendant to be required to pay her £30,000. However, if this happens, the final result will be that the defendant will bear all (and the plaintiff none) of the cost of the risk the couple took for the sake of the relationship. This seems quite unjust. The tendency of estoppel appears to be to portray the representor as the

[80] (1989) 17 NSWLR 343. See also *Ungarian* v *Lesnoff* [1990] Ch 206 where the claimant was held to have acted to her detriment by giving up a secure flat in Poland and the prospect of an academic career in order to move to England. However, the claimant had not even begun her intended doctoral degree so that her academic prospects were rather theoretical. Furthermore, it is debateable whether the prospect of spending the rest of her life (starting in 1968) in a flat in Wroclaw was significantly more attractive than starting a (somewhat less secure) new life in England.

[81] Cf. the view expressed by Mahoney JA (dissenting) *ibid*, 370.

party in the position of power and to assume that, by "inducing" the other party to make a choice to her detriment, the representor is obliged to take all the responsibility for the consequences of that choice. However, where an estoppel arises in the context of an intimate relationship, it might be better to think in terms of an equal sharing of detriment which results from sacrifices undertaken for the benefit of the relationship.[82]

The purpose of the discussion in the previous paragraphs was not to suggest that injustice can never be caused by one party's willingness to subordinate her wishes to the needs of a relationship. The point was simply to highlight the difficulties caused by the need to take account of the subjective preferences of the people concerned and the complexity of an intimate relationship. At a more general level, it is, of course, arguable that these difficulties are not amenable to a solution within the law of estoppel and that the problems could better be addressed in the context of a statutory treatment of the property rights of cohabitees.

3. Reliance

It is not sufficient for a claimant merely to show that she acted to her detriment; it is also necessary to show that the detriment was undertaken *in reliance* on the representation of the legal owner.[83] This requirement of a causal connection between the representation and the detriment has the potential to defeat many claims. For example, in *Taylor Fashions* v *Liverpool Victoria Trustees Co Ltd*,[84] Oliver J held that a tenant who had improved his property had not done so in reliance on an assumption that the lease would be renewed. Oliver J felt that, given the amount of the lease which was left to run, it was likely that the tenant would have undertaken the improvements even without the expectation of a renewal.

---

[82] It has already been pointed out that the requirement of detriment will be satisfied if the claimant's actions, although potentially advantageous to her, would be detrimental if the defendant's representation were not honoured (see text to and following n 66 *supra*). Interestingly, however, the honouring or dishonouring of the representation may not be the only factor which will determine whether a course of action turns out to be detrimental. Imagine that, in the example just discussed in the text, the claimant knew when she gave up her job that she had a 90 per cent chance of obtaining suitable employment in the city to which she was moving. However, as it turns out, the 10 per cent risk eventuates and she is unable to find employment. What detriment has the defendant led her to suffer? Should he only be responsible for the 10 per cent risk she took or must he take the full consequences of the fact that, independently of the dishonouring of his representation, the choice she made turned out badly?

[83] An interesting problem arose in the New Zealand case of *Gibb* v *MacDonnell* [1992] 3 NZLR 475, where Anderson J held that the claimant had acted partly from love and affection for his partner and partly on the basis of the expectation that he would have a permanent home in her house. On this basis, Anderson J gave a remedy of $15,000 on the basis of an expenditure by the claimant of $38,000. Contrast *Wayling* v *Jones* (1995) 69 P & CR 170 where Balcombe LJ, citing the view of Robert Goff J at first instance in *Amalgamated Investment & Property Co Ltd* [1982] QB 84, 104–105, argued that "the promises relied on do not have to be the sole inducement for the conduct; it is sufficient if they are an inducement".

[84] [1982] QB 133n.

The requirement that the detriment have been undertaken in reliance on the representation presents a particularly difficult hurdle in the context of claims by a plaintiff who has worked in the family home or in child-rearing and who has thereby impaired her future financial security and job prospects. *Greasley* v *Cooke*[85] (discussed in the previous sub-section) illustrates the point that, in principle, such conduct is capable of satisfying the requirement of detriment. However, it will be very difficult for a claimant to show that her work in the home was undertaken in reliance on a representation that she would enjoy certain rights over the defendant's land. A court may well hold, as a number of lower English courts have held,[86] that she would have undertaken this conduct even if he had not made such a representation. Here, to some extent, there is a danger of the prejudices of the court interfering with the logic of its conclusion. Certainly, the English decisions appear to indicate a low opinion of work in the home and perhaps a feeling that it represents the kind of conduct which may reasonably be "expected" of a woman.

One possible solution to the problem of an estoppel claimant who relies upon work in the home or in child-rearing is to be found in the judgment of Lord Denning MR in *Greasley* v *Cooke*.[87] Lord Denning suggested that, once a landowner made a representation with the intention that the claimant should act upon it,[88] the burden of proof then lay upon the owner to prove that the actions of the claimant were not undertaken in reliance on the representation. This idea of a presumption of reliance was taken up by Browne-Wilkinson V-C (as he then was) in *Grant* v *Edwards*.[89] Browne-Wilkinson V-C commented as follows:

> "In many cases . . . it is impossible to say whether or not the claimant would have done the acts relied upon as a detriment even if she thought she had no interest in the house. Setting up house together, having a baby, making payments to general housekeeping expenses (not strictly necessary to enable the mortgage to be paid) may all be referable to the mutual love and affection of the parties and not specifically referable to the claimant's belief that she has an interest in the house. As at present advised . . . any act done by her to her detriment relating to the joint lives of the parties is . . . sufficient detriment to qualify . . . [I]n the absence of evidence to the contrary, the right inference is that the claimant acted in reliance [on her partner's holding out that she had a beneficial interest in the house] and the burden lies on the legal owner to show that she did not do so: see *Greasley* v *Cooke* [1980] 1 WLR 1306".[90]

---

[85] [1980] 1 WLR 1306.

[86] See *Stilwell* v *Simpson* (1983) 133 NLJ 894; *Layton* v *Martin* [1986] 2 FLR 227, 235–236; *Coombes* v *Smith* [1986] 1 WLR 808, 820.

[87] [1980] 1 WLR 1306, 1311.

[88] Lord Denning referred (*ibid*) to a representation which was "calculated to influence" the conduct of the claimant. In *Brikom Investments* v *Carr* [1979] QB 467, 482 (relied upon by Lord Denning MR in *Greasley supra*), Lord Denning stated more explicitly that it was necessary that the representation have been made "intending that the other should rely on it".

[89] [1986] 1 Ch 638.

[90] *Ibid*, 657. *Grant* v *Edwards* was decided on the basis of the English "common intention" analysis but, in this part of his judgment, Browne-Wilkinson V-C was discussing a "possible analogy" with proprietary estoppel.

Interestingly, Browne-Wilkinson V-C did not refer to Lord Denning's requirement that the statement of the representor have been made with the intention
that the claimant should rely on it.

Two Privy Council cases have recently been decided without reference to
Lord Denning's suggestion of a presumption[91] and the present position in
England remains unclear. It is, of course, open to courts in other jurisdictions to
follow Lord Denning's view if they so desire. The main difficulty with Lord
Denning's approach is that he appears to have invented the presumption himself, as usual without providing a principled justification or citing convincing
authority.[92] It is submitted therefore that it would be preferable if the courts
ignored Lord Denning's presumption and simply approached the issue of
reliance in an open-minded way, with no preconception that a female claimant
would inevitably have worked without pay in the home in the absence of any
representation.[93]

4. Choosing a remedy: "satisfying the equity"

If the claimant has demonstrated detrimental reliance upon a representation,
then a final issue arises as to the remedy to be afforded to the claimant. At this
point, the courts enjoy a wide discretion. It is normal for judges to speak in
terms of "an equity" being raised in favour of the claimant.[94] The court then
looks at all the circumstances to decide in what manner the equity can be satisfied. Crucially, unlike the situation in relation to promissory estoppel, there is
no rule that proprietary estoppel can be used as a shield but not a sword. In principle, proprietary estoppel can be used as a cause of action and there is no
restriction on the court's choosing from a range of affirmative remedies.[95]
Amongst the options open to the court are the granting of an indefinite license

---

[91] *A-G of Hong Kong v Humphreys Estate (Queen's Garden) Ltd* [1987] 1 AC 114; *Lim Teng
Huan v Ang Swee Chuan* [1992] 1 WLR 113. See Gray, n 1 *supra*, p 333.

[92] Besides his own judgment in *Brikom Investments v Carr* [1979] QB 467, Lord Denning MR
cited *Reynell v Sprye* (1852) 1 De GM & G 660, 708 and *Smith v Chadwick* (1882) 20 Ch D 27, 44.
Since neither of these cases actually involved estoppel, one is left with the suspicion that Lord
Denning MR simply concocted the presumption himself.

[93] For a recent English treatment of the relevant issues, in the context of a homosexual relationship, see *Wayling v Jones* (1995) 69 P & CR 170, discussed by Flynn and Lawson "Gender, Sexuality
and the Doctrine of Detrimental Reliance" [1995] *Feminist Legal Studies* 105 and by Cooke
"Reliance and Estoppel" (1995) 111 LQR 389. The claimant in *Wayling* had conceded in his evidence
that he would have acted in precisely the same manner even if his partner had not represented to him
that he would make provision for him by will. However, the claimant had also stated in evidence
that, if the representation had been expressly withdrawn, he would have left his partner. The majority of the Court of Appeal were satisfied, on the basis of this latter statement, that the reliance
requirement had been satisfied. It is submitted that this reasoning cannot be sustained. The crucial
question is whether the claimant has been led by the representation to act to his detriment. If his
actions have not been influenced by the representation, then it is irrelevant how he might have
reacted to future hypothetical statements by the defendant.

[94] See e.g. *Plimmer v Mayor of Wellington* (1884) 9 App Cas 699, 714; *Crabb v Arun District
Council* [1976] Ch 179, 189F per Lord Denning MR.

[95] See e.g. *Crabb v Arun District Council* [1976] Ch 179, 187E per Lord Denning MR.

to occupy the property in question,[96] the grant of a lease at a nominal rent,[97] the payment of monetary compensation[98] or the grant of the fee simple[99] (or the fee simple remainder)[100] to the claimant. In every case, the court must simply examine all the circumstances and find the appropriate remedy.

Although the court's discretion is broad, one interesting point of principle arises. Should the court seek to erase the detriment suffered by the claimant or to fulfil the expectation raised in the claimant? It is submitted that, in principle, the court should seek to erase the claimant's detriment. Consider a case where a claimant has been led to believe that she will be entitled to remain in a house for the rest of her life. Imagine that, in reliance on that representation, she expends £100 on improving the property.[101] In this kind of situation, the court should order that she be reimbursed her expenditure. This general approach has the advantage of emphasising that the court is not in the business of "enforcing" promises (thus undermining the law of contract) but rather is seeking to compensate for detriment.[102] Naturally, there will be cases where the extent of the detriment is such that, in all the circumstances, the only just solution is to fulfil the expectation which prompted the detrimental conduct.[103] The point is simply that the focus should be, in the first case, upon the detriment rather than the expectation.[104] Unfortunately, although the position outlined above appears to

[96] See e.g. *Vinden* v *Vinden* [1982] 1 NSWLR 618. In relation to the effect of estoppel licences on third parties, see Battersby "Contractual and Estoppel Licences as Proprietary Interests in Land" [1991] Conv 36; Baughnen "Estoppels over Land and Third Parties[:] An Open Question?" (1994) 14 *Legal Studies* 147. See also *Ives* v *High* [1967] 2 QB 379; *Lloyds Bank plc* v *Carrick* [1996] 4 All ER 630, 642 per Morritt LJ; *Habermann* v *Koehler* (1996) 73 P & CR 515; *Silvoi Pty Ltd* v *Barbaro* (1988) 13 NSWLR 466.

[97] See *Griffiths* v *Williams* (1977) 248 EG 947.

[98] See e.g. *Dodsworth* v *Dodsworth* (1973) 228 EG 1115; *Burrows* v *Sharp* (1991) 23 HLR 82.

[99] See e.g. *Pascoe* v *Turner* [1979] 1 WLR 431; *Voyce* v *Voyce* (1991) 62 P & CR 290.

[100] See *Smyth* v *Halpin* [1997] 2 ILRM 38.

[101] See the hypothetical case posited by Deane J in *Commonwealth of Australia* v *Verwayen* (1990) 170 CLR 394, 441 and discussed by Gray, n 1 *supra*, pp 345–346.

[102] Cf. Gray, n 1 *supra*, pp 345–347. This was the view taken in *Commonwealth of Australia* v *Verwayen* (1990) 170 CLR 394, 413 where Mason CJ denied that estoppel has "as its hallmark function the making good of assumptions" and Brennan J commented *ibid*, 429 that "[t]he remedy is not designed to enforce the promise". See also *ibid*, 501 per McHugh J. The Australian approach has logic on its side. The broader the view one takes of estoppel, the greater the danger of an unacceptable trespass on the domain of contract law and the greater the attraction of limiting the remedy to the reversal of detriment.

[103] It seems that there may be some cases where there was an informal bargain between the parties. For example, it might have been understood between them that if they both worked hard in renovating a ruined property they would be equally entitled to its ownership. (See e.g. *Eves* v *Eves* [1975] 1 WLR 1338). In such cases, one might argue that the parties have informally agreed a value for the (generally non-financial) detriment to be incurred by the claimant. If the claimant then fulfils her side of the bargain, it may be just to compensate the detriment at the agreed rate (as it were) by fulfilling the expectation. See further Chapter 5 *infra*, text following n 317.

[104] It is well-established that the expectation generated in the claimant provides an outer limit on the relief which may be awarded. See Pawlowski, n 1 *supra*, p 81; *Lloyds Bank plc* v *Carrick* [1996] 4 All ER 630, 641 per Morritt LJ; *Commonwealth of Australia* v *Verwayen* (1990) 170 CLR 394, 442 per Deane J.

accord with principle, the courts of all jurisdictions display a stubborn fondness for giving effect to expectations.[105]

B. The Mistake Limb of Proprietary Estoppel

There does not appear to have been much consideration of the possible relevance of the mistake limb of proprietary estoppel in the context of family property disputes. However, there are possibilities here which have not been adequately explored.

Many of the issues which have already been discussed in relation to the expectation limb are equally relevant in the context of the mistake limb. The basic difference between the two limbs is that the trigger for the mistake limb is not a representation by the defendant but rather a mistaken belief on the part of the claimant that she has an interest in certain land. As was discussed at an earlier point is this chapter, under the *probanda* laid down in *Willmott* v *Barber*,[106] it was traditionally regarded as necessary that the owner of the land be aware of his own rights and of the claimant's mistaken belief. However, it seems that these two latter requirements are no longer to be applied strictly and are merely relevant factors in the overall inquiry into whether it would be unconscionable for the legal owner to rely on his legal rights.[107]

Once a mistaken belief has been established, it is necessary, just as in relation to the expectation limb, to establish that the claimant has acted to her detriment and that her detrimental conduct was undertaken in reliance on her mistaken belief. The principles discussed in the previous section are equally applicable in this context, as are those relating to the choice of remedy to satisfy the equity which has arisen in favour of the claimant. Since most of the ground has thus been already covered, it is necessary in this section only to examine the possible application of the mistake limb in the context of disputes between cohabitees.

Consider a case where a family home is in the sole name of the male partner to a relationship and the female partner works without remuneration in the home and in rearing the children of the relationship. In doing so, she impairs her future employment prospects and leaves herself in a very vulnerable position should the relationship break down. One might argue that she has most likely acted on the assumption that the relationship would last and has failed to consider the consequences if it were to break down. However, it is also possible that she has assumed that she is entitled to a half share in the home. Even outside

---

[105] See Robertson "Satisfying the Minimum Equity: Equitable Remedies After *Verwayen*" (1996) 20 *Melbourne University Law Review* 805. Cf. Yorio and Thel "The Promissory Basis of Section 90" (1991) 101 *Yale Law Journal* 111. Contrast Hillman "Questioning the 'New Consensus' on Promissory Estoppel: An Empirical and Theoretical Study" (1998) 98 *Columbia Law Review* 580. Cf. Cooke "Estoppel and the Protection of Expectations" (1997) 17 *Legal Studies* 258; Robertson "Reliance and Expectation in Estoppel Remedies" (1998) 18 *Legal Studies* 360.

[106] (1880) 15 Ch D 96. See text to and following n 12 *supra*.

[107] See text following n 15 *supra*.

those Australian jurisdictions where legislation has given certain rights to cohabitees,[108] there appears to be some evidence of a (wholly mistaken) public belief in a concept of "common law marriage" which would protect the property rights of a cohabitee after a certain period of cohabitation.[109] In view of the above, it seems likely that, in some cases at least, a cohabitee could meet the requirement of a mistaken belief that she had an interest in the defendant's land.

Naturally, this would only be the first step to a successful claim. A serious obstacle to a claim based on the mistake limb is presented by the requirement that the claimant have acted to her detriment *in reliance* on her mistaken belief.[110] It might be argued that she would have acted in the same way even if she had been aware that she had no interest in the home; her likely assumption that the relationship would last and that separate ownership would remain irrelevant would be equally likely to have motivated her behaviour. However, where the claimant has made improvements to the family home, it would seem much easier to establish the required link between the claimant's detrimental conduct and her mistaken belief. Thus, the mistake limb might possibly provide a remedy in circumstances such as those in *NAD* v *TD*[111] where the claimant was unsuccessful, despite having contributed heavily to the construction of a house on a site belonging to the defendant.

C. Promissory Estoppel

Having looked in detail at the potential of proprietary estoppel, it is now necessary to address the independent significance of promissory estoppel. This doctrine has featured occasionally in the case law of all jurisdictions.[112] It is submitted that it is difficult to envisage an independent role for promissory estoppel in family property cases. In theoretical terms, the ground is already covered by the two limbs of proprietary estoppel and, if one were honest about it, the contractual flavour of the doctrine of promissory estoppel should generally prevent its application in the context of domestic disputes.

---

[108] See Chapter 1 *supra*, n 96.

[109] See e.g. *Windeler* v *Whitehall* [1990] 2 WLR 505, 513–514. Research into public beliefs in this area is being carried out by the English Law Commission in preparation for a report on the property rights of home-sharers (see *Sixth Programme of Law Reform*, Law Com 234 (London: HMSO, 1995) Item 8). See also Neave "Living Together—The Legal Effects of the Sexual Division of Labour in Four Common Law Countries" (1991) 17 *Monash University Law Review* 14, 56. Note further that New Zealand's Matrimonial Property Bill 1975 originally made provision for applications by couples in de facto relationships. The relevant provision was only removed from the Bill at the Select Committee stage. This appears to explain a widespread misconception in New Zealand that de facto couples have certain legal rights once their relationship has lasted for two years. (See now New Zealand's De Facto Relationships (Property) Bill 1998).

[110] See text to nn 83–93 *supra*.

[111] [1983] ILRM 153.

[112] See e.g. *Maharaj* v *Chand* [1986] AC 898. Promissory estoppel has played a surprisingly large role in the case law of Ireland. See *Cullen* v *Cullen* [1962] IR 268 and *Re JR* (*A Ward of Court*) [1993] ILRM 657.

There are a number of aspects of the doctrine of promissory estoppel which make it unattractive in the domestic context. It has already been seen from the discussion of proprietary estoppel that the requirement of a representation creates a major obstacle for claimants. The problem is even greater under promissory estoppel, where this requirement takes a more strict form. By way of contrast to the fairly loose requirements of proprietary estoppel, it is necessary under promissory estoppel to demonstrate a clear and unambiguous statement of intention[113] which was intended to affect the legal relationship between the parties.[114] It appears that one is looking for a promise which has "the same degree of certainty as would be needed to give it contractual effect if it were supported by consideration".[115] This test is likely to prove very difficult to satisfy in the context of unmarried cohabitation.

A further difficulty lies in the traditional rule that promissory estoppel cannot operate unless there was a pre-existing contractual relationship between the parties. This reflects the origin of the doctrine in *High Trees*[116] in the context of a waiver of rights under an existing contract. This restriction, if taken seriously, would provide a significant limitation on promissory estoppel and would prevent an estoppel resulting from a simple promise made outside the context of any previous contract with the promisee.

However, the requirement under discussion has been diluted to some extent in the case law.[117] Treitel[118] takes the view that, while it is necessary that there be "a relationship giving rise to rights and duties" between the parties, it is not necessary that this relationship be contractual. Significantly for present purposes, the doctrine of promissory estoppel has been applied in the context of the relationship between a cohabiting couple[119] and in other family situations.[120] It appears that, in principle, the requirement of an existing legal relationship between the parties merely reflects the distinct requirement that the promise in question must be *to refrain from enforcing strict legal rights* (which in turn is linked to the principle that promissory estoppel cannot provide a cause of

---

[113] See *Dun and Bradstreet Software Services (England) Ltd* v *Provident Mutual Life Assurance Association* 9 June 1997 (LEXIS, CA); *Engineered Homes Ltd* v *Mason* (1983) 146 DLR (3d) 577 (SCC); *Marine Steel Ltd* v *The Ship "Steel Navigator"* [1992] 1 NZLR 77; Treitel, n 27 *supra*, pp 100–102; Parkinson, n 1 *supra*, p 255ff.

[114] Treitel, n 27 *supra*, p 102. Cf. *Traveller's Indemnity Co of Canada* v *Maracle* (1991) 80 DLR (4th) 653 (SCC).

[115] Treitel, n 27 *supra*, p 103.

[116] *Central London Property Trust Ltd* v *High Trees House Ltd* [1947] KB 130.

[117] See Treitel, n 27 *supra*, pp 101–102, discussing *inter alia Durham Fancy Goods Ltd* v *Michael Jackson (Fancy Goods) Ltd* [1968] 2 QB 839; *The Henrik Sif* [1982] 1 Lloyds Rep 456. Cf. *Revenue Commissioners* v *Moroney* [1972] IR 372; Coughlan "Equity: Swords, Shields and Estoppel Licences" (1993) 15 *Dublin University Law Journal* (ns) 188, 198–201; *Daulat Investments Inc* v *Ceci's Home for Children* (1991) 85 DLR (4th) 248 (Ont Ct of J); *Reclamation Systems Inc* v *Rae* (1996) 27 OR (3d) 419 (Ont Ct of J); *Burbery Mortgage Finance & Savings Ltd* v *Hindsbank Holdings Ltd* [1989] 1 NZLR 356.

[118] See n 27 *supra*, p 100.

[119] See *Maharaj* v *Chand* [1986] AC 898 (PC); *Re JR (A Ward of Court)* [1993] ILRM 657.

[120] See *Cullen* v *Cullen* [1962] IR 268.

action). It is only if the parties are in a pre-existing relationship giving rise to rights and duties that one party has, and therefore can promise not to enforce, strict legal rights against the other.[121] Thus, if one cohabitee is, for example, the licensee of the other, then it might be possible to raise a promissory estoppel to prevent the revocation of the licence.

Even if a promissory estoppel claimant managed to negotiate the obstacles of proving an unambiguous representation and showing that there was a pre-existing legal relationship between the parties, it would still be necessary, as under proprietary estoppel, to show that the claimant relied to her detriment on the representation.[122] Thus, the claimant who relies on promissory, rather than proprietary, estoppel seems to take on additional burdens without deriving any benefit from doing so. Why, then, would any claimant wish to rely on promissory estoppel? There seem to be three possible cases where promissory estoppel might have independent significance. They are as follows:

(1) *Where the expectation limb is given a restrictive application.* Although the *probanda* have largely been discredited in all jurisdictions,[123] there is still some danger (at least at a lower court level) that the application of the expectation limb of proprietary estoppel might be restricted by reference to the logically inapplicable *probanda*. If this were to occur, there might be room for promissory estoppel to fill the gap. This is what happened in the early Irish case of *Cullen v Cullen*,[124] where Kenny J failed to recognise the expectation limb of proprietary estoppel but resolved the case on the basis of promissory estoppel.

(2) *Remedial rigidity.* While proprietary estoppel affords the court a discretion as to which remedy to choose, promissory estoppel is only capable of preventing the promisor from going back on his promise. In certain circumstances, the more rigid nature of promissory estoppel in this respect might constitute an advantage from a claimant's point of view. For example, if one has expended £100 in reliance on a promise of an irrevocable licence to live in an expensive house, one would prefer to prevent the owner from withdrawing his promise than to receive the likely remedy of repayment of the £100 under the more flexible proprietary estoppel regime. However, it would appear that a court might simply decline to find a promissory

---

[121] See generally Finn, n 16 *supra*.

[122] There has been a suggestion in the English case law that promissory estoppel does not require that the claimant have acted to her detriment: see *Brikom Investments v Carr* [1979] QB 467, 482–483 per Lord Denning MR. However, in the proprietary estoppel case of *Greasley v Cooke* [1980] 1 WLR 1306, 1311 Lord Denning MR cited his views in *Brikom* and apparently regarded the position in relation to detriment as identical in both promissory and proprietary estoppel. It appears that Lord Denning did not intend to deny the need for detriment (in a wide sense: see text to and following n 66 *supra*) and may simply have intended to suggest that a presumption of detrimental reliance should be raised in certain circumstances (see text to and following n 87 *supra*). Cf. Parkinson, n 1 *supra*, p 245; Hillman, n 105 *supra* (both stressing the need for detriment).

[123] See text following n 14 *supra*.

[124] [1962] IR 268.

estoppel if there were a sufficient disparity between the detriment suffered by a claimant and the benefit which would accrue to the claimant if the estoppel were to operate. Therefore, it seems likely that there would be a fairly narrow range of cases where a claimant might gain an advantage by opting for promissory rather than proprietary estoppel.

(3) *Where proprietary estoppel is technically unavailable.* Finally,[125] one might mention cases where the representation does not relate to an interest in land. The position is not entirely clear but it seems that proprietary estoppel is inapplicable in cases involving other sorts of property.[126] This point could be relevant in rare cases involving a houseboat, caravan or mobile home which constitutes a family home. If a claimant acted to her detriment in the belief that she would be allowed to remain in occupation of this sort of family home, proprietary estoppel would technically be unavailable. Therefore, resort might have to be had to promissory estoppel.

Proprietary estoppel would also be unavailable to a claimant who acted to her detriment on the basis of her partner's general promise of financial security and support. Unfortunately, promissory estoppel would also be unavailable in such circumstances, given that it cannot be used as an independent cause of action (and therefore cannot operate to compel the fulfilment of the promise). It would only be if one accepted the Australian idea of a unified doctrine of estoppel that a positive remedy could be afforded on the basis of a promise which did not concern an interest in specific land.

To conclude, it may be suggested that promissory estoppel has only a very limited independent significance in this area. From the point of view of theoretical coherence, this is to be welcomed. One hopes that, in future cases, the courts will only resort to promissory estoppel in the most exceptional of circumstances.

D. Estoppel Based on the Relationship?

The foregoing discussion of proprietary and promissory estoppel revealed that the requirement of a representation was particularly damaging to the prospects of a claimant in the context of a cohabitation. In view of this, one might ask whether it would be possible to dispense with this troublesome requirement. Could one recognise a version of estoppel which provided a remedy for a claimant who acted to her detriment, not on the basis of a representation by her partner, but on the basis of an expectation generated by the nature of the

---

[125] As a fourth possible situation where promissory estoppel might be relied upon, it is worth mentioning the scenario in *Maharaj v Chand* [1986] AC 898 where (perhaps unnecessarily) the Privy Council opted for promissory estoppel over proprietary estoppel in circumstances where legislation prevented any proprietary dealing with the property in question.

[126] See n 37 *supra* and accompanying text.

relationship between the parties?[127] The idea would be that the expectation generated by the relationship would fulfil all the functions of a representation under standard estoppel principles (e.g. providing an outer limit on the possible relief for the claimant and providing something upon which the claimant can be said to have relied to her detriment).

One could certainly make a case for the development of the sort of doctrine described above and, indeed, something similar has already occurred in New Zealand.[128] However, it may not be enough simply to dispense with the requirement of a representation by the legal owner. Given that many cohabitees will never have directed their minds to the question of separate property ownership, many claims would still be defeated by a requirement that the relationship have generated an *actual* expectation in the mind of the claimant that she would gain an interest in her partner's property. Because of this problem, the New Zealand courts (led by Cooke P) have based their doctrine on the notion of "reasonable expectations". This has allowed them to grant a remedy to a claimant who has acted to her detriment in circumstances where, given the nature of her relationship with her partner, it *would have been* reasonable for her (had she directed her mind to the question) to have expected to share in her partner's property. This so-called "objective" approach is, in theoretical terms, rather distant from the orthodox principles of estoppel. This is evidenced by the fact that, notwithstanding the *dicta* of Richardson J in the leading case of *Gillies* v *Keogh*,[129] estoppel has generally been seen by the New Zealand courts as only one of a number of theoretical impulses behind the "reasonable expectations" doctrine.

Interestingly, in the New Zealand Court of Appeal in the more recent case of *Lankow* v *Rose*,[130] Tipping J restated the reasonable expectations doctrine in terms which departed from Cooke P's "objective" test and required the claimant to have had an actual (and reasonable) expectation that she would share in her partner's property. This tightening of the requirements of the New Zealand doctrine (as well as potentially limiting its practical scope) moves it somewhat closer to traditional estoppel principles.[131] However, even Tipping J's version of the reasonable expectations doctrine seems too broad to be justified under estoppel principles. A central feature of estoppel is, it is submitted, that *the defendant* has led the claimant to act to her detriment.[132] Where a plaintiff

---

[127] Cf. n 54 *supra*.

[128] Developments in New Zealand will be considered in detail in Chapter 9 *infra*.

[129] [1989] 2 NZLR 327, 344–347.

[130] [1995] 1 NZLR 277, 294.

[131] As will be seen in Chapter 9, there are other differences between New Zealand's doctrine and the conventional estoppel doctrine. For example, Tipping J's formulation in *Lankow* [1995] 1 NZLR 277, 294 requires the claimant to have made "a contribution" to the disputed assets, whereas the emphasis in estoppel terms would be on a more generalised concept of "detriment". Note also that, while there is a wide remedial choice open to the court when applying the principles of estoppel, the New Zealand doctrine generally (but not invariably) leads to a constructive trust.

[132] See *K Lokumal & Sons (London) Ltd* v *Lotte Shipping Co Pte (The "August Leonhardt")* [1985] 2 Lloyds Rep 28, 34 where, in the context of a claim based on estoppel by convention, Kerr LJ insisted that "[a]ll estoppels must involve some statement or conduct by the party alleged to be

claims that she has acted to her detriment on the basis of a particular kind of relationship between herself and the defendant, her argument appears to depend more on the relationship than on her having been "led" to act to her detriment. This in turn suggests that, if such a claimant is to be successful, she would have to rely on a doctrine which, like New Zealand's doctrine but unlike estoppel, focuses strongly on the existence of an intimate relationship between the parties.

III. CONCLUSION

It is clear from the preceding discussion that estoppel, in particular proprietary estoppel, has the potential to play a meaningful role in disputes between cohabitees (even if, in many jurisdictions, much of work is presently performed by the "common intention" constructive trust analysis).[133]

Proprietary estoppel will sometimes be capable of providing a remedy in fact-situations which are not covered by the purchase money resulting trust. The most obvious situations where estoppel may apply are (1) where one partner has carried out improvements to the family home and (2) where one partner has made non-monetary sacrifices in the interests of the relationship, e.g. by giving up a secure home to move in with the defendant or by working in the home at the cost of future employment prospects.

Unfortunately, a number of formidable obstacles face an estoppel claimant in the family situation. The most serious problems lie (i) in proving that there was a representation by the defendant (or a mistaken belief on the part of the claimant) that the claimant would be entitled to some interest in the disputed property and (ii) in showing that the claimant's detriment was incurred *in reliance* upon the relevant representation or mistaken belief. In relation to the latter issue, particularly in the context of non-monetary contributions to a relationship, there is a danger that judicial assumptions concerning appropriate gender-roles may reduce the likelihood of success for a female claimant. Even if a claimant does succeed in establishing an estoppel, the remedy may well be less extensive than a trust over the property; possibilities include the granting of monetary compensation or of an indefinite licence to occupy the family home.

Thus, like the resulting trust, estoppel will sometimes be useful in family property disputes. However, also like the resulting trust, estoppel principles have very serious limitations in this context. It is now proposed to move on, in the next chapter, to an examination of the hybrid analysis of the English courts which aims to combine the strengths of both doctrines.

estopped on which the alleged representee was entitled to rely and did rely". See also *Keen* v *Holland* [1984] 1 WLR 251 (CA); *John* v *George* (1995) 71 P & CR 375 (CA).

[133] This analysis, which draws heavily on the principles of estoppel, will be considered in detail in the next chapter.

5

The English Common Intention Trust

INTRODUCTION

This chapter examines the "common intention" analysis which was first set out in the speech of Lord Diplock in *Gissing* v *Gissing*.[1] This "now classic"[2] analysis represents the favoured approach of the English courts to claims arising upon the termination of an unmarried cohabitation.[3] In the quarter of a century since Lord Diplock's speech, English judges have frequently been called upon to "climb again the familiar ground which slopes down from the twin peaks of *Pettitt* v *Pettitt*[4] . . . and *Gissing* v *Gissing*".[5] Despite the familiarity of the territory, many a judicial expedition has come to grief on these "intellectual steeps".[6] The difficulty experienced by judges reflects the unfortunate reality that, as will be argued in this chapter, the convoluted English approach is fundamentally flawed in both theoretical and practical terms. Nevertheless, this approach must be considered at the outset of any comparative survey since it has provided the starting point for developments in each of the other jurisdictions considered in this book[7] (with the exception of Ireland, where the English approach never became established).[8]

---

[1] [1971] AC 886, 903–911.

[2] *Maharaj* v *Chand* [1986] 1 AC 898, 907 per Sir Robin Cooke.

[3] See generally Hayton *Underhill and Hayton: Law Relating to Trusts and Trustees*, 15th edn (London: Butterworths, 1995) pp 374–390; Gray *Elements of Land Law*, 2nd edn (London: Butterworths, 1993) pp 413–449; Miller *Family Property and Financial Provision*, 3rd edn (Croydon: Tolley Publishing, 1993) pp 30–47; Cretney and Masson *Principles of Family Law*, 6th edn (London: Sweet and Maxwell, 1997) pp 132–148.

[4] [1970] AC 777.

[5] *Grant* v *Edwards* [1986] 1 Ch 638, 646 per Nourse LJ.   [6] *Ibid*, 650.

[7] Although the courts of Australia, Canada and New Zealand have developed their own theoretical approaches to this area, they have not completely discarded the common intention analysis. From a theoretical point of view, the contribution of the Australian courts (in particular those of Victoria) seems to have been most significant. The earlier Australian cases are discussed by Dodds "The New Constructive Trust: An Analysis of its Nature and Scope" (1988) 16 *Melbourne University Law Review* 482. The common intention trust appears to have survived the advent of the "unconscionability" doctrine in *Baumgartner* v *Baumgartner* (1987) 164 CLR 137. See e.g. *Green* v *Green* (1989) 17 NSWLR 343. Contrast *Bryson* v *Bryant* (1992) 29 NSWLR 188, 217 per Sheller JA. By comparison with Australia, the Canadian courts turned more quickly and decisively away from the common intention trust after the landmark decision in *Pettkus* v *Becker* (1980) 117 DLR (3d) 257. However, the English analysis still makes occasional appearances in that jurisdiction. See Hovius and Youdan *The Law of Family Property* (Scarborough, Ontario: Carswell Publishing, 1991) pp 108–109. Cf. the decisions of the Supreme Court of Canada in *Murdoch* v *Murdoch* (1974) 41 DLR (3d) 367; *Rathwell* v *Rathwell* [1978] 2 SCR 436. See also *Gough* v *Fraser* [1977] 1 NZLR 279; *Brown* v *Stokes* (1980) 1 NZCPR 209; *Hayward* v *Giordani* [1983] NZLR 140; Atkin *Living Together Without Marriage* (Wellington: Butterworths, 1991) pp 80–94 (New Zealand); Mee "Trusts of the Family Home: The Irish Experience" [1993] Conv 359 (Ireland).

[8] For detailed discussion of the Irish position, see Chapter 3 *supra*.

Part I of this chapter will discuss the practical operation of the English analysis. The discussion will then turn, in Part II, to a detailed consideration of the theoretical foundations of the doctrine. Naturally, however, this division is purely for the purposes of exposition and one must bear in mind that the parameters of the doctrine have been conditioned by the various theoretical impulses which have contributed to its development. At this preliminary stage, therefore, it is necessary briefly to anticipate the discussion in Part II and to give a general impression of the theoretical basis for the common intention trust.

In this regard, the common intention analysis may be compared to one of the imaginary beasts dreamed up by bored medieval minds, a nightmare synthesis of a number of real creatures. The common intention trust derives its component parts from a range of existing equitable doctrines. Estoppel provides the main driving force of the doctrine, in the form of the central concept of "detrimental reliance"; a distorted version of the presumption of resulting trust allows the courts to interpret the claimant's financial contributions as proof of a representation by the defendant upon which the claimant can be said to have relied; and the influence of the doctrine in *Rochefoucauld* v *Boustead*[9] (combined to a lesser extent with a contract-style "bargain" approach) means that the claimant's remedy is not based on the extent of her detriment but rather takes the form of a trust reflecting the "common intention" of the parties. Of course, if one were designing a modern Ark, one would be ill-advised to reserve a berth for the unicorn or the griffin. It is unfortunate that, in a modern taxonomy of equitable doctrines, space must be wasted on the chimerical common intention trust.

Before moving on to discuss the details of the common intention trust, it is necessary to address the issue of terminology. From the outset, uncertainty has surrounded the juridical nature of this trust. Lord Diplock began his explanation of the new doctrine in *Gissing* with the following famous passage:

> "A resulting, implied or constructive trust—and it is unnecessary for present purposes to distinguish between these three classes of trust—is created by a transaction between the trustee and the cestui que trust in connection with the acquisition by the trustee of a legal estate in land, whenever the trustee has so conducted himself that it would be inequitable to allow him to deny to the cestui que trust a beneficial interest in the land acquired. And he will be held to have so conducted himself if by his words or conduct he has induced the cestui que trust to act to his own detriment in the reasonable belief that by so acting he was acquiring a beneficial interest in the land".[10]

It emerges clearly from this passage that Lord Diplock's trust is triggered by detrimental reliance on a common intention. However, it can also be seen that Lord Diplock evaded the issue of categorising this type of trust as either resulting or constructive. His Lordship's vagueness on the terminological issue was reflected in subsequent judgments and academic discussions of the area which

---

[9] [1897] 1 Ch 196.
[10] [1971] AC 886, 905.

tended to refer to the trust as "resulting or constructive". In more recent years, however, an increasing number of judges and commentators[11] have taken courage and begun to identify the trust as constructive in nature.[12]

In discussing nomenclature, one cannot ignore the question of the uncertain theoretical basis for the common intention trust. It has already been suggested (and will be fully argued in Part II *infra*) that the common intention trust contains elements of (at least) three different legal doctrines. If, as is concluded in this chapter, there is no coherent principle underlying the doctrine, it becomes to some extent a matter of taste as to what label one chooses to apply to it. Arguably, reference to the "spurious" or "supposed" common intention trust would convey a more accurate impression than any of the labels "express", "resulting" or "constructive". However, recognising that the "sticks and stones" adage applies with unusual force when one is disparaging an abstract legal construct, one must content oneself with a more orthodox selection. On this basis, and since this seems the least inappropriate label, the trust will be referred to in the present book as constructive in nature.

I. THE OPERATION OF THE COMMON INTENTION TRUST ANALYSIS

In this Part, it is proposed to examine the practical operation of the common intention trust in the English case law. Once this task has been accomplished, it will then be possible to turn, in Part II, to the more difficult task of seeking a theoretical justification for the doctrine.

According to the English courts, there are three steps in the establishment of a common intention constructive trust:

(1)   There must have been a prior common intention between the parties that the ownership of the property in question would be shared.

---

[11] See e.g. *Lloyds Bank plc v Rosset* [1991] 1 AC 107 (HL); *Drake v Whipp* [1996] 1 FLR 826 (noted by Dunn [1997] Conv 467); Lord Justice Nourse "Unconscionability and the Unmarried Couple—Some Recent Developments in the Commonwealth" in *Law Lectures for Practitioners* (Hong Kong: Hong Kong Law Journal, 1991) p 90; Hayton *Underhill and Hayton* n 3 *supra*, p 374.

[12] Some other commentators have favoured classification as a resulting trust. At first glance, this is a tempting option, since Lord Diplock's trust clearly draws upon the traditional purchase money resulting trust doctrine and since it is predicated on the "common intention" of the parties. However, despite the apparent emphasis on intention, a more crucial element appears to be the fact that the claimant has been led to act to her detriment. In any event, it is submitted that classification as a resulting trust is extremely dangerous, since it invites confusion with the (undoubtedly distinct) purchase-money resulting trust. The second major strand in the common intention analysis, the doctrine in *Rochefoucauld v Boustead*, is supportive of a constructive trust classification (although, depending on one's view of the *Rochefoucauld* doctrine, one might also argue that the trust should be classified as express: see n 245 *infra*). Finally, the estoppel component in the doctrine also points in the direction of a constructive trust categorisation since, when a trust is selected as the appropriate remedy for an estoppel claimant, it is generally categorised as constructive in nature (see *Re Basham* [1986] 1 WLR 1498; *Re Sharpe* [1980] 1 WLR 219). Thus, for what it is worth, the label "constructive trust" seems to be suggested by two of the three doctrines which have been muddled together to form the common intention analysis.

(2) The claimant must have acted to her detriment in reliance on that common intention.

(3) The court will then decide that it would be inequitable for the legal owner to deny the claimant the share which was commonly intended for her. A constructive trust will therefore be imposed.

These three steps will now be examined in turn.

A. Finding a Common Intention

The problem of proving the existence of a common intention was considered in detail by Lord Diplock in *Gissing* v *Gissing*.[13] A relevant common intention will often, but not always, have been formed at the time of the original acquisition of the disputed property.[14] It is clear from his speech, and from the later authorities (in particular the decision of the House of Lords in *Lloyds Bank plc* v *Rosset*)[15] that there are two different methods of proving a common intention: (1) by direct evidence of what was said by the parties and (2) by inference from their conduct.

1. Direct evidence

As Lord Diplock pointed out, it is possible that there could have been an express agreement or understanding between the parties as to how the property would be owned.[16] Before reviewing the relevant cases, it is worth mentioning certain prescient remarks of Lord Reid in *Gissing*.[17] Lord Reid criticised Lord Diplock's requirement of an actual common intention on the basis that "a candid and honest" claimant would agree that the question of ownership had never been considered, whereas "a more sophisticated [claimant] who had been told what the law was would probably be able to produce some vague evidence which would enable a sympathetic judge to do justice by finding in her favour".[18] According to Lord Reid, that "would not be a very creditable state in which to leave the

---

[13] [1971] AC 886. Cf. *Pettkus* v *Becker* (1980) 117 DLR (3d) 257, 269 per Dickson J referring to "the judicial quest for [the] fugitive common intention".

[14] It was accepted by Fox LJ in *Burns* v *Burns* [1984] Ch 317, 327 that a common intention could be formed after the date of acquisition. He instanced the possibility of this occurring on "the discharge of a mortgage or the effecting of capital improvements to the house". This view finds support in *Gissing* v *Gissing* [1971] AC 886, 906D–E per Lord Diplock; 901D per Viscount Dilhorne. See also *Lloyds Bank plc* v *Rosset* [1991] 1 AC 107, 132E–F per Lord Bridge; *Austin* v *Keele* (1987) 61 ALJR 605 (PC); *Clough* v *Killey* (1996) 72 P & CR D22; Gray, n 3 *supra*, p 417. Note the contrary view of Fullagar J in *Thwaites* v *Ryan* [1984] VR 65, 92–93.

[15] [1991] 1 AC 107.

[16] [1971] AC 886, 905.

[17] [1971] AC 886.

[18] *Ibid*, 897.

law".[19] As Waite J conceded twenty years later in *Hammond v Mitchell*,[20] the law is now such that "many thousands of pounds of value may be liable to turn on fine questions as to whether the relevant words were spoken in earnest or in dalliance".[21] Although the discussion will now move on to a detailed consideration of the process of proving common intention by direct evidence, one should bear in mind that the course of the case law (and the "vague evidence" which has decided cases) appears to bear out the concerns expressed by Lord Reid in *Gissing*.

The most obvious method of proving an agreement to share the ownership of the family home would be by reference to direct evidence of what the parties said to each other. According to Lord Bridge in *Lloyds Bank plc v Rosset*,[22] "[t]he finding of an agreement or arrangement in this sense can only, I think, be based on evidence of express discussions between the partners, however imperfectly remembered and however imprecise their terms may have been".[23] Of course, in their conversations with each other, the parties are likely to have expressed their intentions at a general level, without specific reference to the ownership of the home. In this respect, it is important to note the strict view of Lord Bridge in *Rosset*[24] that "neither a common intention by spouses that a house is to be renovated as a 'joint venture' nor a common intention that the house is to be shared by parents and children as the family home throws any light on their intentions with respect to the beneficial ownership of the property".[25]

In some cases, direct evidence of the intentions of the parties must be viewed with suspicion. One such case was *Midland Bank plc v Dobson*.[26] The house in question was in the name of the husband. He had used it as security for a loan obtained by a company of which he was a director. The company ran into financial problems and the bank sought to enforce the charge, claiming possession as mortgagee. The wife argued that she was entitled to a share in the house. She testified that she had always believed that the house belonged to them both jointly, observing that "[m]arriage is a partnership".[27] Similarly, her husband swore that they had always had "a principle of sharing everything in their marriage".[28] Fox LJ commented as follows:

---

[19] *Ibid.*
[20] [1991] 1 WLR 1127.
[21] *Ibid*, 1139.
[22] [1991] 1 AC 107.
[23] *Ibid*, 132.
[24] *Ibid*, 130.
[25] By way of contrast, the Australian courts have sometimes been rather generous in extracting a common intention as to ownership from evidence of a more generalised intention. See e.g. *Hohol v Hohol* (1980) 6 Fam LR 49 (Vic Sup Ct); *Brown v Wylie* (1980) 6 Fam LR 519 (NSW Sup Ct); *Smith v Smith* (1984) 9 Fam LR 1014 (SA Sup Ct). See also *Baumgartner v Baumgartner* [1985] 2 NSWLR 406 (NSW CA), reversed on this point by the High Court of Australia (1987) 164 CLR 137.
[26] [1986] 1 FLR 171.
[27] *Ibid*, 174.
[28] *Ibid.*

"I think that assertions made by a husband and wife as to a common intention formed 30 years ago regarding joint ownership, of which there is no contemporary evidence and which happens to accommodate their current need to defeat the claims of a creditor, must be received by the court with caution".[29]

However, if such evidence were to be accepted, it would suffice to establish a common intention. Therefore, the Court of Appeal did not interfere with the ruling of the trial judge that a common intention had existed.[30]

Rather different problems arise in cases where one party has been deceived by the other. On this point, Lord Diplock stated that:

"[T]he relevant intention of each party is the intention which was reasonably understood by the other party to be manifested by that party's words or conduct notwithstanding that he did not consciously formulate that intention in his own mind or even acted with some other intention which he did not communicate to the other party".[31]

Thus, a dishonest defendant cannot resile from an understanding as to ownership which he has led the claimant to believe he shares.

This principle was applied by the Court of Appeal in a number of subsequent cases. In *Eves* v *Eves*,[32] the defendant told the plaintiff that her name could not appear on the title deeds of their house because she was not yet 21 years of age. He admitted in court that this had merely been an excuse to avoid having to put the house into joint names. Brightman J decided that this raised "a clear inference that there was an understanding between them that she was intended to have some sort of proprietary interest in the house: otherwise no excuse would have been needed".[33] Similarly, an excuse made by the legal owner led to the inference of a common intention in *Grant* v *Edwards*.[34]

The approach to this issue in *Eves* and *Grant* has troubled a number of commentators, notably Gardner.[35] Gardner argues that the reasoning is clearly fallacious and doubts whether even the judges concerned really believed in it. It is submitted, however, that Gardner rather overstates the case.[36] His reasoning is as follows:

---

[29] *Ibid*. Cf. *Re Densham* [1975] 1 WLR 1519 (discussing the effect of a common intention trust in a bankruptcy situation).

[30] In fact, the wife's claim in *Dobson* ultimately failed because she had not acted to her detriment on the basis of the common intention.

[31] [1971] AC 886, 906. Cf. *Marcucci* v *Burns* (1984) 9 Fam LR 599, 600–601 per Mahoney JA (NSW CA).

[32] [1975] 1 WLR 1338.

[33] *Ibid*, 1344.

[34] [1986] 1 Ch 638, 649A–B per Nourse LJ; 653D–G per Mustill LJ; 655G–H per Browne-Wilkinson V-C. For analysis of *Grant*, see Montgomery [1987] Conv 16; Eekelaar [1987] Conv 93; Sufrin (1987) 50 MLR 94; Dixon [1988] *Denning Law Journal* 27. See also *Hammond* v *Mitchell* [1991] 1 WLR 1127 (noted by Lawson [1991] Conv 218) and *Drake* v *Whipp* [1996] 1 FLR 826, which are discussed in the text following n 41 *infra*. Cf. *Risch* v *McFee* [1991] 1 FLR 105, 107E–F.

[35] "Rethinking Family Property" (1993) 109 LQR 263, 264–265, 281–282.

[36] Cf. Glover and Todd "The Myth of Common Intention" (1996) 16 *Legal Studies* 325, 331.

"If I give an excuse for rejecting an invitation to what I expect to be a dull party, it does not mean that I thereby agree to come: on the contrary, it means that I do not agree to come, but for one reason or another find it hard to say so outright".[37]

On this basis, he suggests that the men's excuses constituted a "denial of an entitlement"[38] and accuses the judges of "inventing agreements on women's behalf".[39]

The answer to Gardner's argument (which emerges clearly from the relevant passages in *Grant* and *Eves*) lies in the difference between legal and equitable ownership. Gardner does not appear to advert to the possibility that the woman in each case reasonably understood from her partner's representation that, while it was agreed between the parties that (beneficial) ownership was to be shared, there was some technical obstacle which prevented her being given *legal* ownership of the property. This, after all, is the nature of any "common intention" within the terms of the doctrine under discussion; it is understood between the parties that beneficial ownership is (or will be) shared, notwithstanding the fact that this is not reflected in the legal title. To put the point in Gardner's terms: naturally, the guest's excuse will not make the dull hostess believe that he is really coming to the party; however, depending on the nature of the excuse and the manner in which it is made, she might be led to believe other things about her relationship with the guest, for example, that he finds her company delightful.

It is submitted therefore that, while the judges in *Eves* and *Grant* may have taken a generous view of the facts,[40] their reasoning was certainly not "fallacious".[41] In deciding whether it is appropriate to infer the existence of a common intention from the making of an excuse, it appears that a great deal depends on the facts of the case and on the circumstances in which the excuse was made. Consider, for example, *Hammond v Mitchell*,[42] where, upon purchasing a home in his sole name, the defendant "spontaneously" commented that he had to put the home into his sole name due to tax problems he was

---

[37] See n 35 *supra*, 265.

[38] *Ibid*, 265 n 10.

[39] *Ibid*, 265.

[40] It could be argued that it was more likely that the claimant understood, or should reasonably have understood, that her partner's excuse was merely a "softened way of saying 'no'" (Gardner, n 35 *supra*, 282) to her getting any share in the beneficial interest. However, Gardner was clearly trying to establish a wider point, since he categorises the findings in *Eves* and *Grant* as "necessarily false" rather than as "questionably optimistic" (an epithet which he reserves for certain other English cases). See *ibid*, 265 n 10 (contrasting *Hammond v Mitchell* [1991] 1 WLR 1127 and *Stokes v Anderson* [1991] 1 FLR 391 with *Eves* and *Grant*).

[41] The entire question is made rather more difficult by the fact that Lord Diplock's doctrine is said to turn on "common intention", thus suggesting a requirement of a subjective consensus. However, despite the misleading terminology, the doctrine clearly does not require subjective agreement (and this holds true under all of the various possible theoretical explanations for the doctrine discussed *infra* in Part II of this chapter). Cf. *Grant v Edwards* [1986] 1 Ch 638, 653D–G, where Mustill LJ, while reaching the same substantive conclusion as the other judges, balked at classifying the expectation created in the claimant as a "common" intention.

[42] [1991] 1 WLR 1127.

experiencing.[43] It is possible that the claimant interpreted this comment as a representation that she was to have a share in the beneficial ownership. However, on the same day, the defendant had also promised that "when we are married it will be half yours".[44] A marriage never took place but the claimant did not press her partner on this point since "[b]y then . . . she knew her man well enough to be aware that he was not the type to tie himself down".[45] Against this background, it is arguable that the claimant must have realised at an early stage that her partner had no intention of giving her a share in his property before committing himself to marriage.

Hammond may be contrasted with *Drake* v *Whipp*[46] where the claimant had actively pursued the question of having her name put on the title deeds. Her partner had said that he would have this done "in about a month's time" and, when reminded on a number of later occasions, had said he was busy.[47] The Court of Appeal concluded that this evidence (coupled with a very large direct financial contribution by the claimant) demonstrated the existence of a common intention that the beneficial ownership would be shared. There are, of course, a number of important distinctions between *Hammond* and *Drake*. The cases are placed side by side simply to illustrate the point that the overall strength of the claimant's case will impact on the interpretation of their discussions as to whether the claimant's name should appear on the title. There seems to be a world of difference between an isolated and unprovoked comment by the defendant in *Hammond*, which may have attributable simply to embarrassment or nervousness, and the situation in *Drake*, where the claimant had invested £38,000 in the property and was likely to take drastic action upon a direct refusal by her partner to put her name on the title deeds.

Thus far, the discussion has concentrated on "direct" evidence relating to express conversations which have taken place between the parties. But what if both parties testify that they had a certain intention, albeit that they did not express it to each other verbally (although they may perhaps have expressed it in conversations with other people)?[48] The possibility of a real but unexpressed common intention creates interesting theoretical problems. It would appear that Lord Diplock would have been willing to accept such a common intention, since he prefaced his remarks on the process of inference from conduct by referring to the possibility that the parties "may well have formed a common intention . . . without having used express words to communicate this intention to one another".[49]

---

[43] [1991] 1 WLR 1131.
[44] *Ibid.*
[45] *Ibid.*
[46] [1996] 1 FLR 826.
[47] *Ibid*, 829.
[48] Cf. *Stokes* v *Anderson* [1991] 1 FLR 391, 395–396.
[49] [1971] AC 886, 906. See also *Midland Bank plc* v *Dobson* [1986] 1 FLR 171 where the Court of Appeal made no reference to any express communication between the parties of the intention which (according to their evidence) had existed in each of their minds.

A different approach was suggested by the decision of the Court of Appeal in *Springette* v *Defoe*.[50] In that case, Dillon LJ argued that:

"It is not enough to establish a common intention . . . that each of [the parties] happened at the same time to have been thinking on the same lines in his or her uncommunicated thoughts, while neither had any knowledge of the thinking of the other".[51]

The same view was taken by Steyn LJ[52] and Sir Christopher Slade.[53] Thus far, one cannot disagree. The common intention approach is based on the idea that the legal owner has led the claimant to act to her detriment. If the legal owner has, in no sense, communicated to his partner that she is to get a share in the family home, then it is impossible to say that he has led her to act to her detriment.[54]

However, where one might take exception with the approach in *Springette* is with the Court's rejection of the possibility of a common intention being communicated on a non-verbal level. Steyn LJ was dismissive of counsel's argument that the common intention must have been communicated "at a subconscious level", stating curtly that "[o]ur trust law does not allow property rights to be affected by telepathy".[55] However, with respect, this remark trivialises a difficult issue. Is it really so implausible to suggest that, where a couple both believe that ownership of the family home is to be shared, this belief might transmit itself from one partner to the other over a period of years?[56] One is not dealing here with "telepathy" but with the possibility of conventional, albeit subtle, forms of communication between people who know each other intimately: non-verbal cues, assumptions underlying remarks about other matters, things not said which would otherwise have been said.[57] It is submitted that there is no reason in principle why, albeit probably on rare occasions, communication could not be held to have taken place at a non-verbal level.[58] It is worth bearing in

---

[50] [1992] 2 FLR 388.

[51] *Ibid*, 393.

[52] *Ibid*, 395.

[53] *Ibid*, 397.

[54] See also *Savill* v *Goodall* [1993] 1 FLR 755, 760C–D. However, the decision in *Springette* itself appears to have been incorrect. See Chapter 2 *supra*, text following n 37.

[55] [1992] 2 FLR 388, 394.

[56] Given the acceptance in the case law that a common intention may be formed long after the initial acquisition of the property (see n 14 *supra* and accompanying text), it must logically be sufficient if the non-verbal communication of the parties' intentions takes place at any time prior to the claimant's detrimental reliance.

[57] There is also the alternative (very real) possibility that a claimant might not, by the time of a dispute, be able to remember the chance remarks made by the defendant over the years which contributed to her assumption that she would be entitled to share in the beneficial ownership.

[58] In putting forward a contrary position in *Springette* [1992] 2 FLR 388, 393, Dillon LJ relied on Lord Bridge's insistence in *Rosset* [1991] 1 AC 107, 132F that "direct" evidence must relate to "express discussions between the partners". However, Lord Bridge's main concern at this point seems to have been to distinguish between proof of common intention by means, on the one hand, of direct evidence and, on the other hand, of inference from conduct. Arguably, he was not directing his mind to any distinction which might have been drawn between various forms of "direct" evidence.

mind that, as will be argued later in this chapter, any contention to the contrary runs into serious difficulties in cases where the common intention of the parties is inferred from their conduct.[59]

2. *Inference from conduct*

It is also possible for the court to infer the existence of a common intention from the conduct of the parties. It is important, however, to emphasise at this point that (in theory) the court may not resort to fictions. Although the reasoning process is extremely artificial, it is not regarded as permissible to impute to the parties an intention which they never really had. The relevance of conduct is to shed light on what was actually in the minds of the parties at an earlier point in time. Thus, in a case where the court infers the existence of a common intention from the financial contributions of the claimant, the argument is that (as a matter of probability) she would not have made those contributions if there had not been a prior common intention that she would gain a share. One point of uncertainty, to which the discussion will turn in due course, is the precise nature of the "common intention" which is proven by evidence of the subsequent conduct of the parties: must the conduct evidence a common intention which was actually communicated in words or, on the other hand, can one argue that evidence of conduct proves "the tacit or unexpressed existence"[60] of a prior common intention?

In *Gissing*,[61] Lord Diplock prefaced his consideration of the inferences which could be drawn from particular conduct with the reminder that "[e]ach case must depend on its own facts".[62] Lord Diplock, however, went on to offer detailed opinions on the effect of various forms of conduct.[63] The most obvious form of conduct from which one might infer the existence of a common intention is the making of contributions by the claimant to the acquisition of the house. At this point, Lord Diplock's analysis begins to trespass on the territory of the purchase money resulting trust. Lord Diplock attempted to subsume that doctrine within his wider framework. He felt that the presumption of resulting trust would apply, in the absence of evidence, where the claimant had contributed directly to an outright purchase (made without the aid of a mortgage) or towards the deposit and legal costs where the purchase involved a mortgage.[64] Thus, the presumption of resulting trust would only apply in a rather limited set of circumstances.

[59] See text following n 98 *infra*.

[60] See *Rosset* [1991] 1 AC 107, 110–111.

[61] [1971] AC 886.

[62] *Ibid*, 907. See also *ibid*, 901B per Viscount Dilhorne.

[63] The approach of Lord Diplock in *Gissing* appears difficult to reconcile with his concession in *Pettitt v Pettitt* [1970] AC 777, 822, that in "most of [the cases] which come before the courts, the true inference from the evidence is that [the parties] . . . formed no common intention as to their proprietary rights in the family asset".

[64] [1971] AC 886, 907B–C. It seems to be only in this limited area that the presumption of advancement would play whatever part it could still have in the modern law. See Lord Diplock's comments *ibid*, 907C–D.

Outside these situations, Lord Diplock felt that a more flexible approach would prevail. If there had been an initial contribution to the deposit and legal charges and the claimant had also contributed substantially, whether directly or indirectly, to the mortgage repayments, the likely inference would be that these later contributions were intended to have some effect on the claimant's share. Even if there had been no initial contribution, it might be reasonable to infer that there was a common intention that she should have a share if she made a "regular and substantial direct contribution to the mortgage instalments".[65]

However, unlike direct contributions to the mortgage repayments, Lord Diplock felt that indirect contributions would not normally suffice in themselves to prove a common intention. The only exception would be a case where there had been an adjustment to the contribution to household expenses "which it can be inferred was referable to the acquisition of the house".[66] An example of the sort of adjustment envisaged by Lord Diplock appears to be a case where, upon the purchase of the house, a claimant who had previously worked part-time went into full-time employment in order to relieve the pressure on her partner's finances.[67] In the absence of this sort of adjustment, and of any initial contribution to the purchase, Lord Diplock felt that there was "no material to justify the court in inferring that it was the common intention of the parties that [the claimant] should have any beneficial interest [in the home], merely because she continued to contribute out of her own earnings or private income to other expenses of the household".[68]

Lord Diplock did not directly address the question of whether the conduct of the claimant in working in the home and caring for the children of the relationship could carry evidential weight in the establishment of a common intention that she should have a share in the house. However, given his attitude to indirect financial contributions, it is clear that he would not have been willing to infer a common intention from such conduct. A similar attitude was taken in the later case of *Burns* v *Burns*[69] where Fox LJ observed that:

> "[T]hose facts do not carry with them any implication of a common intention that the plaintiff should have an interest in the house. Taken by themselves they are simply not strong enough to bear such an implication".[70]

Similarly, it would appear that the courts have been unwilling to infer the existence of a common intention to share ownership simply from the making of improvements to the disputed property.[71]

---

[65] *Ibid*, 908.

[66] *Ibid*, 909.

[67] Cf. the facts of *Hargrave* v *Newton* [1971] 1 WLR 1611 and *Hazell* v *Hazell* [1972] 1 WLR 301. Contrast *Allen* v *Allen* [1961] 1 WLR 1186, 1192 per Lord Evershed MR.

[68] [1971] AC 886, 909.

[69] [1984] Ch 317.

[70] *Ibid*, 327–328.

[71] See *Thomas* v *Fuller-Brown* [1988] 1 FLR 237.

In *Lloyds Bank plc* v *Rosset*,[72] the House of Lords had its first opportunity since *Gissing* to comment on the question of inferring a common intention from conduct. With the concurrence of the other Lords, Lord Bridge commented that:

> "[D]irect contributions to the purchase price by the partner who is not the legal owner, whether initially or by payment of mortgage instalments, will readily justify the inference necessary to the creation of a constructive trust. But, as I read the authorities, it is at least extremely doubtful whether anything less will do".[73]

Lord Bridge's approach was more severe than that indicated by a number of previous Court of Appeal decisions. In a number of cases in the 1970s, the Court of Appeal (presided over by Lord Denning MR) had preferred the approach of Lord Reid in *Gissing* to that of Lord Diplock and had held, in effect, that substantial indirect contributions could give rise to a resulting trust.[74] In the later case of *Burns* v *Burns*,[75] Fox LJ (again appearing to be influenced by resulting trust principles) took the view that a common intention could be inferred from indirect contributions which were "referable to the acquisition"[76] of the disputed property. Significantly, this test departs from the approach of Lord Diplock in *Gissing*, where his Lordship referred to the possibility of an "*adjustment* to her contribution to other expenses of the household which it can be inferred was referable to the acquisition of the house".[77] The other judge in *Burns* to express a view, May LJ, simply summarised Lord Diplock's analysis in *Gissing* and only stated a willingness to take account of indirect contributions which were associated with a contribution to the initial deposit.[78] The uncertainty in *Burns* v *Burns*[79] was mirrored in *Grant* v *Edwards*,[80] where Nourse LJ[81] reiterated the "referability" test of Fox LJ in *Burns* but Mustill LJ, without expressing a concluded view, opined that of themselves indirect contributions could not justify the inference of a common intention.[82]

---

[72] [1991] 1 AC 107. For discussion, see Davies (1990) 106 LQR 539; Thompson [1990] Conv 314; Gardner (1991) 54 MLR 126; O'Hagan (1991) 42 NILQ 238. The severity of the approach of the Lords in *Rosset* might be partly explicable on the basis that the claim in that case was a particularly weak one. According to Lord Bridge, it was based on improvements whose monetary value in comparison to the cost of acquiring the property was "so trifling as to be almost de minimus". See [1991] 1 AC 107, 131.

[73] *Ibid*, 133.

[74] See *Falconer* v *Falconer* [1970] 1 WLR 1333; *Davis* v *Vale* [1971] 1 WLR 1022; *Hargrave* v *Newton* [1971] 1 WLR 1611; *Hazell* v *Hazell* [1972] 1 WLR 301; *Cooke* v *Head* [1972] 1 WLR 518. Cf. *Kowalczuk* v *Kowalczuk* [1973] 1 WLR 930.

[75] [1984] Ch 317.

[76] *Ibid*, 328. Note Lord Denning MR's objection to this expression in *Hargrave* v *Newton* [1971] 1 WLR 1611, 1613 and *Hazell* v *Hazell* [1972] 1 WLR 301, 304.

[77] [1971] AC 886, 909 (emphasis supplied). Cf. *Richards* v *Dove* [1974] 1 All ER 888, 894H–J.

[78] [1984] Ch 317, 344–345.

[79] [1984] Ch 317.

[80] [1986] 1 Ch 638.

[81] *Ibid*, 647B.

[82] *Ibid*, 653A–B. No view clearly emerges from the judgment of Browne-Wilkinson V-C, although his close adherence to the speech of Lord Diplock might suggest that he would not have been willing to infer a common intention simply from the making of indirect contributions.

The preceding survey of the case law shows that the position before *Rosset* was anything but clear. In view of this, it is perhaps rather surprising that Lord Bridge felt able to conclude that it was "at least extremely doubtful" that indirect contributions could be taken into account. Presumably, his Lordship took the view that Lord Diplock's approach in *Gissing* was more authoritative than the later opinions expressed in some Court of Appeal cases. Although it is rather unsatisfactory to have the law determined by a passing comment, unsupported by a detailed review of the cases, it seems likely that Lord Bridge's view will dictate the course of future cases.[83]

Thus, to summarise, the English courts seem to have arrived at what Gardner refers to as a "bright-line" test:[84] in general, a common intention may be inferred from direct contributions to the purchase price or to the repayment of a mortgage; other contributions will not suffice. Having outlined the legal position in uncritical terms, it is now necessary to take a more analytical look at the whole process of inferring common intention from conduct. This task will be undertaken in the following sub-sections.

(a) Confusion with the purchase money resulting trust

One of the most audacious aspects of Lord Diplock's speech in *Gissing* was the manner in which he press-ganged the presumption of resulting trust into the service of his "common intention" analysis. It is, of course, well-established that the presumption of resulting trust may be triggered by the making of a financial contribution to the purchase price of property. However, what is being presumed in this situation is a unilateral intention on the part of the contributor to gain a share in the beneficial interest (proportionate to her contribution). It had not been suggested before *Gissing* that the fact of the claimant's contribution to the purchase price justifies an inference that the legal owner of the property had *led her to believe* that she would gain a share in the beneficial interest (which, moreover, is not necessarily proportionate to her contribution).[85] In fact, if there is no additional evidence besides the making of the contribution, there is nothing to disprove the suggestion that the claimant acted on the basis of a self-generated assumption for which the legal owner cannot be held responsible. It is submitted that Lord Diplock was simply wrong to suggest that the claimant's making of a direct financial contribution to the purchase price justifies the raising of a presumption that she was led to act to her detriment. If one accepts this criticism, it is not appropriate to ask the familiar question as to why a common intention cannot be inferred from other conduct such as the making of indirect contributions to the purchase price. The real question is why the courts persist in pretending that "direct" contributions are enough in themselves.

---

[83] See *Ivin v Blake* [1995] 1 FLR 70, 83 (following *Rosset*, indirect contribution through unpaid work in family business insufficient to show common intention). Cf. text following n 153 *infra*.

[84] See n 72 *supra*, 128.

[85] See Section A(4) of this Part *infra* for discussion of the question of "quantifying" the share which was commonly intended by the parties.

The damage created by Lord Diplock's misappropriation of the presumption of resulting trust has been increased by the fact that the House of Lords did not speak with one voice in *Gissing*. Lord Diplock's speech in *Gissing* was, of course, the starting point for the common intention trust. In the same case, Viscount Dilhorne seems clearly to have supported this analysis, although he did not elaborate upon it in great detail. However, Lord Pearson referred back to the speech of Lord Upjohn in *Pettitt* v *Pettitt*[86] and was apparently still thinking in terms of resulting trust principles. Lord Reid, although his speech shows some sensitivity to Lord Diplock's approach, spoke primarily from a resulting trust perspective and was, in any case, putting forward a minority position. Lord Morris, in a very short speech, basically relied on the views he had expressed in *Pettitt*. Against this background, it was all too easy for judges in subsequent cases to create confusion by trying to reconcile Lord Diplock's complex approach (involving some elements of the resulting trust doctrine) with the more straightforward resulting trust approach of Lord Pearson in *Gissing* (and of Lords Morris, Upjohn and Hodson in *Pettitt*).[87]

One specific problem caused by the influence of resulting trust principles on the question of inferring a common intention from conduct has been a tendency to think in terms of a number of discrete categories of conduct (e.g. direct contributions to the purchase price; direct contributions to a mortgage; indirect contributions to a mortgage; the making of improvements; work in the home etc). If one were applying an expanded version of the resulting trust doctrine, it would be sensible to look at each category of conduct and decide whether, in principle, such conduct could constitute a "contribution" to the purchase price. However, if one takes Lord Diplock's analysis seriously, one must concede that it is impossible to develop any fixed rule as to the significance of a certain category of conduct in the process of inferring a common intention. Thus, while a common intention might not normally be inferred from the making of improvements, it could well be sufficient if the claimant had financed the construction of a valuable house on an undeveloped site of comparatively little value. Similarly, it would not seem helpful to give the same treatment to all cases involving "indirect contributions"; a case where a claimant was paying all the legal owner's

---

[86] [1970] AC 777.

[87] See in particular *Burns* v *Burns* [1984] Ch 317. See further the decisions of Lord Denning MR's Court of Appeal cited in n 74 *supra*. Note also that, in briefly discussing the question of inference from conduct in *Lloyds Bank plc* v *Rosset* [1991] 1 AC 107, 133, Lord Bridge commented that the relevant law was set out in the House of Lords' decisions in *Pettitt* and *Gissing*, as "very helpfully analysed" in the judgment of Lord MacDermott LCJ in *McFarlane* v *McFarlane* [1972] NI 59 (NI CA). However, with all due respect, there is no point in pretending that the speeches in *Pettitt* are of any real assistance in determining how to apply the common intention analysis. That analysis was at the time of *Pettitt* only a frustrated glint in the eye of Lord Diplock (whose radically different "imputed common intention" approach had just been rejected by the other Law Lords). Moreover, when considering *Gissing*, it is pointless to look beyond the speech of Lord Diplock (and possibly that of Viscount Dilhorne). It was strange that Lord Bridge described as "helpful" Lord MacDermott LCJ's analysis in *McFarlane supra* given that it gave no attention to the speech of Lord Diplock in *Gissing*, concentrating instead on the conflicting views of Lord Reid and Lord Pearson in that case.

bills except for the mortgage might well merit more favourable treatment than a case where she was merely paying her fair share of expenses (and making a reasonable contribution for her accommodation).

This argument also cuts the other way. The influence of the resulting trust has meant that minor contributions, which technically qualify as "direct" contributions, tend to be treated as giving rise to an automatic inference of common intention. A prime example is the case of *Midland Bank plc v Cooke*,[88] where, as a wedding present, the husband's parents had put £1,100 towards the deposit on a house which was conveyed into the sole name of the husband. Waite LJ concluded that the wedding present had belonged to the couple equally and therefore that the claimant wife had made a contribution of £550 to the purchase of the home (representing less than 7 per cent of the total cost). This direct financial contribution formed the basis of the Court of Appeal's inference of a common intention to share the ownership of the home (ultimately leading to a one-half share for the wife in the beneficial interest). However, putting to one side any question of a "presumption" of common intention, it seems overly generous to infer a common intention from the fact that the wife's share of the wedding present constituted a "contribution" towards the purchase price. The fact that the couple received this particular gift does not change the inherent likelihood that, while the both spouses expected to enjoy the use of the home, they put the ownership into the husband's name because they never contemplated a time when their separate property rights would become important.

The purpose of this section has been to show that the English courts, in purporting to infer the existence of a common intention from the conduct of the claimant, have not always been careful to distinguish the common intention analysis from a simple resulting trust approach. The point has not been to suggest that there is anything inherently inferior in explaining one portion of the common intention doctrine on the basis of resulting trust principles (and resorting to pure estoppel principles to explain cases where there is direct evidence that the claimant was led to act to her detriment). Such an approach is an important theoretical option and, as such, will be given detailed consideration in Part II of this chapter.[89] The problem with the English case law is that there has been no clear recognition of the distinction between this "partitioned" version of the common intention trust and the unitary model put forward by Lord Diplock in *Gissing*. This in turn, has prevented a clear choice being made in favour of either theoretical option.

(b) What precisely is being inferred from conduct?

The next question to consider is the nature of the "common intention" which is being inferred from the conduct of the parties. This fundamental question

---

[88] [1995] 4 All ER 562. See Oldham (1996) 55 CLJ 194; Wragg [1996] *Fam Law* 298; Pawlowski [1996] *Fam Law* 484; Gardner (1996) 112 LQR 378; O'Hagan (1997) 60 MLR 420; Dixon [1997] Conv 66.
[89] See Part II(B)(5) *infra*.

should not be difficult to answer. Within Lord Diplock's theoretical framework, it is clear that the nature of the common intention being proved is precisely the same whatever the nature of the evidence available to the court. This emerges clearly from Lord Diplock's speech in *Gissing* where, having explained the significance of an express common intention, his Lordship went on to note the possibility that the parties "may well have formed a common intention . . . without having used express words to communicate this intention to one another; or their recollections of the words used may be imperfect or conflicting by the time any dispute arises".[90] Lord Diplock believed that "in such a case . . . it may be possible to infer their common intention from their conduct".[91] This passage shows that there is no rigid distinction between an express and an inferred common intention. Thus, for example, if there was a conflict of evidence between the spouses as to whether a common intention had been expressly communicated between them, the court might look to the financial contributions of the claimant to help assess the plausibility of her account of their conversations.[92]

It seems, then, that both types of common intention, "express" and "inferred", partake of the same essential nature. This precludes any suggestion that one could, on the basis of the conduct of the parties, "impute" to them a common intention which was not really in their minds. As has been discussed in an earlier chapter, the House of Lords held in both *Pettitt* and *Gissing* that it was not permissible to operate on the basis of a fictional "imputed" agreement or intention.[93] It follows from this, as Lord Reid went to the trouble of pointing out in *Gissing*, that "[i]f the evidence shows that there was no agreement in fact then that excludes any inference that there was an agreement".[94]

Although the above point is reasonably obvious, it is in danger of being obscured by a tendency to reify the process of inferring common intention from the making of direct financial contributions. A clear example of this is provided by *Midland Bank plc v Cooke*.[95] In this case, as has already been mentioned, the wife was regarded as having made a direct financial contribution to the purchase of the home. Such a contribution was seen by the Court of Appeal as supporting an inference that she and her husband must have had a common intention to share the ownership of the house. However, *both* parties expressly testified in court that they had never had any discussion as to the ownership of the house and had never reached any agreement on the question. The spouses had been

---

[90] [1971] AC 886, 906.

[91] *Ibid.*

[92] See also *Grant v Edwards* [1986] 1 Ch 638, 655B per Browne-Wilkinson V-C. In *Grant ibid*, 655H Browne-Wilkinson V-C felt that the direct evidence was sufficient to establish a common intention but that this was, in any case, "wholly consistent with the contributions made by the plaintiff to the joint household expenses" and with the fact that certain funds, left over after the proceeds of a fire insurance policy had been applied to repairing the house, were lodged to a joint account.

[93] See Chapter 1 *supra*, text following n 59.

[94] [1971] AC 886, 897. See also *ibid*, 897D. A similar point was made by Viscount Dilhorne *ibid*, 900E–F.

[95] [1995] 4 All ER 562.

"just happy, I suppose, you know".[96] This should, of course, have been fatal to the wife's claim under the common intention analysis.[97] The evidence of the wife's contributions suggested that a certain inference of fact was a plausible one; however, the express evidence of the parties made it clear that this inference was unsustainable and that there had never been a common intention. With all due respect, the approach of Waite LJ was clearly indefensible. He does not even appear to have espoused the logically coherent (albeit thoroughly discredited) "imputed" common intention approach. Instead, he suggested that if (and only if) there is some circumstantial evidence suggestive of the existence of a common intention, then the court is entitled to disregard other decisive evidence to the contrary and "presume" the existence of a common intention in the minds of parties who "have been honest enough to admit that they never gave ownership a thought".[98]

Although the approach of Waite LJ has just been criticised, it is important to realise that it is only one degree less defensible than the approach dictated by the orthodox common intention analysis. This point can only be appreciated if one looks more closely at what the courts regard themselves as "inferring" from the conduct of the claimant. Consider a case where the claimant relies on her direct contributions towards the repayment of a mortgage. This evidence of her conduct will allow the court to infer that it is likely that the parties had a common intention. However, if she is cross-examined, is it necessary for her to claim that the common intention was made express in some discussion which took place between her and her partner at some specific time? It would appear that the answer must be negative (notwithstanding the contrary view of Steyn LJ in *Springette* v *Defoe*);[99] such a requirement would have the drastic consequence of depriving the category of "inference from conduct" of any independent significance, so that evidence of conduct would be relevant only to corroborate an assertion that a common intention had been expressed directly. If, then, the claimant is not required to argue that specific express discussions have taken place, and if (as has been argued above in relation to *Cooke*) it is fatal if she concedes that she never gave a thought to ownership, then, by a process of elimination, it appears that the claimant will generally be arguing that it was tacitly understood between her and her partner that she was to get a share.

[96] *Ibid*, 568.

[97] Cf. the similar criticism advanced by Dixon, n 88 *supra*, 71. It is not entirely clear whether a claim to a traditional purchase money resulting trust would be defeated if the claimant admitted that she had never given a thought to ownership. For discussion of the point, see Chapter 2 *supra*, n 58.

[98] [1995] 4 All ER 562, 575. Note Waite LJ's substitution of the word "presumed" for the more obviously unacceptable term "imputed". Of course, the use of the word "presumed" suggests that the confusion with the doctrine of resulting trusts had a role to play in the erroneous approach in *Cooke*.

[99] [1992] 2 FLR 388, 395B–D. (For detailed discussion of *Springette*, see text to nn 50–59 *supra*). There is no trace of support for Steyn LJ's view either in the speech of Lord Diplock in *Gissing* or of Lord Bridge in *Rosset*. Cf. the view of Browne-Wilkinson V-C in *Grant* v *Edwards* [1986] 1 Ch 638, 655B that evidence of contributions could be relevant *inter alia* to corroborate direct evidence *or* "in the absence of direct evidence of intention, as evidence from which the parties' intentions can be inferred".

Thus, it appears that one is reduced to a reliance on non-verbal communication between the parties. However, it is difficult to see how such communication *by the defendant* could be proven merely from evidence of the conduct of the claimant. In *Springette v Defoe*,[100] there was the unusual factor that the female partner admitted that she had always regarded her partner as equally entitled to the home; this made it (just about) arguable that her belief might have transmitted itself to her partner without any express discussion.[101] If, however, a defendant testifies that he always regarded the home as his own, it is difficult to see how it can convincingly be contended that (without his having made some sort of express excuse) he transmitted the opposite view to his partner at a non-verbal level.

The preceding discussion leads one to the conclusion that it is impossible to defend the willingness, on a virtually automatic basis, to infer a common intention simply from the claimant's having made a direct financial contribution. The implausibility of the argument within the terms of Lord Diplock's analysis suggests that, in fact, the English courts have not troubled to examine closely the nature of the common intention which they purport to infer from the conduct of the claimant. It seems likely that, by virtue of a vague appeal to the principles of the resulting trust, they regard the "common intention" inferred from conduct as being somehow essentially different from the "common intention" which is proven by evidence of express discussion between the parties. However, it is obviously unsatisfactory for the English courts to give lip-service to the unified common intention model of Lord Diplock, while reserving the option in difficult cases of retreating into a simple (Irish-style) model based on an extended version of the resulting trust. This latter theoretical option has the major problems which were identified in Chapter 3, while Lord Diplock's model has the (perhaps even greater) theoretical problems which have been pointed out in this and other sections of this chapter. Wriggling back and forth between the two options does not constitute an improvement on a clear adherence to either position.

3. *Is there a requirement of reciprocity?*

This section considers the question of whether a common intention must include an express or implicit understanding that the claimant will provide some *quid pro quo* for the beneficial interest which she is intended to acquire. Lord Diplock appeared to believe so in *Gissing*,[102] suggesting that, to lead to a trust, an agreement must require the claimant to "do something to facilitate [the] acquisition".[103] In *Eves v Eves*,[104] this requirement was taken seriously by

---

[100] [1992] 2 FLR 388.
[101] See text following n 54 *supra*.
[102] [1971] AC 886.
[103] *Ibid*, 905.
[104] [1975] 1 WLR 1338.

Brightman J, who held that it was satisfied on the facts of that case.[105] Later, in *Grant* v *Edwards*,[106] Mustill LJ also considered the possibility of a requirement of reciprocity but expressed no concluded view on the issue. The other two judges in *Grant*, Browne-Wilkinson V-C and Nourse LJ, appear to have made no requirement of reciprocity.

The point arose again at Court of Appeal level in *Lloyds Bank Ltd* v *Rosset*.[107] Nicholls LJ concluded that:

> "[There is] no reason in principle why, if the parties' common intention is that the wife should have a beneficial interest in the property, and if thereafter to the knowledge of the husband she acts to her detriment in reliance on that common intention, the wife should not be able to assert an equitable interest against the husband just as much as she could in a case where the common intention was that, by acting in a certain way, she would acquire a beneficial interest".[108]

The decision of the Court of Appeal was subsequently reversed by the House of Lords.[109] However, although he did not directly address the point, it appears that Lord Bridge accepted Nicholls LJ's view that there was no requirement of reciprocity.[110]

The question of reciprocity is normally discussed in the context of cases where the common intention has been inferred from direct evidence. However, if indeed a requirement of reciprocity existed, it would presumably also apply in cases where the common intention had to be inferred from the conduct of the parties. It is possible that Lord Diplock simply assumed that an element of reciprocity would automatically form part of a common intention inferred in such circumstances. However, such an assumption is questionable. It is already stretching credibility to infer from the financial contributions of the claimant that she was led to believe that she would gain a share in the ownership of the home; it might be too much to expect the court to infer, in addition, that the common intention envisaged that the claimant's share was to be earned by her contributions.

On balance, one may conclude that the English courts have dropped Lord Diplock's requirement in *Gissing* that a common intention must envisage reciprocal obligations.[111] At a later stage in this chapter, an attempt will be made to identify the significance in doctrinal terms of a requirement of reciprocity. It will

---

[105] *Ibid*, 1345.

[106] [1986] 1 Ch 638, 653.

[107] [1989] 1 FLR 51. Note also *Austin* v *Keele* (1987) 61 ALJR 605, 610 (PC) per Lord Oliver (supporting a reciprocity requirement).

[108] *Ibid*, 66.

[109] [1991] 1 AC 107.

[110] See *ibid*, 132 where Lord Bridge discussed the possibility that there might have been an "agreement, arrangement or understanding reached between [the parties] that the property is to be shared beneficially". Lord Bridge did not mention any requirement of reciprocal obligations at this point nor at a later point in his speech (*ibid*) when he briefly stated the requirement that the claimant must have "acted to his or her detriment or significantly altered his or her position in reliance on the agreement".

[111] Cf. Gardner, n 35 *supra*, 266 n 12.

be suggested at that point that the discarding of this requirement, although desirable in practical terms, may have further undermined the theoretical plausibility of the common intention analysis.[112]

4. *What shares were commonly intended?*

Having established a common intention that the claimant should get *some* share, the next stage is to attempt to quantify the share which had been intended for the claimant. Logically, this inquiry forms part of the process of determining the common intention of the parties and is therefore considered at this point. However, it should be borne in mind that, once the claimant has acted to her detriment on the basis of the common intention, the remedy in her favour generally takes the form of a trust reflecting the shares commonly intended. Therefore, a conclusion as to the shares which were commonly intended generally determines the extent of the remedy awarded to the claimant. Notwithstanding this, it is dangerous to collapse the two separate inquiries into one. Doing so conceals certain important questions, for example, the question of whether the remedy should reflect the common intention in cases where the detrimental reliance appears insufficient to justify this. Such questions will be considered in a later section of this chapter.[113]

The discussion, then, will concentrate for the moment on the question of determining the details of the parties' common intention. Once again, different problems arise depending on whether the common intention was proven on the basis of direct evidence or inferred from the conduct of the parties. It will be convenient to consider the two situations separately.

(a) Cases where common intention proven by direct evidence

In some cases where the common intention has been proven by direct evidence, the parties will have made explicit the precise shares which were commonly intended. Whilst in theory any division could be commonly intended, it is most likely that the parties will have indicated an intention to share the property equally.[114] This is consistent with the assumption of partnership and equality underlying many matrimonial and quasi-matrimonial relationships.[115]

It is also possible that, although a general common intention to share has been proven on the basis of direct evidence, it will be necessary to spell out its details by implication from all the relevant circumstances. In *Grant v Edwards*,[116] the common intention had been inferred from the fact that the legal owner had told the claimant that her name should not appear on the title to the property

---

[112] See Part II(B)(3) *infra*, discussing the "bargain model" as a possible rationale for the common intention trust.

[113] See Section C of this Part *infra*.

[114] See for example *Midland Bank plc v Dobson* [1986] 1 FLR 171; *Clough v Killey* (1996) 72 P & CR D22. Cf. *Savill v Goodall* [1993] 1 FLR 755.

[115] Cf. *Gissing* [1971] AC 886, 909A–B per Lord Diplock.

[116] [1986] 1 Ch 638.

because this might prejudice her upcoming divorce proceedings. This gave some indication that the common intention was in favour of equal ownership[117] and this was reinforced by the extent of the claimant's indirect contributions and the fact that the defendant had credited to a joint account the sum of £1,037 which represented the surplus of money paid under a fire insurance policy covering the house. On this basis, the claimant in *Grant* was held to be entitled to a 50 per cent share in the ownership of the house in question.[118]

(b) Cases where common intention proven by inference from the conduct of the parties

Difficult problems of quantification arise where the common intention has been proven by inference from the conduct of the parties. In a case where the inference has been drawn from the making of financial contributions, it is not readily apparent how one is to determine the extent of the shares commonly intended. Lord Diplock gave this question detailed consideration in *Gissing*,[119] suggesting a number of alternative solutions.

He began by stating the view that, in a case where the evidence indicated the existence of a common intention to share, a claim to a trust would not be defeated "merely because . . . there had been no express agreement as to how [the claimant's share] . . . was to be quantified".[120] The court would have to do its best to discover what was the "probable common understanding" about the amount of the claimant's share, even if "that understanding was never expressly stated by one spouse to the other or even consciously formulated in words by either of them independently".[121] It was only if no inference could be drawn as to the probable common intention that the court would be "driven to apply as a rule of law, and not as an inference of fact, the maxim 'equality is equity', and to hold that the beneficial interest belongs to the spouses in equal shares".[122]

---

[117] *Ibid*, 658 per Browne-Wilkinson V-C. This point was not, however, seen as conclusive in itself by Browne-Wilkinson V-C or by Nourse LJ in *Grant* (nor was it mentioned by Waite J in *Hammond* v *Mitchell* [1991] 1 WLR 1127). This may reveal an awareness by the judges concerned of a risk of inconsistency. It is, of course, tempting to suggest that an intention to share equally should be inferred where the claimant was led to believe that her name was omitted from the title deeds only for some technical reason. However, in cases where the property actually *was* taken in joint names, this is generally regarded as proving no more than that the claimant was intended to get *some* beneficial interest. See e.g. *Walker* v *Hall* [1984] FLR 126, 133D per Dillon LJ; *Burns* v *Burns* [1984] Ch 317, 344D per May LJ; *Huntingford* v *Hobbs* [1993] 1 FCR 45, 53E per Sir Christopher Slade. Note, however, *Savill* v *Goodall* [1993] 1 FLR 755, where the evidence showed that the property had been put into joint names in order to give the claimant a feeling of security. Nourse LJ declared (*ibid*, 760G) that "[i]f an ordinary, sensible couple, without more, declare an intention to own their home jointly, they can only be taken to intend that they shall own it equally".

[118] In some cases, it will not be possible to come to any conclusion as to the precise shares which were commonly intended by the parties. For discussion of the remedy appropriate in such cases, see Section C(2) of this Part *infra*.

[119] [1971] AC 886, 908E–909E.

[120] *Ibid*, 908.

[121] *Ibid*.

[122] *Ibid*. In fact, it would appear that such an application of the maxim "equality is equity" would take place at a later stage in the inquiry, that dealing with the remedy which should be afforded to

Lord Diplock then turned to discuss the inferences of fact which might follow in various situations. He first canvassed the possibility that a couple might intend at the time of acquisition "that the beneficial interest should be held by them in equal shares and that each should contribute to the cost of its acquisition whatever amounts each could afford in the varying exigencies of family life to be expected during the period of repayment".[123] Lord Diplock felt that such an inference might be drawn in a case where the relatively smaller size of the claimant's contribution was explicable on the basis of "a reduction of her earnings due to motherhood or some other cause from which the [defendant] benefits as well".[124] His Lordship explained that if the claimant made a smaller contribution for some other (less mutually beneficial) reason, then this might make it more probable that a lesser share was intended for her.

He continued as follows:

"And there is nothing inherently improbable in their acting on the understanding that the wife should be entitled to a share which was not to be quantified immediately upon the acquisition of the home but should be left to be determined when the mortgage was repaid or the property disposed of, on the basis of what would be fair having regard to the total contributions, direct or indirect, which each spouse had made by that date".[125]

Lord Diplock felt that, if this was the most likely inference from the conduct of the parties, "it would be for the court to give effect to that common intention of the parties by determining what in all the circumstances was a fair share".[126]

Of all the possibilities considered by Lord Diplock, the final one seems the most artificial, a fact emphasised by the half-heartedness with which it was advanced by Lord Diplock ("nothing inherently improbable"). It is difficult to imagine that many couples, starting out in life together, would decide that the ownership of their home should depend upon a mechanical calculation of their future financial contributions. This inference of fact would seem more plausible outside the main run of cases, e.g. in family situations involving more than two contributors[127] or in a quasi-commercial context.[128]

the claimant. For this reason, full discussion of the point is postponed until that later stage is analysed. See text following n 184 *infra*.

[123] *Ibid*, 909.

[124] *Ibid*.

[125] *Ibid*.

[126] *Ibid*.

[127] See e.g. *Passee* v *Passee* [1988] 1 FLR 263, noted by Warburton [1988] Conv 361.

[128] Cf. *Bloch* v *Bloch* (1981) 37 ALR 55 (High Ct of Australia). Note also *Stokes* v *Anderson* [1991] 1 FLR 391, 395–396, where the claimant had given £5,000 to the defendant to help him buy out his former wife's interest in the family home. The defendant explained to a family friend that the claimant was "only indirectly buying" the former wife's share and that a later payment of £7,000 had the effect of "increasing her stake" in the disputed property. See also *Drake* v *Whipp* [1996] 1 FLR 826, 829D. This kind of situation does not fully correspond to that postulated by Lord Diplock because the parties do not envisage ongoing contributions and a future valuation on the basis of the total contributions of both parties; rather the claimant, on one or more particular occasions, injects money into the disputed property in a way which is seen as generating an immediate (albeit imprecisely quantified) beneficial interest for the contributor.

However, despite the implausibility of this particular inference of fact, the view appears to have become established following *Gissing* that, where the common intention was inferred only from the making of financial contributions, the shares would necessarily depend on the extent of those contributions.[129] Indeed, some disquiet was expressed by commentators when this assumption was contradicted by the Court of Appeal in *Midland Bank plc v Cooke*.[130] Waite LJ (giving the judgment of the Court) held that, once the common intention had been demonstrated on the basis of direct financial contributions, it was then necessary in quantifying the appropriate shares to take into account all aspects of the case. The claimant in *Cooke* had paid[131] 6.74 per cent of the purchase price and had, at first instance, been awarded a corresponding share in the beneficial ownership. However, as well as her direct contribution to the purchase price, the claimant had over the years contributed her earnings as a teacher to family expenses, had helped to maintain and improve the property and had brought up the children of the marriage. Taking these and other sacrifices into account, Waite LJ decided that the share commonly intended must have been 50 per cent.

It has already been argued that this conclusion was not possible given that both parties in *Cooke* had sworn that they had never considered the question of ownership (thus precluding the inference of any common intention from their conduct). However, it is submitted that, had this factor been absent from the case, there would have been nothing in *Cooke* which was inconsistent with the approach of Lord Diplock. Waite LJ was simply drawing the inference which Lord Diplock had felt would "often" follow in the case of a married couple, i.e. that, despite the different nature of their contributions, the parties intended equal ownership.[132] Following Lord Diplock's speech, Waite LJ was perfectly entitled to "take into consideration all conduct which throws light on the question what shares were intended".[133] In fact, his inference that equal ownership

---

[129] See *Burns v Burns* [1984] Ch 317, 327B (the law "proceeds on the basis" of this inference); *Passee v Passee* [1988] 1 FLR 263; *Risch v McFee* [1991] 1 FLR 105. See also *Brown v Stokes* (1980) 1 NZCPR 209, 212 per Richmond P. Cf. Sparkes "The Quantification of Beneficial Interests: Problems Arising from Contributions to Deposits, Mortgage Advances and Mortgage Instalments" (1991) 11 OJLS 39. See further text following n 191 *infra*.

[130] [1995] 4 All ER 562. Note the views of O'Hagan, n 88 *supra* and Dixon, n 88 *supra*.

[131] See text to and following n 88 *supra*.

[132] Consistent with this, Waite LJ declared in *Cooke* [1995] 4 All ER 562, 576 that he reached his decision "without the need to rely on any equitable maxim as to equality". Cf. *McHardy v Warren* [1994] 2 FLR 338, 340 where, in an *ex tempore* judgment, Dillon LJ declared that it was an "irresistible conclusion that where a parent pays the deposit . . . on the purchase of [the spouses'] first matrimonial home, it is the intention of all three of them that the bride and groom should have equal interests in the matrimonial home". With all due respect, this does not appear to have been a reasonable inference to draw from the evidence. The approach of Dillon LJ is not supported by the previous cases in this area. Both *McHardy* and *Cooke* concerned married couples and it is unclear whether the judges concerned would have taken so generous an approach if the rights of unmarried cohabitees had been at issue.

[133] [1995] 4 All ER 562, 574. Note that Lord Diplock was willing throughout his speech to allow various forms of indirect contributions to "piggy-back" onto direct contributions. See *Gissing* [1971] AC 886, 907F–G (if the claimant has made a contribution to the initial deposit, then it becomes reasonable to take into account subsequent contributions to mortgage repayments);

was intended was surely far more plausible than the alternative suggestion that the parties actually intended the wife to have a share of 6.74 per cent (although, of course, even without the testimony of the parties in *Cooke*, both inferences would have been far less plausible than the suggestion that the parties had had no common intention at all as to ownership).

Why has the approach to quantification in *Cooke* seemed unorthodox to some commentators? Or, putting the question another way, what explains the preference of the courts (prior to *Cooke*) for the inference that the parties intended their shares to be quantified on the basis of their contributions? There appear to be two factors at work here.

The first point is that the focus on the contributions of the parties allows the English courts to refrain from committing themselves to any one theoretical approach. While a contributions-based approach is consistent with Lord Diplock's speech (by reference to the paragraph in his speech beginning "And there is nothing inherently improbable . . ."), it can also be reconciled with competing theoretical impulses. Thus, this kind of quantification fits in perfectly with an extended resulting trust model. It can also be regarded as reflecting the principles of estoppel, in that the remedy matches the detriment of the claimant (albeit as measured rather crudely by the extent of her financial contributions).[134] Finally, advocates of a Lord Denning-style "justice and good conscience" approach[135] may find comfort in the fact that one is awarding the share which appears to the court to be "fair" on the basis of the respective contributions of the parties.

Secondly, it is important to remember that there will be a significant number of cases where a common intention has been proven but it is impossible to draw any inference as to the precise shares which were commonly intended. In this situation, Lord Diplock proposed the application, as a rule of law, of the maxim "equality is equity". However, as will be seen at a later point in this chapter,[136] the courts in subsequent cases have clearly preferred to award a share calculated primarily by reference to the contributions made by the claimant. In order to disguise any conflict with Lord Diplock's speech, the courts have sometimes pretended that the parties actually intended their shares to be quantified on the basis of what would be fair having regard to their subsequent contributions.[137]

Thus, it seems that the concentration on the contributions of the parties is not really dictated by the logic of the common intention analysis but is largely attributable to the confusion of the English courts as to the theoretical basis for their decisions. It is submitted that the share commonly intended should be quantified on the basis of the contributions of the parties only where it seems

907G–H (indirect contributions to mortgage repayments may be taken into account on a similar basis); 908H–909B (arguing, in effect, that work in the home may taken into account when associated with financial contributions).

[134] See *Grant v Edwards* [1986] 1 Ch 638, 657–658 per Browne-Wilkinson V-C.
[135] See Chapter 6 *infra*.
[136] See Section C(2) of this Part *infra*.
[137] As envisaged by Lord Diplock in the *dictum* quoted as text to n 125 *supra*.

most likely that this was really the intention of the parties.[138] In many other cases, it may be more reasonable to infer that the parties intended equal ownership.

B. Proving Detrimental Reliance on the Common Intention

The second step in the common intention analysis is to look for proof that the claimant acted to her detriment in reliance on the common intention. There are two aspects to this requirement: detriment and reliance. These must be considered in turn.

1. *Detriment*

The classic form of detriment under the common intention analysis is the making of financial contributions towards the acquisition of the property.[139] In cases where the common intention has been inferred from the conduct of the claimant in making financial contributions, the same evidence which proves the existence of the common intention is also treated as demonstrating that the claimant has acted to her detriment.

The emphasis on financial contributions has been such that it has occasionally been doubted whether the requirement of detriment can be satisfied by conduct unrelated to the acquisition of the property. Notably, in *Burns v Burns*,[140] May LJ took an extremely limited view of the type of conduct which could suffice, feeling that a claim must fail in the absence of financial contributions to the acquisition of the disputed property. However, it does not appear that this narrow view finds support in the rest of the English cases.

Going back to the origins of the doctrine, Lord Diplock referred in *Gissing* to a common intention requiring the claimant "to do something to facilitate [the disputed property's] acquisition, by contributing to the purchase price or to the deposit or the mortgage instalments when it is purchased upon mortgage or to make some other material sacrifice by way of contribution to or economy in the general family expenditure".[141] This passage seems to envisage a very loose relationship between the detrimental conduct and the acquisition of the disputed property.

A more clear-cut statement of the point came from the Court of Appeal in *Grant v Edwards*.[142] In that case, Nourse LJ commented that, although the

---

[138] As was mentioned in the text following n 136 *supra*, the courts often award a share based on the contributions of the claimant in cases where the evidence permits no inference to be drawn as to the precise shares commonly intended. This, however, occurs at the remedial stage of the theoretical inquiry and, strictly speaking, has nothing to do with the process of inferring a common intention from conduct. See the discussion in Section B(2) of this Part *infra*.

[139] See e.g. *Halifax Building Society* v *Brown* [1996] 1 FLR 103, 109D per Balcombe LJ.

[140] [1984] Ch 317, 344E.

[141] [1971] AC 886, 905.

[142] [1986] 1 Ch 638.

conduct required "can undoubtedly be the incurring of expenditure which is referable to the acquisition of the house, it need not necessarily be so".[143] The approach in *Grant* on this point was confirmed by the House of Lords in *Lloyds Bank plc v Rosset*,[144] where Lord Bridge accepted that, once the common intention has been proven by direct evidence, "it will only be necessary for the [claimant] to show that he or she has acted to his or her detriment or significantly altered his or her position in reliance on the agreement".[145] Lord Bridge made no requirement that the claimant's conduct involve a contribution to the acquisition of the home. Indeed, a central theme of Lord Bridge's speech was that the requirement of detriment could be satisfied by conduct which, in itself, would not have been sufficient to justify the inference of a common intention.

Once it has been conceded that, in principle, any conduct is capable of constituting detriment, it seems reasonable to suggest that one should simply import into the common intention analysis the principles governing detriment in the context of estoppel.[146] However, since the remedy under the common intention analysis is invariably a trust, it is arguable that one should require a greater level of detriment than in relation to estoppel (where the court can also choose from a range of lesser remedies).[147] Given the absence of discussion in the authorities, it remains unclear precisely how one would frame an alternative, and more strict, test of detriment.[148] In any event, even if one concluded that the test for detriment in the "common intention" context should somehow be stricter than in the context of estoppel, it would be difficult to argue against the importation into the "common intention" doctrine of any *limiting* rules developed in the estoppel cases.

Thus, for example, it would be logical to apply the estoppel test of "net detriment", balancing the detriment of the claimant against any advantages which her course of conduct brought to her.[149] Consider a case where, for example, the claimant made direct contributions to the repayment of a mortgage. In principle, one should have to consider whether this detrimental conduct was

---

[143] *Ibid*, 647. Similarly, Mustill LJ noted (*ibid*, 652) that it was "immaterial whether [the detriment] takes the shape of a contribution to the cost of acquiring the property or is of a quite different character". See also *Ogilvie v Ryan* [1976] 2 NSWLR 504, 518 per Holland J.

[144] [1991] 1 AC 107.

[145] *Ibid*, 132.

[146] See generally Chapter 4 *supra*, Part II(A)(2). See text following n 301 *infra* for discussion of the relationship between the common intention analysis and the principles of estoppel.

[147] Cf. *Higgins v Wingfield* [1987] VR 689, 695–696 per McGarvie J. See also Lawson "The Things We Do for Love: Detrimental Reliance in the Family Home" (1996) 12 *Legal Studies* 218, 220 *et seq*.

[148] In fact, rather than tinkering with the rules governing "detriment", it would probably be more sensible simply to scrap the rule which requires that a successful "common intention" claimant automatically be rewarded with a constructive trust. For criticism of the latter rule, see text to and following n 317 *infra*.

[149] See Chapter 4 *supra*, text to and following n 71. Cf. Hayton "Constructive Trusts: Is the Remedying of Unjust Enrichment a Satisfactory Approach?" in Youdan (ed) *Equity, Fiduciaries and Trusts* (Toronto: Carswell, 1989) p 229. Note also the question, discussed in Chapter 4 *supra*, text following n 73, of whether "life-style choices" can be categorised as detrimental conduct.

counter-balanced by any benefits accruing to the claimant (e.g. in the form of rent-free accommodation). However, whatever the strength of the above argument, the courts have shown no signs of applying a "net detriment" approach in the common intention cases.

2. *Reliance*

It has been suggested in the previous section that, provided that the hurdle of establishing a common intention has been surmounted by direct evidence, the detrimental conduct of the claimant need not take the form of direct financial contributions. This opens up the possibility of establishing a constructive trust on the basis of other forms of conduct, such as the payment of general household expenses or the undertaking of work in the home. The remaining difficulty is to demonstrate that the conduct in question was actually undertaken in reliance on the common intention rather than merely on the basis of mutual love and affection. Differing views were expressed on this issue in *Grant* v *Edwards*.[150]

Nourse LJ stated the test for reliance as follows:

"So what sort of conduct is required? In my judgment it must be conduct on which the woman could not reasonably have been expected to embark unless she was to have an interest in the house".[151]

Nourse LJ took the view that "the law is not so cynical as to infer that a woman will only go to live with a man to whom she is not married if she understands that she is to have an interest in their home".[152] Therefore, in the absence of further evidence, such conduct could not be treated as having been undertaken on the basis of the common intention.

Nourse LJ felt that his test for reliance was satisfied on the facts of *Grant* v *Edwards*. It will be recalled that a common intention to share ownership had been inferred from a lie told by the defendant. The plaintiff had contributed substantially to the household expenses. It was impossible to see how the defendant could have kept up the mortgage repayments without her help. Nourse LJ held that her conduct in making these indirect contributions was conduct upon which she could not reasonably have been expected to embark unless she were to have an interest in the house. The learned judge could not see "upon what other basis she could reasonably have been expected to give the defendant such substantial assistance in paying off mortgages on his house".[153]

---

[150] [1986] 1 Ch 638.
[151] *Ibid*, 648. Lawson, n 147 *supra*, 219 interprets this passage as a statement of the test for "detriment" rather than for "reliance". It is certainly arguable that Nourse LJ collapsed the two issues together into a composite test. However, it does appear to the present writer that the thrust of Nourse LJ's reasoning was directed towards the issue of "reliance".
[152] *Ibid*.
[153] *Ibid*, 650.

Nourse LJ's treatment of this point raises a wider issue. It could be argued that Nourse LJ's test could, with equal logic, be applied to the separate issue of inferring the existence of a prior common intention from the conduct of the claimant. If a claimant has engaged in conduct upon which she "could not reasonably have been expected to embark unless she was to have an interest in the house", this would appear sufficient to prove that it was understood that she would get an interest in the house. Is Nourse LJ's test not effectively the same as the test applied to determine whether the claimant's conduct is sufficient to justify the inference of a common intention?[154] Notwithstanding the fact that the two tests appear to be identical, Lord Bridge asserted in *Rosset*[155] that, while the conduct of the claimant in *Grant* was rightly held to constitute sufficient detrimental reliance, it "fell far short of such conduct as would by itself have supported the claim in the absence of an express representation by the male partner that she was to have such an interest".[156] If one accepts Nourse LJ's test for "reliance", it seems impossible to explain how (for example) the making of substantial indirect contributions can amount to "reliance" on an express common intention but fall "far short" of justifying the inference of a common intention.[157]

A different approach to that of Nourse LJ was proposed by Browne-Wilkinson V-C in *Grant*. Browne-Wilkinson V-C was willing to take a more expansive view on the question of detriment, including "[s]etting up house together" and "having a baby" as examples of possible detrimental reliance.[158] Browne-Wilkinson V-C, relying on "an analogy" with proprietary estoppel, went on to suggest that the burden of proof would lie on the defendant to prove that such conduct had *not* been undertaken on the basis of the common intention and, rather, was attributable to mutual love and affection.[159] He supported this suggestion by citing *Greasley* v *Cooke*,[160] where, in the estoppel context, Lord Denning MR had invented a presumption to the effect that the conduct of the claimant had been undertaken in reliance on the representation of the defen-

---

[154] Cf. *ibid*, 652 per Mustill LJ ("a risk of circularity"). See also *Rosset* [1991] 1 AC 107, 131E–F, where Lord Bridge criticised the trial judge's finding that the claimant had engaged in work "upon which she could not reasonably have been expected to embark". However, at this point, Lord Bridge was clearly considering whether or not it was appropriate to infer a common intention. It is revealing that while doing so he employed (albeit within quotation marks) the test devised by Nourse LJ to govern the question of "reliance".

[155] [1991] 1 AC 107.

[156] *Ibid*, 133.

[157] One possible answer is that while the claimant's conduct might show that she was relying on an assumption that she would get a share (satisfying the "reliance" requirement), it might not prove that her partner had given her the impression that he shared that assumption. However, this answer seems to prove too much, since logically it would preclude the inference of a common intention from the making of direct financial contributions (a form of conduct which is undoubtedly treated as sufficient to justify the inference of a common intention: *Rosset* [1991] 1 AC 107, 133).

[158] [1986] 1 Ch 638, 657.

[159] *Ibid*. For discussion of the "possible analogy with proprietary estoppel", see text following n 301 *infra*. See also Chapter 4 *supra*, text following n 87.

[160] [1980] 1 WLR 1306.

dant. There is certainly much to be said for the suggestion that the test for detrimental reliance in the common intention context should be the same as under the principles of estoppel. However, when Lord Denning MR's approach in *Greasley* was discussed in a previous chapter, it was argued that it had no basis in principle and that its status as a matter of authority was questionable.[161] If one accepts this conclusion, then it would seem that the "presumption of reliance" should similarly have no place within the common intention framework. This in turn suggests that, despite its potential to assist claimants who rely on work in the home, Browne-Wilkinson V-C's approach should not be adopted. In any case, the English courts have shown little sign of taking a generous approach to the question of work in the home and it may be concluded that it will be extremely difficult for a claimant to base a successful claim on this sort of conduct.

Having discussed the issues which arise when the common intention has been proven by direct evidence, it is necessary briefly to address the situation where a common intention has been proven by inference from the financial contributions of the claimant. In such cases, as has been seen, the same conduct which proves the common intention is regarded as constituting detrimental reliance on that common intention. It is generally assumed that no issues of "reliance" arise here. This seems reasonable. The existence of a common intention has been inferred on the basis that the claimant would not have acted as she did if there had not been a prior common intention; it appears to follow, as the converse of the previous proposition, that she acted as she did in reliance on the common intention.

C. The Remedial Stage[162]

The final stage of the analysis concerns the remedy to be afforded to a claimant who has acted to her detriment on the basis of a common intention. This aspect of the doctrine is rarely discussed since, following Lord Diplock's approach in *Gissing*, it is generally assumed that the claimant's remedy will invariably be a constructive trust which gives effect to the common intention. However, two important issues do arise in this context. The first concerns the approach to be taken in cases where the detriment incurred by the claimant does not appear sufficient to "earn" the share which was commonly intended. The second question concerns the resolution of cases where there was clearly a common intention between the parties but it is not possible to quantify precisely what shares were intended. These two questions will now be considered in turn.

---

[161] See Chapter 4 *supra*, text to and following n 92.
[162] See generally Hayton *Underhill and Hayton*, n 3 *supra*, pp 382–385.

1. *Cases involving limited detriment*

Difficult issues are raised by the situation where the extent of the claimant's detriment does not appear to justify giving full effect to the common intention of the parties. In cases where the common intention took the form of a "bargain" (as Lord Diplock envisaged would invariably be the case)[163] it would be comparatively easy to determine whether the claimant had "earned" the share commonly intended. One would only have to look at her compliance with her side of the bargain. What, however, if there was no bargain and therefore no *quid pro quo* expressly envisaged in return for the claimant's share (or what if the claimant fulfilled only some of her obligations pursuant to a "bargain")?[164] If the detriment of the claimant appears to be small in comparison to the share she was intended to receive, can the court award her a lesser remedy?

There is little guidance in the case law on this question. The main authority appears to be the early case of *Eves* v *Eves*,[165] where a share was awarded which did not seem to correspond with any common intention of the parties. The common intention in *Eves* had been established on the basis of an excuse made by the defendant for not putting the claimant's name on the legal title. Brightman J (with whom Browne LJ agreed) felt that there had been an informal bargain whereby the claimant would help to renovate the property and, in return, would be entitled to a share in the ownership of the house. According to Browne-Wilkinson V-C in *Grant* v *Edwards*,[166] Brightman J "plainly felt" that the common intention of the parties pointed to the beneficial interests being equal. Despite this, Brightman J described the question of quantifying the remedy as most difficult in the case[167] and concluded that "the court should imply that the plaintiff was intended to acquire a quarter interest in the house".[168]

In *Grant* v *Edwards*,[169] Browne-Wilkinson V-C suggested that the result in *Eves* could be rationalised on the basis of estoppel principles.[170] Browne-Wilkinson V-C pointed out that, "[i]f proprietary estoppel is established, the court gives effect to it by giving effect to the common intention so far as may fairly be done between the parties".[171] For this purpose, "equity is displayed at

---

[163] See text to and following n 102 *supra*.

[164] A "bargain" of the type under discussion might well have an ongoing aspect, as in the case envisaged by Lord Diplock ([1971] AC 886, 909) where the couple agreed that they would each contribute "whatever amounts each could afford in the varying exigencies of family life to be expected during the period of repayment". It is unclear if it would be sufficient if the claimant abided by such an understanding for the duration of a short relationship. On the one hand, she would have kept faith with her partner; on the other hand, it would have originally been envisaged that her contribution would continue for the full term of the mortgage.

[165] [1975] 1 WLR 1338.

[166] [1986] 1 Ch 638, 657 referring to *Eves* [1975] 1 WLR 1338, 1345G.

[167] [1975] 1 WLR 1338, 1345.

[168] *Ibid*, 1346.

[169] [1986] 1 Ch 638.

[170] *Ibid*, 657–658.

[171] *Ibid*, 657.

its most flexible".[172] As Browne-Wilkinson V-C appeared to recognise in *Grant*,[173] the orthodox position is that the remedy for an estoppel claimant should, in general, reflect the extent of her detriment.[174] It is thus tempting to see *Eves* as a case where the remedy was based on the claimant's detriment because the extent of that detriment did not justify fulfilling the common intention of the parties.

One possible problem with this explanation is, however, that Lord Bridge in *Rosset*[175] appears not to have seen *Eves* in these terms, commenting that "[i]n no sense" could the award of a one-quarter share in *Eves* "have been regarded as proportionate to . . . the indirect contributions to the . . . enhancement of the value of the [house] made by the [claimant]".[176] If one were to decide that the result in *Eves* could not be explained as reflecting the detriment incurred by the claimant, then one could only surmise that Brightman J was simply settling on a figure which seemed fair in all the circumstances. It seems plausible to suppose that Brightman J was influenced in this respect by his senior colleague, Lord Denning MR, who (applying his idiosyncratic "new model constructive trust" approach)[177] had suggested that one-quarter would be an appropriate share for the claimant in *Eves*.[178]

It is also worth pointing out that, if one were to take seriously the analogy with estoppel, the remedial discretion of the court would extend to other remedies besides the grant of an equitable interest in the disputed property. Indeed, one might expect that that remedy would be afforded only in rare cases, with the court often favouring less radical solutions such as the award of monetary compensation. For some unexplained reason, however, the "flexibility" envisaged in the common intention context appears to be limited to varying the fraction of the beneficial interest to be awarded to the claimant.

To sum up, it appears that *Eves*,[179] as interpreted by Browne-Wilkinson V-C in *Grant* v *Edwards*, offers some degree of support for an estoppel-style remedial flexibility in the common intention context. However, it is clear that this position has not yet established itself in the English case law. The cases generally show a simple willingness to give effect to the common intention of the parties as soon as the claimant has been shown to have acted to her detriment

---

[172] *Ibid.*
[173] *Ibid*, 657H–658A (explaining that, if one were applying estoppel principles, one could take into account various forms of detriment incurred by the claimant).
[174] See Chapter 4 *supra*, text following n 100.
[175] [1991] 1 AC 107.
[176] *Ibid*, 133.
[177] Cf. *Grant* v *Edwards* [1986] 1 Ch 638, 647G per Nourse LJ. See Chapter 6 *infra* for consideration of the new model constructive trust.
[178] [1975] 1 WLR 1338, 1342H. Another view is that the crucial feature in *Eves* was that it was impossible to draw any inference as to the shares which were commonly intended, thus leaving the court with no option but to award a share based on the detriment incurred by the claimant (or, alternatively, a "fair" share). See Section C(2) of this Part *infra*.
[179] [1975] 1 WLR 1338.

on the basis of that common intention.[180] It seems most likely that, despite *Eves*, cases involving limited detriment would be dealt with by the application of a *de minimus* test.[181] If the claimant's detriment passes the *de minimus* threshold, she would be rewarded to the full extent of the common intention; if not, her claim would fail outright.[182]

One may observe finally that the English courts have evinced no concern over the possibility that giving effect to a common intention might reward a claimant to a greater extent than is merited by her detrimental reliance. This may be explicable on the basis of a general sympathy for claimants in this kind of case. A more specific explanation is that fixing the remedy by reference to the claimant's detrimental reliance on the common intention precludes consideration of other detriment incurred by the claimant which cannot be linked with the common intention. The practice of giving effect to the common intention (which will often be to share equally) may be seen by judges as reflecting more accurately the total detriment incurred by the claimant (both on the basis of the common intention and on the basis of the relationship generally).[183] Of course, this kind of reasoning (if indeed it is influential) it is totally at odds with a doctrine which purports to focus on the fact that the claimant has acted to her detriment *on the basis of* the common intention.

2. *Cases where no common intention can be inferred as to quantification*

A second issue remains to be considered. What remedy will be granted to a claimant where a common intention has been established but, having reviewed all the evidence, it is not possible precisely to quantify the shares which were intended? In *Gissing*, Lord Diplock took it to be clear that the court, "in the exercise of its equitable jurisdiction", would not permit the defendant to retain the full ownership of the disputed property simply because it was not possible to determine exactly what shares were commonly intended.[184] This preliminary conclusion appears incontestable. However, Lord Diplock went on argue that, if no inference as to quantification could be drawn from the evidence, "the court is driven to apply as a rule of law, and not as an inference of fact, the maxim 'equality is equity', and to hold that the beneficial interest belongs to the spouses in equal shares".[185]

---

[180] See *Clough* v *Killey* (1996) 72 P & CR D22 (full transcript on LEXIS) where Peter Gibson LJ took the view that, notwithstanding *Eves* v *Eves* [1975] 1 WLR 1338, it was "only common sense" that the shares awarded to the parties should *prima facie* reflect the shares commonly intended.

[181] See *Rosset* [1991] 1 AC 107, 131G–H.

[182] As will be discussed later in this chapter, this "all or nothing" approach seems to reflect the influence of the view that the common intention trust can be explained, not on the basis of estoppel principles, but rather by reference to the doctrine in *Rochefoucauld* v *Boustead*. See text following n 237 *infra*.

[183] Consider, for example, a case where the claimant worked in the home in addition to making financial contributions.

[184] [1971] AC 886, 908E–F.

[185] *Ibid*, 908.

It appears that this was not a felicitous suggestion. It is undoubtedly reasonable, when applying a resulting trust analysis, to settle on equal ownership in a case where there are evidential difficulties in ascertaining the precise contributions but where it is clear that the claimant has made a very substantial contribution to the purchase price (which may or may not have exceeded one half of the total amount). This approach, authoritatively expressed by Lord Pearson in *Gissing*,[186] can be defended on the basis that there is no other way in which such a case can be resolved. As Lord Upjohn put it in *National Provincial Bank* v *Ainsworth*,[187] the court must use "an equitable knife . . . to sever the Gordian knot".[188] However, by way of contrast, in the common intention situation there *is* an alternative method by which the share of the claimant could be evaluated: by reference to the detriment she has incurred on the basis of the common intention. This appears to provide a more rational solution than an automatic "rule of law" which requires that the claimant be given a one-half share.

In fact, the above argument finds considerable support in the case law. There appears to be no example of a case where a court has applied Lord Diplock's "rule of law". In cases such as *McHardy* v *Warren*[189] and *Midland Bank plc* v *Cooke*[190] the court inferred, as a matter of fact, that equal ownership was intended. In a number of other cases, where in truth it was not possible to determine what shares were commonly intended, the court dodged the issue by holding that the parties had intended their shares to be quantified on the basis of what would be fair having regard to their total contributions to the property.[191] Thus, in *Passee* v *Passee*,[192] Nourse LJ held that the parties "intended, or are taken to have intended" this result. The words used by Nourse LJ reveal an awareness of the fictional quality of the inference of fact which he purported to draw.[193] It is submitted that a more appropriate way to explain the sensible result in cases such as *Passee* would be to concede that it was impossible to infer any common intention as to quantification and that, therefore, the court had to fall back on an evaluation of the shares based on the detriment incurred by the claimant.

A version of the approach suggested above was taken in *Stokes* v *Anderson*.[194] In *Stokes*, Nourse LJ (speaking for the Court of Appeal) gave close consideration to the question under discussion. He put forward the view that:

"[A]ll payments made and acts done by the claimant are to be treated as illuminating the common intention as to the extent of the beneficial interest. Once you get to that

---

[186] *Ibid*, 903.
[187] [1965] AC 1175.
[188] *Ibid*, 1236.
[189] [1994] 2 FLR 338.
[190] [1995] 4 All ER 562.
[191] See text to and following n 125 *supra*.
[192] [1988] 1 FLR 263.
[193] See also *Eves* v *Eves* [1975] 1 WLR 1338, 1346 where Brightman J concluded, surely on a fictional basis, that the claimant "was intended" to acquire a quarter interest in the property. Cf. *Burns* v *Burns* [1984] Ch 317, 327B.
[194] [1991] 1 FLR 391.

stage . . . there is no practicable alternative to the determination of a fair share. The court must supply the common intention by reference to that which all the material circumstances have shown to be fair".[195]

Applying this "fair share" test to the facts of *Stokes*, Nourse LJ decided that the claimant should be entitled to a one-quarter share in the disputed property.[196]

Nourse LJ felt[197] that his approach was supported by the *dictum* of Lord Diplock in *Gissing* (beginning with the words "And there is nothing inherently improbable . . .") which countenanced the possibility of a common intention between the parties that each should ultimately receive a fair share based on their contributions.[198] However, Lord Diplock's *dictum* dealt with a case where the award of a "fair" share was mandated by an actual common intention of the parties; he certainly did not believe that a "fair share" could be awarded where the court could discern no common intention as to quantification.[199] On the other hand, Nourse LJ was probably correct in suggesting that the "fair share" approach was consistent with the results reached in *Eves*[200] and *Passee*[201] and found some support in the judgment of Browne-Wilkinson V-C in *Grant* v *Edwards*.[202]

There are obvious attractions to the approach of Nourse LJ in *Stokes*. One can certainly agree with Nourse LJ's view that, in determining the appropriate share for the claimant, one is not confined to a consideration of contributions to mortgage instalments but may also take into account "all payments made and acts done by the claimant".[203] However, what Nourse LJ does not appear to make sufficiently clear is that one cannot look beyond the detriment incurred by the claimant *on the basis of* the common intention. The claimant may have prejudiced herself in a wide variety of ways which are unrelated to the common intention, e.g. by working in the home and bringing up the children. Furthermore, there may be factors in the case (e.g. the relative wealth of the parties) which make it seem "fair" to favour the claimant. However, within the confines of the common intention doctrine, it is not logical to look beyond conduct which can be linked to the common intention; if it is permissible to leap straight to a "fair" result in this context, then why not in every context?

On a final, and more general point, it is necessary to comment on Nourse LJ's view in *Stokes* that the court was "putting the quantification of the claimant's

---

[195] [1991] 1 FLR 400.

[196] Before the commencement of his relationship with the claimant, the defendant had already been a joint owner of the property in question. (See n 128 *supra*). Nourse LJ felt (*ibid*, 401) that, in the circumstances, it would be "markedly unfair" to order an equal sharing between the defendant and the claimant.

[197] *Ibid*, 399–400.

[198] [1971] AC 886, 909C–E. The relevant passage was quoted as text to n 125 *supra*.

[199] As discussed above, Lord Diplock favoured the imposition of equal ownership in such cases. See text to n 185 *supra*.

[200] [1975] 1 WLR 1338.

[201] [1988] 1 FLR 263.

[202] [1986] 1 Ch 638, in particular 657G–658A.

[203] [1991] 1 FLR 391, 400.

beneficial interest on a more satisfactory footing, a footing which incidentally brings it nearer to proprietary estoppel".[204] It should be remembered that, as was concluded earlier[205] (and as Nourse LJ accepted),[206] quantification depends in the first place on the common intention of the parties and not on the detriment incurred by the claimant. Therefore, the "fair share" (or "detriment-based", as the present author would have it) approach to quantification applies *only* where it is not possible to determine what shares were commonly intended. Thus, while introducing a flavour of estoppel at one point in the analysis, the courts have stopped short of adopting a full estoppel approach to remedies.

II. THE THEORETICAL RATIONALE FOR THE COMMON INTENTION TRUST

A. The Provenance of the Common Intention Analysis

In attempting to identify the theoretical basis for the modern "common intention" analysis, it is a useful preliminary to turn briefly to the cases decided before the old law was swept away by *Pettitt* and *Gissing*. Looking at these antediluvian decisions, one is struck by the fact that there is no trace of the "common intention" analysis as presented by Lord Diplock in *Gissing*. However, this point was not conceded by Lord Diplock in his speech in *Gissing*. Instead, with a clever sleight of hand, Lord Diplock gave the impression that his entirely novel approach had a firm basis in the earlier case law.

In this respect, the key moment in Lord Diplock's speech came immediately after his famous statement of the general characteristics of resulting, implied and constructive trusts.[207] Lord Diplock then stated that:

> "This is why it has been repeatedly said in the context of disputes between spouses as to their respective beneficial interests in the matrimonial home, that if at the time of its acquisition and transfer of the legal estate into the name of one or other of them an express agreement has been made between them as to the way in which the beneficial interest shall be held, the court will give effect to it—notwithstanding the absence of any written declaration".[208]

Lord Diplock went on to argue that "the express oral agreements contemplated by these dicta"[209] were examples of what he termed "common intention". He concluded that "[w]hat the court gives effect to is the trust resulting or implied from the common intention expressed in the oral agreement between the spouses".[210]

---

[204] *Ibid*, 399.
[205] See text following n 179 *supra*.
[206] [1991] 1 FLR 391, 399F–G.
[207] [1971] AC 886, 905, quoted as text to n 10 *supra* ("A resulting, implied or constructive trust—and it is unnecessary for present purposes" etc).
[208] *Ibid*.
[209] *Ibid*.
[210] *Ibid*.

The interesting aspect of this attempt to draw support from what had been "repeatedly said" in earlier cases is that Lord Diplock never actually specified the *dicta* in which it had been accepted that an oral agreement would be enforced. A great deal of ambiguity surrounds the word "agreement". As well as connoting the type of common intention favoured by Lord Diplock, it could also bear any of a number of other meanings. It is submitted that, in the *dicta* indirectly invoked by Lord Diplock, the relevant courts were expressing a willingness to enforce an "agreement" (or "common intention") on a number of widely differing bases, each of them entirely distinct from the one Lord Diplock envisaged. It is worthwhile to demonstrate this point with a brief examination of the attitude of the English courts to "agreement" and "intention" in the early cases.

In the first case in the modern series, *Re Rogers' Question*,[211] Evershed LJ commented that the task of a judge was "to try to conclude what at the time was in the parties' minds and then to make an order which, in the changed conditions, now fairly gives effect in law to what the parties . . . intended at the time of the transaction itself".[212] At first reading, this *dictum* appears to suggest that the court is entitled to give effect to the intentions of the parties irrespective of whether these intentions had manifested themselves in a valid declaration of trust. However, upon a closer examination of the judgments in the case, it becomes clear that the type of intention which the court had in mind was what Bagnall J described in *Cowcher* v *Cowcher*[213] as a "money consensus".[214] Thus, for example, Evershed LJ concluded that "each intended to contribute to the home in the respective proportions found by the judge".[215] Similarly, Asquith LJ emphasised the fact that the wife "never intended in any circumstances to be saddled with any liability"[216] in respect of the portion of the purchase price represented by the mortgage. The conclusion must be that the court was considering the intentions of the parties in relation to the manner in which the mortgage would be paid off and not the intentions of the parties as to how the beneficial ownership would be shared.[217]

A number of later cases relied on the *dictum* of Evershed LJ discussed in the previous paragraph. However, in these cases one clearly sees the influence of the now-discredited "family assets" doctrine and the theory that the courts were given an unfettered discretion by section 17 of the Married Women's Property Act 1882. Thus, for example, in *Rimmer* v *Rimmer*,[218] Denning LJ commented that if it was clear that the spouses "intended to hold [the family home] in defi-

---

[211] [1948] 1 All ER 328.
[212] *Ibid*, 328–329.
[213] [1972] 1 WLR 425.
[214] See generally Chapter 2 *supra*, Part V.
[215] [1948] 1 All ER 328, 330.
[216] *Ibid*. See also *ibid*, 330B and 330G per Lord Greene MR.
[217] Cf. *Diwell* v *Farnes* [1959] 1 WLR 624, 640 per Willmer LJ.
[218] [1953] 1 QB 63.

nite shares, the court will give effect to their intention".[219] However, immediately before this comment, he had asserted that section 17 of the Married Women's Property Act allowed the court to decide the case "as it thought fit" and that "Parliament laid down no principles for the guidance of the courts".[220] Denning LJ made a similar reference to the role of intention in *Fribance* v *Fribance (No 2)*[221] but once more this was on the basis of an analysis which "put . . . the question of contract, gift or trust on one side"[222] and afforded special treatment to "family assets". While one rarely sees any use of the phrase "common intention" in the cases before *Gissing*, when it does occur (notably in the judgment of Diplock LJ in *Ulrich* v *Ulrich and Felton*)[223] it is generally in the context of the "family assets" doctrine or the exercise of the purported discretion under section 17.[224]

A number of other references to the importance of agreement or intention appear to be explicable simply on the basis of long-established principles of trusts law. Thus, for example, in his judgment in *Cobb* v *Cobb*,[225] Romer LJ concluded that the parties were jointly entitled to the beneficial interest in the family home. In reaching this conclusion, he relied on the fact that it had been the intention of the parties at the time of the acquisition of the house that it would be owned jointly. However, given that the disputed home was in the joint names of the parties, Romer LJ's conclusion (and the emphasis on the intentions of the parties, both of whom had contributed to the purchase price) was perfectly reconcilable with orthodox resulting trust theory. Likewise, the references to intention in *Silver* v *Silver*[226] were clearly directed towards the question of whether the plaintiff husband was able to rebut the presumption of advancement. Another orthodox role for "intention" and "agreement" is where it is reflected in an express declaration of the beneficial interests in the home. This clearly explains Lord Upjohn's statement in *Pettitt*[227] that the beneficial ownership of property "must depend upon the agreement of the parties at the time of its acquisition".[228]

A final possible explanation for judicial statements that effect would be given to the agreement or common intention of the parties is, of course, that the judges in question had in mind an enforceable contract between the

---

[219] *Ibid*, 73.
[220] *Ibid*.
[221] [1957] 1 WLR 384.
[222] *Ibid*, 387.
[223] [1968] 1 WLR 180, 189.
[224] See *Rimmer* v *Rimmer* [1953] 1 QB 63, 75 per Romer LJ; *Hine* v *Hine* [1962] 1 WLR 1124, 1132 per Pearson LJ; *Gissing* v *Gissing* [1969] 2 Ch 85, 96 (CA) per Edmund Davies LJ. Cf. *Ward* v *Ward* [1958] VR 68, 75 per Smith J (see n 260 *infra*).
[225] [1955] 1 WLR 731.
[226] [1958] 1 WLR 259, 262 per Lord Evershed MR; 265 per Parker LJ; 266 per Sellers LJ.
[227] [1970] AC 777, 813.
[228] See Lord Upjohn's explanation *ibid*, 813D–E. Cf. *Wilson* v *Wilson* [1963] 1 WLR 601. See the discussion in Chapter 1 *supra*, text following n 152 of the binding effect of an express declaration of the beneficial interests.

parties.[229] Although there are occasional hints of a contractual analysis in the early English cases,[230] there is little explicit discussion of the point. It is interesting, therefore, to consider the Victorian case of *Pearson* v *Pearson*.[231] Having asserted that "[i]f an express agreement is established, of course it prevails",[232] the court went on to reveal its view that such a "bargain" or "mutual intention" is "essentially contractual in its nature and operation, even if opinions may differ as to whether its origin is accurately so characterised".[233]

It seems, therefore, that Lord Diplock was correct in pointing out that the older cases contain many suggestions that a court is entitled to determine ownership on the basis of an agreement (or, less frequently, a "common intention") between the parties. However, it was disingenuous of him to suggest that the older *dicta* could be explained on the basis of his analysis in *Gissing*. In fact, the relevant dicta are susceptible to a variety of alternative explanations (money consensus doctrine, section 17 discretion, family assets doctrine, resulting trust doctrine, express declaration of beneficial interests, enforceable contract). Interestingly, none of the dicta in the older cases make any reference to the modern requirement of detrimental reliance by the claimant. This led Lord Diplock to make the implausible suggestion in *Gissing*[234] that it had been assumed "*sub silentio*" in the relevant *dicta* that the claimant was expected to act to her detriment on the basis of the common intention.

The conclusion which follows from the examination of the older case law in this section is that Lord Diplock's "common intention" analysis can trace its pedigree no further back than *Gissing* v *Gissing*. Of course, while raising one's suspicions, this does not, in itself, justify a negative verdict on the doctrine. It will next be necessary to look more closely at the theoretical foundations of the "common intention" analysis, with a view to seeing whether a coherent rationale can be identified.

B. Possible Theoretical Rationalisations

As was suggested at the outset of this chapter, it is difficult to find a coherent theoretical rationale for the common intention trust. In this section, a number of possible rationalisations are explored.

---

[229] Cf. *Pettitt* v *Pettitt* [1970] AC 777, 799 where Lord Morris stated that "[i]t appears to have been generally accepted that if . . . a judge is able after hearing evidence to come to a conclusion that there was a clear agreement between husband and wife in regard to ownership he must give his adjudication accordingly". It is possible that Lord Morris was referring here to an enforceable contract. This interpretation appears to be supported by his Lordship's remarks *ibid*, 804D–E.

[230] See e.g. *Appleton* v *Appleton* [1965] 1 WLR 25, 28H per Lord Denning MR.

[231] [1961] VR 693 (Full Ct of the Sup Ct).

[232] *Ibid*, 698.

[233] *Ibid*, 700.

[234] [1971] AC 886, 905.

1. *Resulting trust principles*

From its first introduction in the speech of Lord Diplock in *Gissing*, uncertainty surrounded the relationship between the common intention trust and the traditional purchase money resulting trust. This uncertainty is not surprising given the nature of Lord Diplock's project in *Gissing*. In his speech, Lord Diplock clearly aimed to expand the traditional resulting trust and to establish the novel proposition that it merely formed part of a wider doctrine (i.e. the common intention trust analysis). To advance this conclusion, Lord Diplock employed three major strategies in his speech in *Gissing*. The first was to take the resulting trust concept of intention—a contributor's unilateral intention to earn a share—and to transform that into the quite different concept of a "common intention" between the parties that ownership be shared. The second was to embrace the possibility (also alien to the resulting trust doctrine) of establishing intention otherwise than on the simple basis of financial contributions.[235] The final strategy, similar to the second, was to accept conduct other than the making of financial contributions as sufficient to trigger the trust.

These strategies had the knock-on effect of separating two issues which are inextricably linked in the true resulting trust: (1) the establishment of intention (invariably on the basis of financial contributions in the resulting trust) and (2) the quantification of the claimant's share (again always on the basis of the financial contribution in the resulting trust). Thus, Lord Diplock's approach in *Gissing* prefigured the controversial view on quantification taken by the Court of Appeal in *Midland Bank plc v Cooke*.[236]

Lord Diplock's strategies clearly involved the introduction of entirely new elements into the purchase money resulting trust. For example, under the older doctrine the provision of one-quarter of the purchase price will, in the absence of a contrary intention, gain a one-quarter share in the beneficial interest. Yet, under the "common intention" analysis, if there was a common intention that the contributor should get one-half of the beneficial interest, then that common intention may be put into effect even if the contribution still only amounts to one-quarter. Why, if the doctrine depends on resulting trust principles, has it now, after hundreds of years of clear contrary precedent, suddenly become legitimate to award a larger share than that earned by the contributions? This question seems unanswerable. It must be concluded that, assuming that it is legitimate, the "common intention" trust must involve some principle distinct from that underlying the purchase money resulting trust.[237]

---

[235] Thus, as has been discussed in detail in Part I(A)(1) *supra*, Lord Diplock was willing to accept a common intention founded on direct evidence of the statements of the parties.

[236] [1995] 4 All ER 562, discussed in the text to and following n 129 *supra*.

[237] Therefore, there can be no justification in imposing limitations on the new trust simply because they form part of the older doctrine. Thus, one cannot agree with the insistence of May LJ in *Burns v Burns* [1984] Ch 317, 344E that, in order to claim a common intention trust, the claimant must have made a financial contribution to the acquisition of the disputed property. (Cf. the discussion in the text to and following n 140 *supra*).

2. *The principle in* Rochefoucauld *v* Boustead

One alternative to a simple reliance on resulting trust principles is to regard the common intention trust as based on an application of the equitable principle that "a statute cannot be used as an instrument of fraud".[238] The statutory provisions in question here are the modern equivalents of section 7 of the Statute of Frauds 1677. The relevant provision in England is section 53(1)(b) of the Law of Property Act 1925, which requires a trust of real property to be evidenced in writing. The argument (which appears to have fallen somewhat out of fashion in recent years) is that a "common intention" that ownership will be shared is equivalent to an informal declaration of an express trust by the legal owner. Such a trust would *prima facie* fail in the absence of compliance with section 53(1)(b).[239] However, it could be contended that, once the claimant has acted to her detriment on the basis of the common intention, it becomes inequitable for the legal owner to rely on the absence of the statutory formalities. The conclusion would be that a constructive trust is therefore created in favour of the claimant.[240]

There is certainly long-standing authority, outside the family context, for the proposition that an informal trust may be enforced in order to prevent section 53(1)(b) from being used as an instrument of fraud. The relevant principle is often referred to as the doctrine in *Rochefoucauld v Boustead*,[241] after the leading case in the area.[242] The plaintiff in *Rochefoucauld* claimed that certain estates of hers in Ceylon had been purchased by the defendant as trustee for her, subject to a lien for the money he had advanced. The defendant pleaded, *inter alia*, that the trust alleged by the plaintiff was not evidenced in writing signed by him and that therefore the Statute of Frauds provided a defence. Lindley J rejected this argument, saying:

> "[N]otwithstanding the statute, it is competent for a person claiming land conveyed to another to prove by parol evidence that it was so conveyed upon trust for the claimant, and that the grantee, knowing the facts, is denying the trust and relying upon the form of the conveyance and the statute, in order to keep the land himself".[243]

Parol evidence was admitted to establish the trust, which operated as an express trust. However, when the same principle was applied in the more recent case of *Bannister* v *Bannister*,[244] the trust was described as constructive in nature.[245]

---

[238] Cf. *Lincoln v Wright* (1859) 4 De G & J 16; *McCormick v Grogan* (1869) LR 4 HL 82.

[239] Cf. the views of Bagnall J in *Cowcher* v *Cowcher* [1972] 1 WLR 425, 436.

[240] See *Allen v Snyder* [1977] 2 NSWLR 685, 692–693 per Glass JA; Montgomery, n 34 *supra*, 22; Hayton "Remedial Constructive Trusts of Homes" [1988] Conv 259, 264; Miller, n 3 *supra*, p 31; Glover and Todd, n 36 *supra*.

[241] [1897] 1 Ch 196.

[242] See generally Youdan "Formalities for Trusts of Land, and the Doctrine in *Rochefoucauld* v *Boustead*" (1984) 43 CLJ 306. Note also Feltham's response "Informal Trusts and Third Parties" [1987] Conv 246 and Youdan's riposte "Informal Trusts and Third Parties: A Response" [1988] Conv 266. Cf. Thompson "Using Statutes as Instruments of Fraud" (1985) 36 NILQ 358.

[243] [1897] 1 Ch 196, 206.

[244] [1948] 2 All ER 133.

[245] While it appears to make little practical difference whether one categorises the trust as express

The principle in *Rochefoucauld* was expressly invoked in the family context in *Re Densham*.[246] It was clear from the evidence in that case that, at the time of acquisition, a common intention had existed that the house would be owned jointly and that the wife's name had been omitted from the transfer because of "some misunderstanding which arose due to the fact that they married only shortly before the transfer".[247] Goff J considered the view expressed by Bagnall J in *Cowcher* v *Cowcher*[248] that an agreement between the parties as to the sharing of ownership would be unenforceable unless it was in writing or amounted to a specifically enforceable contract. Goff J felt that this view was "contrary to equitable principles".[249] He explained that:

"[O]nce the agreement is found it would be unconscionable for a party to set up the statute and repudiate the agreement. Accordingly, in my judgment, he or she becomes a constructive trustee of the property in so far as necessary to give effect to the agreement. That, in my judgment, was established long ago in *Rochefoucauld* v *Boustead* [1897] 1 Ch 196 and clearly accepted by the House of Lords in *Gissing* v *Gissing*".[250]

There is certainly some support to be found in the speeches in *Gissing* for the approach favoured by Goff J. Although phrased in rather general terms, the following remarks of Viscount Dilhorne (quoted by Goff J)[251] appear to support the application of the *Rochefoucauld* principle:

"Where there was a common intention at the time of the acquisition of the house that the beneficial interest in it should be shared, it would be a breach of faith by the spouse in whose name the legal estate was vested to fail to give effect to that intention and the other spouse will be held entitled to a share in the beneficial interest".[252]

Lord Diplock's speech in *Gissing* might also appear to be founded on the *Rochefoucauld* doctrine. Just after his central statement of principle,[253] Lord Diplock pointed out that the courts had repeatedly stated their willingness to enforce an agreement between spouses as to the manner in which the beneficial

---

or constructive, commentators are divided as to which is preferable from a theoretical viewpoint. See Youdan "Formalities for Trusts of Land", n 242 *supra*, 330–334; Gray, n 3 *supra*, p 379; Dal Pont "Equity's Chameleon—Unmasking the Constructive Trust" (1997) 16 *Australian Bar Review* 46, 68–69; Oakley *Constructive Trusts*, 3rd edn (London: Sweet and Maxwell, 1997) p 53 n 24.

[246] [1975] 1 WLR 1519. See also the explicit application of *Bannister* [1948] 2 All ER 133 by Lord Denning MR in *Neale* v *Willis* (1968) 19 P & CR 836.

[247] *Ibid*, 1525.

[248] [1972] 1 WLR 425, 436.

[249] [1975] 1 WLR 1519, 1525.

[250] *Ibid*.

[251] *Ibid*.

[252] [1971] AC 886, 900. Taken literally, this passage suggests that a trust would follow from the proof of a common intention, without any need to show detrimental reliance. (Cf. Webb "Trusts of Matrimonial Property" (1976) 92 LQR 489, 492; *Re Densham* [1975] 1 WLR 1519; *Thwaites* v *Ryan* [1984] VR 65, 95). However, in *Midland Bank plc* v *Dobson* [1986] 1 FLR 171, 174, Fox LJ doubted that the relevant passage from Viscount Dilhorne's speech "was intended as a comprehensive statement of the position". Fox LJ insisted (*ibid*, 175) that detrimental reliance was necessary to avoid the statutory requirement of evidence in writing. See, however, text following n 273 *infra*.

[253] [1971] AC 886, 905. The relevant passage is quoted as text to n 10 *supra*.

interests in their home would be shared.[254] The courts would do this "notwith-standing the absence of any written declaration of trust".[255] Lord Diplock had earlier pointed out,[256] citing section 53(1) of the Law of Property Act 1925, that in the absence of writing a declaration of trust over land could only take effect as a resulting, implied or constructive trust.

Despite the hints in these rather vague *dicta* that the *Rochefoucauld* principle is the basis for the common intention trust, a closer inspection reveals difficulties in applying *Rochefoucauld* in the family context. The problem is that cases such as *Rochefoucauld* and *Bannister* involved a conveyance which had been made on the basis of an oral declaration of trust. The person who had conveyed the property was permitted to introduce evidence of the true bargain and so benefit from a constructive trust. Thus, if A conveyed property to B on the strength of an oral declaration of trust by B, B would be prevented from invoking the Statute of Frauds to escape his declaration of trust. However, in the family context, the conveyance will not have been made "on the strength of" the informal declaration of trust. The conveyance will have been made, not by the partner seeking to establish a constructive trust, but rather by the former owner of the house, a stranger who will normally have no knowledge of (or interest in) any intention which the new legal owner might have to share the beneficial ownership with his partner. Therefore, in its classic form, the doctrine in *Rochefoucauld* v *Boustead* is not directly applicable to family property disputes.[257]

This is not, however, the end of the matter since one might wish to argue for a wider formulation of the relevant equitable principle. Such an argument could proceed on two alternative bases. The first approach relies on a well-established line of authority demonstrating the courts' willingness to apply *Rochefoucauld* in cases where the defendant has purchased property as agent for the plaintiff. The second approach, more radical but equally unsuccessful, involves an attempt to extend the *Rochefoucauld* doctrine beyond the paradigm of "a conveyance induced by fraud" so as to cover the case of detrimental reliance upon an informal declaration of trust. It is now proposed to examine these two possibilities in turn.

---

[254] *Ibid.*

[255] *Ibid.*

[256] *Ibid*, 905B.

[257] It is necessary to distinguish the situation under discussion from another scenario which has been the subject of controversy. In this other scenario, "A conveys Blackacre to B on an oral under-standing between A and B that it is to be held for the benefit of C" (Feltham, n 242 *supra*, 246). Opinions have varied as to whether this kind of oral understanding may be enforced by either or both of A and C. (See the articles by Youdan and Feltham cited in n 242 *supra*). However, the important point for present purposes is that the above scenario is entirely different from the "family home" situation because it involves an understanding between A (the person conveying the property) and B (the person to whom the property is conveyed). In the family home cases, there is invari-ably no understanding between the original seller of the family home and the purchasing cohabitee as to how the beneficial ownership will be shared as between the cohabiting partners. Cf. Feltham *supra*, 249.

(a) Purchase as agent

The courts have clearly been willing to extend the *Rochefoucauld* principle to cover a situation which bears some resemblance to the family home scenario. This is the case where B purchases property on the basis of an oral agreement with C that he is buying as agent for C. In this situation, it is a matter of indifference to the person selling the property whether or not B adheres to his agreement with C. Nonetheless, on the basis of *Rochefoucauld*, the courts have regarded B as purchasing as trustee for C and have prevented B from setting up the Statute to escape the agreement.[258] A convenient illustration is provided by the facts of *Chattock* v *Muller*.[259]

In *Chattock*, the defendant and the plaintiff were both interested in bidding for a certain property. They reached an understanding that they would each take a portion of the property. On this basis, it was agreed that the defendant would make the purchase as agent for both of them. However, after the purchase had been finalised, the defendant attempted to resile from the agreement and to keep all the land for himself. Malins V-C held that the defendant could not be allowed to perpetrate such a fraud and he therefore compelled the defendant to transfer the agreed portion of the land to the plaintiff (upon the plaintiff's paying the agreed price).

The important question in the present context is whether the extended version of the *Rochefoucauld* principle, developed in cases such as *Chattock*, is sufficiently broad to provide a rationale for the common intention trust in the family context.[260] It is submitted that even the broad version of the principle falls somewhat short in this respect. There are three main problems:

(1) The application of the *Rochefoucauld* principle involves the proposition that the legally owning partner is purchasing the property as agent for himself and his partner. Passing over the artificiality of the notion of agency in this context, one is left with two related difficulties. The first problem is the implication that the common intention must involve an understanding that the claimant will contribute towards the purchase price; otherwise, how could it be said that the legal owner is purchasing on her behalf? However, in practice, the English courts have come down in favour of granting a remedy in cases where the common intention was simply that the beneficial ownership would be shared, without any *quid pro quo* being envisaged.[261]

---

[258] Part of the rationale for equity's intervention in this situation is the feeling that B, by undertaking to acquire the property on behalf of C, may have "lulled" C into not bidding for the property himself. See Youdan "Formalities for Trusts of Land", n 242 *supra*, 329 n 15.

[259] (1878) 8 Ch D 177. See also *Cadd* v *Cadd* (1909) 9 CLR 171; *Pallant* v *Morgan* [1953] Ch 43; *Devine* v *Fields* (1920) 54 ILTR 101; *McGillycuddy* v *Joy* [1959] IR 189; *Gilmurray* v *Corr* [1978] NI 99 and the additional authorities cited by Youdan "Formalities for Trusts of Land", n 242 *supra*, 329 n 14.

[260] Note that in the older case of *Ward* v *Ward* [1958] VR 68, 75, Smith J expressly relied on this version of the *Rochefoucauld* principle.

[261] See the discussion in Part I(A)(3) *supra*.

A remedy has been forthcoming once the claimant has acted to her detriment in some way (not specified in the common intention) on the basis of the assumption that she was entitled to a share in the beneficial ownership. While perfectly explicable on the basis of estoppel principles, such cases cannot be explained on the basis that the legal owner purchased as agent for the claimant.

(2)   The second and related problem is that, if the trust depends on the legal owner purchasing as agent for the claimant, then logically the claimant must subsequently provide part of the purchase price. In other words, one is driven back, by an unexpected route, towards an insistence on a resulting-trust style contribution to the purchase money. As has been explained already,[262] the practice of the English courts is generally to accept any detrimental reliance as sufficient, with no requirement that that conduct should take the form of making a contribution to the purchase price. One must conclude that a reliance on *Rochefoucauld* would lead to an undesirable restriction on the type of conduct which could form the basis of a common intention trust.

(3)   A third, and somewhat different problem, is that, in order to conceptualise a common intention as an agreement to purchase as agent, it is necessary that the common intention have come into existence at, or before, the time of the purchase. Yet the English courts have clearly recognised that, in exceptional cases, a trust may arise from a common intention formed some time after the initial acquisition of the house, for example on the occasion of the making of substantial improvements.[263] Such cases clearly cannot be explained on the basis that the defendant has agreed to purchase the property as agent for the claimant.

(b)   Detrimental reliance on an informal declaration of trust

If one accepts that the "purchase as agent" argument is unsuccessful, then one is forced to contend for a major modification of the *Rochefoucauld* principle to allow it to cover the "common intention" situation. It is worth restating the central problem: in all its manifestations, the *Rochefoucauld* principle "is restricted to situations where a person acquires property subject to a trust".[264] This means, as has been seen, that the principle can only explain cases where the common intention was formed at the time the property was conveyed to the legally-owning partner.[265] In cases where the common intention is formed after acquisition, the legal owner has not acquired the property subject to any trust. He is, at worst, in the position of an absolute owner of property who has made

---

[262] See Part I(B)(1) *supra*.

[263] See n 14 *supra*.

[264] See Youdan "Formalities for Trusts of Land", n 242 *supra*, 325.

[265] Cf. *Thwaites v Ryan* [1984] VR 65, 92–93 where Fullager J's reliance on the *Rochefoucauld* principle led him to deny that a remedy could be based on a common intention formed subsequent to the acquisition of the disputed property.

an informal declaration of trust outside the context of any conveyance of the property in question. Even where the common intention is formed at the time of the conveyance, the truth is that the conveyance is really an irrelevance. Given the indifference of the vendor to the private arrangements of the purchaser and his partner, and given the inapplicability of the "agency" cases, it is simply unrealistic to try to fit the situation into the paradigm of "a conveyance induced by fraud".

The above analysis suggests that any attempt to rely on *Rochefoucauld* can succeed only by jettisoning the attempt to connect the common intention with the vendor's conveyance of the property to the defendant. Instead, it must be contended that a version of the *Rochefoucauld* principle applies where, independently of any conveyance, the defendant makes an informal declaration of trust, thereby leading the claimant to act to her detriment.

This argument faces the initial obstacle that those commentators and judges who have considered the question appear to agree that the *Rochefoucauld* principle has no application to informal declarations of trust which have not, in some way, induced the conveyance of the land to the defendant.[266] "Otherwise", as Gray explains,[267] "there would be no circumstances at all which came within the reach of section 53(1)(b)". However, in response, one would not have to contend that such statements of orthodox principle were wrong; rather, one could make the less onerous argument that they were not consciously directed to cases where there has been detrimental reliance on the declaration of trust.[268]

Conceding for the purposes of argument that a "detrimental reliance" variant of *Rochefoucauld* is not foreclosed as a matter of authority, one is left to consider the merits of such a doctrine. It is submitted that it is indefensible in principle. The objections are as follows:

(1) The first criticism must be that the relevant ground is already fully covered by the principles of estoppel. Under those principles, as has been seen in Chapter 4, an equity is raised in favour of a person who is led to act to her detriment by a representation that she has, or will have, an interest in certain land. The court has a discretion as to how to satisfy the claimant's equity. Given the presence of this comprehensive doctrine, there is no obvious reason to introduce a new doctrine which would apply only in cases where the representation in question took the shape of an informal declaration of trust. Moreover, the new doctrine is demonstrably inferior to the

---

[266] See Ames "Constructive Trusts Based upon the Breach of an Express Oral Trust of Land" (1906–1907) 20 *Harv Law Rev* 549, 549; Youdan "Formalities for Trusts of Land" n 242 *supra*, 325–326; Feltham, n 242 *supra*, 247 n 6 (but see *ibid*, 248); Gray, n 3 *supra*, p 378; *Organ v Sandwell* [1921] VLR 622, 630 per Irvine CJ; *Last v Rosenfeld* [1972] 2 NSWLR 923, 930C, 933A per Hope J; *Wratten v Hunter* [1978] 2 NSWLR 367.

[267] See n 3 *supra*, p 378.

[268] See Feltham, n 242 *supra*, 248 suggesting in passing that in such cases the plaintiff "is not a mere volunteer". Contrast, however, Ames, n 266 *supra*, 549–550.

established one in that it lacks the remedial flexibility of estoppel. The estoppel claimant receives a remedy which is moulded by the extent of her detriment; the "common intention" claimant is automatically rewarded with a constructive trust once her detriment satisfies some ill-defined threshold requirement.[269]

(2)   The reference to "an informal declaration of trust" assumes that one can get over the difficulty in treating a vague (and possibly unspoken) common intention as a declaration of trust which is unenforceable only because it is not evidenced in writing. It is submitted that a "common intention" is likely to fall short of a declaration of trust in a number of other ways besides its informality. It must be remembered that for a valid express trust of land one requires, in addition to the statutory formalities, the presence of the so-called "three certainties" which are essential to any private express trust.[270] In relation to the requirement of certainty of intention, it will often be difficult in a family situation to show that the legal owner intended to subject himself to a legally-binding obligation[271] in the form of a trust.[272] The contention that a "common intention" constitutes an informal declaration of trust seems particularly implausible in cases where the common intention is inferred, not from anything said or done by the defendant, but simply from the claimant's conduct in making financial contributions. There are also likely to be difficulties over certainty of subject matter, in that it may be unclear precisely what share was intended for the claimant under the trust.[273]

[269] See Glover and Todd, n 36 *supra*, 334, referring to the establishment of a trust once the claimant's reliance "is sufficient to overcome the formalities hurdle".

[270] See e.g. Martin *Hanbury and Martin: Modern Equity*, 15th edn (London: Sweet and Maxwell, 1997) pp 89–110. These difficulties do not seem to attach to the contention that a common intention, formed at the time of acquisition, amounts to an agreement that the legal owner will purchase as agent for the claimant. (See the discussion in the text following n 257 *supra*.) It appears from the case law that such an agreement can be relatively informal and need not constitute a declaration of trust; the trust which is ultimately generated in favour of the claimant arises from the fiduciary nature of the agency assumed by the purchaser and not from any actual declaration of trust. See Feltham, n 242 *supra*, 247.

[271] Note, however, the occasionally generous approach of the courts, as illustrated by *Paul v Constance* [1977] 1 WLR 527 (where comparatively flimsy evidence sufficed to prove a declaration of trust over money in a bank account).

[272] A common intention may involve an understanding that, rather than obtain an immediate beneficial interest, the claimant will obtain a share at some point in the future (perhaps conditional on her making some type of contribution). It is arguable that such a postponed or conditional expression of a willingness to share cannot be categorised as a declaration of trust. (Cf. *Jones v Lock* (1865) LR 1 Ch App 25). Nonetheless, the courts are clearly willing to grant a remedy on the basis of the form of common intention discussed above. (Indeed, it has been suggested that the courts might not enforce a common intention *unless* it took the form of a bargain: see text to and following n 102 *supra*). It seems that Glover and Todd would deal with such cases under the principles of estoppel (thus relegating the claimant to a detriment-based remedy). See n 36 *supra*, 332–333; 341–342. However, this approach would involve drawing fine (and apparently arbitrary) distinctions between different types of "common intention".

[273] Note Lord Diplock's discussion in *Gissing* [1971] AC 886, 909 of a common intention that the shares of the partners would be calculated on the basis of their subsequent contributions. See text to n 125 *supra*.

(3)   A related problem concerns the consequences in a bankruptcy context of a decision to categorise a common intention as an informal declaration of trust. Consider the facts of *Midland Bank plc v Dobson*.[274] It will be recalled that this case arose in the context of the husband's bankruptcy and that the spouses persuaded the judge that they had had a common intention to share the ownership of the family home. The Court of Appeal declined to interfere with the trial judge's finding in this respect but held that no constructive trust arose because the wife could not show detrimental reliance.

Here lies the problem. It is well established that the absence of statutory formalities renders a trust of land unenforceable rather than void.[275] In other words, while the beneficiary cannot force the trustee to carry out the trust, the trustee has the option of doing so. The case of *Gardner v Rowe*[276] demonstrates that the trust will become enforceable if the trustee, subsequent to his bankruptcy, brings into existence written evidence of the trust.[277] Thus, if one insists on categorising a common intention as an informal declaration of trust, one would have to accept that the husband in *Dobson* could have ensured the success of his wife's claim simply by acknowledging in writing his previous "declaration of trust". The absence of detrimental reliance would, in those circumstances, have been irrelevant, since the requirements of section 53(1)(b) would have been satisfied and there would have been no need to rely upon any variation of the *Rochefoucauld* principle. This unsatisfactory result[278] can only be avoided, it is submitted, by conceding that most common intentions fall far

---

[274] [1986] 1 FLR 171.

[275] See e.g. Youdan "Formalities for Trusts of Land", n 242 *supra*, 320–322; Gray, n 3 *supra*, p 376.

[276] (1828) 5 Russ 258.

[277] Cf. Hayton "Constructive Trusts: Is the Remedying of Unjust Enrichment a Satisfactory Approach?", n 149 *supra*, p 233 n 130. Youdan "Formalities for Trusts of Land" in *Equity, Fiduciaries and Trusts*, n 242 *supra*, 321 argues for a more narrow interpretation of *Gardner*, suggesting that it is somehow significant that the owner of the land is not subject to an "enforceable" trust until the time that a memorandum comes into existence. Cf. Hayton "Equitable Rights of Cohabitees" [1990] Conv 370, 381. However, Youdan concedes that the statutory requirement is merely evidential and that its lack of fulfilment does not affect the validity of the oral trust. Once this concession is made, it does not seem possible to argue against the proposition in the text to this footnote. Since the written memorandum serves merely as evidence, it must operate to prove something and the thing which is proven is that a trust came into existence at the time of the initial oral declaration of trust. From the point of view of priorities, it is immaterial that, if the dispute had arisen at an earlier stage, the beneficiary would have been unable to supply sufficient evidence to prove her case.

[278] Leaving aside the "common intention" argument, it is most unlikely that one partner would be able to show a genuine oral declaration of trust in favour of his partner. If he could, it might well appear that such a deliberate declaration of trust was made with the intention of defeating the rights of his creditors (thus falling foul of statutory provisions such as s 423 of the English Insolvency Act 1986). However, most couples could come up with the sort of vague evidence which established the "common intention" in *Dobson* [1986] 1 FLR 171 (Sesame Street-style affirmations of the importance of "sharing" and "partnership" in a relationship). Furthermore, the very disparity between this vague sort of "common intention" and a genuine declaration of trust would seem to provide an answer to the allegation that there was an intention to defeat the rights of creditors.

short of constituting informal declarations of trust. This concession, in turn, leads to the conclusion that the common intention analysis cannot be rationalised on the basis of the *Rochefoucauld* principle.

It has been argued in this section that the principle in *Rochefoucauld* v *Boustead* has no application in the family home context, where it is not meaningful to speak in terms of a "conveyance induced by fraud". The suggestion that one should extend the doctrine to cover the case of detrimental reliance on an informal declaration of trust runs into the difficulty that the territory of detrimental reliance is already fully covered by the principles of estoppel. Furthermore, most common intentions do not really constitute informal "declarations of trust" and a willingness to pretend that they do leads to unfortunate consequences in the bankruptcy context. For these reasons, it is submitted that one must reject the principle in *Rochefoucauld* as the basis for the common intention trust.

3. The bargain model

The next possible foundation for the common intention trust may be termed "the bargain model". Put simply, the reasoning behind this model runs as follows: the common intention between the parties amounts to an informal bargain under which the claimant is to receive a share in the home if she acts in a certain manner. Once she has acted in the envisaged manner, it becomes inequitable for the legal owner to resile from the bargain. A constructive trust therefore comes into existence to give effect to the bargain.

In order to understand the bargain model, it is necessary to return to a close examination of the speech of Lord Diplock in *Gissing*. His Lordship attempted a legal analysis, from first principles, of the role of a common intention in the creation of a beneficial interest in the land of another. As a preliminary, he explained[279] that a claim to such a beneficial interest fell to be considered under the law of trusts, in particular the law relating to the creation and operation of resulting, implied or constructive trusts. Having made his famous general comment on the nature of implied, constructive and resulting trusts,[280] Lord Diplock then turned to a more detailed consideration of the path from a common intention to a trust in favour of a claimant.

He began[281] by examining the simple case where there had been an express agreement between the parties which revealed the existence of a common intention. His Lordship noted that it had often been said that the court would give effect to such an agreement notwithstanding the absence of a suitably evidenced declaration of trust.[282] Strictly speaking (he continued) this was too broad a statement "for if the agreement did not provide for anything to be done by the

---

[279] [1971] AC 886, 905.
[280] Quoted as text to n 10 *supra*.
[281] [1971] AC 886, 905.
[282] *Ibid*. Cf. Section A of this Part *supra*.

spouse in whom the legal estate was not to be vested, it would be a merely voluntary declaration of trust and unenforceable for want of writing".[283] Lord Diplock continued as follows:

"But in the express oral agreements contemplated by these dicta it has been assumed *sub silentio* that they provide for the spouse in whom the legal estate in the matrimonial home is not vested to do something to facilitate its acquisition . . . What the court gives effect to is the trust resulting or implied from the common intention expressed in the oral agreement between the spouses that if each acts in the manner provided for in the agreement the beneficial interests in the matrimonial home shall be held as they have agreed".[284]

Lord Diplock went on to explain that the position would be the same if such a common intention could be inferred from the conduct of the parties.[285]

A common intention, under this approach, must therefore constitute an informal bargain whereby the legal owner, whether expressly or by his conduct, makes "the promise of a specified beneficial interest in the land" and this leads the claimant "to act to his or her detriment . . . with the intention of acquiring that beneficial interest".[286] The argument is that when the claimant has fulfilled her side of the bargain, it would be "inequitable" for the legal owner to deny her a beneficial interest in the land and a trust would arise to prevent this and give effect to the common intention.

One obvious difficulty with requiring a bargain, however informal, between the parties is the unlikelihood of a couple striking any sort of bargain when happily beginning their life together in a new home. This reality led, at an early stage,[287] to the rejection of the mainstream law of contract as a useful framework within which to solve disputes of this nature.[288] The artificiality of attempting to infer even an informal bargain from the conduct of the parties is demonstrated in the English case law which attempted to apply the requirement of a bargain suggested by Lord Diplock in *Gissing*.

In *Eves* v *Eves*,[289] it will be recalled, a man led the young woman with whom he was living to believe that she was to have an interest in their house. She had done a lot of work on the house which had been very dirty and dilapidated when it was first purchased. Brightman J (with whom Browne LJ agreed) felt that if "it was part of the bargain between the parties, expressed or to be implied, that the plaintiff should contribute her labour towards the reparation of a house in which she was to have some beneficial interest, then I think that the arrangement

---

[283] *Ibid.*

[284] *Ibid.*

[285] *Ibid*, 906A–B.

[286] *Ibid*, 905.

[287] See the discussion in Chapter 1 *supra*, text following n 59.

[288] Note, however, that in *Pettitt* [1970] AC 777, 822C–D Lord Diplock was more enthusiastic than some of his brethren about using the concept of the exchange of promises as a basis for solving matrimonial property disputes. See Chapter 1 *supra*, text following n 67.

[289] [1975] 1 WLR 1338.

becomes one to which the law can give effect".[290] He noted that what needed to be done when the house was bought was "plain for all to see" and he found it difficult to suppose that she would have worked as hard as she had, including demolishing a large area of concrete with a fourteen pound sledgehammer, except in pursuance of some expressed or implied arrangement.

In *Grant* v *Edwards*,[291] the common intention had also been established on the basis of a lie told by the legal owner. Mustill LJ considered whether this common intention could be fashioned into the shape of a bargain. The claimant in *Grant* had contributed to the family finances, thus enabling the legal owner to pay the mortgage instalments. It was considered legitimate by Mustill LJ to hold that "there must have been an assumption that the transfer of rights to the plaintiff would not be unilateral, and that the plaintiff would play her own part".[292]

In both *Grant* and *Eves*, there is a very artificial flavour to the attempts by the judges to twist the common intention into the shape of a bargain. This probably explains why the English courts now appear to have dropped the requirement that common intention take the form of a bargain which envisages reciprocal obligations for the parties.[293]

There is also another and more crucial difficulty with a reliance on the bargain model. This is the fact that, in any case, there is no satisfactory explanation of how one moves from an informal bargain to a constructive trust. Just like trusts over land, the enforceability of contracts concerning land depends upon compliance with a statutory requirement of evidence in writing. In fact, section 4 of the Statute of Frauds 1677 (requiring a contract concerning land or any interest therein to be evidenced in writing) was treated with more respect by the courts of equity than section 7 (which created a similar formal requirement in relation to trusts over land). The principle that a statute should not be used as an instrument of fraud has generated, in the context of section 4 of the Statute of Frauds, the doctrine of part performance. This doctrine, which has been abolished by statute in England[294] but survives in other jurisdictions,[295] allows a court of equity to decree specific performance in favour of a claimant who has

---

[290] [1975] 1 WLR 1345.

[291] [1986] 1 Ch 638.

[292] *Ibid*, 653.

[293] See Part I(A)(3) *supra*.

[294] The English Law of Property (Miscellaneous Provisions) Act 1989, s 2 repeals s 40 of the Law of Property Act 1925 (which had been based on s 4 of the Statute of Frauds). The effect of s 2 is that the doctrine of part performance no longer applies to contracts concluded on or after 27 September 1989. The new position is that contracts for the sale or other disposition of an interest in land must be in writing (rather than merely being evidenced in writing). An unwritten contract is no longer merely unenforceable but is utterly void. Therefore, as Gray explains (n 3 *supra*, p 258), in the absence of compliance with the statutory formalities, there is "simply no contract in existence in relation to which, and in support of which, acts of part performance can occur".

[295] See e.g. *Hill* v *Attorney General of Nova Scotia* (1997) 142 DLR (4th) 230 (SCC); Dal Pont, n 245 *supra*, 67–68 (discussing the Australian position); *Fleming* v *Beevers* [1994] NZFLR 108; Delany *Equity and the Law of Trusts in Ireland* (Dublin: Round Hall Sweet and Maxwell, 1996) pp 437–441; *MacKey* v *Wilde* [1998] 1 ILRM 449.

"part performed" the contract. Unlike the doctrine in *Rochefoucauld* v *Boustead* which is its parallel in the trust situation, the doctrine of part performance is technical and restricted in its nature and does not rely upon a vague appeal to inequitability. The well-known case of *Maddison* v *Alderson*[296] demonstrates equity's reluctance lightly to subvert the statutory formalities in relation to contracts concerning land.[297]

It seems clear that, despite his reliance on the notion of a bargain, Lord Diplock did not wish to import all the restrictions of the doctrine of part performance into his common intention trust. The common intention trust, as it is portrayed in Lord Diplock's speech and as it has developed in subsequent cases, is clearly far more flexible than the doctrine of part performance.[298] Given this fact, and taking into account the legislative abolition of the doctrine of part performance in England,[299] one might wish to argue that Lord Diplock was relying not on part performance itself but on some related, although distinct, equitable principle.

It is submitted, however, that this simply will not do. If one accepts the bargain model as a theoretical justification, the common intention trust is, just like part performance, based on a willingness to enforce informal bargains in favour of a claimant who has acted on the bargain. The trouble is that it is surely impermissible to employ the very same principle which underlies the doctrine of part performance to justify a new doctrine which would, in many cases, render meaningless the subtleties of the older doctrine. This is the same argument which applies to a possible "resulting trust" explanation for the common intention trust. In both cases the established doctrines would be swept away, not even on the basis of a new principle, but by reference to the very same argument which led the courts to develop those doctrines in the first place. It seems clear, therefore, that some new rationale is required to justify the common intention trust's encroachment on the territory of other doctrines.[300]

This conclusion leads to a consideration of yet another possible theoretical foundation for the common intention trust: the doctrine of equitable estoppel. This is currently the most fashionable rationalisation although, as will be discussed, important features of the common intention trust remain unexplained.

---

[296] 1883) 8 App Cas 467, setting up a requirement that the action of the claimant must be referable to the contract between the parties. Note the more flexible approach taken by the House of Lords in *Steadman* v *Steadman* [1976] AC 536.

[297] This approach is in contrast to the more cavalier approach to s 7 of the Statute of Frauds demonstrated in the cases on informal trusts over land. See Neave "The Constructive Trust as a Remedial Device" (1978) 11 *Melbourne University Law Review* 343, 365–368.

[298] See *Re Gonin* [1979] Ch 16; Hayton "Constructive Trusts: Is the Remedying of Unjust Enrichment a Satisfactory Approach?" n 149 *supra*, p 229; pp 235–236; Hayton *Underhill and Hayton*, n 3 *supra*, pp 386–387.

[299] See n 294 *supra*.

[300] The only remaining role for the bargain model may be within the estoppel framework, where the existence of a bargain might justify the choice of a constructive trust as the claimant's remedy. See text to and following n 317 *infra*.

4. *The estoppel model*

In *Grant* v *Edwards*,[301] Browne Wilkinson V-C explained the requirements for "common intention" trust as follows:

> "If the legal estate in the joint home is vested in only one of the parties ('the legal owner') the other party ('the claimant'), in order to establish a beneficial interest, has to establish a constructive trust by showing that it would be inequitable for the legal owner to claim sole beneficial ownership. This requires two matters to be demonstrated: (a) that there was a common intention that both should have a beneficial interest; (b) that the claimant has acted to his or her detriment on the basis of that common intention".[302]

This approach moves away from the bargain concept and closer to the idea of estoppel. It will be recalled that, in *Gissing*, Lord Diplock referred to a claimant's acting to her detriment "in the reasonable belief that by so acting [she] was *acquiring* a beneficial interest in the land".[303] In many cases where a common intention exists, the claimant would believe, without understanding the legal position, that the house was somehow already joint property. She would act in the assurance that she already owned a share and not in the expectation of earning one by her conduct. The estoppel model is broad enough to cover both conduct intended to acquire a share and conduct based on a belief that a share had already been acquired.

Since the "possible analogy" with proprietary estoppel had not been fully argued before the court in *Grant* v *Edwards*, Browne-Wilkinson V-C felt it safer to rest his judgment on other grounds. However, he did make the following comments:

> "I suggest that in other cases of this kind, useful guidance may in the future be obtained from the principles underlying the law of proprietary estoppel which in my judgment are closely akin to those laid down in *Gissing* v *Gissing* [1971] AC 886. In both, the claimant must to the knowledge of the legal owner have acted in the belief that the claimant has or will obtain an interest in the property. In both, the claimant must have acted to his or her detriment in reliance on such belief. In both, equity acts on the conscience of the legal owner to prevent him from acting in an unconscionable manner by defeating the common intention. The two principles have been developed separately without cross-fertilisation between them: but they rest on the same foundation and have on all other matters reached the same conclusions".[304]

Browne-Wilkinson V-C felt that the law of proprietary estoppel could also provide guidance on the question of quantifying the share of the claimant who had

---

[301] [1986] 1 Ch 638.

[302] *Ibid*, 654.

[303] [1971] AC 886, 905 (emphasis supplied). It is worth mentioning that, despite the current popularity of the estoppel model, Lord Diplock himself never referred explicitly to estoppel in his speech. One must see the estoppel model as a *post hoc* rationalisation of a doctrine which was originally thought to be founded on other principles.

[304] [1986] 1 Ch 638, 656.

relied to her detriment on a common intention. The court would give effect to the common intention "so far as may be fairly done between the parties". Here equity was "displayed at its most flexible".[305]

Since these comments of Browne-Wilkinson V-C, a number of judges have questioned the reality of the distinction between proprietary estoppel and the common intention analysis.[306] Even Lord Bridge, in his very conservative speech in *Lloyds Bank plc v Rosset*,[307] referred on three occasions to the creation of "a constructive trust or proprietary estoppel".[308] Unfortunately, despite some academic debate,[309] there has been no judicial willingness to face up to the consequences of assimilating the two doctrines. If the common intention trust had no independent features, then it would simply collapse into the wider doctrine of estoppel and a great simplification would be achieved. However, upon reflection, one finds that the common intention trust does indeed have independent features and it seems difficult to find any sound theoretical reason for these departures from the restrictions of estoppel.[310]

The most important difference between the doctrines is the willingness, under the common intention analysis, to infer a common intention from evidence of the making of financial contributions to the acquisition of property.[311] This process allows for the award of a remedy in cases where estoppel would be useless. Yet, assuming that the common intention trust is a species of estoppel, what is the justification for the pretence that a representation (sufficient to form the basis of an estoppel) has been made by the legal owner where all that has happened is that his partner has made a financial payment?

It was pointed out earlier in this chapter that this manoeuvre was accomplished by Lord Diplock in *Gissing* under the cover of an analogy with the presumption of resulting trust.[312] Under the traditional purchase money resulting trust, the making of a financial contribution justifies the inference that the contributor intended to gain a share; under the common intention analysis, the making of a financial contribution justifies the inference that the legal owner led the contributor to believe that she would get a share. Thus, effectively, the presumption of resulting trust is being used to manufacture "representations" for

---

[305] *Ibid*, 657. Cf. text to and following n 169 *supra*.

[306] See *Austin v Keele* (1987) 61 ALJR 605, 609 per Lord Oliver (PC) ("in essence . . . an application of proprietary estoppel"); *Lloyds Bank plc v Carrick* [1996] 4 All ER 630, 640 ("a matter of some doubt" whether a distinction exists). See also *Lloyds Bank Ltd v Rosset* [1989] 1 FLR 51, 72A per Nicholls LJ (CA); *Stokes v Anderson* [1991] 1 FLR 391, 399 per Nourse LJ; *Re Basham* [1986] 1 WLR 1498, 1504D–F per Edward Nugee QC.

[307] [1991] 1 AC 107.

[308] *Ibid*, 129D; 132G; 133F. See, however, text to and following n 327 *infra*.

[309] See Hayton "Equitable Rights of Cohabitees", n 277 *supra*; Ferguson "Constructive Trusts: A Note of Caution" (1993) 109 LQR 114; Hayton "Constructive Trusts of Homes—A Bold Approach" (1994) 110 LQR 485. Note also the observations of Gardner "Rethinking Family Property" n 35 *supra*, 266–269 and the extra-judicial remarks of Lord Browne-Wilkinson *Constructive Trusts and Unjust Enrichment* (Birmingham: Holdsworth Club of the University of Birmingham, 1991) pp 5–6.

[310] Cf. Ferguson, n 309 *supra*, 115–123.

[311] Note Gardner's sharp criticism of this process of "invention", n 35 *supra*, 268–269.

[312] See paragraph of text accompanying n 85 *supra*.

the purposes of the doctrine of proprietary estoppel. The result is that the common intention trust is a hybrid, borrowing from both estoppel and resulting trust doctrine (with the principle in *Rochefoucauld* v *Boustead*[313] also being dragged in to explain the choice of a constructive trust as a remedy for the claimant).[314]

There are obvious objections to the creation of a Frankenstein doctrine from the excised parts of other doctrines (each of which has its own distinct rationale). Thus, as was pointed out earlier in this chapter,[315] under the resulting trust doctrine what is presumed from the claimant's contributions is that the *claimant* intended to gain a share; however, under the common intention analysis, what is inferred from the same conduct is that the *defendant* led her to act to her detriment. Furthermore, the better view is that a purchase money resulting trust cannot be triggered by contributions to mortgage repayments.[316] However, it is generally accepted that a common intention may be inferred from such contributions. Thus, in effect, the presumption of resulting trust is being used to achieve results in the common intention context which are impossible under the resulting trust doctrine itself.

Although the greatest difficulty with the estoppel model is the accommodation of the presumption of resulting trust, there are also other problems to be considered. One is the fact that the remedy afforded in the common intention cases is invariably a share in the beneficial interest under a constructive trust,[317] whereas estoppel principles would suggest that the court should have a discretion to select an appropriate remedy. It could be argued that some weight could be borne here by Lord Diplock's notion of the common intention as a bargain. The suggestion would be that, where the parties had envisaged a beneficial interest as the *quid pro quo* for the detrimental conduct of the claimant, this should be treated as the appropriate remedy. It would be as if the parties had agreed a

---

[313] [1897] 1 Ch 196.

[314] It is interesting to observe how the central concept of "*common* intention" has facilitated the blurring of distinct equitable doctrines. It would appear that the inclusion of the word "common" was due initially to Lord Diplock's idiosyncratic desire to retain a contractual element in his analysis. (See Section B(3) of this Part *supra*). Of course, the term "common intention" is rather misleading, since it suggests a necessity for a subjective consensus between the parties. Such a subjective consensus is not, in fact, necessary given that, as Lord Diplock himself pointed out, a person's intention is judged on the basis of what the other person reasonably understood from the first person's words and actions. (See text to n 31 *supra*). However, the notion of "common intention" has given an air of plausibility to the straddling of the doctrines of resulting trust and estoppel. The primary concern of the resulting trust doctrine is with the intention of the *plaintiff* in making her contribution, while estoppel concentrates more on the intention of the *defendant* as reflected in an (objectively understood) representation to the plaintiff. The blanket of "*common* intention" can be laid over the intention of both the plaintiff and the defendant, thus allowing the English doctrine to borrow ideas from both the resulting trust and estoppel. Cf. Hayton "Constructive Trusts of Homes" n 309 *supra*, 486–487; Glover and Todd, n 36 *supra*.

[315] See paragraph of text to n 85 *supra*.

[316] See the discussion in Chapter 2 *supra*, Part I.

[317] Note, however, the unusual case of *Ungarian* v *Lesnoff* [1990] Ch 206 (noted by Sparkes [1990] Conv 223), where the subject matter of the constructive trust was a life interest in the house. Cf. *Bannister* v *Bannister* [1948] 2 All ER 133.

tariff to compensate the claimant's detriment. While there may be some force in this argument, it cannot explain cases where the common intention does not constitute a bargain and where e.g. the claimant has simply acted to her detriment on the assumption that she already owns a share. There appears to be no reason why the remedy for such a claimant should invariably be the declaration of a trust in her favour.[318]

These, and possibly other,[319] unexplained differences lead to the conclusion that the principles of estoppel, although probably the least unsatisfactory explanation, still do not provide a satisfactory theoretical foundation for the common intention trust as it presently operates.

5. Extended resulting trust plus pure estoppel

In this final section, it is necessary to consider a last possible rationalisation for the "common intention" cases. This approach does not actually seek to defend the full "common intention" analysis of Lord Diplock in *Gissing*. Rather, it involves retreating to an alternative, and possibly more defensible, legal position. The suggestion, which has occasionally been raised in the literature, is that cases where a common intention is inferred from financial contributions should be explained in resulting trust terms (with the implication that the claimant's share must always be proportionate to her contributions),[320] while cases where the common intention is proven by direct evidence should be rationalised as examples of pure proprietary estoppel.[321]

It has already been mentioned that there is a great deal of uncertainty in the English case law as to the relationship between the purchase money resulting trust and the common intention analysis (in cases where the common intention

---

[318] A related problem is the fact that a declaration of a common intention constructive trust appears to relate back to the time of the common intention whereas the remedy granted to an estoppel claimant is prospective in nature and would not come into existence until a court decision in favour of the claimant. It could be argued that, from a practical point of view, an estoppel claimant would not be in an inferior position in relation to the establishment of priorities. The argument would be that the claimant's equity exists even before it crystallises in a court order and that this inchoate equity will bind a purchaser of the family home who takes with notice of the facts underlying it. (Cf. the material cited in Chapter 4 *supra*, n 96). However, a difference may remain: under an estoppel analysis, even an inchoate equity would not arise until the claimant had acted to her detriment, whereas it is arguable (on the basis of the *Rochefoucauld* strand of the doctrine) that a common intention trust relates back to the formation of the common intention rather than to the commencement of detrimental reliance upon it. Note the contrary argument of Hayton "The Equitable Rights of Cohabitees" n 309 *supra*, 380–381 and contrast n 277 *supra*.

[319] It may also be pointed out that it is unclear whether the "net detriment" approach developed in the estoppel cases is applied in the common intention context. See text to and following n 149 *supra*. Another point of uncertainty is whether Lord Denning MR's "presumption of reliance" (proposed in the estoppel context in *Greasley v Cooke* [1980] 1 WLR 1306) also applies in common intention cases. See text following n 158 *supra*. However, this latter point is probably of lesser significance given the questionable nature of the relevant presumption.

[320] Cf. O'Hagan, n 88 *supra*; Dixon, n 88 *supra*.

[321] See Warburton "Interested or Not?" [1986] Conv 291; Hayton "Constructive Trusts of Homes", n 309 *supra*, 486 n 10.

is inferred from conduct).[322] One might be tempted to argue that, as in the case of a grammatical error, if a doctrinal "confusion" becomes sufficiently established it takes on the status of orthodoxy and correctness. This could lead to the suggestion that there is now nothing incorrect about what was stigmatised in this chapter as a "confusion" with the resulting trust doctrine.

It is submitted, however, that such a development has not yet taken place. Despite the tendency in some of the cases to borrow from the doctrine of resulting trusts, there is no real authority for dividing up the "common intention" analysis into two parts and explaining each part on the basis of a different doctrine. Such a development would clearly run contrary to the presentation of the doctrine in the speech of Lord Diplock in *Gissing*[323] and in numerous subsequent Court of Appeal decisions (most obviously *Grant v Edwards*).[324]

At first glance, the idea of partitioning the common intention analysis might appear to find some degree of support in the speech of Lord Bridge in *Rosset*.[325] For a start, Lord Bridge was at pains to emphasise the distinction between express and inferred common intention. However, his intention in this regard seems to have been to make the practical point (considered earlier in this chapter)[326] that, where the common intention has been established by direct evidence, the requirement of detriment can be satisfied by conduct which, of itself, would not have justified the inference of a common intention. Admittedly, Lord Bridge did use subtly different terminology when referring to the two different situations: an express common intention was three times said to give rise to "a constructive trust or proprietary estoppel",[327] while an inferred common intention was said to create a "constructive trust".[328] However, this can be explained on the basis that, independently of the common intention trust analysis, an estoppel remedy would clearly be available to a claimant who relied to her detriment on an express representation by her partner that she would have a share in the family home. The same could not be said of a claimant who relied on a common intention artificially inferred from her financial contributions. Therefore, one could argue that there was nothing controversial in Lord Bridge's view that the orthodox doctrine of proprietary estoppel would provide an alternative remedy in one type of common intention case but not in the other. This interpretation of Lord Bridge's speech seems to be supported by the fact that he used the term "constructive", rather than "resulting", to refer to the trust which is created in cases of inferred common intention.[329] The most plausible conclusion

[322] See text to nn 85–89 *supra*.
[323] [1971] AC 886.
[324] [1986] 1 Ch 638.
[325] [1991] 1 AC 107.
[326] See text to and following n 144 *supra*.
[327] [1991] 1 AC 107, 129D; 132G; 133F. See, however, *ibid*, 131G ("constructive trust").
[328] *Ibid*, 133A.
[329] *Cf*, however, *Baumgartner v Baumgartner* (1987) 164 CLR 137, 154 per Gaudron J (contending that applying the label "constructive" to the relevant trust might make it possible, contrary to strict resulting trust theory, to consider contributions to mortgage instalments as contributions to the purchase price).

is that, although perhaps exerting a subliminal influence on some judgments, the rationalisation under discussion is not yet established in the case law.

By way of conclusion, it is vital to stress that, in any case, partitioning the common intention trust by no means constitutes a satisfactory theoretical solution. As has been discussed in detail in an earlier chapter,[330] there is the crucial problem that, if one is to be faithful to principle and authority, contributions to mortgage instalments cannot trigger a purchase money resulting trust. As to the estoppel portion of a partitioned common intention analysis, one is left with difficulty in explaining the various departures from orthodox estoppel principle discussed in the previous section (most significantly, the invariable choice of a constructive trust as the claimant's remedy).[331] The truth is that, if one sacrificed those portions of the common intention doctrine which are not reconcilable with the rationalisation under discussion, one would simply be left with the "extended resulting trust plus orthodox estoppel" regime presently operated by the Irish courts (and discussed in detail in an earlier chapter).[332] It would surely be ironic if, after struggling with the complex contortions of the common intention analysis for twenty-five years, the English courts were finally to settle for such an unpretentious alternative.

III. CONCLUSION ON THE ENGLISH POSITION

It is somewhat surprising that Lord Diplock's "common intention" model so easily attained the status of orthodoxy in England. It seems that this doctrine benefitted from being placed next to Lord Denning's undoubtedly heretical "constructive trust of a new model" (which will be discussed in Chapter 6). One is reminded of the seventeenth century Spanish princesses who included a dwarf in their retinue in the hope of generating a flattering comparison in the eyes of their beholders.[333] Upon close inspection, the "common intention" trust is not a thing of beauty.

As the analysis in this chapter has attempted to demonstrate, the doctrine lacks a coherent theoretical foundation. The English courts have thrown into the pot three distinct doctrines (resulting trust, estoppel and the principle in *Rochefoucauld* v *Boustead*) and have sealed over this unpalatable mixture with a thick crust of confusion, in the form of the misleading phrase "common intention" (with its implications of bargain and subjective consensus). Not surprisingly, even after twenty-five years in the oven, the "common intention" analysis remains stubbornly half-baked. The English courts ignore the fact that the claimant cannot satisfy the full requirements for a remedy under resulting trust principles or estoppel or the *Rochefoucauld* v *Boustead* doctrine, regarding it as

---

[330] See Chapter 2 *supra*.
[331] See text following n 310 *supra*.
[332] See Chapter 3 *supra*, Part II.
[333] Note the painting by Velaquez, "Las Meninas" (1656–57), in the Musee del Prado.

sufficient if the claimant can satisfy *some* (but not all) of the requirements of each of the three distinct doctrines.

It is submitted that this theoretical confusion is simply indefensible. Furthermore, there is the great irony that, despite the liberties it takes with legal principle, the common intention trust analysis can boast very few advantages at a practical level; it is difficult and expensive to apply[334] and provides a remedy for claimants in only a narrow range of cases. Clearly, this ill-conceived doctrine should find no place in the law of England and, *a fortiori*, no place in the legal systems of other jurisdictions which have developed other, more radical, solutions to the problem which the common intention trust analysis tries to solve.[335]

This negative conclusion on the English position leads to a consideration of alternative possibilities. Chapter 6 will consider Lord Denning's unsuccessful attempt to develop a "constructive trust of a new model" to be imposed whenever justice and good conscience requires it. Then, in the remaining chapters of the book, it is proposed to turn to a contemplation of the rather more promising vistas opened up by the courts in Canada, Australia and New Zealand.

---

[334] See the complaints of Waite J in *Hammond* v *Mitchell* [1991] 1 WLR 1127, 1129–1130.

[335] It must not be forgotten that the common intention analysis formed the starting point for developments in Canada, Australia and New Zealand. Its influence has, in fact, been pernicious since its deficiencies have tempted judges to reason that, however dubious the innovation they are considering, it is no more suspect that the "orthodox" common intention trust. See, for example, *Hayward* v *Giordani* [1983] NZLR 140, 148 lines 37–43 per Cooke J.

6

The New Model Constructive Trust

INTRODUCTION

This chapter will examine Lord Denning's efforts in the 1970s to develop "a constructive trust of a new model"[1] which would be "imposed by law whenever justice and good conscience require it".[2] As will be pointed out, Lord Denning's radical proposal never found the full support of his brethren and, since his retirement, has been "comprehensively rejected"[3] by the English courts.[4] Similarly, the courts of Canada, Australia and New Zealand have eschewed Lord Denning's proposal in favour of their own versions of the remedial constructive trust.[5] Despite a dishonourable flirtation with the new model in two recent cases,[6] the Irish courts have, in general, also kept a virtuous distance between themselves and Lord Denning's novelty.

Even though Lord Denning's approach no longer appears to represent the law in any jurisdiction, his unorthodox ideas continue to be a rich source of confusion. It is necessary, as part of the present work's aim of unravelling the general theoretical tangle, that this rogue strand be isolated and traced to its source. The ultimate conclusion of this chapter will be that Lord Denning's doctrine richly deserved its demise and should not be resurrected in any jurisdiction.

I. THE NEW MODEL CONSTRUCTIVE TRUST

A. The Development of the New Model Constructive Trust

In 1965, Lord Denning MR made the following revealing comment in *Appleton* v *Appleton*:[7]

---

[1] *Per* Lord Denning MR in *Eves* v *Eves* [1975] 1 WLR 1338, 1341.

[2] *Per* Lord Denning MR in *Hussey* v *Palmer* [1972] 1 WLR 1286, 1290.

[3] Pearce and Stevens *The Law of Trusts and Equitable Obligations* (London: Butterworths, 1995) p 638.

[4] The English courts have instead favoured Lord Diplock's "common intention" analysis, discussed in detail in Chapter 5 *supra*.

[5] See the detailed consideration in Chapters 7–9 *infra*.

[6] *HKN Invest Oy* v *Incotrade Pvt Ltd* [1993] 3 IR 152; *Murray* v *Murray* [1996] 3 IR 251. See text following n 69 *infra*.

[7] [1965] 1 WLR 25.

"I prefer to take the simple test: What is reasonable and fair in the circumstances as they have developed, seeing that they are circumstances which no one contemplated before?"[8]

Lord Denning adhered to this preference throughout his long career. It will be recalled that in the 1950s and 1960s he made a number of attempts to develop a discretionary approach to family property disputes.[9] However, the House of Lords stamped on these developments in *Pettitt* v *Pettitt*[10] and again, with the other foot, in *Gissing* v *Gissing*.[11] Undeterred, Lord Denning emerged from the wreckage in the early 1970s and proceeded to rebuild his ideas on an even grander scale.

Lord Denning's counter-attack began in a comparatively modest fashion, with a series of judgments rejecting the strict view on indirect contributions which had been taken by the majority of the Lords in *Gissing*.[12] However, Lord Denning soon grew confident enough to proclaim a new, and far more sweeping, doctrine. His new principle first appeared in *Heseltine* v *Heseltine*.[13] The wife in that case had transferred to her husband a number of valuable shares, accepting his advice that this would reduce their possible liability to estate duty. She acted without independent advice but the decision of the Court of Appeal was not founded on the equitable doctrine of undue influence. Lord Denning MR instead held that the husband held these amounts on resulting trust for his wife.

Lord Denning based the trust on the fact that it would have been inequitable for the husband to keep the property for himself. The shares were held on "a resulting trust which resulted from all the circumstances of the case".[14] Lord Denning supported his decision by reference to *Gissing* v *Gissing*[15] and in particular to the following sentence from the speech of Lord Diplock:

"A resulting, implied or constructive trust—and it is unnecessary for present purposes to distinguish between these three classes of trust—is created by a transaction between the trustee and the cestui que trust in connection with the acquisition by the trustee of a legal estate in land, whenever the trustee has so conducted himself that it would be inequitable to allow him to deny to the cestui que trust a beneficial interest in the land acquired".[16]

---

[8] [1965] 1 WLR 28.
[9] See the discussion in Chapter 1 *supra*, text following n 48 of Lord Denning's "family assets" doctrine and his creative interpretation of s 17 of the Married Women's Property Act 1882.
[10] [1970] AC 777.
[11] [1971] AC 886.
[12] See *Smith* v *Baker* [1970] 1 WLR 1160; *Davis* v *Vale* [1971] 1 WLR 1022; *Falconer* v *Falconer* [1970] 1 WLR 1333; *Hazell* v *Hazell* [1972] 1 WLR 301; *Cooke* v *Head* [1972] 1 WLR 518.
[13] [1971] 1 WLR 342.
[14] *Ibid*, 346–347.
[15] [1971] AC 886.
[16] *Ibid*, 905.

On this authority,[17] Lord Denning imposed a trust upon the husband in *Heseltine* because it would have been inequitable, in a non-technical sense of the word, to allow him to keep the property for himself.

In the controversial case of *Hussey v Palmer*,[18] Lord Denning's new trust made a spectacular reappearance.[19] Mrs Hussey, an elderly widow, sold her condemned house and moved in with her daughter and her son-in-law, the defendant. The house was too small for all of them, so the son-in-law, who owned the house, arranged for a bedroom extension to be added on for the use of Mrs Hussey. The cost of the extension was £607 which was paid directly to the builder by Mrs Hussey. Later, she quarrelled with her hosts and left to live elsewhere. She ran short of money and looked to her son-in-law for financial help. When she got a negative response, she brought an action to recover the money she had paid.

Although Mrs Hussey herself referred to the payment she had made as a loan, Lord Denning accepted her counsel's argument that the money had not been lent.[20] He decided that a constructive[21] trust should be imposed.[22] He described the constructive trust as follows:

> "[It] is a trust imposed by law whenever justice and good conscience require it. It is a liberal process, founded upon large principles of equity, to be applied in cases where the legal owner cannot conscientiously keep the property for himself alone, but ought to allow another to have the property or a share in it".[23]

In support of his view, Lord Denning cited *inter alia* a number of his own decisions including *Heseltine v Heseltine*,[24] *Cooke v Head*[25] and *Binions v Evans*.[26]

In the later case of *Eves v Eves*,[27] this time without any support from his

---

[17] Lord Denning failed to quote Lord Diplock's next sentence which was as follows: "And he will be held to have so conducted himself if by his words or conduct he has induced the cestui que trust to act to his own detriment in the reasonable belief that by so acting he was acquiring a beneficial interest in the land". Mahon J in *Avondale Printers and Stationers Ltd v Haggie* [1979] 2 NZLR 124, 146–147 commented that: "It goes without saying that the last sentence wholly negates the construction which Lord Denning places upon the first sentence".

[18] [1972] 1 WLR 1286.

[19] See also *Cooke v Head* [1972] 1 WLR 518; *Binions v Evans* [1972] Ch 359.

[20] [1972] 1 WLR 1286, 1289F, 1291A. Cairns LJ (who dissented) regarded the payment as a loan, and therefore as inconsistent with the creation of a resulting trust, and would have been anxious to allow the plaintiff to amend her particulars of claim and obtain a retrial.

[21] Lord Denning commented that, although a resulting trust had been alleged, he felt that the trust to be imposed would be more in the nature of a constructive trust. However, according to Lord Denning (*ibid*, 1289), this was more a matter of words than anything else, since the "two run together". It is far from surprising that terminological confusion besets the area of trusts of the family home, given that both Lord Diplock and Lord Denning (for their own distinct purposes) were unwilling to distinguish between resulting and constructive trusts.

[22] Contrast *Morris v Morris* [1982] 1 NSWLR 61, illustrating the possibility of applying proprietary estoppel principles in this kind of case. Cf. *In the Marriage of Wright* (1997) 22 Fam LR 89.

[23] [1972] 1 WLR 1286, 1289–1290.

[24] [1971] 1 WLR 342.

[25] [1972] 1 WLR 518.

[26] [1972] Ch 359.

[27] [1975] 1 WLR 1338.

brethren in the Court of Appeal,[28] Lord Denning again argued in favour of his new-style trust. He commented that:

> "Equity is not past the age of child-bearing. One of her latest progeny is a constructive trust of a new model. Lord Diplock brought it into the world [in Gissing] and we have nourished it".[29]

In *DHN Food Distributors v London Borough of Tower Hamlets*[30] Lord Denning and the Court of Appeal once more applied the new model constructive trust, this time in a commercial context. Lord Denning never resiled from his views, and in one of his last judgments (delivered when he was 82 years old), in the case of *Hall v Hall*,[31] he commented that a trust was necessary "as a matter of ordinary common justice"[32] for the plaintiff.

B. Criticisms of the New Model Trust

Traditionally, the constructive trust is imposed in the interests of justice and good conscience *in certain defined circumstances*. The courts of equity have recognised over the centuries a number of categories of case in which a constructive trust will be imposed. As a glance at any textbook on the law of equity will reveal,[33] there will be a constructive trust where a person seeks to derive an advantage from a fiduciary position, in certain cases where a stranger receives or deals with trust property, where a conveyance is obtained by fraud, where a person seeks to profit from his own crime etc. Lord Denning's project was to draw the traditional categories together under one principle and then to use that principle to extend the imposition of the trust to new circumstances. This attempt may be criticised on three different grounds.

The first objection to the "new model constructive trust" relates to the manner of its development. There was virtually no authority for Lord Denning's views.[34] Therefore, in each judgment Lord Denning tended to rely on what he had said in the previous case, his statements growing in generality as time passed. One New Zealand judge described the process by which Lord Denning built up a body of precedent supporting his theory "as a simple violation of the

---

[28] *Eves* is an important authority on the English "common intention" trust. See the discussion in Chapter 5 *supra*, text to and following n 32 and text to and following n 165.

[29] [1975] 1 WLR 1338, 1341.

[30] [1976] 1 WLR 852.

[31] (1982) 3 FLR 379.

[32] *Ibid*, 381.

[33] See e.g. Martin *Hanbury and Martin: Modern Equity*, 15th edn (London: Sweet and Maxwell, 1997) pp 292–317.

[34] The casual nature of Lord Denning's approach may be demonstrated by comparison with another leading case on constructive trusts, *Carl Zeiss Stiftung v Herbert Smith & Co (No 2)* [1969] 2 Ch 276. In the latter case, the Court of Appeal heard argument for five days and considered 28 authorities, none of which was cited in *Hussey v Palmer* which was apparently disposed of in a day. See the editorial note (1973) 89 LQR 2, 5.

principle of stare decisis".[35] Equally flagrant was the manner in which Lord Denning cast Lord Diplock in the role of midwife to "equity's latest progeny", commenting in *Eves* v *Eves*[36] that "Lord Diplock brought it into the world and we have nourished it". Samuels JA in the Australian case of *Allen* v *Snyder*[37] was inclined to attribute the delinquency of the infant to the nourishment lavished upon it by the Court of Appeal, rather than to any attentions from Lord Diplock.[38] Samuels JA felt that "the legitimacy of the new model is at least suspect; at best it is a mutant from which further breeding should be discouraged".[39]

A second objection lies in the nature of the doctrine itself. Mahon J in the New Zealand case of *Carly* v *Farrelly*[40] described it as a "supposed rule of equity which is not only vague in its outline but which must disqualify itself from acceptance as a valid principle of jurisprudence by its total uncertainty of application and result".[41] He continued:

> "It cannot be sufficient to say that wide and varying notions of fairness and conscience shall be the legal determinant. No stable system of jurisprudence would permit a litigant's claim to justice to be consigned to the formless void of individual moral opinion".[42]

The notion of a judge basing his or her decision on his or her own perceptions of justice and good conscience has conjured up in the minds of some commentators the image of a potentate stretched out under a palm-tree, dispensing justice to his subjects upon the whim of the moment. The disadvantages of such a highly discretionary approach were emphasised by Bagnall J in *Cowcher* v *Cowcher*[43] where (in a frequently quoted passage) he said:

> "I am convinced that in determining rights, particularly property rights, the only justice that can be attained by mortals, who are fallible and are not omniscient, is justice according to law; the justice which flows from the application of sure and settled principles to proved or admitted facts. So in the field of equity the length of the Chancellor's foot has been measured or is capable of measurement. This does not mean that equity is past child-bearing; simply that its progeny must be legitimate—by precedent out of principle. It is well that this should be so; otherwise no lawyer could safely advise on his client's title and every quarrel would lead to a law-suit".[44]

---

[35] *Avondale Printers and Stationers Ltd* v *Haggie* [1979] 2 NZLR 124, 152 per Mahon J.

[36] [1975] 1 WLR 1338, 1341.

[37] [1977] 2 NSWLR 685.

[38] Lord Diplock's very different approach has already been discussed in detail (see Chapter 5 *supra*).

[39] [1977] 2 NSWLR 685, 701.

[40] [1975] 1 NZLR 356.

[41] *Ibid*, 367.

[42] *Ibid*.

[43] [1972] 1 WLR 425.

[44] *Ibid*, 430. As evidence of the danger that personal prejudice will influence the result when the court is allowed an unlimited discretion, one may refer to *Cooke* v *Head* [1972] 1 WLR 518, 519 where Lord Denning was impressed that the claimant had done "quite an unusual amount of work for a woman" in the construction of a house.

A final point militating against this use of the constructive trust to achieve justice *inter partes* is the possible injustice to third parties.[45] In the event of the insolvency of the constructive trustee, the beneficiary under the trust will take priority over the unsecured creditors of the trustee. It seems wrong that rights which have been acquired for valuable consideration should be prejudiced merely in order to do justice *inter partes*. However, it is possible that this objection to the new model trust, if it were the only one, could be overcome with a little ingenuity. It could be argued that, in deciding on the basis of justice and good conscience, a judge would naturally have to consider the rights of third parties. Presumably, it could be provided in an appropriate case that the trust would operate only from the date of the judgment, thus reducing the possible prejudice to third parties.[46]

C. The Status of the New Model in the Various Jurisdictions

Whatever about the merits of the new model, it appears to have no future in the common law world, at least in its original form. In England, a number of *dicta* have called it into question. In the important case of *Grant v Edwards*,[47] Nourse LJ described Lord Denning's reasoning in *Eves v Eves* as "at variance" with the principles enunciated by the House of Lords in *Pettitt* and *Gissing*. In the earlier case of *Re Sharpe*[48] Browne-Wilkinson J regarded the notion of the remedial constructive trust as "a novel concept in English law" and said that "in order to provide a remedy the court must first find a right which has been infringed".[49] More recently, in *Springette v Defoe*[50] Dillon LJ commented that "[t]he Court does not as yet sit, as under a palm tree, to exercise a general discretion to do what the man in the street, on a general overview of the case, might regard as fair".[51]

The English position appears to be well summarised by Oakley[52] who suggests that "it is unlikely that much more will be heard of *Hussey v Palmer*". He goes on to assert that:

[45] See Oakley "Has the Constructive Trust Become a General Equitable Remedy?" (1973) 26 CLP 17, 19.

[46] Lord Denning may have hinted in *Hussey v Palmer* [1972] 1 WLR 1286, 1290A that the court had a discretion to decide when the constructive trust would come into effect (but see the convincing argument to the contrary by O'Connor "Happy Partners or Strange Bedfellows: The Blending of Remedial and Institutional Features in the Evolving Constructive Trust" (1996) 20 *Melbourne University Law Review* 735, 757). Cf. the comments of Deane J in *Muschinski v Dodds* (1985) 160 CLR 583, 615 (discussed in Chapter 8 *infra*, text following n 138) and see also *Re Densham* [1975] 1 WLR 1519.

[47] [1986] 1 Ch 639, 647.

[48] [1980] 1 WLR 219.

[49] *Ibid*, 225.

[50] [1992] 2 FLR 388.

[51] *Ibid*, 393. See also *Haslemere Estates Ltd v Baker* [1982] 1 WLR 1109, 1119 per Megarry V-C; *Ivin v Blake* [1995] 1 FLR 70, 75 per Glidewell LJ.

[52] *Constructive Trusts*, 2nd edn (London: Sweet and Maxwell, 1987) p 44. See also *ibid*, 3rd edn (London: Sweet and Maxwell, 1997) pp 59–84 which takes the same general view on the "short existence of the 'new model' constructive trust" (p 83).

"[T]he proposition that a constructive trust may be imposed whenever the result of a case would, otherwise, be inequitable cannot be supported either as a matter of precedent or as a matter of principle and it is to be hoped that such authority as there is in support of this proposition will be overruled by the House of Lords when a suitable opportunity arises".[53]

In Canada,[54] the notion of a "remedial" constructive trust has been accepted after an initial struggle. The Canadian remedial constructive trust will be considered in detail in the next chapter. For the moment, however, it will suffice to note that, although the Canadian courts were undoubtedly influenced by Lord Denning's judgments, their model differs considerably from Lord Denning's creation and is closer to the unjust enrichment remedy of American law. As Dickson J explained in the leading case of *Pettkus* v *Becker*,[55] three elements are required to establish an unjust enrichment: "an enrichment, a corresponding deprivation and absence of any juristic reason for the enrichment". Furthermore, it is necessary to demonstrate a "causal connection" between the contributions and the disputed asset.[56] If all these requirements are satisfied then a constructive trust will be imposed.[57]

As emerges from the above brief explanation of the Canadian remedial constructive trust, it is rather more "scientific" than Lord Denning's trust.[58] Interestingly, in *Hussey* v *Palmer*, Lord Denning described his constructive trust

---

[53] *Ibid*, p 47.

[54] Cf. Meagher, Gummow and Lehane *Equity: Doctrines and Remedies*, 2nd edn (Sydney: Butterworths, 1984) p 384, commenting in a different context on the tendency of the Canadian courts to take up "with reverential wonder" each new heresy of Lord Denning.

[55] (1980) 117 DLR (3d) 257, 274.

[56] See also *Sorochan* v *Sorochan* (1986) 29 DLR (4th) 1.

[57] Interestingly, in *Soulos* v *Korkontzilas* (1997) 146 DLR (4th) 214 a majority of the Supreme Court of Canada held that unjust enrichment was not the sole basis for the constructive trust. McLachlin J (for the majority) identified "good conscience" as the "unifying concept underlying constructive trust" (*ibid*, 225). In so doing, she drew some comfort from Lord Denning's views in cases such as *Hussey* v *Palmer* [1972] 1 WLR 1286. While noting ((1997) 146 DLR (4th) 214, 225) that "[m]any English scholars have questioned Lord Denning's expansive statements on constructive trust", she asserted that "he is not alone". However, as it turned out, the only company she could muster for Lord Denning was Bingham J (in the commercial case of *Neste Oy* v *Lloyds Bank plc* [1983] 2 Lloyds Rep 658). On the whole, for a number of reasons, it does not seem that McLachlin J's formulation is supportive of the new model constructive trust. In the first place, she suggested ((1997) 146 DLR (4th) 214, 229) that (outside the unjust enrichment context) a trust would arise on the basis of "wrongful acts like fraud and breach of duty of loyalty". This emphasis on "wrongful conduct" (in a rather technical sense: see *ibid*, 230) is inconsistent with the unlimited jurisdiction envisaged by Lord Denning. Secondly, she stressed (*ibid*, 227) that a judge "will have regard not merely to what might seem 'fair' in a general sense, but to other situations where courts have found a constructive trust". Her conclusion (*ibid*) was that "[t]he goal is but a reasoned, incremental development of the law on a case-by-case basis". Finally, as well as quoting Lord Denning, McLachlin J also relied on the far more conservative position of Edmund Davies LJ in *Carl Zeiss Stiftung* v *Herbert Smith & Co (No 2)* [1969] 2 Ch 276 ("want of probity" as the unifying feature of constructive trusts). In the end, it appears that McLachlin J's position is simply a liberal Canadian version of the English textbook view that "good conscience" is, at a very general level, the central feature of constructive trusts. For further discussion of *Soulos*, see Chapter 7 *infra*, n 12. Cf. *LeClair* v *LeClair Estate* (1998) 159 DLR (4th) 638.

[58] The Canadian model suffers from its own problems of vagueness and uncertainty. See generally Chapter 7 *infra*.

as "an equitable remedy by which the court can enable an aggrieved party to obtain restitution".[59] Thus, it might seem that Lord Denning was using the constructive trust to remedy unjust enrichment, along the lines of the American practice. However, Lord Denning's trust is to be imposed "whenever justice and good conscience require" and its application is not limited by the principle of unjust enrichment. However, by hinting at the American analogy, Lord Denning gained some degree of plausibility for his completely discretionary trust.

The new model was decisively rejected at an early stage in Australia (*Allen* v *Snyder*)[60] and in New Zealand (*Carly* v *Farrelly*[61] and *Avondale Printers and Stationers Ltd* v *Haggie*).[62] Given the vehemence of these rejections, it is somewhat surprising that the courts in these jurisdictions have gone on to develop doctrines which bear at least a superficial resemblance to Lord Denning's innovation. The Australian courts are now willing to impose a constructive trust to remedy unconscionable conduct.[63] However, this remedy differs significantly from Lord Denning's new model in that it focuses on the acceptability of the defendant's conduct, while the new model aimed to achieve a fair result in the circumstances irrespective of the nature of the defendant's conduct.[64] Moreover, the Australian doctrine claims a specific theoretical foundation in the analogy with the rules applicable upon the termination of a premature joint venture between the parties.[65] Similarly, the modern New Zealand doctrine, while clearly sharing some of the ideology of Lord Denning's new model,[66] is comparatively specific in its focus and turns upon the "reasonable expectations of the parties" in the light of their respective contributions.[67]

On the whole, it does not seem that the "new model" constructive trust has been accepted in Ireland. While there may have been some (not very clear-cut) support for the doctrine in the early High Court case of *Heavey* v *Heavey*,[68] later decisions of the Irish Supreme Court have taken a more strict view.[69]

---

[59] [1972] 1 WLR 1286, 1290.

[60] [1977] 2 NSWLR 685, 693–695 per Glass JA; 700–701 per Samuels JA; 706–707 per Mahoney JA. This was confirmed by the High Court of Australia in *Muschinski* v *Dodds* (1985) 160 CLR 583, 594–595 per Gibbs CJ; 608 per Brennan J; 615–616 per Deane J. Cf. *Arthur* v *Public Trustee* (1988) 90 Fed LR 203, 213 per Asche CJ: "Darwin may be truly blessed with a colourful array of palm trees. But they are not there for the judges of this court to sit under".

[61] [1975] 1 NZLR 356.

[62] [1979] 2 NZLR 124.

[63] See *Muschinski* v *Dodds* (1985) 160 CLR 583; *Baumgartner* v *Baumgartner* (1987) 164 CLR 137.

[64] Note the editorial comment n 34 *supra*, 6 that it would have been "a harsh judgment" on the defendant in *Hussey* v *Palmer* [1972] 1 WLR 1286 to describe him as wanting in probity.

[65] See the detailed discussion of the Australian doctrine in Chapter 8 *infra*.

[66] See Chapter 9 *infra*, n 5 and accompanying text. Cf. *Elders Pastoral Ltd* v *Bank of New Zealand* [1989] 2 NZLR 180 (NZ CA).

[67] For detailed discussion, see Chapter 9 *infra*.

[68] (1974) 111 ILTR 1 (Kenny J). See also *CB* v *SB*, 17 May 1983, unreported (High Court) p 5 of the transcript per Barron J.

[69] See *BL* v *ML* [1992] 2 IR 77 and *EN* v *RN* [1992] 2 IR 116 (discussed in Chapter 3 *supra*, Part II). In those cases, the Supreme Court applied a narrow version of the purchase money resulting trust

Interestingly, in two recent Irish cases, *HKN Invest Oy* v *Incotrade Pvt Ltd*[70] and *Murray* v *Murray*,[71] Lord Denning's moribund creation was beginning to show alarming signs of life.[72] Fortunately, the latest Irish case, *Dublin Corporation* v *Ancient Guild of Incorporated Brick and Stone Layers*[73] appears to have put an end to the doctrine's unexpected recovery in Ireland.[74]

To summarise, it appears that the new model has been discreetly discarded in England and (probably) Ireland, while it has been transmuted in Canada, Australia and New Zealand into more sophisticated forms of the remedial constructive trust.

II. CONCLUSION

The new model constructive trust is no longer a serious theoretical option. It has been rejected in England and throughout the Commonwealth. Even those who support a more creative use of the constructive trust generally recoil from the untrammelled judicial discretion afforded by the new model. Put simply, the looseness of Lord Denning's new model is seen as giving the remedial constructive trust a bad name. One cannot expect to resolve complex legal issues on the basis of a simple appeal to abstract notions of equity and fairness.

Having dismissed Lord Denning's doctrine, it remains to consider the remedial constructive trust as it has evolved in Canada, Australia and New Zealand. The developments in these jurisdictions, which certainly owe something to Lord Denning's failed innovation, represent the cutting edge of equity's response to the problem of family property. They are considered in detail in the next three chapters.

which took account of neither contributions to the improvement of property nor of work in the home. It is surely inconceivable that the judges of the Supreme Court would have failed even to mention the new model constructive trust if they had considered that it formed part of Irish law. See also *NAD* v *TD* [1985] ILRM 153, 163 per Barron J ("the question is not . . . what is fair").

[70] [1993] 3 IR 152.

[71] [1996] 3 IR 251.

[72] See the criticism in Mee "Palm Trees in the Rain—New Model Constructive Trusts in Ireland" (1996) 1 [Irish] *Conveyancing and Property Law Journal* 9.

[73] 6 March 1996, unreported (LEXIS, High Court).

[74] Unfortunately, the problem of interpreting this case is made more difficult by Budd J's failure to come to clear conclusions on important issues. However, one can only assume, from the material he quoted and from his own direct comments, that Budd J did not regard the new model constructive trust as forming part of Irish law. The decision of Budd J was reversed by the Supreme Court *sub nom Dublin Corporation* v *Building and Allied Trade Union* [1996] 1 IR 468 (noted by O'Dell "Restitution and *Res Judicata* in the Irish Supreme Court" (1997) 113 LQR 245). The Supreme Court did not find it necessary to discuss the new model constructive trust but Keane J did comment ([1996] 1 IR 468, 484) that the law had avoided the dangers of "palm-tree justice" by identifying a number of specific categories of unjust enrichment. Although not directly in point, this comment would appear, in its tenor, to be antagonistic to Lord Denning's entirely discretionary trust.

7

The Canadian Unjust Enrichment Approach

INTRODUCTION

The next three chapters analyse the comparatively radical approaches which have been taken in a number of Commonwealth jurisdictions. It will be seen that, on the surface at least, there are significant distinctions between the doctrines employed in each of the jurisdictions examined. Thus, the Canadian courts speak in terms of unjust enrichment, the Australian courts of unconscionable conduct and the New Zealand courts of reasonable expectations. On the other hand, there is the common feature that the constructive trust is, in each case, being used to provide a remedy for a perceived injustice. This, coupled with the rather vague nature of all of the doctrines, makes it plausible to suggest that the three approaches are linked in a broad sense. As one New Zealand judge suggested, it is possible that the doctrines are "all driving in the same direction".[1]

Upon close inspection, the cases in all three jurisdictions prove something of a disappointment. Although the judges are vehement in their rejection of Lord Denning's wholly discretionary "new model" constructive trust, it is difficult to avoid the feeling that they protest too much. The proverbial palm-tree casts its shadow over all three doctrines. For example, the insistence that the Canadian constructive trust is based on the rational principle of unjust enrichment becomes less comforting when one finds no correlation between orthodox restitution theory and the practice of the Canadian courts in family cases. As will emerge in later chapters, similar doubts surround the theoretical credibility of the Australian and New Zealand approaches.

The present chapter will begin with a general discussion of the philosophy behind using the constructive trust as a remedy. It is then proposed to go on to consider in detail the unjust enrichment doctrine developed by the Canadian courts. This approach is the longest established of those under discussion, having become established in 1980,[2] and has also generated the most case law and academic comment. In the next chapter, the discussion will turn to Australia, where the constructive trust has been used as a remedy against unconscionable conduct. This departure is more recent than its Canadian counterpart, with the

---

[1] *Per* Cooke P in *Pasi* v *Kamana* [1986] 1 NZLR 603, 605.
[2] See *Pettkus* v *Becker* (1980) 117 DLR (3d) 257.

decisive authority coming in 1987.[3] Finally, in Chapter 9, it will be necessary to turn to an examination of the equally radical "reasonable expectations" approach of the New Zealand courts.

I. THE REMEDIAL CONSTRUCTIVE TRUST[4]

As a preliminary to examining the development of the constructive trust in Canada, it is necessary to sidestep a rather sterile controversy which crops up frequently in the literature. This is the issue of whether the constructive trust is a "remedy" or "a substantive institution". This "unintelligible and infinitely damaging dispute"[5] has obscured the important questions in this area and has therefore inhibited theoretical progress. Basically, the controversy comes down to a competition between two alternative views of the constructive trust.[6] One tradition, strong in English law, is to treat the constructive trust as "an analogous institution to the express trust arising in certain definite situations such as the assumption of trustee duties by a stranger to a trust, the participation in the fraud of a trustee by a stranger, and reception and dealing with trust property by a stranger in ways inconsistent with the trust".[7] In these situations, "a man against his will is brought within the express trusteeship institution".[8] Thus, the constructive trust is explained by reference to the paradigm of the express trust.

A different view of the constructive trust has, however, long been favoured in the USA[9] and has been accepted in Canada in the line of family property cases which will be discussed in this chapter. Rather than focusing exclusively on the analogy with the express trust, the constructive trust is seen as a "remedial mechanism"[10] to be used in situations which have nothing to do with an

---

[3] See *Baumgartner* v *Baumgartner* (1987) 164 CLR 137.

[4] See generally the essays collected under this title in Birks (ed) *The Frontiers of Liability* (Oxford: Oxford University Press, 1994) Vol 2 pp 165–226. See also *Muschinski* v *Dodds* (1985) 160 CLR 583, 612–615 per Deane J.

[5] Birks *An Introduction to the Law of Restitution*, revised edn (Oxford: Clarendon Press, 1989) p 89.

[6] A third position is adopted by Elias in *Explaining Constructive Trusts* (Oxford: Clarendon Press, 1990) who argues that the various forms of constructive trust are neither based on confused and capricious rules nor can they be united under the heading of unjust enrichment. Instead, he advances the argument that constructive trusts operate to further three rational aims: perfection of intended transfers, reparation for loss caused to another and restitution of gains from another.

[7] *Rathwell* v *Rathwell* [1978] 2 SCR 436, 453–454 per Dickson J.

[8] *Ibid*, 454.

[9] See generally the *Restatement of the Law of Restitution: Quasi-Contracts and Constructive Trusts* (St Paul: American Law Institute Publishers, 1937). Cf. *Beatty* v *Guggenheim Exploration Co* (1919) 225 NY 380, 386 per Cardozo J. See also Elias, n 6 *supra*, pp 155–164.

[10] *Rathwell* v *Rathwell* [1978] 2 SCR 436, 454. See also Waters "The Nature of the Remedial Constructive Trust", ch. 13 in *The Frontiers of Liability*, n 4 *supra*. Cf. the lack of enthusiasm for the remedial constructive trust in *Re Goldcorp Exchange Ltd* [1995] 1 AC 74 (PC); *Halifax Building Society* v *Thomas* [1996] Ch 217 (Eng CA); *Re Polly Peck International plc (in administration) (No 2)* [1998] 3 All ER 812 (Eng CA); *Fortex Group Ltd* v *MacIntosh*, [1998] 3 NZLR 171 (NZCA). Note also Lord Browne-Wilkinson's view in *Westdeutsche Landesbank Girozentrale* v *Islington LBC* [1996] AC 669, 716 that the remedial constructive trust might one day form part of English law.

existing trust or other fiduciary relationship. Unfortunately, merely to identify the constructive trust as a remedy is uninformative and confusing.[11] One is entitled to ask what is being remedied. The answer, in the United States and Canada[12], is unjust enrichment.[13] Thus, at a logically prior stage to the possible imposition of a constructive trust, lies the principle of the law of restitution that unjust enrichment must be reversed. It is only if this principle is accepted that one is free to consider the methods (including the constructive trust) by which such an enrichment can be reversed.[14] With this point out of the way, it will be possible to proceed directly to the crucial issue: are the Canadian courts correct in their view that the law of restitution can provide a remedy (whether by means of a constructive trust or otherwise) for claimants in family property disputes?

II. THE EMERGENCE OF THE LAW OF RESTITUTION

As has just been mentioned, the Canadian doctrine has been firmly anchored to the law of restitution and in particular to the principle against unjust enrich-

[11] In a sense, a remedy is given to the plaintiff in many of the traditional categories of constructive trust recognised in English law. The point of difference with the North American position is that in England the principle of unjust enrichment is not recognised as a basis for a remedy by way of constructive trust. It is also possible that an emphasis on the "remedial" aspect of the constructive trust might lead to a re-examination of the consequences which flow from the imposition of such a trust. Traditionally, the beneficiary under a constructive trust automatically gains (1) priority over unsecured creditors of the trustee, (2) the right to trace the subject matter of the trust and (3) a proportionate benefit from any increase in the value of the subject matter. One leading Canadian supporter of the remedial constructive trust, Waters (see n 10 *supra* and "The Constructive Trust in Evolution: Substantive *and* Remedial" in Goldstein (ed) *Equity and Contemporary Legal Developments* (Jerusalem: Hebrew University of Jerusalem, 1992) especially pp 499–505) suggests that it may be appropriate for the courts to "unpack" this set of outcomes and to exercise a discretion in each case as to which of them should attach to a constructive trust. (Cf. Chapter 8 *infra*, text following n 138, discussing Deane J's suggestion in *Muschinski* v *Dodds* (1985) 160 CLR 583, 615 that the court could impose a constructive trust with prospective effect). See, however, Gardner "The Element of Discretion", ch. 14 in *The Frontiers of Liability*, n 4 *supra*, discussing the problems associated with the creation of judicial discretion in this area.

[12] In *Soulos* v *Korkontzilas* (1997) 146 DLR (4th) 214, a majority of the Supreme Court of Canada held through McLachlin J (*ibid*, 222–223) that "[t]his Court's assertion that a remedial constructive trust lies to prevent unjust enrichment . . . should not be taken as expunging from Canadian law the constructive trust . . . where its availability has long been recognised". Thus, the majority took the view that, while unjust enrichment provides a unifying concept behind one type of constructive trust, such a trust may also be imposed in situations where the defendant has engaged in wrongful conduct. Cf. Hoegner "How Many Rights (or Wrongs) Make a Remedy? Substantive, Remedial and Unified Constructive Trusts" (1997) 42 *McGill Law Journal* 437. See also Chapter 6 *supra*, n 57.

[13] In the next two chapters, it will be necessary to consider the use of the constructive trust in Australia as a remedy for "unconscionability" and in New Zealand to give effect to "reasonable expectations". Cf. *Fortex Group Ltd* v *McIntosh* [1998] 3 NZLR 171, 178 per Gault, Keith and Tipping JJ ("reasonable expectations" constructive trust classified as institutional rather than remedial).

[14] The Canadian judges, particularly in the early cases, have not always been clear on this point. Thus, in *Rathwell* v *Rathwell* [1978] 2 SCR 436, 454, Dickson J asserted that "[t]he constructive trust amounts to a third head of obligation, quite distinct from contract and tort". Contrast *Peter* v *Beblow* (1993) 101 DLR (4th) 621, 644b per McLachlin J.

ment.[15] It is therefore necessary to consider the status of that principle. This involves an examination of the developing law of restitution. One may state at the outset that, in recent years, the law of restitution has emerged as a distinct and reputable branch of the law. Due largely to the pioneering textbook by Goff and Jones,[16] and to the subsequent endeavours of Birks towards developing a theoretical structure for the subject,[17] it has become clear that restitutionary principles form part of English law.[18] There has been a similar process of acceptance in Australia,[19] Ireland[20] and (less clearly) in New Zealand.[21]

In light of the above, one is left to conclude that, if the liberal Canadian approach to family property disputes were actually mandated by restitutionary principles, there would be a very strong case for its acceptance into the legal systems of the other jurisdictions under discussion. It is worth dwelling on this point for a moment. Having seen the inadequacies in the theoretical approaches discussed so far in this book, what one is looking for is a legal principle which, without the need to make arbitrary concessions to the family situation, can generate a more socially acceptable range of outcomes. It will be seen in the next Part that the Canadian approach provides a remedy in a wide variety of circumstances. Unlike the traditional resulting trust or the English common intention trust, the remedial constructive trust is available to claimants who have engaged in domestic labour and child-rearing. Moreover, other forms of relief (most likely a monetary payment) are also available in cases where the facts do not justify the imposition of a constructive trust. From the point of view of a claimant, the doctrine seems almost too good to be true. If it is truly consistent

---

[15] See the leading Canadian case of *Delgman* v *Guaranty Trust Co of Canada* [1954] SCR 725. See also Klippert *Unjust Enrichment* (Scarborough, Ontario: Butterworths, 1983); Maddaugh and McCamus *The Law of Restitution* (Aurora, Ontario: Canada Law Book Inc, 1990); Fridman *Restitution*, 2nd edn (Scarborough, Ontario: Carswell, 1992). Cf. Justice McLachlin "Restitution in Canada", ch. 18 in Cornish, Nolan, O'Sullivan and Virgo (eds) *Restitution Past Present and Future* (Oxford: Hart Publishing, 1998).

[16] *The Law of Restitution*, 1st edn (London: Sweet and Maxwell, 1966). See now, 4th edn (London: Sweet and Maxwell, 1993).

[17] See in particular *An Introduction to the Law of Restitution*, n 5 supra. Note also a later textbook, Burrows *The Law of Restitution* (London: Butterworths, 1993).

[18] See the decisions of the House of Lords in *Lipkin Gorman* v *Karpnale Ltd* [1991] 2 AC 548; *Woolwich Equitable Building Society* v *IRC* [1993] AC 70.

[19] See *Pavey and Matthews Pty Ltd* v *Paul* (1986) 162 CLR 221; *Australia and New Zealand Banking Group Ltd* v *Westpac Banking Corp* (1988) 164 CLR 662; *David Securities Pty Ltd* v *Commonwealth Bank of Australia* (1992) 175 CLR 353; Mason and Carter *Restitution Law in Australia* (Sydney: Butterworths, 1995) p 4 *et seq*.

[20] See the decisions of the Irish Supreme Court in *East Cork Foods Ltd* v *O'Dwyer Steel Co Ltd* [1978] IR 103; *Murphy* v *Attorney General* [1982] IR 241; *Rogers* v *Louth Co Co* [1981] ILRM 144; *Dublin Corporation* v *Building and Allied Trade Union* [1996] 1 IR 468. See also O'Dell "The Principle Against Unjust Enrichment" (1993) 15 *Dublin University Law Journal* (ns) 27.

[21] See e.g. the High Court cases of *Daly* v *Gilbert* [1993] 3 NZLR 731; *Equiticorp Industries Group Ltd* v *The Crown* [1996] 3 NZLR 586, 611; *National Bank of New Zealand Ltd* v *Waitaki International Processing (NI) Ltd* [1997] 1 NZLR 724. (Contrast *Avondale Printers and Stationers Ltd* v *Haggie* [1979] 2 NZLR 124). There are also a number of *dicta* from the New Zealand Court of Appeal suggesting general support for the Canadian unjust enrichment approach to family property cases. See e.g. *Hayward* v *Giordani* [1983] NZLR 140, 148 per Cooke; *Lankow* v *Rose* [1995] 1 NZLR 277, 289 per Gault J.

with the law of restitution, then the Canadian approach should be welcomed into the law of other jurisdictions.

It will be the task of this chapter to test the theoretical credentials of the new doctrine[22] and to see whether its breadth and flexibility can be justified as a matter of legal principle. The discussion will give particular attention to the most radical aspect of the Canadian doctrine, i.e. its ability to award a remedy on the basis of work in the family home and in the rearing of children. It will ultimately be concluded that, unfortunately, the Canadian cases do not pass the test of consistency with the law of restitution. It will be suggested that, in the normal run of cases in the area, a remedy in restitution can only be made available if one is willing to do extreme violence to the principles of unjust enrichment. For this reason, it will be suggested that the Canadian doctrine does not provide an acceptable solution to the problem of finding a legal doctrine which can generate a just set of outcomes.

Before turning to a close examination of the relationship between the Canadian doctrine and the orthodox law of restitution, it will be helpful to examine the historical development of the doctrine and to gain a general idea of the manner in which it operates. Once this examination (which is undertaken in the next Part) is complete, it will be possible to consider the foundations of the doctrine in Restitution theory.

III. THE DEVELOPMENT OF THE CANADIAN DOCTRINE

The evolution of the remedial constructive trust in Canada[23] must be seen in the context of that jurisdiction's initial acceptance of Lord Diplock's approach in *Gissing* v *Gissing*.[24] Thus, in the early Supreme Court case of *Murdoch* v *Murdoch*,[25] the majority judges rejected the plaintiff's claim on the basis that there was no common intention that the plaintiff should share in the ownership of the disputed property. The plaintiff had relied upon the physical labour she had contributed towards her husband's ranching operations. However, referring to Lord Diplock's speech in *Gissing*, Martland J emphasised the fact that the claimant had made no financial contribution to the acquisition of the property and had merely done "the work done by any ranch wife".[26]

---

[22] This task will be somewhat hampered by the fact that the English texts on restitution pay surprisingly little attention to the Canadian developments. For example, Goff and Jones, n 16 *supra*, p 13 n 71 relegate the leading Canadian family property cases to a passing reference in one footnote.

[23] See generally Dewar "The Development of the Remedial Constructive Trust" (1982) 60 *Canadian Bar Review* 265; Litman "The Emergence of Unjust Enrichment as a Cause of Action and the Remedy of Constructive Trust" (1988) 26 *Alberta Law Review* 407; Hovius and Youdan *The Law of Family Property* (Scarborough, Ontario: Carswell Publishing, 1991) ch. 7.

[24] [1971] AC 886. See generally Chapter 5 *supra*.

[25] (1974) 41 DLR (3d) 367. For an earlier insistence on orthodoxy, see *Thompson* v *Thompson* (1960) 26 DLR (2d) 1.

[26] *Ibid*, 376.

Despite the orthodox approach of the majority in *Murdoch*, a clear dissatisfaction with the English analysis was apparent in the dissenting judgment of Laskin J. Laskin J appealed to the role of the constructive trust in the law of the USA, quoting the view expressed in *Scott on Trusts*[27] that "a constructive trust is imposed where a person holding title to property is subject to an equitable duty to convey it to another on the ground that he would be injustly enriched [*sic*] if he were permitted to retain it".[28] In Laskin J's opinion, the plaintiff wife had "established a right to an interest which it would be inequitable to deny and which, if denied, would result in the unjust enrichment of her husband".[29] Laskin J's judgment brought to prominence, for the first time in the family property context, the principle of unjust enrichment.[30] However, it is worth noting his willingness to appeal also to a more vague notion of "inequitability".

The movement towards change took on more momentum in the next Supreme Court decision, *Rathwell v Rathwell*.[31] In *Rathwell*, five of the nine judges of the Court found in favour of the claimant. Three of the majority judges, speaking through Dickson J,[32] supported the "unjust enrichment" approach of Laskin J in *Murdoch*. However, the other two majority judges[33] decided the case on the basis of resulting trust principles and found it unnecessary to comment on the appropriateness of the unjust enrichment approach. Moreover, the four dissenting judges[34] strongly rejected the latter approach. When the heads are counted, one sees that the new approach was rejected in *Rathwell* by four votes to three, with two abstentions.

Despite the minority status of his views in *Rathwell*, the judgment of Dickson J has been the enduring legacy of that case. Dickson J put forward a detailed defence of the use of the constructive trust as a remedy for unjust enrichment. Dickson J, like Laskin J before him, relied[35] on *Scott on Trusts*.[36] Once more, however, it is worth noting that the reference to unjust enrichment was bolstered by a more general appeal to fairness and good conscience. Immediately after referring to *Scott*, Dickson J quoted Lord Denning MR's assertion in *Hussey v Palmer*[37] that the constructive trust should be imposed "whenever justice and good conscience require it". Dickson J had earlier referred to the constructive trust as "an obligation of great elasticity and generality".[38] In the event

---

[27] Scott and Fratcher *The Law of Trusts*, 3rd edn (Boston: Little Brown, 1967) Vol 5 p 3215.
[28] (1974) 41 DLR (3d) 367, 388.
[29] *Ibid*, 389.
[30] Cf. Lord Reid's dismissive reference to the principle in *Pettitt v Pettitt* [1970] AC 777, 795G–H.
[31] [1978] 2 SCR 436.
[32] Laskin CJ and Spence J concurring.
[33] Ritchie and Pigeon JJ.
[34] See the judgment of Martland J, with whom Judson, Beetz and de Grandpre JJ concurred. Significantly, the leading judgments in *Thompson* (1960) 26 DLR (2d) 1 and in *Murdoch* (1974) 41 DLR (3d) 367 were given by Judson and Martland JJ respectively.
[35] [1978] 2 SCR 436, 454, 455.
[36] See n 27 *supra*.
[37] [1972] 1 WLR 1286, 1290.
[38] [1978] 2 SCR 436, 454.

that a constructive trust were imposed, according to Dickson J, the court would "assess the contributions made by each spouse and make a fair, equitable distribution having regard to the respective contributions".[39] These aspects of Dickson J's judgment do not indicate a clear distinction between his approach and Lord Denning's new model constructive trust.[40]

However, in one vital paragraph of his judgment, Dickson J moved away from Denning-style generalities and stated a three-part test for a remedy based on unjust enrichment. He commented that:

> "[F]or the principle to succeed, the facts must display an enrichment, a corresponding deprivation, and the absence of any juristic reason—such as a contract or disposition of law—for the enrichment".[41]

This, admittedly very general, outline of the elements of a successful claim has been central to the subsequent Canadian jurisprudence in the area.

A full acceptance of the unjust enrichment approach finally came in the famous case of *Pettkus v Becker*.[42] An unmarried couple had lived together for nineteen years and had built up a bee-keeping business through their joint efforts. On the break-up of their relationship, the woman claimed a half-share in the business and in certain lands. The Supreme Court of Canada unanimously upheld her claim and, on this occasion, six of the nine judges supported the imposition of a constructive trust to remedy unjust enrichment. Again, it was Dickson J who gave the key judgment.

Dickson J began his legal analysis with a discussion of the English "common intention" analysis. He noted that the English approach involved a "judicial quest for [a] fugitive common intention".[43] Having pointed out the artificiality of the "meaningless ritual"[44] of searching for a "phantom intent",[45] Dickson J concluded that no common intention could be inferred on the facts of the case before him. It was therefore necessary to consider whether a remedy could be granted in the form of a constructive trust.[46]

According to Dickson J, "[t]he principle of unjust enrichment lies at the heart of the constructive trust".[47] He argued that unjust enrichment had "played a role in Anglo-American legal writing for centuries".[48] Reiterating the three-fold test for unjust enrichment which he had outlined in *Rathwell* (enrichment, cor-

---

[39] [1978] 2 SCR 436, 454.

[40] Cf. *Re Polly Peck International (in administration) (No 2)* [1998] 3 All ER 812, 832 per Nourse LJ.

[41] [1978] 2 SCR 436, 455.

[42] (1980) 117 DLR (3d) 257.

[43] *Ibid*, 269.

[44] This phrase actually comes from Dickson J's judgment in *Rathwell* [1978] 2 SCR 436, 443.

[45] *Pettkus* (1980) 117 DLR (3d) 257, 270.

[46] Contrary to the modern English view (see Chapter 5 *supra*, n 12 and accompanying text), Dickson J assumed that the "common intention" trust was resulting, rather than constructive, in nature.

[47] *Pettkus* (1980) 117 DLR (3d) 257, 273. Cf. n 12 *supra*.

[48] *Ibid*.

responding deprivation and absence of juristic reason), Dickson J asserted that this approach was "supported by the general principles of equity that have been fashioned by the Courts for centuries, though, admittedly, not in the context of matrimonial property controversies".[49] Significantly, Dickson J did not cite any authority which directly supported his three-fold test.[50] He did stress, however, that "it is not enough for the Court simply to determine that one spouse has benefited at the hands of another and then to require restitution".[51] It was necessary in addition that the retention of the benefit would be "unjust", an issue addressed by Dickson J's requirement that there be "no juristic reason for the enrichment".

In relation to the dispute before him, Dickson J was satisfied that the first two parts of the test (enrichment and corresponding deprivation) were satisfied: "Mr Pettkus has had the benefit of 19 years of unpaid labour, while Miss Becker has received little or nothing in return".[52] In relation to the third requirement, i.e. "absence of any juristic reason for the enrichment", Dickson J held that:

> "[W]here one person in a relationship tantamount to spousal[53] prejudices herself in the reasonable expectation of receiving an interest in property and the other person in the relationship freely accepts benefits conferred by the first person in circumstances where he knows or ought to have known of that reasonable expectation, it would be unjust to allow the recipient of the benefit to retain it".[54]

In this brief passage (the implications of which will be considered in detail in a later section)[55] lies the kernel of the new Canadian approach to disputes over family property.

Once the test of unjust enrichment was satisfied there was, according to Dickson J,[56] one further hurdle to be surmounted. It was necessary to show a "causal connection" between the deprivation of the claimant and the acquisition of the disputed property. However, on the facts of *Pettkus*, this further test was

---

[49] *Ibid.*

[50] See further n 101 *infra*.

[51] (1980) 117 DLR (3d) 257, 274.

[52] *Ibid.*

[53] Dickson J went on (*ibid*, 276) to insist that the remedial constructive trust was general in its application and could not be restricted to the marital context. Interestingly, the converse problem later arose in *Rawluk v Rawluk* (1990) 65 DLR (4th) 161, where it was contended that the remedial constructive trust could not be invoked by a married person because her position was covered by a detailed legislative code. Ontario's Family Law Act (RSO 1990, c F-3) provided for a scheme of "equalization of net family property" under which the spouses' property was to be valued at the date of separation. The majority of the Supreme Court of Canada, speaking through Cory J, held that the wife was entitled to the property under a remedial constructive trust and therefore, as equitable owner, could share in any increase in value between the date of the separation and the time of the trial. The judgment of the minority (delivered by McLachlin J) took the view that the statutory regime displaced the remedial constructive trust. See generally Rickett [1991] Conv 125. Cf. *LeClair v LeClair Estate* (1998) 159 DLR (4th) 638.

[54] (1980) 117 DLR (3d) 257, 274.

[55] See text to nn 113–162 *infra* (discussing the unjust factor of free acceptance invoked by Dickson J).

[56] (1980) 117 DLR (3d) 257, 277.

satisfied because the plaintiff's "indirect contribution of money and . . . direct contribution of labour [were] clearly linked to the acquisition of [the] property".[57] In view of this "clear link" with the property in question, Dickson J concluded that it was appropriate to impose a constructive trust over the defendant's farm and bee-keeping business.[58]

In the cases following *Pettkus*, the unjust enrichment doctrine has been consolidated and expanded. In the subsequent Supreme Court case of *Sorochan* v *Sorochan*,[59] there was a significant weakening of the "causal connection requirement" applied in *Pettkus*. In his judgment in *Sorochan*, Dickson CJ (as he had then become) noted that the disputed property had already belonged to the defendant at the time the plaintiff moved in with him. Therefore, it could not be argued that the plaintiff's work had helped him to *acquire* the property. This was not, however, fatal to her claim since all that was required was "a clear proprietary relationship" between the services rendered and the disputed property. As Dickson CJ explained:

> "While it is important to require that some nexus exist between the claimant's deprivation and the property in question, the link need not always take the form of a contribution to the actual acquisition of the property. A contribution relating to the preservation, maintenance or improvement of property may also suffice".[60]

A further important development occurred in *Sorochan* concerning the status of work in the family home and in child-rearing. The claim in *Sorochan* was based not only on unpaid labour on the husband's farm or in his business (as in *Murdoch*, *Rathwell* and *Pettkus*) but also on the fact that the claimant had, during a forty-two year cohabitation, done all the domestic labour in the family home and had cared for the six children of the relationship. The Supreme Court of Canada, following earlier lower court decisions,[61] found no difficulty in recognising a claim of unjust enrichment arising from this type of work. This conclusion has more recently been reiterated, and the law further liberalised, by the Supreme Court of Canada in *Peter* v *Beblow*.[62] As will be discussed later in this chapter,[63] *Peter* effectively created a presumption that the performance of domestic services will give rise to a claim for unjust enrichment.

Another point which has been clarified in the cases following *Pettkus* is that the constructive trust is only one of the possible remedies for unjust enrichment.

---

[57] (1980) 117 DLR (3d) 257, 277.

[58] Note that the *Pettkus* v *Becker* litigation had a tragic sequel. The claimant committed suicide in 1986, having failed to recover anything (beyond one payment which went towards legal fees) on foot of the judgment in her favour. See Welstead "Domestic Contributions and Constructive Trusts: The Canadian Perspective" [1987] *Denning LJ* 151, 151.

[59] (1986) 29 DLR (4th) 1. Cf. *Palachik* v *Kiss* [1983] 1 SCR 623.

[60] *Ibid*, 10.

[61] See e.g. *Herman* v *Smith* (1984) 42 RFL 154; *Murray* v *Roty* (1983) 147 DLR (3d) 438. Contrast the view of Laskin J in his dissent in *Murdoch* v *Murdoch* (1974) 41 DLR (3d) 367, 389 ("mere housekeeping chores").

[62] (1993) 101 DLR (4th) 621 (the facts of which are discussed in the text following n 208 *infra*).

[63] See text following n 105 *infra* (for McLachlin J's reliance on a general presumption in favour of restitution) and text following n 143 *infra* (for the free acceptance approach of Cory J).

While the Canadian courts still accept Dickson J's contention in *Pettkus* that "unjust enrichment lies at the heart of the constructive trust",[64] there has been an insistence that the reverse does not follow. In other words, "[t]he constructive trust does not lie at the heart of the law of restitution".[65] It has been emphasised that the constructive trust is, in fact, the remedy of last resort and will only be available where it is clear that other possible remedies (such as a monetary award)[66] are inadequate.[67]

Finally, it is important to note that the *Pettkus v Becker* principle has been applied by the Canadian courts outside the context of family disputes.[68] Wilson J observed in *Hunter Engineering Co v Syncrude Canada Ltd*,[69] that "unjust enrichment giving rise to a constructive trust is by no means confined to [family] cases".[70] She felt that the imposition of such a limitation would "impede the growth and impair the flexibility crucial to the development of equitable principles".[71] These sentiments were adopted by La Forest J in *Lac Minerals Ltd* v *International Corona Resources Ltd*.[72]

It is, of course, arguable that a great deal of the flexibility of the Canadian doctrine would have to be sacrificed if it were to be generally applicable. However, there have been suggestions that, even if a more strict approach is necessary in the commercial context, the doctrine should continue to be applied in a relaxed manner in the family context.[73] This view gains some support from Dickson J's original emphasis in *Pettkus v Becker*[74] on the existence of "a relationship tantamount to spousal".[75]

The clearest expression of the view that family relationships should be treated differently is to be found in the minority judgment of Cory J in *Peter v Beblow*.[76] Dealing with the specific issue of showing a deprivation of the claimant, Cory J suggested that, although "it may well be essential in a commercial relationship

---

[64] But see n 12 *supra*.

[65] *Per* La Forest J in *Lac Minerals Ltd v International Corona Resources Ltd* (1989) 61 DLR (4th) 14, 48.

[66] For an example in the family context, see *Everson v Rich* (1988) 53 DLR (4th) 470. See also *Sorochan* (1986) 29 DLR (4th) 1 (constructive trust combined with monetary award).

[67] See e.g. (1989) 61 DLR (4th) 14, 51 per La Forest J; 76 per Sopinka J. See further text following n 235 *infra*.

[68] See generally Fridman "The Reach of Restitution" (1991) 11 *Legal Studies* 304; Waters "The Nature of the Remedial Constructive Trust", n 10 *supra*, 180–182.

[69] (1989) 57 DLR (4th) 321 (SCC).

[70] *Ibid*, 383. See also *Lac Minerals Ltd v International Corona Resources Ltd* (1989) 61 DLR (4th) 14 (SCC); *Atlas Cabinets and Furniture Ltd v National Trust Co Ltd* (1990) 68 DLR (4th) 161 (BC CA); *Regional Municipality of Peel v Canada* (1993) 98 DLR (4th) 140 (SCC).

[71] *Ibid*.

[72] (1989) 61 DLR (4th) 14, 49. See, however, *ibid*, 75–76 per Sopinka J.

[73] Interestingly, most Canadian commentators concede that special rules must be applied in the family situation. See Hovius and Youdan, n 23 *supra*, p 124; Scane "Relationships 'Tantamount to Spousal', Unjust Enrichment and Constructive Trusts" (1991) 70 *Canadian Bar Review* 260, 304–306; Fridman, n 68 *supra*; Farquahar "Unjust Enrichment—Special Relationship—Domestic Services—Remedial Constructive Trust: *Peter v Beblow*" (1993) 72 *Canadian Bar Review* 538, 543.

[74] (1980) 117 DLR (3d) 257.

[75] *Ibid*, 274.

[76] (1993) 101 DLR (4th) 621. L'Heureux-Dube and Gonthier JJ concurred with Cory J.

to closely scrutinise the contributions made by each of the business partners to the acquisition of property, such an approach would be unrealistic and unfair in the context of a family relationship".[77] According to Cory J, "[t]he nature of the relationship, its duration and the contributions of the parties must be considered".[78] He concluded that "[e]quity and fairness should form the basis for the assessment".[79] A somewhat more strict view was, however, taken in the majority judgment of McLachlin J in the same case.[80] Concerned about being trampled in Cory J's "rush to substantive justice", she argued that it would be unwise to create separate categories of family and commercial cases in applying unjust enrichment principles. Echoing the comments of Wilson J in *Hunter*,[81] McLachlin J felt that to do so "might have an adverse effect on the development of this emerging area of equity".[82]

It is possible that the view of McLachlin J will prevail. This is because, as will emerge from the discussion in the next Part of this chapter, judges desiring to favour claimants in the family context may do so on the basis of generous interpretations of the facts, without the need to admit openly that special legal principles apply.[83] On the other hand, it must be said that recent Canadian cases appear to show an increased concern with the nature of the relationship between the parties. Where the court regards the parties as having a "relationship tantamount to spousal" (or sometimes merely a sexual relationship),[84] the claimant appears to have a very strong likelihood of success.[85] Outside this kind of relationship, the courts have looked with less favour on claimants.[86]

---

[77] *Ibid*, 635. Cf. *Murray* v *Roty* (1983) 147 DLR (3d) 438, 444 per Cory JA (as he then was).

[78] *Ibid*.

[79] *Ibid*. Note also Cory J's assertion (*ibid*, 639) that, in selecting the remedy for unjust enrichment, the constructive trust might be invoked more freely in the family context than in a business setting.

[80] La Forest, Sopinka and Iacobucci JJ concurred with McLachlin J.

[81] (1989) 57 DLR (4th) 321.

[82] (1993) 101 DLR (4th) 621, 650. Somewhat surprisingly, the Canadian courts have always acted on the assumption that the law of restitution is "equitable" in character. See, however, the detailed discussion by Fridman, n 68 *supra*, 305–310 of the common law's central contribution to the development of the law of restitution.

[83] Note also that, despite her denial that family cases should be given special treatment, McLachlin J appeared to believe that the causal connection requirement should be applied in a more generous manner in the family situation. See text to and following n 230 *infra*.

[84] Note the surprising success of the claimant in *Nowell* v *Town Estate* (1997) 30 RFL (4th) 107 (Ont CA) reversing (1994) 5 RFL (4th) 353 (24-year affair without cohabitation).

[85] Even where the factual basis of the claim appears weak, the claimant often emerges with at least a monetary award. An extreme example is *Baird* v *Iaci* (1997) 18 ETR (2d) 103 (BC SC) where (*ibid*, 117) "the Defendant gave and gave and gave and the Plaintiff took and took and kept on taking". The plaintiff, a lawyer, had deliberately "inveigled" the defendant into a relationship with a view to "extracting" money from him. Romilly J's view was that "[f]ar from suffering any deprivation from the relationship, the Plaintiff benefitted financially". The plaintiff had also assaulted, falsely accused and stolen from the defendant (whom she referred to as her "sugar daddy"). In the circumstances, she had to be content with an award of $40,000.

[86] Note the failure of the claims in the following cases: *Livingston* v *Lisowski* (1986) 64 AR 286 (Alta QB) (friends); *O'Brien* v *O'Brien* (1990) 30 RFL (3d) 249 (BC CA) (estranged spouses living apart); *Hesjedal* v *Granville Estate* (1993) 109 DLR (4th) 353 (Sask QB) (housekeeper and employer); *Hammond* v *Hammond* (1995) 7 ETR (2d) 280 (BC SC) (parent and child); *Strudwick* v *Strudwick*

Notwithstanding the lip-service given to restitutionary principles, it is difficult to escape the impression that the Canadian courts regard themselves as having a discretion to redistribute the wealth of an unmarried couple[87] at the end of their relationship.[88]

Having observed the development and general scope of the Canadian doctrine, it will now be possible to move on in the next Part to test the validity of that doctrine against the principles of the law of restitution. Before doing so, it is worth making one further observation. One suspects that many restitution scholars would rather sweep the tricky question of family property under the carpet of "social policy".[89] However, one must remember Derrida's insight that the situation which is marginalised as exceptional may well turn out to be the one which is in fact truly "central".[90] It is possible that, by attempting rigorously to apply orthodox restitution principles in the difficult context of family property disputes, one might conceivably learn something about the limitations of those principles as well as about family property. A theory which explains only the easy situations is not an entirely satisfactory theory.

IV. THE RELATIONSHIP OF THE CANADIAN DOCTRINE TO THE LAW OF
RESTITUTION[91]

A. Locating the Canadian Approach Within the Law of Restitution

In a seminal text, *An Introduction to the Law of Restitution*,[92] Birks attempted to impose a theoretical structure on the law of restitution. His ideas have not found complete acceptance with other commentators. Nonetheless, his influence has been undeniable and his structure provides a useful starting point for discussion. In his text, Birks divides the subject initially into two parts,

---

Estate (1996) 21 RFL (4th) 185 (BC SC) (parent and child); *Gensig* v *Hutchings* (1996) 23 RFL (4th) 11 (BC CA) (primarily a business relationship). Contrast the success of a step-child in *Clarkson* v *McCrossen Estate* (1995) 122 DLR (4th) 239 (BC CA).

[87] Including pension entitlements. See e.g. *Bigelow* v *Bigelow* (1995) 15 RFL (4th) 12 (Ont Ct of J (Div Ct)); *Thibert* v *Thibert* (1992) 39 RFL (3d) 376 (BC CA); *Dorflinger* v *Melanson* (1994) 3 RFL (4th) 261 (BC CA); *Brand* v *Brand* (1996) 186 AR 205 (Alta QB).

[88] Cf. text to and following n 242 *infra*.

[89] Cf. Birks, n 5 *supra*, pp 127–128 (writing in 1985 when the influence of Lord Denning's Court of Appeal was stronger than it is today).

[90] See the discussion in Culler *On Deconstruction: Theory and Criticism after Structuralism* (London: Routledge and Kegan Paul, 1983) p 110 *et seq* and see also *ibid*, p 140.

[91] See generally Hovius and Youdan, n 23 *supra*, p 120 *et seq*; Rotherham "The Contribution Interest in Quasi-Matrimonial Property Disputes" (1991) 4 *Canterbury Law Review* 407, 409–413; Narev "Unjust Enrichment and De Facto Relationships" (1991) 6 *Auckland University Law Review* 504; Gardner "Rethinking Family Property" (1993) 109 LQR 263, 269–274, 283–286 (cf. Gardner "The Element of Discretion", n 11 *supra*, p 189 n 28); Spillane "Unjust Enrichment and De Facto Relationships: The End of a Marriage of Convenience" (1997) 12 *Auckland University Law Review* 301.

[92] See n 5 *supra*.

"restitution for unjust enrichment" and "restitution for wrongs".[93] Given the reliance of the Canadian courts on the principle of "unjust enrichment", it is clear that the doctrine under discussion falls within Birks' first category. Birks subdivides his analysis of "unjust enrichment" into a consideration of (1) the problem of showing an "enrichment" and (2) that of showing that this enrichment was "unjust". For the moment, the present discussion will focus on the word "unjust" which, as Birks points out, "binds together all the most difficult questions and, in sheer quantity, the greater part of the whole subject".[94] In a later section, it will be necessary to consider issues related to "enrichment", the other half of "unjust enrichment".[95]

When will an enrichment be unjust? Birks insists that:

> " 'Unjust' . . . does not look up to an abstract notion of justice but down to the cases and statutes. It is merely a general word expressing the common quality of those factors which, when present in conjunction with an enrichment, have been held to call for restitution".[96]

The above passage reflects the view that there are a number of identifiable "unjust factors" which will trigger a restitutionary remedy. On this traditional view, the Canadian doctrine will be acceptable only if it is based on a recognised unjust factor.[97] At one level, the Canadian courts have accepted the need for an unjust factor. In *Pettkus v Becker*,[98] Dickson J identified the operative factor as "free acceptance". It will be recalled that Dickson J stated the key principle as follows in *Pettkus*:

> "[W]here one person in a relationship tantamount to spousal prejudices herself in the reasonable expectation of receiving an interest in property and the other person in the relationship *freely accepts benefits conferred by the first person in circumstances where he knows or ought to have known of that reasonable expectation*, it would be unjust to allow the recipient of the benefit to retain it".[99]

Given this explicit reliance on free acceptance, it will shortly be necessary to consider carefully both the role of this concept in the law of restitution and its treatment in the Canadian cases. Before doing so, however, it is necessary to dis-

---

[93] *Ibid*, p 99 *et seq*.

[94] *Ibid*, p 99.

[95] See text following n 162 *infra*.

[96] See n 5 *supra*, p 99.

[97] Birks divides the factors rendering an enrichment unjust into three categories: (a) non-voluntary transfer; (b) free acceptance; and (c) others. The second of his two categories, free acceptance, is relevant to the Canadian doctrine and will be discussed in detail in the text to nn 113–162 *infra*. Birks' first category, non-voluntary transfer, embraces transfers made as a result of e.g. duress, mistake or undue influence, as well as transfers made on the basis of some condition (such as the existence of a valid contract) which has not been satisfied. One unjust factor under this heading, "failure of consideration", is not considered in the Canadian cases but is nonetheless of possible relevance in the family situation. Failure of consideration will be analysed in due course in the context of the Australian cases. See Chapter 8 *infra*, text following n 182. Birks' third category is a miscellaneous one and is of no relevance in the present context.

[98] (1980) 117 DLR (3d) 257.

[99] *Ibid*, 274 (emphasis supplied).

cuss a second, and far more radical, approach which also features strongly in the Canadian cases.

B. A Presumption in Favour of Restitution

The more radical approach dispenses with the need for any identifiable "unjust factor". Instead, it trades on the language used by Dickson J in his classic tripartite formulation of the elements of unjust enrichment.[100] It will be recalled that Dickson J looked for (1) an enrichment; (2) a corresponding deprivation; and (3) the absence of a juristic reason for the enrichment. The third part of this formulation, read literally, places the burden on the recipient to justify his retention of the enrichment (e.g. by reference to a contract or a gift).[101]

As a number of commentators have pointed out,[102] the above approach involves turning the crucial question on its head. It assumes that a person who has received property is under a duty to make restitution unless he can explain why he is entitled to retain it (i.e. unless he can point to a "juristic reason" for his enrichment). However, the approach of the common law has always been that, if a person is claiming property which belongs to another person, then it is up to her to demonstrate a convincing reason why that property should be surrendered to her.[103] In the family context, an emphasis on "absence of juristic reason" effectively puts the burden of proof on the defendant to show that the plaintiff's contribution was intended as a gift to him.[104] Given the normally hazy nature of the intention of a person providing domestic services, the location of the burden of proof is likely to make a decisive difference in many cases.[105]

---

[100] Dickson J first put forward this formula in *Rathwell* [1978] 2 SCR 436, 455 and repeated it in *Pettkus* (1980) 117 DLR (3d) 257, 274.

[101] The learned judge cited no authority for his statement of the elements of unjust enrichment. It appears that the notion of "absence of juristic reason" finds its origins in the civil law tradition. Dickson J was clearly influenced by *Cie Immobliere Viger Ltee v Laureat Giguere Inc* [1977] 2 SCR 67 (decided the year before *Rathwell* and subsequently cited by Dickson CJ in *Sorochan v Sorochan* (1986) 29 DLR (4th) 1, 5) where the Supreme Court of Canada placed the same three elements at the heart of unjust enrichment in Quebec's civil law system. Dickson J was a member of the Court in *Cie Immobliere Viger* but, as would be normal for a common law judge in a case involving the civil law, did not himself give a judgment. For discussion of the Quebecois version of unjust enrichment, now codified as Art 1493 of the Code Civil du Quebec, see *Code Civil Du Quebec: Loi Sur L'Application de la Reformee du Code Civil* (Montreal: DAFCO, 1994) p 500 *et seq*.

[102] See e.g. Gardner "Rethinking", n 91 *supra*, 270 n 31. Contrast Litman, n 23 *supra*, 431 *et seq*.

[103] Note Lord Diplock's denial of the existence in English law of any "general doctrine" of unjust enrichment in *Orakpo v Manson Investments Ltd* [1978] AC 95, 104. Cf. Burrows, n 17 *supra*, pp 55–56.

[104] Note Dickson J's observation in *Pettkus v Becker* (1980) 117 DLR (3d) 257, 274 that there was no evidence to indicate that the defendant had ever informed the plaintiff that her work was being performed on a gratuitous basis. By implication, it was irrelevant that the plaintiff had never informed the defendant that she expected recompense for her work.

[105] Cf. n 146 *infra*.

Looking at the reasoning of the judges in the leading Canadian family property cases, one sees clearly the influence of the idea of "absence of juristic reason". The most notable example is the judgment of McLachlin J (speaking for the majority of the Supreme Court of Canada) in *Peter v Beblow*.[106] Making no attempt to identify a specific "unjust factor", McLachlin J regarded it as sufficient to assert that the claimant had been under no *obligation*, contractual or otherwise, to perform the domestic services in question.[107] However, the defendant resisting a claim of unjust enrichment is clearly not arguing that he could have sued his partner if she had stopped her work in the home. His contention may simply be that his partner had an intention inconsistent with the availability of a restitutionary remedy. The analysis is skewed in favour of the claimant by the willingness of the Canadian courts to grant a remedy in the absence of affirmative proof of a binding contract or an intention to make a gift.

It is submitted that there is little possibility of the adoption in other jurisdictions of the "presumption" in favour of restitution which the Canadian courts sometimes adopt. As the law of restitution is currently seen in England,[108] Australia,[109] Ireland[110] and (presumably) New Zealand, it is clearly necessary for the claimant to point to some factor justifying restitution. Therefore, there is comparatively little general significance to the strand of Canadian thinking which relies on a presumption in favour of restitution. As a result, the discussion in the following sections will concentrate on free acceptance, the unjust factor identified by Dickson J in *Pettkus v Becker* as central to the Canadian doctrine.[111] In the discussion which follows in the next section, it will be seen that a number of commentators have cast serious doubts upon the status of this unjust factor. Given the aim of this chapter to test fully the theoretical foundations of the Canadian doctrine, it will be necessary to examine the competing arguments and to venture a judgement as to whether "free acceptance" is indeed a valid "unjust factor" in the law of restitution.

Before proceeding to test the Canadian doctrine against orthodox principles of the law of restitution, it must be stressed that the Canadian courts themselves have never sought to test their doctrine in this manner. A number of judges, as has just been discussed, assume that there is a presumption in favour of restitution and those who are unwilling to make this assumption are content with

---

[106] (1993) 101 DLR (4th) 621.

[107] *Ibid*, 646. See also *Sorochan v Sorochan* (1986) 29 DLR (4th) 1, 7 per Dickson CJ. Contrast *Toronto Dominion Bank v Carotenuto* (1998) 154 DLR (4th) 627, 637.

[108] See *Woolwich Equitable Building Society v IRC* [1993] AC 70, 172C–D per Lord Goff; *Banque Financiere de la Cite v Parc (Battersea) Ltd* [1998] 2 WLR 475, 479 per Lord Steyn; *Kleinwort Benson v Lincoln City Council* [1998] 3 WLR 1095, 1104H–1105B per Lord Browne-Wilkinson; 1125A per Lord Goff; 1134A per Lord Lloyd; 1146H–1147A per Lord Hope.

[109] *David Securities Pty Ltd v Commonwealth Bank of Australia* (1992) 175 CLR 353, 379 per Mason CJ, Deane, Toohey, Gaudron and McHugh JJ.

[110] *Dublin Corporation v Building and Allied Trade Union* [1996] 1 IR 468, 484 per Keane J.

[111] (1980) 117 DLR (3d) 257, 274.

Dickson J's vague invocation of "free acceptance" in *Pettkus*.[112] Therefore, the theoretical inquiry which follows must proceed without any great assistance from the Canadian judges themselves.

C. Free Acceptance in the Law of Restitution

Birks explains that the unjust factor of "free acceptance" is unusual in that it focuses on the state of mind of the defendant rather than merely on the qualified or vitiated intent of the plaintiff to make a transfer.[113] Perhaps for this reason, free acceptance has been the subject of great controversy. Birks suggests that "[a] free acceptance occurs where a recipient knows that a benefit is being offered to him non-gratuitously and where he, having the opportunity to reject, elects to accept".[114] In his initial discussion of the principle of free acceptance, Birks utilised the following example which he then regarded as "clear and simple":

> "Suppose that I see a window-cleaner beginning to clean the windows of my house. I know that he will expect to be paid. So I hang back unseen till he has finished the job; then I emerge and maintain that I will not pay for work which I never ordered. It is too late, I have freely accepted the service. I had my opportunity to send him away. I chose instead to let him go on. I must pay the reasonable value of his work".[115]

Although Birks' view finds support in Goff and Jones *The Law of Restitution*[116] (where the phrase "free acceptance" was in fact coined),[117] a number of other commentators have strongly disputed the role of free acceptance as an unjust factor.

Burrows argues that the major authorities relied upon by Birks and Goff and Jones[118] are explicable on the basis of other principles. Burrows' argument is

---

[112] In fact, the Canadian courts have not clearly distinguished between the two approaches. Thus, for example, in his minority judgment in *Peter v Beblow* (1993) 101 DLR (4th) 621, 635, Cory J devoted some attention to the idea of free acceptance as expressed by Dickson J in *Pettkus* (1980) 117 DLR (3d) 257, 274. (See text to and following n 143 *infra*). However, Cory J was clearly also influenced to some extent by the notion of a presumption in favour of restitution (see (1993) 101 DLR (4th) 621, 636: "[t]here was no juristic reason for the enrichment, that is to say there was no obligation of any kind upon the appellant to provide the services to the respondent").

[113] See n 5 *supra*, p 265. See generally *ibid*, p 104, pp 114–116, pp 265–293.

[114] *Ibid*, p 265. See also the definition offered by Goff and Jones, n 16 *supra*, p 19.

[115] *Ibid*.

[116] See n 16 *supra*, pp 18–22.

[117] 1st edn (1966) pp 30–31, quoted by Burrows, n 17 *supra*, p 11.

[118] These authorities (which are not compelling) are listed by Burrows, n 17 *supra*, p 317. See now Aldous J's support (*obiter*) for the principle of free acceptance in the English case of *BAGS v Gilbert* [1994] FSR 723, 743. See also *Angelopolous v Sabatinos* (1995) 65 SASR 1, discussed by Bryan "The Acceptance World" [1995] LMCLQ 337. Note that Birks regards the equitable doctrine of estoppel by acquiescence as explicable on the basis of free acceptance (n 5 *supra*, pp 277–279) as do Goff and Jones (n 16 *supra*, p 20). See, however, Burrows "Free Acceptance and the Law of Restitution" (1988) 104 LQR 576, 583–586 (see also the "lightly-updated" version of this essay in Burrows *Understanding the Law of Obligations* (Oxford: Hart Publishing, 1998) p 72 *et seq*); Simester "Unjust Free Acceptance" [1997] LMCLQ 103, 115–116. Cf. Birks "In Defence of Free

that the window-cleaner in Birks' example is merely a risk-taker who has gambled on the house-owner's willingness to pay.[119] For Burrows "the plaintiff's risk-taking cancels out any shabbiness in [the house-owner's] free acceptance".[120] Mead[121] has also criticised the idea of free acceptance, suggesting that it is inconsistent with well-established common law principles and is too uncertain in its application.

Birks has attempted to modify his position to meet the various criticisms of free acceptance[122] but his attempt at "fine-tuning" has not satisfied his critics. In a later contribution to the debate, Burrows argues that any support which free acceptance enjoys in the cases "is not sufficiently strong to avoid marginalisation and reclassification".[123] His conclusion is that:

> "[A]s a matter of principle, even the minor and 'last resort' role to which Birks now confines free acceptance as an unjust factor seems overgenerous. At least at the present time burial is more apt for his troublesome creature than imprisonment in a tiny cell".[124]

Having briefly sketched the arguments on both sides, it is now necessary to make a judgement on the status of free acceptance in the law of restitution. In the end, it must be concluded that "free acceptance" does not constitute a valid "unjust factor". The authority on the matter is clearly slender and the issue comes down to a question of basic principle. At this level, there is no answer to Burrows' simple point that the moral balance is equal as between the person who provides unrequested services and the recipient who declines to express his unwillingness to pay. This absence of a moral imbalance between the parties entirely undercuts the purported basis of free acceptance.

Acceptance", ch. 5 in Burrows (ed) *Essays on the Law of Restitution* (Oxford: Clarendon Press, 1991) p 109. See also n 175 *infra*.

[119] Birks points out (*Introduction* n 5 *supra*, pp 266–267) that matters might be different if the window-cleaner had acted in the mistaken belief that the householder had asked for the windows to be cleaned. His mistake might then provide him with an "unjust factor". Interestingly, in his discussion of mistake as an unjust factor (*ibid*, p 147), Birks points out that a mere "misprediction" cannot be equated to a mistake justifying restitution. However, in advocating the principle of free acceptance, Birks appears to admit mispredictions into the law of restitution through the back door (see *ibid*, pp 278–279 and see also n 175 *infra*). For example, he stresses ("In Defence of Free Acceptance" n 118 *supra*, p 121) that the person who freely accepts a service is aware that the claimant "was proceeding on a wrong estimate of the probability of that expectation's being fulfilled". However, this is not necessarily true. The person who cleans windscreens at a set of traffic lights may correctly estimate that, on average, 50 per cent of motorists will pay him. He is not making a series of individual predictions (half of which are wrong); rather he is relying on one general prediction which is a reasonable one. See Simester, n 118 *supra*, 109.

[120] "Free Acceptance and the Law of Restitution", n 118 *supra*, 578. Note the traditional resistance of the law to the idea of "free acceptance" reflected in the famous *dictum* of Pollock CB in *Taylor v Laird* (1856) 25 LJ Ex 329, 332: "One cleans another's shoes. What can the other do but put them on?"

[121] "Free Acceptance: Some Further Considerations" (1989) 105 LQR 460.

[122] See "In Defence of Free Acceptance", n 118 *supra*. Birks' refinements (for example, reclassifying a number of cases under the alternative unjust factor of failure of consideration) are not of direct relevance in the present context.

[123] *The Law of Restitution*, n 17 *supra*, p 320. See also Simester, n 118 *supra*.

[124] *Ibid*.

Burrows' point is brought out clearly by the following example, which builds on an exchange between Birks and Mead[125] on the question of when it will be reasonable to expect the recipient of the services to speak out. Consider the case of a female motorist stopped at traffic lights. A waiting male begins to clean her windscreen.[126] The motorist realises that the man expects payment. The principle of free acceptance suggests that, if she does not wish to pay, she must take a reasonable opportunity to make this clear to the man. Therefore, it may seem reasonable to require her to wind down the window and speak to the man. But what if she is listening to the radio, which at that moment is providing her with a piece of information vital to her business? Or if she is listening to a favourite piece of music which she has not heard in years? Or if she has recently sprained her wrist and will find it slightly painful to wind down the window? Or if she finds it unpleasant to allow the pollution of the city into her car? The point, which goes somewhat beyond Mead's,[127] is simply that it is counter-intuitive to require *any* effort or sacrifice on the part of the motorist. She owes nothing to the person who, based on his own calculation of the profitability of the strategy, has taken it upon himself to wash people's windscreens without asking them. If *any* trouble is too much to expect from the recipient, this suggests that the moral balance already lies in her favour and that it will *never* be reasonable to expect her to speak out, even if (as in Birks' extreme example) virtually nothing would be required of her.[128]

Therefore, it is submitted that, in principle, free acceptance should not be recognised as an unjust factor in the law of restitution.[129] However, it must be conceded that, as a matter of authority, the point has not yet been resolved in England, Ireland, Australia or New Zealand. Moreover, the Canadian courts certainly appear to accept the concept. Given that an argument can still be made in its favour, it is proposed in the next section to assume the validity of free acceptance as an unjust factor. This will facilitate an assessment of the compatibility of the Canadian cases with that unjust factor. If the Canadian courts have

---

[125] See n 121 *supra*.

[126] This situation, very common in real life, has threatening overtones and has been deliberately chosen for this reason. In many cases where someone provides an unrequested service in the hope of payment, there will be some degree of coercion, threat or moral blackmail. At a minimum, the person who chooses to provide an unrequested service is relying on the power of inertia to ensure a reasonable rate of return. Society's instinct against such tactics is reflected in many jurisdictions in legislation discouraging the inertia selling of goods and services.

[127] Mead argued (n 121 *supra*, 464–466) that it is difficult to tell when one is reasonably required to speak out and, as a result, those who are impecunious will be compelled to take unreasonable steps simply to avoid the risk of becoming involved in costly litigation. See Birks' (not entirely convincing) response "In Defence of Free Acceptance", n 118 *supra*, p 126. Cf. Simester, n 118 *supra*, 116–120.

[128] Note that Birks' example gained some of its intuitive force from the undignified behaviour (hiding in the hope of obtaining a benefit) which he attributed to the recipient of the service.

[129] This is not to deny that there might still be a more complex function for free acceptance to perform in the law of restitution. See, for example, the argument of Simester, n 118 *supra*, 120–127. Note also the possible role of "free acceptance" in establishing enrichment, discussed in the text following n 170 *infra*.

strayed beyond the limits of even the questionable principle of "free acceptance", their doctrine would not appear to merit adoption in other jurisdictions.

D. Free Acceptance and the Canadian Cases

Assuming then, for the purposes of argument, that "free acceptance" constitutes a valid unjust factor, it remains to be considered whether the Canadian cases can be rationalised on the basis of this factor. In order to undertake this consideration, one must examine the elements of free acceptance. Birks, while conceding that "the detailed requirements for a free acceptance have not yet been fully worked out", suggests[130] that it is necessary that:

(1)   The defendant had the opportunity to reject the service;
(2)   the plaintiff had a "non-gratuitous intent" in providing the service;
(3)   the defendant was aware of this "non-gratuitous intent"; and
(4)   the defendant neglected his opportunity to reject the service in circumstances which are "sufficient to draw him into responsibility for the transfer of value to him".[131]

It is submitted that these requirements, at least when stated at this level of generality, are not particularly controversial. As a result, they provide a useful method of testing the consistency of the Canadian doctrine with orthodox restitution theory.[132] It is now proposed to consider whether the above requirements are likely to be met in the family situation. This task will be somewhat complicated by the fact that (not surprisingly) the Canadian cases do not explicitly rely on Birks' requirements for free acceptance but rather on Dickson J's famous paragraph beginning with "[W]here one person in a relationship tantamount to spousal prejudices herself . . .".[133]

1. *The opportunity to reject*

The first requirement, the opportunity to reject, will normally be satisfied. In relation to the provision of domestic services, the defendant will presumably be able to choose to do his own share of the domestic work or to pay someone else to undertake this work. A similar conclusion would appear to apply in relation

---

[130] *An Introduction*, n 5 *supra*, pp 279–286. In his discussion, Birks considers together points (2) and (3) below. However, they have been separated here for convenience of discussion.

[131] *Ibid*, p 283.

[132] It is important to stress the obvious point that the views of one English commentator cannot be of decisive importance. Birks' four headings have been chosen as a convenient basis for analysis because, as a matter of logic, they capture the essentials of the principle of free acceptance. The discussion throughout relies on principle, rather than simply on Birks' views, to determine the details of a possible doctrine based on free acceptance.

[133] Quoted as text to n 99 *supra*.

to other contributions such as the making of improvements to the defendant's property.[134]

2. Non-gratuitous intent

More difficulty is raised by the second requirement, that of a "non-gratuitous intent". Birks explains that this is "an intent other than to give a gift".[135] In other words, the person providing the service must intend to receive something in return for her work. It is worth considering some possibilities within the range of possible intentions on the part of a contributor of domestic services:[136]

(1)   She may have expected some form of recompense for her work, either in the form of money or, more likely,[137] in the form of a share in accumulated assets in the event that the relationship were to break down.

(2)   She may never have thought about the possibility of the relationship's ending and therefore never considered receiving anything in return for her services.

(3)   She may have believed that she was already entitled to a share in her partner's assets, or that, under some imaginary doctrine of common law marriage, she would be entitled to a share if the relationship were to break down.[138]

(4)   She may have believed that if the relationship ever broke down, her partner would behave honourably and, despite the absence of a legal obligation, would provide for her.[139]

(5)   Being uncertain as to her partner's intention with regard to the sharing of assets, she may have chosen not to bring up the question for fear of damaging the relationship.

(6)   She may have understood that her partner had no intention of sharing his property with her but have continued to provide domestic services because she wished the relationship to continue and was willing to take the risk of being left with nothing if it was to break down.

---

[134] In a sense, the defendant could "reject" the service simply by informing the plaintiff that he has no intention of paying for it. This issue is considered further in the text following n 153 *infra*.

[135] See n 5 *supra*, p 281. Birks' framing of the issue hints at a willingness to reverse the burden of proof in relation to the establishment of a gift. Cf. text to and following n 100 *supra*.

[136] Cf. the discussion of the question of "reasonable expectations" by Eekelaar "Non-Marital Property", ch. 15 in *Frontiers of Liability*, n 4 *supra*, pp 208–210.

[137] See *Peter v Beblow* (1993) 101 DLR (4th) 621, 652a per McLachlin J.

[138] See Scane, n 73 *supra*, 274 n 37 arguing that one should attribute to a claimant a mistaken belief that she was earning a share in the defendant's assets. This would, he suggests, bypass the problems (identified in the previous section of the text) surrounding the principle of free acceptance. The drawback of Scane's suggestion is that it appears to involve the unexplained attribution of a convenient intention to claimants. Moreover, Scane does not develop in detail the argument for restitution in favour of a claimant who actually does make the kind of mistake he identifies. For discussion of mistake as an unjust factor, see Birks, n 5 *supra*, pp 146–173; Burrows, n 17 *supra*, pp 94–138. See also *Kleinwort Benson v Lincoln City Council* [1998] 3 WLR 1095.

[139] This seems to have been the belief of the plaintiff in *Lankow v Rose* [1995] 1 NZLR 277, 283.

It is submitted that, with the exception of the first one, these intentions do not really correspond with a non-gratuitous intention, i.e. an intention to receive something *in return for the particular service which she is providing*.[140]

The Canadian courts have not been disconcerted by the problem raised in the previous paragraph.[141] It will be recalled that Dickson J spoke in *Pettkus* in terms of a partner prejudicing herself "in the reasonable expectation" that she would be recompensed.[142] One would have thought that, in this context, the word "reasonable" was intended to exclude from a remedy a claimant whose expectation of recompense, although actually present, was unreasonable. However, without apparent embarrassment, leading Canadian judges have used the word "reasonable" to connote an expectation which, although not actually present in the claimant's mind, would have been a reasonable one for her to have had. Thus, Cory J in *Peter* v *Beblow*[143] commented as follows on the test laid down by Dickson J:

> "The test put forward is an objective one. The parties entering a marriage or a common law relationship will rarely have considered the question of compensation for benefits. If asked, they might say that because they loved their partner, each worked to achieve the common goal of creating a home and establishing a good life for themselves. It is just and reasonable that the situation be viewed objectively and that an inference be made that, in the absence of evidence establishing a contrary intention, the parties expected to share in the assets created in a matrimonial or *quasi*-matrimonial relationship, should it end".[144]

As emerges from the above passage, Cory J was clearly willing to grant a remedy to a claimant on the basis of a hypothetical non-gratuitous intent.[145] The

---

[140] Obvious practical difficulties lie in the way of a defendant who argues that his partner had no intention of obtaining recompense for her labours. For example, in *Pettkus* v *Becker* (1980) 117 DLR (3d) 257, 265 Ritchie J noted the trial judge's comment that the claimant's contribution during the early years of the relationship "was in the nature of risk capital invested in the hope of seducing a younger defendant into marriage". Ritchie J described this conclusion as "gratuitously insulting" to the claimant, while Dickson J upheld the plaintiff's claim, commenting only on the lack of "gallantry" in the trial judge's comments. The assumption of the Supreme Court appears to have been that it could never happen that one partner to a relationship, being in a weaker position, performed certain work without expectation of recompense in the hope of preserving the relationship. Unfortunately for defendants, the nature of the Canadian doctrine means that, to resist a claim, it may be necessary for a defendant to ascribe unflattering motives to the plaintiff and callous motives to himself.

[141] Note, however, that the problem of intention was taken seriously in earlier (now discredited) cases such as *Kshywieski* v *Kunka* [1986] 3 WWR 472 (Man CA); *Parent* v *Therrien* (1987) 76 NBR (2d) 279 (NB CA); *Stanish* v *Parasz* (1989) 35 ETR 227 (Man QB). Cf. *Kainz* v *Bleiler Estate* (1993) 108 DLR (4th) 483, 490c per Newbury J (BS SC).

[142] (1980) 117 DLR (3d) 257, 274.

[143] (1993) 101 DLR (4th) 621. In her majority judgment in *Peter*, McLachlin J did not address the issue of free acceptance and relied instead on the existence of a presumption in favour of restitution. See text following n 105 *supra*.

[144] *Ibid*, 635.

[145] Cory J's qualification of this rule, i.e. that it will give way to evidence establishing a contrary intention, has limited practical significance; the claimant is most likely not to have given any thought to the consequences of her actions, so that it will not be possible to prove that she affirmatively intended a gift.

word "objective" is used to conceal a shameless legal fiction, the attribution of an intention to a claimant which, according to Cory J, she probably would not have formed even if an "officious bystander" had asked her if she was expecting recompense.[146]

Thus, one may conclude that the Canadian doctrine, at least in the important context of domestic services, demonstrates an unacceptably lax approach to the question of "non-gratuitous intent". The Canadian courts are prepared to attribute to a claimant the intent of a fictional reasonable person. It will be recalled from an earlier chapter of this book that courts have generally repudiated any suggestion that a judge can "invent or devise" a legal result.[147] This explains the rejection of Lord Denning's "family assets" doctrine, Lord Reid's imputed contract theory and the imputed common intention theory propounded by Lord Diplock in *Pettitt* v *Pettitt*.[148] If it is impermissible, despite the worthy social objectives which might motivate such an endeavour, to "cheat" on the strict legal rules of contract, trusts and property, why then is it permissible to "cheat" on the law of restitution?

3. *Defendant's awareness of the non-gratuitous intent*

This requirement is also down-played by the Canadian courts. Dickson J's formulation in *Pettkus* v *Becker*[149] requires that the defendant "knows or ought to have known" of the non-gratuitous intent. Thus, it will not avail a defendant to argue that he honestly, but unreasonably, believed that the services of the plaintiff were being offered without expectation of recompense.

It is very difficult to accept that constructive knowledge can trigger a free acceptance. Goff and Jones are happy to accept that services can be freely accepted where the defendant "as a reasonable man, should have known that the plaintiff . . . expected to be paid for them".[150] Although Birks has been less committal, it seems that he regards it as necessary for the defendant to "know" that the service is being offered non-gratuitously.[151]

---

[146] Contrast the more strict approach favoured by Newbury JA in *Ford* v *Werden* (1996) 25 RFL (4th) 372, 381–382 (BC CA). See also Scane, n 73 *supra*, 276–279, anticipating Cory J's approach in *Peter* v *Beblow* by suggesting that the Canadian approach could be rationalised by raising a rebuttable presumption that a person providing domestic services expected some form of recompense. He defends this suggestion by analogy with the traditional presumption of resulting trust. The difficulty with his suggestion is the following: when equity first created the presumption of resulting trust, it clearly constituted a *realistic* prediction of people's actual intentions (see Chapter 2 *supra*, n 14). While this prediction may have become outmoded over the centuries, the point remains that equity never took the conscious step of inventing a presumption which (while serving some worthwhile social agenda) was from the start *unrealistic*. It is submitted that Scane's suggested presumption does not actually reflect reality because it ignores the fact (central to the law's difficulty in dealing with such cases) that people who provide domestic services rarely do so with the intention of earning recompense.

[147] See Chapter 1 *supra*, text following n 59.

[148] [1970] AC 777.

[149] See text to n 99 *supra*.

[150] See n 16 *supra*, p 19.

[151] See his original definition of free acceptance in *An Introduction*, n 5 *supra*, p 265 (quoted as text to n 114 *supra*). See also *ibid*, p 282; "In Defence of Free Acceptance", n 118 *supra*, e.g. pp 123–124.

As a matter of principle, bearing in mind also the questionable status of free acceptance as an unjust factor, it seems clear that free acceptance cannot take place in the absence of knowledge of, or wilful blindness to, the plaintiff's non-gratuitous intention. To return to Birks' original example, if the house-owner honestly but unreasonably believed that the window-cleaner was doing him a kindness by cleaning his windows, it seems rather harsh to suggest that he should be liable to pay the cleaner the reasonable value of his service. Surely the cleaner, who chose to perform the service without consulting the house-owner, should bear the risk of the house-owner's failing to divine his motives. It may be concluded that the Canadian approach to this issue is highly questionable.

4. *Neglect of the opportunity to reject in circumstances sufficient to draw the defendant into responsibility*

This final requirement, perhaps because of the uninformative label he puts on it, is the most obscure of Birks' four points. He explains it as follows:

> "[T]he key to free acceptance is that it prevents the defendant from driving the plaintiff back to bear the risk which he took. If this is right, it follows that the circumstances of the acceptance must be such as to make the plaintiff a party to that risk. The question must be: Does the acceptance, in the given circumstances, disable the defendant from that retort?"[152]

Thus, what Birks has in mind here is the possibility that the circumstances may be such that the defendant's acceptance does not prevent him from denying the claimant restitution.[153] Although this point is not discussed by Birks, it appears that, for present purposes, the most important possibility covered by this fourth heading is that the claimant might be aware of the defendant's unwillingness to compensate her.

Consider a case where a man and a woman live together. She contributes domestic services without payment but with, let it be assumed, the requisite non-gratuitous intent. The defendant knows, or ought to know, that his partner intends to get something in return. What if she, in her turn, knows that he has no intention of giving her any recompense? Here, surely, she should be denied a remedy based on free acceptance. Knowing the view of her partner, she nonetheless continues to confer benefits upon him without recompense. Her knowledge of his intention destroys the foundation of any argument based on free acceptance and means that she must accept the risk (or more accurately, the certain knowledge) that she will not be recompensed.[154]

The Canadian courts have not taken seriously the possibility of a claim being undermined by the plaintiff's knowledge of her partner's attitude. To take a

---

[152] See n 5 *supra*, p 283 (footnote omitted).
[153] See the cases (including *Hussey v Palmer* [1972] 1 WLR 1286) considered by Birks, n 5 *supra*, pp 284–285.
[154] Cf. *BAGS v Gilbert* [1994] FSR 723, 743 per Aldous J.

clear example from one of the leading cases, in *Sorochan v Sorochan*[155] the Court noted that, eleven years before the claim was made, the plaintiff had asked the defendant to transfer to her a share in the disputed farm. He had refused. The Supreme Court of Canada concluded from this, not that the plaintiff knew from then on that her partner intended her to have no share in the farm, but rather that the defendant knew of the plaintiff's expectation of recompense for her work.[156] Similarly, in *Harrison v Kalinocha*[157] the trial judge had found that the claimant had been aware that the defendant had no intention of sharing ownership of his house with her.[158] Notwithstanding this finding of fact, the British Columbia Court of Appeal simply proceeded to grant her a constructive trust without further reference to the issue.

Assuming that, as must surely be the case despite the relaxed approach of the Canadian cases, knowledge of the defendant's unwillingness to share his assets is fatal, what of constructive knowledge? What if, from all she knows of his attitudes and behaviour, the plaintiff ought to know her partner's views? Given that the Canadian courts have held that constructive knowledge of the plaintiff's non-gratuitous intention should be attributed to the defendant,[159] it seems incontestable that they should similarly attribute constructive knowledge to the claimant of the defendant's unwillingness to share his assets.

However, there is no trace in the leading Canadian cases of an application of constructive knowledge in this situation. In many of the cases, it is easy to see that the court views the defendant as selfish. For example, the defendant in *Pettkus v Becker* was asked whether he would have generated as much wealth as he did without the assistance of the plaintiff. He replied, with alarming honesty, that if he had not had the plaintiff, he "would have had somebody else".[160] It therefore appears that the defendant was a man who took an uncompromisingly selfish attitude to his relationship. Was this fact really unknown to his partner? In this and similar cases, can one assume that the plaintiff has remained entirely unaware of her partner's callousness, only to be devastated by his

---

[155] (1986) 29 DLR (4th) 1, 7.

[156] See Scane, n 73 *supra*, 294–295. Scane goes on to make the argument that in a spousal or truly quasi-spousal relationship, "a continuation of the supply of benefits after such an overt refusal [of compensation] is still not 'voluntary', in the sense that bars restitution". Scane's suggestion is that the possible damage to the relationship caused by the withdrawal of services constitutes a "threat" to the claimant, such that she continues to provide the services under the equivalent of duress. While Scane's argument seems somewhat extravagant, it clearly raises important issues. For example, it is significant that in *Sorochan* the refusal to provide compensation was made *after* the claimant had provided services for over 30 years. In such a case, there seems to be justice in the argument that, since she had already prejudiced herself irrevocably, it was too late to expect her to risk losing her home by ending the relationship. It is unclear, however, how this type of argument could be accommodated within a restitution law framework. Cf. *Hopkins v Sturgess* (1988) 4 FRNZ 639 (NZ High Ct).

[157] (1994) 112 DLR (4th) 43.

[158] *Ibid*, 46.

[159] See text to and following n 149 *supra*.

[160] See the judgment of Wilson JA in the Ontario Court of Appeal in *Becker v Pettkus* (1978) 87 DLR (3d) 101, 105. Once is entitled to speculate that, in applying a doctrine as vague as the one under discussion, ugly character traits will in practice count against a defendant. Cf. n 140 *supra*.

sudden change of character at the end of the relationship? It is submitted that, to the contrary, it will often be arguable that the plaintiff knew, or certainly ought to have known, that her partner had no intention of sharing any of his assets with her. The conclusion must be that, in the interests of favouring claimants, the Canadian courts have often found a free acceptance in circumstances where the claimant's knowledge (actual or constructive) should have precluded any claim based on unjust enrichment.

E. The Compatibility of the Canadian Approach With the Unjust Factor of Free Acceptance

When one looks at the role of free acceptance in the Canadian doctrine, one can only conclude that the cases stray very far from the approach suggested by strict restitution theory. The outer reaches of the doctrine, as it is applied in Canada, may (with only a slight element of caricature) be stated as follows:

> A defendant may be liable to make restitution where he did not know, but should have known, of a non-gratuitous intention which the claimant did not actually have, but would as a reasonable person have had, even though the plaintiff knew, or should have known, that the defendant had no intention of giving her any recompense for her services.

Even before one takes into account the preference for plaintiffs shown in the courts' interpretation of the facts, the legal doctrine itself is, without theoretical justification, heavily stacked in favour of the plaintiff.

At a more general level, the Canadian approach appears to offend against the principle of encouraging the parties to regulate their own affairs. If a woman is living with a selfish man who has no intention of rewarding her contribution to their relationship, surely it would be better if she found this out at the outset, rather than at the end, of a long cohabitation. In the absence of statutory intervention regulating property entitlements in the area, the law should, it is submitted, encourage the parties to an unmarried cohabitation to discuss their rights and to ascertain each other's expectations.[161] As Canadian law now stands, one could argue that there is no incentive for a claimant to bring up the question of the consequences of her work. If the matter is discussed, her partner might well make it clear that he has no intention of sharing his assets, leaving her with the choice of terminating the relationship or continuing to contribute without reward. On the other hand, if nothing is said, the courts will presume that she intended to receive something in return and that she was unaware of her partner's contrary intention.[162]

---

[161] See Chapter 1 *supra*, Part III.

[162] Of course, it could equally be argued that the approach suggested in the text would encourage reticence on the part of defendants, who would be protected if nothing were discussed. There is certainly some force in this point. However, the ownership of the property under dispute is vested in the defendant; there is arguably a greater onus to establish agreement on a person who seeks an informal transfer of another's property than on a person who merely seeks to retain ownership.

F. Questions Related to "Enrichment"

The previous sections examined the Canadian treatment of the requirement that the enrichment of the defendant be "unjust". In this section, it is proposed to look at the issues related to "enrichment", the other half of the principle against unjust enrichment.

Birks writes of "enrichment (by subtraction)",[163] thus emphasising the point that the sort of enrichment at issue is that which occurs as a result of a corresponding subtraction of value from the plaintiff. At first glance, the Canadian requirements of "enrichment and corresponding deprivation" appear to cover the same ground. However, when one examines the leading Canadian cases, one discovers that, on these issues also, the Canadian approach differs very significantly from an orthodox restitution approach. It will be helpful to examine the issues under the headings of (1) Enrichment and (2) At the expense of the plaintiff.

1. *Enrichment*

This issue has not presented many problems for the Canadian courts. In a situation where a claimant has made financial contributions or has provided unpaid services, it seems clear that the defendant is enriched as a result. It will be recalled that in *Pettkus v Becker*[164] Dickson J simply pointed out that the defendant had received the benefit of the plaintiff's unpaid labour for the previous nineteen years.[165] The courts have reasoned with similar brevity in cases involving the provision of domestic services.[166]

Despite the equanimity displayed by the Canadian courts, however, it is necessary to consider an important theoretical issue in relation to enrichment through the provision of services. This is the possibility of "subjective devaluation". The point is that, whatever the position in relation to transfers of money or goods, the provision of a service will not enrich the recipient unless that person values the service. If someone cleans my windows without asking me, I might not be enriched. Perhaps I like, or am indifferent to, or have deliberately chosen not to spend my money on cleaning my dirty windows. For most

---

[163] See n 5 *supra*, in particular p 132 *et seq*.

[164] (1980) 117 DLR (3d) 257.

[165] *Ibid*, 274.

[166] See e.g. *Peter v Beblow* (1993) 101 DLR (4th) 621, 631 per Cory J. Note also that the Canadian courts have been willing to accept a wide range of conduct as "enriching" the defendant. See e.g. *Peter v Beblow ibid*, 634 (*inter alia* helping the defendant's children to make Christmas gifts); *MacDonald v Adams* (1989) 64 DLR (4th) 476 (guaranteeing defendant's bank loan without being required to pay on guarantee); *Harrison v Kalinocha* (1994) 112 DLR (4th) 43 (urging defendant to buy a certain property (with defendant's own money)); *Forrest v Price* (1992) 48 ETR 72, 80 (BS SC) ("overseeing [the defendant's] general health and welfare"). Cf. *Hammond v Hammond* (1995) 7 ETR (2d) 280, 297 (BS SC) (many of the services performed by plaintiff son deemed by judge to fall into the "piddly" category).

commentators, it is a basic principle of the law of restitution that, subject to certain exceptions, the recipient of a service is entitled to "subjectively devalue" that service. In other words, he can say that, whatever attitude other people might take, he puts no value on the service he has received and so has not been enriched by it. There is a respectable school of thought which holds that it will rarely be possible to overcome the subjective devaluation argument in the context of "pure" services.[167] Other commentators, however, take a wider view, recognising a number of possible answers to subjective devaluation.[168] The two which are of possible relevance in the present context are "free acceptance" and "incontrovertible benefit".[169] These will now be considered in turn.[170]

(a) Free acceptance

Free acceptance is regarded by Birks as having a dual function in the law of restitution. As well as constituting a possible "unjust factor", Birks feels that free acceptance may also be relevant to show that the defendant has been enriched. Birks argues that, if the recipient has freely accepted a service, he is precluded from raising the subjective devaluation argument.[171] This position has been strongly attacked on the basis that the defendant's inaction does not necessarily prove that he values the service; he might equally be indifferent to its performance[172] or might not wish to spend money on it as a present priority.[173] Birks has responded with the argument that the free acceptance does not establish that the recipient actually values the service but merely makes it unconscientious for him to raise the subjective devaluation argument.[174] This argument appears to bring us back to the points discussed previously in relation to free acceptance as an unjust factor. It will only be unconscientious for the recipient to raise the subjective devaluation argument if his free acceptance creates a moral imbalance between him and the provider of the service; however, as was argued in detail in an earlier section, no such moral imbalance is in fact created.[175] Thus, it appears

[167] See Beatson "Benefit, Reliance and the Structure of Unjust Enrichment" (1987) 40 CLP 71.

[168] See generally Birks, n 5 *supra*, p 114 *et seq*; Burrows, n 17 *supra*, pp 9–16; Goff and Jones, n 16 *supra*, pp 16–31.

[169] See also Birks, n 5 *supra*, p 124 *et seq* discussing a number of cases under a miscellaneous third heading.

[170] For other discussions of "enrichment" in the family context, see Rotherham, n 91 *supra*, 411–412; Narev, n 91 *supra*, 518–523; Gardner, n 91 *supra*, 283–284; Spillane, n 91 *supra*, 303–318.

[171] See n 5 *supra*, pp 114–115. A similar view is taken by Goff and Jones, n 16 *supra*, p 41. Cf. *Brenner v First Artists' Management Pty Ltd* [1993] 2 VR 221.

[172] See Burrows, n 17 *supra*, pp 12–14.

[173] See Garner "The Role of Subjective Benefit in the Law of Restitution" (1990) 10 OJLS 42, 44.

[174] "In Defence of Free Acceptance", n 118 *supra*, p 128 *et seq*.

[175] See text following n 124 *supra*. See also Burrows *The Law of Restitution*, n 17 *supra*, p 13. Birks relies on an example ("In Defence", n 118 *supra*, p 131) where the defendant sees the claimant building a garage on his land and, knowing of his neighbour's "mistake or misprediction", decides to stay silent until the work is finished. Birks feels that, on these facts, it would be "outrageous" if the defendant could use the subjective devaluation argument to show that he was not enriched. Unfortunately, the apparent force of this example is due to Birks' blurring of the line between a mistake and a misprediction (cf. n 119 *supra*). The moral quality of the defendant's silence is entirely different in the following two situations: (1) where he knows that the claimant mistakenly believes

that free acceptance cannot be accepted as a means of establishing enrichment in the family situation.[176]

(b) Incontrovertible benefit

The second possible answer to subjective devaluation lies in the notion of "incontrovertible benefit". Birks takes the view that the recipient of a service is enriched if "no reasonable person" would say that he has not been enriched.[177] Birks identifies two situations where, in his view, no reasonable person would deny the existence of an enrichment: (1) where the service provided to the defendant anticipates an expenditure which the defendant was obliged (by law or factual circumstance) to make and (2) where the service confers a benefit which has been realised in money by the defendant.

It is necessary first to consider the question of the anticipation of necessary expenditure.[178] The idea is that a service which saves the defendant "necessary expenditure" confers upon him a "negative benefit". The classic example is where the plaintiff discharges a debt of the defendant. In the family context, it could plausibly be argued that the defendant is saved a necessary expense if the plaintiff contributes towards mortgage instalments or pays more than her half of essential family expenses. The issues are, however, more tricky in relation to child-care and other domestic services.

What if the defendant argues that, had the claimant not made her contribution, he would have done the housework[179] and taken care of the children himself?[180] It seems reasonable to argue that a person is not enriched by a service if he could have performed it himself.[181] In response to this point, one might argue that, as a practical matter, many defendants would choose to pay for child-care

that she is building on her own land (a standard case of estoppel by mistake) and (2) where he knows that the claimant is consciously building on someone else's land in the hope that the owner will choose to pay her for her work (the free acceptance scenario).

[176] Burrows ("Free Acceptance and the Law of Restitution", n 118 *supra*, 582) argues that a defendant can be said to be enriched where he has "bargained for" the services provided by the plaintiff. However, it is unlikely that this concept could be useful in the family context, given that it depends on there being a void, unenforceable, incomplete or anticipated contract between the parties. See also Spillane, n 91 *supra*, 311.

[177] See n 5 *supra*, pp 116–124.

[178] Some of the problems surrounding this rather slippery concept are explored in *Regional Municipality of Peel v Canada* (1992) 98 DLR (4th) 140, 156 *et seq* per McLachlin J (accepting, for the purposes of argument, the principle of "incontrovertible benefit").

[179] One must bear in mind the partly self-serving nature of domestic work. If the male partner goes out to work and leaves the woman to carry out all the domestic work, he is enriched by only *half* of the value of that work. The other half of the work was always the responsibility of his partner. See Deech "The Case Against the Legal Recognition of Cohabitation" (1980) 29 ICLQ 480, 486–487. It is not apparent that this point is always, or ever, considered by the Canadian courts. (See e.g. the trial judge's approach in *Peter v Beblow*, discussed by McLachlin J in the Supreme Court of Canada (1993) 101 DLR (4th) 621, 652h).

[180] Or would have asked his parents to do it or would, as Lothar Pettkus tried to argue (see text to n 160 *supra*), have found another lover who would have done it for nothing? Note also that if the claimant is the mother of the children, matters will be complicated by the fact that she also shares legal responsibility for their rearing. Cf. Scane, n 73 *supra*, 271–273.

[181] Cf. Beatson, n 167 *supra*, 77.

and house-keeping services rather than give up their jobs in order to perform the work themselves. This counter-argument is not particularly convincing in a case where the defendant has no children to be looked after; a defendant is under a legal obligation to take care of his children but not to live in a tidy house or to eat well-prepared food. Furthermore, even if there are children, one can imagine situations where the defendant has been saved no expense by his partner's work. Consider the case of a retired defendant who had been taking care of his children until the claimant moved in and who resumed the task when she moved out. Such a defendant could convincingly argue that, in the absence of the claimant, he would simply have performed the work himself. Furthermore, even if there are children and even if the defendant's career prevents him from looking after them himself, he could still argue that his legal obligation extends only to doing the bare minimum for his children, e.g. hiring a young au pair to work for board and a small wage. This suggests that the enrichment of a defendant will not necessarily correspond with the market value of the claimant's work. One may conclude that, in the context of a claim based on the provision of domestic services, the concept of "anticipation of necessary expenditure" argument may not always be sufficient to establish enrichment (and, arguably, will rarely be sufficient to establish enrichment to the extent of the full market value of the claimant's services).

Birks' second subcategory of "incontrovertible benefit" is where the service received has resulted in a benefit to the defendant which has been realised in money (e.g. where a property which has been improved by the claimant is sold at an increased price by the defendant).[182] This notion of realisation in money, if accepted as an answer to subjective devaluation, might sometimes apply in the family context where a claimant has improved the defendant's property. However, the expenditure of money on "improving" a property will not always increase the market value of the property (and certainly not always to the full extent of the money invested). Moreover, Birks' test of "realisation in money" involves the requirement that the property have already been sold at the time of the claim for unjust enrichment, something that will not always have occurred in the family context.[183]

Thus, one sees that it might sometimes be possible to utilise the idea of "incontrovertible benefit" to establish enrichment in the family context. The "anticipation of necessary expenditure" may be applicable in the context of financial contributions and the performance of domestic services and the notion of "realisation in money" may be relevant where the claimant has contributed towards improvements. However, it is important to note that the relevant

---

[182] See generally n 5 *supra*, pp 121–124.

[183] Note that Goff and Jones, n 16 *supra*, pp 144–149 take a wider view, accepting as an enrichment a benefit which, although not realised, is "readily realisable". Burrows *The Law of Restitution*, n 17 *supra*, p 10 suggests that the test should be whether the benefit has been realised or is "reasonably certain" to be realised in the future.

arguments are not entirely clear-cut and have been given no attention in the Canadian cases. Neither has there been any sensitivity to the possibility of special features in the facts of a case which might, if the orthodox principles of restitution were taken seriously, preclude a finding of enrichment. One's general conclusion must be that, although even greater problems exist at other points in the analysis, some doubt is cast on the Canadian approach by an examination of issues relating to enrichment.

2. *Enrichment at the expense of the plaintiff*

It is a prerequisite to a claim in unjust enrichment that the defendant's enrichment have occurred "at the expense of" the plaintiff. The purpose of this requirement is primarily to identify the appropriate plaintiff. The mere fact that X has been enriched is no reason to allow A, B or C to sue him; an action is only available to the person (if any) at whose expense the enrichment has occurred. At first glance, it would appear that the same ground is covered by the Canadian requirement that the enrichment of the defendant be matched by a "corresponding deprivation" on the part of the plaintiff. However, the word "deprivation" is a loaded one and its use in Canadian discourse has contributed to two problems which are evident in the case law.

The first problem is that the Canadian courts have tended, on occasion, to make too much of the requirement of a "corresponding deprivation" of the claimant. The point is not really a difficult one: if the defendant is held to have been enriched by a service provided by the claimant, then it follows that the claimant has been correspondingly deprived by having provided the relevant service.[184] Although it is sometimes recognised in the Canadian cases that "benefit and deprivation are essentially two sides of the same coin",[185] one can still detect a tendency to view the two questions as, in some way, distinct. Thus, for example, in *Sorochan v Sorochan*,[186] having held that the male partner was enriched by his partner's years of unpaid labour, Dickson CJ solemnly devoted a further paragraph to reaching the conclusion that the claimant was correspondingly deprived by having provided the services.

If one begins to invest the test of "corresponding deprivation" with a life of its own, then a second (and related) problem emerges. There is an almost irresistible temptation to take into consideration the cost to the claimant of

---

[184] It seems that the difficulties experienced by the Canadian courts in relation to "corresponding deprivation" are, in part, attributable to an underlying artificiality in orthodox restitution theory: the problem of trying to fit the provision of services into a restitutionary model. It is relatively straightforward to discern "enrichment and corresponding deprivation" in relation to the payment of money. However, in relation to services, tricky questions arise in establishing "enrichment". There is the potential for great confusion if these questions are given different answers when they arise again under the heading of "corresponding deprivation".

[185] *Peter v Beblow* (1993) 101 DLR (4th) 621, 631 per Cory J.

[186] (1986) 29 DLR (4th) 1, 6.

providing the service in question.[187] Thus, in *Pettkus* v *Becker*[188] Dickson J explained that the claimant, although she weighed only eighty-seven pounds, regularly assisted in moving bee hives weighing eighty pounds. From the viewpoint of restitution, it is irrelevant what effort it cost the claimant to provide the service; the enrichment of the defendant is judged simply by the value he has received. Therefore, one cannot agree with the argument of Cory J in *Peter* v *Beblow*[189] that the courts should take into account the opportunity costs of the claimant e.g. in giving up her career and diminishing her earning capacity. While an estoppel approach is well adapted to take account of this type of "detriment", the same cannot be said of a restitutionary approach which focuses on the "enrichment" of the defendant.

Unfortunately, the Canadian courts tend to smuggle the concept of "detriment" or "sacrifice" into their analysis under the cover of the notion of "deprivation" (ignoring the vital qualification that this deprivation must "correspond" to an enrichment of the defendant). The following comments of Goldie JA in *Thibert* v *Thibert*[190] show how the concept of "deprivation" has broken free from its association with "enrichment":

> "Mrs Thibert's role as a homemaker and mother had a twofold effect: she contributed time and undertook responsibilities without remuneration, and as she remained out of the workforce her employment skills atrophied. Mr Thibert was benefited by the first, and Mrs Thibert experienced a corresponding deprivation from the second".[191]

It is, in fact, a crucial weakness of the Canadian approach that (if its theoretical basis is taken seriously) it is incapable of taking account of "detriment" to the plaintiff which does not enrich the defendant. What one sees in *Thibert* and similar cases[192] is an attempt to cover this weakness by playing on a fortuitous ambiguity in the word "deprivation". While this tactic serves to increase the practical scope of the Canadian doctrine, it further undercuts the plausibility of the claim that it is founded on the principles of unjust enrichment.

---

[187] The concept of "deprivation" has also played a role in the recognition of "passing on" as a defence to unjust enrichment in Canada. See *Air Canada* v *British Columbia* (1989) 59 DLR 161 (SCC). Contrast *Kleinwort Benson* v *Birmingham City Council* [1996] 4 All ER 733 (CA); *Commissioner of State Revenue* v *Royal Insurance Australia Ltd* (1994) 182 CLR 51.

[188] (1980) 117 DLR (3d) 257, 277.

[189] (1993) 101 DLR (4th) 621, 634h–635a. Cf. Hovius and Youdan, n 23 *supra*, p 138.

[190] (1992) 39 RFL (3d) 376 (BC CA).

[191] *Ibid*, 388.

[192] For another clear example, see *Clarkson* v *McCrossen Estate* (1995) 122 DLR (4th) 239 (BC CA) (claimant had looked after her step-father; she suffered "deprivation" by continuing in low-paid employment as a hair-dresser and giving up the opportunity to live with her lover in Chicago). See also *Ford* v *Werden* (1996) 25 RFL (4th) 372 (BC CA) (claim rejected partly because claimant had suffered no loss of career opportunities). Cf. *Single* v *Macharski Estate* (1996) 11 ETR (2d) 1 (Man CA) (unjust enrichment trespassing on the natural territory of estoppel).

G. Benefits Received by the Claimant

In this section, it is proposed to consider the problem of countervailing benefits. In virtually all cases in this area, the claimant will have received significant benefits from the defendant. She may, for example, have been able to live rent-free in a house which belongs to the defendant, as well as receiving financial benefits in terms of the payment of food and living expenses.

This issue of countervailing benefits straddles the categories into which the theoretical discussion has thus far been divided. In other words, it can influence the question of whether an enrichment has been "unjust" as well as the question of whether (and to what extent) there has been an "enrichment" at all. The significance of countervailing benefits appears to depend on the attitude taken by the parties. There are three relevant possibilities: (1) both parties accepted that the benefits received by the claimant would offset the benefits she conferred on the defendant; (2) while the defendant assumed that the claimant's work was to be compensated by the benefits which she received, the claimant did not share this assumption; (3) neither party believed that the work of the claimant would be offset by the benefits which she received. These three possibilities will now be considered in turn.

(1) *Both parties assumed that the benefits would cancel each other out.* In this situation, it would appear that there is no unjust enrichment. One can point to a "juristic reason"[193] for the enrichment of the defendant—the fact that the benefits were passed to him pursuant to an informal bargain giving countervailing benefits to the claimant.[194]

(2) *Only the defendant believed that the benefits would cancel each other out.* Even in this situation, where there was no agreement between the parties, there is still an argument that the enrichment of the defendant is not unjust. The key question on the facts of each case is whether the benefits which the defendant conferred made it reasonable for him to assume that his partner expected nothing further for her efforts. If it was reasonable for him to make that assumption, then it cannot be said that he ought to have known of the claimant's "non-gratuitous intention" (i.e. to gain more than the benefits she received) and, therefore, one of the key elements of a free acceptance is missing. On the other hand, if the defendant's belief was unreasonable, there is no obstacle to the finding of a free acceptance. However, the defendant would be in no worse a position than he would be

[193] From a strict restitution law perspective, one could argue that only a valid contract acts as a bar to unjust enrichment. On this view, one would reach the result suggested in the text by a slightly different route. One would argue that, while the informal bargain did not constitute a sufficient "juristic reason" for the transfer to the defendant, there is neither an enrichment nor a corresponding deprivation because the parties subjectively valued the benefits exchanged as equal.

[194] In the absence of undue influence or an unconscionable bargain, it would not appear to be relevant in this situation if it appears to the court that (from an objective standpoint) the benefits accruing to the defendant exceed those accruing to the claimant.

under heading (3) (which will be discussed shortly). Therefore, he would be able to raise an argument that the claimant has herself been unjustly enriched to the extent of the benefits he conferred upon her.

(3)   *Neither party regarded the benefits provided as linked to each other.* Where neither the defendant nor the claimant believed that the benefits would cancel each other out, there is no argument that the enrichment of the defendant has not been unjust. Nonetheless, the countervailing benefits received by the claimant are still important. In attempting to pin down their precise significance, it is tempting to argue that the receipt of benefits automatically indicates that the defendant has been enriched to a correspondingly lesser degree. However, assuming that the parties did not link the benefits in their own minds,[195] this approach seems overly simplistic. If a defendant has received benefits from the claimant, he has clearly been thereby enriched. If, over the same period of time, there has been a transfer of value by the defendant to the claimant, then she too has been enriched. It now seems to be accepted by the Canadian courts (albeit not yet at Supreme Court level)[196] that in such situations there are two separate claims for unjust enrichment. As a matter of principle, the issues raised by each claim are distinct.[197]

Some interesting consequences flow from the separation of the two claims of unjust enrichment. The first is that, in theory, it might be possible for a claimant to argue that, while her contributions were made with a non-gratuitous intent, her partner's intention in conferring benefits was to make a gift to her.[198] This argument might seem more plausible where the defendant's contributions consisted of isolated transfers of value, e.g. the conveyance of a family home into joint names or the making of occasional substantial "gifts" of valuable

---

[195] Cases where the benefits were linked have already been considered in the text above under heading (1).

[196] See e.g. *Naiker* v *Naiker Estate* (1995) 6 ETR (2d) 98 (BC SC); *Pickelein* v *Gillmore* (1997) 27 RFL (4th) 51 (BC CA) (discussed in detail in the text following n 201 *infra*). See also *Ford* v *Werden* (1996) 25 RFL (4th) 372, 379 (para 13) per Newbury JA (BC CA). Cf. Parkinson "Beyond *Pettkus* v *Becker*: Quantifying Relief for Unjust Enrichment" (1993) 43 *University of Toronto Law Journal* 217, 226.

[197] Note, however, that this view does not appear to be widely accepted by restitution scholars. McKendrick "Total Failure of Consideration and Counter-Restitution: Two Issues or One?", ch. 8 in Birks (ed) *Laundering and Tracing* (Oxford: Clarendon Press, 1994) p 232 states that "a plaintiff cannot both get back what he has parted with and keep what he has received *in return*" (emphasis supplied). Cf. Birks, n 5 *supra*, p 415 *et seq* analysing the problem in terms of the claimant being obliged to make "counter-restitution". It is assumed by Birks and McKendrick that the benefits conferred by the defendant will have a causal link with the benefits he received. (Cf. *Westdeutsche Landesbank Girozentrale* v *Islington LBC* [1994] 4 All ER 890, 929 per Hobhouse J). This will, of course, be the normal situation in commercial cases, e.g. involving transfers under invalid contracts. In the family situation, however, it will often be the case that the benefits have not been consciously linked by the parties. In such cases, it is more important to see the claim for "counter-restitution" as truly a separate claim for unjust enrichment. Note that McKendrick *supra*, p 232 n 61 presents as "an alternative analysis" the position which is advocated in the text.

[198] This gambit was tried without success in *Hesjedal* v *Granville Estate* (1993) 109 DLR (4th) 353, 361 (Sask QB).

jewellery. In such a case, it does seem likely that the defendant's intention was truly gratuitous. From a theoretical perspective, it is unclear why the fact that the defendant is being required to disgorge his benefits should somehow entitle him to counter-restitution despite his initial gratuitous intention.[199] From a practical perspective, however, justice appears to dictate that the defendant be allowed credit for the benefits he conferred on the claimant.[200] Thus, one is left with a serious problem in applying the Canadian doctrine in the family situation: while it is (relatively) plausible to attribute a non-gratuitous intent to a partner who provides domestic services, it will often be far more artificial to attribute such an intent to her partner.

A second consequence of the "two claims" analysis is the surprising one that a remedy may be available to a claimant even where her contributions were fully matched by those of her partner. This emerges from the decision of the British Columbia Court of Appeal in *Pickelein v Gillmore*.[201] On the facts of *Pickelein*, the court accepted that the parties had contributed equally to the relationship, both in financial terms *and* in providing household and child-care services.[202] The female partner claimed an interest in her partner's property on the basis of unjust enrichment and, not surprisingly, he counterclaimed for a share in her property on the same basis. The trial judge upheld both claims and, to the dismay of the parties, awarded each a constructive trust over half of the other's property.[203] On appeal, the British Columbia Court of Appeal overturned this verdict and instead awarded $56,000 to the female partner.[204]

The Court was not willing to regard the reciprocal contributions as cancelling each other out[205] (nor to infer that the parties had intended this result). Instead, the Court (through Huddart JA) held that each party had been unjustly enriched by the other. The enrichment in each case was linked to various properties which the enriched party had been able to acquire by virtue of the joint family enterprise. This link entitled each claimant to share in the increased value of the

---

[199] The answer may lie in an examination of another unjust factor, that of "failure of consideration". One could argue that the defendant made his gifts on the assumption that his partner was conferring her benefits with a similarly non-gratuitous intent. However, it is by no means clear that this argument is sustainable. See Chapter 8 *infra*, text following n 182 where an attempt is made to assess a more general form of the "failure of consideration" argument i.e. that the claimant conferred benefits on her partner on the basis that their relationship would continue.

[200] Interestingly, the Canadian analysis has not proved receptive to claims by a plaintiff who, in reliance on the relationship between the parties, transferred a property into joint names (or into the sole name of the defendant). In contrast to the long-term provision of domestic services, such "once-off" transfers tend to be treated as gifts which may justly be retained by the recipient. See e.g. *Berdette v Berdette* (1991) 81 DLR (4th) 194 (Ont CA); *Biljanic v Biljanic Estate* (1995) 10 ETR (2d) 148 (BC CA); *Spence v Mitchell* (1993) 1 RFL (4th) 28 (Ont Ct of J) (aff'd (1997) 33 RFL (4th) 147). Contrast the Australian position, discussed in Chapter 8 *infra*, n 14.

[201] (1997) 27 RFL (4th) 51 (BC CA).

[202] *Ibid*, 62–63.

[203] Cf. *Partridge v Moller* (1990) 6 FRNZ 147.

[204] This award was partly explained by the fact that the court took into account an additional contribution to one property by the female partner's mother.

[205] Cf. *Strachan v Brownbridge* (1997) 31 RFL (4th) 101, 114 per Errico J (BS SC).

other party's assets.[206] However, over the course of the relationship, the man's property had appreciated in value to a greater extent than the female partner's property.[207] Therefore, the final result in the case was not a rejection of both claims of unjust enrichment but a monetary award which equalised the benefits they received from the relationship.

Before concluding this section, it is worth pointing out that, whatever their approach to the theoretical questions, the Canadian courts often seem to display a bias in favour of claimants when it comes to the practical question of valuing countervailing benefits. Two examples will serve to illustrate the point. Consider first the facts of *Peter v Beblow*.[208] In 1973, the claimant and her four children (from a previous relationship) moved into the defendant's property. The parties lived together for twelve years. The last of the defendant's children left the house in 1977, four years into the cohabitation, while the last of the claimant's own children left in 1980. Except for the first year of the relationship, the claimant worked as a cook from June to October and received unemployment benefits during the winter months. The claimant performed all the domestic work as well as looking after the children. The defendant "generated most of the family income and helped with the maintenance of the property".[209] The claimant managed to save some money over the course of the relationship and was able to buy a property of her own. Reversing the British Columbia Court of Appeal, and restoring the order of the trial judge, the Supreme Court of Canada unanimously held the claimant entitled to the entire beneficial interest in the family home.[210]

Significantly, neither of the judgments in the Supreme Court of Canada provided a convincing refutation of the view of the British Columbia Court of Appeal that the claimant's domestic work, together with her "relatively minor gardening activities",[211] were compensated for by the rent-free accommodation and financial support she had received for herself and her four children (who remained in the home for longer than the defendant's two children).

Even more surprising was the decision of the majority of the British Columbia Court of Appeal in *Crick v Ludwig*.[212] The claimant in *Crick* had enjoyed a lav-

[206] Huddart JA relied on the "value surviving" approach to calculating the remedy for unjust enrichment. See text to and following n 215 *infra* and see also n 240 *infra*.

[207] See (1997) 27 RFL (4th) 51, 63 (para 14).

[208] (1993) 101 DLR (4th) 621.

[209] *Ibid*, 654 per McLachlin J.

[210] By the time of the trial, the defendant had retired to his houseboat, leaving the disputed property empty. The claimant, on the other hand, was living on welfare in "a trailer court". It seems clear that the decision of the Supreme Court was influenced by the relative economic position of the parties, a factor which is not directly relevant to the application of the principle of unjust enrichment. Cf. *Nowell v Town Estate* (1997) 30 RFL (4th) 107 (Ont CA) (defendant extremely wealthy; apparently undeserving plaintiff awarded $300,000).

[211] Cf. *Strachan v Brownbridge* (1997) 31 RFL (4th) 101, 107 (BS SC) (gardening "one of the major recreational pursuits of middle-aged persons"). It is a testimony to the unpredictability of the Canadian doctrine that one appellate court in *Peter v Beblow* classified the plaintiff's gardening work as "relatively minor" while another saw it as a significant part of a successful claim to the entire beneficial interest in the home.

[212] (1994) 117 DLR (4th) 228. See the discussion of this case in Chapter 1 *supra*, text to and following n 112.

ish life-style by virtue of the relationship (going on numerous expensive holidays funded by her partner)[213] and her only contribution of substance appears to have been to take two months off work to be with her partner when he was recovering from cancer. Nonetheless, she was awarded $45,000, a sum representing 10 per cent of the increase in the value of the defendant's house after renovations undertaken during the relationship.

It must be concluded that cases such as *Peter* and *Crick* demonstrate a tendency on the part of the Canadian courts not to give sufficient practical weight to the countervailing benefits received by a claimant.

H. The Remedy for Unjust Enrichment

From the point of view of the law of restitution, it is clear that a defendant who receives a service is enriched (at most) to the value of that service. Assuming that the enrichment was unjust, the remedy should serve to reverse the enrichment. The Canadian courts have, however, separated two issues which restitution theory treats as identical: the question of the extent of the defendant's enrichment and the question of the extent of the remedy appropriate to reverse that enrichment.[214] When it comes to assessing the appropriate remedy, the courts ignore the issues which they regarded as relevant under the headings of "enrichment" and "corresponding deprivation" and look instead at the assets in the defendant's hands at the end of the relationship. Thus, they are willing to impose a constructive trust over the family home (thereby allowing the claimant to share in the increased value of what is generally the defendant's most important asset) or to grant a monetary remedy reflecting the increase in value of the defendant's general assets. As will be discussed in more detail shortly, this means that the remedy covers not only the enrichment at the expense of the plaintiff (the value of her work) but also enrichments which did not occur at her expense.

In *Peter* v *Beblow*,[215] the Supreme Court of Canada attempted to rationalise their approach on the basis of a distinction, indirectly borrowed from the work of Birks,[216] between two possible approaches to the remedying of unjust

---

[213] During the relationship, the claimant had been away from her work as an air hostess and had been receiving disability benefits. Therefore, the defendant had to contribute heavily to her expenses. Scane, n 73 *supra*, 284 argues that it is inappropriate to bring into the equation "life-style benefits" which each party enjoyed by virtue of the relationship. Scane believes that such benefits should be dismissed as "sunk costs" for which neither party expected compensation. However, this approach seems quite arbitrary and, applied to a case such as *Crick*, it involves the unexplained assumption that, while the claimant expected recompense for her efforts, her partner expected no credit for all the money he spent on her.

[214] See Birks' "Proprietary Rights as Remedies", ch. 16 in *Frontiers of Liability*, n 4 *supra*, p 222; Barker "Rescuing Remedialism in Unjust Enrichment Law: Why Remedies are Right" (1998) 57 CLJ 301, 315–316.

[215] (1993) 101 DLR (4th) 621, 641–642 per Cory J; 651–652 per McLachlin J.

[216] See n 5 *supra*, p 75 *et seq*. Birks' work was not actually cited in either of the judgments in *Peter* v *Beblow*. However, it was discussed in some detail by Scane, n 73 *supra* in an article which was

enrichment. These two different measures of restitution are the "value received" and the "value surviving" approaches. Birks explains that the first of these, "value received", is "much the more common".[217] It looks to the benefit which has been transferred to the defendant. For example, in relation to the provision of domestic services, one would simply put a value on the services provided. "Value surviving", however, looks to "what the defendant has left".[218] This may be relevant if the defendant has consumed or dissipated goods or monies received, so that they are no longer available to be recovered. Or it may be that the defendant has converted what he received into other property, in which case the claimant may be able to trace her original property into the new property which has been substituted for it. In his text, Birks discusses in detail the situations in which the "value surviving" approach will be appropriate.[219] It is clear from this discussion that he regards the "value surviving" approach as applicable only in relation to transfers of goods or money. When a pure service is at issue, it will not be intelligible to talk of part of that service having been dissipated or of it having been converted into other property. The benefit of the service will simply have been received by the defendant and, as a matter of principle, the measure of restitution should be the value of that service.[220]

The Canadian courts, however, despite sheltering behind Birks' terminology, have developed a far more sweeping idea of "value surviving". They regard this approach as entitling them to look at all the property which the defendant has accumulated over the period when the claimant's contribution was being made and to measure the restitutionary remedy by reference to this "enrichment". However, it is clear that the assets accumulated by the defendant will have come into his hands only partly as a result of the claimant's contribution. First, it must be remembered that, inherent in living together, there will generally be mutual savings resulting from the sharing of grocery and accommodation expenses.[221] This reduction in his expenses will undoubtedly increase the defendant's ability to accumulate assets during the relationship. However, any resulting enrichment of the defendant is not "at the expense of" the claimant; the claimant, while gaining a similar advantage from the arrangement, suffers no deprivation

cited by Cory J ((1993) 101 DLR (4th) 621, 637) and which also appears to have influenced the judgment of McLachlin J.

[217] See n 5 *supra*, p 76.

[218] *Ibid.*

[219] See n 5 *supra*, pp 358–401 (discussing the rules of tracing at common law and in equity).

[220] Thus, it seems clear that the value surviving approach of the Canadian courts cannot be explained on the basis of the conventional principles of tracing. See Scane, n 73 *supra*, 289–291. Interestingly, Cory J referred in *Peter v Beblow* (1993) 101 DLR (4th) 621, 638–639 to the argument that, even where the traditional tracing rules are not satisfied, it might be permissible to impose a constructive trust on the basis that the defendant's assets have been "swollen" by the receipt of the claimant's property. Note, however, that the swollen assets heresy has been comprehensively discredited. See Smith *The Law of Tracing* (Oxford: Clarendon Press, 1997) pp 270–274; 310–320.

[221] See Rotherham, n 91 *supra*, 19. Many of the cases (e.g. *Peter v Beblow* (1993) 101 DLR (4th) 621 and *Harrison v Kalinocha* (1994) 112 DLR (4th) 43) involved partners who had children from previous relationships. For such cohabitees, who may not have any further children as a result of the new relationship, obvious economic benefits flow from a cohabitation.

corresponding to the benefit to her partner. This problem seems to be over-looked when the Canadian courts choose to base the claimant's remedy on the assets "surviving" in the defendant's hands.

A second point to consider is that the defendant will often have accumulated assets because of his superior earning capacity. Consider the following example. A man who earns £1,000 a week lives with a woman who provides full-time domestic services worth £200 a week. Over the period of the relationship, the man accumulates assets worth £50,000. A strict restitutionary approach (the "value received" approach) would restrict any remedy to the value of the ser-vices provided by the claimant. The "value surviving" approach would concen-trate instead on the £50,000. The argument would be that the male partner would not have been able to accumulate this amount of money without the help of his partner. It therefore becomes plausible to allow her an equal share in the accumulated assets. However, this approach appears to ignore the differential value of different kinds of work in our society. The man's work in this example is valued by society at a far higher rate than the work done by the woman.[222] How does a restitutionary argument allow her to participate equally in his wealth? If the two lived next door to each other, rather than together, society would tolerate his more favourable earning power. When they live together, why should the neutral principle of restitution for unjust enrichment operate to accomplish a forced equalisation of the value of their respective work? It is impossible to see how, within a restitution framework, the claimant can answer the argument that the defendant could have purchased her services from some-one else at £200 a week, instead of the £500 a week which he is retrospectively being compelled to pay to her.

A final point may be made in relation to increases in the value of a defendant's real property. From a practical point of view, the appreciation in the value of a family home is one of the most important mechanisms by which a family can accumulate wealth. However, this appreciation is generally attributable to the nature of the housing market rather than to any improvements (which may of course add to the underlying tendency to increase in value) or work of the claimant in "maintaining and preserving" the home.[223]

The preceding discussion suggests that, in itself, a conventional restitution analysis provides no justification for basing the claimant's remedy in a family case on the assets "surviving" in the defendant's hands. Therefore, if the

---

[222] Her claim in unjust enrichment is not based, as an estoppel claim might be, on the income she has foregone in staying in the home. It is instead based squarely on the fact that she provided ser-vices without recompense.

[223] Cf. *Bruyninckx* v *Bruyninckx* (1995) 13 RFL (4th) 199, 212 (BC CA). Perhaps it is worth point-ing out that real property is not as fragile as some of the *dicta* in the Canadian cases appear to sug-gest. Cory J in *Peter* v *Beblow* (1993) 101 DLR (4th) 621, 640 referred to the plaintiff's contribution "to the maintenance and the preservation" of the home. She had (*ibid*) "painted the fence, planted the cedar hedge, installed the rock garden and built the chicken coop". In fact, her activities prob-ably did very little to increase the value of the property. Providing that a house is not allowed to dete-riorate at a structural level, it is likely to continue to increase in value in the face of a fair degree of neglect.

Canadian approach is to be justified, it is clearly necessary to construct some theoretical "bridge" between the actual enrichment of the defendant (the "value received") and a share in the wealth accumulated by the defendant (the "value surviving").[224] Of course, at one level, this bridge is provided by the device of the constructive trust.[225] However, it is clearly insufficient simply to say that a constructive trust should be imposed over certain of the defendant's assets. One must explain *why* this proprietary remedy has been chosen.

The Canadian courts have, on a number of occasions, discussed the pre-requisites of a proprietary remedy. Unfortunately, they have tended to lay down requirements to be satisfied without explaining why the satisfaction of these requirements actually justifies a proprietary remedy. The following discussion attempts first to establish the test presently applicable in Canadian law. Once this has been achieved, it will be possible to assess the explanatory power of the relevant test.

The first test proposed in the Canadian case law was the notion of a "causal connection" put forward by Dickson J in *Pettkus v Becker*.[226] It will be recalled that Dickson J originally required a causal connection between the contribution of the plaintiff and the acquisition of the disputed assets.[227] This causal connection requirement was diluted in *Sorochan v Sorochan*,[228] so that all that was necessary was a causal connection with the "preservation, maintenance or improvement" of the disputed property. Furthermore, Cory J took the attitude in *Peter v Beblow*[229] that, since the provision of domestic services "seeps throughout all the assets of the defendant", there was no need for this kind of contribution to be linked directly to a specific property. At first glance, it appears that McLachlin J took a more strict approach in *Peter*, insisting that the claimant must establish "a direct link to the property which is the subject of the trust".[230] However, she subsequently took an extremely broad view of the "property" to which the claimant's contribution had to be linked; it would be sufficient if there was a link with "the assets of the family enterprise".[231] Once a

---

[224] Note that, in *Rawluk v Rawluk* (1990) 65 DLR (4th) 161, 191d–f, McLachlin J rejected the idea of imposing a constructive trust at the behest of the *defendant* where the defendant's property had, in fact, decreased in value. Thus, it appears that only the plaintiff will be allowed to cross any theoretical "bridge" between her contributions and the assets of the defendant. However, it seems unjust to allow the plaintiff to claim a proportionate share in her partner's property when it has increased in value, while allowing her the option of claiming on a "value surviving" basis (or simply walking away) if it has decreased in value. (Cf. *Harrison v Kalinocha* (1994) 112 DLR (4th) 43, 51a–b per Taylor JA). Note McLachlin J's apparent assumption in *Rawluk supra*, 191e–f that a person who has been unjustly enriched is necessarily a wrongdoer who cannot "come to equity with clean hands".

[225] This remedy has an in-built tendency towards the "value surviving" approach; a share under a constructive trust in specific property will allow the claimant to share in the increase in its value over the years. Cf. n 240 *infra*.

[226] See text to and following n 56 *supra*.

[227] See *Pettkus v Becker* (1980) 117 DLR (3d) 257, 277.

[228] (1986) 29 DLR (4th) 1, 10.

[229] (1993) 101 DLR (4th) 621, 637–638.

[230] *Ibid*, 649.

[231] *Ibid*, 653–654.

link could be shown at this general level, it would be legitimate to impose a constructive trust over whichever one of "the family assets" seemed appropriate.[232]

In *Sorochan*, Dickson CJ also suggested that the nature of the remedy for the plaintiff depended, to some extent, on a second consideration: whether the plaintiff had a "reasonable expectation" of obtaining a proprietary interest in the defendant's property.[233] Unfortunately, Dickson CJ did not explain clearly the relationship between this test and the causal connection requirement.[234] In any case, given that "causal connection" has now been diluted to almost homeopathic proportions in the family context, it is difficult to see any need to provide a claimant with an alternative path to proprietary relief. Therefore, it is perhaps not surprising that there was no mention of "reasonable expectation" in McLachlin J's discussion of the remedial issue in *Peter v Beblow*.[235]

Although McLachlin J seems to have discarded the concept of "reasonable expectation" in *Peter*, she did not feel that "causal connection"[236] was the sole determinant of the availability of a proprietary remedy. It was also necessary, according to McLachlin J, to show that a monetary remedy would be inadequate.[237] This reflects statements in earlier Canadian unjust enrichment cases arising outside the family context.[238] In the family situation, it seems that it would rarely occur that the claimant would succeed in passing the causal connection test but would be denied a proprietary remedy on the basis that a monetary remedy would be adequate. This is because, according to McLachlin J, the proprietary remedy should be calculated on the value surviving basis while a monetary award should be calculated on the (generally less favourable) value received approach.[239] Since the proprietary remedy will generally have more financial value than a monetary remedy, the latter will generally not be

---

[232] See *ibid*.

[233] (1986) 29 DLR (4th) 1, 12.

[234] On this point, see Litman, n 23 *supra*, 458–460; Scane, n 73 *supra*, 302; Farquahar "Causal Connection in Constructive Trusts after *Sorochan v Sorochan*" (1989) 7 *Canadian Journal of Family Law* 337, 348–349; Farquahar "Unjust Enrichment—Special Relationship", n 73 *supra*, 547–550. Dickson CJ also failed to clarify whether he required an actual expectation on the part of the claimant or if it would suffice if it *would have been* reasonable for her to have held the relevant expectation. The second possibility seems more likely given Dickson CJ's approach to "reasonable expectation" at another point in his analysis (see text following n 140 *supra*). See also Scane, n 73 *supra*, 292–297.

[235] (1993) 101 DLR (4th) 621, 649 *et seq*. However, in his minority judgment in *Peter*, Cory J laid substantial emphasis on the "reasonable expectations" of the parties (see *ibid*, 637e, 639e–640a). Cory J's ultimate conclusion (*ibid*, 640) was that the choice of remedy in family cases should be based on "common sense and a desire to achieve a fair result for both parties".

[236] In fact, McLachlin J formulated this requirement in somewhat different terms, referring to the need for a "link" or "nexus" between the claimant's contribution and the disputed property.

[237] (1993) 101 DLR (4th) 621, 650d–e, 652a. Cf. the list of relevant factors suggested by Hovius and Youdan, n 23 *supra*, p 147 and quoted with approval by Cory J (1993) 101 DLR (4th) 621, 640.

[238] See text to nn 64–67 *supra*. For discussion of the question of the adequacy of a monetary remedy, see Gardner "The Element of Discretion", n 11 *supra*, p 191 ("adequacy is the deceptively bland name for a clearly normative exercise").

[239] (1993) 101 DLR (4th) 621, 651f–g.

"adequate".[240] Therefore, in the family context, as McLachlin J appeared to accept,[241] little is added to the causal connection requirement by the insistence that the claimant must also demonstrate the inadequacy of a monetary remedy.

The above survey of the case law suggests that, following the majority judgment of McLachlin J in *Peter v Beblow*, the claimant will be entitled to a constructive trust[242] if she establishes a link or causal connection between her contribution and the disputed assets (and also, for what this added requirement is worth, that a monetary remedy will be inadequate). One is, however, still left wondering as to the rationale behind the causal connection requirement. Why does the existence of some vague link between the claimant's contribution and the assets of the defendant[243] entitle her, through the medium of a constructive trust, to recover more than the value of the defendant's enrichment? It is submitted that, in fact, "causal connection" is only one part of the story and that (sometimes at a subliminal level) the Canadian courts justify their choice of remedy on the basis of a "partnership" view of cohabitation. The parties to a cohabitation are seen as participating in a joint "family enterprise" and, therefore, as being entitled to share the profits of that enterprise in the proportions of their respective contributions.

Admittedly, this point is more clearly articulated in the academic literature[244] than in the cases themselves. However, the more recent case law does contain some revealing *dicta*. For example, in *Peter v Beblow*,[245] Cory J explained that the "value surviving" approach "apportions the assets accumulated by the couple on the basis of the contributions made by each".[246] Similarly, in the later case of *Pickelein v Gillmore*,[247] Huddart JA commented that:

> "In a marriage-like relationship where each contributes equally to the partnership, . . . it is reasonable to presume . . . that each expected to share in whatever wealth they created during their relationship".[248]

---

[240] Cf. Gardner "The Element of Discretion", n 11 *supra*, p 191 text to n 49. Unfortunately, there appears to be a degree of inconsistency in McLachlin J's judgment. She asserted ((1993) 101 DLR (4th) 621, 652) that, in considering whether to award a trust or a monetary remedy, the court could take into account factors such as the probability of a monetary award being paid by the defendant. However, given her insistence that a monetary remedy must be calculated on the value surviving basis, this appears to suggest that the defendant's ability to meet a monetary award might serve to downgrade the claimant's remedy to one calculated on the (generally less favourable) "value received" basis. In fact, contrary to McLachlin J's view, there appears to be no reason why a monetary award could not, in a suitable case, be calculated on the value surviving basis. This was the view taken by Huddart JA in *Pickelein v Gillmore* (1997) 27 RFL (4th) 51, 67ff (BC CA).

[241] (1993) 101 DLR (4th) 621, 650d.

[242] Or, perhaps, a monetary remedy calculated on the value surviving basis. See n 240 *supra*.

[243] Note also that, in practice, the Canadian courts exaggerate the extent of the link between the claimant's contribution and the wealth accumulated by the defendant. See the discussion in the text to and following n 220 *supra*.

[244] See Scane, n 73 *supra*, p 279 *et seq*; Parkinson, n 196 *supra*.

[245] (1993) 101 DLR (4th) 621.

[246] *Ibid*, 641.

[247] (1997) 27 RFL (4th) 51 (BC CA).

[248] *Ibid*, 64.

The approach suggested by these *dicta* resembles a "super" version of the purchase money resulting trust;[249] the parties are treated as "contributing" to the "purchase" of the wealth accumulated during their relationship and therefore that wealth is shared between them in the proportions of their contributions. Thus, as emerges from *Pickelein* v *Gillmore*,[250] equal contributions by the parties will not cancel each other out (as they might under an orthodox restitution analysis) but will instead lead to an equal sharing of the total assets acquired by the parties. Obviously, all of this goes well beyond the traditional purchase money resulting trust doctrine. However, this expansion of the law is seen as justified on the basis that there is something analogous to a "partnership" between cohabitees whereby they pool their resources to acquire the "assets of the family enterprise".[251]

This partnership model of cohabitation has undoubted attractions and, as will be seen in the next two chapters, is at the heart of the unconscionability doctrine developed by the Australian courts.[252] What is unsatisfactory about the Canadian approach is that the partnership model is presented as being relatively peripheral to a doctrine based primarily on other principles. The partnership analogy is only brought into play *after* the claimant has satisfied the requirements of enrichment, corresponding deprivation and absence of juristic reason and then it merely serves as a "bridge" between the enrichment of the claimant and a particular form of remedy.[253] In theoretical terms, this is surely profligate. If the partnership line of reasoning were truly acceptable, then it would be sufficient in itself to justify the practice of the Canadian courts in family cases and one could dispense entirely with the pretence that the doctrine of unjust enrichment is being applied in this context.

It must be concluded that the remedial policy of the Canadian courts cannot be defended within the terms of their unjust enrichment analysis. The only plausible theoretical justification for the Canadian approach to remedies involves the adoption of a "partnership" view of cohabitation and, if this step could justifiably be taken, the rest of the Canadian doctrine would effectively be rendered otiose.

---

[249] Note the resulting trust-style focus on acquisition in the original version of the causal connection test. See *Pettkus* v *Becker* (1980) 117 DLR (3d) 257, 277.

[250] (1997) 27 RFL (4th) 51.

[251] Note that the concept of a "family enterprise" was central to McLachlin J's treatment of the remedial issue in *Peter* v *Beblow* (1993) 101 DLR (4th) 621.

[252] See Chapter 8 *infra*. The "partnership" model is considered further in Chapter 10 *infra*, Part II. Note also that the concept of "reasonable expectation", which plays a comparatively minor role in the Canadian analysis (see text following n 232 *supra*), is regarded by the New Zealand courts as sufficient to underpin their entire doctrinal structure in this area. See Chapter 9 *infra*.

[253] Admittedly, in *Peter* v *Beblow* (1993) 101 DLR (4th) 621, 635, the minority judgment of Cory J placed some weight on the nature of the relationship between the parties in determining whether there had been an absence of juristic reason for the defendant's enrichment. However, McLachlin J began her majority judgment by stating (*ibid*, 642) that she differed from Cory J *inter alia* in relation to the requirement of absence of juristic reason. It was only in relation to the remedial issue that she put any emphasis on the concept of a "family enterprise".

V. CONCLUSION ON THE CANADIAN APPROACH

It will be recalled that, at the outset of this chapter, emphasis was laid on the credibility lent to the Canadian doctrine by its reliance on the law of restitution. It was stated that, if mandated by the principle of unjust enrichment, the Canadian doctrine would be likely to be welcomed into the legal systems of other jurisdictions. Unfortunately, it has emerged from the preceding detailed consideration that the Canadian doctrine has no real foundation in restitution theory. Leaving aside the various concessions made to claimants in terms of the interpretation of the facts, three crucial theoretical problems can be identified. The first difficulty relates to the reason for restitution; the Canadian doctrine relies either on a sweeping assumption that restitution must follow in the absence of a "juristic reason to the contrary"[254] or else on a extremely loose version of the already questionable unjust factor of "free acceptance".[255] Secondly, there is the problem that, under the cover of the concept of "corresponding deprivation", the Canadian courts have taken into account "detriment" incurred by the claimant which in no way enriches the defendant. The final problem is that, at the remedial stage, the Canadian doctrine involves an unexplained redistribution of the parties' accumulated wealth with no reference to the enrichment which triggered the remedy.

One is left to conclude that the Canadian courts have effectively arrogated to themselves a statutory-style discretion providing for the adjustment of the property rights of cohabitees upon the ending of their relationship.[256] Whether the rule they have chosen reflects the social conditions and expectations of people in Canada is a matter for speculation.[257] The important point appears to be that the discretion the Canadian courts have created for themselves does extreme violence to the principles of the law of restitution. Yet, if a court had the stomach for such violence, similar results could be achieved with almost equal ease by taking the hatchet to a more familiar area of the law such as contract or trusts.[258] Thus, one's conclusion must be that the appeal to the principles of unjust enrichment provides no easy answer to the problem of property disputes between unmarried couples.

Now that the Canadian approach has been judged, and found wanting, it remains only to consider the developments in Australia and New Zealand. This task will be attempted in the next two chapters.

---

[254] See text to and following n 100 *supra*.

[255] See text to nn 113–162 *supra*.

[256] Cf. Birks, n 214 *supra*, p 219.

[257] The extremely liberal approach to the property rights of unmarried couples may be influenced to some extent by recent case law under the Canadian Charter of Rights and Freedoms 1982. Note McLeod's suggestion (annotation to *Pickelein* v *Gillmore* (1997) 27 RFL (4th) 51, 56) that, in view of cases such as *M* v *H* (1996) 142 DLR (4th) 1 (Ont CA), it is arguable that "all current matrimonial property statutes violate the [Canadian Charter of Rights and Freedoms] by discriminating against non-married family spouses". See also *Taylor* v *Rossu* (1998) 161 DLR (4th) 266 (Alberta CA) (cf. Chapter 1 *supra*, n 16).

[258] Cf. Chapter 1 *supra*, text following n 59.

8

The Constructive Trust as a Remedy for Unconscionability in Australia

This chapter considers the Australian version of the remedial constructive trust. As will be discussed shortly, the Australian "unconscionability" doctrine is founded upon an analogy with the rules applicable on the termination of a partnership or contractual joint venture. The Australian doctrine is a comparatively recent development and there is still some uncertainty as to its scope. However, it is clear that, like its Canadian counterpart, the Australian doctrine has the potential to deliver a remedy in a wide range of situations. In keeping with the objective of this book, it will be necessary in this chapter to test the theoretical credentials of the Australian doctrine and to see whether it reflects a coherent principle which could be adopted by the courts in other jurisdictions. After a detailed consideration of the Australian case law, it will be concluded that, unfortunately, the Australian unconscionability doctrine lacks a basis in the principles of equity. For this reason, one cannot accept that it should be adopted in other jurisdictions.

The Australian approach developed against a doctrinal background similar to the present English position. The Australian courts had rejected Lord Denning's early[1] and later[2] attempts to establish a discretionary approach to family property disputes. They were, however, willing to accept the "common intention" trust analysis put forward by Lord Diplock in *Gissing* v *Gissing*.[3] For a time, the Australian judges contented themselves with the development of a moderately generous version of this English analysis.[4] However, like the

---

[1] See *Wirth* v *Wirth* (1956) 98 CLR 228 and *Hepworth* v *Hepworth* (1963) 110 CLR 309 where the High Court of Australia rejected the suggestion that Australian legislative provisions similar to s 17 of the Married Women's Property Act 1882 could be used to afford a wide discretion to the courts to rearrange the property entitlements of spouses upon the breakdown of the relationship. See further Chapter 1 *infra*, text following n 48.

[2] The constructive trust of a new model was decisively rejected in *Allen* v *Snyder* [1977] 2 NSWLR 685. See further Chapter 6 *supra*, n 60 and accompanying text. Note, however, that even now there is an occasional judicial tendency to treat "unconscionability" (the central concept in the modern Australian doctrine) as merely an aggravated form of "unfairness and injustice". See e.g. the comments of Walsh J in *Bennett* v *Tairua* (1992) 15 Fam LR 317, 341 (WA Sup Ct).

[3] [1971] AC 886.

[4] For discussion of the relevant Australian cases, see Dodds "The New Constructive Trust: An Analysis of its Nature and Scope" (1988) 16 *Melbourne University Law Review* 482.

Canadian courts,[5] the Australian courts ultimately tired of the restrictiveness (and artificiality) of the common intention trust.[6] Perhaps as a reaction to the restraint they had shown for so many years, the Australian courts eventually opted for a new, and far more radical, approach.[7]

The turning point was the decision of the High Court of Australia in *Muschinski* v *Dodds*.[8] In this case, Deane J drew an analogy with the rules applicable in the context of a commercial joint venture which fails without fault on the part of either party. In such a situation, the courts of equity would regard it as unconscionable for one party to retain benefits which had been transferred to him on the assumption that the joint venture would continue. Deane J felt that it was permissible to apply this approach even where the joint venture was less formal in nature. On this basis, he was able to provide a remedy in the context of a non-marital cohabitation. However, the facts of *Muschinski*[9] (which will be discussed shortly) were unusual in that the parties were involved in a quasi-commercial project. It remained unclear for a time whether Deane J's new approach was applicable in the more normal context of a straightforward dispute between cohabitees, with no commercial element to their relationship.

The uncertainty was resolved by the High Court of Australia in 1987 in *Baumgartner* v *Baumgartner*.[10] In *Baumgartner*, the High Court made it clear

---

[5] See Chapter 7 *supra*.

[6] Interestingly, the "common intention" analysis has continued to be applied in the Australian courts, alongside the modern unconscionability principle. See *Green* v *Green* (1989) 17 NSWLR 343; *Bennett* v *Tairua* (1992) 15 Fam LR 317, 322–323 per Rowland J; *Rasmussen* v *Rasmussen* [1995] 1 VR 613; *Bell* v *Elliot*, 26 November 1996 (LEXIS, NSW Sup Ct). Note also a number of cases which appear to blur the boundaries between the English approach and the modern unconscionability doctrine: *Lipman* v *Lipman* (1989) 13 Fam LR 1, 20–21; *Woodward* v *Johnston* (1991) 14 Fam LR 828; *Miller* v *Sutherland* (1990) 14 Fam LR 416; *Bell* v *Bell* (1995) 19 Fam LR 690. See also Bryan "Constructive Trusts and Unconscionability in Australia: On the Endless Road to Unattainable Perfection" (1994) 8 *Trust Law International* 74, 74–75. Contrast Sheller JA's apparent hostility to the common intention analysis in *Bryson* v *Bryant* (1992) 29 NSWLR 188, 217.

[7] For commentary on the modern Australian approach, see (in addition to the articles cited elsewhere in this chapter) Black "*Baumgartner* v *Baumgartner*, The Constructive Trust and the Expanding Scope of Unconscionability" (1988) 11 *University of New South Wales Law Journal* 117; Hayton "Remedial Constructive Trusts of Homes: An Overseas View" [1988] Conv 259; Parkinson "Intention, Reliance and Contribution in the De Facto Cases" (1991) 5 *Australian Journal of Family Law* 268.

[8] (1985) 160 CLR 583.

[9] *Ibid*.

[10] (1987) 164 CLR 137. Three years before *Baumgartner*, the legislature of New South Wales had passed the De Facto Relationships Act 1984. This Act allows the courts to adjust the property rights of cohabitees upon the termination of their relationship. (*Baumgartner* itself was a New South Wales case but, since the Act is not retrospective, was not covered by its provisions). See generally Astor and Nothdurft "Report of the New South Wales Law Reform Commission on De Facto Relationships" (1985) 48 MLR 61 and the materials referred to by Chisholm, Jessep and O'Ryan "De Facto Property Decisions in NSW: Emerging Patterns and Policies" (1991) 5 *Australian Journal of Family Law* 241 n 4. See also *Evans* v *Marmont* (1997) 42 NSWLR 70. Four other Australian jurisdictions have since passed legislation based on the New South Wales model: see Victoria's Property Law (Amendment) Act 1987, adding a new Part IX to the Property Law Act 1958 (new regime applicable only to real property); the Northern Territory's De Facto Relationships Act 1991; the Australian Capital Territory's Domestic Relationships Act 1994 and the South Australian De Facto Relationships Act 1996. See generally Parkinson "The Property Rights of Cohabitees—Is Statutory

that the new approach was applicable even in cases lacking a commercial aspect.[11] However, having abstracted Deane J's approach from the fact situation which had originally lent it plausibility, the High Court left unresolved a number of basic issues relating to the application of the new doctrine. Although *Baumgartner* has been followed in a long line of Australian cases since 1987, few of these major issues have been clarified. Despite the ritualistic condemnations by the Australian judges of Lord Denning's new model constructive trust, it is not easy to identify an intelligible principle which separates the Australian approach from Lord Denning's creation.[12] The ultimate conclusion of this chapter will be that the Australian "unconscionability" approach does not provide a satisfactory theoretical solution to the problem with which this book is concerned.

It is now proposed to examine the modern Australian approach in detail. It will be helpful to begin, in Part I, with a discussion of *Muschinski* and *Baumgartner*, the two cases which revolutionised Australian law in this area. Next, Part II will consider the practical operation of the modern Australian doctrine. It will then be necessary in Part III to attempt an assessment of the viability of the theoretical foundation for the doctrine. Finally, Part IV will be devoted to some concluding reflections on the Australian approach.

I. THE DEVELOPMENT OF THE UNCONSCIONABILITY APPROACH

A. Muschinski v Dodds[13]

In 1972, Mrs Muschinski and Mr Dodds began living together in a house belonging to Mrs Muschinski. Both parties had been married to other partners. After four years, they decided to purchase a new property which was located at Picton. Their plan was to build a prefabricated home for themselves on the property and to restore an old cottage on the land for use in a crafts business

---

Reform the Answer?", ch. 21 in *Frontiers of Family Law* (Chicester, West Sussex: John Wiley & Sons Ltd, 1995); Bailey-Harris "Property Disputes in De Facto Relationships: Can Equity Still Play a Role?" (with "Commentary" by Neave), ch. 7 in Cope (ed) *Equity[:] Issues and Trends* (Sydney: Federation Press, 1995). Surprisingly, the existence of wide-ranging legislation has not blunted the enthusiasm of the Australian courts for innovation in this area of the law. Indeed, the equitable jurisdiction has developed to such an extent that the legislative provisions are sometimes rendered superfluous. See e.g. *Miller v Sutherland* (1990) 14 Fam LR 416 (constructive trust declared, Cohen J concluding in a single paragraph that the same result would have followed under the De Facto Relationships Act 1984). Cf. text following n 237 *infra*.

[11] Compare the occasional references in the early English case law to the notion of a family "joint venture". See e.g. *Silver v Silver* [1958] 1 WLR 259, 263 per Lord Evershed MR; *Diwell v Farnes* [1959] 1 WLR 624, 639–640 per Willmer LJ; *Hine v Hine* [1962] 1 WLR 1124, 1129 per Donovan LJ.

[12] Cf. Mason "The Place of Equity and Equitable Remedies in the Contemporary Common Law World" (1994) 110 LQR 238, 249–250.

[13] (1985) 160 CLR 583. See Evans "De Facto Property Disputes: The Drama Continues" (1986) 1 *Australian Journal of Family Law* 234; Meagher "Constructive Trusts: High Court Developments and Prospects" (1988) 4 *Australian Bar Review* 67.

which Mrs Muschinski wished to establish. Mrs Muschinski provided the whole of the purchase price. However, it was agreed that Mr Dodds would pay for the renovation of the cottage and for the erection of the prefabricated house. Since he was going to make a substantial investment in the property, Mr Dodds insisted that his name should appear on the title. On the advice of their solicitor, the property was conveyed to the couple as tenants in common in equal shares.[14]

Unfortunately, a number of difficulties arose with the project. A property settlement upon which Mr Dodds had been relying to fund his contribution proved less substantial than expected. Planning permission was refused for the construction of the prefabricated home. Ultimately, the couple's personal relationship collapsed and they separated. In the meantime, a certain amount of work had been done on the property. As Deane J explained, "the parties were left as equal legal owners of the project property towards the overall costs of which Mrs Muschinski had contributed approximately ten-elevenths . . . while Mr Dodds had contributed but the remaining one-eleventh".[15]

It was contended on behalf of Mrs Muschinski that a constructive trust should be imposed "based on broad notions of fairness"[16] or on the ground of unjust enrichment. These avenues were, however, firmly rejected by Deane J in the leading judgment in the case. In relation to the argument based on fairness, Deane J stressed that "[t]he mere fact that it would be unjust or unfair in a situation of discord for the owner of a legal estate to assert his ownership against another provides, of itself, no mandate for a judicial declaration that the ownership in whole or in part lies, in equity, in that other".[17] Significantly, Deane J went on to deny that "general notions of fairness and justice have become irrelevant to the content and application of equity".[18] According to Deane J, such notions "remain relevant to the traditional equitable notion of unconscionable conduct which persists as an operative component of some fundamental rules or principles of modern equity".[19] As for unjust enrichment, Deane J took the view that, whatever the future might hold, unjust enrichment was not yet in Australian law "an established principle constituting the basis of decision of past and future cases".[20]

---

[14] A distinctive feature of the Australian jurisprudence is the number of cases where a remedy has been afforded to a person who has paid the purchase price of property but has allowed it to be conveyed into joint names. See e.g. *Muschinski v Dodds* (1985) 160 CLR 583; *Jasco v Vuong* (1988) 12 Fam LR 615; *Atkinson v Burt* (1989) 12 Fam LR 800; *Medley v McHenry*, 21 March 1990 (LEXIS, NSW Sup Ct). Contrast the Canadian position discussed in Chapter 7 *supra*, n 200. Note also the views of Judge Kaye QC in *Rhoden v Joseph*, 6 September 1990 (LEXIS, Ch D).

[15] (1985) 160 CLR 583, 611.

[16] *Ibid*, 612 per Deane J.

[17] *Ibid*, 616. Cf. *Stern v McArthur* (1988) 165 CLR 489, 514 per Brennan J. See also n 2 *supra*.

[18] *Ibid*.

[19] *Ibid*. Interestingly, Deane J here cited authorities on equitable estoppel and on the equitable jurisdiction to overturn unconscionable bargains.

[20] *Ibid*, 617. For the subsequent development of unjust enrichment in Australia, see *Pavey and Matthews Pty Ltd v Paul* (1986) 162 CLR 221; Mason and Carter *Restitution Law in Australia* (Sydney: Butterworths, 1995) pp 28–34.

Having discounted "fairness" and "unjust enrichment", Deane J found it necessary to consider whether there was "any narrower and more specific basis on which,
independently of the actual intention of the parties, Mrs Muschinski can claim to be
entitled to relief by way of constructive trust".[21] Deane J found this "narrower and
more specific basis" for relief in the rules "applicable to regulate the rights and duties
of the parties to a failed partnership or contractual joint venture".[22] Deane J
explained that these rules provided that "to the extent that the joint funds allow, the
joint venturers are entitled to the proportionate repayment of their capital contributions to the abortive joint venture".[23] These rules, according to Deane J, were
"properly to be seen as instances of a more general principle of equity".[24]

Deane J explained that this general principle, "[l]ike most of the traditional
doctrines of equity", operated "to prevent a person from asserting or exercising
a legal right in circumstances where the particular assertion or exercise of it
would constitute unconscionable conduct".[25] In a crucial passage, Deane J then
made the following comment on the relevant principle:

> "[T]he principle operates in a case where the substratum of a joint relationship or
> endeavour is removed without attributable blame and where the benefit of money or
> other property contributed by one party on the basis and for the purposes of the rela-
> tionship or endeavour would otherwise be enjoyed by the other party in circumstances
> in which it was not specifically intended or specially provided that that other party
> should so enjoy it. The content of the principle is that, in such a case, equity will not
> permit that other party to assert or retain the benefit of the relevant property to the
> extent that it would be unconscionable for him so to do: cf *Atwood* v *Maude*[26], and
> per Jessel MR, *Lyon* v *Tweddell*[27]".[28]

Deane J went on to consider whether, in the circumstances, it would be
unconscionable for Mr Dodds to assert his one-half legal interest in the land
without making allowance for Mrs Muschinski's greater contribution. Deane J
accepted that there might be special considerations in the context of a personal
relationship which could prevent the application of the relevant equitable principle. For example, if the parties stayed together for a number of years "direct
contributions in money or labour" might be offset by "indirect contributions in
other forms such as support, home-making and family care".[29] However, Deane

---

[21] *Ibid.*
[22] *Ibid*, 618.
[23] *Ibid*, 619.
[24] *Ibid.* For discussion of the authorities upon which Deane J relied, see Part III *infra*.
[25] *Ibid*, 619–620.
[26] (1868) LR 3 Ch App 369, 374–375.
[27] (1881) 17 Ch D 529, 531.
[28] (1985) 160 CLR 583, 620.
[29] *Ibid*, 622. See Chapter 7 *supra*, Part IV(G) for discussion in the Canadian context of the significance of countervailing benefits received by the claimant. This issue has not attracted a great deal
of attention in the Australian case law. However, as is demonstrated by the comments of Deane J
quoted as text to this footnote, no claim should be possible under the Australian doctrine if the contributions of the claimant were matched by the benefits she received from her partner. Cf. *Vitas* v
Petrovic, 7 February 1996 (LEXIS, NSW Sup Ct).

J pointed out that, on the facts before him, there was "no consideration or combination of considerations arising from the personal relationship between the parties which could properly be seen as negating or overriding the unconscionable character of Mr Dodds' conduct".[30] He ordered that the parties hold the property on a constructive trust under which their respective contributions would be repaid to them and "the residue" would be held in equal shares.[31]

Although Deane J's approach carried the day and has determined the course of the later cases, it is worth noting that the High Court of Australia was by no means united behind him in *Muschinski*. Only Mason J concurred with Deane J's judgment. While Gibbs CJ was content to agree with the order proposed by Deane J, his judgment was in fact based on an entirely different interpretation of the law.[32] Brennan J, with the concurrence of Dawson J, dissented and expressly stated the view that no analogy could be drawn between the parties' relationship and a legal partnership.[33] Thus, it was by the barest of margins that Deane J's view prevailed.

B. Baumgartner v Baumgartner[34]

For a time, it remained unclear what effect *Muschinski* would have on this area of Australian law.[35] Then, in *Baumgartner* v *Baumgartner*[36] in 1987, the High Court of Australia used *Muschinski* as the platform for a wide-ranging new doctrine. The facts of *Baumgartner* were rather different to those in *Muschinski* and the case was, in fact, much closer to the normal run of disputes arising upon the termination of an unmarried cohabitation.

The parties met in 1978 and, after a few months, began to cohabit in a house belonging to the male partner. As Kirby P pointed out in the Court of Appeal of New South Wales, the relationship between the parties was "rocky from the start" and the claimant left her partner some seven or eight times during the course of their four-year cohabitation.[37] After a time, apparently after the option of marriage had been rejected by her partner,[38] the claimant changed her name by deed poll to that of her partner. A baby was planned and was born in

---

[30] (1985) 160 CLR 583, 622.

[31] *Ibid*, 624.

[32] Gibbs CJ felt that, because the parties had had a joint contractual liability to pay the purchase price, the fact that Mrs Muschinski had paid everything entitled her to a right of contribution from Mr Dodds. See Parkinson "Doing Equity Between De Facto Spouses: From Calverley v Green to Baumgartner" (1988) 11 *Adelaide Law Review* 370, 374–381.

[33] (1985) 160 CLR 583, 609.

[34] (1987) 164 CLR 137.

[35] Note that the decision in *Muschinski* was warmly welcomed by Meagher, n 13 *supra*. One presumes that Meagher, virulent critic of Denning-style discretionary justice, did not foresee what the Australian courts would later do in the name of *Muschinski*.

[36] (1987) 164 CLR 137.

[37] (1985) 2 NSWLR 406, 409.

[38] (1987) 164 CLR 137, 142 per Mason CJ, Wilson and Deane JJ.

early 1980. Meanwhile, the male partner suggested the purchase of another property upon which he would build a new house for the family. The new property was purchased in the name of the male partner and was financed by the sale of his original property. The cost of building the house was borrowed by him on a mortgage. The claimant worked throughout the relationship, with the exception of a three-month period at the time of the birth of their child. Every week, she handed over her pay-packet to her partner, who took most of the responsibility for financial decisions.

In 1982, the claimant left finally, taking with her the child of the marriage and an amount of furniture. She claimed an equitable share in the home. Overturning the conclusion of the Court of Appeal of New South Wales, the High Court of Australia held that, on the evidence, there had been no common intention between the parties that the ownership of the new property would be shared. However, according to the High Court, this did not conclude the matter and the court unanimously held that a constructive trust should be imposed independently of intention.

In the leading judgment, given by Mason CJ, Deane and Wilson JJ, reliance was placed on the "joint venture" principle identified in *Muschinski*. The three judges expressed their central conclusion in the following terms:

> "The case is accordingly one in which the parties have pooled their earnings for the purposes of their joint relationship, one of the purposes of that relationship being to secure accommodation for themselves and their child. Their contributions, financial and otherwise, to the acquisition of the land, the building of the house, the purchase of furniture and the making of their home, were on the basis of, and for the purposes of, that joint relationship. In this situation the [man's] assertion, after the relationship had failed,[39] that the Leumeah property, which was financed in part through the pooled funds, is his sole property, is his property beneficially to the exclusion of any interest at all on the part of the respondent, amounts to unconscionable conduct which attracts the intervention of equity and the imposition of a constructive trust at the suit of the [woman]".[40]

The other two members of the Court in *Baumgartner* gave brief judgments. Toohey J agreed that a constructive trust should be imposed. However, he put forward the view that this result could equally have been achieved through the application of the principle against unjust enrichment. Toohey J argued that the notion of unjust enrichment "is as much at ease with the authorities and is as capable of ready and certain application as is the notion of unconscionable

---

[39] Note that a number of the Lords in *Pettitt v Pettitt* [1970] AC 777 were at pains to emphasise that the ownership of family property could not be affected by the ultimate breakdown of the relationship between the parties. See *ibid*, 793H–794A per Lord Reid; 803F–G per Lord Morris; 825D per Lord Diplock. (Cf. *B v B*, 25 July 1978 unreported (Irish High Court); *AL v JL*, 27 February 1984 unreported (Irish High Court). The approach in *Baumgartner* is difficult to reconcile with *Pettitt*, in that (as will emerge from the discussion in this chapter) it effectively treats the property arrangements of the parties as having been conditional upon the continuation of the relationship.

[40] (1987) 164 CLR 137, 149. For further discussion of the remedy in *Baumgartner*, see text to and following n 130 *infra*.

conduct".[41] He suggested that in a situation "where two people have lived together for a time and made contributions towards the purchase of land or the building of a home on it, an approach based on unconscionable conduct or one based on unjust enrichment will inevitably bring about the same result".[42]

Gaudron J agreed with the joint judgment of Mason CJ, Deane and Wilson JJ. However, she added some brief comments of her own. First, she discussed the relationship between the new unconscionability-based constructive trust and the traditional purchase money resulting trust. According to Gaudron J, in determining the extent of the constructive trust, it might on some occasions "be sufficient to treat the contributions to mortgage repayments as if they were contributions to the consideration for the purchase of the asset".[43] Thus, in the view of Gaudron J, the "new" form of constructive trust might simply allow the Australian courts to escape from the strict view taken in *Calverley* v *Green*[44] and to recognise contributions to mortgage instalments for the purposes of the purchase money resulting trust (along the lines of the Irish practice).[45]

However, Gaudron J did envisage a more radical approach in other situations, suggesting that "in the context of domestic relationships it is relevant to inquire whether the asset was acquired for the purposes of the relationship, and whether non-financial contributions should be taken into account".[46] She explicitly stated that the contribution of the claimant should be increased by reference to the amount she would have earned but for her absence from work around the time of the birth of her child.[47]

II. THE OPERATION OF THE UNCONSCIONABILITY DOCTRINE

The previous Part considered the two decisions of the High Court of Australia upon which the unconscionability doctrine is founded. It was seen that the High Court was willing to grant a remedy to a claimant upon the termination of a cohabitation on the basis that it would be unconscionable for her partner to retain the benefits he received pursuant to the "joint venture"[48] between the parties. In this Part, it will be necessary to examine the more detailed development of the doctrine in cases subsequently decided by the lower Australian courts.

---

[41] *Ibid*, 153.

[42] *Ibid*, 154. The unjust enrichment approach has received rather limited support in the later Australian cases. See *Public Trustee* v *Kukula* (1990) 14 Fam LR 97; *Re Toohey* (1991) 14 Fam LR 843; *Bryson* v *Bryant* (1992) 29 NSWLR 188, 205–209 per Kirby P dissenting. Note also the more negative comments of Sheller JA in *Bryson ibid*, 223.

[43] *Ibid*, 156.

[44] (1984) 155 CLR 242. See Chapter 3 *supra*, text following n 1. Cf. Hayton "Constructive Trusts: Is the Remedying of Unjust Enrichment a Satisfactory Approach?" in Finn (ed) *Equity, Fiduciaries and Trusts* (Sydney: Law Book Co, 1989) p 243.

[45] See Chapter 3 *supra*, Part II.

[46] (1987) 164 CLR 137, 156.

[47] *Ibid*, 157.

[48] For closer examination of the concept of a joint venture in this context, see Part III(B) *infra*.

The discussion will focus on a number of key issues concerning the operation of the unconscionability doctrine. It is proposed to begin by considering what types of contributions are capable of triggering the doctrine. Later sections will consider whether the doctrine may be applied where there has been no premature collapse in the personal relationship of the parties, whether a remedy should be denied to a claimant who is to blame for the termination of the relationship, what is the role of the intention of the parties and what is the extent of the remedial discretion of the court.

A. What Types of Contribution Can Trigger the Doctrine?

1. *Contributions to mortgages and improvements*[49]

The cases show a clear acceptance of the following contributions as sufficient to trigger the unconscionability doctrine: direct contributions to the repayment of a mortgage,[50] indirect contributions to a mortgage through the payment of other family expenses[51] or the provision of unpaid work in the legal owner's business[52] and contributions of money and labour towards the making of improvements.[53]

2. *Contributions in the form of domestic labour*

There has been less certainty in relation to "non-financial contributions" such as the performance of domestic labour. The approach in *Baumgartner* itself was somewhat ambivalent. It will be recalled that the High Court took into account the contribution of the claimant during a three-month absence from work

---

[49] Direct contributions to the purchase price, made at the time of the purchase, are, of course, capable of creating a resulting trust. See e.g. *Atkinson v Burt* (1989) 12 Fam LR 800; *Ammala v Sarimaa* (1993) 17 Fam LR 529; *Harmer v Pearson* (1993) 16 Fam LR 596. Cf. *Jasco v Vuong* (1988) 12 Fam LR 615.

[50] *Carville v Westbury* (1990) 102 Fed LR 223; *Kais v Turvey* (1994) 17 Fam LR 498. See also *Bell v Bell* (1995) 19 Fam LR 690, 693. Contrast the failure of the claim in *Tory v Jones*, 30 July 1990 (LEXIS, NSW Sup Ct).

[51] *Baumgartner* (1987) 164 CLR 137; *Hibberson v George* (1989) 12 Fam LR 725; *Lipman v Lipman* (1989) 13 Fam LR 1; *Renton v Youngman* (1995) 19 Fam LR 450; *Bell v Bell* (1995) 19 Fam LR 690. See also *Stowe and Devereaux Holdings Pty Ltd v Stowe* (1995) 19 Fam LR 409, 418 per Ipp, Owen and White JJ. Cf. *Bennett v Tairua* (1992) 15 Fam LR 317, 339. Note also the failure of the claim on the unusual facts of *Arthur v Public Trustee* (1988) 90 Fed LR 203.

[52] *Lipman v Lipman* (1989) 13 Fam LR 1.

[53] *Miller v Sutherland* (1990) 14 Fam LR 416, 424; *Booth v Beresford* (1993) 17 Fam LR 147; *Kidner v Secretary, Department of Social Security* (1993) 31 Admin Law Decisions 63; *Kais v Turvey* (1994) 17 Fam LR 498 (see, however, the note at (1994) 11 WAR 357, 357: claimant undertook not to enforce relevant portion of judgment in the face of High Court of Australia's indication that it would grant leave to appeal in respect of this point). Cf. *Stowe and Devereaux Holdings Pty Ltd v Stowe* (1995) 19 Fam LR 409, 418–419 per Ipp, Owen and White JJ. Note also *Carville v Westbury* (1990) 102 Fed LR 223 (defendant allowed credit for improvements he had made to property held on constructive trust for claimant).

around the time of the birth of the child of the relationship. However, interestingly, the credit was not measured by the value of her labour; rather it was based on the amount she would have earned had she continued in her normal employment. The High Court did not explain its approach to this issue, which appears to have involved an appeal to the broad argument that it would have been unfair of the man to deny his partner credit for earnings she lost, as it were, in the service of the relationship. It remained unclear from *Baumgartner* whether contributions through domestic labour could only be recognised if they were associated, as in *Baumgartner* itself, with other "financial" contributions.[54]

The subsequent case law has done little to clarify the position on this important practical issue. The most important authority[55] is the decision of the New South Wales Court of Appeal in *Bryson v Bryant*.[56] The facts of *Bryson* raised the issue under discussion in a particularly clear manner. A couple had eloped and been married in 1927 and had lived together happily until their deaths within a few months of each other in 1988 and 1989. A number of years after the marriage, a site was purchased in the name of the husband. He provided the full purchase price in cash. With the help of friends, a house was built on the site. Although after so many years the evidence was limited, it appeared that the wife had provided some assistance with the construction, in the form of cleaning up rubbish and camping on the site with her husband for a number of weeks. There were no children of the marriage. Over the sixty years for which the marriage lasted, the wife provided "substantial, enduring and faithful"[57] domestic services for her husband who "couldn't even cook a sausage".[58] Although the evidence was again limited, it appeared possible that she might also have been the main breadwinner for a short period during the Depression.

Shortly before the wife's death, while her husband was in hospital suffering from advanced dementia, she had made a will leaving all her property to her

---

[54] Note that this appears to have been the view of the Full Court of the Supreme Court of South Australia in *Stowe and Devereaux Holdings Pty Ltd v Stowe* (1995) 19 Fam LR 409, 418–419. See also *Re Sabri* (1996) 21 Fam LR 213, 223. Cf. Neave "The New Unconscionability Principle—Property Disputes Between De Facto Partners" (1991) 6 *Australian Journal of Family Law* 185, 201–202. One source of confusion in the Australian case law lies in the much-quoted passage from the judgment of Mason CJ, Deane and Wilson JJ in *Baumgartner* (1987) 164 CLR 137, 149 which begins "The case is accordingly one in which the parties have pooled their earnings for the purposes of their joint relationship . . .". Given that the reasoning in *Baumgartner* is not entirely clear, judges in subsequent cases (e.g. *Stowe supra*) have tended to focus on the wording of this passage and to attribute special significance to the concept of pooling. The implication is that the making of contributions might be insufficient unless there had been a "pooling" of resources. Unfortunately, no coherent explanation has been advanced as to the function of "pooling" within the unconscionability doctrine. Cf. *Hibberson v George* (1989) 12 Fam LR 725, 742 where the majority of the Court of Appeal of New South Wales held that "pooling" did not necessarily involve a physical aspect. See further Chapter 10 *infra*, text to and following n 47 where the concept of "pooling" is given detailed consideration.

[55] See also *Balnaves v Balnaves* (1988) 12 Fam LR 488, 495 (Full Ct of Fam Ct of Aus); Spry (1997) *Australian Property Law Journal* 86, discussing *Dunne v Turner*, 20 August 1996, unreported (Queensland CA).

[56] (1992) 29 NSWLR 188.

[57] *Ibid*, 204.

[58] *Ibid*, 214 per Sheller JA (quoting one of the witnesses).

brother. Not long afterwards, a caveat was lodged on her behalf against the husband's legal title to the family home. Upon her death, the brother claimed that he should be entitled to a share in the property on the basis that a constructive trust had arisen in favour of his sister. The Court of Appeal of New South Wales rejected his claim by a majority of two to one.

Kirby P, in a vigorous dissent, favoured the recognition of a constructive trust based on the domestic contributions of the claimant. Kirby P argued that:

> "It is important that the 'brave new world of unconscionability'[59] should not lead the court back to family property law of twenty years ago by the back door of a pre-occupation with contributions, particularly financial contributions, made by claimants of beneficial interests and at the time of the acquisition of the property in question . . . Nor should . . . [those] who have provided 'women's work' over their adult lifetime . . . be told condescendingly, by a mostly male judiciary, that their services must be regarded as 'freely given labour' only or, catalogued as attributable solely to a rather one-way and quaintly described 'love and affection', when property interests come to be distributed".[60]

Taking into account the wife's other contributions,[61] Kirby P took the view that she should be entitled to a one-half share under a constructive trust.

The views of Sheller JA, the first of the majority judges, are more difficult to discern. Sheller JA refused the claim on the basis that, given the likely intentions of the parties during their lifetimes, there was nothing unconscionable in the husband's estate retaining the property after the wife's death.[62] In his brief discussion of the issue, he appeared to assume, at least for the purposes of argument, that if the parties had "pooled their resources, both financial and otherwise, for the purposes of their joint relationship", they would each have enjoyed an equitable interest in the property during their joint lives.[63] However, the reference to contributions "financial and otherwise" leaves open the possibility of recognising domestic contributions only when they are combined with other financial contributions.

The final judge, Samuels A-JA, also rejected the claim, this time on the basis that the domestic work of the claimant could not be related to the improvement or acquisition of the property. He insisted that the case was "not about providing rewards or fair recompense to a spouse who has loyally and for sixty years discharged the burdens and enjoyed the benefits of a long marriage".[64] Noting that the division of domestic functions in their marriage was far from unconventional at the time, he commented that:

---

[59] See Bryan "The Conscience of Equity in Australia" (1990) 106 LQR 25, 27.

[60] (1992) 29 NSWLR 188, 203–204.

[61] Kirby P commented (*ibid*, 204) that "if the mercantile obsessions of our law require us to focus exclusively on financial contributions, they are readily to be found in this case". According to Kirby P (*ibid*), the wife had contributed financially during the period when "by inference, for a time, at least, she was the sole breadwinner during the Depression".

[62] Cf. n 85 *infra*.

[63] (1992) 29 NSWLR 188, 222.

"Whether or not the way in which they lived together is desirable or is fair to the aspirations of women, or anything else of that kind, it was not unusual and her adherence to it does not distinguish Margaret [the wife] as some kind of social heroine".[65]

Samuels A-JA concluded his judgment in the following terms:

"[I]f a declaration is sought to be made in the present case, it would seem to follow that in any marriage of the conventional pattern or of the pattern which was conventional at the time [the parties] married, the wife would become entitled to any property acquired by the husband merely because she carried out her role as the homemaker. As far as I am aware, there is no principle of law which is capable of producing that result. To produce such a result would, in my opinion, carry the Court beyond the furthest confines of judicial activism. I do not know whether the community at large would, in any case, welcome such a change. It is a matter for the parliament".[66]

Unfortunately, it remains unclear from his judgment whether Samuels A-JA would have been willing to grant a remedy based on a contribution of domestic labour made, for example, during a period when a mortgage was being repaid.

To conclude, *Bryson* provides no clear answer to the question of the status of domestic contributions. On the one hand, only one judge supported the wife's claim on the facts. On the other hand, neither of the majority judges rejected domestic contributions *in limine*; Sheller JA concentrated on the fact that there had been no unexpected collapse in the relationship and Samuels A-JA emphasised the absence of a link with the acquisition or improvement of the property. Given the dearth of other relevant authorities, the law remains unclear as to the status of a claim based purely on domestic labour. However, on the basis of *Baumgartner* itself, it seems clear that domestic contributions can be taken into account (at least to a limited degree) when combined with financial contributions.

3. Contributions unrelated to mortgage repayments or improvements

The final issue relates to contributions, whether to family expenses or in the form of unpaid domestic or other labour, which cannot be related (even indirectly) to the purchase of a property or the making of improvements. It will be recalled that in *Muschinski v Dodds*[67] Deane J referred to "money or other property contributed . . . on the basis and for the purposes of the relationship or endeavour".[68] Similarly, in *Baumgartner*,[69] Mason, Wilson and Deane JJ commented that the contributions of the parties were made "on the basis of, and for the purpose of, [their] joint relationship".[70] These comments leave open the

---

64 *Ibid*, 225.
65 *Ibid*.
66 *Ibid*, 231.
67 (1985) 160 CLR 583.
68 *Ibid*, 620.
69 (1987) 164 CLR 137.
70 *Ibid*, 149. See also the comment (*ibid*) that the parties had arranged "that their earnings would be expended for the purposes of their relationship and for their mutual security and benefit".

possibility of taking account of contributions "to the relationship" even if they are unrelated to the acquisition or improvement of the disputed property.

A different approach was taken by Toohey J[71] in *Baumgartner*. Toohey J suggested that:

> "[I]t is not enough that one spouse has benefitted from the contributions of another. What is required is that the contributions of one spouse have enabled or assisted in enabling the other to acquire the asset in dispute".[72]

Toohey J was stating the rules relating to unjust enrichment as developed by the Canadian courts. What is presently under consideration is the position under the Australian unconscionability doctrine, which, despite Toohey J's argument in *Baumgartner*, has remained distinct from the Canadian unjust enrichment approach. In any case, the Canadian courts have in recent years broadened their doctrine to allow a remedy on the basis of any contribution which, in a very loose sense, assists in the "acquisition, maintenance or preservation" of the asset in question. In addition, they have been willing to grant a monetary remedy where no connection, however tenuous, can be established with a particular asset.[73]

There has been a great deal of uncertainty in the subsequent Australian cases that have considered the question of contributions unrelated to acquisition or improvement. Some cases have favoured the recognition of such contributions,[74] while other cases, relying on Toohey J's dictum, have taken the opposite view.[75] It remains to be seen which view will establish itself. However, while one cannot be certain, there would seem to be a strong likelihood that the future trend in Australian law will be towards taking account of "unrelated" contributions. After all, the Canadian courts (treated in Australia as supporting a strict approach) have clearly liberalised their approach and are now willing to

---

[71] The final judge in *Baumgartner* was Gaudron J. Her brief judgment expresses no definite view on the issue under discussion. However, perhaps more than Mason CJ, Wilson and Deane JJ, she concentrated her reasoning on the "acquisition of the land and the subsequent building of the house" (*ibid*, 157). This might suggest that she would have been unwilling to take account of contributions unrelated to the acquisition or improvement of property.

[72] *Ibid*, 153.

[73] See Chapter 7 *supra*, text to nn 64–67.

[74] See *Bennett v Tairua* (1992) 15 Fam LR 317, 324–325 per Nicholson J (Walsh and Rowland JJ not expressing a view on this precise point); *Bryson v Bryant* (1992) 29 NSWLR 188, 204 per Kirby P (dissenting in the result); 222 per Sheller JA (*semble*). In the later case of *Stowe and Devereaux Holdings Pty Ltd v Stowe* (1995) 19 Fam LR 409, 418–419, the Full Court of the Supreme Court of Western Australia seemed to take the view that, once there were contributions to the acquisition or improvement of property, other unrelated contributions could also be taken into account. This curious "parasitic" approach appears to have been influenced by the similarly mysterious approach of the High Court to the claimant's domestic contribution in *Baumgartner* (see text following n 53 *supra*). See also *Re Sabri* (1996) 21 Fam LR 213, 223.

[75] *Public Trustee v Kukula* (1990) 14 Fam LR 97, 102 per Handley JA (but see his remarks *ibid*, 99, quoted as supporting the opposing viewpoint by Nicholson J in *Bennett v Tairua* (1992) 15 Fam LR 317, 325); *Bryson v Bryant* (1992) 29 NSWLR 188, 231 per Samuels JA. See also *Hibberson v George* (1989) 12 Fam LR 725, 738–739 per Mahoney JA dissenting (the majority not expressing a view); *Booth v Beresford* (1993) 17 Fam LR 147, 151 where, although Toohey J's *dictum* was not mentioned, the judges seem clearly to have opposed the recognition of "unrelated" contributions.

grant a remedy in the case of such contributions.[76] It is probably only a matter of time before the Australian courts also decide that the constructive trust is only one possible remedy for "unconscionability" and are willing to award a monetary remedy where there is no connection with a particular asset.[77]

B. Is the Breakdown of the Relationship a Prerequisite of a Remedy?

Most of the cases in this area concern the premature termination of the relationship between the parties. However, as has been noted in an earlier chapter,[78] in a number of contexts outside the breakdown of a relationship it may become important to determine the separate property rights of the parties. The most obvious cases are where one of the parties dies or the legal owner of the family home becomes bankrupt.[79] In these situations, it will be relevant to decide whether the premature termination of the relationship is an essential prerequisite for the grant of a remedy. The fundamental statements of principle in *Muschinski*[80] and *Baumgartner*[81] place a strong emphasis on the fact that the relationship between the parties had collapsed prematurely.[82] This suggests that there may be a problem in affording a remedy in a case where there has been no such collapse.

It will be helpful to examine separately the problems arising in the case of the death of one of the partners and in the case of the bankruptcy of the defendant or the intervention of his creditors.

1. *The death of one of the partners*

The issues which arise upon the death of one of the partners are neatly illustrated by the facts of *Bryson* v *Bryant*.[83] It will be recalled[84] that *Bryson* concerned a married couple who, until their deaths in 1988 and 1989, had lived together happily for sixty years in a house owned by the husband. The wife's brother, the sole beneficiary under her will, claimed that the wife had been entitled to a share in the family home under a constructive trust. Interestingly, although the claim in *Bryson* was ultimately unsuccessful, neither of the major-

---

[76] See text to n 73 *supra*.

[77] Cf. the discussion of the question of remedial flexibility in the text to nn 146–151 *infra*.

[78] See Chapter 1 *supra*, text following n 90.

[79] Australian cases have also arisen in the context of disputes over taxation or the entitlement to a state pension. See *Kidner* v *Secretary, Department of Social Security* (1993) 31 Admin Law Decisions 63; *AAT Case No 9763* (1994) 29 ATR 1151.

[80] (1985) 160 CLR 583.

[81] (1987) 164 CLR 137.

[82] Deane J referred specifically in *Muschinski* ((1985) 160 CLR 583, 621) to "the special circumstances of the unforeseen and premature collapse of a joint relationship or endeavour". See also *Baumgartner* (1987) 164 CLR 137, 149 per Mason CJ, Wilson and Deane JJ.

[83] (1992) 29 NSWLR 188.

[84] See text following n 56 *supra*.

ity judges based their decision on the fact that the relationship between the parties had not come to a premature end.[85] Moreover, Kirby P, in his dissenting judgment, also assumed that a constructive trust could arise in favour of the claimant during the currency of the relationship.[86]

Thus, in *Bryson* none of the judges believed that the premature breakdown of the relationship was an essential element in a successful claim. This is very difficult to reconcile with the "premature failure of a joint venture" analogy which purportedly underpins the Australian doctrine. One possible rationalisation is that it was crucial in *Bryson* that the wife had asserted her claim during her lifetime.[87] The argument would be that, by her request to her husband to hand over her rightful share, the wife altered the nature of their joint relationship and shattered the previously prevailing assumption that their separate property rights were irrelevant. The "joint venture" in the relevant sense was over, even if the parties might still have continued to have contact with each other.[88] From that point onwards, it would have been unconscionable for the husband (or his executors) to deny her a share.

Therefore, it appears that the premature failure of the personal relationship between the parties is not an essential requirement for the creation of a constructive trust. Instead, it is sufficient if the claimant seeks the transfer of her rightful share (or, perhaps, if the conditions for a finding of unconscionability are created by some other "precipitating event").[89] If, however, the eventual

---

[85] Only Sheller JA specifically addressed the significance of the fact that the relationship had not broken down. He commented ((1992) 29 NSWLR 188, 222) that "[t]he relationship did not collapse so that a situation arose which neither party would have foreseen". However, Sheller JA did not, in fact, refuse to apply the unconscionability doctrine on this ground. Instead, he reasoned that the likely intention of a married couple would be to acquire their assets for their mutual enjoyment and to allow those assets to be enjoyed by the survivor when they were separated by death. Since the husband had been the survivor, Sheller JA felt that he would have been intended to enjoy the property exclusively, so that there was nothing unconscionable in its retention by his estate. Sheller JA felt (*ibid*) that if the husband had died first it might have been necessary to impose a constructive trust in favour of the wife "at least to the extent of a beneficial interest in the subject property for her life". Therefore, Sheller JA clearly did not see as an essential element in a finding of unconscionability the fact that the relationship had come to a premature end. This is confirmed by his comment (*ibid*) that, assuming sufficient contributions on the part of the wife, "during their lives each enjoyed an equitable interest in the subject property".

[86] He expressly stated (*ibid*, 210) that her interest, "having vested before her death", was "available to be disposed of by her will" and "survived her death".

[87] She had placed a caveat on the disputed property (*ibid*, 192) and had purported to leave it to her brother by her will. Note the (mild) emphasis placed by Kirby P (*ibid*, 211) on the fact that the wife had asserted her entitlement during her lifetime.

[88] It is submitted that it would not make sense to require a claimant, in addition to asserting her claim, to terminate her personal relationship with the defendant. It is quite possible that a claimant, having been denied any share in the family property, will be in no position financially to set up a separate household. See also n 104 *infra* and accompanying paragraph of text.

[89] The phrase was used by Barry J in *AAT case No 9763* (1994) 29 ATR 1151, 1158. Barry J suggested (*ibid*) that it might constitute unconscionable conduct if the defendant were to sell the disputed property without reference to the claimant's rights. It might be possible to conceptualise such an event as the termination of the joint venture by the defendant.

death of one of the parties brings a natural end to the relationship,[90] it is not easy to see how one can apply the analogy of a joint venture which fails prematurely.

It is difficult to know what conclusion to draw from the difficulty in applying the Australian doctrine in the context of the death of one of the partners. While to some this might seem to be a drawback of the doctrine, it might also be argued that equitable intervention is unwarranted in a case where the parties' relationship has ended because of the death of the "claimant".[91] If she never asserted a claim during her lifetime, it is unclear why equity should step in to divert the wealth of the relationship from her partner to her successors. However, as Sheller JA pointed out in *Bryson v Bryant*[92] there may be a stronger argument for intervention in the case of the death of the legally-owning partner. It would appear to constitute a weakness of the Australian doctrine if, when applied in a manner consistent with its theoretical foundation, it were unable to provide a remedy in this situation.

2. *Bankruptcy or the intervention of third party creditors*

Tricky problems also arise when the legally-owning partner becomes bankrupt (or one of his creditors attempts to enforce a security over his property).[93] Some Australian courts have refused to apply the unconscionability doctrine in these circumstances, arguing that there has been no premature termination of the joint venture between the parties and no unconscionable conduct on the part of the legal owner.[94] Other courts, however, have been willing to impose a constructive trust on the basis that, given the contributions of the claimant, it *would have been* unconscionable for the defendant to deny her an interest *if* their relationship were to break down.[95]

Given the uncertainty in the Australian case law, it is necessary to try to find a way through this complex issue. One begins with the proposition that, as has

---

[90] Serious problems also arise in the situation where the legally-owning partner dies suddenly. Would it be unconscionable for his executors to refuse his partner's demand for a share? It is not easy to decide when a death will bring a "premature" end to a relationship, given that, in a sense, almost all deaths will be seen as premature. Cf. n 167 *infra*.

[91] Cf. *Novick v Miller* (1989) 58 DLR (4th) 185 (Sask CA).

[92] (1992) 29 NSWLR 188, 222. See n 85 *supra*.

[93] Two of the leading Australian cases, *Re Osborn* (1989) 25 FCR 547 and *Re Popescu* (1995) 55 FCR 583, show a marked hostility towards the application of the unconscionability doctrine in the bankruptcy context. See e.g. *Re Popescu supra*, 590 per Einfeld J. Contrast *Re Sabri* (1996) 21 Fam LR 213. See generally Housego "Bankruptcy and Family Law: Is There An Equitable Solution?" (1991) 5 *Australian Journal of Family Law* 57; Parkinson "Property Rights and Third Party Creditors—the Scope and Limitations of Equitable Doctrines" (1997) 11 *Australian Bar Review* 100.

[94] *Re Osborn* (1989) 25 FCR 547, 553–554 per Pincus J; *Re Popescu* (1995) 55 FCR 583, 589–590 per Einfeld J; *National Australian Bank Ltd v Maher* [1995] 1 VR 318, 325–326 per Fullagar J; 335–336 per Ormiston J.

[95] See *Kidner v Secretary, Department of Social Security* (1993) 31 Admin Law Decisions 63, 75–76 per Drummond J, followed in *Re Sabri* (1996) 21 Fam LR 213, 228–230 per Chisholm J. Cf. *Bryson v Bryant* (1992) 29 NSWLR 188, 226B-D, 228B per Samuels A-JA.

been argued above,[96] a breakdown in the parties' personal relationship is not an essential prerequisite for the application of the unconscionability doctrine. It is sufficient if the claimant requests her rightful share. Even in the bankruptcy situation, there will have been such a request, occurring at the latest when the claimant makes a legal claim to a share. Therefore, in theory, there is no reason why a constructive trust could not arise in a bankruptcy situation. However, and this is the important point for practical purposes, it is submitted that the trust cannot come into existence prior to the claimant's request for a transfer of her share.

Consider a case where the joint enterprise of the parties is proceeding smoothly. They are content to leave the legal ownership of the family's property in the sole name of the male partner. It then happens that the defendant runs into financial problems. The claimant requests him to hand over her share. Assume that, given the claimant's prior contributions to the joint enterprise, it would be unconscionable for the defendant to refuse to make the transfer. From that time onwards, equity sees the claimant as entitled to her rightful share of the family property and, even if the defendant refuses to make the transfer,[97] equity will "see as done that which ought to be done" and treat her as equitable owner.[98] However, *before* the claimant has made her request, how can she be seen as equitable owner of the property? At this stage, for the purposes of their joint venture, the parties have seen fit to leave the property in the defendant's name. They may gain certain advantages from doing so. The defendant's being the legal and beneficial owner may facilitate his carrying out business transactions for the benefit of the family enterprise, enabling him (without deceiving his creditors) to give security over the property. Moreover, if the *claimant* were to become bankrupt at this point, *her* creditors would be unable to make any claim over the assets in her partner's name.[99] How can equity say at this stage that, despite the advantages which the couple may be gaining from their arrangement, the defendant "ought" to transfer the property to his partner? To do so would be to suggest that there was something objectionable per *se* about the

---

[96] See n 88 *supra* and accompanying text.

[97] Note the interesting situation which arose in *Re Osborn* (1989) 25 FCR 547 where, shortly before his bankruptcy, a husband transferred a share in the matrimonial home to his wife (who had made very substantial contributions to the relationship). This transfer was successfully challenged by the creditors of the husband on the basis of the applicable bankruptcy legislation. Pincus J denied the wife's claim to be entitled in any event under a constructive trust on the basis that (*ibid*, 554) the husband had never acted unconscionably because the transfer to her had been "in accordance with the dictates of his conscience and established equitable principle". This seems a curious approach since it implies that the claimant, having demanded her share, would be in a better position if the defendant dishonestly refused her request than if he honestly complied with it. The position taken in the text is that the claimant should be in the same situation in both cases i.e. her interest should date from the time of her request for a share and not from the time of her contributions to the joint venture.

[98] Subject to the discretion of the court to postpone the operation of the constructive trust until the date of the court hearing (or the publication of the court's reasons). See the *dicta* of Deane J in *Muschinski* (1985) 160 CLR 583, 615, discussed in the text following n 138 *infra*.

[99] Cf. *Malone v McQuaid*, 28 May 1998 (LEXIS, Irish High Court).

manner in which the parties have chosen (or been content) to hold their property during the course of their joint venture.

The argument in the previous paragraph, if accepted, leads to the conclusion that, in principle, the earliest the Australian-style constructive trust can take effect is the time of the termination of the joint venture (which includes the claimant requesting her share) and *not* the time at which the contributions of the claimant were made.[100] This means that in a dispute involving third party creditors, the Australian doctrine would be less favourable for a claimant than other doctrines (e.g. the common intention doctrine which is invariably retrospective in its operation).[101] Of course, on one view, this constitutes an advantage of the doctrine since it is able to do justice between the cohabitees without creating prejudice to third party creditors.

C. Should a Remedy be Denied to a Claimant Who is Responsible for the Failure of the Relationship?

It will be recalled that in *Muschinski*[102] Deane J regarded the unconscionability doctrine as operating "where the substratum of a joint relationship or endeavour is removed *without attributable blame*".[103] This rule, an inconvenient legacy of the analogy with partnerships and joint ventures, has proven remarkably difficult to apply and, in practice, has almost universally been ignored by the Australian courts.[104]

As Parkinson explains, the question of blame "does not transfer easily to the context of de facto relationships where the reasons for the breakdown of relationships are varied and complex".[105] Moreover, there has been a trend in

---

[100] This conclusion does not depend on the vexed question of whether one regards the "unconscionability" constructive trust as being "institutional" or "remedial" (cf. Chapter 7 *supra*, text following n 4). Even an "institutional" constructive trust cannot come into existence until its "defining conditions occur" (*Re Sabri* (1996) 21 Fam LR 213, 224). If its theoretical basis is taken seriously, the defining conditions for the unconscionability constructive trust are not satisfied simply by the making of contributions to a joint venture; it is also necessary that there be a (premature) termination of that joint venture such that it would be unconscionable for the defendant to retain the benefit of the contributions. Until there is a termination of the joint venture (which, it has been suggested, includes the claimant's demanding her share), there is no basis for the imposition of a constructive trust. Thus, it may not make much difference in a bankruptcy situation if, following Deane J's *dictum* in *Muschinski* (see n 98 *supra*), the court chooses to postpone the operation of the constructive trust until the date of the trial. It might well happen that, even without any postponement, the constructive trust would come into operation too late to gain priority over the defendant's creditors.

[101] See Chapter 5 *supra*, n 318.

[102] (1985) 160 CLR 583.

[103] *Ibid*, 620 (emphasis supplied).

[104] It is particularly difficult to make sense of this requirement because, as was argued in n 88 *supra*, the breakdown of the parties' personal relationship is not a necessary element in a successful claim. Presumably, one must interpret the rule as denying a remedy in cases where the relationship has, in fact, collapsed and where the claimant was to blame for this.

[105] "Doing Equity Between De Facto Spouses: From Calverley v Green to Baumgartner" (1988) 11 *Adelaide Law Review* 370, 392.

modern family law legislation to move away from an exclusively fault-centred approach to such issues as the grounds for divorce and the criteria for the reallocation of property between the spouses upon the breakdown of their relationship.[106] Thus, any attempt to allocate "blame" for the breakdown of a relationship meets with both practical and policy difficulties.

In only a handful of the Australian cases is there a passing reference to the allocation of blame for the termination of the relationship[107] and in no case is any practical result made to turn on the issue. It appears that the case law is bearing out Parkinson's prediction that "the notion of blame will quietly disappear as a meaningful requirement".[108]

The refusal of the Australian courts to enter into the issue of blame removes one practical obstacle to the smooth functioning of their unconscionability doctrine. However, their pragmatic approach involves further distancing the unconscionability doctrine from the principle applied in the context of partnerships and joint ventures. It is also arguable that injustice may result if a remedy is available irrespective of fault. As Mahoney JA pointed out (in a somewhat different context) in the Court of Appeal of New South Wales in *Baumgartner*,[109] it is possible to question the "justice or social expediency" of the assumption that the court is free to "disregard the fact that, as it may be, the termination of the relationship has been brought about by one party against the will of the other and in circumstances which, according to social or moral attitudes, are wrong".[110] It may increase the bitterness of a "wronged" partner to endure the imposition of a constructive trust upon his assets on the grounds that it is unconscionable for *him* to deny his partner a share.

D. The Role of Intention

In this section, it is proposed to examine the role of intention within the Australian theoretical structure. It will be recalled that, in *Muschinski*,[111] Deane J felt that the court would impose a constructive trust upon the collapse of a joint relationship where property contributed by one party "would otherwise be

---

[106] *Ibid*, 392–393. Cf. *Evans v Marmont* (1997) 42 NSWLR 70, 79 per Gleeson CJ and McLelland CJ in Equity.

[107] See *Re Osborn* (1989) 25 FCR 547, 554; *Bennett v Tairua* (1992) 15 Fam LR 317, 321–322 per Rowland J; *Harmer v Pearson* (1993) 16 Fam LR 596, 600–601 per Pincus JA. Cf. *Carson v Wood* (1994) 34 NSWLR 9, 27–28 per Sheller JA. The most detailed discussion appears at first instance in *Schmutz v Aras*, 8 August 1996 (LEXIS, NSW Sup Ct) p 50 where Bryson J concluded that "no great severity is . . . appropriate in applying the concept of attributable blame". (The point was not discussed on appeal: *Aras v Schmutz*, 9 December 1997, unreported (NSW CA)).

[108] See n 105 *supra*, 393. Note that fault is by no means an invariable bar to restitution. See e.g. Birks *An Introduction to the Law of Restitution*, revised edn (Oxford: Clarendon Press, 1989) pp 234–242.

[109] (1985) 2 NSWLR 406.

[110] *Ibid*, 426.

[111] (1985) 160 CLR 583.

enjoyed by the other party in circumstances in which it was not specifically intended or specially provided that that other party should so enjoy it".[112] The implication is that no remedy should be available where it was intended by the parties that the disputed property should remain with the legal owner, even after the termination of the relationship. In practice, it is most likely that it will be the legal owner who has the "intention" to retain the property. However, if, from the start, the other party was aware of this intention,[113] it is submitted that there should be no scope for a constructive trust over that property.[114]

The Australian courts have, however, been reluctant to give any weight to the intentions of the legal owner. One clear example of this attitude is provided by *Hibberson* v *George*.[115] The family home in *Hibberson* had been "purchased by Mr George with his own money and he intended that it should be his alone".[116] As the trial judge had held, the claimant "knew or must have known this at all times".[117] However, this finding of fact in no way disconcerted the majority judges.[118] McHugh JA (with the concurrence of Hope JA) cheerfully noted the trial judge's assertion that the defendant was not "the sort of person who would pay the whole deposit and commit himself under a mortgage to pay the balance of the purchase price with the intention that the [claimant] should have equal rights of ownership".[119] He dismissed this finding with the comment that "the issue is not what the respondent's intention was but whether a constructive trust should be imposed".[120] McHugh JA proceeded to declare that the claimant was entitled to 40 per cent of the beneficial interest in the house.

An even more surprising case is *Kais* v *Turvey*.[121] The claimant in *Kais* had taken on himself to discharge the outstanding mortgage debt on the defendant's home. He had ignored the advice of friends and the defendant's father, as well as the defendant's frequent reminders that he would gain no beneficial interest from his gift. He had described the gift as "an early birthday present" for the defendant and, according to the trial judge, had enjoyed boasting to his friends about his generosity.[122] Nonetheless, the Supreme Court of Western Australia unanimously upheld his claim.[123]

---

[112]   (1985) 160 CLR 620.

[113]   It might also be sufficient if the claimant had constructive notice of her partner's intention. In such circumstances, the defendant could argue that he should not be bound by the claimant's unreasonable misunderstanding of the nature of their joint venture.

[114]   However, difficult problems arise if, during the course of the relationship and after the claimant has prejudiced herself, the legal owner belatedly makes clear his intentions. See the discussion of this issue in the Canadian context, Chapter 7 *supra*, n 156.

[115]   (1989) 12 Fam LR 725.

[116]   *Ibid*, 733 per Mahoney JA (dissenting).

[117]   *Ibid*.

[118]   Contrast the emphasis on the question of intention in Mahoney JA's dissenting judgment in *Hibberson*. See also *Tory* v *Jones*, 30 July 1990 (LEXIS, NSW Sup Ct) p 26.

[119]   (1989) 12 Fam LR 725, 743.

[120]   *Ibid*.

[121]   (1994) 17 Fam LR 498.

[122]   He had also been influenced by the fact that the defendant had agreed to become engaged to him (in the hope that he would "shut up about getting married"). However, it would appear

In a revealing passage, Malcolm CJ explained the situation as follows:

"In the present case the respondent made it clear at all times that she regarded the home unit as hers. It is clear that there was no common intention that the appellant by making the gifts he did should acquire any legal or equitable interest in the home unit. He raised the matter from time to time, but the response was always in the negative. In my opinion, this was no obstacle to the existence of a constructive trust".[124]

Malcolm CJ proceeded to rely on Deane J's observation in *Muschinski*[125] that the constructive trust was a remedial institution imposed "regardless of actual or presumed agreement or intention".[126] This statement of the familiar proposition that the constructive trust does not turn on intention was used by Malcolm CJ to justify the conclusion that the legal owner's intentions are simply irrelevant in determining whether such a trust should be imposed. In fact, as has been argued above, it is quite possible that the intention of the legal owner, if known by the claimant, could be of decisive importance in determining whether it would be unconscionable for the legal owner to retain the disputed property.[127]

Interestingly, while ignoring intention in making a finding of unconscionability, the Court in *Kais* appears to have taken the issue into account in formulating the appropriate remedy for the claimant. Instead of a beneficial interest in the property, the claimant had to be content with an equitable charge to secure the return of the money he had put towards the property. Thus, by departing from the orthodox remedy of the constructive trust, the Court in *Kais* managed to avoid the full consequences of ignoring the clearly expressed intention of the legal owner.[128]

that, of themselves, promises to marry cannot become the ground for the grant of equitable relief. Note the comment of Handley JA in *Public Trustee* v *Kukula* (1990) 14 Fam LR 97, 101 that "a constructive trust cannot arise, Phoenix-like, from the ashes of the common law cause of action for breach of promise" (which was abolished in Australia by s 111A of the Marriage Act 1961 (Cth)). Cf. *Stowe and Devereaux Holdings Pty Ltd* v *Stowe* (1995) 19 Fam LR 409, 417–418.

[123] Contrast the *dictum* of Deane J in *Commonwealth of Australia* v *Verwayen* (1990) 170 CLR 394, 440 to the effect that equitable estoppel, also founded on the notion of "unconscionability", exists to protect people from being victimised by others rather than from the consequences of their own folly. See Haines "Unconscionability in Constructive Trusts and Remedies Therefor" (1991) 5 *Australian Journal of Family Law* 206, 216.

[124] (1994) 17 Fam LR 498, 501.
[125] (1985) 160 CLR 583.
[126] *Ibid*, 614.
[127] It seems that another source of confusion evident in the passage quoted from Malcolm CJ in *Kais* (see text to n 124 *supra*) was his concern to reject the English requirement of a subjective common intention (see Chapter 5 *supra*). Malcolm CJ slipped from the proposition that intention was no longer an essential prerequisite of a remedy to the assumption that it was a complete irrelevance.
[128] See also *Booth* v *Beresford* (1993) 17 Fam LR 147 where a constructive trust was imposed upon a defendant who had been extremely wary about protecting his ownership of the family home. However, as in *Kais*, the "trust" was limited to the amount of the claimant's financial contribution. Note also the very similar case of *Renton* v *Youngman* (1995) 19 Fam LR 450. See further text to nn 146–151 *infra*, discussing the trend towards remedial flexibility in the Australian cases. A final example of a willingness to allow the intentions of the parties to impact upon the remedy for unconscionability is provided by the judgment of Sheller JA in *Bryson* v *Bryant* (1992) 29 NSWLR 188. See n 85 *supra*.

One may conclude that the Australian courts have, in determining whether certain conduct was unconscionable, paid insufficient attention to the intention of the parties, in particular that of the legal owner. In some cases the courts have compensated for this (without express explanation) by employing a flexible remedial strategy. However, this is not a complete solution. It would be preferable if the issue were expressly considered by the courts, both at the stage of making a judgement that the defendant has behaved unconscionably and then in choosing a remedy.

E. Remedies Available under the Doctrine

1. *The constructive trust*

There has been an assumption in most of the Australian cases that the remedy for unconscionability will inevitably be a constructive trust. Thus, even on the unusual facts of *Muschinski*, the majority of the High Court held that a constructive trust was the appropriate medium to restore to the parties their respective contributions to the joint venture.[129] Of more significance for the future course of the case law was the approach of the High Court of Australia in *Baumgartner*.[130] It will be recalled that the couple in *Baumgartner* had pooled their earnings to pay all their family expenses, including mortgage repayments. In their joint judgment, Mason CJ, Wilson and Deane JJ indicated a preference for equal ownership of the disputed property. They commented as follows:

> "Equity favours equality and, in circumstances where the parties have lived together for years and have pooled their resources and their efforts to create a joint home, there is much to be said for the view that they should share the beneficial ownership equally as tenants in common, subject to adjustment to avoid any injustice which would result if account were not taken of the disparity between the worth of their individual contributions either financially or in kind".[131]

On the facts, however, the court decided that it was necessary to depart from the presumption in favour of equality. Although the case was "close to the borderline", they felt that it was not possible to treat the contributions of the parties as approximately equal in value. The male partner had contributed 55 per cent of the family budget as against 45 per cent contributed by the claimant. Since there was no suggestion that this substantial disparity was off-

---

[129] (1985) 160 CLR 583, 624 per Deane J.

[130] (1987) 164 CLR 137.

[131] *Ibid*, 149–150. Toohey J, despite his reliance on the doctrine of unjust enrichment, appeared to be at least as enthusiastic an advocate of equal sharing (see *ibid*, 154). Note also the remarks of Gaudron J *ibid*, 157.

set by the claimant's contributions in other areas,[132] the judges decided to impose the trust in the proportions of 55 per cent to the male and 45 per cent to the female.[133]

Later cases have faithfully recognised the existence of a presumption in favour of equality,[134] although almost all the cases have found reason to depart from that presumption.[135] It is submitted that the approach of the High Court in *Baumgartner* is inconsistent with the aim of ensuring the return of contributions upon the breakdown of a relationship. Rather than operating a presumption of equality which will be decisive only where the contributions happen to be equal, it would be far more sensible to begin with the rule that the remedy will depend on an approximate assessment of the contribution of the claimant.[136]

While (despite the references to a presumption of equality) the Australian courts have generally focused on the contributions of a claimant, it is important to realise that, like the Canadian courts, they have (effectively) adopted a "value surviving" approach to determining what remedy should flow from those contributions.[137] In other words, they have looked to the wealth "surviving" in the hands of the defendant and have given a remedy to the claimant which reflects her contribution to the accumulation of that wealth. As in Canada, this approach has been facilitated by the extensive use of the constructive trust remedy. Thus, despite the lip-service given to the restitutionary idea of "returning" her contributions to a claimant, the Australian doctrine has, in practice, simply shared out the wealth of the relationship. Interestingly, the Australian courts

---

[132] It will be recalled that the claimant had already been given credit for the amount she would have earned during her absence from work around the time of the birth of their child.

[133] The judges also ordered that various other adjustments be made in the interests of justice. Most significantly, they dealt with the male partner's contribution to the purchase of almost $13,000, representing the proceeds of sale of his previous property. However, this contribution did not earn the male partner a proportionate share in the increase in value of the new property. Instead, the judges ordered that he should simply be repaid the amount in question. None of the judges in the High Court defended this approach in logical terms and it is submitted that it is indefensible. The male partner had already owned a property which was likely to appreciate in value; his contribution of this equity to the acquisition of a new property was treated merely as a loan to be refunded without interest. Cf. the similar approach taken by the majority in *Hibberson v George* (1989) 12 Fam LR 725 (NSW CA).

[134] See *Hibberson v George* (1989) 12 Fam LR 725, 743 per McHugh JA; *Miller v Sutherland* (1990) 14 Fam LR 416, 422 per Cohen J; *Bennett v Tairua* (1992) 15 Fam LR 317, 323 per Rowland J; 327 per Nicholson J; *Bryson v Bryant* (1992) 29 NSWLR 188, 209 per Kirby P.

[135] See *Hibberson v George* (1989) 12 Fam LR 725 (40 per cent share in family home); *Miller v Sutherland* (1990) 14 Fam LR 416 (25 per cent share in family home); *Bennett v Tairua* (1992) 15 Fam LR 317 (30 per cent share in family home and lands). See also *Lipman v Lipman* (1989) 13 Fam LR 1 (one-half share awarded in two residential properties but not in other assets).

[136] Cf. the rejection of the presumption of equality by the New Zealand courts (see, for example, *Lankow v Rose* [1995] 1 NZLR 277, 295 per Tipping J). Of course, there may be practical sense in the High Court's view in *Baumgartner* (1987) 164 CLR 137, 150 that the courts should not waste time in pursuing complex factual issues which are unlikely greatly to affect the respective shares of the parties. This, however, is really an argument for a broad-brush approach to assessing the extent of the contributions, rather than a reason for favouring equality as a starting point.

[137] Cf. Chapter 7 *supra*, Part IV(H).

have devoted even less analysis to this question than their Canadian counterparts, their only effort in this direction being the occasional mention of the Canadian notion of a "causal link" between the claimant's contribution and the disputed property.[138]

A final issue concerning the constructive trust remedy relates to the time at which it should come into effect.[139] Deane J made the interesting suggestion in *Muschinski*[140] that a constructive trust might be framed so as to operate only "from the date of judgment or formal court order or from some other specified date".[141] He ultimately held that, "[l]est the legitimate claims of third parties be adversely affected, the constructive trust should be imposed only from the date of publication of reasons for judgment of this Court".[142]

Surprisingly, there has been little analysis of the issue in the subsequent case law.[143] None of the judgments imposing constructive trusts has stated that the trust should operate on a prospective basis only.[144] One is left to conclude that, where there is no evidence of the existence of third party claims, the Australian courts have simply allowed constructive trusts their normal retrospective application.[145] It remains to be seen whether a further judicial initiative will revive interest in Deane J's suggestion in the future.

---

[138] This has occurred in the particular context of claims based on contributions which did not assist in the acquisition or improvement of the disputed property. See text to nn 67–77 *supra*.

[139] See generally Stone "The Reification of Legal Concepts: *Muschinski v Dodds*" (1986) 9 *University of New South Wales Law Journal* 63; O'Connor "Happy Partners or Strange Bedfellows: The Blending of Remedial and Institutional Features in the Evolving Constructive Trust" (1996) 20 *Melbourne University Law Review* 735, 751–761. Cf. Birks "Proprietary Rights as Remedies", ch. 16 in Birks (ed) *Frontiers of Liability* (Oxford: Oxford University Press, 1994) Vol 2 p 214.

[140] (1985) 160 CLR 583.

[141] *Ibid*, 615. The remedial flexibility proposed by Deane J contrasts sharply with the conventional view that a trust carries with it "a fixed bundle of incidents" (see O'Connor, n 139 *supra*, 738). Under the conventional view, if a court imposes a trust, certain "doctrinally pre-determined" consequences follow, one of which is the retrospective operation of the trust. Deane J wished to do some limited unpacking, treating the retrospectivity question as a separate one which could be dealt with on the facts of each case. See generally Austin "The Melting Down of the Remedial Trust" (1988) 11 *University of New South Wales Law Journal* 66. One attractive feature of Deane J's approach is that the burden of imposing a trust may be lightened; with the risk of prejudice to creditors reduced, one might be able to grant a remedy in a wider range of circumstances. Cf. the argument of Hayton "Equitable Rights of Cohabitees" [1990] Conv 370, 380–385.

[142] *Ibid*, 623.

[143] See, however, the consideration of the point in *Re Osborn* (1989) 25 FCR 547 where, in the context of a bankruptcy, Pincus J refused to award any constructive trust, whether prospective or retrospective in nature. See also the detailed discussion in *Re Sabri* (1996) 21 Fam LR 213.

[144] The language normally used is that the court "declares" that the defendant "holds" the property on constructive trust in certain proportions. See e.g. *Baumgartner* (1987) 164 CLR 137, 150; *Lipman v Lipman* (1989) 13 Fam LR 1, 25; *Hibberson v George* (1989) 12 Fam LR 725, 744; *Atkinson v Burt* (1989) 12 Fam LR 800, 805. Cf. the apparent assumption that the remedy would be retrospective in nature in *Bryson v Bryant* (1992) 29 NSWLR 188, 210 per Kirby P; 222 per Sheller JA.

[145] See also *Re Sabri* (1996) 21 Fam LR 213 where a constructive trust was imposed retrospectively so as to defeat the rights of third parties. Chisholm J relied *inter alia* on *Re Jonton Pty Ltd* [1992] 2 Qd R 105, where Mackenzie J held that a constructive trust took priority over the interest of a mortgagee. However, the constructive trust in *Jonton* owed its existence to a common intention between the parties and, therefore, it seems that its retrospective effect was simply in keeping with the orthodox common intention trust analysis. See also n 100 *supra* and accompanying text.

2. *Other remedies*

Despite the general preference of the Australian courts for a constructive trust remedy, one can detect, in some of the cases following *Baumgartner*, a dissociation between liability and remedy.[146] In other words, a finding of liability based on unconscionability is no longer automatically followed by a declaration of a constructive trust.[147] Rather, the courts have felt free to resort to various other remedies. This trend has yet to receive explicit consideration in the judgments but could have important implications for the future development of the doctrine.

The flexible approach to the choice of remedy has been seen mostly in cases falling outside the *Baumgartner* pattern of a pooling of earnings to meet household expenses. In particular, the constructive trust has often been eschewed in cases involving contributions to improvements.[148] The normal approach has been to impose a charge to secure the return of the amount expended on the improvements.[149]

It is possible that a wider approach to remedies could influence the substantive development of the unconscionability doctrine. It will be recalled that there are conflicting authorities on the subject of contributions which cannot be related to the acquisition or improvement of property.[150] It seems likely that the lack of a connection with particular property would no longer be fatal if the Australian courts, following their Canadian counterparts,[151] were willing to grant a purely monetary remedy.

---

[146] See O'Connor, n 139 *supra*, 745–750.

[147] Cf. *Bathurst City Council v PWC Properties Pty Ltd* (1998) 72 ALJR 1470, 1479 (High Ct). For discussion of a parallel development in the Canadian unjust enrichment doctrine, see Chapter 7 *supra*, text to nn 64–67 (constructive trust no longer seen as central to the law of restitution).

[148] See also the unusual facts of *Kais v Turvey* (1994) 17 Fam LR 498 (discussed in the text to and following n 121 *supra*).

[149] See *Hibberson v George* (1989) 12 Fam LR 725 (contributions to improvements treated separately from indirect contributions to mortgage; charge imposed on property to enforce refunding of cost of improvements); *Booth v Beresford* (1993) 17 Fam LR 147, 155 (property held on trust "to the extent of $7500"; question of imposition of a charge left open); *Kais v Turvey* (1994) 17 Fam LR 498 (charge imposed; see, however, (1994) 11 WAR 357, 357: leave to appeal denied by High Court of Australia upon claimant's undertaking not to enforce aspect of judgment relating to improvements). Note also the complex remedy ordered by Needham J in *Nichols v Nichols*, 12 December 1986 (LEXIS, NSW Sup Ct). Even in cases involving a pooling of earnings, the Australian courts do not invariably employ the traditional remedy of a proportionate share in the equitable ownership. See *Renton v Youngman* (1995) 19 Fam LR 450 (constructive trust to the extent of $5,000) and *Bryson v Bryant* (1992) 29 NSWLR 188 where Sheller JA (*ibid*, 222) commented that, had the facts been slightly different, it might have been necessary to impose a trust "at least to the extent of a beneficial interest in the property for [the claimant's] life". Note also that in *Miller v Sutherland* (1990) 14 Fam LR 416, the value of the claimant's one-quarter interest was fixed at a particular sum (based on the current value of the house), so that she would not benefit from any increase in the value of the property in the period before it was sold.

[150] See text to nn 67–77 *supra*.

[151] See text to n 73 *supra*.

3. *Conclusions on the question of remedies*

The foregoing discussion shows that the Australian courts have devoted comparatively little analysis to the question of the remedies for unconscionability. The case law has failed to build upon Deane J's suggestion in *Muschinski* that an innovative approach be adopted to the time of operation of the constructive trust. However, the later cases show a trend towards the development of a different type of flexibility, which would look beyond the constructive trust as the sole remedial option. Within the terms of the Australian doctrine, this development would be a logical one and might help to resolve some other points of uncertainty within the doctrine.[152] Unfortunately, however, because of the lack of analysis in the cases, the position remains somewhat unclear. What is probably necessary now is a fresh decision of the High Court of Australia to consolidate the progress which has been made and to point the way to future development.

III. THE THEORETICAL BASIS OF THE UNCONSCIONABILITY DOCTRINE

The previous Part was dedicated to a detailed analysis of the parameters of the Australian unconscionability doctrine. Now that this work has been accomplished, this Part will look more closely at the theoretical basis for the doctrine. Once the theoretical viability of the doctrine has been tested, it will be possible to form a conclusion on the question of whether it can provide useful guidance for the courts of other jurisdictions.

It is clear from Deane J's statement of principle in *Muschinski*[153] that the unconscionability doctrine is founded on an analogy with the rules applicable upon the premature termination of a formal partnership or a commercial joint venture. The first task of this Part will be to consider the validity of the analogy drawn by Deane J in *Muschinski*. It will be suggested that the material relied upon by Deane J does not support the doctrine which he developed. The argument will then be made that, in *Baumgartner* and subsequent cases, the joint venture analogy has been further stretched and its credibility further strained. These considerations will support this chapter's ultimate conclusion that the Australian doctrine lacks a convincing theoretical basis and, therefore, cannot provide useful guidance for the courts in other jurisdictions.

A. The Basis for the Analogy with a Joint Venture

In *Muschinski*,[154] Deane J conceded that the parties were not, strictly speaking, partners and that the arrangement between them "while consensual, was a non-

---

[152] Cf. text to n 151 *supra*.
[153] (1985) 160 CLR 583, 620.
[154] (1985) 160 CLR 583.

contractual one".[155] Nonetheless, he felt that the rules applicable upon the failure of a partnership or contractual joint venture might "be relevant in the search for some more general or analogous principle applicable in the circumstances of the collapse of the consensual commercial venture and personal relationship in the present case".[156] Deane J proceeded to consider the rules of equity and the common law applicable "where money or other property is paid or applied on the basis of some consensual joint relationship or endeavour which fails without attributable blame".[157] His ultimate conclusion was that, underlying the specific rules developed by the courts over the years, there was a "more general principle of equity".[158] It will be recalled[159] that this principle would operate "where the substratum of a joint relationship or endeavour is removed without attributable blame" and would prevent one party retaining property transferred "on the basis and for the purposes of" the joint relationship "to the extent that it would be unconscionable for him to do so".[160]

To justify his identification of this new principle, Deane J adverted to three different sets of legal rules. These were the rules governing the premature dissolution of partnerships, those governing the premature collapse of a commercial joint venture and finally[161] those related to the frustration of contracts. It is now necessary to consider these rules in turn.

1. *The premature collapse of a partnership*

The first set of legal rules invoked by Deane J were those governing the premature dissolution of partnerships. Deane J pointed out that "the prima facie rule of equity on premature dissolution is . . . that the parties are, after the discharge of partnership debts, entitled to be repaid their respective capital contributions".[162] This point is, it is submitted, largely blunted by the fact that, as Deane J conceded, the same rules would apply "in the case of an ordinary dissolution".[163] In other words, the approach of equity to a premature dissolution is dependent on the nature of a legal partnership rather than on the underlying equitable principle for which Deane J was arguing. In any case, Deane J regarded as "[m]ore important for present purposes" the fact that "if a premium has been paid by a fixed term partner who is not to be held responsible for the premature dissolution, an equity court will order a refund or partial refund of

---

[155] *Ibid*, 618.

[156] *Ibid*.

[157] *Ibid*. Deane J explained (*ibid*) that the rules he was considering had no application if the parties themselves had expressly or impliedly provided for the premature termination of the enterprise.

[158] *Ibid*, 619.

[159] See text to n 28 *supra* for a full quotation of the relevant passage from Deane J's judgment.

[160] (1985) 160 CLR 583, 620.

[161] In fact, Deane J mentioned this last set of rules first but, for convenience, the discussion which follows will be presented as if he had referred to them last.

[162] (1985) 160 CLR 583, 619.

[163] *Ibid*.

the premium to the extent that its retention by the other partner would be unconscionable: cf *Atwood* v *Maude*[164]".[165]

The case of *Atwood* v *Maude*,[166] upon which Deane J relied heavily in *Muschinski*, concerned a solicitor, Maude, who had agreed to go into a seven-year fixed-term partnership with Atwood. To compensate him for the inexperience of his new partner, Maude extracted a premium of £800. Differences arose between the partners and the partnership came to an end after only two years. The English Court of Appeal held that Atwood was entitled to the repayment of a proportionate amount of his premium.[167]

It is submitted that there is no justification in Deane J's implication that the principles applying to the property affairs of legal partners are somehow of general application. The crucial point is that the relationship between partners is fiduciary in nature.[168] Although the term "fiduciary" is a vexed one, bearing different meanings in different contexts, in the partnership context it usefully signifies the fact that the decision of the parties to enter into a formal partnership has wide-ranging implications for the management of their property.[169] Outside the special relationship of partnership, however, the applicable legal principles are clearly different.

This is demonstrated by the contrast between *Atwood* and the case of *Whincup* v *Hughes*,[170] decided only three years later. In *Whincup*, a premium of £25 had been paid on behalf of a boy who was to be apprenticed to a watchmaker for a period of six years. The watchmaker died after only one year. Recovery of the money was denied on the basis that there had not been a total failure of consideration. The boy had got the benefit of one year of his apprenticeship and, on the grounds of this partial performance of the contract, was denied restitution. Naturally, it is legitimate to question the inflexible "total failure of consideration" rule applied in *Whincup* (and numerous other cases).[171] The point, however, is that outside the sheltered context of a formal partnership, one is in the domain of the general law.[172] Probably the boy in *Whincup*

---

[164] (1868) LR 3 Ch App 369.

[165] (1985) 160 CLR 583, 619.

[166] (1868) LR 3 Ch App 369. See also the similar case of *Lyon* v *Tweddell* (1881) 17 Ch D 529 which was also relied upon by Deane J in *Muschinski* (1985) 160 CLR 583, 620.

[167] The effect of this case was given legislative form in the English Partnership Act 1890. See the discussion in Banks *Lindley and Banks on Partnership*, 17th edn (London: Sweet and Maxwell, 1995) p 736 n 16. Interestingly, there is no entitlement in English law to the return of a premium upon the death of either partner, this being seen as "a contingency which all persons entering into partnership know may unexpectedly put an end to it". See *ibid*, pp 737–738.

[168] See generally Finn *Fiduciary Obligations* (Sydney: Law Book Co, 1977); Shepherd *The Law of Fiduciaries* (Toronto: Carswell, 1981).

[169] Note that the court has jurisdiction to dissolve a partnership on equitable grounds (see Banks, n 167 *supra*, p 710 *et seq*), a power which clearly could not be translated into the context of a personal relationship.

[170] (1871) LR 6 CP 78.

[171] See n 183 *infra*.

[172] Note that when *Atwood* v *Maude* (1868) LR 3 Ch App 369 was cited in argument in *Whincup*, Bovill CJ interjected ((1871) LR 6 CP 78, 80) to point out that the question in *Atwood* had arisen "on a bill praying for a dissolution of partnership". One may infer that Bovill CJ regarded *Atwood* as

should, in a rational legal system, have been able to recover on the ground of "partial failure of consideration"; however, the argument cannot be strengthened by a vague analogy with the special rules governing partnerships.[173]

2. *Collapse of a commercial joint venture*

The second set of legal rules invoked by Deane J concerned equity's treatment of the premature collapse of "a contractual joint venture for the pursuit of some commercial advantage".[174] Deane J explained the *prima facie* rule of equity applicable to this situation in the following terms:

> "[T]o the extent that the joint funds allow, the joint venturers are entitled to the proportionate repayment of their capital contributions to the abortive joint venture. This is so notwithstanding that it was the common understanding or agreement that the funds advanced were to be applied for the purposes of the joint venture and that the return from them would take the form, not of a repayment of capital contributed but of a share in the proceeds of the joint venture when it was carried to fruition: cf, eg, *Allen* v *Kent*[175]; *Ewen* v *Gerofsky*[176]; *Legum Furniture Corporation* v *Levine*[177]; and cf, generally, "Joint Ventures", *Corpus Juris Secundum*, vol 48A, pp 452–453, 463".[178]

A closer look at the American authorities invoked by Deane J demonstrates that joint ventures in American law are treated as constituting simply a less formal kind of legal partnership.[179] Thus, nothing new is added to Deane J's argument by his noticing that the American courts have extended some of the rules of partnership to a similar business arrangement.[180] It is also worth mentioning

turning on the particular rules governing partnerships. Note also that another case relied upon by Deane J in *Muschinski* (1985) 160 CLR 583, 620, *Hirst* v *Tolson* (1850) 2 Mac & G 134, was severely criticised by a unanimous Court of Common Pleas in *Whincup supra*. Bovill CJ ((1871) LR 6 CP 78, 83) described *Hirst* as "based on a misapprehension of the law" and (*ibid*) as not being "a satisfactory authority or one by which we are bound". Similarly, Willes J regarded its authority (*ibid*, 84) as "very doubtful". Note Pearson J's acceptance in *Ferns* v *Carr* (1885) 28 Ch D 409 of counsel's argument (*ibid*, 410) that *Hirst* had been "in effect overruled by *Whincup*".

[173] As Brennan J noted, (1985) 160 CLR 583, 609, the couple in *Muschinski*, having received legal advice, had deliberately decided not to form a legal partnership. Brennan J concluded simply (*ibid*) that "no analogy can be drawn between a partnership and the present case".

[174] *Ibid*, 619.

[175] (1957) 136 A (2d) 540, 541.

[176] (1976) 382 NYS (2d) 651, 653.

[177] (1977) 232 SE (2d) 782, 785–786.

[178] (1985) 160 CLR 583, 619.

[179] As the matter is put in one of the authorities cited by Deane J, *Corpus Juris Secundum* Vol 48A (1981) p 399: "The relation of the parties to a joint venture is so similar to that in a partnership that their rights, duties, and liabilities are usually tested by partnership rules, and in numerous decisions it has been held that both joint venture and partnership are governed by the same rules of law". (Footnotes omitted).

[180] Note that, in the family context, unlike in the commercial/contractual context, the parties often do not expect "a share of the proceeds of the joint venture when it was carried into fruition" ((1985) 160 CLR 583, 619 per Deane J). Consider the case where a couple acquire a family home, take the legal ownership in the sole name of the man and eventually succeed in paying off the mortgage associated with the purchase. In this situation, where the joint venture of acquiring the property has not failed, the parties have nonetheless left the property in the sole name of one of the

that the approach in the American case law is dependent upon a willingness (not shared by the Australian courts) to regard joint venturers as being subject to fiduciary duties similar to those of formal partners.[181] There is again no justification for ignoring the absence of a fiduciary element in the relationship between the parties to a domestic relationship.[182]

3. *The frustration of contracts*

The final point to be considered is Deane J's reference to the rules applicable where a contract was frustrated without attributable fault on either side. In this situation, according to Deane J, "the present tendency of the common law is that contributions made should be refunded at least if there has been a complete failure of consideration in performance".[183] It is submitted, however, that this rule of the law of restitution offers no support for the analogy which Deane J wished to draw.

parties. The point is that the emphasis on the "premature" failure of the joint venture is potentially misleading; in the family context, even if the joint venture does not fail, the parties may still believe that their relationship renders irrelevant their separate property entitlements. If the parties have not contracted for the success of the venture, why should equity impose a contractual solution upon its failure? (The above point is complicated by the widening, in the cases following *Muschinski*, of the concept of "joint venture" (see Section B of this Part *infra*)).

[181] See *Allen v Kent* (1957) 136 A (2d) 540, 541 per Williamson CJ; *Ewen v Gerofsky* (1976) 382 NYS (2d) 651, 654 per Fein J. Contrast *United Dominions Corp Ltd v Brian Pty Ltd* (1985) 157 CLR 1, where (subsequent to *Muschinski*) the High Court of Australia rejected the American position on this issue. See also *Auag Resources Ltd v Waihi Mines Ltd* [1994] 3 NZLR 571. See generally Bean *Fiduciary Obligations and Joint Ventures* (Oxford: Clarendon Press, 1995).

[182] A somewhat different way of making the same point is to emphasise the importance of whether or not the parties have governed their relationship by contract. While, at first glance, it might seem plausible to equate a "contractual joint venture" with a "consensual non-contractual joint venture", it is necessary to look more closely at the matter. Where else in the law is it permissible simply to ignore the absence of a contract? Consider the case of an agreement (irrespective of its subject matter) where all the elements of a contract are present except for an intention to create legal relations. In this context, one cannot argue that the case is "analogous" to one where there is a valid contract. The one difference which exists, the fact that the parties chose not to bind themselves legally, is sufficient to distinguish the two cases. It is submitted that the same vital distinction exists between contractual joint ventures and non-contractual family arrangements.

[183] (1985) 160 CLR 583, 618 citing *Fibrosa Spolka Akcyjna v Fairbairn Lawson Combe Barbour Ltd* [1943] AC 32; *Denny, Mott and Dickson Ltd v James B Fraser and Co Ltd* [1944] AC 265, 275. The requirement of a "total failure of consideration" was established by the House of Lords in *Fibrosa supra* and has constituted a serious restriction on this area of the law of restitution. The effect of the requirement is that if one party has received any benefit (however inadequate) pursuant to the contract, he will be denied restitution of property he himself transferred under the contract. Moreover, it is unclear whether restitution is ever possible in this situation if the benefits transferred do not consist of money. It seems that these restrictions may be attributable to the difficulties the law has traditionally experienced in valuing non-monetary benefits. The leading restitution writers argue that, with the increased sophistication of restitution theory, these difficulties surrounding the notion of "enrichment" should not create an automatic bar on restitution. See generally Birks, n 108 *supra*, pp 238–248; Burrows *The Law of Restitution* (London: Butterworths, 1993) pp 259–261; Goff and Jones *The Law of Restitution*, 4th edn (London: Sweet and Maxwell, 1993) pp 400–416. The law now seems to be moving strongly away from the requirement of total failure of consideration. See *Goss v Chilcott* [1996] AC 788 (PC). See also Edelman "The New Doctrine of Partial Failure of Consideration" (1996–97) 15 *Australian Bar Review* 229.

The availability of restitution upon the frustration of a contract is explicable on the basis of the need to prevent unjust enrichment. As was explained in the previous chapter in the context of a discussion of the Canadian cases, it is necessary in every case to identify a specific basis to ground the assertion that a particular enrichment is "unjust".[184] In the context of frustrated contracts, the relevant unjust factor is known as "failure of consideration".[185] The parties to the contract have acted on the basis that a valid contract exists between them and, upon the frustration of the contract, the consideration for any transfer has failed. Therefore, a restitutionary remedy will be available to secure the return of property transferred pursuant to the contract.

Since, in the context presently under discussion, there is no contract between the parties, there would seem, at first glance, to be no role for the unjust factor of "failure of consideration". However, the law of restitution may require one to take a wider view of the concept of "consideration". Birks has argued[186] that, in this context, one must understand the word in its older sense of "a matter considered". In other words, "the reason for the act, the state of affairs contemplated as its basis".[187] This wider idea of "failure of basis" offers more possibilities in the present context.

It appears that an argument based on "failure of basis" could lead in two directions in the present context. The first possibility would be to suggest that, in a case like *Muschinski*, the parties have made their contributions on the basis of their "consensual but non-contractual" joint venture and that they should be entitled to the return of those contributions when that basis fails.

The difficulty with this argument is that it really restates, at a higher level of abstraction, the argument that a non-contractual joint venture should be accorded some special status which would allow it to form the "basis" of the parties' dealings in a way similar to a formal partnership or a contractual joint venture. The arguments based on the analogy with partnership and contractual joint venture have already been answered at a specific level in the previous two sections. At a more abstract level, the answer to the "failure of basis" argument[188] appears to be that, in order for a state of affairs to constitute a "basis" in the relevant sense, that state of affairs must be agreed upon by both parties as constituting the legal basis of their actions. In the absence of any framework agreed between the parties, it is not meaningful to speak of a basis which has failed or of

---

[184] See generally Chapter 7 *supra*, text following n 101.

[185] See the discussion in Birks, n 108 *supra*, p 219 *et seq*; Burrows, n 183 *supra*, p 250 *et seq*; Goff and Jones, n 183 *supra*, p 400 *et seq*.

[186] See n 108 *supra*, p 223.

[187] *Ibid*.

[188] Unfortunately, restitution law writers have taken very little interest in the untidy questions arising in the context of family property. Therefore, one is in the somewhat unsatisfactory situation of inventing the argument which afterwards one will claim to have defeated. It is possible that, as the law develops, other writers may develop a more sophisticated "failure of basis" argument, presented from a wider restitution law perspective, which might be more difficult to meet.

a gap which must be filled by the law of restitution.[189] Putting it colloquially, it would be like speaking about a hole in the absence of a surrounding Polo Mint.

The second possible argument based on a wider conception of "failure of basis" would be to look to the rules governing conditional gifts which, arguably, provide another illustration of this principle.[190] The law has long recognised that it is possible for a donor to attach a condition to his generosity. Such a condition will be enforced by the courts provided that it is neither contrary to public policy[191] nor too uncertain.[192] The argument in the family context would be that the transfer of benefits from the claimant to the defendant was conditional upon the continuation of their relationship and that, therefore, the claimant is entitled to the return of those benefits upon the premature termination of the relationship. Although the Australian courts have not been attracted to this rationalisation of the unconscionability doctrine,[193] it is still necessary to consider its viability from a theoretical point of view.

It appears that a crucial problem is presented by the simple requirement that a condition must actually have been attached to the gift by the donor.[194] People have many motives for their actions and are likely to have intended to further certain goals by the making of a gift. However, the law cannot fasten on every assumption, motive or hope underlying a gift and elevate it to the level of a binding condition. The donor must consciously decide to qualify his generosity by providing that in certain circumstances (the non-satisfaction of the condition) the donee will not enjoy the property. Moreover, it is not sufficient if the donor privately resolves that a certain condition should attach to his gift; it is necessary that he communicate this condition to the donee.[195] Unless the donor has

---

[189] Note, however, the wider view of failure of consideration canvassed by Lord Browne-Wilkinson in *Woolwich Equitable Building Society* v *IRC* [1993] AC 70, 197 in the (rather different) context of the recovery of a wrongly extracted tax payment.

[190] See Birks, n 108 *supra*, pp 223–226. However, it would not seem possible to classify as restitutionary a case such as *Messenger* v *Andrews* (1828) 4 Russ 478 (see n 195 *infra*).

[191] Cf. *Zapetal* v *Wright* [1957] Tas SR 211.

[192] See e.g. *Re Brace (dec'd)* [1954] 1 WLR 955. It is also possible, it appears, to have a condition which imposes a merely personal obligation. See *Messenger* v *Andrews* (1828) 4 Russ 478; *M'Mahon* v *M'Mahon* [1901] IR 489; *Duffy* v *Duffy* [1920] 1 IR 122.

[193] See Deane J's express rejection of this avenue in *Muschinski* (1985) 160 CLR 583, 612. See further n 197 *infra*. Note also the suggestion of Malcolm CJ in *Kais* v *Turvey* (1994) 17 Fam LR 498, 501–502 that the rules on conditional gifts are merely part of the larger unconscionability principle (rather than *vice versa*).

[194] Cf. the comment of Birks, n 108 *supra*, 219: "The essence of the matter is that the plaintiff specified the basis of his giving".

[195] The security of transactions would be seriously undermined if every gift were liable to be reclaimed on the basis of a condition which the donor claims to have secretly attached to the gift. It could also be argued that it would be unfair to deny the donee knowledge of the condition which must be satisfied if he is to retain ownership of the property in question. His lack of knowledge may lead him to breach the condition and, unexpectedly, find himself without property which he imagined was his absolutely. Furthermore, it is clear that the donee must be given the option of refusing to accept the gift on the donor's terms, which may be very onerous. See e.g. *Messenger* v *Andrews* (1828) 4 Russ 478 (having accepted a bequest conditional on the payment of certain debts, the defendant was obliged to fulfil the condition even though the debts far exceeded the amount of property bequeathed to him).

imposed a condition and communicated this decision to the donee, the donor simply takes the risk that events may turn out otherwise than he hoped, assumed or intended.[196]

Therefore, in their traditional form, the rules governing conditional gifts will not often have a meaningful role to play in family property disputes. Those living together in an intimate relationship will not normally impose conditions upon their willingness to contribute to family expenses or to undertake domestic labour.[197] If they think at all about their separate property entitlements, it is far more likely that they will negotiate for the transfer of a share in the legal ownership of the family home or other family property.

In attempting to develop the existing law to meet the special problems of the family situation, one might try to reach a wider position by looking, not for a condition for which the donor consciously stipulates, but rather at the motive or purpose underlying the gift. When one uses the terminology of "failure of basis", it is not too difficult to slip over to the assumption that the "basis" of a gift means the donor's purpose or motivation in making the gift.[198] There may be a hint in Birks' account of the law on qualified giving[199] to the effect that the mere fact that the donor made a gift with a particular purpose or motive is sufficient to make the gift conditional upon that purpose or motive.[200] However, such a suggestion is contrary to principle and is not supported by the authorities.[201] From a practical point of view, as Birks concedes, there is an "obvious

[196] See Birks, n 108 *supra*, 219. Cf. *Re Adams and the Kensington Vestry* (1884) 27 Ch D 394.

[197] There will, however, be some exceptional cases, mostly occurring in the context of a transfer to the defendant of a share in the legal ownership. See e.g. *Muschinski* (1985) 160 CLR 583 itself, where Brennan and Dawson JJ concluded that the transfer of the property to the defendant had been made conditional on his providing the intended contribution. However, Deane J held (somewhat colourfully) that the parties had not provided for the possibility that the proposed venture "would crumble under the yoke of inauspicious stars" (*ibid*, 612). Gibbs CJ (*ibid*, 593) and Mason J (*ibid*, 599) took a similar approach. See also *Kais v Turvey* (1994) 17 Fam LR 498; *Jasco v Vuong* (1988) 12 Fam LR 615; *Medley v McHenry*, 21 March 1990 (LEXIS, NSW Sup Ct); *Ryan v Hopkinson* (1993) 16 Fam LR 659, 666–667 per Priestly JA; *Hancock v Gibson* [1996] NZFLR 289. See further *RF v MF* (1985) [1995] 2 ILRM 572 where, instead of applying the rules governing conditional gifts, the Irish Supreme Court made an ill-advised attempt to accommodate a conditional intention to benefit within the doctrine of resulting trusts. Cf. *Atkinson v Burt* (1989) 12 Fam LR 800; *Jenkins v Wynen* [1992] 1 Qd R 40, 47, lines 36–40.

[198] In fact, it might be more precise, if perhaps inelegant, to speak of "failure of stipulated basis".

[199] See n 108 *supra*, p 224.

[200] However, the example given by Birks involves a gift expressed to be made on the occasion of a marriage. This is a special situation because equity is willing to grant specific performance of contracts made in consideration of marriage (see e.g. Baker and Langan *Snell's Equity*, 29th edn (London: Sweet and Maxwell, 1990) pp 126–127). The cases cited by Birks, *Essery v Cowlard* (1884) 26 Ch D 191 and *Re Ames' Settlement* [1946] Ch 217, were decided on the basis that, when the marriage failed to take place, there was a total failure of consideration in respect of the contract.

[201] Besides the marriage cases discussed in the previous footnote, the other authority mentioned by Birks is *Burgess v Rawnsley* [1975] Ch 249, where the failure of the purpose motivating the creation of a trust was held to give rise to a resulting trust. The reasoning in this case (which is not, in any case, directly in point) is convincingly criticised by Bandali "Injustice and the Problems of Beneficial Joint Tenancy" (1976) 41 Conv 243, 252–257. Note also *Rhoden v Joseph*, 6 September 1990 (LEXIS, Ch D), where Judge Kaye QC responded as follows to an argument based on *Burgess v Rawnsley* [1975] Ch 249: "The suggestion is, in effect, that one partner should be able to say to the

danger of uncertainty in implied specification of basis".[202] Moreover, since it is difficult to see how one could logically limit the situations in which one would elevate a motive into a binding condition, there could be unfortunate results in the commercial context.[203] For these reasons, it seems that one must resist the temptation to suggest that, because one party's contributions to a personal relationship were made on the basis of the relationship, it automatically follows that they were conditional on the indefinite continuation of that relationship. This means that the law on conditional gifts is unlikely to be of practical assistance in a property dispute between cohabitees.

4. Conclusion

Having inspected the foundations of Deane J's "more general principle of equity", it is necessary to consider whether that principle can stand up to critical analysis. Following the preceding discussion, the conclusion must be that the principle is not supported by the material relied upon by Deane J (i.e. one aspect of the law of unjust enrichment, involving the unjust factor of "failure of consideration", combined with the special rules governing the fiduciary relationships between legal partners or contractual joint venturers). It is submitted that the flaw in Deane J's reasoning is one which is all too common in this area of the law. The search for a unifying "deeper" principle of equity leads only to an oversimplification. Deane J's principle puts to one side the rules of the law of restitution in favour of a principle requiring the return of benefits "unconscionably

---

other: 'You are to remain here with me in this property for life and, if you do not, then I shall be able to say, at any time hereafter, that the whole purpose of the trust for which I have given you a share in my property has failed, and in those circumstances you shall have nothing, or less than you might otherwise have'. I, for my part, find that somewhat repugnant". See also *Rushworth* v *Parker* (1981) 7 Fam LR 342, 357–358 (NSW Sup Ct); *Walmsley* v *Stanton*, 27 February 1997 (LEXIS, NSW Sup Ct).

[202] See Birks, n 108 *supra*, p 452. It is not entirely clear from Birks' brief discussion (which is contained in an endnote) what he means by "implied" specification of basis. On the one hand, he requires (*ibid*) that "the implication must be absolutely clear in content and strictly a genuine inference from conduct". This may suggest that Birks supports the view advanced in the text that there must be a conscious decision by the donor to impose a binding condition and that this must be communicated to the donee, whether expressly or impliedly. On this view, "implied" specification would simply cover the rare case where the existence of a binding condition is conveyed to the donee without the need for words. On the other hand, having discussed implied specification, Birks goes on to comment (*ibid*) that *Muschinski* v *Dodds* involved restitution "on a ground similar to this". In his subsequent discussion of the case (*ibid*, pp 462–463), Birks explains the approach of the majority as a recognition of "the wide concept of failure of consideration" for which his treatise had argued. However, since no condition was actually imposed by Mrs Muschinski, Birks' comments seem to suggest that he does not object to the elevation of a person's motives to the level of a condition. Cf. Birks "Trusts Raised to Reverse Unjust Enrichment: The *Westdeutsche* Case" [1996] *Restitution Law Review* 3, 6 n 16; Birks "Equity in the Modern Law: An Exercise in Taxonomy" (1996) 26 *Western Australian Law Review* 1, 95.

[203] If the motive underlying a gift can create a binding condition on that gift, it is difficult to see why the motive for entering a contract should not be given similar treatment. However, problems would obviously arise if e.g. my mentioning that I am buying your product with the intention of reselling it to X Ltd automatically made our contract conditional on X Ltd's staying in business.

retained". The vagueness of this concept, and the absence of detailed rules and safeguards for individual autonomy (e.g. the possibility of "subjective devaluation" of non-monetary benefits),[204] leads to an impressionistic approach to the subject similar to that favoured by Lord Denning. Despite Deane J's lengthy protestations to the contrary,[205] there is much force in the conclusion of Brennan J in *Muschinski* that the argument for a constructive trust "proves, on analysis, to be a plea for the return of the interest given on the ground of fairness".[206] It is revealing that, after Deane J established his "joint venture" analogy in *Muschinski*, the point has not come up again in any of the reported Australian cases on family property. Content with Deane J's rationalisation of the principle, judges in later cases have attempted to work out the parameters of the new doctrine without reference back to its purported basis in authority and principle.

B. A Shift in the Definition of a "Joint Venture"

1. *Introduction*

Thus far, the argument has been directed towards the approach of Deane J in *Muschinski*. However, in the line of subsequent cases, beginning with *Baumgartner*,[207] the Australian courts have considerably developed his "joint venture" doctrine. In these later cases, it is possible to detect an unheralded but crucial shift in the nature of the "joint venture" to which the unconscionability doctrine is applied. The position originally taken by Deane J in *Muschinski* involved a "joint venture" between the parties to acquire and/or improve certain property. The personal relationship between the parties merely provided the context for this more narrow joint venture. By contrast, *Baumgartner* and later cases have focused instead on the personal relationship of the parties and have treated this, in itself, as the relevant "joint venture" for the purposes of the unconscionability doctrine. In order to illustrate the shift which has taken place, it will now be necessary to look more closely at the concept of "joint venture" as understood by Deane J in *Muschinski* and as then modified in *Baumgartner* and later cases.

2. *Deane J's view in* Muschinski

In *Muschinski*, Deane J clearly took a narrow view of the concept of "joint venture". From the start of his judgment, Deane J focused on "the joint project"[208]

---

[204] See Chapter 7 *supra*, text following n 166.
[205] (1985) 160 CLR 583, 615–616.
[206] *Ibid*, 609.
[207] (1987) 164 CLR 137.
[208] (1985) 160 CLR 583, 610.

(or, as he also described it on a number of occasions, "the overall arrangement" between the parties) to purchase and develop the land.[209] Deane J clearly regarded this "joint project" as being distinct from the personal relationship between the parties. This is demonstrated, for example, by his identifying, as one of the reasons for the failure of the "joint project", the fact that the "de facto relationship between the parties came to an end".[210]

3. *The approach of the High Court in* Baumgartner

In *Baumgartner*, the High Court of Australia greatly increased the scope of the unconscionability doctrine. This was achieved by means of (what might be called in literary criticism) a "strong misreading" of Deane J's judgment in *Muschinski*.[211] In their joint judgment in *Baumgartner*, Mason CJ, Wilson and Deane JJ[212] took full advantage of the word "relationship" in Deane J's key formulation of principle in *Muschinski*.[213] Having quoted the relevant passage,[214] the judges proceeded to argue that the parties in *Baumgartner* had "pooled their earnings for the purposes of their joint relationship, one of the purposes of that relationship being to secure accommodation for themselves and their child".[215] Thus, the "relationship" upon which the judges concentrated was the personal relationship between the parties, a relationship clearly distinct from the subsidiary "purpose of that relationship" which was to secure accommodation for the family. The judges in *Baumgartner*, applying the words of Deane J's formulation in *Muschinski*, went on to assert[216] that the parties had made their various contributions "on the basis of, and for the purposes of, that joint relationship". The final step in the reasoning in *Baumgartner* was to conclude that, "after the relationship had failed"[217] (clearly meaning the personal relationship) it was unconscionable for the man to assert his exclusive ownership in the family home.[218]

---

[209] See *ibid* where he outlined the contributions which it was envisaged that each would make to this project.

[210] There are numerous other indications to the same effect throughout the judgment of Deane J. See e.g. *ibid*, 618 where Deane J noted that "the overall arrangement between them, while consensual, was clearly non-contractual", a comment which would not make sense if he were referring to the personal relationship between the parties. See also *ibid*, 620, 622. In fact, on Deane J's analysis, the personal relationship between the parties constituted a possible obstacle to the success of Mrs Muschinski's claim. See text following n 28 *supra*.

[211] Of course, Deane J was one of the judges who, in *Baumgartner*, gave a very wide scope to the doctrine he had developed in *Muschinski*. However, this sheds little light on Deane J's intentions at the time of *Muschinski*.

[212] It is difficult to discern from their judgments the views of Gaudron and Toohey JJ on the issue under discussion.

[213] See the text to n 28 *supra* ("the principle operates where the substratum of a joint relationship or endeavour is removed without attributable blame . . .").

[214] (1987) 164 CLR 137, 148.

[215] *Ibid*, 149.

[216] *Ibid*.

[217] *Ibid*.

[218] It should be noted that, although it achieved a highly significant shift from a *Muschinski*-style

4. *The concept of "joint venture" in the later cases*

One of the earliest post-*Baumgartner* cases was *Hibberson v George*,[219] where, without expressly adverting to the issue, the majority of the Court of Appeal of New South Wales appears to have taken the *Baumgartner* approach of focusing on the personal relationship of the parties. McHugh JA, with whom Hope JA concurred, emphasised on a number of occasions that the claimant had "spent her money for the benefit of the joint relationship".[220] In these comments, and in his discussion of the consequences of the breakdown of the "relationship", it is obvious that McHugh JA intended to refer to the personal relationship between the parties rather than to any joint undertaking to purchase or improve certain property.[221]

Although unfortunately the issue has never been confronted explicitly,[222] the later cases appear to follow the line of the majority in *Hibberson*.[223] Furthermore, it is revealing to refer back to the discussion, earlier in this chapter,[224] of the treatment of indirect contributions which cannot be related to the acquisition or improvement of property. It will be recalled that those judges who opposed the recognition of such contributions as the source of a constructive trust appear to have done so on the basis of the difficulty in linking them to the disputed property.[225] In none of the cases was it suggested that the problem was the absence of a relevant joint venture between the parties. This suggests,

---

joint venture to purchase/improve property over to a purely personal "joint venture", the leading judgment in *Baumgartner* did envisage a subsidiary role for the more narrow conception of "joint venture". This is evident in the fact that, as was mentioned earlier, the judges saw fit to emphasise (*ibid*) that "one of the purposes" of the parties' relationship was to "secure accommodation" for the family and that the contributions the parties had made had been "to the acquisition of the land, the building of the house, the purchase of the furniture and the making of their home". The point seems to be that contributions to the narrow project of acquiring/improving the home of the parties can readily be seen as having been made "for the purposes of" their wider joint relationship and therefore as justifying a remedy.

[219] (1989) 12 Fam LR 725.

[220] *Ibid*, 743.

[221] See, however, the vigorous dissent of Mahoney JA (especially *ibid*, 735–739) and note also the comments of the same judge in *Green v Green* (1989) 17 NSWLR 343, 369 on the effect of the majority judgment in *Hibberson*.

[222] See, however, *National Australian Bank Ltd v Maher* [1995] 1 VR 318, 335–336 per Ormiston J (Appeal Division of Vic Sup Ct) (in determining whether the joint venture between the parties has failed "it would be highly artificial to confine the joint venture or relationship assumed for these purposes to the acquisition of the house and the two lots of land"). Cf. *ibid*, 326 per Fullagar J.

[223] See e.g. *Bryson v Bryant* (1992) 29 NSWLR 188, 202 where Kirby P referred to the imposition of a constructive trust on the basis of "contributions to the resources of the relationship". He also insisted (*ibid*, 202–203) that the unconscionability principle should apply to married couples as well as unmarried couples, thus suggesting that he regarded the principle as applying to the personal relationship of the parties. Sheller JA similarly emphasised (*ibid*, 222) the question of "contributions to the relationship", again obviously referring to the personal relationship of the parties. See also *Miller v Sutherland* (1990) 14 Fam LR 416, 425 ("each contributed to their joint welfare").

[224] See text to nn 67–77 *supra*.

[225] See in particular *Public Trustee v Kukula* (1990) 14 Fam LR 97, 102 per Handley JA; *Bryson v Bryant* (1992) 29 NSWLR 188, 231 per Samuels A-JA.

by strong implication, that the Australian courts have been content to accept the personal relationship of the parties as the focus for the joint venture analogy.

5. *The implications of the wider conception of joint venture*

From the foregoing analysis, it must be concluded that the Australian courts have accepted the shift to a definition of "joint venture" which can be satisfied simply by the existence of an intimate personal relationship between the parties.[226] However, once the concept of a joint venture is watered down to include "joint venturers . . . in the journey of life",[227] the analogy with a true commercial venture, purportedly the foundation for the entire Australian doctrine, loses much of its credibility.

On the other hand, whatever the theoretical disadvantages, the modification of the notion of "joint venture" has significant practical implications. It opens up the possibility of granting a remedy based simply on contributions made "to the relationship" rather than to the acquisition and improvement of specific property. This in turn could allow the Australian doctrine the same extremely wide scope as its Canadian counterpart. As was discussed earlier in this chapter,[228] this opportunity has not yet been fully taken up. However, the potential is clearly there and, as was suggested previously,[229] it is probably only a matter of time before the Australian courts further develop their doctrine.

IV. CONCLUDING REFLECTIONS ON THE AUSTRALIAN DOCTRINE

Having looked in detail at both the practical operation, and the theoretical basis, of the Australian doctrine, it is now possible to venture a general conclusion. In the end, it seems that the Australian unconscionability doctrine has much in common with the Canadian unjust enrichment doctrine examined in the previous chapter. Both doctrines appear, at first sight, to offer great promise. Admittedly, in terms of generating a liberal set of outcomes, the Australian doc-

---

[226] The Australian courts have not given close consideration to the precise nature of the personal relationship required to trigger their doctrine. In order to justify the application of the joint venture analogy, it would seem to be necessary that the parties had some expectation that their relationship would continue indefinitely. Otherwise, it could not be argued that the claimant had neglected to protect her separate property entitlements on the basis of the relationship. Cf. *Renton* v *Youngman* (1995) 19 Fam LR 450 (where, in the context of a short relationship, Wallwork J emphasised the fact that the defendant had once said that he would like to have children with the claimant). It would not appear necessary that the parties should actually cohabit but, in practical terms, it is less likely that relevant contributions will be made in a case where the parties are not cohabiting. Cf. the failure of the claim in *Public Trustee* v *Kukula* (1990) 14 Fam LR 97. There is no logical reason to confine the doctrine to heterosexual relationships. See *Harmer* v *Pearson* (1993) 16 Fam LR 596 (doctrine applied to a homosexual relationship; note, however, the relatively harsh treatment of the claim on the facts).

[227] *Bell* v *Bell* (1995) 19 Fam LR 690, 694 per Nathan J.

[228] See text to nn 67–77 *supra*.

[229] See text to n 77 *supra*.

trine has not yet reached its full potential. However, it is a relatively new doc-trine and there appears to be no reason to doubt that, in due course, it will become as broad as the Canadian doctrine.

Unfortunately, the Australian unconscionability doctrine also shares with its Canadian counterpart the absence of a convincing theoretical foundation. It looks for legitimacy to the joint venture analogy developed by Deane J in his ground-breaking judgment in *Muschinski*.[230] However, in the preceding discus-sion in this chapter, this claim to legitimacy was challenged on two grounds. First, an attempt was made to show that the authorities relied upon by Deane J do not actually support the position he reached.[231] Secondly, it was argued that in the later Australian cases, beginning with *Baumgartner*,[232] the joint venture analogy has been distorted so as to apply simply to the personal relationship between the parties.[233] This distortion, while increasing the practical utility of the doctrine, has further diminished the plausibility of the joint venture analogy upon which it was founded. Indeed, it is clear from the recent cases that the Australian judges prefer to refrain from further consideration of the theoretical basis of their doctrine. Their idea appears to be that the matter was considered once by Deane J in *Muschinski* and that further reflection on the matter might be counter-productive.

It is worth noting, however, that the Australian doctrine does have certain advantages over the Canadian approach. Unlike the Canadian doctrine, which threatens to turn on its head the general law of unjust enrichment,[234] the uncon-scionability approach is expressly tied to the intimate relationship between the parties. Therefore, there is less likelihood of the general law being contaminated by a generous approach suitable only in the family context.[235] Moreover, the Australian doctrine does not require the court to make improbable inferences concerning the intention of the claimant.[236] Its focus is on the heart of the mat-ter; the fact that one party neglected to consider her separate property rights because she put her faith in her relationship with the defendant.

---

[230] (1985) 160 CLR 583.

[231] See Part III(A) *supra*.

[232] (1987) 164 CLR 137.

[233] See the discussion in Part III(B) *supra*.

[234] See the discussion in Chapter 7 *supra*, Part IV(B) of the suggestion in the Canadian cases that restitution should follow "in the absence of a juristic reason" for an enrichment.

[235] There has, however, been a number of cases where the unconscionability doctrine has been pleaded outside the family context. Most of these pleas have been unsuccessful: see *Re Australian Elizabethan Theatre Trust* (1991) 102 ALR 681; *Australian National Industries Ltd v Greater Pacific Investments Pty Ltd (No 3)* (1992) 7 ACSR 176; *Bluebird Investments Pty Ltd v Graf* (1994) 13 ACSR 271; *KT & T Developments Pty Ltd v Tay* (1994) 13 WAR 363. See, however, *Carson v Wood* (1994) 34 NSWLR 9 (successful claim in context of business joint venture). Note also *Keogh v Burnside CC* (1992) 75 LGRA 163; *Bathurst City Council v PWC Properties Pty Ltd*, (1998) 72 ALJR 1470. Cf. *Re Toohey* (1991) 14 Fam LR 843, 856 per McCall J.

[236] As is necessary under the English common intention analysis (discussed in Chapter 5 *supra*) or if one seeks to explain the Canadian approach in terms of restitution on the basis of the unjust factor of "free acceptance" (see Chapter 7 *supra*). However, as was discussed in detail in Part II(D) *supra*, the Australian courts have, like their Canadian counterparts, given insufficient weight to the intention of the legal owner.

While it has just been pointed out that the Australian doctrine is not without merit, and is arguably superior to the Canadian doctrine, it is submitted that this is not enough to recommend it to other legal systems. It cannot be sufficient simply for the courts to observe that an intimate cohabitation has some of the features of a joint venture and to move directly from that generalised observation to a statutory-style regime of redistribution of property upon the termination of such a cohabitation. Such a development could only be legitimate if it had the imprimatur of the democratically elected legislature. Ironically, many Australian legislatures have, in fact, intervened to provide a statutory remedy upon the collapse of a de facto relationship.[237] Mahoney JA observed in *Wallace v Stanford*[238] that the subsequent development of the law in *Baumgartner* may have removed "many of the reasons" for the intervention of the legislature.[239] Surely, however, the reverse is the case. The initiative of various Australian State legislatures exposes as unwarranted judicial legislation the attempts of the Australian courts to solve the problem on their own.

Now that a review of Canadian and Australian developments has been completed, it remains only to consider the contribution of the New Zealand courts. The next chapter addresses that task.

---

[237] See n 10 *supra*.
[238] (1995) 37 NSWLR 1.
[239] *Ibid*, 8.

9

New Zealand's "Reasonable Expectations" Approach

INTRODUCTION

In this chapter, it is necessary to consider the approach taken by the New Zealand courts. Thus far in this book, rather than attempting to present a statement of the law prevailing in any particular jurisdiction, the discussion has focused on an analysis of the various doctrinal options. It is a mere coincidence that, unlike in many other areas of law, each of the jurisdictions considered has taken a distinctive theoretical approach. The New Zealand case law, however, presents special difficulties. The problem is that the New Zealand courts have been unable to detect any real difference between the English, Canadian and Australian doctrines. This conclusion has led them to put forward an approach which purportedly "draws upon and encompasses the principal features of the various approaches canvassed in the authorities in Commonwealth jurisdictions".[1] They have identified the concept of "reasonable expectations" as a central element in all the relevant doctrines. While the "reasonable expectations" approach has some independent features worthy of discussion, the New Zealand courts' refusal to disavow any of the other competing doctrines has somewhat reduced the extent of their contribution to the theory of this area.

In general, it may be suggested that the New Zealand courts have taken a distinctly anti-theoretical approach, concentrating firmly on the instrumentalist goal of achieving a broad adjustive discretion. Their willingness to view all the other doctrines as co-extensive is, to the extent that it is not due simply to misunderstanding, explicable on the basis that their focus is primarily on the results generated by the doctrines. Stripping away the veneer of theory, the New Zealand courts have looked through to the underlying social concerns of the Australian, Canadian and (to a lesser extent) English judges. When Cooke P asserted in *Pasi* v *Kamana*[2] that "we are all driving in the same direction",[3] he demonstrated that his concern was with the destination rather than with the name (or mechanics) of the "conceptual vehicle"[4] in which he travelled. This attitude clearly has much in common with that of Lord Denning, as is confirmed

---

[1] *Per* Gault J in *Lankow* v *Rose* [1995] 1 NZLR 277, 287–288.
[2] [1986] 1 NZLR 603.
[3] *Ibid*, 605.
[4] See Cooke P's remarks in *Phillips* v *Phillips* [1993] 3 NZLR 159, 167–168.

by Cooke P's approving reference in *Phillips* v *Phillips*[5] to "Lord Denning's frank reliance on justice, good conscience and fairness".

Effectively, the result of the New Zealand case law has been the creation (with even less concessions to doctrinal development than in Canada or Australia) of a wide judicial power to adjust property entitlements upon the breakdown of a quasi-matrimonial relationship.[6] It is, of course, arguable that this approach is justified by social attitudes and conditions in New Zealand. However, the nakedly instrumental approach of the New Zealand courts requires no doctrinal clothes, making it difficult to see what the courts in other jurisdictions might decently borrow. Nonetheless, there are clearly some useful lessons to be extracted from the New Zealand cases.

Part I of this chapter will consider the development of the present New Zealand position over a series of cases including *Hayward* v *Giordani*,[7] *Gillies* v *Keogh*[8] and *Lankow* v *Rose*.[9] Part II will examine the operation of the "reasonable expectations" approach, with an attempt being made to probe whatever points of theoretical tension can be identified in such an amorphous doctrine. Finally, in Part III, a number of conclusions will be ventured on the state of New Zealand law in this area.

I. THE DEVELOPMENT OF THE DOCTRINE

A. The Doctrinal Background

As with the other Commonwealth jurisdictions considered in this work, New Zealand began with the inheritance of the English common intention trust. This doctrine was accepted as the appropriate basis of decision by the New Zealand Court of Appeal in *Gough* v *Fraser*[10] and the doctrine was applied to the facts

---

[5] *Ibid*, 168. Cf. the audacious attempt by McMullin J in *Pasi* v *Kamana* [1986] 1 NZLR 603, 607 to turn the tables on critics of a liberal approach: "Expressions such as 'the formless void of individual moral opinion' may be quaint but like many legal metaphors they do little to clarify". Cf. text to n 18 *infra*.

[6] Interestingly, Cooke P commented in *Lankow* v *Rose* [1995] 1 NZLR 277, 281 that "the present New Zealand case law represents an attempt to ensure justice while recognising that there is a basic difference between legal marriage and de facto union". While he felt (*ibid*, 280–281) that legislation might be desirable to lay down "some more hard-and-fast approach", he doubted whether "ideally, any law can aim for more" than was achieved by the cases. Note also the earlier calls for legislation in *Gillies* v *Keogh* [1989] 2 NZLR 327, 348 per Richardson J; 349 per Casey J; *Partridge* v *Moller* (1990) 6 FRNZ 147, 153 per Tipping; *D* v *A* (1992) 9 FRNZ 43, 48 per Doogue J. Cf. Cooke P's original preference for proceeding without legislation, expressed in *Pasi* v *Kamana* [1986] 1 NZLR 603, 605. See now the De Facto Relationships (Property) Bill 1998: proposed regime to apply to heterosexual couples living together for at least three years (with shorter relationships being covered in exceptional circumstances); family home and chattels to be shared equally and other family property to be shared on the basis of contributions to the relationship.

[7] [1983] NZLR 140.

[8] [1989] 2 NZLR 327.

[9] [1995] 1 NZLR 277.

[10] [1977] 1 NZLR 279. See also *Brown* v *Stokes* (1980) 1 NZCPR 209.

in an orthodox manner. Richmond P distinguished *Cooke v Head*[11] and *Eves v Eves*,[12] somewhat improbably explaining away[13] Lord Denning MR's judgments in those cases in terms consistent with the orthodox approach of Lord Diplock in *Gissing v Gissing*.[14]

Lord Denning MR's "new model constructive trust" was given a more direct consideration by Mahon J in *Carly v Farrelly*.[15] As has already been discussed in a previous chapter,[16] Mahon J was sharply critical of the new model constructive trust in *Carly*, emphasising its "total uncertainty of application and result"[17] and the manner in which it consigned litigants to "the formless void of individual moral opinion".[18] Four years after *Carly*, Mahon J returned to the attack in *Avondale Printers and Stationers Ltd v Haggie*.[19] In *Avondale*, the focus was on the status of the principle of unjust enrichment in New Zealand law. Counsel relied on *Hussey v Palmer*,[20] where Lord Denning MR had sought respectability for his "new model constructive trust" by associating it with the law of restitution as applied in the USA. Mahon J's view was that whether all the relevant legal doctrines and remedies were "assembled under the rubric of a law of restitution or a doctrine of unjust enrichment does not seem to matter, so long as the forms of relief remain settled and definable".[21] However, for Mahon J, "the point of departure occurs when justice in its truly legal sense is supplanted by unfairness and misfortune, and when the maxim aequum et bonum succumbs by free translation to mean subjective judicial opinion as to where the merits lie".[22] Thus, Mahon J was not opposed to the gradual development of the existing rules of the law of restitution. However, he clearly rejected the expansive notion of unjust enrichment which was, soon afterwards, heralded in Canada by *Pettkus v Becker*.[23]

In *Brown v Stokes*[24] (decided in 1980), the New Zealand Court of Appeal expressly left open the question of whether or not it was possible further to develop the constructive trust in the area of family property disputes.[25] Although the omens were not favourable, it will be seen in the next section how

---

[11] [1972] 1 WLR 518.

[12] [1975] 1 WLR 1338.

[13] [1977] 1 NZLR 279, 283.

[14] [1971] AC 886.

[15] [1975] 1 NZLR 356.

[16] See Chapter 6 *supra*, text following n 39.

[17] [1975] 1 NZLR 356, 367.

[18] *Ibid*.

[19] [1979] 2 NZLR 124. See McKay "Avondale Printers v Haggie: Mr Justice Mahon and the Law of Restitution" [1980] *New Zealand Law Journal* 245. Note that neither *Carly* [1975] 1 NZLR 356 nor *Avondale* involved family disputes.

[20] [1972] 1 WLR 1286, 1290.

[21] [1979] 2 NZLR 124, 153.

[22] *Ibid*.

[23] (1980) 117 DLR (3d) 257. Note the view of Hammond J in *Daly v Gilbert* [1993] 3 NZLR 731, 739 that Mahon J had "set a long face" against this kind of approach.

[24] (1980) 1 NZCPR 209.

[25] *Ibid*, 211 per Richmond P; 213 per Cooke J.

the New Zealand courts, inspired by the judgments of Lord Robin Cooke (as he has now become), quickly discarded their conservative views and braved "the formless void of individual moral opinion".

B. The "Reasonable Expectations" Approach[26]

The origins of the new doctrine can be traced to *Hayward v Giordani*.[27] The case involved a de facto relationship which lasted for five years before the untimely death of the female partner. The male claimant had done "a tremendous amount of work" on a cottage which his partner owned in her sole name. He had also handed over all his earnings to his partner, who was "the exchequer" of the relationship. The relationship had been a happy one and the female partner had suggested on a number of occasions that she should put the property into joint names. However, the claimant was "in some respects perhaps a little unusual",[28] in that he was not materialistic, and had brushed aside such suggestions. His partner had made a will leaving all her property to the claimant "houe has been so wonderfull [*sic*] to me and given me so much happiness".[29] Unfortunately, this will had not been witnessed and so was invalid. At law, the deceased's property passed to a former friend under a will made four years before she had met the claimant.

The Court of Appeal unanimously held that the claimant was entitled to a one-half interest in the property. All three judges felt that this conclusion could be justified under the common intention analysis. Therefore, it was not, strictly speaking, necessary for the Court to consider any wider issues of principle. However, Cooke J decided, for the benefit of High Court judges in future cases, to give "some indication . . . of the direction in which thinking in this Court is tending".[30] He stressed that his comments reflected merely his "personal preference" and did not "represent a final commitment".[31]

---

[26] See generally, Atkin "De Factos Engaging our Attention" [1988] *New Zealand Law Journal* 12; Peart "A Comparative View of Property Rights in De Facto Relationships: Are We All Driving in the Same Direction?" (1989) 7 *Otago Law Review* 100; Narev "Unjust Enrichment and De Facto Relationships" (1991) 6 *Auckland University Law Review* 504; Atkin *Living Together Without Marriage* (Wellington: Butterworths, 1991) ch. 5 (especially pp 99–104); Gardner "Rethinking Family Property" (1993) 109 LQR 263, 278–279; Atkin "Husband and Wife" Vol 13 in *The Laws of New Zealand* (Butterworths: Wellington, 1995) pp 91–93; Chalmers and Dal Pont *Equity and the Law of Trusts in Australia and New Zealand* (North Ryde, New South Wales: LBC Information Services, 1996) pp 706–707; Richardson "De Facto Property Disputes in New Zealand" (1996) 7 *Canterbury Law Review* 369. See also *Report of the Working Group on Matrimonial Property and Family Protection* (October, 1988); *De Facto Marriages: Property Law Reform* (Dept of Justice, April 1995).

[27] [1983] NZLR 140.

[28] *Ibid*, 142 per Cooke J, quoting the trial judge.

[29] See *ibid*, 141.

[30] *Ibid*, 145 per Cooke J.

[31] *Ibid*.

In the remarks which Cooke J went on to make in *Hayward*, one sees the beginning of the tendency to treat the competing theoretical possibilities as interchangeable. Cooke J began by referring "to Lord Denning MR's proposition in *Cooke v Head*[32] . . . and other cases that whenever two parties by their joint efforts acquire (or improve) property to be used for their joint benefit the Courts may impose or impute a constructive or resulting trust".[33] According to Cooke J, Lord Denning was "in substance" putting into effect the approach of Lords Reid and Diplock in *Pettitt v Pettitt*.[34] It will be recalled[35] that Lord Reid had been willing to "ask what the spouses, or reasonable people in their shoes, would have agreed if they had directed their minds to the question of what rights should accrue to the spouse who has contributed to the acquisition or improvement of property owned by the other spouse".[36] Similarly, Lord Diplock had invoked "the familiar legal technique" whereby the court "imputes to the parties a common intention which in fact they never formed and it does so by forming its own opinion of what would have been the common intention of reasonable men".[37] Cooke J pointed out that, although these views had not prevailed in England, the New Zealand courts were not under the same constraints of precedent and were free to adopt them.[38]

Cooke J went on to suggest that "essentially the same approach" had been taken by "other distinguished overseas Judges".[39] He referred in particular to *Pettkus v Becker*[40] where Dickson J had applied the doctrine of unjust enrichment to the family context.[41] Cooke J conceded that the scope of that doctrine was unsettled in New Zealand.[42] However, he pointed out that "[t]he law of unjust enrichment—and the principles of equity more generally—cannot have ceased growing at some climactic date in England, any more than tort law stopped before *Donoghue v Stevenson*".[43] Ultimately, Cooke J was content to observe that he regarded the approach in *Pettkus* as "very helpful".

Cooke J went on to make a final point, directed against the "lingering sense" that the law should not recognise relationships falling short of marriage as having any bearing on property rights. According to Cooke P:

---

[32] [1972] 1 WLR 518.

[33] [1983] NZLR 140, 145.

[34] [1970] AC 777.

[35] See the discussion in Chapter 1 *supra*, text following n 59.

[36] [1970] AC 777, 795.

[37] *Ibid*, 823.

[38] [1983] NZLR 140, 146.

[39] *Ibid*, 147.

[40] (1980) 117 DLR (3d) 257.

[41] See Chapter 7 *supra* for discussion of the Canadian approach. Cooke J also referred to the rather more conservative opinion of Mahoney JA in the Australian case of *Allen v Snyder* [1977] 2 NSWLR 685, suggesting that this and the judgment of Dickson J in *Pettkus* should be "read as a whole".

[42] For the modern New Zealand position on unjust enrichment, see Chapter 7 *supra*, n 21.

[43] [1983] NZLR 140, 148.

"[A] function of the Courts must be to develop common law and equity so as to reflect the reasonable dictates of social facts, not to frustrate them. While not alone enough to justify imposing a constructive trust, a stable de facto union provides a background in which one will tend to arise much more naturally than as between strangers".[44]

Cooke J felt that the common intention trust analysis already involved "judicial creativity" and, "[b]y comparison it would seem only a small step to eliminate the need to strain for proof of a common intention".[45]

The other judges in *Hayward* gave shorter concurring judgments. Richardson J commented that there was "considerable force" in the argument "that given the realities of contemporary family life the property interests of parties should not turn upon an elusive and often vain search for indications of a common intention".[46] He felt, however, that it was unnecessary to resolve the issue of whether the constructive trust should be developed to "reflect the direct and indirect contributions of the parties".[47] The final judge, McMullin J, inclined to the view that in this area "policy considerations should not inhibit the Courts from developing [the law] to meet different circumstances and relationships and changing social conditions".[48] However, he too felt that it was unnecessary to reach a conclusion on the matter.

The Court of Appeal next commented on the issue in *Pasi v Kamana*.[49] The claim in this case was particularly weak and was speedily and unanimously rejected by the Court. However, Cooke P (as he had then become) took the opportunity to restate his views. He pointed out that, in the absence of legislation governing the property rights of de facto spouses, it was necessary to focus on whether there had been sufficient direct or indirect contributions to the property in question to carry an interest in it. He went on to state that:

"In conducting that inquiry I respectfully doubt whether there is any significant difference between the deemed, imputed or inferred common intention spoken of by Lord Reid and Lord Diplock (and now by the English Court of Appeal in *Grant v Edwards*)[50] and the unjust enrichment concept used by the Supreme Court of Canada. Unconscionability, constructive or equitable fraud, Lord Denning's "justice and good conscience" and "in all fairness": at bottom in this context these are probably different formulae for the same idea. As indicated in *Hayward v Giordani*,[51] I think we are all driving in the same direction".[52]

---

[44] [1983] NZLR 140, 148 Cf. *Hamilton v Jurgens* [1996] NZFLR 350 where a cohabitation between two men, involving "an intense loving bond" but no sexual activity, was considered by Anderson J to be within the principles developed by the Court of Appeal in the cases following *Hayward*.

[45] *Ibid*.

[46] *Ibid*, 149.

[47] *Ibid*.

[48] *Ibid*, 153.

[49] [1986] 1 NZLR 603.

[50] [1986] Ch 638.

[51] [1983] NZLR 140.

[52] [1986] 1 NZLR 603, 605.

Having asserted that all the doctrines amounted to the same thing, Cooke P went on to indicate what he understood that thing to be:

"One way of putting the test is to ask whether a reasonable person in the shoes of the claimant would have understood that his or her efforts would naturally result in an interest in the property. If, but only if, the answer is Yes, the Court should decide on an appropriate interest—not necessarily a half—by way of constructive trust, as indicated in *Gissing* v *Gissing*[53]".[54]

Thus was born the "reasonable expectations" test. This test was further refined by the Court of Appeal in the important case of *Gillies* v *Keogh*.[55] The de facto relationship in *Gillies* had lasted for approximately three years. The defendant's previous marriage had broken down and she felt that she had been "done in the eye" in relation to the resulting property settlement. She made it clear to her new partner that the money she had received under this settlement was sacrosanct and was to be used for the purchase of a new house for her. The claimant conceded that, when this house had ultimately been purchased, he had agreed to it being in her name only. During their relationship, the parties had pooled their earnings to meet household expenses and outgoings associated with the house. The claimant also contributed to extending and improving the house and developing the gardens. When the original house was sold, and another purchased in the sole name of the defendant, the claimant again helped in cleaning up the house and grounds. He claimed to be entitled to a 40 per cent share in the house. The Court of Appeal were unanimous in rejecting this claim.

Cooke P welcomed the opportunity "to add expressly one element of certainty in an field where it is sometimes said to be lacking and complaints of 'palm-tree justice' are voiced".[56] The "element of certainty" envisaged by Cooke P was that "an interest or monetary right by way of constructive trust cannot arise if a reasonable person in the claimant's position would have understood that he or she was not to receive one".[57] This "freedom to stipulate against any trust or obligation" was seen by Cooke P as analogous to the "contracting-out" provisions of section 21 of New Zealand's Matrimonial Property Act 1976.[58] Since the claimant in *Gillies* had been fully aware that the defendant regarded the house as hers entirely, he could have had no reasonable expectation of an interest in the property and therefore would not be entitled to a remedy under any of the relevant doctrines.

As well as dealing with the central reason for denying a remedy on the facts before him, Cooke P again discussed the principles of law generally applicable

---

[53] [1971] AC 886.

[54] [1986] 1 NZLR 603, 605.

[55] [1989] 2 NZLR 327. Note also *Oliver* v *Bradley* [1987] 1 NZLR 586 (CA).

[56] *Ibid*, 330.

[57] *Ibid*.

[58] *Ibid*, 334. Cf. Cripps "Contracting Out of the Matrimonial Property Act 1976" (1978) 9 *Victoria University of Wellington Law Review* 101.

in this area.[59] He insisted once more that it normally made "no practical difference" which doctrine one applied,[60] the only change in his position being that he now added promissory and proprietary estoppel to the list of indistinguishable doctrines.[61]

Cooke P also identified two further[62] factors which would have to be weighed in "grey area cases".[63] The first factor was the degree of sacrifice by the claimant, notably in terms of other opportunities in life which she has foregone.[64] While the length of the union might be a relevant factor in this respect, this would not always be the case and it would clearly be inappropriate to insist on an arbitrarily selected number of years as a prerequisite for a remedy. Cooke P went on to point out that:

> "[A] second and equally obvious major factor to be weighed is the value of the broadly measurable contributions of the claimant by comparison with the value of the broadly measurable benefits received".[65]

These two factors ("sacrifice" and "contributions") arguably exhaust the possible range of conduct upon which a claimant could rely in a case of this sort. Cooke P went on to confirm more explicitly that he was unwilling to exclude any type of relevant conduct. He pointed out that, while the law required "contributions to assets", these contributions could be indirect.[66] He expressly accepted that they could include "domestic services or the care of children".[67] Cooke P concluded his discussion of the law by pointing out that, in some cases, a monetary remedy would be "the most appropriate way of satisfying the

---

[59] It is interesting that in the previous two cases discussed (*Pasi* [1986] 1 NZLR 603 and *Gillies* [1989] 2 NZLR 327), there was little doubt that the claim should fail. (See also *Hayward* [1983] NZLR 140, where the claim could simply have been upheld under the common intention trust analysis). It seems that the judges in question were politically astute in pushing forward the boundaries of their doctrine while, at the same time, giving the impression of moderation by denying a remedy on the facts before them. Cf. Atkin *Living Together Without Marriage*, n 26 *supra*, p 101.

[60] [1989] 2 NZLR 327, 330. See also *Partridge* v *Moller* (1990) 6 FRNZ 147, 153 per Tipping J ("[a]ll . . . roads lead to Rome") and *Williams* v *Tedcastle* [1994] 1 NZLR 85.

[61] [1989] 2 NZLR 327, 330–331. The most puzzling element in Cooke P's judgment was his insistence (*ibid*, 333) that the English courts were not "significantly out of line with the rest of the Commonwealth in this field". Cf. *Phillips* v *Phillips* [1993] 3 NZLR 159, 168–169 per Cooke P. Contrast the more realistic views of Tipping J in *Lankow* v *Rose* [1995] 1 NZLR 277, 293.

[62] A third factor, discussed by Cooke P at this point, was the issue of whether there had been any "contracting-out" by the parties. This issue has already been discussed in the text following n 56 *supra*.

[63] [1989] 2 NZLR 327, 332.

[64] See further text to and following n 195 *infra*.

[65] [1989] 2 NZLR 327, 334. Cooke P went on (*ibid*) to explain that: "Contributions to household expenses, or to maintenance, repairs or additions, may amount to no more than fair payment for board and lodgings and the advantages of a home for the time being. More than that is commonly needed to justify an award". In the spirit of this *dictum*, New Zealand courts have been willing to take into account any benefits received by the claimant as a result of her relationship with the defendant. See e.g. *Harvey* v *Bindner* (1991) 8 FRNZ 560, 564 per Barker J; *Wech* v *Linnell* (1993) 11 FRNZ 569, 573–574 per Thorp J; *Lankow* v *Rose* [1995] 1 NZLR 277, 282 per Hardie Boys J.

[66] *Ibid*, 335.

[67] *Ibid*.

equity or the requirements of conscience in giving effect to reasonable expectations".[68]

Gillies v *Keogh* is also important for the judgment of Richardson J. Richardson J confessed himself "less than comfortable with treating fairness in the round as the ultimate test and with some of the judicial attempts to structure a framework within which it is to operate".[69] While accepting the reasonable expectations approach, he sought to find for it a "principled basis in law".[70] Richardson J's solution lay in "the well-settled principles of estoppel".[71]

For an outside observer, it seems somewhat surprising that Richardson J believed that the sweeping reasonable expectations approach could be deduced from conventional estoppel doctrine.[72] It will be recalled[73] that there are two main obstacles in the path of an estoppel claim in the family context; first, the unlikelihood of any relevant representation actually having been made and, secondly, the difficulty in proving that the claimant acted to her detriment *in reliance on* such a representation, rather than on the basis of her affection for the defendant or her belief that the relationship would last indefinitely. Obliquely addressing these problems, Richardson J argued, somewhat unconvincingly, that it would not be fatal if the parties had never turned their minds to the question of beneficial interests in family property. He felt that the problem could be surmounted if the court were to "focus on their attitudes to the family property while the relationship enured [*sic*], and for that purpose draw appropriate inferences from the way they led their lives together".[74] Richardson J also stressed the need to recognise that "individual expectations within relationships must be affected by changing attitudes in society".[75] He went on to comment that:

> "Whatever the position in other countries, it seems to me that social attitudes in New Zealand readily lead to expectations, by those within apparently stable and enduring de facto relationships, that family assets are ordinarily shared, not the exclusive property of one or the other, unless it is agreed otherwise or made plain".[76]

Like Cooke P, Richardson J believed that financial contributions should not be accorded special status, commenting that "domestic services may be as significant or more significant than any financial contributions" and that, when it came to determining the nature and quality of the remedy, there was "no presumption that a direct contribution of a monetary nature to particular property is of greater value . . . than any other contribution".[77]

---

[68] *Ibid.* See further text following n 203 *infra.*
[69] *Ibid*, 344.
[70] *Ibid.*
[71] *Ibid.*
[72] See generally Chapter 4 *supra*, Part II(D).
[73] See Chapter 4 *supra*, Part II.
[74] [1989] 2 NZLR 327, 346.
[75] *Ibid*, 347.
[76] *Ibid.*
[77] *Ibid*, 346. The other two judges in *Gillies*, Casey and Bisson JJ, gave shorter concurring

The most recent major Court of Appeal pronouncement on the area is *Lankow* v *Rose*.[78] In direct contrast to *Pasi*[79] and *Gillies*,[80] the claimant in *Lankow* had a very strong case. The relationship had lasted for ten years, during which time she had worked outside the home and contributed her earnings to the household, had undertaken "thousands and thousands of dollars" worth of unpaid work on behalf of her partner's business and had performed the housework. Over the course of the relationship, the defendant had moved from a position of having no net wealth to a net worth of $650,000. The Court of Appeal unanimously upheld the trial judge's view that the claimant was entitled to a half-share in the family home and in certain chattels.

An unusual feature of *Lankow* was the fact that counsel for the defendant, a Mr Gazley, "criticised . . . without moderation"[81] the decision in *Gillies*.[82] The particular focus of counsel's antagonism, Cooke P,[83] retorted that the attack "might have been wounding but for the hyperbole of its language".[84] Nonetheless, perhaps slightly ruffled after all, Cooke P refrained from further comment on the law, leaving it to his colleagues to defend the honour of the "reasonable expectations" approach.[85]

The judgments in *Lankow* demonstrated that, twelve years after *Hayward*,[86] "the exact basis" of New Zealand law was "not yet finally settled".[87] While none of the judges questioned New Zealand's orthodox heterodoxy, which insists that "it is not necessary to choose between the various approaches",[88] Gault J did suggest that, if required to choose, he would be inclined to favour the Canadian unjust enrichment approach.[89] Tipping J, on the other hand,

judgments. Interestingly, in the later case of *Phillips* v *Phillips* [1993] 3 NZLR 159, where constructive trust issues were incidental to the main dispute, Cooke P took the opportunity to undermine Richardson J's estoppel approach. While Cooke P did "not question its potential value", he felt (*ibid*, 168) that it was "an indirect and abstruse way of creating rights" and that "the notion of an implied representation or acquiescence and acting upon it has a fictional quality reminiscent of inferred common intention".

[78] [1995] 1 NZLR 277. See also the subsequent decisions of the Court of Appeal in *Gormack* v *Scott* (1995) 13 FRNZ 43; *McMahon* v *McMahon* [1997] NZFLR 145; *Smyth* v *Tremain* [1998] NZFLR 97. Cf. *Ball* v *Fawcett* [1997] 1 NZLR 743 (Master Faire).

[79] [1986] 1 NZLR 603.

[80] [1989] 2 NZLR 327.

[81] [1995] 1 NZLR 277, 287 per Gault J.

[82] [1989] 2 NZLR 327.

[83] Cf. Gazley "Do I Ultracrepidate?" [1990] *New Zealand Law Journal* 108, criticising Cooke P's extra-judicial contribution "Fairness" (1989) 19 *Victoria University of Wellington Law Review* 421.

[84] [1995] 1 NZLR 277, 280. Cooke P went on to comment (*ibid*) that "[p]hrases such as 'meaningless leguleian judicial activism", although synthetic, have an entertainment quality which robs them of all sting".

[85] Note also Tipping J's response (*ibid*, 297) to counsel's suggestion that the concept of "reasonable expectations" enjoyed "the same lack of substance as proved to be the case with Charles Dickens' *Great Expectations*": "The only relevance of the work of that great author to this case is that it was written at a time when [counsel's] reactionary submissions may have found greater favour".

[86] [1983] NZLR 140.

[87] [1995] 1 NZLR 277, 281 per Hardie Boys J.

[88] *Ibid*, 289 per Gault J.

[89] *Ibid*.

found the prevention of unconscionability to be "the most convincing rationale".[90] Hardie Boys J did not venture a preference, instead stressing how
important it was "that whatever the legal rubric there should be clear criteria for
the imposition of constructive trusts in the area of de facto relationships".[91]
Remarkably, Hardie Boys J appeared to see no connection between the clarifi-
cation of the appropriate "legal rubric" and the establishment of clear criteria
for the granting of a remedy.

Partly because of the absence of Cooke P's voice in *Lankow*,[92] the judgments
in that case may reflect a somewhat different approach from that of the earlier
cases. In this respect, the most important feature of *Lankow* was the restatement
by Tipping J of "the essential conclusions to be derived"[93] from the earlier
Court of Appeal authorities. Tipping J summarised his approach by stating that
a claimant must show:

(1) contributions, direct or indirect, to the property in question;
(2) the expectation of an interest therein;
(3) that such expectation is a reasonable one;
(4) ·that the defendant should reasonably expect to yield the claimant an inter-
     est.[94]

This formulation of the law represents a departure in that it appears to require
an actual expectation of an interest on the part of the claimant. Earlier statements of principle by Cooke P had insisted that it was legitimate to impute to
the claimant the intention which it would have been reasonable for her to have.
On the facts of *Lankow*, the difference was of no practical effect, since the
claimant had testified that she had indeed had an expectation of sharing in her
partner's assets. However, it is clear that the point could be of importance in
other circumstances and, in the analysis which follows later in this chapter, it
will be necessary to explore this issue in detail.

Having traced the development of the doctrine, it is now necessary to attempt
a theoretical analysis of the reasonable expectations approach. It will be convenient to begin with an examination of the requirement of a contribution by the
claimant and its role within the doctrine. The discussion will then move on to
an issue at the heart of the doctrine, the question of "reasonable expectations".
In this context, an attempt will be made to determine whether the judgment of
Tipping J in *Lankow v Rose*[95] is likely seriously to change the course of New
Zealand law in the area. The analysis of the reasonable expectations approach
will then be completed by a consideration of the remedies generated by the
doctrine.

[90] *Ibid*, 294.
[91] *Ibid*, 282. Cf. *Cook v Stark* (1992) 8 FRNZ 419, 427 per McGechan J ("[t]he doctrinal basis is
of fading importance").
[92] [1995] 1 NZLR 277.
[93] *Ibid*, 293.
[94] *Ibid*, 294.
[95] [1995] 1 NZLR 277.

II. THE APPLICATION OF THE "REASONABLE EXPECTATIONS" APPROACH

A. Contributions

It is clear from all formulations of the reasonable expectations approach that it is necessary for the claimant to demonstrate that she has made "contributions". It appears that such contributions perform two related functions within the doctrine: first, they provide the basis for a "reasonable" expectation[96] and, secondly, they provide the further element of unjust enrichment (also conceptualised as detrimental reliance or unconscionability) which triggers the imposition of a constructive trust.

For the most part, the New Zealand courts have been in general agreement on the nature of the contributions which will trigger their doctrine. Clearly acceptable are direct financial contributions to the purchase price of property[97] or to the repayment of mortgage instalments,[98] indirect financial contributions through the payment of family expenses,[99] contributions to improvements,[100] unpaid work for the benefit of the legal owner's business[101] and contributions in the form of child-rearing and domestic labour.[102]

Interestingly, the New Zealand courts have identified one restriction on the range of "qualifying contributions".[103] As Cooke P pointed out in *Gillies* v *Keogh*,[104] the law of constructive trusts is concerned with "contributions to assets".[105] Therefore, as was reiterated by Tipping J in *Lankow* v *Rose*[106] "[a] contribution to the relationship will not qualify unless it is also . . . a contribution to [the property at issue]".[107] In a similar vein, Hardie Boys J insisted in

---

[96] Note the view of Cooke P in *Gillies* [1989] 2 NZLR 327, 332 that "it is difficult to imagine a case in which a reasonable person would expect a benefit without having conferred anything in return". It would also appear that, in *Pettitt* v *Pettitt* [1970] AC 777, both Lord Reid (*ibid*, 795D) and Lord Diplock (*ibid*, 824F) assumed that an agreement or common intention would be imputed only if the claimant had made some form of contribution to the acquisition or improvement of the property.

[97] See e.g. *Phillips* v *Phillips* [1993] 3 NZLR 159 (contribution towards deposit).

[98] See e.g. *Fitness* v *Berridge* (1986) 4 NZFLR 243.

[99] See the facts of *Lankow* v *Rose* [1995] 1 NZLR 277 and the *dicta* of Tipping J *ibid*, 295. See also e.g. *Murray* v *Murray* (1986) 2 FRNZ 134; *Harvey* v *Bindner* (1991) 8 FRNZ 560; *Smyth* v *Tremain* [1998] NZFLR 97.

[100] See e.g. *Hayward* v *Giordani* [1983] NZLR 140; *Oliver* v *Bradley* [1987] 1 NZLR 586; *Gillies* v *Keogh* [1989] 2 NZLR 327; *Cook* v *Stark* (1992) 8 FRNZ 419.

[101] See e.g. *Phillips* v *Phillips* [1993] 3 NZLR 159; *Lankow* v *Rose* [1995] 1 NZLR 277.

[102] See e.g. *Partridge* v *Moller* (1990) 6 FRNZ 147; *Phillips* v *Phillips* [1993] 3 NZLR 159; *Nash* v *Nash* (1994) 12 FRNZ 446 (CA); *Lankow* v *Rose* [1995] 1 NZLR 277. See also *Oliver* v *Bradley* [1987] 1 NZLR 586, 590 per Cooke P; *Gillies* v *Keogh* [1989] 2 NZLR 327, 335 line 6 per Cooke P. Cf. *McMahon* v *Mahon* [1997] NZFLR 145, 150 ("[o]ccasional mowing of the lawns . . . far from adequate").

[103] The phrase is that of Tipping J in *Lankow* [1995] 1 NZLR 277, 295.

[104] [1989] 2 NZLR 327.

[105] *Ibid*, 335. Cf. *Pasi* v *Kamana* [1986] 1 NZLR 603, 608 lines 16–17.

[106] [1995] 1 NZLR 277.

[107] *Ibid*, 294. See also *ibid*, 297–298 per Tipping J.

Lankow that it was dangerous to draw an analogy with New Zealand's Matrimonial Property Act 1976[108] because under that Act "the Court will tend to look to contributions to the marriage partnership; whereas for a constructive trust the Court must look to contributions to assets".[109]

It is somewhat surprising that the New Zealand courts insist that qualifying contributions must be linked to the assets of the defendant. Following modern Canadian decisions,[110] one would have expected that, where the absence of a sufficient link between the contributions and any particular property precluded the imposition of a constructive trust, a monetary remedy would nonetheless have been available.[111] It is possible that the narrowness of the New Zealand approach is an adverse consequence of the project of assimilating all the other Commonwealth doctrines.[112] In order to bolster the argument that the Canadian unjust enrichment doctrine could be fitted under the "reasonable expectations" umbrella, Cooke P drew attention in *Gillies v Keogh* to the use by the Canadian courts of the phrase "reasonable expectations".[113] Since, in Canada, the presence of a "reasonable expectation" of a proprietary interest is a factor pointing to a constructive trust rather than a monetary remedy,[114] the New Zealand courts are led to tie their "reasonable expectations" doctrine exclusively to the constructive trust remedy. This concentration on the proprietary remedy, in turn, leads the New Zealand courts to focus on contributions to specific assets.[115]

Having seen that the New Zealand courts require a link between the contributions of the claimant and the assets of the defendant, it remains to consider

[108] Contrast *Wech v Linnell* (1993) 11 FRNZ 569.

[109] [1995] 1 NZLR 277, 286. Cf. *ibid*, 282 per Hardie Boys J. For an earlier expression of a contrary view, see the judgment of Fisher J in *Cossey v Bach* [1992] 3 NZLR 612, 630–631 ("[t]he sources of jurisdiction relied upon [in *Gillies*] contain no such inherent limitation").

[110] See e.g. *Everson v Rich* (1988) 53 DLR (4th) 470.

[111] It is still possible that New Zealand law will develop in this direction. See text following n 203 *infra*. However, it appears that this type of monetary remedy would be seen as deriving from the general law of restitution rather than the reasonable expectations doctrine. See n 208 *infra*.

[112] Another possible explanation lies in the desire of the New Zealand courts to distinguish the type of contributions relevant under New Zealand's Matrimonial Property Act 1976 (contributions to the relationship) from those relevant under the "reasonable expectations" doctrine (contributions to assets). Cf. text following n 180 *infra*.

[113] [1989] 2 NZLR 327, 332. Cooke P argued (*ibid*) that the comparatively minor role of "reasonable expectations" in Canadian statements of principle was "largely and perhaps entirely a matter of the formal arrangement of the whole proposition". See also n 114 *infra*.

[114] See Chapter 7 *supra*, text following n 232. The term "reasonable expectations" also occurs in Dickson J's famous statement of principle in *Pettkus v Becker* (1980) 117 DLR (3d) 257, 274, which provided that a remedy would be available whenever "a person in a relationship tantamount to spousal prejudices herself in the reasonable expectation of receiving an interest in property". In this context, "reasonable expectation" was really part of a wide formulation of the restitutionary unjust factor of "free acceptance". This appears to be what Cooke P had in mind in *Gillies* [1989] 2 NZLR 327, 332 where (echoing Dickson CJ in *Sorochan v Sorochan* (1986) 29 DLR (4th) 1, 10) he stated that "reasonable expectations" in Canada were treated as "part and parcel" of the requirement of "absence of any juristic reason for the enrichment". Cf. *Peter v Beblow* (1993) 101 DLR (4th) 621, 645g per McLachlin J (in determining whether there was an absence of juristic reason for the enrichment of the defendant, "the fundamental concern is the legitimate expectations of the parties").

[115] See also text following n 203 *infra*.

the strength of the required link. There were two statements of the relevant test in *Lankow*. Tipping J put forward the following view:

> "I would allow as a contribution any payment or service by the claimant which either:
> (1)   of itself assists in the acquisition, improvement or maintenance of the property or its value or
> (2)   by its provision helps the other party acquire, improve or maintain the property or its value".[116]

Hardie Boys J's formulation borrowed more strongly from the language of the Canadian courts. He required "a causal relationship between the contributions and the acquisition, preservation or enhancement of the defendant's assets".[117]

In interpreting the above tests, the Canadian experience is obviously of potential relevance. It will be recalled[118] that the Canadian courts have taken a very generous view of the requisite "causal connection". Thus, they have been willing, for example, to accept that domestic services "seep" into all the assets acquired or improved by the defendant.[119] They have further drained the causal connection requirement of significance by reference to the vague ideas of "maintenance" and "preservation" of the defendant's assets, concepts employed in the formulations of Tipping and Hardie Boys JJ respectively. However, some indication that the New Zealand courts will not be as generous as their Canadian counterparts is to be found in the interesting case of *Nuthall* v *Heslop*.[120]

The facts of *Nuthall*, although unspectacular in themselves, might have been deliberately constructed to test the outermost limits of the remedial constructive trust. The parties cohabited for five years, with the claimant contributing some $15,000 above her share of family and living expenses. However, no new assets were acquired during the relationship nor did the defendant's assets increase in value.[121] The claimant's argument was that she had supported her partner, thus

---

[116] [1995] 1 NZLR 277, 295.

[117] *Ibid*, 282. Interestingly, Hardie Boys J went on to assert (*ibid*) that the contributions need not be "to particular assets" but could be "to the defendant's assets in general". The switch to general assets, rather than the specific property claimed, contrasts with the view of Tipping J (who spoke of contributions to "the property", by which he surely meant "the property claimed"). It is also at odds with *dicta* in previous New Zealand cases (and, it would seem, with the approach of the Court of Appeal in the subsequent case of *McMahon* v *McMahon* [1997] NZFLR 145, 150–151 (see n 203 *infra*)). Hardie Boys J went on to comment (*supra*, 286) that where the contributions are to assets generally, the court should "determine an appropriate award" which "can then be given effect by the imposition of a trust on an appropriate asset". Hardie Boys J did not indicate how (except by resort to a test of "causal connection" with a particular asset) one would select an "appropriate" asset upon which to fix the constructive trust. The approach of Hardie Boys J appears to have been influenced by that of McLachlin J in *Peter* v *Beblow* (1993) 101 DLR (4th) 621. Cf. *ibid*, 638e per Cory J. See further Chapter 7 *supra*, text to and following n 230.

[118] See generally Chapter 7 *supra*, text following n 227.

[119] Cf. the similar view expressed by Gault J in *Nash* v *Nash* (1994) 12 FRNZ 446, 450.

[120] [1995] NZFLR 755, noted by Richardson "Constructive Trusts and 'Contributions'" [1996] *New Zealand Law Journal* 4.

[121] The only exception was that the family home, a cottage owned by a company in which the defendant held preference shares, had increased in value by $3,000. The defendant was willing to pay $2,000 to the claimant in respect of this increase, thus relieving Tipping J of the need to consider whether the increase in value of the cottage had actually increased the value of the defendant's shares.

enabling him to "maintain" his assets. Tipping J rejected the claim, explaining that he had not had this kind of situation in mind when he wrote his judgment in *Lankow*.[122] Although the claimant had helped the defendant to keep his assets intact, this "indirect" maintenance was of a passive rather than an active kind. Tipping J felt that potentially intractable problems could arise if the courts used the constructive trust "to adjust retrospectively the way the parties have chosen to run their domestic finances".[123] He was particularly concerned about the possibility that a male partner who had paid more than his share of the living expenses in a de facto relationship would be able to claim a share in any assets of the economically weaker party upon the termination of the relationship.[124] Tipping J concluded that the matter involved social policy and was therefore one for parliament.[125]

The approach of Tipping J in *Nuthall* suggests that New Zealand law requires a genuine causal link between the claimant's contributions and the acquisition of new assets or the improvement/enhancement of existing assets. It remains to be seen whether other New Zealand judges will take an equally strict view.

B. Reasonable Expectations

Now that the question of "qualifying contributions" has been considered, it is possible to tackle the concept at the heart of the New Zealand jurisprudence, that of "reasonable expectations". Since the case law indicates that it is relevant to consider the reasonable expectations of both parties, it will be helpful to look at the question first from the claimant's perspective and then from that of the defendant.

1. *Reasonable expectations of the claimant*

In considering the question of "reasonable expectations", it is necessary, at the very outset, to confront an ambiguity which recurs throughout this area of the law. A reference to a claimant's "reasonable" expectation may mean either one which was both actually and reasonably held by the claimant or else one which, although not actually held, *would have been* a reasonable one for the claimant

---

[122] [1995] NZFLR 755, 757. Contrast *Sorochan* v *Sorochan* (1986) 29 DLR (4th) 1, 10 per Dickson CJ (claimant succeeded on the basis of a contribution "to the maintenance and preservation of the farm preventing asset deterioration or divestment").

[123] *Ibid*, 759. Tipping J did concede (*ibid*, 761) that there might be "unusual cases" where "by dint of what has been said or understood between the parties, it may be reasonable for one at the end of a relationship to expect a retrospective re-accounting between them".

[124] *Ibid*. Cf. *Novick* v *Miller* (1989) 58 DLR (4th) 185 (Sask CA) (a cohabitee had supported her seriously ill partner for a number of years; upon the death of both parties, the court carried out the sort of retrospective re-accounting to which Tipping J objected in *Nuthall*).

[125] *Ibid*.

to have held.[126] It is beyond doubt that Cooke P, in his seminal judgments in the cases before *Lankow*,[127] envisaged the second, "objective", meaning of "reasonable expectations". This was clear as early as *Hayward v Giordani*,[128] where Cooke J (as he then was) relied on the imputed common intention approach of Lord Reid and Lord Diplock in *Pettitt v Pettitt*.[129] Furthermore, Cooke J went on in *Hayward* to affirm expressly that a trust could arise "even if [the parties] had not applied their minds to the precise question".[130] Cooke P adhered to this position in *Oliver v Bradley*[131] and *Gillies v Keogh*,[132] before strongly reiterating the point in *Phillips v Phillips*:[133]

> "What was and is clear . . . is that [none of the available doctrines] treat the actual intentions formed by the parties as decisive. The latter are sometimes spoken of as "subjective" intentions, an adjective which is strictly superfluous but has value for emphasis".[134]

Cooke P had earlier criticised Richardson J's estoppel approach in *Gillies* "as an indirect and abstruse way of creating rights which a system of law claiming to be based on integrity of principle should be prepared to acknowledge more candidly".[135] However, upon reflection, it is clear that Cooke P's "objective" reasonable expectations approach is itself rather "indirect and abstruse" in the way in which it creates rights.[136] It requires one to determine the expectations of a reasonable person in the shoes of the claimant (on the assumption that such a person would direct her mind to the question). It seems clear that a reasonable person would expect to receive what she was entitled to, no more and no less. And how would she judge the extent of her entitlement? Presumably, not on the basis of any of the private prejudices which even a reasonable person (or judge) may be permitted to harbour but on the basis of contemporary society's attitude to the entitlement of a de facto partner (in her particular circumstances) upon the break-up of her relationship. Thus, by a circuitous route, we come to the proposition that "reasonable expectations" equate with "reasonable entitlements in today's society". However, the use of the phrase "reasonable expectations" allows the court to pretend that the decisive issue is what was expected

---

[126] Cf. Chapter 7 *supra*, text following n 141.
[127] [1995] 1 NZLR 277.
[128] [1983] NZLR 140, 145–146.
[129] [1970] AC 777.
[130] [1983] NZLR 140, 148.
[131] [1987] 1 NZLR 586, 589 lines 9–13.
[132] [1989] 2 NZLR 327, 331 lines 3–4; 333 lines 16–17. The point was perhaps slightly obscured in *Gillies* by Cooke P's misguided attempt (*ibid*, 332–333) to argue on the basis of *Grant v Edwards* [1986] Ch 638 that the English cases also supported his "reasonable expectation and objective test approach". See also Cooke P's comments in *Gillies supra*, 333 lines 21–37.
[133] [1993] 3 NZLR 159.
[134] *Ibid*, 168.
[135] *Ibid*.
[136] Cf. the comment of Atkin *Living Together Without Marriage*, n 26 *supra*, p 99 that "the phantoms of common intention . . . may simply be replaced by the phantoms of reasonable expectation".

by *the claimant* in advance of the separation as opposed to what, after the separation, *the court* thinks the claimant deserves in the circumstances.[137]

Whatever the merits of Cooke P's totally "objective" approach, it is, in any case, by no means clear that the other leading New Zealand judges have always supported it. The distinct approach of Richardson P in *Gillies v Keogh*[138] was the first challenge to the supremacy of Cooke P's doctrinal vision. It appears that Richardson J's attempt to reconcile the "reasonable expectations" doctrine with orthodox estoppel principles required him to insist on the claimant having an actual expectation of an interest in property, albeit an expectation which would readily be inferred in the circumstances of a long-term de facto relationship.[139] More recently in *Lankow*, where Cooke P was uncharacteristically silent, Hardie Boys J (while not adopting a full-scale estoppel approach) endorsed Richardson J's view that an actual intention was required but could easily be inferred.[140]

A more direct challenge to the fully objective approach was mounted by Tipping J in *Lankow*.[141] It will be recalled that Tipping J stated a four-part test for the availability of a remedy.[142] The second requirement was that the claimant have an "expectation of an interest" and the third requirement was that "such expectation [be] a reasonable one".[143] Thus, in the clearest possible terms, Tipping J showed that he was interpreting "reasonable expectations", not in Cooke P's artificial "objective" sense, but rather simply to mean an actual expectation which is also reasonable.

At first glance, one would have thought that there was a substantial divergence between Tipping J's view and that previously expressed by Cooke P, with potentially serious practical implications. Would Tipping J's requirement of a subjective expectation not defeat a large number of claims? Upon further reflection, it becomes clear that, for a number of reasons, Tipping J's divergence from "objectivity", although undoubtedly important, is not quite as radical as it first appears.[144]

---

[137] It will later emerge that the New Zealand courts regard it as reasonable that an unmarried claimant should receive a remedy corresponding to the extent of her contributions. See text to and following n 182 *infra*.

[138] [1989] 2 NZLR 327.

[139] See *ibid*, 346–347 per Richardson J. Cf. n 77 *supra*.

[140] [1995] 1 NZLR 277, 282 lines 38–41. Note, however, Hardie Boys J's earlier use of language with an "objective" flavour (*ibid*, 282: "must be taken reasonably to have expected"). Note also that, in the subsequent Court of Appeal case of *Gormack v Scott* (1995) 13 FRNZ 43, 49, Hardie Boys J referred to the "objective approach that must be taken" when determining reasonable expectations. One of the other judges in *Lankow*, Gault J, appears to have supported Cooke P's "objective" approach (*supra*, 288: "the reasonable expectations of the parties determined objectively"). The final judge, McKay J, agreed fully with the reasoning of Tipping J (which is discussed in the next paragraph of text).

[141] [1995] 1 NZLR 277.

[142] *Ibid*, 294, quoted as text to n 94 *supra*.

[143] *Ibid*.

[144] Cf. Watts "De Facto Relationships" [1994] *New Zealand Recent Law Review* 432: *Lankow* "did not raise any new issue, and there is little new in the judgments". See also Watts "Domestic Relationships and Constructive Trusts" [1990] *New Zealand Recent Law Review* 343, 345 *et seq* (arguing for a continuing role for "implied actual agreement").

The first point to note is that, although Tipping J required an actual expectation on the part of the claimant, it was not necessary (as it would be in England) that this expectation should have been communicated to her partner.[145] Secondly, in determining whether she had this (possibly unilateral and unspoken expectation), it will be necessary to look at all the circumstances of the relationship in the light of social attitudes to cohabitation in New Zealand. As Richardson J pointed out in *Gillies*, "social attitudes in New Zealand readily lead to expectations, by those within apparently stable and enduring de facto relationships, that family assets are ordinarily shared".[146] The point is that a claimant who asserts that she expected a share in her partner's assets is more likely to be telling the truth in New Zealand than in (say) England.[147]

Problems remain in two situations. The first case, presumably very common even in New Zealand,[148] is where the claimant had never directed her mind to property questions. Although a dishonest claimant may be believed if she pretends to have had the requisite expectation, what of the honest claimant who admits that she had no actual expectation? Hardie Boys J in *Lankow*,[149] following Richardson J in *Gillies*[150] on this point, boldly contended that absence of conscious thought did not preclude the inference of an expectation.[151] However, insofar as those judges also contend that the requisite expectation must be an actual one, they are clearly slipping into artificiality at this point. Tipping J, on the other hand, gave no such hostages to fiction. He simply asserted that a constructive trust cannot be imposed in favour of the claimant if "for any reason" she had no expectation of an interest in property.[152] He found in favour of the claimant on the ground that she had "stated quite clearly and directly that she did expect an interest and why that was".[153] It remains unclear what approach Tipping J would take in the (perhaps more usual) case where the claimant had not given conscious thought to property questions.

---

[145] Contrast *Springette v Defoe* [1992] 2 FLR 388, discussed in Chapter 5 *supra*, text to nn 50–54. A further point of departure from the English approach comes in relation to the treatment of the expectations of the defendant. The focus in New Zealand is on what it would have been reasonable for the defendant to have expected, rather than, as in England, on what (on an objective interpretation) the defendant had communicated to the claimant by his conduct. Cf. text following n 161 *infra*.

[146] [1989] 2 NZLR 327, 347.

[147] It is noteworthy that in *Lankow* [1995] 1 NZLR 277, 291 McKay J felt that it would have been "surprising indeed", and Tipping J (*ibid*, 300) that it would have been "extraordinary", if the claimant had not expected an interest on the facts. Note also Hardie Boys J's comment (*ibid*, 283) that "an assertion [of an expectation] is easily made after the event, but in this case it is entirely credible and reasonable".

[148] Cf. *Partridge v Moller* (1990) 6 FRNZ 147, 154 per Tipping J.

[149] [1995] 1 NZLR 277, 282.

[150] [1989] 2 NZLR 327, 346.

[151] Hardie Boys J argued in *Lankow* [1995] 1 NZLR 277, 282 that the inference of a reasonable expectation would follow unless there was some "particular feature" to the case, as in *Gillies* where the defendant had made clear her unwillingness to share the ownership of her property.

[152] *Ibid*, 294.

[153] *Ibid*, 296.

The second problem situation is one where a claimant admits that she did consider the question of property entitlements but that the expectations she formed were lower than they might "reasonably" have been.[154] Such cases might not be all that rare. One may consider the case of a claimant who under-values her own contribution (perhaps because of the dismissive attitude of her partner). Also, as has been explained by Eekalaar,[155] what a person expects may be different from what she feels she deserves. What of a woman who believes she has made a valuable contribution but expects that her selfish partner would leave her with nothing if they broke up?

The cases contain no detailed discussion of the problem of the claimant who admits to modest expectations.[156] However, one judge in *Lankow*,[157] McKay J, did address the converse problem of an expectation which exceeded what was reasonable. He noted that the claimant in *Lankow* had described her expecta-tion as extending beyond a half-share in the family home and chattels to include a payment of $70,000 to reflect her contribution to her partner's business. McKay J took the view that "the test of reasonableness relates to the expecta-tion of an interest in the property, not the extent of the particular interest claimed".[158] McKay argued that, whether or not her particular expectations were reasonable, it was "sufficient that it was reasonable for her to have an expectation of *some* interest in the property in question".[159] It would then be for the court to quantify an "appropriate interest" for the claimant based on the respective contributions. It is arguable that one could apply McKay J's approach to prevent the overly modest claimant from being penalised. However, there is clearly some force in the contrary argument that, in a doctrine based on actual expectations, the expectations of the claimant should form an upper limit on her ultimate entitlement.[160] In any case, McKay J's reasoning

---

[154] This situation is to be distinguished from a *Gillies*-type scenario, where the defendant has made clear to the claimant that she is to gain no interest in the property, thus precluding any rea-sonable expectations to the contrary. (See text following n 161 *infra*). In the situation under discus-sion in the text, the claimant forms a modest expectation without agreeing it with her partner as the basis upon which their relationship proceeds.

[155] "Non-Marital Property", ch. 15 in Birks (ed) *Frontiers of Liability* (Oxford: Oxford University Press, 1994) Vol 2 pp 208–210.

[156] See, however, *Harvey v Bindner* (1991) 8 FRNZ 560 where the claimant admitted that she had been "pleased and touched" by (and had "accepted") a statement by the defendant that she would be entitled to 10 per cent of the disputed property. Despite accepting her evidence concerning this conversation, Barker J ultimately found that the claimant was entitled to a 20 per cent share. Significantly, the defendant had denied that the relevant conversation had ever taken place, thus seriously diminishing his practical chances of relying on it to restrict the extent of the claimant's share. Cf. *Smyth v Tremain* [1998] NZFLR 97 (CA) (claimant conceded that she had had no expec-tation of sharing in defendant's superannuation fund; Tipping J held that, following *Lankow*, this was fatal to her claim to share in this asset).

[157] [1995] 1 NZLR 277.

[158] *Ibid*, 289.

[159] *Ibid*, 290 (emphasis supplied).

[160] Cf. Chapter 4 *supra*, n 104 (the expectation induced in the claimant represents the outermost limit of relief under the principles of estoppel).

would be of no assistance to a claimant who had *no* expectation of benefit whatsoever and would therefore fall at the first hurdle.

In the end, the conclusion appears to be that the requirement of an actual "expectation" is not a helpful one. The problem is that such an expectation will be acceptable even if it is unilaterally held by the claimant and never communicated to her partner. If the claimant alleges that she had such an intention, the only way of testing her claim will be to see if it was reasonable in the circumstances. This suggests that, if one is willing to go as far as the New Zealand courts have gone, it would be cleaner and more honest simply to base one's approach on "objective" reasonable expectations. The alternative approach of Tipping J (if taken seriously) would really punish only the honest claimant who draws attention to her unusually modest expectations.[161]

2. *Reasonable expectations of the defendant*

The final element of Tipping J's formulation in *Lankow*[162] was that "the defendant should reasonably expect to yield the claimant an interest". This suggests that it is necessary to look at "the other side of the coin"[163] and consider matters also from the viewpoint of the defendant. Although this approach reflects *dicta* in earlier cases,[164] it is not easy to see the independent significance of the added requirement. It is clear that the subjective expectations of the defendant will be of no relevance if they are not deemed "reasonable" by the court. As Tipping J explained in *Lankow*, "[i]n that respect the Court stands as his conscience".[165] What is difficult to imagine is a case where the claimant is deemed to have had a reasonable expectation of benefit and yet it is nonetheless deemed reasonable for the defendant to refuse to yield up a benefit. It would appear that the New Zealand courts have created two requirements where only one truly exists.

One possible function for the focus on the defendant's expectations would be to give effect to the *ratio* of *Gillies*, i.e. that there can be no constructive trust where the defendant has made clear to the claimant that he is unwilling to share the property. However, such an express communication will impact on the

---

[161] Of course, even within Cooke P's objective model of "reasonable expectations" it is necessary to confront the potential for divergence between what the court deems reasonable and what a claimant actually expected. However, the convenient solution of simply ignoring the claimant's actual expectations (except where they affect the reasonable expectations of her partner) is more easily adopted in a doctrine which does not highlight actual expectations by making them an essential prerequisite for a remedy. Cf. *Gormack v Scott* (1995) 13 FRNZ 43, 47 per Cooke P; 50 per Hardie Boys J (evidence of an actual *common* intention between the parties is relevant in determining the reasonable expectations of the parties; if such a common intention were expressed with sufficient clarity, it would render unnecessary a consideration of reasonable expectations).

[162] [1995] 1 NZLR 277, 294.

[163] *Gillies* [1989] 2 NZLR 327, 334 per Cooke P.

[164] See *Oliver v Bradley* [1987] 1 NZLR 586, 589 per Cooke P; *Gillies v Keogh* [1989] 2 NZLR 327, 334 per Cooke P; 344 per Richardson J.

[165] [1995] 1 NZLR 277, 294.

reasonableness of the expectations of both parties. Once the defendant has made his position clear, it will no longer be reasonable for the claimant to expect to receive a benefit.[166] Therefore, it would appear that a separate requirement relating to the defendant's expectations is simply otiose. However, despite its logical deficiencies, the requirement under discussion may serve a practical function in drawing attention to the defendant's ability to "contract-out" of any liability to the claimant. It will, therefore, be convenient to discuss this feature of New Zealand law under the present heading.

It will be remembered that in *Gillies* the Court of Appeal had been pleased to introduce "one element of certainty" by holding that a claim would fail if the defendant had made it clear that he intended to retain sole ownership of the home.[167] Interestingly, however, this "element of certainty" has come into question in two later cases.[168]

The first sign of weakness came in *Gibb v MacDonnell*.[169] The defendant, concerned about her financial security, had expressly stated that the disputed house was to be purchased in her sole name to ensure the preservation of her sole proprietary ownership. Thus, the claimant faced "the same impediment as prevented relief . . . in *Gillies v Keogh*".[170] Anderson J pointed out that it would sometimes be possible for a constructive trust to arise despite specific assertions of sole ownership by the defendant. He had in mind "the hypothesis of a de facto union which, with the passage of time and the actual conduct of the parties throughout its span, indicates the arising of reasonable expectations notwithstanding initial assertions".[171] However, Anderson J did not feel that this exception applied on the facts before him. Nonetheless, he concluded that the parties had had "a clear expectation" that the house would be "their permanent home; a place they would share together permanently".[172] Since the claimant had had a reasonable expectation of a *possessory* interest in the property, Anderson J (citing *Gillies* and a number of estoppel authorities) was willing to grant him a remedy.[173]

The second relevant case is *Daly v Gilbert*,[174] where once more the defendant had made clear that she was unwilling to share the ownership of the disputed residential property. Nonetheless, her partner made various contributions in the

---

[166] See *Gillies* [1989] 2 NZLR 327, 340 per Cooke P.

[167] See text to n 56 *supra*.

[168] See also *Harvey v Bindner* (1991) 8 FRNZ 560; *D v A* (1992) 9 FRNZ 43. Cf. the earlier case of *Hopkins v Sturgess* (1988) 4 FRNZ 639 (a number of years into the relationship, the defendant made clear that he planned to leave the disputed property to his sons; Wallace J held that it was not permissible to take into account contributions made by the claimant after that date).

[169] [1992] 3 NZLR 475.

[170] *Ibid*, 479.

[171] *Ibid*. Cf. *Gormack v Scott* (1995) 13 FRNZ 43, 47 per Cooke P; 49 per Hardie Boys J (reasonable expectations may change over the course of a relationship; the court must look to the whole circumstances and history of the relationship).

[172] *Ibid*.

[173] Anderson J (*ibid*, 481) ordered the payment of $15,000 "as if it were equitable damages".

[174] [1993] 3 NZLR 731.

form of labour and materials in respect of the building of the house. He had also, on the occasion of a temporary resumption of their relationship, spent a substantial sum on carpets and curtains for the house. The defendant conceded a liability to recompense the claimant for most of his contribution. However, in relation to the carpets and curtains, she relied on the fact that she had warned her partner that she simply could not afford to pay for them and that he proceeded at his own risk. Hammond J held that, while there had been no "reasonable expectation" of an interest in the property, it was nonetheless possible for the claimant to obtain a monetary remedy under the law of unjust enrichment.[175] He upheld the claim in relation to the building work but not the carpets and curtains.

To sum up, the implication from *Gibb* v *MacDonnell*[176] and *Daly* v *Gilbert*[177] is that, in order to protect his[178] position completely, a defendant must make clear that he will concede neither a proprietary nor a possessory interest in the property nor any monetary or other form of recompense. As was held in *Gillies*, the absence of a reasonable expectation of an interest in the property will preclude the declaration of a constructive trust; however, other doctrines (such as estoppel and unjust enrichment) may provide alternative remedies in some cases.[179]

C. Remedies

The final question to be considered is that of determining the appropriate remedy for the claimant who has satisfied the requirements of the New Zealand

---

[175] Cf. the comment of Gault J in *Lankow* [1995] 1 NZLR 277, 289 that the Canadian unjust enrichment doctrine might be applied in New Zealand "where there has been enrichment even though there was a clear understanding that a proprietary interest in particular property would not be obtained".

[176] [1992] 3 NZLR 475.

[177] [1993] 3 NZLR 731.

[178] Interestingly, the defendants in *Gillies* v *Keogh* [1989] 2 NZLR 327, *Gibb* v *MacDonnell* [1992] 3 NZLR 475 and *Daly* v *Gilbert* [1993] 3 NZLR 731 were all, in fact, female. See also the English case of *Thomas* v *Fuller-Brown* [1988] 1 FLR 237. It is unclear whether the success of female defendants in protecting the beneficial ownership of their property is indicative of a judicial bias in their favour or whether it is explicable on the basis that, because of their greater economic vulnerability in society, women are more likely to take active steps to protect their property entitlements.

[179] One point not addressed in the text is whether (as under the common intention or estoppel analyses) it is necessary that the claimant's contributions have been made *in reliance* on her reasonable expectation of an interest in the disputed property. The point arose in *Lankow* [1995] 1 NZLR 277, where the claimant had admitted in cross-examination that her motivation in acting as she did had been simply to help out her partner rather than to gain an interest in his property. None of the judges in *Lankow* considered this relevant. Hardie Boys J, stressing (*ibid*, 283) that the "constructive trust is not a reward only for the calculating", noted the "essential difference between motive and expectation". According to Hardie Boys J, the claimant's motivation was not inconsistent with the existence of an expectation on her part that she would share in her partner's assets. (Cf. the similar comments of Gault J *ibid*, 287 and Tipping J *ibid*, 296). This approach was not surprising since, as has already been discussed (see text following n 126 *supra*), many New Zealand judges feel entitled to impute to a claimant "reasonable expectations" which she never had. If the expectations are fictional, it would clearly be unreasonable to require the claimant to have acted in reliance upon them.

doctrine. The focus on "reasonable expectations" might suggest the possibility of the courts' exercising a broad remedial discretion. In particular, it might be suggested that it could be reasonable for a claimant in a stable de facto relationship of long duration to expect an equal share in her partner's assets. This suggestion, however, has a practical disadvantage stemming from the particular legislative background in New Zealand. New Zealand's Matrimonial Property Act 1976 operates on the basis of a strong presumption of equal sharing.[180] The nature of New Zealand's matrimonial property regime provides a neat method of distinguishing the judicially-created "reasonable expectations" jurisdiction from the statutory regime. By restricting the de facto claimant's remedy to one which reflects the extent of her contributions, and eschewing any suggestion of creating equality, judges can claim to be exercising restraint and avoiding any trespass on the territory of the legislature.[181]

The concentration on contributions, and the policy-motivated desire to distinguish clearly between de facto and married couples, can be seen from an early stage in the Court of Appeal's treatment of this area of the law. In *Gillies*,[182] Cooke P considered the manner in which the reasonable expectations test had functioned in practice. After a hint of self-congratulation (a recurrent feature in this area of New Zealand law),[183] Cooke P commented that:

> "Awards, when made, have been moderate and less than would be expected in matrimonial property cases. This is appropriate: a de facto union is not to be treated as the full equivalent of marriage".[184]

When this passage was called into question in *Phillips* v *Phillips*,[185] Cooke P went on to affirm that "a de facto union is fundamentally different in the eyes of society and law from a legal marriage". He explained that equal sharing could conceivably result in a de facto case "where the contributions were particularly meritorious".[186] However, "a strong case would be needed to justify the court in going so far".[187] The two main features of Cooke P's approach in *Phillips*, i.e. that de facto couples were not to be treated on the same basis as married

---

[180] Marital property will be shared equally by the spouses except in cases where the marriage is of a short duration or there are other "extraordinary circumstances" which render an equal sharing repugnant to justice (or where the parties have chosen to "contract out" of the legislative regime). Note also the Matrimonial Property Amendment Bill 1998.

[181] See e.g. *Phillips* v *Phillips* [1993] 3 NZLR 159, 171 per Cooke P. This argument would not make sense in a jurisdiction such as England where there is a strong (but by no means exclusive) emphasis on the respective contributions of the spouses in the legislation governing the distribution of property upon the termination of a marriage. See s 25 of the English Matrimonial Causes Act 1973.

[182] [1989] 2 NZLR 327.

[183] *Ibid*, 332 ("the law has been working reasonably well"). Cf. *Phillips* v *Phillips* [1993] 3 NZLR 159, 170 per Cooke P; *Lankow* v *Rose* [1995] 1 NZLR 277, 280 per Cooke P (judges have achieved "workable and wise solutions").

[184] *Ibid*.

[185] [1993] 3 NZLR 159. Counsel had cited *D* v *A* (1992) 9 FRNZ 43, where Doogue J had quoted the above passage from Cooke P in *Gillies* and asked rhetorically: "Why not?".

[186] *Ibid*, 171.

[187] *Ibid*.

couples and that their remedy would depend on contributions, were reiterated explicitly by the Court of Appeal in *Lankow v Rose*[188] and again, for good measure, in the later case of *McMahon v McMahon*.[189] As Hardie Boys J held (in effect) in *Lankow*,[190] the only expectation which a de facto spouse can reasonably hold is that her contributions will be recompensed; an expectation of equality will not be deemed reasonable by the court.

Thus, New Zealand has clearly rejected the High Court of Australia's suggestion in *Baumgartner v Baumgartner*[191] that there should be a presumption of equality in the case of long-term de facto relationships. As Tipping J explained in *Lankow*:

> "In the case of a de facto union, the claimant does not start from a presumptive half-share but rather from nothing. A de facto claimant must demonstrate first a case for an interest and then what that interest should be. The interest must broadly reflect the contributions. Arithmetical precision will generally be unattainable and is in any event not necessary. The Court must, however, do its best to reflect in the assessed shares the value of the claimant's contributions".[192]

Tipping J went on to explain that the "contributions must be judged from a proprietary point of view" and ultimately "the Court must assess as closely as reasonably possible what weight the claimant's contributions have had against the contributions of the defendant in the acquisition, improvement or maintenance of the property or its value".[193] This approach is broadly similar to that favoured by the Canadian courts.[194]

Two areas of uncertainty remain. The first relates to the role of "sacrifice" on the part of a claimant. It will be recalled that in *Gillies*[195] Cooke P had identified the degree of sacrifice on the part of the claimant as a factor ranking alongside "contributions" in deciding "grey area cases". However, in *Lankow*,[196] Tipping J simply assumed that the contributions of the claimant represented "the amount of the unjust enrichment accruing to the defendant which in turn is the amount of the claimant's sacrifice".[197] Accordingly, his approach to quantification concentrated exclusively on contributions. What of the many forms of "sacrifice" (including "other opportunities in life foregone")[198] which do not, in

---

[188] [1995] 1 NZLR 277, 286 per Hardie Boys J; 295 per Tipping J. But see *ibid*, 290 per McKay J.

[189] [1997] NZFLR 145, 150 per Blanchard J.

[190] [1995] 1 NZLR 277, 286.

[191] (1987) 164 CLR 137, 149–150 per Mason CJ, Deane and Wilson JJ.

[192] [1995] 1 NZLR 277, 295.

[193] *Ibid*. Contrast the approach suggested by Fisher J in *Cossey v Bach* [1992] 3 NZLR 612, 632. Cf. the comment of Anderson J in *Hamilton v Jurgens* [1996] NZFLR 350, 358: "Broadly measurable contributions compared with broadly measurable benefits, evaluated in the context of reasonable expectations, tends to synthesise the norms of human behaviour with the imperatives of equity".

[194] See generally Chapter 7 *supra*, Part IV(H).

[195] [1989] 2 NZLR 327, 333–334.

[196] [1995] 1 NZLR 277.

[197] *Ibid*, 295.

[198] See *Gillies* [1989] 2 NZLR 327, 334 per Cooke P. See also *Fleming v Beevers* [1993] NZFLR 13.

themselves, translate directly into an enrichment of the defendant?[199] As the Canadian experience demonstrates,[200] it is unclear how, without artificiality,[201] such estoppel-style "detriment" can be accommodated within an unjust enrichment analysis.[202] It remains to be seen whether the supremely flexible New Zealand approach, with its claim to encompass *inter alia* the principles of estoppel, can cope adequately with a claim based on "detriment" rather than "contributions".[203]

The second uncertainty is whether a purely monetary remedy may be awarded in New Zealand even if the requirements of the "reasonable expectations" doctrine are not satisfied. The picture is clouded by the fact that all judges appear to agree that, once the conditions for a constructive trust are established, there is no difficulty in awarding a monetary payment as a method of "implementing" that trust.[204] What appears to be undecided is whether a monetary remedy can be awarded in a case where no constructive trust can be made out. In *Gillies*,[205] Cooke P appeared to support the possibility of such a remedy, relying on the Canadian authorities and on "what has been decided about equitable compensation in a broader field" in New Zealand.[206] Tipping J did not address this issue directly in *Lankow* but the tone of his judgment perhaps suggests that he would have been opposed to the idea. One of the other judges in *Lankow*, Hardie Boys J, expressly left the question open,[207] while Gault J implied that, since the Canadian doctrine formed part of New Zealand law, the option of a "purely" monetary remedy would be open.[208] The problem, which

---

[199] Cf. *Nuthall v Heslop* [1995] NZFLR 755, 761 (expenditure on improvements which did not translate into increased value).

[200] See Chapter 7 *supra*, text to and following n 189.

[201] See *Cossey v Bach* [1992] 3 NZLR 612, 637 per Fisher J (the claimant had given up her home to move in with her partner, giving an "intangible benefit to [him] in that he presumably wanted her there"). Cf. *ibid*, 631 lines 7–17.

[202] It is possible that the New Zealand courts would simply deal with such a case on the basis of the conventional doctrine of proprietary estoppel: see e.g. *Stratulatos v Stratulatos* [1988] 2 NZLR 424. See also *Gibb v MacDonnell* [1992] 3 NZLR 475 (in view of *Gillies v Keogh* [1989] 2 NZLR 327, absence of express representation regarded as no obstacle to estoppel remedy).

[203] Note the hardening attitude of the Court of Appeal (*per* Blanchard J; Richardson P and Henry J concurring) in *McMahon v McMahon* [1997] NZFLR 145, 150–151: "[I]t is insufficient, when unable to point to the requisite contributions to the property which is the subject matter of a claim, to base a case on hardship or prejudice to the claimant either generally or in relation to other property".

[204] See *Lankow v Rose* [1995] 1 NZLR 277, 294 per Tipping J. This kind of remedy has been awarded in many New Zealand cases. See e.g. *Partridge v Moller* (1990) 6 FRNZ 147; *Nash v Nash* (1994) 12 FRNZ 446.

[205] [1989] 2 NZLR 327, 332. Cf. *Cossey v Bach* [1992] 3 NZLR 612, 631; *Daly v Gilbert* [1993] 3 NZLR 731, 738–740.

[206] Cf. *Day v Mead* [1987] 2 NZLR 443.

[207] [1995] 1 NZLR 277, 282 lines 8–10, lines 49–51.

[208] *Ibid*, 289 lines 14–15, lines 23–24. The tendency in the cases has been to assume that, if such a remedy were available, it would not arise under the reasonable expectations doctrine but under some independent doctrine of unjust enrichment. See *Daly v Gilbert* [1993] 3 NZLR 731, 738–739 per Hammond J. See also text to and following n 174 *supra*.

may eventually force the New Zealand courts to confront the nature of their cause of action,[209] remains to be authoritatively resolved.

III. CONCLUSION

New Zealand's approach suffers from precisely the opposite defects to that taken in Ireland, the other small jurisdiction considered in this book.[210] While the Irish courts have blinkered their vision, ignoring developments in other jurisdictions, the New Zealand judges have voyaged too widely and had their heads turned by the ways of foreign lands. Despite their own avowedly instrumentalist approach,[211] the New Zealand courts have failed to realise that the doctrines developed in England, Canada and Australia also have an instrumentalist rather than a doctrinal basis. Therefore, they are each doctrinally flawed and acceptable (if at all) only because they achieve a degree of justice for vulnerable members of society. A major failing of the New Zealand courts has been to believe all the doctrinal falsehoods, when just one would have achieved the desired result. As a result, one has the absurdity of Gault J's suggestion in *Lankow* that a claimant may formulate a case on any one of (at least) eight separate bases.[212] This contrasts sharply with Cooke P's emphasis in *Phillips*[213] on "the desirability of a simply explainable law".[214] It is as if, wanting to look especially well at a party, a guest arrived wearing all her frocks at once.

On another level, detrimental consequences have followed from the failure to channel intellectual resources (limited in a relatively small jurisdiction) into working out fully the parameters of any one theory. The preceding discussion has identified a number of points of uncertainty[215] which might have been cleared up if a doctrinal basis had been identified and worked through. The greatest degree of uncertainty has been created by the decision in *Lankow*, where an exceptionally aggressive counsel mounted a wide-ranging attack on the "reasonable expectations" doctrine and may have wrought some concessions from Tipping and Hardie Boys JJ. Those judges appear to have added a

---

[209] *Ibid*, 282 lines 7–10 per Hardie Boys J.

[210] See Chapter 3 *supra*.

[211] One advantage of New Zealand's instrumentalist approach is that there is little danger of the broad "reasonable expectations" approach to de facto disputes leading to the "infection" of other areas of law. See *Gillies v Keogh* [1989] 2 NZLR 327, 333 per Cooke P ("a truism that certainty is particularly valued in commercial law").

[212] [1995] 1 NZLR 277, 289 ("contract, express, implied or resulting trusts, common intention, unconscionability, estoppel and unjust enrichment"). Gault J insisted (*ibid*, 288) that each of these approaches was "firmly based in principle". Revealingly, however, the only defence he seemed able to muster for them (*ibid*, 288–289) was that each had been criticised and that none was more vague than any other.

[213] [1993] 3 NZLR 159.

[214] *Ibid*, 168.

[215] Is an actual expectation necessary (see text to and following n 138 *supra*)? What recognition will be accorded to "sacrifice" on the part of the claimant (see text following n 194 *supra*)? Is a purely monetary remedy available (see text following n 203 *supra*)?

requirement of an actual expectation on the part of the claimant and to have focused the quantification of the remedy firmly on the contributions of the claimant. It may be that *Lankow*, coupled with Cooke P's subsequent retirement from the New Zealand courts, will signal a period of mild retrenchment in the future.

In the end, the New Zealand doctrine may be simply too broad and ill-defined to appeal to courts in other jurisdictions. The social climate in New Zealand has produced an approach which (because it purports to combine them all) is potentially wider than any of the others discussed previously in this book. Unfortunately, this sweeping doctrine appears to lack any independent theoretical basis. Nonetheless, the New Zealand case law does provide some interesting lessons on the outermost limits of the remedial constructive trust. Moreover, the concept of "reasonable expectations", although insufficient to carry the full weight of the New Zealand doctrine, does represent a genuine contribution to the theoretical debate in this area.

10

Conclusion

This book has examined the equitable rules governing the property rights of cohabitees in five jurisdictions. This concluding chapter will attempt to draw together a number of themes running through the various doctrines which have featured in the case law. It will also be necessary to consider whether it might be possible, by a process of synthesis, to develop an "ideal" doctrine which could successfully address the difficult problems which arise in this area. It will be seen that it is possible to identify a doctrinal structure which would, in a more straightforward and rational manner, accomplish the results achieved by the existing doctrines. However, such an "ideal doctrine" avoids artificiality primarily because it does not pretend to be founded on legal principles of general application. Instead, it relies on an overt assumption that the special circumstances of an intimate cohabitation justify the application of special rules to ensure the just sharing of the wealth accumulated by the parties. The difficulty is that it is questionable whether it is for the courts, rather than for the legislature, to make such policy judgments. Therefore, the ultimate conclusion of this chapter will be that the better solution would be to proceed by way of legislation (the nature and timing of which would, of course, have to depend on the social and political climate in each individual jurisdiction).

Before proceeding to these wider questions, it will be useful to begin with an attempt to identify, in summary form, the main features of each of the competing doctrines. Instead of concentrating on each doctrine in turn, as did the discussion in the previous chapters, it is proposed now to take a more thematic perspective and to examine the treatment of a number of key issues under the various doctrines. The discussion will be divided into four sections; the first concentrating on the question of "Contributions"; the second dealing with "Intention"; the third section addressing the issue of the "Quantification" of the remedy awarded to the claimant; and the final section attempting an overall assessment of the "Strengths and Weaknesses of Each Doctrine".

I. A THEMATIC SUMMARY OF THE COMPETING DOCTRINES

A. Contributions

1. *Ireland: modified resulting trust*

The Irish position, although in many respects conservative, nonetheless does reflect some degree of development from the absolutely unyielding position at common law from which all the jurisdictions began. As well as contributions to the purchase price of property (always capable of giving rise to a resulting trust), the Irish courts will recognise direct contributions to a mortgage[1] as well as "indirect" contributions to the repayment of a mortgage[2] (through the payment of other household expenses[3] or unpaid work in the legal owner's business[4]). However, this has been the limit of the generosity of the Irish courts. Indirect contributions to a purchase in the form of domestic labour have been rejected as the basis of a resulting or constructive trust,[5] as have contributions towards improvements[6] and other contributions which take place after the acquisition of the disputed property.[7] Claimants relying on the above "excluded" contributions may, in theory, invoke the doctrine of proprietary estoppel (any form of conduct being capable of satisfying the requirement of detriment under that doctrine). However, the development of estoppel theory in Ireland has been slow and this, coupled with the inherent limitations of the estoppel analysis, explains why there has been no successful reliance on estoppel principles in a mainstream family property dispute.[8]

2. *England: common intention analysis*

The English doctrine, because of its close links with estoppel, is theoretically capable of rewarding all forms of contribution. In cases where the common intention is established by direct evidence of the parties' conversations, this flexibility constitutes a clear strength of the doctrine.[9] In other cases, however, the practical impact of this theoretical advantage is severely limited. As will be discussed in due course, the common intention necessary to trigger a remedy will be inferred only from a very narrow range of contributions (direct financial contributions to the purchase price of property or to the repayment of a mortgage representing that price). Therefore, a claimant who relies on e.g. indirect contributions to the repayment of a mortgage will (in the absence of direct evidence of common intention) be left without a remedy.

---

[1] *C v C* [1976] IR 254. Note also that it is treated as immaterial whether the mortgage represents the purchase price of the disputed property: *EN v RN* [1992] 2 IR 116.

[2] *McC v McC* [1986] ILRM 1.

[3] See e.g. *R v R* [1979] ILRM 1.

[4] *EN v RN* [1992] 2 IR 116.

[5] *BL v ML* [1992] 2 IR 77.

[6] *EN v RN* [1992] 2 IR 116.

[7] See *McGill v S* [1979] IR 283.

[8] But see *Re JR (A Ward of Court)* [1993] ILRM 657.

[9] See e.g. *Green v Green* (1989) 17 NSWLR 343, where despite the existence of Australia's radical "unconscionability" doctrine, the court found it expedient to resort to the common intention analysis.

3. *The position in Canada, Australia and New Zealand*

It is convenient to consider together the position under the more radical doctrines developed in Canada ("unjust enrichment"), Australia ("unconscionability") and New Zealand ("reasonable expectations"). All three doctrines take account of a wide range of contributions. As well as direct and indirect financial contributions to the purchase price, recognition has also been accorded to contributions (whether in money or labour) towards the making of improvements to the disputed property. Contributions through domestic labour have clearly been embraced by the Canadian[10] and New Zealand[11] courts. The Australian position on such contributions is less certain but they clearly can be taken into account in at least some circumstances.[12]

A major point of contention in all three jurisdictions has been contributions which cannot be related to the acquisition or improvement of the disputed property. The Canadian courts, who have had the most experience in the matter, appear to have reached a resolution satisfactory to themselves. They have limited the availability of the constructive trust remedy to cases where there was a causal connection between the contribution of the claimant and the acquisition or the "preservation, maintenance or improvement" of the disputed property. This test has been watered down in practice by a willingness to interpret widely the notion of the "preservation or maintenance" of property and to regard domestic contributions as "seeping into" all the assets of the defendant. In cases where even this loose kind of "causal connection" is absent, the Canadian courts have been willing to grant a purely monetary remedy. Neither the Australian nor the New Zealand courts have fully resolved this issue and there is still some doubt as to whether any remedy can flow from contributions unrelated to the acquisition or improvement of the disputed property. Moreover, the decision of Tipping J in *Nuthall v Heslop*[13] suggests that, in determining whether to declare a constructive trust, the New Zealand courts may take more seriously than their Canadian counterparts the concept of the "maintenance or preservation" of the defendant's assets.

A final point relates to sacrifice on the part of the claimant, i.e. conduct which is to her detriment but which does not, strictly speaking, enrich the defendant in any way[14] (or does not enrich him to the full extent of the claimant's detriment).[15] This type of conduct may clearly be relevant as "detriment" under estoppel principles and, under those principles, may provide a remedy in any of the three jurisdictions under discussion (just as it might in England or Ireland).

---

[10] See e.g. *Sorochan v Sorochan* (1986) 29 DLR (4th) 1; *Peter v Beblow* (1993) 101 DLR (4th) 621.
[11] See e.g. *Phillips v Phillips* [1993] 3 NZLR 159; *Lankow v Rose* [1995] 1 NZLR 277.
[12] See *Baumgartner v Baumgartner* (1987) 164 CLR 137.
[13] [1995] NZFLR 755.
[14] A claimant might, for example, give up a secure home in order to live with the defendant.
[15] For example, a claimant might have sacrificed a promising career (and a salary of (say) £1,000 per week) in order to bring up the children of the relationship (a contribution having a market value of (say) only £200 per week).

What is less clear is whether, in the many cases where estoppel will provide no remedy,[16] successful resort can be had to the new doctrines developed in the family situation.

It seems that the Canadian unjust enrichment doctrine, expressly premised on "enrichment" of the defendant, is logically incapable of compensating pure sacrifice on the part of the claimant. However, logic and theoretical purity have not been the strong suits of the Canadian courts in this area and a remedy may sometimes be granted even if the defendant has not actually been enriched.[17] In theory, the Australian unconscionability doctrine operates to return "contributions" made on the basis of the joint venture between the parties. Therefore, there should once more be no room for a remedy in cases where the claimant has made a sacrifice which did not contribute to the wealth of the claimant. The position in New Zealand is unclear. Although in *Gillies* v *Keogh*[18] Cooke P identified "sacrifice" as a relevant factor,[19] the New Zealand courts now appear to be moving towards a position where "contributions to assets" are a prerequisite of a remedy, thus excluding "sacrifice" from the ambit of the reasonable expectations doctrine.[20]

B. Intention

Even where the claimant has established that she has "contributed" to the property of the defendant (or that she has acted to her detriment), it is still necessary to address the problems surrounding the intentions of the parties. Outside the special circumstances of intimate cohabitations, it is clear that the property rights of individuals (who have not committed any form of equitable fraud) are not to be altered without their agreement. The paradigmatic example of the consensual alteration of legal entitlements is by means of a contract agreed between the parties. When one looks at the more traditional doctrines of equity which have been applied in the family context, the purchase money resulting trust and proprietary estoppel, one sees that these doctrines do not radically depart from the "agreement" model. The purchase money resulting trust arose at a time when it was extremely common for property to be held by a nominee "to the use of" its true owner. Where X had contributed to the purchase price of property held at law in the name of Y, equity presumed (realistically, at the time) that it had been agreed between the parties that the beneficial ownership would be shared in the proportions of the contributions. Similarly, the doctrine of estoppel turns on the creation by the defendant of an expectation in the

---

[16] For example, where there has been no representation or where the claimant is shown not to have acted *in reliance* on the representation.

[17] See e.g. *Clarkson* v *McCrossen Estate* (1995) 122 DLR (4th) 239.

[18] [1989] 2 NZLR 327.

[19] *Ibid*, 333–334.

[20] See, in particular, the judgment of Tipping J in *Lankow* v *Rose* [1995] 1 NZLR 277.

claimant that she will share in his property; it can be fitted into the "agreement" model because it operates when the claimant understands reasonably from the defendant's conduct that he agrees that she is to get a share.

The modern doctrines of the five jurisdictions under consideration were developed precisely because the traditional doctrines of equity, with their strict focus on the intentions of the parties, were seen as inadequate to do justice in family property disputes. As will be discussed shortly, these doctrines handle the problem of intention in different ways. However, before continuing the discussion further, it may be helpful to represent the problem in diagrammatic form.

Table 10.1: Range of Possible Intentions in the Family Context

(A) *Intention to share*	(B) *No intention*	(C) *Intention not to share*
(Joint understanding that there will be sharing)	(No understanding one way or the other as to sharing)	(Joint understanding that there will be no sharing)

The above diagram shows, in simplified form, the range of possible intentions in a family property dispute. The focus is on the joint understanding of the parties; in other words, a person's intention is taken to be that which the other party reasonably understands it to be on the basis of the first person's words and conduct.[21] If the parties share the same assumption but have never communicated it to each other (at any level) there is no joint understanding and therefore the case falls within Category B ("No intention") in the above diagram.[22]

It is clear that no difficulty arises in cases falling into Category A (Intention to share). If the claimant acts to her detriment on the basis of the joint understanding that ownership will be shared, a remedy may be available under the doctrine of proprietary estoppel.[23] Therefore, at least in respect of the issue of intention, no extension to the scope of traditional equitable doctrine is needed to cover this first category. Similarly, one would expect to find few problems with Category C (Intention not to share). Here the defendant has communicated to the claimant his unwillingness to share the legal ownership of his property and, if she contributes to that property thereafter, she does so at her peril.[24]

---

[21] See the remarks of Lord Diplock in *Gissing* v *Gissing* [1971] AC 886, 906, quoted in Chapter 5 *supra* as text to n 31.

[22] It is arguable that, in the context of an intimate cohabitation, communication between the parties at a non-verbal level should be sufficient to satisfy the requirements of equity. The opposite view was, however, taken by the English Court of Appeal in *Springette* v *Defoe* [1992] 2 FLR 388.

[23] The remaining obstacle for a claimant is to show that she acted to her detriment in reliance on the joint understanding that property ownership would be shared.

[24] See *Gillies* v *Keogh* [1989] 2 NZLR 327. Of course, it is possible to imagine cases where it might be morally objectionable for a defendant to deny the claimant a share despite making his attitude

Admittedly, as is demonstrated by the New Zealand authorities,[25] there are some additional complexities to consider, e.g. whether the defendant has sufficiently excluded the possibility of providing monetary compensation to the claimant. However, it would appear that all jurisdictions[26] accept the general principle that the defendant's expressing his unwillingness to share should prevent the imposition of a resulting or constructive trust.

The main theoretical battleground is therefore Category B (No intention), where the parties have never discussed (nor possibly ever privately considered) their separate property entitlements. Before the recent doctrinal developments, this apparent "no-man's land" of intention was, in fact, securely occupied by the defendant. In the absence of some reason (generally involving an element of intention) for depriving him of his property rights, the defendant was allowed to enjoy those rights in full. However, each of the new doctrines under discussion uses a distinct strategy to encroach on the "No intention" category and claim some territory for the plaintiff. It will now be useful to review, in turn, the strategies employed by each of the doctrines.

1. *Ireland: extended presumption of resulting trust*

The Irish courts have built on the traditional presumption of resulting trust. This presumption was always raised where a claimant contributed directly to the purchase price of property. As was mentioned earlier, the presumption, in the turbulent times in which it was developed, initially represented a realistic prediction of the likely intention of the contributor. In modern times, however, it is more questionable whether the presumption reflects social reality. Nonetheless, it is firmly entrenched in the law and has provided the Irish courts with a plausible foundation for development. The Irish courts' extension of the presumption to cover direct and indirect contributions to the mortgage could be defended on the basis that the extended presumption is (almost) as likely to represent an accurate prediction of intention as in the traditional case of a direct contribution to the purchase price itself.

2. *England: inference of common intention from conduct*

The English approach, it will be recalled, focuses on whether the claimant has acted to her detriment on the basis of a common intention. To make inroads

clear to her, for example, if he were to gain benefits at the expense of an emotionally weaker partner who was unwilling to risk terminating the relationship. However, unless the problem could be accommodated within a developing doctrine of undue influence/relief against unconscionable bargains (see *Louth* v *Diprose* (1992) 175 CLR 621), it would appear to be beyond the scope of judicial development and to be remediable only by legislation.

[25] *Gibb* v *MacDonnell* [1992] 3 NZLR 475; *Daly* v *Gilbert* [1993] 3 NZLR 731.

[26] With the possible exception of Australia: see *Hibberson* v *George* (1989) 12 Fam LR 725; *Kais* v *Turvey* (1994) 17 Fam 498. There are also some Canadian decisions which (without express discussion) appear to ignore the principle under discussion. See *e.g. Harrison* v *Kalinocha* (1994) 112 DLR (4th) 43. *Cf McC* v *McC* [1986] ILRM 1 (agreement to the contrary prevents resulting trust).

into Category B, where the parties never actually discussed their rights, the English courts have developed a rule that the making of direct contributions to the repayment of a mortgage will entitle the court to infer that there must have been an actual common intention between the parties that ownership would be shared. This rule clearly owes something to the original presumption of resulting trust although the presumption is being applied in a setting far removed from its original doctrinal context. The English courts have, however, been unwilling to recognise other forms of contribution as sufficient to justify the inference of a common intention.

3. *Canada: "reasonable" expectation and unjust enrichment*

In Canada, two distinct strategies have been developed to address the problem of missing intention.[27] The first is by means of the introduction of an "objective" element into the unjust factor of "free acceptance" in the law of restitution. The focus is placed, not on whether the claimant actually expected to be compensated for her efforts, but whether it *would have been* reasonable for her to expect such compensation. This is combined with a similarly "objective" approach to the intentions of the defendant, who is liable if "he knew or ought to have known" of the claimant's imaginary reasonable intention to receive compensation. The emphasis on objectively-determined "reasonable" intention neatly sidelines the problem of missing subjective intention.

The second Canadian strategy is more crude and potentially more damaging to the wider Canadian legal framework. It is simply to rest the entire law of restitution on the principle that, in general, restitution must follow upon an enrichment unless the defendant can establish a juristic reason for his enrichment. In the family property situation, this reversal of the burden of proof leaves the defendant in the unenviable position previously occupied by the plaintiff. Since the parties never formed any intentions, it will not be possible for him to prove affirmatively that his partner intended to make a gift of her services to him. Therefore, restitution must follow. The drawback of this second strategy is that it clearly broadens the general law of restitution, with potentially disastrous results in the commercial context.

4. *Australia: conditional intention*

The Australian approach comes closest to honesty on the question of intention, in that it acknowledges that the situation has been transformed by the unexpected breakdown of the relationship. The Australian "unconscionability" doctrine takes on board, and turns to its advantage, the point that the parties will probably not have contemplated the possibility of a breakdown of their rela-

---

[27] The relationship between these two strategies is not entirely clear. It appears that Cory J leant towards the first in his minority judgment in *Peter* v *Beblow* (1993) 101 DLR (4th) 621, while McLachlin J appeared to favour the second in her majority opinion in the same case.

tionship. The Australian courts use this proposition to discount those intentions which the parties actually have demonstrated, for example by putting or leaving the property in one or other partner's name. The Australian position is that, upon the termination of the relationship, it would be unconscionable for the defendant to retain any benefits which have come into his hands by virtue of that relationship. Thus, the gap in the parties' intentions before the breakdown is rendered irrelevant by the insistence that any such intentions can be ignored because they were conditional on the assumption that the relationship would last indefinitely.

5. *New Zealand: reasonable expectations*

The New Zealand courts have taken a very direct approach to the problem under discussion. They have, at an even more basic level than the Canadian courts, relied on the substitution of objectively-determined "reasonable" expectations for the actual intentions of the parties.[28] The concept of "reasonable expectations" is seen as sufficient in itself to resolve the theoretical problems surrounding intention, without any need to delve in detail into the theory of restitution (or any other area of) law.[29]

C. Quantification of the Remedy

It is next necessary to consider the respective treatments of the question of quantifying the remedy ultimately granted to the claimant under each of the doctrines.

1. *Ireland: a share based on contributions to the purchase*

As a result of the Irish courts' reliance on the traditional resulting trust, the remedy available will generally take the form of a trust reflecting the proportion of the purchase price represented by the claimant's contribution. However, in the context of contributions to mortgage instalments, the Irish courts have achieved

---

[28] The judgment of Tipping J in the leading case of *Lankow* v *Rose* [1995] 1 NZLR 277 appears to suggest a more subjective approach, requiring the existence of an actual expectation on the part of the claimant. However, it does not seem necessary that this expectation have been communicated to the defendant, so that the New Zealand doctrine would still cover at least part of Category B ("No intention").

[29] Probably because of the existence of the overlapping "common intention" analysis, there has been little attempt to overcome the problem of "missing intention" in the context of estoppel. It has already been pointed out that estoppel may be applicable in cases falling into Category A (joint understanding of sharing, communicated between the parties). See text to n 23 *supra*. However, it is possible to imagine an expanded form of estoppel which would afford a remedy on the basis of an expectation generated by the relationship between the parties notwithstanding the absence of any representation on the part of the defendant. See the discussion in Chapter 4 *supra*, Part II(D).

a somewhat more generous position by virtue of an idiosyncratic approach to the mathematics of the question.

2. *England: the share commonly intended*

Whatever compensation there is for the overly complex nature of the English approach comes at the point of quantifying the claimant's remedy. The English courts regard themselves as entitled to award the share which was commonly intended. Although in practice the award will sometimes simply reflect the contributions,[30] there have been a number of leading cases where a half-share has been awarded on the basis of lesser contributions.[31] Thus, it is clear that the English approach generates results which are sometimes more generous than the Irish approach and, occasionally (it seems), more generous even than under the Commonwealth doctrines.[32]

3. *Canada: restitution in a loose sense*

The Canadian approach is founded on the law of restitution and, therefore, one would expect that a successful claimant would be entitled merely to restitution of the amount by which the defendant had been enriched at her expense. However, the Canadian courts have been willing to go much further than this and to allow the claimant to share in the increased wealth of the defendant. This is achieved by imposing a constructive trust over specific real property on the basis that there has been a "causal connection" between the claimant's contribution and the "acquisition" or the "preservation, improvement or maintenance" of the disputed property. Given the tendency of real property to increase in value over the course of a relationship, the imposition of a constructive trust allows the claimant to extract from the defendant far more than the amount by which, under strict restitution theory, he was enriched.

Unlike the Irish and English doctrines discussed above, the Canadian unjust enrichment doctrine allows for the award of a purely monetary remedy in cases where the requirements for the imposition of a constructive trust are not satisfied.

---

[30] See e.g. *Passee v Passee* [1988] 1 FLR 263.

[31] *Grant v Edwards* [1986] 1 Ch 638; *Midland Bank plc v Cooke* [1995] 4 All ER 562.

[32] In at least some of the relevant English cases, it is arguable that the court simply took into account contributions falling outside the narrow band from which a common intention can be inferred in England. Thus, in *Midland Bank plc v Cooke* [1995] 4 All ER 562, where the claimant was awarded a one-half share despite having made a financial contribution of only 6.74 per cent of the purchase price, she had worked in the home for many years and quite probably would have received a comparable share in, say, Canada. On the other hand, in *Grant v Edwards* [1986] 1 Ch 638 it does seem that the share commonly intended went beyond the extent of the claimant's contributions (however broadly defined).

4. *Australia: return of contributions*

Under the Australian doctrine, the claimant's remedy is expressed to be the return of benefits unconscionably retained by the defendant after the termination of the relationship. Although one might have expected the remedy to be limited to the value of the claimant's contributions, the Australian courts (like their Canadian counterparts) have been willing to "return" to the claimant the share of the defendant's wealth represented by her contributions. The High Court of Australia went further in *Baumgartner* v *Baumgartner*[33] and suggested that a presumption of equality arises in the circumstances of a long-term de facto relationship.[34] However, this presumption was said to give way to evidence that the contributions had been unequal and, therefore, may rarely be of decisive effect.

There have been a number of Australian cases where the court did not impose a constructive trust but instead ordered a monetary payment to the claimant. It is not entirely clear whether such a payment was simply a convenient method of giving effect to an underlying constructive trust or whether, as in Canada, a monetary remedy is an independent remedial option.

5. *New Zealand: a remedy based on contributions*

The position in New Zealand is similar to that in Canada. Provided that there has been a "causal connection" with the disputed property, the court will impose a constructive trust calculated by reference to the respective contributions of the parties. The New Zealand courts have strongly repudiated the Australian notion of a presumption of equality and insist that the remedy must correspond to the extent of the claimant's contributions to the disputed asset. The New Zealand courts have expressly reserved their position on the question of the availability of a "purely" monetary remedy in cases where the requirements for a constructive trust have not been satisfied.

6. *Estoppel*

The better view appears to be that, under an estoppel analysis, the remedy will generally reflect the detriment suffered by the claimant.[35] In a family property dispute, this may be co-extensive with the extent of her contributions to the disputed property. However, it may also include other sacrifices unrelated to that property. The Court has a wide discretion in fixing the appropriate remedy, equity being "at its most flexible" in the context of "satisfying the equity" which has arisen in favour of the claimant. Therefore, although the imposition of a

---

[33] (1987) 164 CLR 137.

[34] *Ibid*, 149–150 per Mason CJ, Deane and Wilson JJ.

[35] The competing view, which still has a strong body of support, is that the remedy should fulfil the expectation induced in the claimant.

constructive trust is one possibility, the court may well prefer to order a monetary payment or other remedy.

D. Strengths and Weaknesses of Each Doctrine

This final section of the thematic summary of the doctrines looks briefly at each doctrine and attempts to identify its strengths and weaknesses from both a practical and a theoretical perspective.

1. *Ireland*

The Irish approach involves little in the way of elaborate theoretical footwork. In essence, there have been two developments: (1) the extension of the purchase money resulting trust to cover contributions to mortgage instalments and (2) the further step of recognising "indirect" financial contributions to mortgage instalments. To justify the latter step, the Irish courts have made reference to "the family pool". It will later be argued that the "pooling" concept (a concept not, of course, unique to Irish law) may have an important contribution to make to the general theory of this area of law.[36]

The primary weakness of the Irish approach is the limited nature of the contributions it recognises. It excludes *inter alia* contributions in the form of domestic labour and contributions to improvements. As well as limiting the practical prospects of claimants, the preferential treatment of one type of contribution (financial contributions to a purchase) creates problems of inconsistency at a theoretical level. For example, there appears to be no defence for Irish law's willingness to reward unpaid work in the legal owner's business, while ignoring unpaid domestic labour.

2. *England*

The common intention analysis has very little to recommend it. From a claimant's point of view, the one advantage is the possibility that she might gain a remedy beyond that indicated by her contributions.[37] However, the theoretical price is simply too high. The doctrine involves an unjustifiable scrambling of a number of distinct doctrines (resulting trust, proprietary estoppel, doctrine in *Rochefoucauld* v *Boustead*[38]) and therefore has created confusion across a wide swathe of the law of equity. Unfortunately, the contagion of the common intention analysis has been passed on to Canada, Australia and New Zealand (but not, it seems, to Ireland). Its inadequacies may well have skewed the development of the law in those jurisdictions, making even dubious doctrinal develop-

---

[36] See text following n 47 *infra*.
[37] See text to n 31 *supra*.
[38] [1897] 1 Ch 196.

ments appear plausible in comparison. One can only hope that the common intention trust suffers a speedy demise. This prospect is perhaps more likely in jurisdictions outside England, although it is not impossible that the Law Commission might recommend its abolition as a first step towards the reform of the law of home-sharing.[39]

3. *Canada*

By way of contrast with the Irish and English positions, the Canadian unjust enrichment doctrine provides a remedy in a wide range of situations. One major limitation is its inability to take account of sacrifice on the part of the claimant which, although contributing to the relationship, does not actually enrich the defendant.[40]

From a theoretical point of view, there are many problems with the Canadian approach. As has been pointed out already, it relies either on an extremely expansive version of the already questionable unjust factor of "free acceptance" or on a general principle that all enrichment must be reversed unless it occurs because of some identifiable juristic reason. Both explanations, but in particular the second, leave open the possibility of other areas of law being destabilised by rules which are really only designed to operate in the family context.

Leaving aside this point, the Canadian doctrine generates its results in a rather contorted fashion. The focus is purportedly on the enrichment of the defendant at the expense of the claimant. However, in order to find that there has been a net enrichment of the defendant[41] it is necessary, in many cases, to gloss over the question of countervailing benefits (e.g. accommodation and financial support) which pass from the defendant back to the claimant. Once the enrichment has been determined in this artificially inflated manner, it is then transformed into a proprietary remedy by reference to the existence of a "causal connection" with the disputed property.[42] Unfortunately, no satisfactory explanation is offered for the functioning of this convenient concept of "causal connection". Ultimately, then, the underlying problem with the Canadian analysis is that, in theory, it is concerned with reversing unjust enrichment but, in practice, it operates to share between the parties the wealth generated by the relationship.

4. *Australia*

In some ways, the Australian analysis is the most promising yet developed. It focuses usefully on the unexpected breakdown in the intimate relationship

---

[39] See *Sixth Programme of Law Reform*, Law Com 234 (London: HMSO, 1995) Item 8.

[40] See, however, text to n 17 *supra*.

[41] But see the more complex approach suggested in *Pickelein* v *Gillmore* (1997) 27 RFL (4th) 51 (BC CA).

[42] Or sometimes on the basis that the claimant had a "reasonable expectation" of proprietary relief. See *Sorochan* v *Sorochan* (1986) 29 DLR (4th) 1, 12 per Dickson CJ.

between the parties, the factor which is at the heart of the commonly held intuition that a claimant in these cases should be entitled to some remedy for her contributions. The difficulty with the Australian doctrine is that the legal materials upon which it is purportedly founded, those considered by Deane J in *Muschinski* v *Dodds*,[43] simply do not provide adequate support for it. Beyond this, there is the problem that it is said to be based on the analogy with a joint venture which fails prematurely, thus creating confusion in cases where the relationship ends "naturally" upon the eventual death of one of the parties. Moreover, the stated basis for the doctrine (the return of contributions upon the failure of the joint venture) is at odds with the results actually generated by the doctrine (the sharing of the wealth generated by the relationship). As will be argued in more detail shortly, it would probably be more satisfactory to base the doctrine on an analogy with a joint venture which *succeeds*, thus providing a logical justification for allowing the parties to share in the fruits of that venture in the proportion of their contributions to its success.[44]

5. New Zealand

New Zealand's reasonable expectations doctrine appears to be close in scope to the Canadian unjust enrichment doctrine, with the difference that the New Zealand courts have not yet resolved the question of the availability of purely monetary relief. Unfortunately, the New Zealand judges have failed to clarify the doctrinal basis of their analysis, thus severely damaging its credibility as an option to be imitated elsewhere.

6. Estoppel

Finally, it is necessary to comment on the principles of estoppel. These principles are extremely flexible and allow the court to take account of all forms of relevant conduct and to respond in whatever way seems appropriate. Unfortunately, there are two major limitations on the practical utility of estoppel in the family context.

The first problem is that of showing that the defendant represented to the claimant that she would be entitled to an interest in the disputed property. The second is in showing that the actions of the claimant were undertaken in reliance on the representation and not merely on the basis of her love for her partner or her assumption that the relationship would subsist indefinitely. Although future developments may conceivably reduce the significance of these two problems, for the moment the doctrine of estoppel will not often be capable of providing a remedy in the type of case under discussion.

---

[43] (1985) 160 CLR 583.

[44] However, there appears to be no way of defending the "presumption of equality" put forward in *Baumgartner* (1987) 164 CLR 137, 149–150 and this presumption should simply be dropped.

II. WHAT IS THE BEST WAY FORWARD?

When one comes to discuss the possible future development of the law, it is obviously necessary to take into account the differing positions from which the various jurisdictions start. England and Ireland begin from a relatively conservative position. The question in relation to these jurisdictions is whether it would be appropriate to adopt one of the radical Commonwealth doctrines (or some variation thereon). In the three Commonwealth jurisdictions, however, the toothpaste is already out of the tube and it is difficult to imagine a return to the conservative position of England or Ireland. The more realistic question in relation to Canada, Australia and New Zealand is whether it is possible to devise some more satisfactory theoretical foundation for the broad powers which the courts have created for themselves.

In order to answer the two questions identified in the previous paragraph it is necessary to form some judgment as to the credibility of the Commonwealth doctrines. As emerges from the preceding summary of the main features of the competing doctrines, each of them leaves a lot to be desired. The problem is not only the absence of a firm theoretical basis for any of the doctrines but also the fact that they do not make the most of the doctrinal licence they have taken. This suggests the following preliminary conclusions: first, that the English and Irish courts should not adopt any of the Commonwealth doctrines in their existing form and, second, that it would not be unreasonable for the courts of Canada, Australia and New Zealand to consider alternative theoretical possibilities which might better explain the broad jurisdiction they have become accustomed to exercising.

Consequent upon the preceding conclusions, it is now proposed to attempt a synthesis of the ideas underlying doctrines developed in Canada, Australia and New Zealand. The aim will be to develop an "ideal" version of the Commonwealth doctrines which will share their broad scope but, unlike them, will at least be founded on a principle consistent with the results it generates. It should be stressed that no attempt is being made at this point to suggest that even this "ideal" doctrine is necessarily acceptable.[45] The idea is simply that the identification of an "ideal" doctrine, stripped of the arbitrary weaknesses and internal contradictions of the existing versions of the remedial constructive trust, will allow for a more straightforward assessment of the merits and demerits of a solution broadly along the lines explored in Canada, Australia and New Zealand.

---

[45] Therefore, in the present context, the word "ideal" should not be understood in the sense of "a conception of something which is perfect". What is intended is more an "ideal construction", a phrase which connotes "a mental conception formed by abstracting properties found in experience and recombining or developing them". See *Oxford English Dictionary*, 2nd edn (Oxford: Clarendon Press, 1989) Vol VII p 615.

A. An Ideal Synthesis of the Commonwealth Doctrines

Looking to the substance of the Commonwealth doctrines, leaving aside minor variations across the jurisdictions, it would appear that they operate like a glorified version of the traditional purchase money resulting trust. They look to the parties' respective contributions to the wealth which has been generated by the relationship and award the claimant a share proportionate to her contribution. One obvious difference from the traditional purchase money resulting trust is that the "super resulting trust" is not concerned merely with financial contributions to the *purchase* of property; rather, it is concerned with the accumulation of wealth through the acquisition[46] of new assets and the improvement of existing ones. Another difference lies in the nature of the contributions which can be taken into account; a broad view is taken which recognises all forms of contribution to the ability of the family to generate wealth. This means that there is no difficulty in taking account of domestic labour nor should there be any problem with giving credit for sacrifice which one party has had to undergo for the benefit of the relationship.

In order to rationalise the "super resulting trust", it is clearly insufficient to invoke the concept of unjust enrichment (as in Canada) or of returning contributions (as in Australia).[47] Instead, one must have resort to the concept of "pooling". This idea already plays a significant role in the modern Australian and Irish doctrines. Unfortunately, the precise function of the concept has been inadequately explained in the Australian case law. Therefore, it may be more useful to examine the concept of "pooling" in the context of the Irish doctrine. Consider the following simplified example:

> Jack and Jill have lived together for a number of years in a stable relationship. The family home is held in the sole name of Jack. It is subject to a mortgage which is paid every month from Jack's bank account. Every month, Jack pays 75 per cent of the family expenses (which expenses are taken here to include the mortgage) and Jill contributes 25 per cent.

If one approaches this problem from an unjust enrichment point of view, it may not be possible to see why Jill should get any remedy. She has contributed less than Jack and (although this does not inevitably follow) she may well have received more in terms of benefits (e.g. accommodation and food) than she has transferred to Jack. However, under the Irish approach, which postulates the existence of a "family pool", Jill is permitted to share in the ownership of the family home which is being acquired over the period of time in which she is making her contribution. Her contribution to the family purse represents 25 per

---

[46] The word "acquisition" conceals an important ambiguity; it can mean either a resulting trust-style purchase of property or, in the much broader sense in which it is used in the text to this footnote, it can refer to the accumulation of money and other assets, not necessarily by means of a purchase.

[47] New Zealand's concept of "reasonable expectations" is simply uninformative.

cent of the total and therefore she is entitled to credit for 25 per cent of the mortgage instalments paid over the time she has contributed.

What is presently being advocated is to transplant this pooling logic to a wider setting. It is necessary to shed the limitations of the Irish approach and to take into account all forms of contributions and all forms of wealth accumulation. One may then consider a situation where a claimant has contributed one-quarter of the total input into the relationship (in terms of all forms of contributions and sacrifices[48] made for the benefit of the relationship). The argument is that, since she has contributed to this extent to the relationship, she should share in the same proportion in the economic fruits of the relationship. Therefore, she should be entitled to one-quarter of the assets accumulated by the partners during the course of the relationship.

It is clear that this approach involves treating an intimate cohabitation as, in effect, an economic partnership.[49] Obviously, there is a clear departure from traditional legal reasoning in this willingness to afford a special status to a social relationship other than marriage. However, the ideal model which is being put forward in this section goes no further than the existing Australian model, which, it will be recalled, relies on an analogy between a personal relationship and a commercial joint venture. The model presently being advanced really only attempts to apply the analogy in a more helpful manner; instead of focusing the analogy, as the Australian courts do, on "a joint venture which prematurely fails", the suggestion is to look to "a joint venture which succeeds". This revised analogy better explains the results generated in the case law of Australia and, indeed, is also capable of explaining the case law of Canada and New Zealand (where, of course, different rationalisations have been advanced).

It should finally be noted that, under an ideal doctrine which turns on the notion of economic partnership, it must be possible for the defendant to show that the parties did not, in fact, regard themselves as partners in the required sense. This is, of course, the familiar issue of "contracting out" of the judicial property regime. The ideal doctrine would require the courts to consider evidence of statements and other conduct of the parties which showed that their relationship did not fall within the paradigm of an economic partnership. The

---

[48] Although the status of "sacrifice" is somewhat uncertain under the existing doctrines (see text to and following n 14 *supra*), there appears to be no logical justification for treating it on a different footing to "contributions".

[49] Some commentators have argued that the partners to a cohabitation may be treated as standing in a fiduciary relationship to one another. See Gardner "Rethinking Family Property" (1993) 109 LQR 263, 286–289; Morris "Equity's Reaction to Modern Domestic Relationships", ch. 12 in Oakley (ed) *Trends in Contemporary Trust Law* (Oxford: Clarendon Press, 1996) pp 312–313. However, it is questionable whether important theoretical problems can be solved by what Lord Browne-Wilkinson once described as "the reach me down a fiduciary syndrome" ("Equity in a Fast Changing World", an address by his Lordship to the New Zealand Law Conference on 10 April 1996; see (1996) 70 *Australian Law Journal* 674). Given the general uncertainty surrounding the concept of "fiduciary" in our law, it would probably be best not to rely on it in the present context. Cf. *Re Goldcorp Exchange Ltd* [1995] 1 AC 74, 98 per Lord Mustill; Birks "Equity in the Modern Law: An Exercise in Taxonomy" (1996) 26 *Western Australian Law Review* 1, 17–18.

New Zealand cases, in particular, provide useful guidance as to the circumstances where one party has sufficiently communicated to the other an unwillingness to share his assets. Under the ideal doctrine, as under the presently existing Commonwealth doctrines, the burden of proof would lie on the defendant[50] to show that he has made the position clear.[51] Although the Australian and Canadian cases have not always done so, it would also be important to give due weight to the manner in which the parties have chosen to regulate their financial affairs. Therefore, for example, in the absence of any other convincing explanation, the presumption of an intention to share ownership could be displaced by the fact that a house purchased during the relationship was conveyed into the sole name of one of the partners.[52]

B. Disadvantages of the Ideal Doctrine

Having completed the preliminary step of identifying an ideal doctrine, it is now necessary to discuss the potential disadvantages of the adoption of such an approach.

1. *The problem of uncertainty*

It is first necessary to consider one of the traditional objections to judicial activism in this area of the law, that of uncertainty. The requirement of certainty was always strongly emphasised by opponents of Lord Denning's various discretionary doctrines. Interestingly, however, it seems that uncertainty may not be such a problem with the ideal doctrine discussed above. While Lord Denning perpetrated isolated outrages against the established order, the ideal doctrine involves far more revolutionary changes. Paradoxically, it seems that the broader the doctrine the less the uncertainty.

Imagine, for the sake of argument, a doctrine which gave a cohabitee the automatic right to share equally in her partner's assets in all cases, irrespective of her contributions. Such a doctrine could be criticised on a number of grounds but it could surely not be said to be uncertain. In any given case, it will be comparatively easy to predict the result in advance. Although the ideal doctrine is a very different proposition to the extreme approach considered above, its broad approach eliminates many possible points of uncertainty; all contributions to the relationship, including work in the home and contributions which take the form of a sacrifice, are clearly recognised as capable of generating a share. The

---

[50] This assumes that the court has, at a prior stage in the inquiry, determined that their relationship was of such a nature as to trigger the presumption of economic partnership. See text to and following n 53 *infra*.

[51] Cf. n 24 *supra*.

[52] Contrast the approach of the Court of Appeal of New South Wales in *Hibberson v George* (1989) 12 Fam LR 725.

share awarded will always reflect the proportion borne by the claimant's contribution to the total contributions to the relationship. It seems from the existing Commonwealth cases that, except in relation to one issue, unpredictability would not be a major problem with the new doctrine.

The problematic issue[53] relates to the nature of the relationship necessary to trigger the doctrine. This issue has not been much ventilated in the Commonwealth cases. This is partly because, except in Australia, the existing doctrines do not explicitly identify as central the relationship between the parties. However, the reported decisions seem to suggest that it is not very difficult to determine whether a given relationship should be categorised as an economic partnership. A (perhaps too glib) explanation might be that the type of contributions and sacrifices necessary to trigger a remedy are unlikely to have been made except in the context of an intimate relationship in which the parties have intertwined their economic fortunes. Nonetheless, there will be cases,[54] where the relatively short and casual cohabitation between the parties seems to fall outside the paradigm of an economic partnership. It would appear that the courts would have to deal with this issue on a case by case basis, examining carefully the parties' commitment to the relationship and the degree to which they have neglected to protect their separate property interests on the basis of the relationship.[55]

2. *Effect on the rights of married couples*

The second problem to be considered is the effect of an expansive doctrine of "economic partnership" on the position of married couples. The difficulty is that the legislature in each of the countries under discussion has regulated the property rights of married couples upon the termination of their relationship. It would clearly be unfortunate if this legislative choice were undermined by a judicially-created doctrine designed to deal with a different social problem. Already, this issue has arisen in the Australian[56] and Canadian[57] cases.[58] However, upon further reflection, it appears that this problem may not be insurmountable. Unlike in Ontario, for example, where the matrimonial regime

---

[53] Admittedly, some degree of uncertainty may also surround the concept of a sacrifice made for the benefit of the relationship. However, the issues raised here are really identical to those arising under the well-established doctrine of proprietary estoppel and, therefore, should not be sufficient to disqualify the ideal doctrine from acceptance.

[54] See e.g. *Crick* v *Ludwig* (1994) 117 DLR (4th) 228 (BC CA).

[55] Cf. Rotherham "The Contribution Interest in Quasi-Matrimonial Property Disputes" (1991) 4 *Canterbury Law Rev* 407, 424–425. As will be argued at a later stage (see text to and following n 70 *infra*), this whole question could more easily be addressed in the context of a legislative solution to the overall problem.

[56] See *Bryson* v *Bryant* (1992) 29 NSWLR 188.

[57] See *Rawluk* v *Rawluk* (1990) 65 DLR (4th) 161.

[58] But not, however, in New Zealand due to the fact that the relevant legislation (the Matrimonial Property Act 1976) operates as an exclusive code and precludes the application of the equitable rules to the marital situation.

proceeds on the basis of a principle of "equalization" of property entitlements (which operates independently of the respective contributions to the relationship),[59] the matrimonial legislation in England, Ireland and Australia already turns largely on the respective contributions and sacrifices.[60] Thus, it does not seem likely that a spouse in these countries could get a better settlement by relying on the principles of equity and, in any case, if he or she could, the other spouse could presumably make an application under the relevant matrimonial property legislation and have the property re-distributed, this time on the basis of the statutory criteria. Obviously, as the Canadian experience has shown, the problem is greater in jurisdictions which rely on an equalisation of matrimonial property. However, such jurisdictions could simply follow the lead of New Zealand[61] and include in their matrimonial legislation a specific provision restricting the extent to which the statutory regime could be affected by the operation of equitable doctrines.

3. *The rights of third parties*

Another problem relates to the rights of third parties. Obviously, a broad doctrine of economic partnership could impact on the rights of third parties such as banks and other creditors. However, a possible solution to this problem has been signalled in the Australian case law. As Deane J suggested in *Muschinski* v *Dodds*,[62] it is possible for the court to exercise control over the extent to which a proprietary remedy afforded to a claimant will be allowed to impact upon the rights of third parties. Although this suggestion has not been given much consideration in subsequent Australian cases, it would appear to offer a method whereby the rights of third parties could be adequately protected. Although Deane J may have intended the court to exercise a discretion on the facts of each case, there is much to be said for the simple proposition that a remedy under the ideal doctrine should *never* give the claimant priority over the general creditors of the defendant.[63] If a couple choose, for reasons internal to their relationship, to allow the ownership of their property to rest in the hands of one partner, why should they not take the consequences of this arrangement upon the bankruptcy of the legally-owning partner? After all, if the non-legally owning partner had

---

[59] See Ontario's Family Law Act (RSO 1990, c F-3), ss 4–5.

[60] Difficulty has been caused in Australia by a quirk in the "unconscionability" doctrine, i.e. the presumption of equality favoured by the High Court of Australia in *Baumgartner* v *Baumgartner* (1987) 164 CLR 137. The result has been that a more favourable result (equality) might be obtained under the unconscionability doctrine than would prevail under the matrimonial regime. However, since the presumption of equality is indefensible as a matter of principle, it finds no place in the "ideal" doctrine discussed in this chapter. Therefore, the problem presently experienced in Australia is no impediment to the adoption of the ideal doctrine.

[61] See n 58 *supra*.

[62] (1985) 160 CLR 583, 615.

[63] Cf. Gardner, n 49 *supra*, 298 n 141. Contrast the position of Paccioco "The Remedial Constructive Trust: A Principled Basis for Priority Over Creditors" (1989) 68 *Canadian Bar Review* 315. See also *Fortex Group Ltd* v *McIntosh* [1998] 3 NZLR 171, 175 line 35—176 line 44 per Gault, Keith and Tipping JJ.

become bankrupt during the course of the relationship, her creditors would have had little chance of gaining access to the assets in her partner's hands.[64]

4. *The problem of legitimacy*

The next problem is a fundamental one. It has thus far been tacitly assumed that it would be a legitimate enterprise for the courts to seek a "just" solution to the social problem posed by the breakdown of unmarried cohabitations. However, very serious issues arise in relation to the entitlement of unelected judges to make law in this area. It could plausibly be argued that the legislative role of judges should be "interstitial" in nature, involving the filling of (comparatively minor) gaps in the legislative structure of things.[65] The creation of a regime allowing for the adjustment of property between unmarried couples could be seen as going well beyond the legitimate function of judges. A number of Australian jurisdictions have already introduced legislation permitting the adjustment of the property entitlements of cohabitees. New Zealand is on the point of introducing similar legislation.[66] It is difficult to see why, if social and political conditions were favourable, the legislatures of other jurisdictions could not follow suit. If, however, there would be insufficient support in a given juris-diction to allow the introduction of legislation, why then should the courts take it upon themselves to change the law?

It is also worth remembering that in England, in the marital context, the apparently harsh decisions in *Pettitt* v *Pettitt*[67] and *Gissing* v *Gissing*[68] soon led to legislative reform in the shape of the Matrimonial Proceedings and Property Act 1970.[69] It is arguable that the courts should not be too ready to facilitate the legislature in its desire to avoid confronting controversial social problems. Furthermore, if the legislature does intervene, it will be extremely difficult for it to undo the work of equity. Thus, wide-ranging equitable doctrines developed to meet a specific problem are likely to outlast their purpose, unnecessarily com-plicating the law and potentially undermining the distinctions drawn by the leg-islature.

---

[64] See e.g. *Malone* v *McQuaid* 28 May 1998 (LEXIS, Irish High Court). Contrast *Clark Drummie and Co* v *Ryan* (1997) 146 DLR (4th) 311.

[65] See generally Bell *Policy Arguments in Judicial Decisions* (Oxford: Clarendon Press, 1985). Cf. Lord Reid's reference in *Pettitt* v *Pettitt* [1970] AC 777, 795 to the distinction between "lawyer's law" and law which implements social policy and which should be dictated by parliament.

[66] See the De Facto Relationships (Property) Bill 1998. Note that the English Law Commission is at present considering this matter (see *Sixth Programme for Law Reform*, Law Com No 234 (1995)) and is expected to produce a consultation paper in Spring 1999.

[67] [1970] AC 777.

[68] [1971] AC 886.

[69] Of course, *Pettitt* and *Gissing* came at the end of more than two decades of reported decisions on the area. It is possible, however, that Lord Denning's well-meaning exertions in the Court of Appeal in the 1960s merely postponed the crisis and resulting legislative intervention.

5. *The superiority of a legislative solution*

Even ignoring for a moment the issue of legitimacy, it appears that (if one had the choice) a legislatively-imposed scheme would be preferable to a judicially-imposed one. One of the most important advantages of legislation is that the legislature could provide a clear definition of the circumstances in which the regime would apply.[70] Thus, for example, the New South Wales regime[71] applies to de facto relationships which have subsisted for at least two years, subject to exceptions for cases where the relationship has produced a child or where the applicant has made substantial contributions (or has care of the respondent's child) and serious injustice would be caused by a strict application of the two-year threshold.[72] It is clear that no court could invent an arbitrary threshold of two years; this sort of line-drawing is clearly within the province of the legislature.[73] The value of a threshold is obvious; it allows a couple to know when their (previously entirely informal) relationship has moved into the realm of legal regulation.

Associated with this point is the fact that the passing of an Act could give rise to an information campaign targeted at those members of society likely to be affected by its provisions. A new judicial direction is unlikely to be heralded in this way. The result is that, if a legislative solution were adopted, there would be a greater likelihood that the parties would actually understand their legal positions.[74] Moreover, the legislature could provide a clearly defined pro-

[70] Also a legislative regime could conceivably go beyond a consideration of the contributions and sacrifices of the parties and have regard to wider issues such as "fault, needs, maintenance, compensation, expectation [and] reliance". Cf. *Evans* v *Marmont* (1997) 42 NSWLR 70, 97–98 per Meagher JA.

[71] Established by the De Facto Relationships Act 1984.

[72] See *ibid* s 17. As well as laying down a threshold for the duration of the relationship, the New South Wales Act also provides a definition of the nature of the relationship covered by the Act. This question has previously been identified (see text to and following n 53 *supra*) as one of the areas of uncertainty remaining in even an "ideal" synthesis of the existing doctrines. The choice open to a legislature is clearly a wide one, as is illustrated by the contrast between the definition in s 3 of the New South Wales Act ("relationship of living or having lived together as husband and wife on a bona fide domestic basis although not married to each other") and that in s 3 of the Australian Capital Territory Domestic Relationships Act, 1994 ("a personal relationship (other than a legal marriage) between 2 adults in which 1 provides personal or financial commitment and support of a domestic nature for the material benefit of the other, [including] a *de facto* marriage").

[73] Of course, one might not like the lines which a legislature chose to draw. While it would be difficult for a court to justify the exclusion of same sex couples from a judicially-created property regime, the legislature is obliged to defend its decisions only at the level of political expediency. Thus, for example, the New South Wales De Facto Property Act 1984 applies only to those living together "as husband and wife . . . although not married to each other". Note, however, that this kind of discrimination might possibly offend the equality/anti-discrimination provisions contained in the Canadian Charter of Rights and Freedoms 1982, the New Zealand Bill of Rights Act 1990 and the Irish Constitution of 1937.

[74] This ties in with the argument previously advanced concerning legitimacy. The present law in the Commonwealth countries reflects the philosophy that "no one should expect spousal services for free". However, in the absence of legislation, one could also argue that no-one should expect a share of another's property without ever discussing the issue with him. The advantage of legislation would be that it would, with authority, place the onus on the defendant. He would then realise that, unless

cedure whereby a couple could contract out of the provisions of the Act (if such a possibility were thought appropriate) with the added possibility of attaching formalities (independent legal advice, written consent etc) to any such contracting-out.[75]

6. *Questioning the basic premise of the partnership paradigm of cohabitation*

The ideal doctrine involves the assumption that an unmarried cohabitation may appropriately be analogised to an emotional and economic partnership. This assumption allows one to ignore (for the most part) the inconvenient question of the intentions of the parties and to concentrate entirely on the more easily verifiable issue of the contributions and sacrifices of the parties.[76] But is every cohabitation really a "partnership" in the relevant sense? Are such relationships invariably characterised by what Gardner describes as "the values of trust and collaboration" and "communality"?[77]

It is arguable that the ideal doctrine falls into the trap of imposing a matrimonial paradigm on unmarried cohabitation.[78] As was argued in Chapter 1,[79] not all unmarried cohabitations can properly be regarded as marriages in everything but name. If the parties really are guided by the ethic of "trust and collaboration" or "communality", why then do they not share out the ownership of their property in a manner which reflects that ethic? The stock answer is, of course, that the legal ownership of property is not crucial for ordinary people and that "the lack of thinking associated with emotional relationships"[80] prevents the parties from giving consideration to their separate property entitlements. However, as was mentioned in Chapter 1, those involved in cohabitations have often been through the acrimonious breakdown of a previous relationship and the cases show at least some examples of an unromantic concern by cohabitees (male and female) to protect their individual rights.[81]

Moreover, even if one of the parties neglects to consider her financial position, can one assume that equity should step in to make things right? Consider the following hypothetical example of two people of the opposite sex who do

he contracted out of the provisions of the relevant Act, he would not be entitled to treat the contributions of his partner as freely given.

[75] See e.g. Part IV of the Australian Capital Territory Domestic Relationships Act 1994 which governs agreements between the parties to a domestic relationship. This provides that if the agreement is in writing, signed by the person against whom it is sought to be enforced and was made after a solicitor provided a certificate stating that he or she had advised both parties independently as to the matters listed in s 33(d), then the court cannot (in normal circumstances) make an order inconsistent with the terms of the agreement.

[76] Cf. Neave "Three Approaches to Family Property Disputes—Intention/Belief, Unjust Enrichment and Unconscionability", ch. 10 in Youdan (ed) *Equity, Fiduciaries and Trusts* (Toronto: Carswell, 1989) p 253.

[77] See n 49 *supra*, 282–297.

[78] See generally Chapter 1 *supra*, Part II(B)(1) and (2).

[79] See Chapter 1 *supra*, Part II(B)(2).

[80] See Gardner, n 49 *supra*, 289.

[81] See Chapter 1 *supra*, text following n 103.

not share any kind of emotional or sexual relationship. The male, who works in a highly paid job, has managed to save a reasonably large sum of money. Being interested in financial matters and in improving his own personal position, he purchases a second house and rents it out. His tenant (a stranger) is a younger woman who earns less than he does and is rather less worldly in her outlook. She is content to live in rented accommodation for the time being, effectively paying her landlord's mortgage for him. Due to a boom in the property market, the value of the house doubles in a relatively short time. The landlord decides to sell at a large profit and his tenant, unable to afford to get into the housing market at current levels, moves on to other rented accommodation.

The above example shows a case where a hard-headed man profits "at the expense of" a less sophisticated woman. Very few would argue that equity should intervene in such a case. People who do not give sufficient thought to their financial future, like the tenant in the previous example, are generally made to suffer the consequences of their insouciance. Obviously, the cohabitation situation is distinguishable because of the sexual relationship of the parties. However, one is entitled to ask whether this should really make all the difference. Women suffer from various inequalities in our society and, to take one example, on average earn substantially less than men. It seems dangerous to focus attempts to eliminate these inequalities on cases where the women in question has entwined her fortunes with those of a male partner.[82] The result could be to perpetuate women's dependence on men and to discriminate against those women who choose not to enter into a cohabitation with a male partner.

The case could also be made that it is desirable to allow some freedom from legal regulation for people who do not wish to marry.[83] It is not necessarily progressive to impose a matrimonial model on all human relationships. There is certainly some irony in the fact that, in the Commonwealth countries, the traditional philosophy of marriage has won a sort of victory. As the point has been put in another context, "no longer bothering to look down on its adversaries, [marriage] has transformed them in its own image".[84]

On balance, one might not be convinced by the arguments in this section. However, they are not trivial and, in the present author's view, there is much to be said for the proposition that it is for the legislature to make the decision to override them.

---

[82] One could argue that the crucial feature in the cohabitation context is the unequal division of child-care responsibilities between the sexes. However, if child-rearing is the key issue, then a partnership model of cohabitation seems a somewhat indirect method of approaching the question. Compare Eekelaar's interesting suggestion of a legislative jurisdiction explicitly linked to the question of child-rearing (see "Non-Marital Property", ch. 15 in Birks (ed) *Frontiers of Liability* (Oxford: Oxford University Press, 1994) Vol 2 p 210 *et seq*).

[83] See Deech "The Case Against the Legal Recognition of Cohabitation" (1980) 29 ICLQ 480.

[84] See Glendon *State, Law and Family* (Amsterdam: North-Holland Publishing Co, 1977) p 91 (quoting Scapel "Que reste-t-il de la 'paix des familles' apres la reforme du droit de la filiation" *Juris-Classeur Periodique* (1976) No 2757).

C. What is the Best Way for Equity to Develop in This Area?

1. *Canada, Australia and New Zealand*[85]

It has already been mentioned that, because the genie has already been allowed out of the bottle in Canada, Australia and New Zealand, there is little point in considering whether it would be appropriate for the courts in those countries to move to a more conservative position.[86] Once the courts have gone as far as they have in Canada, Australia and New Zealand (even if they should not have done so in the first case), the most logical progression would probably be to discard the existing unsatisfactory doctrinal structure and to adopt some variation on the ideal doctrine discussed above. Then, because equity's intervention would be based explicitly on the special nature of an intimate cohabitation, it would be possible to minimise the damage to the wider theoretical structure of the law. Furthermore, it would also be possible to eliminate certain arbitrary limitations on the scope of the existing doctrines.[87]

2. *England and Ireland*

Due to the relatively conservative starting points in these jurisdictions, the stakes are somewhat higher when one comes to consider possible future developments. The logical conclusion from what has been said earlier in this chapter is that the courts in England and Ireland should resist the temptation to adopt any of the doctrines favoured in the Commonwealth jurisdictions or the so-called ideal doctrine and should leave the question of reform to the legislature.

Of course, this approach will not attract everyone. Some may feel that the issue of democratic legitimacy is outweighed by the need to do justice to primarily female claimants who are left at an unfair disadvantage upon the termination of a relationship. Similarly, those campaigning for the rights of lesbians and gay men could very reasonably argue that any legislation which emerges is quite likely to exclude same sex couples from its ambit.[88] These are weighty

---

[85] Cf. Parkinson "The Property Rights of Cohabitees—Is Statutory Reform the Answer?", ch. 21 in *Frontiers of Family Law* (Chicester, West Sussex: John Wiley & Sons Ltd, 1995); Bailey-Harris "Property Disputes in De Facto Relationships: Can Equity Still Play a Role?" (with "Commentary" by Neave), ch. 7 in Cope (ed) *Equity: Issues and Trends* (Sydney: Federation Press, 1995).

[86] The Australian experience has shown that, even in those jurisdictions where relevant legislation has been enacted, the doctrines of equity have remained as vigorous as before.

[87] For example, as the law stands in Australia, it is not clear that contributions of domestic labour can be taken into account in all circumstances.

[88] This has happened in four of the five Australian jurisdictions which have enacted legislation in this area (the exception being the Australian Capital Territory). It may well also happen in New Zealand. See the De Facto Relationships (Property) Bill 1998. Admittedly, the English Law Commission is presently working on possible reforms of the law on "home-sharing", a focus which is not (on the face of it) likely to lead to discriminatory legislation. Cf. Neave "Commentary" on Bailey-Harris "Property Disputes in De Facto Relationships: Can Equity Still Play a Role?", n 85 *supra*, p 220 (absence of systemic role division in homosexual partnerships seen as reducing the need

arguments and the discussion in the earlier part of this book (which concentrated primarily on matters of legal doctrine) has not adequately prepared the ground for an attempt to assess them.

In the present context, therefore, one must be content to offer the view that, while the ideal doctrine discussed above would represent an improvement on any of the existing Commonwealth doctrines, the optimum solution would be the introduction of legislation which would reflect a considered view of how the society in question wishes to regulate the property rights of cohabitees, heterosexual and homosexual. If the optimum solution is not available, then it will be necessary to make a choice between a number of less desirable alternatives. In respect of this difficult choice, all the present book can offer is the conclusion that the existing Commonwealth doctrines[89] are not based on any existing principle of the law of equity and effectively constitute judicial legislation. What one makes of this conclusion depends on one's view on the underlying questions of social justice and on the importance one attaches to the notion that social change should come about on the basis of political consensus and not unilateral judicial intervention.

III. CONCLUSION TO THE CONCLUSION

This book has concerned itself with a complex social problem. Although there are many aspects to that problem, and to the law's response, this book has concentrated on only one aspect: the potential of the doctrines of equity to provide a solution. Naturally, other areas of concern have intruded upon the inquiry, particularly in the Conclusion where the discussion has proceeded at a higher level of generality, and it has been necessary to consider briefly the possibility of legislative and other solutions. However, the ultimate contribution of the book can relate only to its essential subject matter, the doctrinal options favoured in Ireland, England, Canada, Australia and New Zealand. The conclusion has been reached that, despite their express claims to doctrinal respectability, the various doctrines lack a convincing theoretical foundation.

At this final stage, it may be appropriate to venture some comments on the wider lessons to be drawn from equity's attempts to provide a remedy for claimants upon the termination of a cohabitation. When one looks across the five jurisdictions, one can only conclude that, in terms of legal doctrine, equity's performance has been far from impressive. One is reminded of the opening sentence of *Anna Karenina*: "Happy families are all alike; every unhappy family is unhappy in its own way".[90] When all judges are attempting faithfully to apply a set of legal principles in a consistent manner, one has some hope of a pattern

for statutory regulation; note, however, that these comments were made on the assumption that a broad equitable jurisdiction would be available to the parties to such relationships).

[89] As well as the "ideal" synthesis of those doctrines discussed above.

[90] Translated by Constance Garnett (London: Pan Books Ltd, 1977) p 7.

emerging in the law. However, when judges decide to depart from principle in order to obtain a result which seems just, it is quite fortuitous which particular rule they choose to bend. Therefore, instead of one departure from principle, one ends up with endless different forms of theoretical misery. In the context of disputes over family property, one can identify a dozen theoretical approaches: the purported section 17 discretion, the "family assets" doctrine, the extended resulting trust, Lord Reid's imputed contract theory, Lord Diplock's imputed common intention approach, Bagnall J's money consensus analysis, the common intention trust, Lord Denning's new model constructive trust, Canada's unjust enrichment analysis, the Australian unconscionability doctrine and New Zealand's reasonable expectations approach (including Richardson J's estoppel-based approach).[91]

What has happened is that, on a grand scale, a hard case (the special situation of cohabitees) has created bad law.[92] The common intention trust has so confused the law in England that in one of the leading authorities, *Springette* v *Defoe*,[93] the Court of Appeal wrongly decided a simple resulting trust case. The entire Canadian law of restitution was set on an independent course in *Rathwell* v *Rathwell*[94] and *Pettkus* v *Becker*,[95] when, without citing any authority, Dickson J fixed on something he remembered from a civil law case with which he had recently been involved.[96] The examples could be multiplied. The unsatisfactory doctrinal position examined in this book should give some pause to those who "exaggerate . . . the mission of equity to do unanalysed justice".[97] In the Commonwealth jurisdictions, there is a danger that, having "solved" the problem of the property rights of cohabitees, equity will, like Alexander, go looking for new worlds to conquer. In the view of the present author, a greater degree of modesty would become equity (and its sometimes over-enthusiastic proponents). It is all too easy to cast aside legal principle and precedent in favour of discretionary justice. However, if equity tries to smooth out all of the

---

[91] While some of these theoretical innovations were prompted by the problem of the property rights of cohabitees, others originated in the context of disputes between married couples. It may happen that, as legislation is introduced in various jurisdictions to govern the rights of heterosexual cohabitees, only same sex couples will be affected by the rules of equity. Therefore, one might see a third wave of equitable development, with the existing rules being, once more, adapted to meet a new social context.

[92] There is a clear danger that, in any case with a vaguely "family" flavour, lower courts will treat cases such as *Pettkus* v *Becker* (1980) 117 DLR (3d) 257, *Baumgartner* v *Baumgartner* (1987) 164 CLR 137 and *Gillies* v *Keogh* [1989] 2 NZLR 327 as magic wands capable of banishing any inconvenient doctrinal requirements. Moreover, given the frequency with which these intoxicating authorities are cited outside the family context, it would appear that they have had a generally suppressing effect on equity's inhibitions.

[93] [1992] 2 FLR 388.

[94] [1978] 2 SCR 434.

[95] (1980) 117 DLR (3d) 257.

[96] See Chapter 7 *supra*, n 101.

[97] Birks, n 49 *supra*, 24. See also Parkinson "The Conscience of Equity", ch. 2 in Parkinson (ed) *The Principles of Equity* (Sydney: LBC Information Services, 1996) p 51.

inequities resulting from human relationships,[98] there is a real danger that vulnerable individuals will be drawn unnecessarily into the painful business of litigation. Sometimes, though by no means all the time, it might be better if the Chancellor kept his big feet out of people's lives.

---

[98] See *Allen* v *Synder* [1977] 2 NSWLR 685, 706 per Mahoney JA. See also *Hibberson* v *George* (1989) 12 Fam LR 725, 734 per Mahoney JA (dissenting) (equitable jurisdiction not designed to "avoid all the ordinary abrasions of life"). The view of the present author is that, if the special problem of cohabitation were satisfactorily dealt with by legislation, one could appropriately rely on the traditional rules of equity (including the principles of estoppel) to deal with disputes arising in the context of other personal relationships (including the relationship between children and elderly parents).

Index